**Great Lakes
Archaeology**

NEW WORLD ARCHAEOLOGICAL RECORD

Under the Editorship of
James Bennett Griffin
Museum of Anthropology
University of Michigan
Ann Arbor, Michigan

Published:

Ronald J. Mason, Great Lakes Archaeology
Dean R. Snow, The Archaeology of New England
Jerald T. Milanich and Charles H. Fairbanks, Florida Archaeology
George C. Frison, Prehistoric Hunters of the High Plains

Great Lakes Archaeology

Ronald J. Mason

*Department of Anthropology
Lawrence University
Appleton, Wisconsin*

ACADEMIC PRESS

A Subsidiary of Harcourt Brace Jovanovich, Publishers
New York   London   Toronto   Sydney   San Francisco

Cover design by James Laughlin

COPYRIGHT © 1981, BY ACADEMIC PRESS, INC.
ALL RIGHTS RESERVED.
NO PART OF THIS PUBLICATION MAY BE REPRODUCED OR
TRANSMITTED IN ANY FORM OR BY ANY MEANS, ELECTRONIC
OR MECHANICAL, INCLUDING PHOTOCOPY, RECORDING, OR ANY
INFORMATION STORAGE AND RETRIEVAL SYSTEM, WITHOUT
PERMISSION IN WRITING FROM THE PUBLISHER.

ACADEMIC PRESS, INC.
111 Fifth Avenue, New York, New York 10003

United Kingdom Edition published by
ACADEMIC PRESS, INC. (LONDON) LTD.
24/28 Oval Road, London NW1 7DX

Library of Congress Cataloging in Publication Data

Mason, Ronald J.
    Great Lakes archaeology.

  (New World archaeological record)
  Bibliography: p.
  Includes index.
    1. Indians of North America--Great Lakes region--
Antiquities. 2. Great Lakes region--Antiquities.
3. Indians of North America--Great Lakes region--History.
I. Title. II. Series.
E78.G7M37   977'.01   80-2340
ISBN 0-12-477850-X   AACR2

PRINTED IN THE UNITED STATES OF AMERICA

81 82 83 84   9 8 7 6 5 4 3 2 1

Contents

Preface	ix
Acknowledgments	xiii
List of Illustrations	xv

Chapter 1
AT THE END
The Beheading of Prehistory   1

The Great Lakes Indians upon Discovery: An Approximation	4
Stones Knives and Old Ways	13
The Unseen World	24
Society: The Proto-Ojibwa Way	27
Society: A Potawatomi Model	32
Society: Iroquoian Themes	36
Tribal Grandparents: Into Prehistory	46
References	48

Chapter 2
THE INLAND SEAS
Their Geology and Biology   49

The Biological Environment	56
The Ice Age and the Rise of the Great Lakes	61
References	79

Chapter 3
THE INFILTRATORS
The Paleo-Indians of 9500–8000 B.C.

81

Chapter 4
INTERREGNUM
The Late Paleo-Indian or Early Archaic Period

111

    Components of the Late Paleo-Indian Tradition   115
    Early Archaic Contemporaries and Successors   126
    References   139

Chapter 5
TRANSFORMATION ACHIEVED
The Late Archaic Period

141

    Lamoka   147
    Laurentian   160
    The Old Copper Culture   181
    And Morrison's Island-6   195
    References   199

Chapter 6
A QUICKENING PACE
The Archaic–Woodland Transition of 1500–100 B.C.

201

    The Frost Island Culture   205
    Meadowood and Middlesex   209
    Red Ocher and Some Thematic Variations   219
    The Leimbach Culture   227
    References   235

Chapter 7
THE MIDDLE WOODLAND PERIOD
Circa 200 B.C.–A.D. 500

237

    The Great Lakes Southern Tier:
    Hopewellian Middle Woodland Cultures   244

Middle Tier Middle Woodland Cultures 259
The Northern Tier: Laurel 284
References 292

Chapter 8
FARMERS WITHOUT PLOWS, WARRIORS WITHOUT SWORDS 295
The Last Act of Prehistory

Late Woodland I 300
Late Woodland II: Lower Lakes 324
Late Woodland II: Upper Lakes 350
References 371

Chapter 9
AFTER THE END 373
Historic Indian Archaeology to the Close of the Eighteenth Century

REFERENCES 407
INDEX 421

Preface

Cheetahs loped across the western grasslands and mastodons lumbered about in the spruce-fir tangles of the East when migrating people first set squinting eyes on the sweet water seas of the North American continent. After some 113 centuries, great cities now stand on the shores of the lakes; giant ore-carriers and small pleasure-craft plow through or skim over their waves; and strange fish share their now less-innocent depths with native species. The remote descendants of the first people are at last relegated to scattered enclaves or to obscure commingling with later migrants in unanticipated urban guise, their cultural independence a thing of the past.

Personal experience as a field archaeologist, museum worker, and college professor has made me keenly aware of the great interest of many Americans and Canadians, as well as foreign visitors, in the Great Lakes and the people who originally inhabited their shores. Probably, most people have some inquisitiveness about things historical and archaeological; a great many are fascinated. Yet, most history books have treated the indigenous people of the continent as a kind of background noise to be noted in the first chapter or two and, thereafter, either ignored or consigned to the surviving ethnic minorities, so troublesome to advocates of national integration. Although most people generally realize that the opening chapters of the national-state histories coincide, as cause to effect, with the closing chapters of the autonomous cultural careers of the native societies, few people are more than only dimly aware of the antiquity or complexity adhering to the latter. This book is addressed to those inquiring people who sense something more than cacophony in the "background noises" of our national histories and who are willing to put a little effort into discovering just what that something is.

Although my desire that my professional colleagues in archaeology, anthropology, and history will find something of interest in what follows, my main concern in these pages is with the wider community of reflective people in all walks of life who would like to learn something short of encyclopedic about the lakes and their indigenous people. It is also my hope that some contemporary Native Americans may find in these pages reason to awaken or renew their interest in the experiences of their ancestors who, but for the shovel of the archaeologist, would remain unknown and mute. The historical experience of a significant portion of humanity is of interest beyond its own time and place and is part of the patrimony of us all. The time is long past to reject as equally indefensible the view of some Americans and Canadians of European extraction that Native American history and prehistory are somehow irrelevant to our current understanding of humanity and the argument of some Indians that their cultural past is nobody's concern but their own.

This book is an introduction to the archaeology of the Great Lakes. It is a guide, not a catalog. Necessarily, much has been summarily treated or omitted altogether. No claims are advanced of either completeness or finality, but rather of a careful, selective examination of representative cultures, assemblages, and sites which together are believed to provide a fair and balanced picture of who the people of the Great Lakes were and what happened to them. In doing this, an attempt has been made to vary the pace by addressing somewhat different problems when describing diverse cultures and dealing with different time periods and areas. Of course, it would certainly have been possible at almost every point to have selected sites other than those I chose to describe, to have emphasized this problem instead of that, or to deal with another regional culture in addition to or instead of those I included. The structure of Great Lakes archaeology that emerges on the following pages reflects my own view. While it is probably in general accord with "what really happened," the many uncertainties, lacunae, and issues of legitimate disagreement among specialists are necessarily presented, if not resolved, according to my own appreciation of pertinent fact and theory. In such matters it should surprise no one that professional colleagues might well arrive at different conclusions.

Because this is addressed to a wide audience rather than my professional peers, I have rejected as too cumbersome the otherwise preferable practice of citing radiocarbon dates with their statistical margins of probability error and their laboratory sample numbers. The usefulness of the dates is as order of magnitude approximations against which to scale natural and cultural events. The general readers need some handholds on the chronological ladder and should not be distracted from looking around as they ascend or descend. Those who may be interested in greater specificity will be able to indulge themselves by consulting the pertinent references. By the same token, every effort has been taken to hold the lists of references to a minimum and to avoid wherever possible works that are out of print, were published in not readily available journals, or that would otherwise be difficult for a nonspecialist reader to locate. Similarly, I have not listed unpublished manuscripts, doctoral dissertations, papers read at meetings, or private communications. Anyone wanting more bibliographical information will be able to find it by consulting the references cited in the works I have listed.

Born on the Canadian side of the Detroit River in Windsor, Ontario, living part of my boyhood in Toronto, and spending golden summers at my cousins' home on the shore of Lake St. Clair's Anchor Bay in Michigan, I suppose that I could make a case for a natural affinity for the Great Lakes. I remember the feeling of delicious adventure when we made night crossings on the ferry between Sarnia, Ontario, and Port Huron, Michigan—cautiously approaching with my father and mother and kid sister the awesome fall-off of the Scarborough Bluffs over Lake Ontario, and singing with childhood friends, anxious mothers, and the assistant rector "Pack Up Your Troubles in Your Old Kit Bag," while our Sunday school excursion boat felt its way through clutching fog for the safety of the Toronto harbor, and home. A door dramatically opening on a sense of antiquity accompanied a grade-school field trip to the Royal Ontario Museum, and there a personal commitment was instantly and irrevocably given. And just a few years later in Philadelphia the purchase of a little book in the neighborhood five-and-ten-cent store disclosed the wonder of a world I had not been particularly aware of before: the world of the North American Indian (bless you, Lillian Davids Fazzini, whoever you were). Then came my introduction to the riches of the University of Pennsylvania's University Museum. I had come to know that moccasined feet had preceded my own on the Scarborough Bluffs and that bark canoes had known the Detroit River and Lake St. Clair in another time when the world was young. Others have experienced the majesty and the mystery of the lakes, though they have responded in tongues not my own. I am still amazed at the wonder of it all. My hope is that in the following pages the reader will learn many interesting and worthwhile things and arrive at the end with sense of wonder intact, if not enhanced.

A sense of wonder may provide the motive power, but it will not deliver the means for studying the past if something more than amusement or entertainment is wanted of the exercise. So even though this is not a treatise for specialists, it is intended as a serious study aimed at a scientific and historical understanding of past events. To borrow a phrase from the great evolutionary biologist George Gaylord Simpson, this is a piece of "historical science." This simply means that although our concern is with tracing the origin, development, and fate of Indian societies of the Great Lakes—a unique historical chain of events—we will seek to do so only with proven and testable means and with the stipulation that our assumptions and conclusions must always be conformable with, or at least not in contradiction of, physical, biological, and sociocultural laws that govern comparable phenomena in the contemporary world and are believed by the uniformitarian principle to have operated throughout prehistory as well.

Acknowledgments

I would like to extend my gratitude to the many people who in one way or another helped make possible the merits of the ensuing pages. Even though I declined to follow many good suggestions and have adhered to my own interpretations of certain matters where others may have proffered respectable alternatives, my feeling of debt to those colleagues and friends is no less great. My intellectual indebtedness is, of course, much greater than the formal testimony of the bibliography.

I am especially beholden to the four archaeologists whose influence has been greatest in molding, correcting, or enriching my understanding of the aboriginal peoples of the prehistoric and early historic Great Lakes: my wife, colleague, best friend, critical proof reader, and implacable foe of misplaced commas, Carol I. Mason; and my esteemed friends James B. Griffin, William A. Ritchie, and James V. Wright. To these stalwart four I am forever and gratefully in debt. James B. Griffin not only initially suggested that I write this book, but his meticulous criticism of the manuscript, in many instances not acted upon (but never ignored), supplied a prod to rethinking certain propositions and strengthened anew my appreciation of his justly celebrated comparative memory.

The following individuals and institutions graciously provided the illustrations here published as well as some I was unable to use because of space or other considerations: William D. Finlayson, Richard I. Ford, Robert E. Funk, James B. Griffin, Charles F. Hayes III, William M. Hurley, Elden Johnson, Mike McLeod, David F. Overstreet, William A. Ritchie, Daniel M. Seurer, Orrin C. Shane III, Peter L. Storck, David M. Stothers, George Stuber, James W. VanStone, and James V. Wright; the Archaeological Survey of Canada, National Museum of Man, National Museums of Canada, Ottawa; the John Carter Brown Library, Brown University, Providence, Rhode Island; the Field Museum of Natural History, Chicago; the Great Lakes Archaeological Research Center, Inc., Waukesha, Wisconsin; the Illinois State Museum, Springfield; the Department of Anthropology, Lakehead University, Thunder Bay, Ontario; the Department of Anthropology, Lawrence University, Appleton, Wisconsin; the National Oceanic and Atmospheric Administration, Washington, D.C.; the Neville Public Museum, Green Bay, Wisconsin; the New York State Museum and Science Service, Albany; the Oshkosh Public Museum, Oshkosh, Wisconsin; the Rochester Museum and Science Center, Rochester, New York; the Royal Ontario Museum, Toronto; the Science Museum of Minnesota, St. Paul; the Thunder Bay Historical Society Museum, Thunder Bay, Ontario; The Toledo Area Aboriginal Research Society, Inc., Toledo, Ohio; the University of Michigan, Museum of Anthropology, Ann Arbor; the University of Minnesota, Department of Anthropology, Minneapolis; the University of Toledo, Laboratory of Ethnoarchaeology, Toledo, Ohio; the University of Toronto, Department of Anthropology, Toronto; and the University of Western Ontario, Museum of Indian Archaeology, London, Ontario. I am entirely responsible for all of the photographs of materials in the collections of Lawrence University, the Neville Public Museum, and the Oshkosh Public Museum.

Win Thrall of Central Services, Lawrence University, took my sketch maps and worked them into form suitable for the public eye.

Finally, thanks to the editorial staff at Academic Press for its labors in seeing the manuscript through to published form.

List of Illustrations

Maps

MAP 1-1. *Approximate locations of major Great Lakes tribal groupings when first mentioned in the annals of European exploration.* 7

MAP 1-2. *The "Joliet Map of 1674."* 28-29

MAP 2-1. *The drainage basin of the Great Lakes.* 52-53

MAP 2-2. *Major biotic provinces of the Great Lakes.* 58

MAP 2-3. *The Great Lakes region during Late Woodfordian (Port Huron) times.* 73

MAP 2-4. *The Great Lakes region during recessional Valderan (Algonquin Stadial) times.* 75

MAP 2-5. *The Great Lakes during the Chippewa-Stanley low water stage.* 77

MAP 2-6. *The Great Lakes during the Nipissing high water stage.* 78

MAP 3-1. *Paleo-Indian sites discussed in the text.* 83

MAP 3-2. *Strandline of Glacial Lake Algonquin in southwestern Ontario showing locations of Early and Late Paleo-Indian sites.* 95

MAP 4-1. *Interregnum (Late Paleo-Indian and Early Archaic) sites discussed in the text.* 113

MAP 5-1. *Approximate ranges of Archaic cultures and locations of Archaic sites mentioned in the text.* 142

xvi List of Illustrations

MAP 6-1. *Principal distributions of the Frost Island, Leimbach, Meadowood, and Red Ocher cultures, and locations of Transitional Period (Archaic-Woodland transition) sites mentioned in the text.* 203

MAP 7-1. *Middle Woodland cultures and sites (numbered) mentioned in the text.* 240

MAP 8-1. *Major cultural groupings in the Late Woodland I Period and archaeological sites mentioned in the text.* 301

MAP 8-2. *Major cultural groupings in the Late Woodland II Period and archaeological sites mentioned in the text.* 325

MAP 9-1. *Locations of Protohistoric and Historic archaeological sites mentioned in the text.* 374

Table

TABLE 8-1. *Correlations of Ontario and New York Proto-Iroquoian cultures with the Western Basin or Younge Tradition.* 349

Plates

PLATE 1-1. *Common types of bone and stone fishing gear from various archaeological sites in Ontario.* 18

PLATE 1-2. *Western Algonquian pottery of the Blackduck style common in northern Minnesota, northwestern Wisconsin, and western Ontario.* 30

PLATE 1-3. *Reconstructed early historic or protohistoric Potawatomi vessel from Rock Island Site II, Door County, Wisconsin.* 34

PLATE 1-4. *Iroquoian-style clay smoking pipes from Ontario.* 38

PLATE 1-5. *Artist's reconstruction of the protohistoric Huron Draper site near Pickering, Ontario.* 41

PLATE 1-6. *Late prehistoric or protohistoric Huron artifacts from sites in southern Ontario.* 44

PLATE 3-1. *Fluted points from southeastern Ontario.* 87

PLATE 3-2. *Paleo-Indian artifacts from the Fisher site, Simcoe County, Ontario.* 96

PLATE 3-3. *Fluted points and double-spurred graver from sites in northwestern Ohio and southeastern Michigan.* 100

PLATE 3-4. *Fluted point in simulated hafting with foreshaft.* 106

List of Illustrations

PLATE 4-1. *Eden and Scottsbluff projectile points from the Renier site, Brown County, Wisconsin.* 118

PLATE 4-2. *Scottsbluff points from the Renier site, Brown County, Wisconsin.* 119

PLATE 4-3. *Scottsbluff and Eden points from eastern Wisconsin.* 122

PLATE 4-4. *Taconite bifaces from the Brohm site near Thunder Bay, Ontario.* 126

PLATE 4-5. *Late Paleo-Indian projectile points, preforms or biface blades, end-of-blade scraper, and denticulate tool from the Cummins site near Thunder Bay, Ontario.* 127

PLATE 4-6. *Tool blanks and other bifaces from the Cummins site near Thunder Bay, Ontario.* 128

PLATE 4-7. *Early Archaic side-notched projectile points from eastern Wisconsin.* 130

PLATE 4-8. *Various styles of bifurcate-stemmed and other Early Archaic points from southern Ontario.* 134-135

PLATE 5-1. *Bannerstone (spear-thrower weight?) from Waupaca County, Wisconsin.* 144

PLATE 5-2. *Two examples of Late Archaic three-quarter grooved axes from eastern Wisconsin.* 146

PLATE 5-3. *Lamoka projectile points, knives, scrapers, drills, and celts and adzes from the Scottsville, Geneva, and Lamoka Lake sites, New York.* 148-149

PLATE 5-4. *Lamoka hammerstones, abradingstones, choppers, notched sinker, grooved mauls, and mortar and pestle from the Scottsville, Geneva, and Lamoka Lake sites, New York.* 152-153

PLATE 5-5. *Lamoka bone and antler artifacts from the Scottsville and Lamoka Lake sites, New York.* 156-157

PLATE 5-6. *Laurentian hafted beaver incisor tool, gouges, celt, flint drills, and adze, and a Lamoka type beveled adze from various sites in Ontario.* 162-163

PLATE 5-7. *Brewerton Laurentian flint projectile points, bone points, and bannerstone from various sites in New York.* 164-165

PLATE 5-8. *Brewerton Laurentian projectile points, scrapers, knives and drills, bone flaking tool?, biface blades and choppers, and rough stone implements from New York.* 168-169

PLATE 5-9. *Brewerton Laurentian scrapers, drawshaves, chisel, drills, and bifaces and rough stone tools from New York.* 170-171

PLATE 5-10. *Brewerton Laurentian beaver incisor tools and celts, adzes, and gouges from sites in New York.* 173

List of Illustrations

PLATE 5-11. *A Frontenac Phase burial (No. 50) at the Frontenac Island site, Cayuga County, New York.* 175

PLATE 5-12. *Frontenac Phase celts, adzes, and gouges, unfinished and finished bannerstones, grooved plummets, ground slate points and ulu fragment, and native copper awls and possible compound fishhook components from the Frontenac Island site, Cayuga County, New York.* 176-177

PLATE 5-13. *Frontenac bone and antler artifacts from the Frontenac Island site, Cayuga County, New York.* 178-179

PLATE 5-14. *Frontenac bone, antler, and shell artifacts from the Frontenac Island site, Cayuga County, New York.* 182-183

PLATE 5-15. *Old Copper Culture adze, gouge, and socketed spearpoints from various sites in eastern Wisconsin.* 184

PLATE 5-16. *Copper tanged points, ulu or crescentic knife, bracelet, awls, large fishhook or gaff, asymmetrical tanged knife exhibiting punch marks of unknown significance, notched tanged point, and "rat-tailed" tanged point from various sites in eastern Wisconsin.* 187

PLATE 5-17. *Old Copper serrated-tanged and split or notched-tanged spearpoints from northeastern Wisconsin.* 189

PLATE 5-18. *Old Copper "rat-tailed" tanged points from northeastern Wisconsin and the Upper Michigan Peninsula.* 190

PLAT 5-19. *Old Copper socketed ax or adze blades ("spuds") from northeastern Wisconsin and the Upper Michigan Peninsula.* 195

PLATE 5-20. *Old Copper crescentic knives from the Upper Michigan Peninsula and northeastern Wisconsin.* 196

PLATE 6-1. *Rare carved soapstone bowl from southern Ontario.* 208

PLATE 6-2. *Cache of 243 mortuary blades (Feature 1) from the Meadowood site at Red Lake, Jefferson County, New York.* 213

PLATE 6-3. *Meadowood grave goods from the Muskalonge Lake and Red Lake sites, Jefferson County, New York.* 214-215

PLATE 6-4. *Red Ocher Culture white flint mortuary knife from the Dyer Farm site, Lake County, Indiana.* 221

PLATE 6-5. *Red Ocher Culture turkey-tail and stemmed blades of southern Indiana or southern Illinois flint from sites in eastern Wisconsin.* 223

List of Illustrations   xix

PLATE 6-6. *Artifacts from the Transitional Period Williams cremation burial site, Wood County, Ohio.*   225

PLATE 6-7. *Ground slate birdstones from Transitional Period sites in southern Ontario.*   228

PLATE 6-8. *Rimsherds of the pottery type Leimbach Thick from the Leimbach site, Lorain County, Ohio.*   230

PLATE 6-9. *Stemmed Leimbach Phase projectile points from the Leimbach site, Lorain County, Ohio.*   231

PLATE 6-10. *Schultz Thick interior-exterior cordmarked potsherds from the Schultz site, Saginaw County, Michigan.*   233

PLATE 7-1. *Hopewellian vessel from western Michigan.*   241

PLATE 7-2. *Hopewellian vessel from western Michigan.*   242

PLATE 7-3. *Mound H at the Hopewellian Norton Mound Group, Kent County, Michigan, before excavation.*   246

PLATE 7-4. *The central burial area in Norton Mound M of the Norton Mound Group, Kent County, Michigan.*   248

PLATE 7-5. *Set of corner-notched projectile points found with Burial 3 in Norton Mound M.*   249

PLATE 7-6. *Grave goods from Burial 3 in Norton Mound M.*   250

PLATE 7-7. *Pottery vessel of the type Norton Zoned Dentate Stamped from Burial 17, Norton Mound C.*   252

PLATE 7-8. *Marine shell (Busycon contrarium) ladles or containers from burials 16 and 17, Norton Mound C.*   253

PLATE 7-9. *Hopewellian (Tittabawassee Ware) rimsherds from the Schultz site, Saginaw County, Michigan.*   255

PLATE 7-10. *Hopewellian (Green Point Ware) rimsherds from the Schultz site, Saginaw County, Michigan.*   257

PLATE 7-11. *Saugeen Culture burials (GB-GF) at the Donaldson site, Bruce County, Ontario, showing extended, flexed, and bundle styles of inhumation.*   262

PLATE 7-12. *Grave offerings from directly beneath the bundle burial in the group GB-GF at the Donaldson site, Bruce County, Ontario.*   263

PLATE 7-13. *Cache of biface blades at the Donaldson site.*   264

List of Illustrations

PLATE 7-14. Saugeen vessel from the Donaldson site with pseudo-scallop shell stamping above a rocker stamped body. 265

PLATE 7-15. Saugeen pseudo-scallop shell stamped rimsherds from the Donaldson site. 267

PLATE 7-16. Saugeen dentate stamped rimsherds from the Donaldson site. 268

PLATE 7-17. Artifacts of bone and teeth from the Donaldson site. 270

PLATE 7-18. Point Peninsula antler combs from the Jack's Reef, Avon or Durkee, and Kipp Island sites, New York, and from the Bay of Quinté and Port Maitland, Ontario. 274

PLATE 7-19. Point Peninsula artifacts from various sites in southeastern Ontario. 275

PLATE 7-20. North Bay Linear Stamped vessel from Rock Island Site II, Door County, Wisconsin. 279

PLATE 7-21. North Bay projectile points from the Mero site, Door County, Wisconsin. 280

PLATE 7-22. North Bay cordwrapped-stick decorated and plain and dentate stamped pottery from the Mero and Porte des Morts sites, Door County, Wisconsin. 281

PLATE 7-23. North Bay Linear Stamped, corded stamped and stab-and-drag, annular punctated, incised-over-cordmarked, and pseudo-scallop shell stamped sherds from the Porte des Morts and Mero sites, Door County, Wisconsin. 282

PLATE 7-24. Hopewell (Baehr) rimsherd, three Laurel or Laurel-like rimsherds, four water-rolled North Bay sherds, and a plain and two cordmarked North Bay sherds from the Porte des Morts and Mero sites. 283

PLATE 7-25. Laurel Culture platform pipe of polished stone from western Ontario. 285

PLATE 7-26. Laurel rimsherds from northern Minnesota. 287

PLATE 7-27. Laurel artifacts from various sites in western Ontario. 288

PLATE 7-28. Laurel vessel from site EaJf-1 on the Wabinosh River, Lake Nipigon, Ontario. 291

PLATE 8-1. Heins Creek Ware rimsherds from the Heins Creek site, Door County, Wisconsin. 302

PLATE 8-2. Reconstructed Madison Ware cordmarked vessel from the Effigy Mound Culture Sanders site, Waupaca County, Wisconsin. 304

PLATE 8-3. Point Sauble Collared rimsherds from the Heins Creek, Mero, and Porte des Morts sites, Door County, Wisconsin. 307

List of Illustrations

PLATE 8-4. *Cord and fabric reconstructed from impressions on a Point Sauble Collared rimsherd from the Effigy Mound Sanders site, Waupaca County, Wisconsin.* 308

PLATE 8-5. *The Madison Ware type Aztalan Collared as represented by rimsherds from the Aztalan site, Jefferson County, Wisconsin, and from sites on the Wisconsin Door Peninsula.* 309

PLATE 8-6. *Madison Cord Impressed and the closely related Madison Fabric Impressed rimsherds from the Sanders site, Waupaca County, Wisconsin.* 310

PLATE 8-7. *Effigy Mound Culture celt, broken gorget, and adzes from the Sanders site, Waupaca County, Wisconsin.* 311

PLATE 8-8. *Rimsherds of the Blackduck Culture from sites in northern Minnesota.* 314

PLATE 8-9. *Blackduck Culture vessel from the Martin Bird site (DbJm-5), Whitefish Lake, Ontario.* 316

PLATE 8-10. *Artifacts from the McCluskey and other western Ontario Blackduck sites.* 317

PLATE 8-11. *Mackinac Banded vessel, Mackinac Phase, Juntunen site, Bois Blanc Island in the Straits of Mackinac, Michigan.* 320

PLATE 8-12. *Princess Point Complex pottery from the Middleport site, Haldimand County, Ontario.* 322

PLATE 8-13. *Stratification of Princess Point Complex occupations at the Cayuga Bridge site, Haldimand County, Ontario.* 323

PLATE 8-14. *Pottery vessel of the Owasco Canandaigua Phase from the Bates site, Chenango County, New York.* 327

PLATE 8-15. *Owasco Canandaigua Phase rimsherds from the Bates site, Chenango County, New York.* 328

PLATE 8-16. *Representative Owasco bone and antler artifacts from New York.* 331

PLATE 8-17. *An Oak Hill Phase proto-Iroquois vessel of the type Oak Hill Corded from the Clark site, Broome County, New York.* 333

PLATE 8-18. *Early Ontario Iroquois (Glen Meyer Culture) pottery of the types Ontario Oblique and Glen Meyer Oblique from sites in southern Ontario.* 335

PLATE 8-19. *Early Ontario Iroquois (Glen Meyer Culture) vessel from southern Ontario.* 337

PLATE 8-20. *Early Ontario Iroquois (Pickering Culture) pottery from the Bennett site near Hamilton, Ontario.* 338

List of Illustrations

PLATE 8-21. *Middle Ontario Iroquois (Middleport) artifacts from sites in southern Ontario.* 339

PLATE 8-22. *Site plan of the Middleport sub-stage Nodwell site at Port Elgin, Bruce County, Ontario, showing longhouse outlines, concentrations of midden, and the encircling palisades.* 341

PLATE 8-23. *Plan of one of the Middleport longhouses at the Nodwell site at Port Elgin, Bruce County, Ontario, showing postmolds, pits, and other features of the house floor.* 342

PLATE 8-24. *Late prehistoric Neutral or Neutral-Erie artifacts from the Lawson and other sites in southern Ontario.* 343

PLATE 8-25. *Rivière au Vase type vessel of the Younge (Western Basin) Tradition from the MacNichol site, Wood County, Ohio.* 345

PLATE 8-26. *Younge Phase Western Basin pottery from the Petrie site, Lucas County (Toledo), Ohio.* 347

PLATE 8-27. *Upper Mississippian-related Late Woodland II pottery from the Fort Meigs site, Wood County, Ohio.* 348

PLATE 8-28. *Ossuary (Feature 11) of the Juntunen Phase occupation at the Juntunen site in the Straits of Mackinac, Michigan.* 351

PLATE 8-29. *Partly restored Juntunen Phase pot from the Juntunen site in the Straits of Mackinac, Michigan.* 352

PLATE 8-30. *Rare Middle Mississippian (Ramey Incised-like) pottery from the Juntunen site in the Straits of Mackinac, Michigan.* 354

PLATE 8-31. *Ocean shell gorget with face and "weeping eye" motif from the Anker site, Cook County, Illinois.* 360

PLATE 8-32. *Oneota bone awls, pins, and needles from the Pipe site, Fond du Lac County, Wisconsin.* 361

PLATE 8-33. *Oneota disc-shaped catlinite pipes from Wisconsin.* 362

PLATE 8-34. *Green Bay Phase (Mero Complex) Oneota rimsherds from the Mero site, Door County, Wisconsin.* 363

PLATE 8-35. *Oneota vessel from Rock Island Site II, Door County, Wisconsin.* 364

PLATE 8-36. *Lake Winnebago Phase Oneota pottery from the Lasleys Point site, Winnebago County, Wisconsin.* 365

List of Illustrations

xxiii

PLATE 8-37. *Lake Winnebago Phase Oneota pottery from the Lasleys Point site, Winnebago County, Wisconsin.* 366

PLATE 8-38. *Lake Winnebago Phase Oneota rough stone tools from the Lasleys Point site, Winnebago County, Wisconsin.* 367

PLATE 8-39. *Lake Winnebago Phase Oneota triangular arrowheads from the Lasleys Point site, Winnebago County, Wisconsin.* 368

PLATE 8-40. *Lake Winnebago Phase Oneota end-scrapers from the Lasleys Point site, Winnebago County, Wisconsin.* 368

PLATE 8-41. *Lake Winnebago Phase Oneota bone and shell artifacts from the Lasleys Point site, Winnebago County, Wisconsin.* 369

PLATE 9-1. *Plan of the Draper site near Pickering, Ontario.* 376

PLATE 9-2. *Early historic period artifacts from southern Ontario Iroquois (Huron, Petun, Neutral) sites.* 377

PLATE 9-3. *Early historic Seneca burial (No. 61) at the Dutch Hollow site, Livingston County, New York.* 379

PLATE 9-4. *Turtle-shell rattles and cut animal jaws from the Dutch Hollow site, Livingston County, New York.* 380

PLATE 9-5. *Carved antler anthropomorphic figurines from the Dutch Hollow site, Livingston County, New York.* 381

PLATE 9-6. *Early historic Seneca pottery of the type Seneca Barbed from the Dutch Hollow site, Livingston County, New York.* 382

PLATE 9-7. *Protohistoric and historic Huron artifacts from sites in southern Ontario.* 385

PLATE 9-8. *Ontario Iroquois bird effigy smoking pipes.* 387

PLATE 9-9. *Soil profile at Rock Island Site II, Door County, Wisconsin, showing the physical stratification of old humus zones, living surfaces, and wind-blown sand.* 397

PLATE 9-10. *Bone and antler artifacts from Rock Island Site II, Door County, Wisconsin.* 399

PLATE 9-11. *Trade goods and associated artifacts from Rock Island Site II, Door County, Wisconsin.* 401

PLATE 9-12. *Huron style vessel from Rock Island Site II, Door County, Wisconsin.* 403

At the End
The Beheading of Prehistory

1

The French sailed up the broad St. Lawrence and anchored at Quebec among the incredible forests of Canada. Lowering their sails like an alighting seagull folding its wings, they reembarked upriver in the bark canoes that skimmed the shallower depths like waterbugs. In these light, tough craft they undertook journeys that would rival in distance and hardship the sail from Europe to Quebec itself. And in these fabulous journeys of sail and paddle they met a new race of men—men who literally stepped out of prehistory to help haul their boats ashore. As in Massachusetts and Virginia, in Florida and the Caribbean islands, in Mexico and Panama and Peru, men of two hemispheres came face to face on the St. Lawrence and learned of a branch of the family of man whose existence neither had had previous inkling.

Both were the inheritors of long histories. But one lacked writing and continually contracted its historical tail as generation followed generation; its oral myths and ceremonies recalled only a recent past. It was accordingly left to the ocean-crossers, who had writing and a literate tradition tied to a fixed calendar, to record those meetings. Despite a common humanity these were vastly different worlds that met, and incomprehension obscured the understanding of those whose long-separated paths now came together. But men being men, there were some things all held in common. This fact not only permitted communication to be successfully initiated in the first place, it also suggested in one's interpretation of the other where certain advantages might lie.

When the French went up the St. Lawrence and then ventured into the Ottawa River valley—the first of these rivers providing entry into the lower Great Lakes via the Thousand Islands, the second into the upper lakes by way of Georgian Bay—they blundered into an appreciation that the Indian societies of these inland seas and the network of streams giving access to them were both numerous and diverse. They also perceived that to approach each of these societies and establish effective, friendly relations required patience, diplomacy, and at least outward accomodation to foreign protocols they only rarely and incompletely came to understand. Always following the first landfalls, the Europeans learned of interior tribes through the ties established with the local people encountered on first coming ashore. Amazed at the technology and what must be the awesome spiritual prowess of people who came so confidently so far with such strange and wonderful accouterments, the Indians who first met the French were usually as anxious to monopolize the newcomers as the French were to make contacts and to exclude other European powers from doing the same.

As they set up trading stations and then missions and the first tentative colonies of immigrants, the newcomers found themselves becoming the allies and clients of the local people. The latter sought to maintain themselves between the Europeans and the interior tribes. By doing this they hoped to advantage themselves by developing a middleman position in the nascent fur trade. Realizing through direct exchange the benefits of the French contact, these Indians also realized their own vulnerability and moved to protect their interests by seeking to block, or at least control, French access to neighboring and more remote tribes. As middlemen, the contact Indians could represent (or claim to represent) the French interests in dealing with the interior tribes even (especially) as they frustrated direct French approaches to those tribes. To the French they could claim to act as agents of the other tribes, while at the same time persuading—with threats if need be—their native neighbors to rely on their good offices in any business with the newcomers. The middleman position inevitably shifted, of course, as the Europeans came to know more about the New World and its resources and peoples. Relations with the indigenous peoples necessarily altered as French numbers slowly increased and as the tribes with whom they were in direct contact became increasingly dependent on the trade for tools and weapons and, eventually, even clothing and foodstuffs. Inevitably, Indian middlemen suffered military reverses at the hands of traditional or novel coalitions of enemies, and experienced severe population losses as European endemic diseases commenced new and more ferocious careers in the new lands. Direct European influence then took another great step deeper into the continent. Tribes once remote and formerly dependent on the now defunct or irrelevant middlemen now moved more distinctly into the French orbit. Some of them, in turn, tried to set themselves up as successor middlemen, intervening between the French and tribal societies even more remote. Thus on their historic way to their epochal trading and military alliance with the Huron Confederacy, the

French had to work through and eventually by-pass such persistent actual and would-be middlemen as the Montagnais, Stadaconans, and Hochelogans in the St. Lawrence Valley and then the sundry bands of the Algonkins in the Ottawa Valley.

French contacts with nonmiddleman tribes were necessarily more infrequent and under less predictable control. The middlemen naturally sought to limit such contacts because they threatened to undermine their advantageous position as guides, translators, trouble-shooters, and general economic and diplomatic go-betweens. Well played, the role of such cultural brokers paid off handsomely at both ends. But the walls that Indian middlemen attempted to build between other Indians and the growing European presence had many holes even in the best of times. There were too many alternate routes into the interior countries, and there was the pressure to honor traditional trading rights inherited from prehistoric times involving trade in shells, copper, chert, corn, animal skins, and other commodities. These factors, added to curiosity, the desire for the wonders of the new technology, and the general and widespread Indian sense of freedom, independence, and usufruct, combined on the Indian side to make the middleman's barriers only occasionally effective.

When the first Huron Indians descended the Ottawa River to meet the strange new people they had heard about from friends among the eastern tribes, they could only come as guests of their traditional trading partners among the Ottawa River Algonkins. French access to the Huron country had to be acquired through travel privileges controlled by the Algonkins as the recognized social, and not simply geographic, intermediaries. As time would prove, the Algonkins were ultimately dwarfed by the power and mutual interests of the Hurons and the French. In time the latter two traded directly regardless of Algonkin desires, though the ritual courtesies were observed whenever possible. Although the Algonkins by virtue of geography, ancient custom, and a sometime sufficiency of numbers of warriors controlled the Ottawa River and the movement of all those people on it who did not want to rupture friendly relations with them, their need of the Hurons as allies against Iroquois incursions from the south tempered their disapproval of the strengthening ties between their white and red neighbors.

Whenever the French or Dutch or English came into direct contact with hitherto remote tribes, they discovered that their arrival had been long preceded by rumors purporting to describe them and by sometimes fairly numerous examples of their industrial prowess. Via the Indian middlemen, the interior tribes had had some access to the brass kettles, iron knives and hatchets, glass beads, and woven blankets which were highly regarded as symbols of friendship with the potent new people and which were perceived by the Indians to be superior to the native products they replaced. The importance of this recurring fact of the precedence of European influence, though translated and mitigated by Indian intermediaries before the physical arrival of European men, is that social and cultural changes, however subtle, had already commenced to shift native societies away from what they had been before the first European ever had opportunity, let alone inclination, to jot down his observations.

There is something of a mystery—an inescapable and pervasive quality of uncertainty—variable in intensity from region to region and time to time, regarding the precise nature of the indigenous societies whose careers were so dramatically redirected, if not terminated, by the coming of European man. Indian societies had started to change in adjustment to that coming before the actual event in any given instance following the initial landfall. Ideas, manufactured items, and disease organisms were carried by Indian middlemen to interior regions in advance of the ocean-crossers who were their source. What were the Algonkins (or Hurons or Iroquois or Ojibwas or Potawatomis) like when at last encountered by flesh-and-blood Frenchmen? How did they correspond to the Algonkins who had lived *immediately before* the first rumor ever reached them that there were new men in the world? In actual fact, prehistory was beheaded with the European discovery of America. The most we can know about what the Great Lakes Indians were truly like at the threshold of history is only an approximation. This approximation is a compound of ethnohistory (the study of the earliest documents describing the aborigines), ethnography and social anthropology (what has been learned about the nature of comparable societies elsewhere in the world), and archaeology. In general outlines and many matters of substance, the approximation is pretty clear. It is the details that are elusive, the details such as preoccupy us with our contemporaries. It is like seeing a head in shadows and not being quite able to make out the face.

The Great Lakes Indians upon Discovery: An Approximation

At the time when the agents of the French king and the Christian God first looked upon the shoreless horizons of Lakes Huron and Ontario and saw wealth squandered in anarchy and souls in the thrall of Satan, the lands surrounding the Great Lakes were peopled by a population divided into innumerable small-scale and politically autonomous societies, each of which, in at least some small measure, had its own distinctive culture. Many neighboring tribes spoke separate dialects or even mutually unintelligible languages as distantly related as modern English and Chinese. These societies varied so much in size, structure, and way of life, as well as language, that the term *tribe* when applied to them must be used in a loose sense to signify an ethnic group whose members *maximally* thought of themselves as a people distinct from other such groups. Furthermore, *tribe* implies the sharing of a common culture and language, and the occupation of a more or less circumscribed territory. They were not nation-states in the political sense, despite the confusion of European observers. Centralization of authority, let alone power, was virtually nonexistent both in concept and actuality, and the social boundaries separating tribes were remarkably permeable. Alliances were even more unstable than among European states.

The Algonkin Indians exemplify some of the problems of indigenous Great Lakes sociology. Making up the Algonkin tribe in early historic times were a variable number of often separately named and socially and territorially distinguished subtribes, or *bands,* all of which enjoyed an incredible propensity for uncoordinated, independent action. These seem gradually to have disappeared or coalesced with the passage of time, people, and larger events. Counted as Algonkins were such named groups as the Weskarini, Onontchataronon, Kichesipirini (the latter infamous to many an early traveler on the middle Ottawa River, Indian and Frenchman alike, because they levied tolls with a heavy hand on all up- and downriver traffic), and the Otaguottouemin. Still other divisions of the Algonkins lived elsewhere on the Ottawa River and its tributaries or resided along the St. Lawrence above the Montagnais Indians in Quebec.

There were three major linguistic stocks represented among the multitude of separate languages and dialects of the Great Lakes region. These have come to be called Iroquoian, Algonquian, and Siouan. They must not be confused with the ethnic or tribal groups called Iroquois, Algonkin, and Sioux, though each of these spoke languages of the appropriate stock. Others spoke these languages, too.

Languages of the great Iroquoian family were spoken over a vast part of the lower Great Lakes. The most famous Iroquoian-speakers to readers of American and Canadian history were the Iroquois and Huron Indians. Iroquois was really the name of an alliance or confederation of five important and quite independent tribes. These member tribes of the League of the Iroquois all dwelt south of Lake Ontario in what is now New York State. From east to west these were the Mohawks, the "keepers of the eastern door" whose villages were located in the river valley still bearing their name, the Oneidas, the Onondagas ("keepers of the central fire"), the Cayugas, and, south of present day Rochester in the Genessee valley, the Senecas, "guardians of the western door of the great longhouse of the League." Well after the establishment of relations with European powers, the League accepted into membership a sixth "nation" composed of displaced southerners: the Tuscaroras. The constituent tribes of the Iroquois confederacy also had a remarkable facility for the large-scale absorption of fragments of other, sometimes formerly antagonistic, tribes. Because of their critical geographic position and their far-flung wars, the Iroquois exercised an influence in northeastern North America greatly disproportionate to the size of their homeland or the weight of their numbers.

West of the Senecas toward the Niagara River and the falls were an Iroquoian-speaking people barely known to Europeans: the Wenros or Wenroronans, unaffiliated with the League Iroquois. Other independent and more powerful Iroquoian-speaking peoples were located far to the south in the lower Susquehanna Valley in Pennsylvania (the Susquehannocks), to the southwest along the southeastern shore of Lake Erie (the Eries, or "Cat Nation"), and to the west on the Ontario Niagara Peninsula westward to the valley of the Grand River and up around the west end of Lake Ontario (the Neutrals, either a numerous tribe or a confederacy of closely related tribes).

Well north of the Iroquois and intervening Lake Ontario were the Hurons situated between Lake Simcoe and the Georgian Bay arm of Lake Huron. Like "Iroquois," the name Huron belonged to a confederation of autonomous Iroquoian-speaking tribes: the Arendarhonon on the east, the Attignawantan on the Penetanguishene Peninsula in the west, and the Attigneenongnahac and Tahontaenrat between. A fifth group, the Ataronchronon, may have been an "unofficially" affiliated tribe or an unusually prominent division of the Attignawantan tribe. To the south and west of the Hurons, and inalnd to the Blue Mountains from Nottawasaga Bay at the south end of Georgian Bay, were the close linguistic cousins of the Hurons, the Petun Indians (also called Tionnontaté and Tobacco Nation). Although there was an oral tradition that in earlier years there had been war between them, the Petuns and the much more powerful Hurons were friendly when and after initial French contact was made. Both allied themselves with the Ontario Algonquian-speaking tribes and with the French, and they both shared destruction or dispersal in 1649 with the unprecedentedly sustained winter campaigns of the Iroquois. Intermarrying with the Algonquian-speaking Ottawas, the refugee Hurons and Petuns merged in the lands of their diaspora and formed a new tribe which took the name Wyandot.

Except for portions of Minnesota and Wisconsin, the rest of the Great Lakes country during the early historic period was home to speakers of the Algonquian family of languages (it is important not to confuse the linguistic label "Algonquian" or "Algonkian" with the tribal designation "Algonkin"). The Algonquians included a great many separately named societies ranging from well-integrated, stable tribes to amorphous societal fragments whose precise nature is difficult to make out. Many of the latter are historical will-o'-the-wisps, making brief and transitory appearances ir traders' or missionaries' accounts, and then vanishing without later report. It seems likely that some of these groups were given disparate names by different reporters. Some groups which should have been recognized as

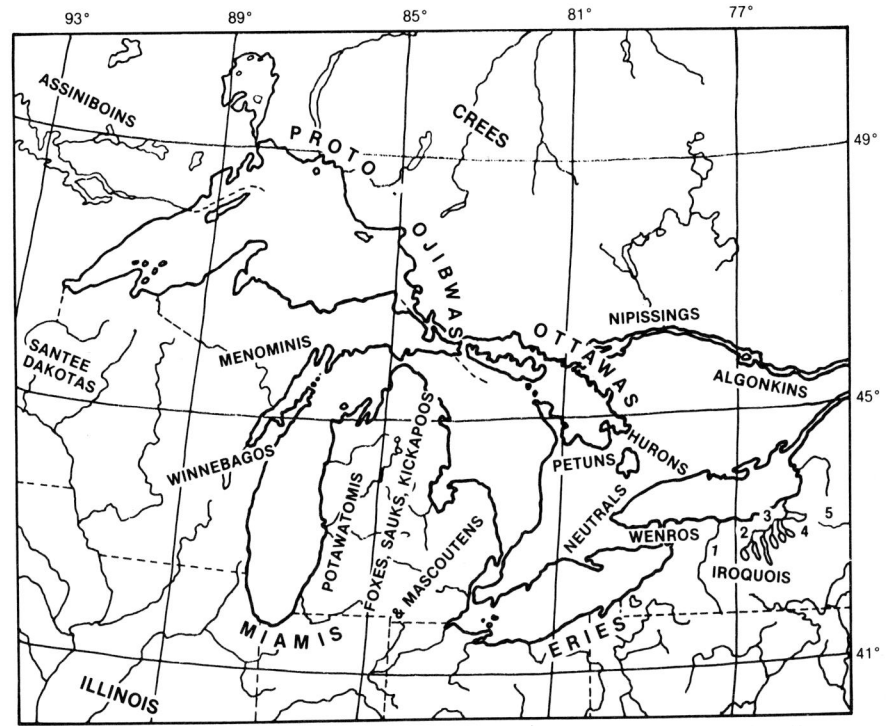

MAP 1.1. *Approximate locations of major Great Lakes tribal groupings when first mentioned in the annals of European exploration. The numbered Iroquois tribes are: (1) Seneca; (2) Cayuga; (3) Onondaga; (4) Oneida; and (5) Mohawk.*

separate peoples were ignorantly confused and erroneously given an inclusive rubric. Many surrendered great portions of their autonomy and individuality between their first appearance in French ethnic cognition and later French and British accounts. Indeed, many disappeared as separate peoples, either becoming extinct or amalgamating with others as a result of population losses and ejection from their traditional homelands due to the vicious circle of economic rivalries, wars, disease, and threat of social disintegration ultimately deriving from the irreversible growth of European interest in the New World. Still other Algonquians appeared and disappeared in the obscurity of fragmentary first accounts, and no one knows what happened to them.

Although in the strictest sense not a Great Lakes people because their Ottawa Valley homeland drains into the St. Lawrence River below the debouchment of Lake Ontario, the Algonquian-speaking Algonkins were important in Great Lakes history. They were among the first aboriginal peoples to be met by the French in Canada, and for many years they controlled access to the Huron country and the upper lakes. In addition, they were potent military and trading allies of the Hurons, French, and other northern Algonquians, and upon occasion individuals and entire Algonkin extended families went to live with friends and trading partners among the Hurons and the Great Lakes Algonquian tribes. We have already mentioned some of the subtribes or bands of which the Algonkin tribe was constituted.

Much of southern Ontario in the early historic period appears to have been distinctly underpopulated, even by Indian standards. It seems to have been a no man's land in which people from different tribes hunted, but rarely settled. The first groups of Algonquian tribes west of the Algonkins were thus neighbors of the Hurons and true Great Lakes dwellers. In the rugged country surrounding Lake Nipissing northeast of where Georgian Bay makes its great westward bend were the Indians known as the Nipissings or Nipissiriniens. About the central and northern shores of Georgian Bay and the north coast of Lake Huron westward to Sault Ste. Marie and the Straits of Mackinac, and then along the rocky northern coast of Lake Superior lived two related great peoples: the Ottawas (mainly in the southeastern portions of this range) and the Ojibwas or Chippewas (tending northward and westward).

Like the Algonkins, the Ottawas and the Ojibwas were really great folk societies or aggregations, each composed of a number of politically independent smaller subtribes, bands, and villages. These had their own headmen and occupied a generally respected home territory whose exact boundaries were more often than not in a state of readjustment as seasons progressed, years passed, and fortunes altered. For example, the Ottawa tribe included not only such major groups as the Kiskakons, Sables, Nassauaketons, Sinagos, and Keinouches, but from time to time even unrelated people came temporarily to be known as Ottawas because they joined forces with them in fishing expeditions, overwintered in their territory, or were invited to participate in the trading activities for which the Ottawas were famous.

The sundry divisions of the Ottawa when the French first learned of their existence lived along the shores of Georgian Bay, including the Bruce Peninsula, to Manitoulin Island—the giant reclining at the north end of Lake Huron. Within this immense domain of lakes, rushing rivers, rocks, and forests the individual segments of the larger society wandered in highly knowledgeable response to the shifting seasonal resources on which life depended. They tended to congregate in the easy months of summer and to disperse in small family units for the ardors of interior winter hunting and trapping. As part of a general aboriginal adjustment to colonization and an unrelenting westward movement of formerly more eastern tribes, the Ottawas gradually retreated from their eastern ancestral estates and expanded their western frontiers. Depending on the date, few or many Ottawas came to dwell west of the Sault along the southern shore of Lake Superior as far away as Chequamegon Bay in northwestern Wisconsin.

Others lived for a while on the Door Peninsula in the northern Lake Michigan basin or roamed extensive areas of the lower peninsula of Michigan. At any given time following their withdrawal from their former haunts, there were some Ottawas living hundreds of miles away from other Ottawas and sometimes with Indians of other ethnic affiliations occupying interposed terrain. A general consequence of these movements was the inevitable blurring and loss of once important social and cultural distinctions whereby the Ottawa peoples had once more locally and unequivocally identified themselves.

The Ojibwa Indians are a classic example of a tribe originally constituted of quite separate and jealously independent smaller tribes. Usually called Chippewas in the United States, the Ojibwas, like their close relatives the Ottawas, never really existed as a tribal unit until some time after the beginning of the historic period and the coming of the Europeans. Originally, the ancestors of the Ojibwa tribesmen lived in small hunting, fishing, and gathering societies, each inhabiting its own traditional domain. Although they shared a fundamentally similar way of life, had much the same world view, spoke the same language, and intermarried frequently, they possessed their own names by which they identified themselves and were known to others. Significantly, these were most often the names of animals (e.g., Bear, Beaver, Catfish, Crane, Snapping Turtle). And their members typically felt, when all was said and done, that they were the truest and bravest men in all the world. Tragically, these brave little societies disintegrated under the combined blows of war and disease and the demoralization that sets in as traditional answers had to be squared with new questions. Among the survivors, many coalesced with others of their kind from far and near, and ultimately, phoenix-like, there arose the new, larger, and more formidable tribe known to history as the Ojibwa.

The small proto-Ojibwa tribes included the Amikwas, Missisaugas, Maramegs, Noquets, Ouasouarinis, Nopemings, Saulteurs, Mikinacs, Outchibous, and others whose names, if they survive at all, do so as labels on road signs—like fossils protruding from a rock. Some of the luckier proto-Ojibwa societies were later transfigured and became the great clans of the Ojibwa tribe, attaining through the extension of kinship ties a postponement of the mortality the others experienced more abruptly and unequivocally. Thus, while the Noquets (People of the Bear) lost their status as a separate people, they were not without survivors; their legacy is the Noka Clan (the Bear Clan) of their Ojibwa descendants. Similarly, the Amikwas (People of the Beaver) and the Ouasouarinis (Fish People), although long extinct as discrete ethnicities, survived as the Ahmik (Beaver) and Auwausee (Fish) clans of their merged and renascent inheritors.

In prehistoric and early historic times these precursors of the Ojibwa tribal people were thinly spread over an enormous country along the southern reaches of the Canadian Shield along and inland from the northern coasts of Lakes Huron and Superior and along a portion of the northwestern shore of Lake Michigan. Many ranged at least seasonally beyond this country. As the proto-Ojibwa societies amalgamated and an integrated Ojibwa tribe emerged, the frontiers of the homeland contracted in the east, recoiling from the traumas associated with that direction, and enormously expanded in the west, frequently at the expense of older resident societies. In response to fishing opportunities along the St. Marys River at the Sault, trade at the Straits of Mackinac, and hunting and war booty at Chequamegon Bay near the west end of Lake Superior (whence their eruption into northwestern Wisconsin and adjoining Minnesota) large groups of Ojibwas came to play increasingly important roles in intertribal and Indian–European affairs far west of their ancestral hearths.

In the lower peninsula of Michigan between Lakes Huron and Michigan, there were initially greater population densities than in most areas to the north. Wars and consequent emigration in the early historic period reduced them markedly and for a time made the region a virtual no man's land. Some of the indigenous peoples were later able to return; others finally established new homes as far afield as Mexico! Some of the best known central Algonquian tribes were natives of Michigan when they first came into historical focus. These were the Potawatomis, Foxes, Sauks, Mascoutens, and Kickapoos. They seem to have possessed somewhat more solidly organized tribal structures, and each seemed better able than the northerners to act more as a unit when benefits for doing so were perceived.

Following the abandonment of most of the lower Michigan peninsula in the early to mid-seventeenth century, eastern Wisconsin became a favorite refuge and a new home for many. One reason for this is that there seems to have been at this time a marked power imbalance between the two sides of Lake Michigan. This imbalance was either the result of an incredible collapse of the Siouan-speaking Winnebagos, supposedly the dominant tribe in eastern Wisconsin when that country first came to the attention of the French, or because they never had the power usually credited them. The other eastern Wisconsin natives, the Menominis, were also Algonquian-speakers and were a relatively small tribe generally friendly to the newcomers. In this new setting, increasing intermarriage and adoption among all of these tribes took place so that ethnic identities were considerably altered and social organizations correspondingly realigned.

In the eighteenth century, numbers of Potawatomis and other former inhabitants drifted back into Michigan or took over vast tracts of northern and central Indiana and Illinois. In many of their southern Lake Michigan camps they welcomed transient groups of Delawares and Shawnees—fragments of tribes earlier dispossessed of their ancestral estates further east. Again, intermarriage was not infrequent.

Unlike the Great Lakes Algonquians to the north and east who either planted few crops or none at all, the Potawatomis, Kickapoos, and other lower Michigan tribes were importantly agriculturalists in at least some portions of their lands. However, they still placed very heavy reliance on hunting and the systematic collecting of wild vegetable foodstuffs. The mixture of subsistence efforts changed over time, of course, and was also partly a function of where the people were in their migrations. Sometime after they had moved to northeastern Wisconsin, the Potawatomis extended their "homeland" well to the south and west despite the protests of Indians with older claims to those regions. In doing this many Potawatomis adopted the use of the horse and even took up buffalo hunting, Plains style, on the prairies beyond the Mississippi. At least after European contact, individuals, families, or whole villages of these tribes might travel enormous distances and dwell in quite diverse ecological regions within the span of a few years. Groups of Sauk Indians, for example, are known to have overwintered on the south shore of Lake Superior, traded on the Door Peninsula in the northern Lake Michigan basin, hunted buffalo on the prairies of Iowa and Missouri, settled for a time at Detroit, and waged war in Ontario, Ohio, Indiana, Illinois, and on southwestward into Kansas. At the height of their military power in the eighteenth century, the Potawatomis sent war parties as far away as New England and Mississippi.

The indigenous Algonquians of Wisconsin, as mentioned in another connection, were the Menominis. They lived west of Green Bay and on up into the upper Michigan peninsula. The closely related and even smaller Noquet tribe, already described as one of the proto-Ojibwa groups, was nearby. Prehistorically, they may have occupied part of the upper peninsula of Michigan and some of the islands at the mouth of Green Bay. The Menominis planted fields near their villages in corn and squash but retained a heavy dependence on hunting, fishing, and gathering as well. Additionally, they were among the major harvesters of wild rice in the western Great Lakes. This latter characteristic was due much more to natural availability of that highly nutritive cereal than to a peculiarly intensified "taste." Where the Ojibwas had access to rich stands of wild rice in northwestern Wisconsin and in Minnesota, they, too, capitalized on it. The homeland of the Menominis was especially blessed in this fine natural grain; it provided an increased cushion against the threat of starvation when the domesticated crops failed.

Living in villages on and landward of the south and southwestern shores of Lake Michigan in Wisconsin, Illinois, and Indiana were the Miamis. These Algonquian-speakers were divided into several groups, some of which, like the Weas and the Piankashaws, eventually split away and for a time were thought of as being separate tribes in their own right. Very successful farmers enjoying the benefits of rich soils and a long growing season, the Miamis also paid a lot of attention to the biological diversity, particularly in big game, which the interfingering prairies introduced into their homeland; elk and bison hunting provided excitement as well as a supply of red meat. Because they were the most prairie-oriented of the Great Lakes Indians, the Miamis not surprisingly made little use of canoes. They felt much more at ease dry-shod on firm ground.

At various times the Miamis went north to Green Bay to trade with the Indians there as well as with the French. But they were usually found much further south. Indeed, they claimed territory reaching well into the Ohio–Mississippi drainage. When the expansion of the Potawatomis took place, the Miamis were among those who lost the most. A neighboring people who sometimes camped with them, the Illinois (actually a confederacy of the Cahokias, Kaskaskias, Peorias, and others), were not a Great Lakes group although they sometimes turned up in the early history of the western lakes. They occasionally sent trading parties to Green Bay and even Lake Superior, and they blocked or facilitated French movements between the lakes and the Mississippi Valley as they fancied. They fought the Winnebagos and the Iroquois, and they were eventually dispossessed of their ancestral estate by the Potawatomis, Kickapoos, and other formerly more northern and eastern tribes.

Except for the Winnebagos in northeastern Wisconsin, there were no Siouan-speakers habitually resident in the Great Lakes. Some eastern divisions of the Sioux, or Santee Dakota, occupied lands with ill-defined and fluctuating boundaries which, over many centuries, repeatedly brought limited numbers of them into the westernmost reaches of the Great Lakes system. After the westerly movements and ethnic consolidations of the southern Ojibwas brought those people in force to the hunting lands south of Lake Superior, an initial period of mutually beneficial interaction was followed by bitter and prolonged warfare between the Ojibwas and the Sioux. The latter were gradually forced out of any and all countries draining into the Great Lakes (always before only a small and marginal part of their customary haunts anyway) and retired westward. Those early documents relating to the Great Lakes that speak of the Siouan-speaking Ioways and Assiniboins are referring to hunting or trading parties briefly entering the drainage basin; they were not long-time residents like the Winnebagos.

When the French first heard of the Winnebagos through their Algonquian connections in the upper lakes (Champlain dispatched Jean Nicolet in 1634 to meet them), they were reported as arrogant and contemptuous of outsiders. As potential middlemen in a developing trade, the Algonquians were probably not adverse to portraying the Winnebagos as more inhospitable than they really were (Nicolet, it seems, was well received). However that may be, news of their eating Ottawa and Illinois visitors did little to enhance their reputations. Their relations with the Menominis, at least, appear to have been marked by tolerance if not cordiality. Despite their language, the Winnebagos were not greatly dissimilar to their Algonquian neighbors, particularly the Miamis. Like the latter they were expert farmers. They also hunted, fished, gathered river mussels, and collected the natural plant resources of their aboriginal estate, including wild rice. Just a few years after Nicolet's mission, the Winnebagos lost much of their land to the incoming Michigan tribes, and most of their remaining population was absorbed in intertribal marriages.

Stone Knives and Old Ways

In more than technology the Great Lakes Indians were Stone Age people. But to take material attributes first, the sometime use of a regionally abundant metal in ways only quasi-metallurgical removes none of the force of the generalization. Native copper was obtained by shallow surface mining on Isle Royale and along the shores of Lake Superior where unusually pure deposits could be worked out with a little digging and a lot of prying and hammering. Usable chunks of the metal could also be picked up from time to time in the ubiquitous gravel plains and hills left behind by Ice Age glaciers. Given the pattern of its distribution, it is not surprising that copper was more used by the westerners than by the Indians of the eastern lakes. Unalloyed, unsmelted, and never cast, copper was hammered either cold or after heating in a fire, then turned into such ornaments as beads, tubes for stringing on braids of hair, and bracelets, or such implements as awls or bodkins, knives, fishhooks, and gorges. Some copper was traded eastward to the lower lakes. It is reasonable to assume that when the French and their Indian associates extended the fur trade westward, they were following ancient routes of trade.

Everything else with which the Indians manipulated their world was made more or less directly out of raw materials more widely distributed. Stone is the most conspicuous of these other materials because on many archaeological sites it is all that has survived to bear witness to man's onetime presence. "Stone Age" is really a convenient abbreviation for "Stone–Bone–Antler–Wood–Bark–Hide–Sinew Age."

Throughout the lakes country, cherts and other flinty stones were worked into knife blades, scrapers, and drills which were usually hafted in wooden, bone, or antler handles. Arrowheads were almost always triangular in shape but showed a wide range in workmanship from crudely trimmed slivers of chert to precisely crafted equilateral or isosceles triangles beautifully thinned on both faces. Some wedging and graving tools were shaped strictly for or as the result of use and were not modified in any way to accord with aesthetic considerations. Heavy-duty tools such as hammers and celts (grooveless axes) were laboriously pecked and ground out of basalts, gabbros, and other tough nonflinty rocks. Stone also had more passive uses: for heat storage and radiation in roasting pits and sweat baths or, grooved or notched, as sinkers for fish nets and as weights for holding down wigwam covers. It is commonly assumed that men did all the stone-working in Great Lakes Indian societies, but no one really knows. Surely there must have been many a woman who replaced a broken knife or scraper blade with one of her own making when she needed one and the men were away hunting.

Pottery occured throughout the Great Lakes. However, it was much more common along and inland the southern reaches of the lakes than the northern. Indeed, some Ottawas and Ojibwas made pottery only infrequently—and then borrowed notions about how it ought to look from their neighbors—or they supplied their needs in this commodity by trading for it. Many Ottawas, for example, either got their pottery directly from the Hurons or they made their own, copying Huron fashions. The fanciest pottery was made by the Iroquoian tribes around the lower lakes and by Algonquian-speaking groups influenced by them. The Mahican in the Hudson Valley and the Munsee, the northern Delawares in the upper valley of that name, both Algonquian peoples, made excellent and beautifully decorated earthenware pots, some examples of which are difficult to distinguish from the Iroquoian models. Not surprisingly, there was stylistic variation in pottery manufacture from tribe to tribe. Much Mohawk pottery was distinctive enough in many subtle ways to make the total character of the final product recognizably different from that of, say, the Cayugas. While sharing basic vessel architecture, manufacturing and finishing techniques, and even most decorative motifs, Seneca pottery was divergent enough from Onondaga or Neutral pottery that only the simpler versions of their wares might be confused. Whereas Huron pots often looked just like Petun examples, neither would ever be confused with Seneca or Susquehannock vessels.

As recorded in early missionary and other accounts, all of the Great Lakes peoples shared a basic type of clothing, though each tribe emphasized some peculiarity of style that set it apart. Almost all clothing at that time was made of animal skins. After stitching (a laborious process before the eyed steel needle) the garments were left plain or they were embellished with painted designs or with copper or shell beads or dyed porcupine quills. This was good clothing with thousands of years of trial and error in its design behind it. However, many items, particularly woolens, even though of Old World origin, rapidly made their way into the Indian wardrobe soon after their introduction. Such items would have to be deducted from any reconstruction of aboriginal attire, of course, even if the result differed from our traditional biases.

Men usually wore a breechcloth tied over a belt so that an extra flap, or apron, hung down in front and back. In warm weather and in camp this was often the sole bit of clothing. Among some tribes even this was omitted. Leggings, fringed or otherwise, were often worn, especially in cold weather, and were tied to the belt. Pull-over shirts or jackets were common. In the winter months an animal skin robe would be worn with the hair inside to provide extra warmth. Moccasins had soft soles and were sometimes supplied with ankle covers. Tribal differences in foot gear took the form of the way moccasins were cut, how the toes were gathered or puckered, and the style and manner in which decoration was applied. These things began to change very early under the influence of European materials and concepts of style. Much of the curvilinear, floral patterns in beadwork, for example, seem to owe as much to Europe as to native antecedents.

Women wore skirts and were bare above the waist, or they wore dresses which covered them from shoulder to knee. They also often wore leggings and, of course, moccasins. Like the men they, too, wrapped themselves in winter in fur robes with the hair inside. The outsides (hairless side) of these robes were sometimes finely decorated with porcupine quillwork, beadwork, or painting. They often doubled as blankets at night. Bags with shoulder straps were used by both sexes and were often beautifully embellished; knives, scrapers, needles, extra arrowheads, a fire-making kit, a pipe, and personal lucky charms were carried in such bags. More often than not children went entirely naked.

Women wore their hair loose, braided, or tied up in a loose knot. A common men's style (and the one by which Great Lakes and other northeastern Indians became stereotyped in popular concept) was the shaven head with braided or knotted scalp lock. Often a roach was worn down the center of the head with a couple of large feathers and a string of beads protruding at the back. Notwithstanding the practices of many of those who perform Indian rituals for the modern public, the Great Lakes tribes did not make or use the famous eagle-feather warbonnet. Face and body painting and even tattooing were common in the Great Lakes, although this cultural trait was not as highly elaborated as in the southeastern United States and lower Mississippi River valley where it probably originated. Allowing facial hair to grow out was avoided by all the tribes; the European habit of wearing moustaches and beards was thought ludicrous if not disgusting.

Great Lakes Indian houses showed variation in architecture, size, and permanence depending on tribe, location, season, and function. At the simplest end of the scale were single- or double-sided lean-tos such as a hunter might make or a family might construct on an overnight berry-picking expedition or trip to a neighboring community 2 days away. These were made of a few slabs of bark leaned against a makeshift pole frame; they represented such a slight investment of material and effort that they were abandoned after one night's use. Much more meticulous individuals might take along a couple of rolls of sewn birchbark to throw over a makeshift lean-to frame, the next morning abandoning the frame but retrieving the bark rolls. In good weather, or if there were some reason to avoid attention (as in a war party), people thought nothing of sleeping without benefit of artificial shelter.

More permanent, true domiciles were double lean-tos with closed back and circular dome-shaped or conical tentlike wigwams. The latter was fashioned by screwing poles or even freshly cut saplings several inches to a foot into the ground and tying them together at the top. Partly depending on the area, such frames were then covered with overlapping sheets of bark, animal skins, or bullrush or other woven mats. A smokehole was left at the top and the entranceway was closed, if needed, with more of the same material or with a blanket or even a boardlike rawhide. Such structures were meant to shelter single families, perhaps accompanied by an odd friend or relative. They rarely exceeded 4.6 m (15 ft) in diameter. In breaking camp the wigwam cover was removed, rolled up, and carried to the next campsite. Alternatively, it might be cached if the people were laden with the rewards of a successful hunt or if returning from a fishing trip. The pole frames were left standing.

In the larger and more sedentary villages, the houses tended to be more carefully constructed, and here also were found the largest domiciles. Architecturally, the most impressive were the famous Iroquoian longhouses. Actually, the longhouse was by no means confined to Iroquoian-speaking tribes, though it was most common among them; also, it was not the only style of house they built. There were many minor variations on the longhouse theme in the Great Lakes area. For example, Mohawk and other League Iroquois longhouses were square-ended, while those made by the Hurons tended to be round at both ends. But the common function of the longhouse was to serve as home for several closely related families. Like the wigwam, it was a pole-frame building. It usually had an entrance at both ends and was covered with birch, elm, or cedar bark which was sometimes supplemented with pieces of hide or some sewn rush mats. In summer months sections of covering were removed to allow easier access to cool breezes and more light. In winter they were closed as tightly as possible. Although this helped to retain welcome heat from the several cooking fires maintained along the centerline of the longhouse, it likewise hindered the escape of smoke. Chronic eye ailments were a time-immemorial accompaniment of winter quarters. The combination of jostling human bodies, scratching dogs, hustling mice, and biting lice and fleas, all congested in a winter longhouse where red fires and greasy smoke obscured the air, drove one desperate Jesuit missionary to liken a visit to such an abode as a veritable descent into Hell.

Pole-frame benches lined the walls of the longhouse. Covered with bark, woven rush mats, and fur robes, these served as seating accomodations during the day (though the ground was often used for this purpose) and as beds at night. Most longhouses appear to have been internally partitioned into a series of small compartments or cubicles on either side of the central aisle. In many cases the central fires were shared by the two families occupying opposite compartments. Dogs as well as people roamed the longhouse, so the rafters were employed to store food, skins, ritual paraphernalia, and items of personal value. Storage pits were also dug into the dirt floor.

Great Lakes longhouses ranged upwards in size to about 6 or 8 m wide by 15, 24, 31, or even 61 m long (20 or 25 ft by 50, 80, a 100, or 200 ft). They were clustered together, often inside a wooden palisade for protection from attack, and were adjacent to or even surrounded by the community's corn fields. Such towns were exceedingly vulnerable to fire, and even if they did not burn down, they had to be abandoned every 8–15 years due to soil exhaustion, overhunting of the local game, and depletion of ready supplies of firewood and building materials. Many Iroquoian villages required 15,000–25,000 stakes to be enclosed within a palisade. These were usually circular with the entranceway framed by overlapping walls. The French and British did not think highly of these primitive fortifications, and they were sometimes able to induce their Indian allies to build more defensible squares, pentagons, and hexagons, sometimes with corner bastions.

All of the Indians of the Great Lakes hunted, fished, and gathered wild plant foods. But whereas the northern Algonquians relied on the natural munificence of wild foods almost entirely, or traded for corn and dried squashes, such lower lake peoples as the Ontario and League Iroquoians were mainly farmers who sought out the produce of the forest to supplement and vary their diet as well as to provide a little insurance against a bad crop. Corn or maize was easily the dominant domesticated plant, but squashes (including pumpkin), beans, and sunflowers were also grown. Invariably, while men did the strenuous labor of clearing lands for cultivation, the actual planting, tending, and harvesting was women's work. Men, however, raised tobacco. Children were useful in chasing away birds and squirrels and other pests to agriculture, and by their chatter provided company.

The Central Algonquians in Michigan and Wisconsin and in northern Ohio, Indiana, and Illinois had dual subsistence economies. They planted extensively, but they also went off on extended hunting expeditions with sometimes whole villages—men, women, and children—actually migrating into the prairie lands to spend weeks or even months hunting elk and buffalo. They then returned in late summer or early autumn to harvest what the insects and birds had left of their crops. Entire communities of Miamis and Siouan-speaking Winnebagos annually migrated across the Mississippi to communally hunt buffalo. This pattern was especially developed after the introduction of the horse made large-scale movements

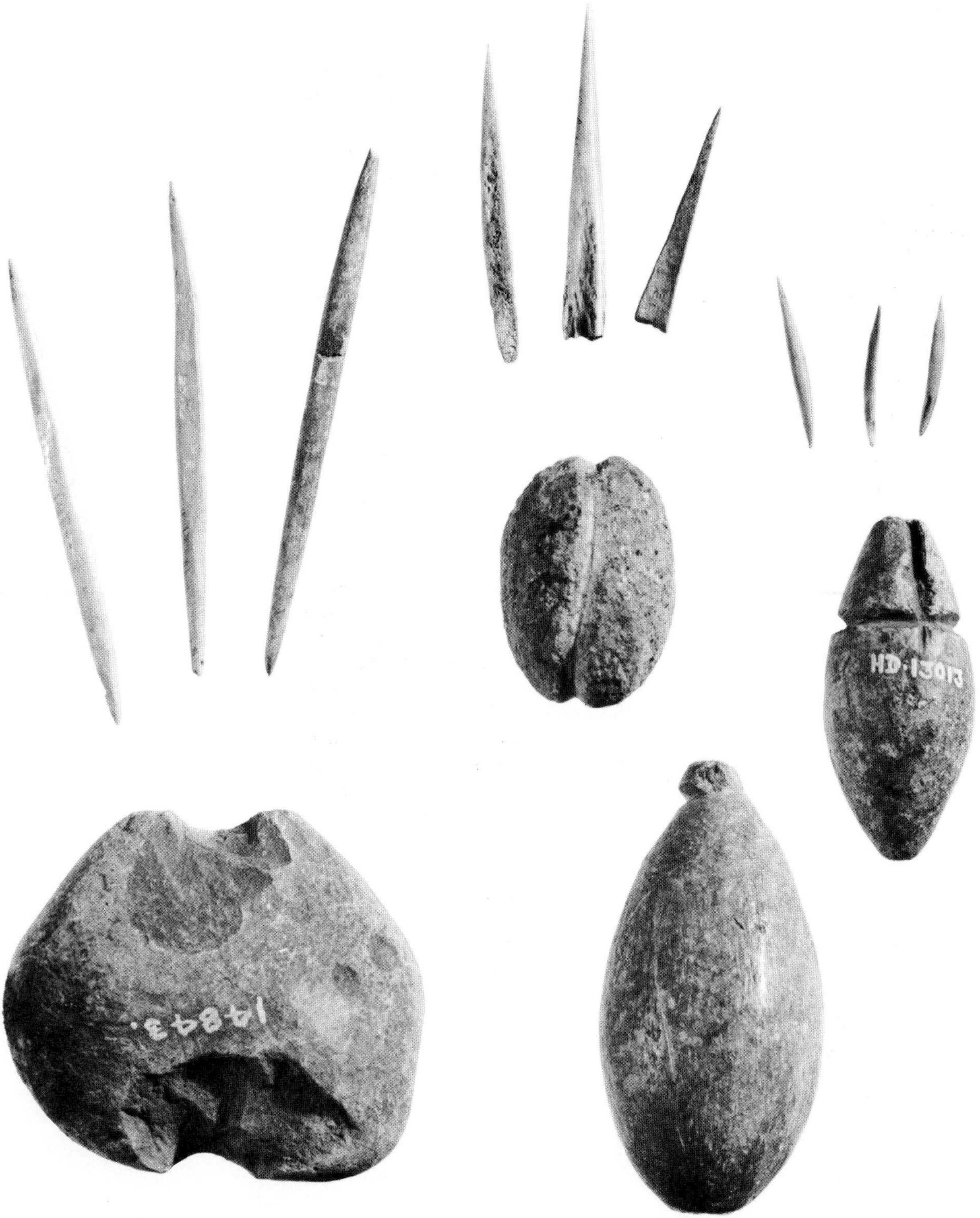
HD·13013
14843.

over great distances more feasible. Where fish were unusually abundant and large catches predictable, people from many different tribes would travel a long way to peacefully congregate and harvest the waters' bounty. The churning waters of the St. Marys River at Sault Ste. Marie were widely celebrated in this regard.

Individual tribes relied on their own particular combinations of subsistence resources interpreted in the light of their traditional needs and their present circumstances. These resources varied, of course, from season to season and from one year to the next in concert with the ebb and flow of natural cycles. Moose and woodland caribou were vital to the boreal forest dwellers along the north shore of Lake Superior. Yet in some years of changing animal populations, bears assumed particular importance in the food quest. Here and in some other parts of the Great Lakes during and following the times of fish runs and spawning activity, many thousands of Indians lived entirely on fresh, dried, or smoked fish for several months. Deer were the single most important source of red meat for the tribes in the broadleaf forests of the central and southern Great Lakes country. Elk at least seasonally replaced deer along forest–prairie edges. With the sometime exception of people like the Miamis, buffalo hunting was unusual in the Great Lakes and was limited to the approaching prairies on the southern and western margins.

In early spring, wherever good stands of maple were to be found, entire camps labored to collect prodigious quantities of maple sap and to process it into syrup and sugar. This activity really flourished after the fur trade began, when copper, brass, and iron kettles became available. Individual camps of Menominis, Ottawas, Potawatomis, and other tribes consumed unbelievable quantities of this good food and natural candy during and following the maple tapping season. We know from personal accounts of white people captured and forced to live with the Indians how important this resource could be. In the eighteenth century (and thus a time when trade kettles were in use), some Ojibwas near Sault Ste. Marie consumed over 2 kg of maple sugar per day per person for several weeks. An individual's monthly consumption in this group could be as much as 17 kg (37.5 lbs.). Although this example should not be thought of as typical, neither is it exceptional. The liquid fruit of the sugar maple was widely available and was a major subsistence resource locally.

Strawberries, raspberries, cranberries, and many other varieties of

---

PLATE 1.1. *Common types of bone and stone fishing gear from various archaeological sites in Ontario: probable bone leister prongs from fishspears (upper left); possible bone points from compound fishhooks (upper middle); bipointed bone fish gorges (upper right); notched pebble net-sinker (lower left); grooved cobble net-sinker (center); plummets or fishline weights (lower middle and lower right). (Shown actual size.) (Courtesy Peter L. Storck and the Royal Ontario Museum, Toronto, Canada.)*

natural fruits grew better in some localities than in others, and over generations women had learned to condition many of their movements so as to take maximum advantage of them. The endless cycle of hunting and fishing and farming and gathering meant that all but the most intensive and successful cultivators scheduled their lives in highly knowledgeable and deliberately planned movements so as to make the most of the natural sequencing of resources. There were always some people trekking or canoeing from base camp or multifamily village to smaller berry-picking, acorn-gathering, fishing, maple-tapping, wild-rice-collecting, duck- and geese-trapping, or hunting camps, and back again. These movements were the result of the accumulation and oral transmission of centuries of hard experience with the intricate mosaic of land and water and the complex interrelations of plants and animals. Within the restrictions of available technology, they were both efficient and demanding. But there was much leisure in this life, too. Indeed, a recurring European complaint lodged against the Indians was that they enjoyed their leisure too much and could not see that work had a virtue of its own. The inexorable limiting factor was the inevitability of the year when game became scarce, the fish runs diminished below expectations, and poor winter snows and prolonged summer drought combined. Then, as Hobbes has said, was man's life brutal and brief.

What people could not find or produce for themselves was obtained through trade. By modern per capita standards aboriginal trade was unimpressive before the advent of the fur trade. What trade that occurred was conducted in a highly formal and ceremonialized way with ritual trading partners. The exchange of goods and services among tribes, because it involved transactions with people who were not kin and were therefore potentially enemies, required the exact following of ancient formalities that were understood and subscribed to by all tribes. Money and markets in any modern sense were lacking until Europe introduced them. Economic exchanges took place under the guise of social relations and were subordinated to them. Ritual friendships and fictive kinship relations had to be established, usually between men who initiated the intertribal contacts; women rarely if ever participated directly. Typically, they then passed on the rights to the trade to their sons (in patrilineal tribes) or their sisters' sons (in matrilineal tribes). Because headmen were the individuals who commonly spoke for their kin group, village, or tribe, they were normally the men who were the principal actors in the trade. This offered them further opportunity to exercise their leadership roles and to reinforce them. The unspoken laws governing kinship-structured societies such as the Great Lakes tribes required that all tribesmen benefit from the success of any of their members and, reciprocally, share in any burden of loss. Furthermore, the pervasive ethic of generosity was expected to find expression nowhere more uncompromisingly than in the actions of headmen. Prerequisite to esteem was generosity. When trading was undertaken between tribes, it was mutually with anticipation of benefits for all, not just the active trading partners. Between trading partners themselves, gifts were given and every effort was made to imbed the economic transactions in the more comfortable and humane structure of social relations. More commonly than not, before wholesale accomodations to the European market system, strictly economic considerations were subordinated to social ones. Haggling was insulting and was something only Europeans did.

Some tribes were better situated by geography for trade than were others. The Hurons, for example, lived near the border between two great environmental provinces. They themselves were supremely successful farmers. Their native land consisted in good part of gently rolling sandy soils nourished with the decaying litter of broadleaf forest. Even though located over 160 km (100 mi) north of the north shore of Lake Erie, the climate of Huronia was admirably suited to the needs of Indian agriculture. The combination of excellent soils, warm and sufficiently long summers with only infrequent early frosts, and adequate precipitation meant that in most years the Hurons were able to raise more corn than they needed for their own subsistence. A surplus was thus at hand which could be employed in exchange for products they were unable to produce at home or of which their local production was insufficient to meet felt needs. Their near Algonquian neighbors, the Nipissings, Ojibwas, and Ottawas, ranged over the southern parts of the Canadian Shield. Here soils were thin and poor. Bedrock was exposed at the surface over much of the country. Lakes and wild, immature streams abounded. Here, too, the broadleaf forests mixed with and were replaced by the evergreen boreal forest. Farming was a chancy, hence marginal, thing for the northerners. Either they did not attempt it at all, or they planted small ragged gardens and rejoiced when the first killing frosts were late and they were enabled to harvest anything. On the other hand, fishing was exceptional if you knew where to be at the right time, hunting in thinly occupied country could pay off handsomely for small groups, and beaver robes and other furs and skins could be garnered with relative ease. Over generations a mutually beneficial trade was established between these northern Algonquians and the Hurons (and their neighbors, the Petuns). Corn, tobacco, Indian hemp, woven fish nets, and sometimes even clay pots went north in return for dried meat and fish, skins, and furs. This trade received an enormous boost when European manufactures were injected into it. Other tribes, like the Seneca, were surrounded by tribes with the same subsistence base and following essentially the same way of life as themselves. They also engaged in trade but, understandably, it was significantly less valuable and important to them. Again, this was altered when Europeans and their goods insinuated themselves into the picture.

Another kind of intertribal involvement having economic as well as social implications was warfare. Aboriginal warfare, that is, before its transformations under European influence, was relatively small scale and, except for the unfortunates who were maimed, captured, or killed, minimally destructive. But it was endemic. As testified by the excavation of prehistoric palisaded towns, warfare involving whole communities was firmly established in the cultural patterns of Indians long before the white man contributed new technologies and additional motivations to its pursuit. Before heavy European contact Indian warfare was low-level, if persistent; it was a chronic condition of Great Lakes life.

War was fought by small parties of warriors (from 3 or 4 to perhaps 50 men, rarely more than 100) who bore a grudge against their prospective targets, usually because of a killing sometime in the past. The killing of a person required that his kinsmen receive satisfaction either in the form of a public payment or in the death of the killer or one of his kinsmen. When a killing was the deed of someone outside the tribe, blame might be so diffused by confusion that the slaughter of any member of that tribe would suffice as retribution. But this in turn placed an obligation on the new survivors to seek revenge. Like a feud between families, it was usually impossible to pinpoint other than proximate causes of the hostilities, and where original blame should be placed was lost in time and passion. And also like a feud, this kind of warfare was almost immune to rational analysis by any of the participants and it tended to be endless.

Besides being engaged in to right the wrong of an antecedent killing, war was one of the principal, and easily the most dramatic, arenas in which young men could gain prestige and the esteem of their elders. Excitable youths with their tendency to act first and think later rarely needed much persuasion to seek revenge for the loss of a kinsman or friend. In fact, older and wiser men had ample reason to complain in stereotypic terms of the difficulties in restraining the young men for the good of the community. In Great Lakes societies young men could "get ahead" by sharpening their hunting skills, by not shirking their labor responsibilities in clearing land for cultivation, in being generous and self-effacing in their intercourse with others, and in honoring the traditional values by which family and village lived. An unusual male, say one born with a deformity (if he had not been killed at birth) or with a proclivity to sense deeper and more mysterious meanings in events than others, could find his fulfillment in the arduous role of medicine-man, or shaman. But for the great majority of young men the path of the warrior was wide open, offering blandishments difficult to resist. Particularly in some societies where certain males were born into families having hereditary rights to headmanships, those not so favored saw that warfare offered a more thoroughgoing egalitarian road to the young man anxious to make a name. The admiration of one's fellows—not to mention that of young women—and the gaining of a reputation among other tribesmen rewarded the successful warrior.

With regard to the Iroquoians in particular, it appears that warfare was also involved with ideas of a partly religious nature. The taking of prisoners, for example, had high priority. If not adopted or kept for ransom, prisoners were ritually tortured to death and their bodies eaten, for it was believed that some of the decreased prisoners' admirable qualities would be absorbed by the participants. Ideally, a captive being tortured should be made to suffer as much and as long as possible and should not be allowed to die until in the full light of the rising sun. This may have had some tenuous connection through the southern United States with religious ideas more complexly developed in Mexico—or so some scholars have speculated.

Indigenous warfare in the Great Lakes was pursued to gather personal glory, to satisfy the needs of revenge, and to fulfill certain partly religious obligations. It probably also, though quite unconsciously, functioned to help space the distribution of communities with respect to natural resources and to act as a check on population where other mechanisms were also at work. Some of these included high rates of infant and maternal deaths, long lactation periods with accompanying sexual abstinence, and periodic starvation due to abnormal perturbations in natural cycles.

Before its awful transformation into naked competition for trading advantages and control of diminishing sources of fur by European-supported tribal coalitions armed with guns and iron hatchets and arrowheads, aboriginal warfare had stressed individual feats in a context of small numbers. War involved sneak raids on unsuspecting villages or it emphasized boisterous confrontations between gaudily made up and haranguing groups of warriors. Bluff and insult played a big role. Less than half a dozen people might actually be killed, for aboriginal military technology helped to limit the damage. Contemptuous as Europeans were of the fortified Indian towns, it remains a fact that they had long proved fairly effective against small groups of besiegers armed with stone-tipped spears and arrows. Some Indians even wore a primitive sort of armor made of wood slats tied together and worn on the trunk, legs, and upper arms; this was reasonable protection against all but the direct, close-up discharge of an arrow or a spear thrust. Steel-tipped arrows and guns soon rendered such armor obsolete. Finally, even under ideal conditions, the aboriginal tribes lacked the supporting manpower and subsistence reserves to field large bodies of men for extended periods. Changing these factors had to await European underwriters and new perceptions about the nature and economic possibilities of war.

Still, Stone Age warfare was lethal enough that palisaded villages were common in the Great Lakes. And although initially small scale, it was fought with a savagery to equal anything men were capable of anywhere else. Women and children were killed in addition to men. Old people and babes-in-arms were equally fair game for a war party. Every effort was made to capture enemies and bring them back alive. The ritual torture of war captives was developed to a sadistic level and intensity unparalleled elsewhere in North America and rarely approached outside the hemisphere. Cannibalism invariably followed the captive's death. To date, no one has offered a satisfactory explanation for this darker side of the Great Lakes Indian character.

The Unseen World

For Indians religion was a more diffuse, but also more pervasive, affair than was the case with Europeans. Although the Great Lakes natives had part-time religious specialists and quasi-secret organizations that took charge of directing certain ceremonies, they strongly believed that religion was a highly individualized matter and that what was proper belief and practice for one group was not necessarily the best for another. Naturally, though, the time-honored observances of one's own group were usually thought to be more reasonable than those of others. The European insistence that all other peoples must renounce their traditional practices and accept theirs was incomprehensible to Indians. Most viewed conversion as an act of politeness to the missionaries and as adding religious lore to what one already had; it was not a substitution.

Religion and the practice of medicine were so intertwined that the conventional European distinctions between the two makes no sense when applied to Indian culture. In theory and in much actual practice, the Indians of the Great Lakes did not dichotomize the world the way European did into the natural and the supernatural, or the corporeal and the incorporeal. Allowing for tribal differences in many specifics, all Great Lakes Indians had an essentially holistic concept of the nature of the universe. Man was no more foreign to the universe than were stars, rocks, lakes, trees, porcupines, or mosquitos. He was not placed above these things. Animals and plants and inanimate things such as rocks and waterfalls were not only tangible, physical entities, but at the same time they had an inner quality that was just as real as what the observer could see with his eyes, hear with his ears, or feel with his hands. And this was not idle philosophizing. Indeed, so real was this inner quality, this nonphysical essence of the thing, that the truly perceptive man, sensitized by ceremony and by individual spiritual acumen, could sometimes see it with his inner eyes, hear it with his soul's ears, and even grapple with it with incorporeal hands. Animals and plants and features of the physical world were sentient and had souls just like men. These souls interacted among themselves and with human souls; they were very much interested in what men did. Animals sometimes transformed themselves and assumed the guise of men. A powerful shaman could turn himself into an animal. The inner and outer qualities of things interacted; the process was age-old and on-going.

When a hunter killed an animal, he not only did injury to the physical world, he assaulted the spiritual. The death of an animal, or a man, ended nothing more than the phenomenal aspect of that being; its inner aspect, or soul, persisted. It followed a separate course. Because all things had their being in these two separate ways and because the one influenced the other in reciprocal fashion, hunting pitted not only body against body, but equally, soul against soul. In war the enemy you saw was only part of what you were up against. As mortal a threat, and much more difficult to cope with, was your enemy's soul. If not effectively dealt with, that soul would effect revenge.

With such a perception of the world it is hardly surprising that religious leaders and medical practitioners inevitably were the same persons. The two ways or aspects of being were not really separable. People who would effectively deal with the problems of the world must operate more or less concurrently in these two areas. The Jesuits and other missionaries could condemn or worse the shamanistic practices they saw as superstitious nonsense only because their own spiritual eyes were so ethnocentric and they were ignorant of the cultural underpinnings of the world into which they intruded themselves.

Conformably, dreams were serious matters because they were glimmerings of the inner reality. Dreams foretold the future and they provided clues to a person's illness. Supernatural forces could communicate with people as they dreamed. Souls often left people's bodies during sleep and had adventures in that other world; dreams were memories of such escapades. Indian shamans paid close attention to dreams. They realized that dreams only rarely communicated their significance directly, and that interpretation of their symbolism was required. Long before Sigmund Freud introduced Europeans to the nontriviality of dreams, Indian shamans had made the crucial distinction between manifest and latent dream content, and were working with their patients in what can only be called psychotherapy. Due to the circumstance that a majority of human illnesses are either psychosomatic or have an important psychosomatic component, the Indian shamans were vastly more effective in their ministrations than missionaries ever credited them.

As already suggested in the discussion of why the warrior's path was so attractive, individuals of unusual sensitivity or with out-of-the-ordinary personalities or a physical peculiarity (dwarfs especially) might be attracted to shamanism. The role offered socially acceptable outlets for people unable or unwilling to operate in the more mundane channels of the majority. It offered a refuge for the moody and introspective as well as the psychological virtuoso with a gift for empathy. Someone cured of a serious illness might feel that his recovery was a sign that he should somehow associate himself with the curer or even become a shaman himself. This matter of dealing with sickness, trying to see into the future, interpreting sensitive dreams, and dealing with powerful unseen forces was a potentially dangerous business and not to be undertaken lightly. As in handling electricity, naiveté ran the risk of a bad jolt. Shamans, as everybody knew, made mistakes. And the dividing line between eccentricity and witchcraft was obscure and shifting. The shaman who was a witch could be killed without fear of community reprisal.

In most Great Lakes tribes the shaman worked alone or with a few apprentices and associates. Reputations waxed and waned with successes and failures. In some tribes there were also medicine societies whose members tried to achieve collectively what solitary practitioners did in other tribes. The Midewiwin, or Grand Medicine Lodge of the Algonquians, and the Society of False Faces of the Iroquois are two of the most famous examples. The former was almost certainly a product of the post-contact, or historic, period. The False Face Society more likely had prehistoric roots. Through the cherishing and recitation in ceremony of efficacious myths, the donning of fantastic dream-inspired masks, the shaking of rattles and beating of sticks, and the communication to the patient that a concerned body of knowledgeable people were working in cooperation with unseen forces on his behalf, the society relieved much genuine suffering. Because it drew its membership from different houses, lineages, and clans, the society also functioned to tighten the bonds of social solidarity. Many people became curers because of the society's activities. Upon joining the society, they found themselves with new horizons of knowledge and responsibility and friendship. There were other curing societies as well, but none so famous as the Society of False Faces.

Although culturally highly stereotyped, the religious life of the individual man or woman had an inescapable idiosyncratic quality due to the cultural stress on one-on-one experience of supernatural power. The key to spiritual power was a direct encounter. Not all people achieved this ideal, of course. The individual vision-quest was important—and essential for aspiring shamans; it facilitated a powerful personal contact with the unseen world, and it might come in a dream or during the course of an illness. There were deities and spirits, benevolent and malevolent, whose wills might be apprehended and turned to accord with human needs. And in the world at large there was a limitless reservoir of impersonal power which sensitivity informed by wisdom might temporarily harness. Any man or woman might tap this force; success commonly manifested itself in consistently productive hunts or bountiful harvests or unusual prowess at arms or healing the sick, or simply in a remarkable run of good luck. There was little religious concern with moralistic questions of right and wrong such as seemed to preoccupy Christians. Religion in the Great Lakes was much more bound up with aiding people with a Stone Age technology to extract a full, meaningful, and satisfying life from the inner as well as outer conditions of their existence.

Society: The Proto-Ojibwa Way

The native peoples who lived on and inland from the shores of North America's unique inland seas followed ways of life so different in so many ways from that of Europeans that even long after initial introductions each had difficulty in comprehending in more than a superficial way the values and points of view of the other. The monarchies, nation-states, monetary systems, abstract philosophies, and the missionizing world religion of the Europeans were as foreign and bizarre to the Indians as was the basic nature of aboriginal society to the Europeans. The differences were so fundamental, we are still coming to an appreciation of them.

Throughout the Great Lakes the indigenous peoples lived in small-scale, relatively simply structured societies based largely on principles of kinship and with a marked emphasis on the independence of family and the individual. There was little or no hierarchical ordering of these societies.

All Great Lakes Indians lived in familistic societies. Members of a particular tribe differentially participated in a common culture, depending on their age and sex, and thus shared a basic core of habits, ways of thought, customs, etiquettes, and ideas. Appropriate to their age and sex they dressed alike, shared aesthetic perceptions, and subscribed to most of the same beliefs. They also spoke the same dialect of one language and lived in a generally recognized territory. But most importantly, tribesmen believed that they were bound together, however loosely, because, ultimately, they were kinsmen—family. In these societies a man could inevitably orient himself in an unfamiliar camp or village of his tribe because it was always possible to find someone with whom there were connections established by marriage or descent from a shared ancestor. Through such a connection a stranger could then socially align himself with more remotely related persons. The networks of kinship in these societies were incredibly intricate and wide, so wide in fact that the stranger who could not be tied into the networks, however tenuously, must be a potential enemy.

Probably the smallest and most simply organized Great Lakes societies

---

MAP 1.2. *The "Joliet Map of 1674." Although long attributed to Louis Joliet, famed explorer and* maître d'hydrographie *in Canada, this may instead be the product of a copier (Tucker 1942, Plate IV). This is a reproduction from the photographic copy in the Illinois State Museum; the original map is in the collections of the John Carter Brown Library, Brown University. (Courtesy Illinois State Museum and John Carter Brown Library, Brown University.)*

Nouvelle Decouverte de Plusieurs Nations Dans la Nouuelle France

MER GLACIALE

BA...

Les sauuages habitans de l'Isle

Lac Sup...

LA

LA FRONTENACIE

Riviere de la Siene ou Pointcine

A Monseigneur
Le Comte de Frontenac Conseiller en ses conseils Gouuerneur et lieutenant General pour sa ma.té en Canada Acadie Isle de Terreneue et autres pays de la nouuelle France

Monseigneur

[body of dedication letter — illegible manuscript cursive]

Monseigneur

...vostre tres humble et tres obeissant seruiteur

Jolliet

Mer Vermeille ou est La Californie par ou on peut aller au Perou au Japon et a la Chine

Le Mexique

La Nouuelle Grenade

LE SEIN DE M...

1673 & 1674

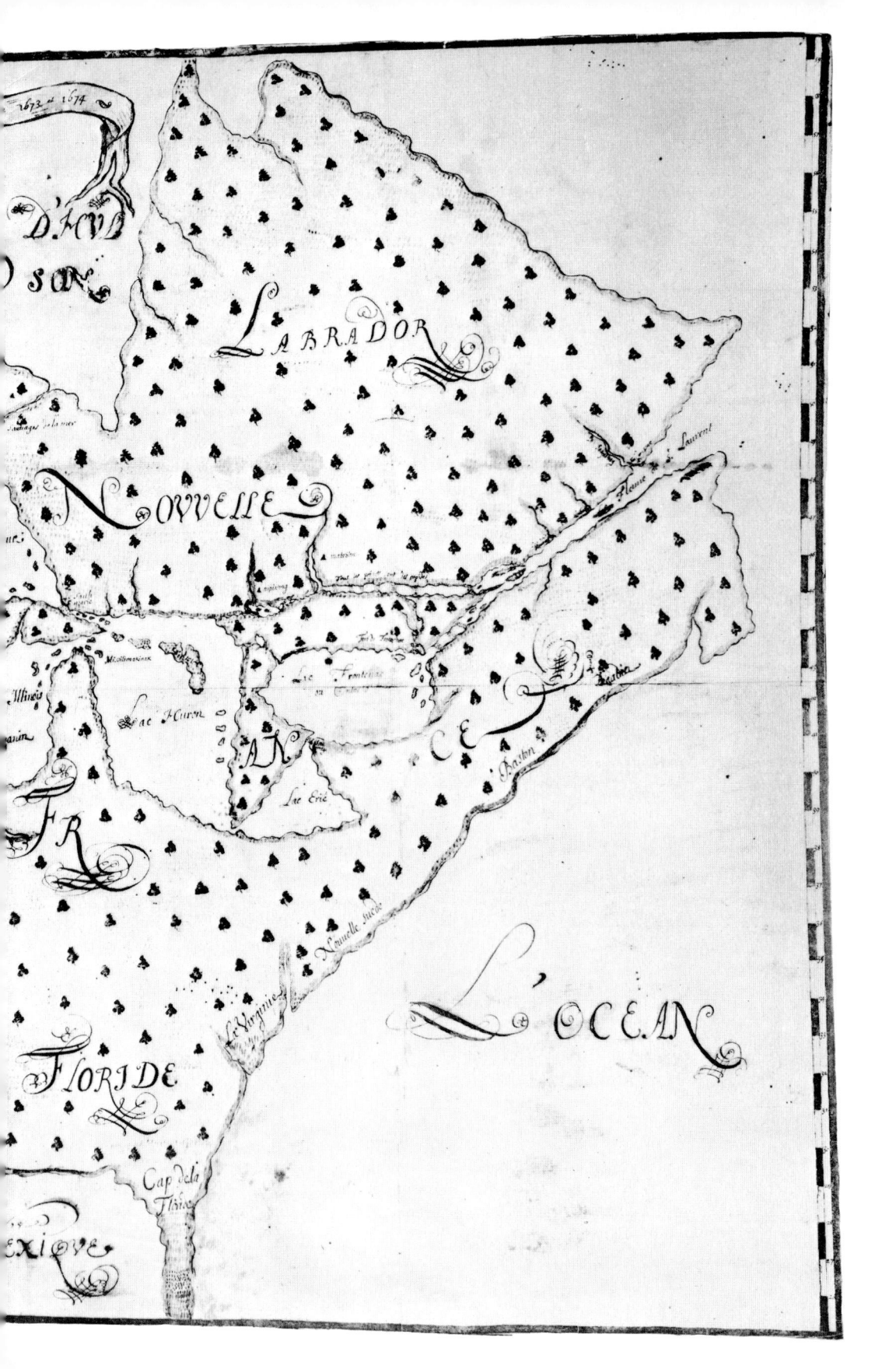

D'HVD
)SON

LABRADOR

NOUVELLE

Laurent
Fleuve

Mistassins
Anglois
Fort de Nos. de la paix
Lac Frontenac
ou Ontario
Boston

Mississakioux
Lac Huron
Illinois
Lac Erié
FRAN CE
Boston

Nouvelle Suede
La Virginie

L'OCEAN

FLORIDE

Cap de la
Floride

MEXIQVE

were those of the original northern Algonquians. Unfortunately, those societies underwent rapid and significant changes before anyone could record much about them in their pristine condition. Reconstruction is tricky; it must be pieced together with scraps of information from historical sources guided by anthropological theory and what is known of other societies in similar environments and with comparable population levels and technologies.

It was certainly the case among the proto-Ojibwas, Ottawas, Nipissings, and similar people that almost all tasks and problems were traditionally met and handled by local coalitions of closely related families. Typically, these families seem to have consisted of a residential core of kinsmen who shared a "blood" relationship (and hence had rights to the inheritance of family names, traditions, kinship support, perhaps some preferential access to certain hunting lands, and so on) and others who had entered the family by marriage. Kinship was recognized through both father and mother, although with a decided male bias. Among the proto-Ojibwas, for instance, each local geographic society was a community of people who were related among themselves because each person had either been born into the group or married into it. Members could also be adopted. Of course, kinship ties were recognized with the outside groups from which spouses had been recruited. It seems likely that males remained in their

PLATE 1.2. *Western Algonquian pottery of the Blackduck style common in northern Minnesota, northwestern Wisconsin, and western Ontario. These examples, shown half actual size, are from Ontario. (Courtesy Peter L. Storck and the Royal Ontario Museum, Toronto, Canada.)*

natal group throughout their lives while women usually moved out of theirs upon marriage and went to live with their husbands. This tendency to *patrilineal* inheritance reckoning and *patrilocal* selection of residence made a great deal of sense among these northern hunting people. These practices served to keep the men who were vital to the local community as hunters and warriors in the community and thus to preserve the male cooperative enterprises which fed and defended it.

The bonds of kinship cemented social relations and established beyond reasonable question people's rights and reciprocal obligations. Within these small societies, such as the Amikwas, Missisaugas, Ouasouarinis, Nopemings, and the other proto-Ojibwa tribes mentioned earlier (often named after an animal), all except outside visitors were in some important sense "family." It seems that these groups normally produced all of the food, goods, and services they required and that they consumed most of what they produced. There appear to have been no internal markets through which things circulated, and thus no buyers or sellers. From what has been learned of these and comparable societies elsewhere, there is every reason to believe that goods and services were freely exchanged in the form of gifts, that gift-giving was continuous and stimulated by reciprocity, and that decent behavior was ensured through the unrelenting pressure of public opinion. In keeping with both a pre-market economy and a wide interpretation of kinship, generosity was a vital ideal; its realization in actual behavior was of such common occurrence and magnitude as to amaze Europeans.

Headmen in proto-Ojibwa and other northern Algonquian tribes were pretty ephemeral: outstanding personalities called into temporary prominence more by circumstance than any authority of office. Headmen were often great hunters or respected elders who were able to persuade other people to their point of view. Although it is far from clear, it does seem that some family lines had stronger "rights" to put forward headman candidates than did others. However that may be, a "chief" or headman was only as effective as the consensus of the group would permit. All people were regarded as essentially equal when it came to the matter of governing, the main distinctions among people being based on age, sex, and individual ability and temperament. Everybody seems to have recognized that, although all were equal socially and not to be put upon by others, some men were simply superior hunters or warriors compared with other men; some women for reasons no one could explain conducted themselves in all they did in such a way as to excite the admiration and respect of all who knew them, and there were those women who could not make a clay pot without its cracking. The mystery of personality made some men reassuring, attractive, even inspiring to others, while most men were of the type who never seek a leadership role and who reject it if offered. A headman carried responsibility easily and he had an authority that was more personal than official. A headman often seems to have been one who in times of stress could get others to let him act for the collectivity. Without a free consensus there could be no headman.

Notwithstanding the extraordinary emphasis Great Lakes Indians placed on the autonomy of the local residence units and the freedom of the individual, these tribes were far removed from the primitive societies romantic proponents of "self-realization" have written about. Individuals were indeed remarkably free from the arbitrary imposition of another's wishes. Even the greatest headman could not issue a command to anyone; if he had tried he would have been pointedly ignored, if not laughed at; if he persisted in authoritarian directions, people would repudiate him. The individual was permitted to do as he wished when he wished—provided that he did not violate traditional values and that he observed and participated in the customary rules of mutual support and reciprocal obligations due his kinsmen. Despite the fact that adults were not subject to the orders of a superior, and children were almost never subjected to corporal punishment (much to the disgust of missionaries), these were all "tight" little societies where everyone had to conform to group expectations or suffer the consequences. Children were expected to respect their elders, wives were subordinate to their husbands. The power of public opinion, while invisible and usually subtle, was pervasive and inescapable in such restricted face-to-face groups. People who followed their own idiosyncratic inclinations too far risked gossip and the sting of ridicule. It took an unusual personality to persist in behavior his kinsmen disapproved of or found ridiculous. Those whose deviance from customary norms came to be judged particularly offensive or detrimental to the general good faced shunning or physical exile; they could even be killed. Since there could be no human life outside of society, shunning and exile were tantamount to a sentence of death. People who were actually killed were usually those suspected of witchcraft and who had so alienated their kinsmen that their murder would not provoke outcry and trigger a feud. Such killings were rare and would not be attempted without the tacit support of the rest of the community.

Society: A Potawatomi Model

More socially complex than the Ojibwas, Ottawas, and other northern Algonquians were the hunter–farmers of the lower peninsula of Michigan, northern Ohio, Indiana, Illinois, and eastern Wisconsin. The Potawatomis, for instance, at the time of our first glimmerings of them in the early seventeenth century, were probably not as conspicuously divided as their northern neighbors. Whereas the latter were composed of a number of vaguely related, territorially distinct, autonomous little tribes or bands, the Potawatomis were not only more sedentary but were probably close to constituting a more unified, if still loose, tribal structure. This was made up of several relatively permanent villages which, besides sharing a common language and culture, shared kinsmen through cross-cutting and interlocking clan organizations.

In their original homeland somewhere in the central and western part of the lower Michigan peninsula, the early historic Potawatomis lived in a number of large semipermanent villages of dome-shaped, bark or mat-covered wigwams, frequently surrounded for protection by log stockades. Settlements were sometimes deliberately located along natural boundary areas where forest and prairie met in order to take advantage of the resources of both environments. These towns were largest and had their most numerous occupants during the summer months except during an expedition onto the prairies for the communal hunting of buffalo; their residents tended to divide into dispersed smaller villages and camps for the winter hunting.

The residential core of a Potawatomi village was a group of male kinsmen who shared a number of generations of fathers and, ultimately, a primal "father" from whom all the succeeding generations had sprung. Individual adult men with their wives maintained their own separate wigwams into which the children were born. Oftentimes, however, a number of such households of brothers lived in a household cluster associated with the house of the brothers' father or fathers. Because, for the Potawatomis, the term *father* also applied to the men we would describe as father's brothers (paternal uncles) and the husbands of mother's sisters, such a patrilocal household cluster could easily include several dozens of people. Residing with the men, of course, would be their wives, unmarried sisters, and young children. Equally "mother" to any child of such an extended family were all of mother's sisters as well as the wives of father's brothers. By definition, orphans were rare in such societies.

The logic of kinship by which the descending generations of such an extended family were tied together was based on the father–son succession. This kind of inheritance of social identification was thus patrilineal and constituted a type of lineage. In a sense, the lineage expressed the kinship logic by which fathers, sons, brothers, and sisters identified themselves in the social networks of Potawatomi society. The lineage was constantly changing in its passage of the generations, adding new personnel as babies came along, and gradually sloughing off the old with death and, inevitably, faltering social memory. But in the lifetime of any individual the permanent rather than the transitory aspect of lineage was normally paramount. Deaths hurt, but the lineage went on; it was the family's immortality.

A person was born into a lineage and remained a part of it throughout his or her life. Even though a woman upon marrying normally went to live in the household of her husband and any of his kin with whom he happened to reside, she never relinquished her membership in the lineage into which she had been born; she physically left her natal household but she brought with her into her new home the prestige and protection of her patrilineage. Like any man, the Potawatomi woman retained perpetual rights in the lineage that had given her birth: The other members of her

PLATE 1.3. *Reconstructed early historic or protohistoric Potawatomi vessel from Rock Island Site II, Door County, Wisconsin (shown half actual size). (Collections of Department of Anthropology, Lawrence University, Appleton, Wisconsin.)*

lineage were no less her blood kinsmen than they were her brothers', and she always had a moral claim on them for help and support in time of need. Would-be exploiters of a new woman in the patrilocal household had to reckon with the fact that her natal kinsmen took a strong family interest in her proper treatment at the hands of her new householders (who had become new relatives to her kinsmen).

Just as a number of families were related by remembered patrilineal descent and constituted lineages traceable back to an honored male ancestor several generations removed, so the Potawatomi lineages recognized themselves to be constituents of even larger, though more amorphous, "superfamilies." These were the clans. Like the lineages, clans proscribed internal marriage; they were exogamous and their members had to find spouses in clans other than their own. Unlike lineages, the patrilineal linkages among families and over generations were assumed by custom rather than demonstrated by geneology. The clans were named, usually after animals. Although a special relationship might exist with the animal of the clan's name, members of the clan did not necessarily believe that they were in fact descended from that animal and they were not prohibited from killing and eating it. While none of the clan names are unambiguously preserved from the time of the Europeans' first encounter with Potawatomis, after the tribe's migration to Wisconsin in the mid-seventeenth century they had such names as Sturgeon, Rabbit, Turtle, Bear, Wolf, and Beaver. Also unlike lineages, which had some tendency to be localized in particular villages, clans cut across settlement boundaries and claimed members throughout the Potawatomi domain. Because a member of, say, the Rabbit clan, could expect to find some Rabbit clansmen in a village he had never visited before, the clan system was a powerful and pervasive influence making for tribal unity.

Extended family, lineage, and clan provided the individual Potawatomi and his immediate family with social identity. And beyond a much more dilute sense of Potawatomi tribalism, nothing more was needed until their subjugation to foreign interests. The patrilineal bonds of descent so expressed tied each person to a great family tradition. They inexorably linked him with by-gone generations as well as with the succeeding. Symbols of this social-aligning function of lineage and clan were the rights and obligations of kinsmen, the inheritance rights to personal names, and access to supernatural power through community visions, ritual practices, and sacred paraphernalia. While pots, bows and arrows, harpoons, wigwam covers, canoes, and so on, were typically owned by individuals or their nuclear or extended families, common lineage or clan membership made these things more directly and freely available than would usually be the case with more distantly related people. The individual was never alone, even in a strange Potawatomi village; always with him was the mystique of family.

The Potawatomis were not ignorant of ties to their mother's kinfolk. Indeed, they recognized close affinities with their mothers and their families by acknowledging a special relationship with mother's father. This dual lineage system of primary affiliation through father and secondary affiliation to another group of kinsmen through mother's father gave the individual Potawatomi access to the friendship, cooperation, and support of a great many people. Because the Potawatomis were heavily engaged in farming (women's work once the land was cleared) as well as hunting, trading, and warfare (men's responsibilities) this was important for further guaranteeing the availability and perpetuation of relatively large men's and women's work groups.

Potawatomi tribal structure grew stronger and more cohesive after the middle of the seventeenth century and their migration to northeastern Wisconsin. Here the Potawatomis quickly established themselves as one of the dominant tribes of the western Great Lakes. In their new setting, enriched by growing access to trade goods, they elaborated their culture through a unique fusion of native and European ideas and technologies. They soon enjoyed enormous success in their trading and military ventures and for a time came to occupy an immense territory in Wisconsin, Illinois, Indiana, and Michigan. It was probably in these expansionist times that the Potawatomis adopted the Midewiwin, or Grand Medicine, Society. This great medical–religious organization, by recruiting a membership without regard to residence or clan affiliations, was an effective device fostering an increased sense of tribal unity. For example, it was one of the principal means whereby the Ojibwas evolved an integrated tribal structure out of the multiple ethnicities of the proto-Ojibwas. There are good reasons for believing that the Midewiwin Society was in large part a development of forces put into motion by European contact and tribal dislocations; it is very doubtful that anything very like it existed in prehistoric times.

Society: Iroquoian Themes

In the early historic period the Iroquoian-speakers seem to have had the most complexly developed societies of any of the Great Lakes peoples. Their networks of kinship reckoning were at least as complicated as those of any Algonquian or Siouan groups, and they were further extended in nascent political forms unusual elsewhere. The Iroquoians nurtured inter-tribal confederations of an effectiveness and permanence not seen anywhere else in the Great Lakes.

It was Iroquoians who pushed native agriculture to its limit. In their world hunting, fishing, and gathering were strictly secondary in rounding out subsistence. Population levels and densities anywhere in the lake country probably never exceeded those of the Iroquois, Hurons, Neutrals, and other Iroquoians except spasmodically at such uniquely rich and mainly single resource cornucopias as the fisheries of the St. Marys River at Sault Ste. Marie. But the Iroquoians were far more sedentary, more territorially rooted and bounded. While infamously difficult to verify, the best-documented population estimates for some of the Iroquoian peoples include: about 12,000 for the Neutrals, between 2000 and 4000 for the Petuns, 18,000–21,000 for the Hurons, and perhaps 20,000 for the Iroquois. These figures are believed to approximate the population levels of these tribes or confederacies shortly before the decimating effects of introduced European diseases to which the Indians had had no prior exposure and thus little or no natural immunity. They may well be far off the mark, but they are the best we will probably ever get.

The Iroquoians were more fully committed to the land-binding ways of the farmer, whose overriding allegiance can no longer be that of the age-old harvesters of the uncultivated wilderness. They were putting labor into the land in new and uniquely intensive ways; they had come to place their main reliance on converting the ancient forest and glens into gardens. Red meat came from deer, mainly, but also from bears and smaller animals—including, not unimportantly, dogs—and it seems to have come in rather modest quantities, considering the demand. While the broadleaf forests of the Iroquoian country were richer in game than the evergreen forests of the northern Algonquians, human populations were also denser and appear to have brought about game depletion in areas surrounding the larger settlements. Communal deer drives involving the construction of miles of converging brush lines that led into a trap or corral sometimes brought in small mountains of welcome meat. But most times meat seems to have been much less available than people would have liked. It was a high-prestige food provided by the men, and they probably ate more of it than did the women and children. But it was the "three sisters"—corn, beans, and squash—that were the real "meat and potatoes" of the Iroquoian way of life. It has been estimated that these domesticated plants provided up to 80% of the food of the Senecas and the Hurons.

The very heavy reliance on farming was predictably reflected in many aspects of Iroquoian culture. Most anthropologists believe they see its influence in social organization itself, in the details of division of labor by sex, and in the way Iroquoians conducted themselves in many of their activities.

Farming was of the variety called "swidden horticulture"; except for its magnitude and per capita importance, it was essentially like that practiced elsewhere in aboriginal eastern North America. Clearing forest lands for cultivation was hard and exhausting work where the efficiency deficit of stone versus steel axes had to be made up for in muscle. Work parties of a village's able-bodied men did this labor. Smaller trees and brush were cut down and piled up for burning. Large trees, especially where the land had never been cultivated before (as in climax forest), were girdled by prying away the bark near the base; these trees, left to die and then dry, were later burned when the new land was put to the torch. But many of the largest trees were simply left standing and little attempt was made to remove any but the more rotten stumps. Because of the magnitude of this kind of work

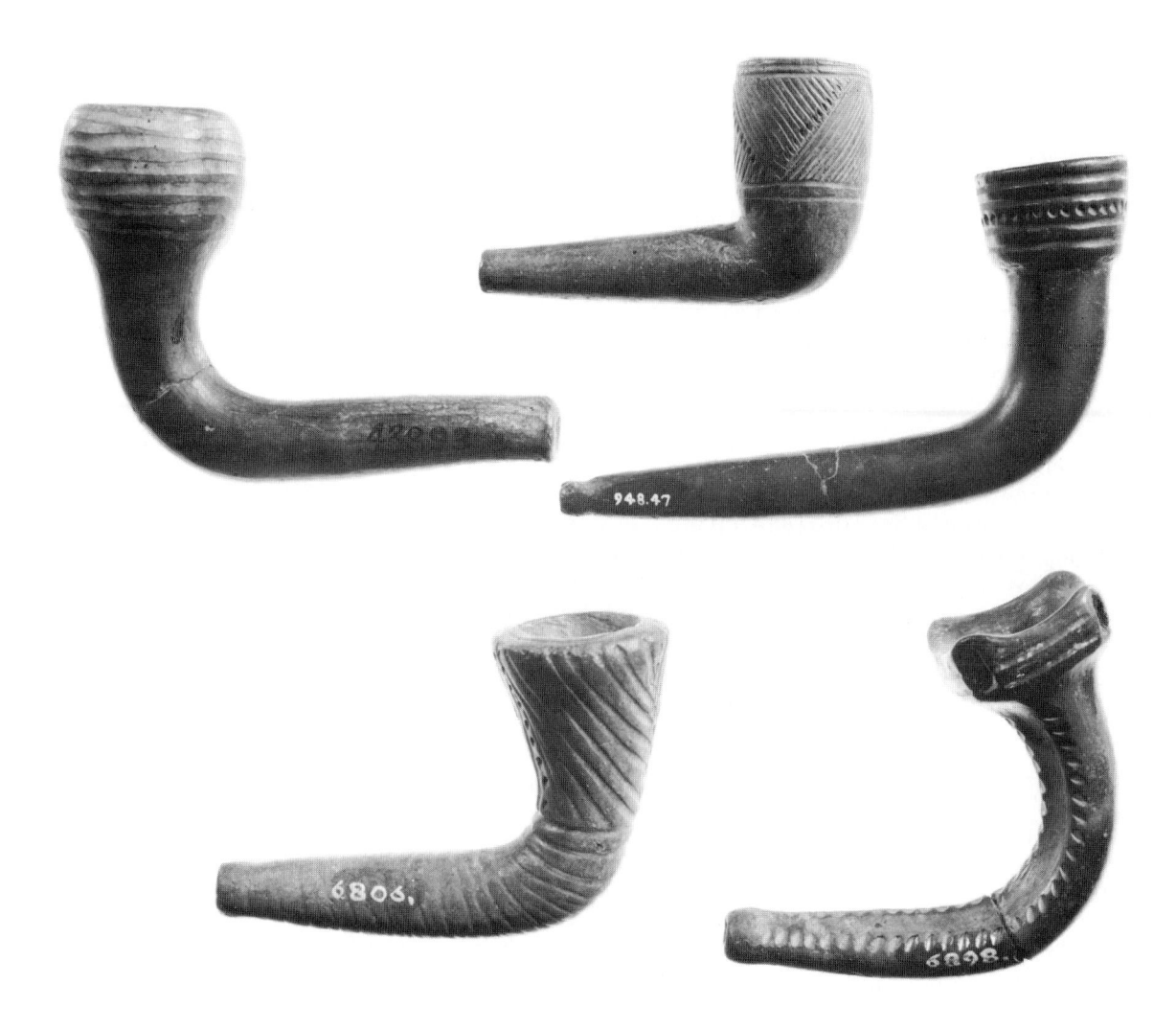

PLATE 1.4. *Iroquoian-style clay smoking pipes from Ontario (shown two-thirds actual size). (Courtesy Peter L. Storck and the Royal Ontario Museum, Toronto, Canada.)*

and the fact that green wood required some time to dry out before efficient firing could be relied upon, community leaders tried to have new lands cleared ahead of immediate need. Inasmuch as soil exhaustion usually occured within little more than a decade, if not sooner, some new land clearing was perpetually underway. The wholesale removal of a village was necessary when suitable areas for cultivation had been exhausted. The old fields were then allowed to revert to a wild state and to regain their fertility by natural means. Great Lakes Indians never fertilized their gardens beyond the incidental addition of ashes from the land-clearing fires. Popular mythology notwithstanding, the New England Algonquians who aided the Pilgrims probably did not fertilize either. Even after several decades such abandoned fields were easy to recognize and far easier to clear than primary mature forest. Such formerly opened-up tracts yielded another harvest in that they tended to attract greater than usual numbers of deer.

The planting and subsequent tending and harvesting of the crops was done by the women working singly or in groups. Among the Hurons the actual farming seems to have been carried out by many small groups of women, each tending individual family plots. Mothers and daughters and sisters formed informal work groups and, talking and laughing, did things together whenever possible. The New York Iroquois appear to have been a little more formal in their arrangements. Garden plots at least seem to have been more conspicuously identified with particular lineages. These tracts were communally tended by the women residents of the longhouse or longhouses associated with the lineage. Children, especially girls, helped in the fields at such chores as weeding and chasing away birds, squirrels, rabbits, and other garden pests.

Corn, beans, squashes, and sunflowers were grown on low ridges or groups of mounds made by scraping up the surrounding soil with digging sticks and hoes equipped with wood, bone, or shell blades. Such light instruments precluded extensive tilling of heavy soils, so the gardens were usually situated in sandy loams if possible. The seeds were dropped in holes punched in the little mounds and ridges with a dibble, or digging stick. Even though their tops were only a few inches to a couple of feet higher than the hollows and furrows between them, these slight elevations helped to protect the plants from the earliest frosts by providing intervening traps for cold, low-lying air. Some idea of the scale of all of this work may be gained from the fact that Iroquoian villages usually had from a few hundred to as many as a few thousand people residing in them. The most recent studies of soil conditions and the nature of aboriginal horticulture among the early historic-period Hurons suggest that a village of a thousand inhabitants would have had to have access to approximately 145 ha (360 acres) of cleared land.

Except for the heavy labor of land-clearing operations which, as we have just seen, was the task of men, the cultivation of domesticated crops—and thus supplying of the major part of the Iroquoian diet—was the responsibility of women. Fishing was at least as important as hunting, and in some places much more so, in augmenting the food supply and in introducing animal fats and proteins. These activities necessarily took men away from their villages for frequent and extended periods of time. The other major men's affairs, warfare and trading, also took them away from home and brought them into contact with alien people and unfamiliar customs. Because sexual division of labor was exclusive in most things the Great Lakes Indians did and because the principal roles of women (child rearing, house tending, pottery making, farming) were by their nature more locally and inwardly directed than those of the men, women in Iroquoian societies were more immediately involved on a continuing day-to-day basis in household and internal village affairs. It was women who most consistently provided continuity and stability in representing, preserving, and extending family interests, whereas men tended to concerns of a more intervillage, tribal, and even intertribal character. Women accordingly were normally more conservative than men in Iroquoian society. Repeatedly, the opinions and actions of the women validated their more central roles as conservators and exemplars of family life.

The primary family of husband, wife, and children although in theory the minimal family unit, was in actuality so thoroughly integrated with other groups of its kind into the multifamily longhouse and multigeneration lineage that an independent existence was virtually precluded. As already described, the Iroquoian longhouse was a localized extended-family domicile built around a core of closely related females. While bilaterality in kinship was recognized with duties and responsibilities owed kinsmen through fathers as well as mothers, it was the maternal side which expressed its paramountcy in principles of descent and in preferential residence arrangements.

The lineages were *matrilineal,* and the affairs of the longhouse were run by the women of child-bearing age and the senior matrons. At marriage, a man customarily left his natal household and moved into that of his wife and her female blood relatives. Even though he never relinquished his membership in his (his mother's) lineage, he was from now on expected to morally and materially support the household into which his marriage had brought him. Signification of the continuing and indissoluble tie with his own matrilineage was a man's special obligation to contribute food to his sisters and to take formal interest in the raising and training of his sisters' sons. As may be imagined, this sometimes amounted to a kind of social schizophrenia for some of the men involved. But it also was a powerfully integrative social mechanism that effectively served to suppress other than trivial quarrels between longhouses and lineages linked by marital ties.

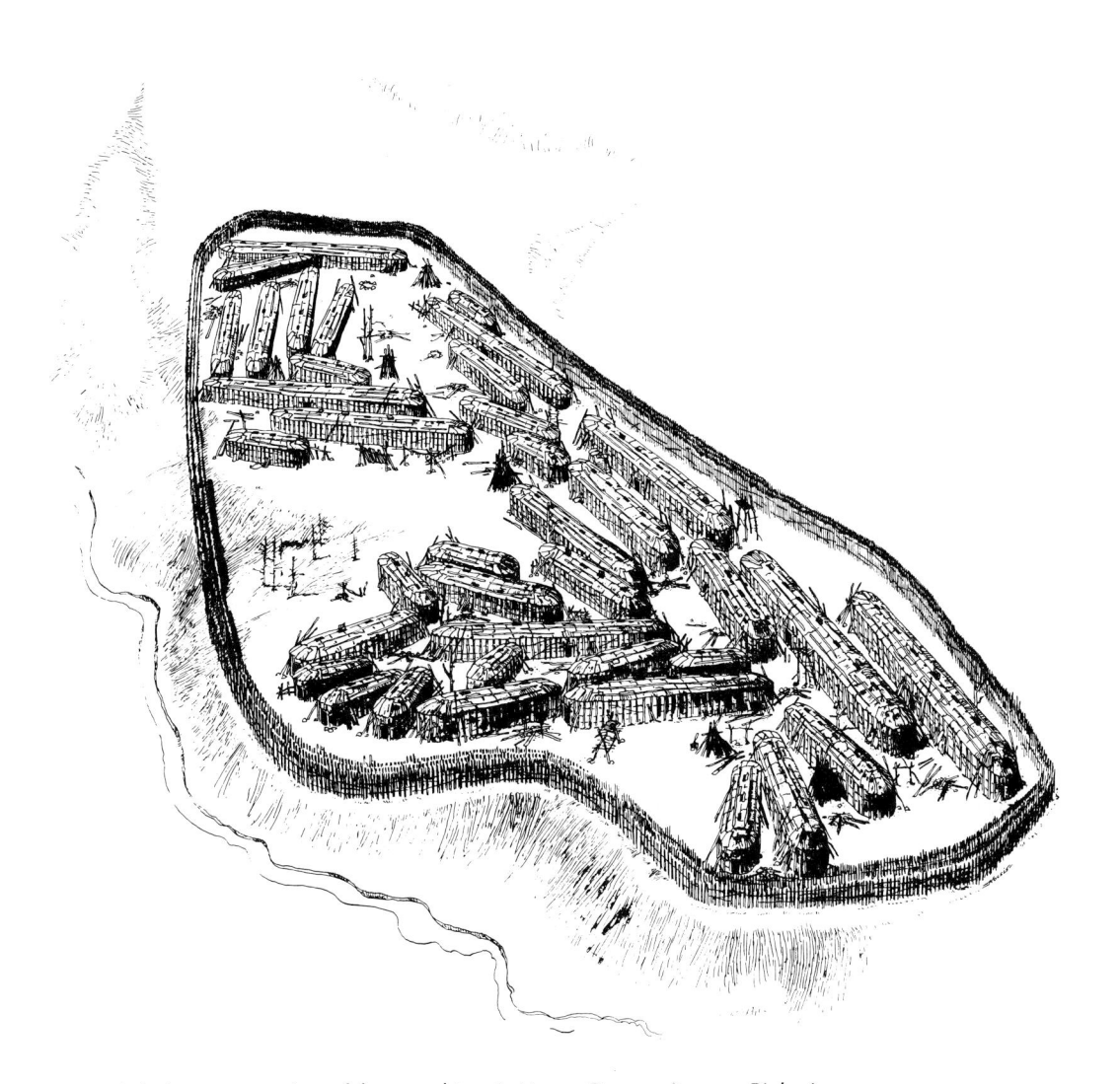

PLATE 1.5. *Artist's reconstruction of the protohistoric Huron Draper site near Pickering, Ontario (Ivan Kocsis, artist). The site plan of this community is reproduced as Plate 9.1. (Courtesy William D. Finlayson and the Museum of Indian Archaeology, University of Western Ontario, London.)*

Within a particular Iroquoian village the lineages were grouped into the larger and more amorphous entities that anthropologists call clans. Like the Potawatomi clans already described, the Iroquoian analogs gathered in kinsmen on the assumption, rather than the actual genealogical tracing, of kinship. The common ancestor at the apex of the generational pyramid was likewise mythological, though no less sociologically real because of that.

While clansmen tended to live near each other in a village, they lacked the tangible residential expression of the longhouse and lineage. They were exogamous, and because they had "local chapters" in more than one village, the clans made the tribe more strongly knit.

The number of clans varied from tribe to tribe, and certainly also over time. While the Mohawks, for example, had only three clans, the Seneca had eight. The Hurons likewise had eight clans; they were named Deer, Bear, Beaver, Porcupine, Wolf, Snake, Turtle, and Hawk. Among some of the Iroquoian peoples all of the clans were in turn grouped into two grand tribal divisions (moieties) or into three or more such maximal units (phratries). The Huron clans appear to have been divided among three phratries. The exact nature and the functions of these superclan groupings are very imprecisely understood, and they virtually disappeared following initial European contacts. They do seem to have operated in the conducting of reciprocal ceremonies and games.

Iroquoian clans operated essentially like those of the other Great Lakes tribes, except that they were matrilineal: as great family associations or sororities offering and demanding mutual aid and support to all clansmen and as regulators of marriage. They also provided the basis for government. Thus, typically, within each village, each clan had two chiefs or headmen. These were a civil, or "peace," chief and a war chief. The former was responsible for overseeing the organization of condolence ceremonies for other clans, adjudicating arguments among clansmen, and trade and friendly relations with foreign tribes. The civil chief, at least, was selected by consensus from a particular lineage having hereditary rights to the position. Inheritance of chiefly titles remained within the lineage and, characteristically, passed from brother to brother or uncle to sister's son and never from father to son. Many lineages had no rights to the clan chieftainship. For the men of such lineages, war typically offered the way to the high achieved status of a leader, as the "pine tree" chiefs of the Iroquois. Those men who succeeded to the lineage inheritance of a clan chieftainship ("sachems" among the Iroquois) not only had to be born into that lineage, they had to demonstrate the abilities and personality people would respect. Great prowess as a hunter, generosity, a gift for oratory, and a facility for making people willing to follow their advice were all prerequisites of a chief. Once a chief, a man led by example and was sustained by the power of public opinion. However, the women, invariably influenced by the opinions and desires of their husbands and especially their brothers could recall an unsatisfactory sachem and replace him.

Clan chiefs and male lineage spokesmen formed a village council. It seems that in some communities one of the clans enjoyed traditional seniority over the other clans. The chief of such a "senior" clan acted also in the capacity of village chief. Meetings were held in his house; he usually presided over trading matters affecting the village as a whole; and he represented his people before foreign emissaries. But certainly a prime function of the village chief, perhaps more often assumed than made explicit, was to act as a model for the conduct of all. He was expected to ensure that peace and cooperation continued uninterrupted among the kin and residence constituents of the community. Interestingly, there is ethnohistoric evidence to show that chiefs inheriting office were one of the exceptions to the general ideal of matrilocal residence. Some chiefs, it seems, brought their wives to live with them in their house or in that of their mother's brother.

At a higher level, though in a basically similar fashion, the clan and village chiefs from each community met as a tribal council to maintain peace among the villages and to discuss and decide issues affecting them all. The tribal council never interjected itself except cautiously and indirectly into matters intrinsically internal to a particular village or clan or lineage. Internal autonomy, "home rule," was jealously maintained. In most cases there does not seem to have been a clearcut paramount or tribal chief such as characterized many of the tribes of the southeastern United States. Rather, great men rose to positions of persuasive paramountcy within the tribal council, and by public support and by success in their undertakings they filled a role rather than a continuing office. Here again, however, options were effectively narrowed by traditional deference to senior lineages and clans having time-honored rights to a special hearing. But the rights of even the least honored could not be trampled on in meetings of the tribal council. All matters brought to the council had to be decided unanimously or not at all. No man, regardless of his status, could impose his will on another. Of course, there were often ferocious pressures for people holding minority opinions to yield to the weight of the prevailing view. Even the largest Iroquoian tribes were pretty small scale, and public opinion in such relatively homogeneous contexts was a benign despot.

Finally, most Iroquoian tribes were in turn voluntarily affiliated with others in a confederation. Many Algonquian tribes also formed confederacies, but none of them in the Great Lakes country approached the size, stability, and effectiveness of such Iroquoian models as the Huron confederacy or the famous League of the Iroquois. In effect, the confederacies did for the affiliated tribes what the tribal councils did for their constituent villages: They operated primarily to subdue blood feuds and to ensure peace among their members. In times of unusual stress and atypical agreement in emotionally laden issues, such confederacies might even present a united front to a common enemy. Through coordination they could wield a power greater than any of the tribes acting alone could hope to muster. Such occasions were exceedingly rare. Most of the time the confederacy councils had their hands full trying to preserve some degree of peace among their constituents while the individual tribes pursued their own foreign policies largely independently. These were fragile, immature

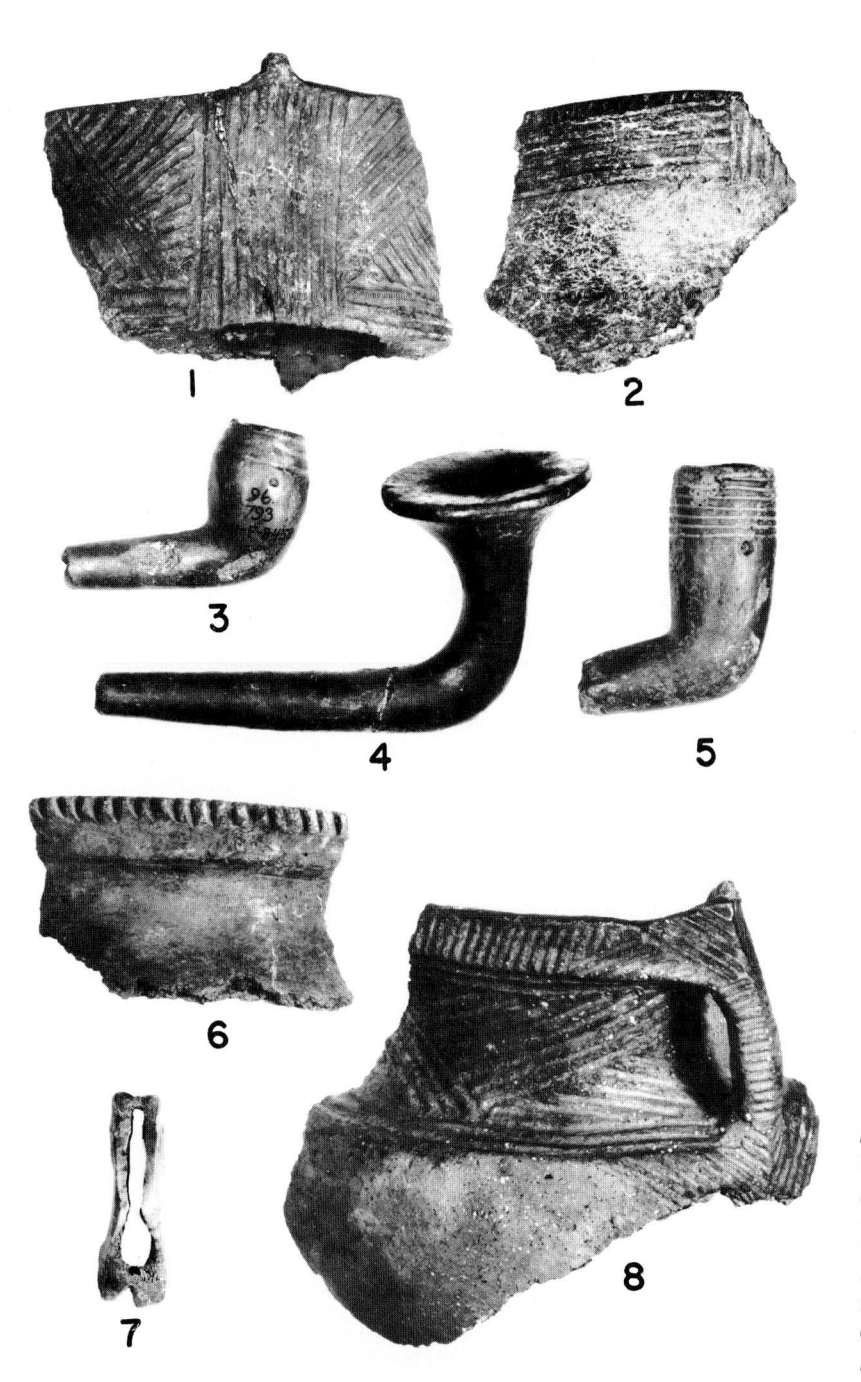

PLATE 1.6. Late prehistoric or protohistoric Huron artifacts from sites in southern Ontario: pottery (1, 2, 6, 8); clay smoking pipes (3–5); and a toggle of worked deer toe bone (7). (Courtesy James V. Wright and the Archaeological Survey of Canada, National Museum of Man, Ottawa.)

coalitions, and no one knows if they were born in prehistory or were children of cultural miscegenation. Given the abundant evidence of prehistoric warfare, it would not be surprising that some of the Indian confederacies were truly indigenous, their further development having been stimulated by the special circumstances of the European discovery of the New World.

Meetings of confederacy councils were held at least annually and were run on the principle of unlimited debate until decisions became unanimous. This effectively checked the potential exploitation of member tribes with relatively small representations in the confederacy councils by tribes with larger delegations. The need to reach unanimity also protected the less from the more prestigious. Just as there were senior and more honored clans within a tribe, so not all tribes even in a freely constituted confederation were socially fully equal. The Attignawantan was the commonly regarded "senior" tribe in the Huron confederacy, as well as the biggest. In council meetings which were usually held in the longhouse of the senior chief of the Attignawantans, the representatives of that tribe sat along one side of the longhouse looking across the fires at the delegates from the other three tribes. Size, however, had no necessary correlation with prestige or seniority. The "senior" member of the League of the Iroquois was the Onondaga, one of the smaller tribes in the confederacy. The idea of seniority was rationalized by appeals to the great oral traditions by means of which the past was recalled and put at the service of present need. Presumably, the Attignawantans and Onondagas were the first, or the most prestigious among the first, to join their respective confederacies.

Confederacy council meetings were public occasions. Intense interest focused on issues to be discussed and on the personalities and reputations of the delegates who traditionally numbered 50 in both the Iroquois and Huron confederacies. A highly stylized language of diplomacy was used in the meetings; skill and elegance in handling ideas and language were much admired; and good humor and tolerance of opposing views expected of all. Inasmuch as numerous relatives and friends often accompanied the delegates to the village where the council was being held, usually the principal town of the Onondagas for the Iroquois, the meetings were also occasions for the lower level intercourse of gossip, seeing new people, and exchanging gifts among old friends and distant kinsmen. Under the scrutiny of so many interested observers—not to mention commentators, for every individual had his own opinion and thought highly of it—the confederacy representatives were under considerable pressure to conduct themselves so as to bring credit to their efforts and to the people for whom they spoke. The emphasis on effective public speech, particularly in a society lacking writing and utterly dependent on oral replication of important points on which earlier councils had turned, makes the early and often repeated European comments on the poise and eloquence of many Indian leaders more understandable. They not infrequently outshone the French and British diplomats sent by those royal courts to negotiate with them.

Tribal Grandparents: Into Prehistory

Interpretive and selective, the foregoing sketches of Indian life in the Great Lakes have been drawn as closely as possible to what the state of indigenous culture and society are believed to have been like in the early days just past the threshold of history. As for the last moments of prehistory, a detailed portrayal remains a goal and not an accomplishment. Deliberately, material culture has been underrepresented in the foregoing descriptions because it will be picked up and closely examined in most of the following chapters.

It is a truism that societies in general have some sensitivity to changes in their environments. We have seen that Great Lakes societies were already in the process of adjusting themselves to the indirect influence of Europe before most actual first encounters. This is not meant to imply that Indian societies before the European discovery were somehow fixed or unchanging. Even a cursory glance at the archaeological record will dispel that notion. The importance of the coming of Europeans, for our interests, lies not in that their coming caused changes in aboriginal institutions (these were always changing anyway, if not so quickly and fundamentally), but that it has proved so difficult to distinguish those social alterations uniquely attributable to European presence from those precipitated out of the internal workings of the indigenous societies themselves. This perplexing question is in one way or another at the heart of the old and still current controversies in history and the social sciences concerning the relative importance of autochthonous innovation and cultural evolution, diffusion as prime mover in social and cultural change, trajectories of cultural change, adaptation, destiny, and so on.

But the main purpose of this chapter has been simply to provide at least a glimpse of the richness and complexity of the human drama of Great Lakes Indian life as close as possible to the already retreating horizon of prehistory. When the pages of the very earliest historical accounts are read and closed and we pick up shovel and trowel, screening tables and cameras, and step back into prehistory, it is like entering a vast, gray vault darkening before us and listening to the diminishing echoes of a great door closed upon our heels. It is exciting and a little scary. Now, suddenly, the noise of actually seen and recorded people is gone, and the vault is silent as a tomb—for that indeed is what it is, the eternally deepening abyss of all creation past. The color of personality is now vanished and, if we search hard and are lucky, we will find bones. Why venture into such a place?

Because it contains whatever is left of whatever was. Our remoter ancestors are here. And though we will never hear their voices nor touch their individuality, we can learn something about them in not wholly impersonal ways. We are their grandchildren, and together we are humanity. We want to know those other parts of ourselves.

In examining and thinking about the archaeological record of the North American Great Lakes or anywhere else, it is easy to become so fascinated by the physical remains and their time and space relations that the people behind these relics come to be thought of as products of their physical remains rather than the other way around. But then, this can, in its way, be a fruitful point of view. People are, after all, inclined to act and think and organize in ways compatible with the environment in which they live and the technology available for its manipulation. But this is certainly an incomplete view. As others have observed, history makes men, but men also make history. Rarely are cause-and-effect relations clear in human affairs. Things get muddled; creativity coexists with mindless replication; mistakes abound; interpretations of who did what vary with the interpreter. Explanation by abracadabra, so endemic in dogmatic theology and in too much of social science, is capable of attractive disguise and too facilely slips in explanations of human behavior when the subjects are dead. When prehistory is entered and the infinite complications of articulate speech cease, and the dreams and aspirations of equally infinite personalities evaporate, what is left behind is an enormous simplification of what once was. Unfortunately, this survival of the elemental has encouraged simple minds to think that that is all there ever was.

Nevertheless, though simplification through erosion it may be, the archaeological record is still rich, complex, and ever challenging; it is yielding ever new kinds of insights into past human behavior with each development of novel ways to examine that record. But it remains a partial record, one dependent on those activities that sufficiently modified the environment so that vestiges of their effects are still discernible. As will be apparent in later chapters, many of these environmental modifications are amazingly persistent in resisting obliteration, and many seemingly abstract qualities of what people do have quite incidentally, but in patterned ways, brought about physical changes which archaeologists can detect and trace back to some of the circumstances of their initiation. Even such incorporeal stuff as social organization and ideology, subtle and variable as they are, have some physical results in the marks people leave on the land. So something even of society and once-held beliefs is recoverable. But only something. Even a sketch of part of what we know to have been the symbolic opulence of early historic Indian life will not only remind us of this, but it should prove enlightening when it comes to understanding what archaeologists have excavated. We should see something more than bones, potsherds, and stone tools.

References

On the general ethnographic background:

Callender 1962 and 1978; Castile 1979; Hodge, editor, 1907–1910; Leacock and Lurie, editors, 1971; Murdock and O'Leary, editors, 1975; Oswalt 1973 (especially Chapter 6: "The Fox," and Chapter 11: "The Iroquois"); Quimby 1960b; Ritzenthaler and Ritzenthaler 1970; Spencer, Jennings, *et al.*, 1965 (especially Chapter IX: "Tribes of the Northeast"); Sturtevant and Trigger, editors, 1978; Swanton 1953.

For early historical accounts of the nature and affairs of Great Lakes Indian societies and interpretive commentaries on them:

Blair, editor, 1911–1912; Fitting 1970 (especially Chapter VII: "Those Who Were There," and Chapter VIII: "The Archaeology of History"); Greenman 1961; Kellogg, editor, 1917; Kinietz 1965; R. J. Mason 1976; Quimby 1966a; Thwaites, editor, 1896–1901, and 1902.

For detailed ethnohistorical studies of the Proto-Ojibwas, specifically:
Hickerson 1962, 1970, and 1971.

For detailed ethnohistorical studies of the Potawatomis, specifically:
Clifton 1977 and 1978; Deale 1958.

For detailed ethnohistorical studies of the Iroquoian peoples specifically:
Bonvillain, editor, 1979; Fenton 1940, 1971, and 1978; Heidenreich 1971; Hunt 1940; Tooker 1964; Trigger 1969 and 1976.

On the race and physical anthropology of the Indians:
Stewart 1973.

On the indigenous Great Lakes languages:
Goddard 1978; Lounsbury 1978.

On correlations of cultural and natural areas:
Kroeber 1953.

On European comprehension of Indian psychology:
Trigger 1976 and 1978; Washburn 1964.

For Great Lakes state- and provincial-level archaeological overviews see:
For Illinois: Bluhm, editor, 1959; for Indiana: Kellar 1973; for Michigan: Fitting 1970; for Minnesota: Johnson 1969; for New York: Ritchie 1969; for Ohio: Potter 1968; for Ontario: J. V. Wright 1972a; for Pennsylvania: Kent, Smith, and McCann, editors, 1971; for Wisconsin: Stoltman (ed.), in preparation.

The Inland Seas
Their Geology and Biology

2

It is always with a sense of awe that I clamber along the still wild and forested coast of northern Lake Michigan on Wisconsin's Door Peninsula. First attracted to this rocky, irregular shore by our research interests, my wife and I now have a summer cottage here. Standing at water's edge at night without a single light other than from our cottage to puncture miles of blackness, it seems incredible that millions of lights are holding that blackness at bay at the southern end of the same lake. Hearing no sounds the Indians did not hear, I cannot convincingly recall to memory's ear the municipal and industrial noise of the lake's southern basin. But I have heard that noise and seen those lights. They, too, are real. How paradoxical that the same lake which in its vastness girdles the Door Peninsula is itself half-girdled in concrete, asphalt, and steel. After all, 240 km south sprawls Milwaukee, and then Racine and Kenosha, and then Illinois with Waukegan, Evanston, and the giant, Chicago. The same lake then curves eastward, nudged by the dirty steel and chemical works of the Indiana shore: Hammond, East Chicago, Gary.

If a natural feature is defined in some important measure by its surroundings, as a flower in a garden, an oasis in a desert, or a mountain in a plain, then, surely, the greasy effluents of Wolf Lake and Lake Calumet beneath the Chicago Skyway and the connecting west terminus of the Indiana East–West Toll Road (Interstate 90) belong to a different lake than that breaking so clean on the sand and limestone shore of the Door Peninsula. The map claims they are one lake. And I know they are. What I am seeing and trying to reconcile with my sense of the wholeness of things is change, change in its aspect of horizontality. My cottage in the woods is on a shore little changed from what the first French explorers saw: a coastal fringe of boreal forest outflanking for a short distance the more typical mixed evergreen–broadleaf forest of more interior parts. In that sense it is representative of the past and a fitting enough summer abode for archaeologists. Milwaukee and Chicago and the west Indiana shore belong to a different time. Going from one end of the lake to the other is something like experiencing a time-warp in science fiction. When the southenders begin their annual swarming for their summer invasion of the north, and the northenders start labeling their garnered junk "antique," the fact is demonstrated that some part of my view is socially perceived and not just personal.

Change is most often thought of as taking place in time; but what changes, of course, whether it be glaciers or human institutions, moves through space as well. A common evolutionary result of this movement across space as well as time is the phenomenon I have alluded to in the foregoing as being so paradoxical—the phenomenon of stasigenesis: the survival into later times of ancestral forms more typical of earlier times. Portions of the Door Peninsula shore and that off Lake Shore Drive in Chicago 360 km to the south could hardly be more different as reflections of change; stasigenesis has preserved one in an older state while the other has become the apotheosis of modernity.

Change—today people know it is so insistent and unrelenting that it may more often be perceived as a threat than a promise. Yet, ironically, the very intrusiveness and concreteness of so many of the products of change foster the contradictory illusion of permanence and stability. How difficult it is today to visualize Chicago minus the John Hancock Center or the Sears Tower, let alone the Tribune Building or the Merchandise Mart. Yet we know that these are structures of recent vintage. I saw the Sears and the Hancock skyscrapers when they were being built—and it seems like yesterday. And there are believable old photographs of Chicago that do show the metropolis as it was before the Sears Tower or the Merchandise Mart, or before Soldiers' Field, or even before the Great Fire. Yet despite our knowing otherwise, dynamic, bustling places like Chicago and Cleveland and Toronto, as they are today, radiate an aura of permanence, of having arrived and intending to remain. We all use them as points of reference in our individual and collective lives. Such places seem eternally fixed even as they generate innovation and novelty. But Chicago is only a couple of centuries old, and the skyline we marvel at today is only a creation of the last few years. What a contrast to the rate and magnitude of change at the northern end of the lake.

If Chicago, the celebrated rail center and one-time hog-butcher of the world, seems of only a sham permanence, then surely the lake that sustains it possesses a genuine quality of longevity. That lake is over 480 km long and, at its widest, is 190 km across; it is almost 305 m deep at its deepest point. Except for the reversal of the flow of the Chicago River and the diversion of lake water into the Chicago Sanitary and Ship Canal, pollution problems, and the introduction of such marine fishes as alewives, Coho salmon, and lamprey eels, the lake is as it was when the French first dipped their paddles in its icy waters. Even the oldest Indian guide showed the French a land unchanged from the days of his grandfathers. Warriors and great shamans had come and gone, but the lake was as fixed as the stars.

In human terms, Lake Michigan has indeed been around for a long time. Within the history of human interaction with the lake, it has even been bigger than it is today. A minimal idea of how much bigger it has been may be gained by tracing out the 8-m contour above modern lake level on a topographical map and seeing what extensive shorelands would be inundated by a rise in water of that magnitude. Furthermore, expansions of the lake in its northern basin must have the effects of formerly glacier-depressed land surfaces added to absolute increases in lake surface altitude. On the other hand, there were also episodes in the natural history of the basin when water levels fell 110 m below the modern average of 180 m above mean sea level. At such times two lakes occupied the basin. So the lake is no more permanent in its size and configuration than the city, even if it has experienced a far longer tenure. Lake Michigan has had a long and complicated history. It is also but one lake in an interconnected group, and its history but a part of the evolution of the world's greatest system of lakes.

European explorers were dumbfounded at the colossal size of the North American Great Lakes. The lakes seemed to go on forever. Nothing in their previous experience had prepared them for such freshwater seas. When, finally, shores constricted and a "fond du lac" was sighted after days or even weeks of coastal paddling, a new river or strait would appear. Once through it, the forested shores might suddenly recoil and the horizon once more explode onto the flat vastness of sky-bounded water. Mirror calm or gently heaving, within a time uncomfortably short for making emergency landfall, the lakes could become like the North Sea: white flecked and ominous gray, erupting in ragged, mountainous waves.

Today a ship taking the most direct route between the eastern and westernmost lake ports will steam just over 1900 km. For Indians and early Europeans the distance was greater because, for reasons just alluded to, bark canoes were rarely taken out of easy reach of land, and water routes were only slightly less irregular than the coasts they guided by. And even though most of the early travel between the French settlements in the St. Lawrence Valley and the upper Great Lakes followed the Ottawa River–Mattawa River–Lake Nipissing–French River–Georgian Bay route, thus cutting off the lower lakes altogether, the reduction in distance and effort was less than a glance at a map might suggest. The rivers twist and turn, and impossible falls and heart-stopping rapids required dozens of laborious portages.

The Great Lakes, including the myriad smaller lakes and innumerable

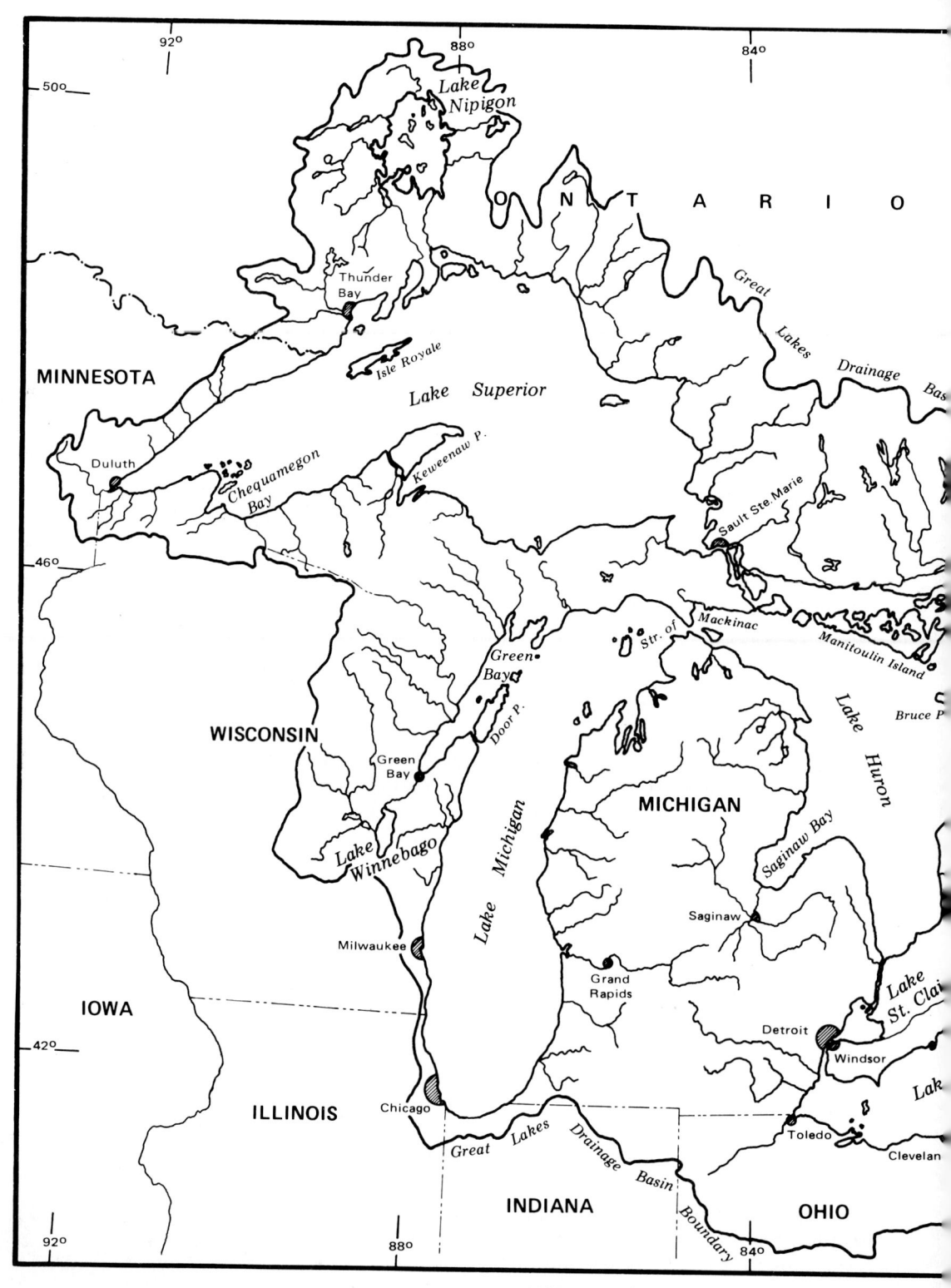

MAP 2.1. *The drainage basin of the Great Lakes.*

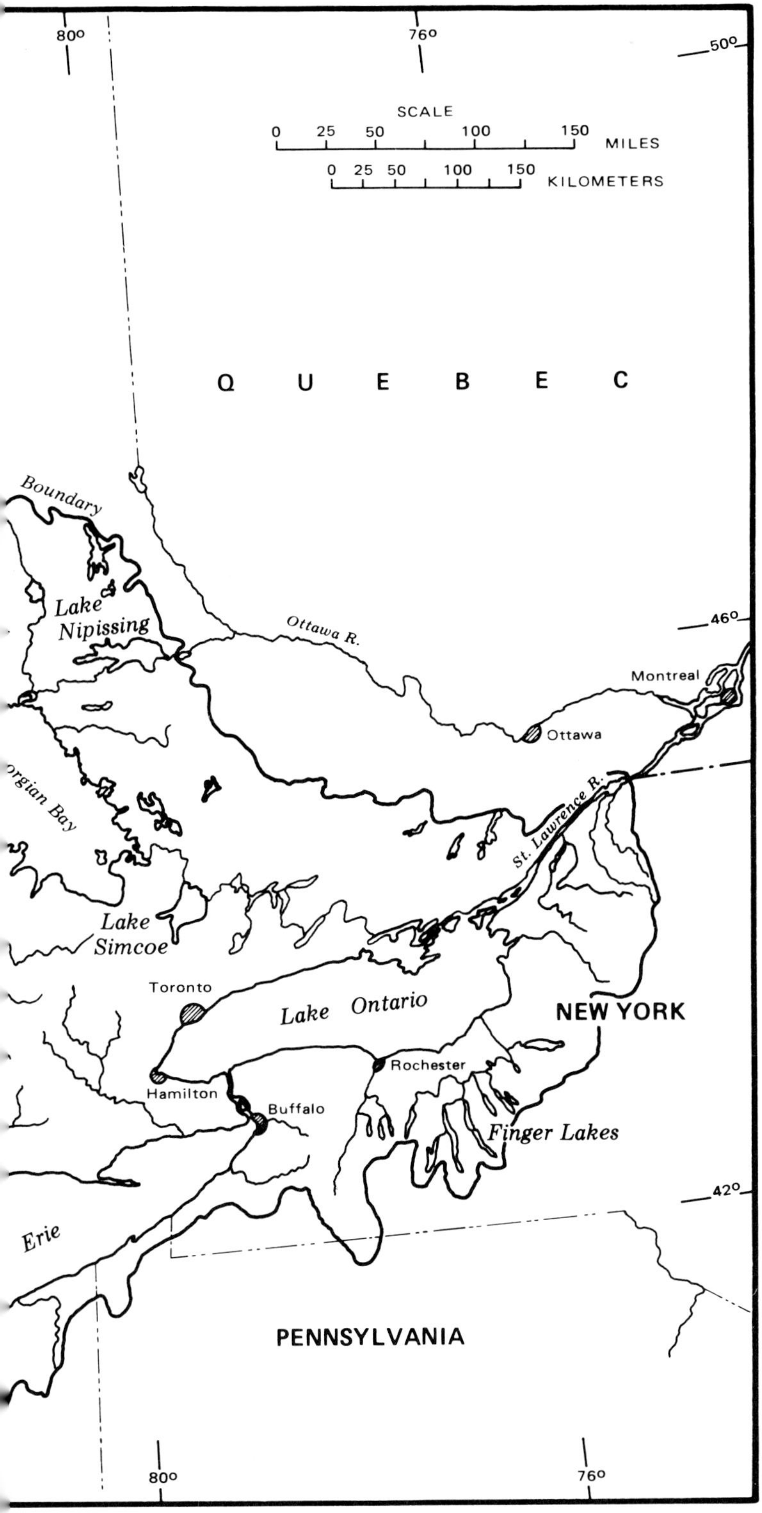

80°
76°
50°
SCALE
0 25 50 100 150 MILES
0 25 50 100 150 KILOMETERS
Q U E B E C
Boundary
Lake Nipissing
Ottawa R.
46°
Montreal
Ottawa
orgian Bay
St. Lawrence R.
Lake Simcoe
Toronto
Lake Ontario
NEW YORK
Rochester
Hamilton
Buffalo
Finger Lakes
42°
Erie
PENNSYLVANIA
80°
76°

rivers and creeks emptying into them, sprawl over almost 650,000 km² (almost 300,000 sq. mi) of the North American land mass. This is a country bigger than Texas, as large as the combined territories of California and Oregon plus half of Washington; it is half the size of Alaska. The Great Lakes occupy a drainage basin only slightly smaller than the combined areas of France and West Germany. And well within the time for which there is archaeological proof of the presence of man, these lakes have been both enormously larger and surprisingly smaller than they are now. They have grown and contracted in phase with the continent's changing climatic regimen.

Superior, with a surface area of almost 83,000 km², is not only the biggest of the five Great Lakes, it is also the largest body of fresh water in the world. The smallest of the Great Lakes is Ontario, almost 20,000 km² in extent. Huron and Michigan are each approximately 57,000 km², while Lake Erie is not quite 26,000. Together, these five giants have just under 18,000 km of shoreline. But it is usually overlooked that there are other lakes in the Great Lakes drainage system which, while small in comparison with the big five, are still large by the standards of most of the rest of the world. Lake Nipigon, for example, which sits atop Lake Superior and drains southward into it, embraces 4800 km²; it is not only bigger than the much more famous Great Salt Lake, it is in fact the thirty-second largest lake in the world—and that on a list including such salt water "lakes" as the Caspian and Aral Seas of Asia. And such Great Lakes "dwarfs" as Lake Saint Clair (1190 km²), Lake Nipissing (850 km²), Lake Simcoe (725 km²), and Lake Winnebago (560 km²) are individually impressive-sized bodies of fresh water.

The five Great Lakes contain a major portion of the world's fresh surface water. Maximum depths of the lakes range from 397 m in Lake Superior to 64 m in Lake Erie. Average depths are considerably less, of course. The extreme example in this regard, Lake Erie, with an average depth of only 18 m, is by far the shallowest of the lakes. It still contains the appreciable volume of 148,000 m³ of water. Lake Superior contains 30 times more. Lake Ontario, which receives all the overflow of the other four lakes, except for a relatively small volume diverted at Chicago to the Des Plaines–Illinois–Mississippi river system, delivers the discharge of the Great Lakes to the St. Lawrence River at an average rate a little in excess of 6 million liters per sec. An enormous amount of water is also given up directly to the atmosphere through evaporation. Approximately 5 m of Lake Superior's depth is lost each year to evaporation, perhaps one of Erie's. Rain and snow on the lakes themselves and over their watersheds more than compensate for evaporation losses over the long term. With an average overall rate of 79 cm, annual precipitation varies in the Great Lakes from 74 cm on Lake Superior to 86 cm on Lakes Erie and Ontario.

The average altitude of the surface of Lake Superior is 184 m above mean sea level. Lakes Michigan and Huron are at 177 m, while Erie and Ontario are at 174 and 75 m, respectively. Of course, the lakes are constantly fluctuating about these averages from season to season and from year to year. Depending on precipitation, relative cloud cover, extent and duration of winter ice, and other variables, seasonal changes in the levels of the Great Lakes generally are of a magnitude of .3–.6 m. The lake surfaces are essentially the visible portions of the basin's water table. They are very sensitive over both the short and the long term to variations in amount of precipitation. Over intervals of several years the maximum overall fluctuations between high and low levels are 1 m on Lake Superior to over 2 m on Lake Ontario. Temporarily and locally, these differences in surface levels may be significantly exaggerated in either direction by storms.

Largely contained within the 75th and 93rd parallels between 41 and 50° north latitude, the Great Lakes basin occupies the east–central part of the Great Central Lowlands of North America. These extensive lowlands, together with the Great Plains, intervene between what geographers call the Cordilleran Highlands (the Rocky Mountains and coastal ranges) and the Appalachian Mountains–Labrador Plateau. The lakes drain through the middle of the latter via the St. Lawrence lowlands. With very few and geographically quite limited exceptions, all of the country immediately surrounding the Great Lakes is less than 300 m in elevation above sea level. Around Lake Ontario the altitude is below 150 m. Just inland of the lakes in large areas of Ontario, New York, Pennsylvania, Wisconsin, and Minnesota, elevations between 300 and 600 m are common and extensive. Only east of Lake Ontario in the Adirondack Mountains does the watershed exhibit heights in excess of 1500 m.

Thoroughly scoured by Ice Age glaciers in geologically recent time, all of the Great Lakes country has been sculptured out of very old materials. The rock surfaces exposed so dramatically along the north shores of Lakes Superior and Huron and along all but the eastern third of Superior's south shore are Precambrian in age. These very hard rocks represent the southern apron of the enormous Laurentian, or Canadian, Shield. This consists of granites, conglomerates, quartzites, gneisses, slates, and a few other mainly igneous and metamorphic rocks, the youngest of which are older than 570 million years. Everywhere else the Great Lakes are bounded and underlain by Paleozoic rocks formed of sediments laid down by ancient transgressions of the sea. Typical of these younger rocks, which date between approximately 570 and 225 million years ago, are limestones, dolomites, sandstones, and shales. There are also deeply buried salt beds up to 300 m in thickness. Except for the relatively thin veneer of the last, or Pleistocene, age, erosion has removed whatever deposits may have been laid down in the Great Lakes region within the last 225 million years. The actual Pleistocene land forms which so dominate the Great Lakes country today, while incorporating such ancient rocks, are themselves only tens and hundreds of thousands of years old. And the lakes date to the very end of this period.

The Biological Environment

Geographers refer to the prevailing climate of the Great Lakes region as a "humid continental," one with warm to hot summers and cold winters. But obviously, splayed out over such a wide and deep area as they are, the lakes exhibit considerable variations in the length and intensity of summer heat and winter cold. These regional temperature differences, combined with geographic discrepancies in precipitation, soils, and other natural factors, are reflected in the distributions, associations, and densities of plants and animals. These in turn were of primary concern to Indians in their adaptations to the environment. In terms of diversity, for example, plant and animal resources tend to be richer in the southern reaches of the lakes although they are comparatively impoverished in the northernmost parts, where fewer species prevail over immense tracts. The numbers of frost-free days are significantly dissimilar within the basin to have exercised a major effect on the range and success of agriculture and thus to some degree on aboriginal social institutions.

There are a number of overlapping and cross-cutting schemes that have been offered by botanists, zoologists, geographers, and others for recognizing and classifying the natural areas of the Great Lakes. One of these simply distinguishes between needle-leaf (evergreen or coniferous) and broad-leaf (deciduous) forests and notes similarities and differences in associated animal populations. Another trifurcates the Great Lakes into more or less latitudinally parallel zones that exemplify midcontinental segments of three out of seven "transcontinental life zones." These and some others, useful for certain studies, are too broad-scale to be of much value in this instance.

The classification followed here divides the Great Lakes into four great "biotic provinces," "biomes," or biological "communities." It is based on dynamic interrelations of plant and animal communities and climate. Like all classifications seeking to comprehend very complex phenomena, this one, too, suggests a false simplicity and unreal neatness. It is no less true for being a commonplace observation that nature is opportunistic and ever changing. Sharp boundaries exist in classifications and on maps, rarely in the real world. More often than not, great natural communities or associations of trees, shrubs, herbs, fungi, mammals, birds, reptiles, and arthropods so intergrade along their boundaries with other biological communities as to form, in effect, another natural or biotic division in that overlapping boundary area. Such overlapping zones sharing the attributes of the neighboring divisions are sometimes called "ecotones." Frequently they are biologically richer than the biotic provinces they buffer. Their boundaries in turn may be anything but sharp and clearcut. But the following biotic provinces, with major representation in the Great Lakes country, have the virtue of being pretty clearly recognizable and distinctive in the centers of their respective ranges, even if there are legitimate grounds for arguing over exactly where their boundaries ought to be drawn. At least these divisions have currency and are meaningful to most biologists and geographers, even if they have their own favored alternatives. Unlike marriages made in heaven, classifications are the products of fallible men. The question then is not so much whether a particular scheme is right or wrong, but how useful it is for the purposes for which it was constructed.

One other complication should be mentioned. The biotic provinces described in the following are believed to have formed the principal terrestrial biological communities in the Great Lakes at the time of European discovery. Unfortunately, they were massively disturbed, if not largely destroyed, before they could be studied by trained observers. As the natural scientists who constructed these classificatory divisions intended, they are approximations; they are reconstructions of what natural conditions are believed to have been just before the steel axe came upon the forests like locusts upon the wheat. This is sometimes forgotten by archaeologists in their anxiety to causally relate past cultural practices and environmental variables. Relating reconstructed cultures of reconstructed societies to reconstructed environments is a sobering task as we shall see.

The northernmost of the biotic provinces with representation in the Great Lakes is one of the most widespread in North America, although it embraces only a small part of the lakes country itself. This is the Hudsonian Biotic Province, or the Spruce–Fir–Moose–Caribou Biome. In botanical terms, this is the taiga or boreal coniferous forest. Although it encompasses only the central part of the north shore of Lake Superior and some isolated pockets to the south, it extends northward to the tree line and stretches transcontinentally from Newfoundland to Alaska. Most of this province may be referred to as subarctic.

Typical of the Hudsonian Biotic Province are long, severe winters and short, warm summers. Heavy snowfalls are common. Soils are thin, and extensive exposures of naked bedrock unremarkable. Characterized by an immature drainage, the province is covered with a complex network of rivers, bogs, and lakes. Many a canoeist has set out on these confusing waterways and has had to fight panic in order to work his way out again. Overland travel is exceedingly difficult due to often impenetrable forests and, in the summer, sometimes maddening plagues of mosquitos and biting flies.

Black spruce is the major tree, but also important are white spruce, balsam fir, white birch, jack pine, tamarack, and sometimes cedar, willow,

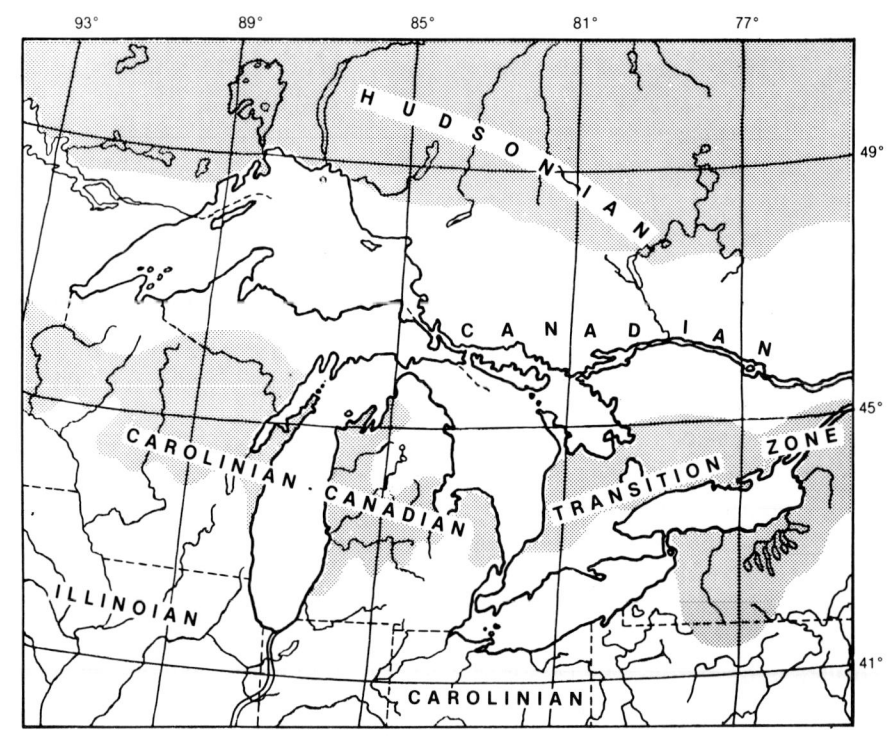

MAP 2.2. *Major biotic provinces of the Great Lakes. (After Cleland 1966.)*

and poplar. Red pine, white pine, and hemlock are regionally prominent, if intrusive, members of the boreal forest in its southernmost parts along Lake Superior and in the lower St. Lawrence Valley. The most important animals, from the human perspective, are moose, caribou, black bear, wolf, lynx, wolverine, marten, fisher, red fox, porcupine, beaver, and snowshoe hare. With local and seasonal exceptions, game tends to low population densities. Together with limited wild plant foods, a restricted aboriginal technology, and severe climate, the low densities of game kept human populations low and dispersed through much of the year.

An especially vital resource in an area where terrestrial hunting is often unsupportive of large groups is fish. Although most of the same fish that were available to Indians in Lake Superior and the lakes and streams tributary to it were also present throughout the Great Lakes generally, few localities could rival the seasonal productivity of the fish runs at Sault Ste. Marie between Lakes Superior and Huron. The most important fish in the Great Lakes were bass, pike, pickerel, whitefish, lake trout, sturgeon, smelt, perch, bullhead catfish, sucker, and sheepshead or fresh-water drum. In some places the lakes also yielded sufficient turtles, frogs, and clams to augment local diets seasonally.

The Canadian Biotic Province surrounds most of the Lake Superior basin and the northern parts of the Lake Michigan and Lake Huron basins, including most of Georgian Bay. But there are enclaves of true boreal forest deep in this province in such places as the upper Michigan peninsula and northern Wisconsin. This is also formerly heavily glaciated country, and many of the soils are derived from glacial tills and old lake beds and outwash plains; these soils tend to be deeper and richer in organic content than those in the Hudsonian Biotic Province. Long, cold winters are the norm while summers are somewhat longer and warmer than in the Hudsonian.

The forest type of the Canadian Biotic Province is the Lake Forest. It is under the climatically ameliorating influence of the immense lakes around which it evolved. All of the Hudsonian or boreal forest trees are present here also, but they are intermixed with greater quantities of cedar, white and red pine, Norway pine, alder, yellow birch, beech, elm, hemlock, aspen, basswood, and sugar maple. The Canadian Biotic Province, although identifiable in its own right, is in many important ways a broad ecotone, or transitional or overlapping zone, between the much larger Hudsonian and Carolinian provinces to the north and south. This intergradational character is so gradual over such a wide zone as to make attempts at drawing boundaries arbitrary.

To gain an idea of the importance of the plant resources of these biotic provinces to the Indians, it may be noted that in the Upper Great Lakes alone, mainly comprising portions of the Canadian and bordering Hudsonian and Carolinian provinces, at least 373 native plants are known to have been utilized. Because only part of the aboriginal plant lore was ever recorded, it is estimated that probably close to 500 plants were actually used. Of the recorded practices (bearing in mind that some species had more than one use), 130 native wild plants were treated as sources of food (sample: sugar maple, wild onion, pepperroot, jack-in-the-pulpit, strawberry, red-berried elder, wild black currant, wild rice, raspberry, hazelnut, bunchberry, butternut, crab apple, paw-paw, black walnut, puffed shield lichen). Eighteen plants were employed in making beverages and for flavoring other foods (for example, wild ginger, wintergreen, sassafras, Labrador tea), while 68 plants were collected to make medicinal infusions (such as balsam fir, red baneberry, black cherry, and small cranberry). Other known uses of wild plants were as medicines (207 varieties of plants): witch hazel, sweet fern, hemlock, wild bergamot, honeysuckle; as charms (31): sweet flag, dragon root, wild vetch or pea; for smoking, with or without the admixture of tobacco, and frequently for ritual purposes (27): bearberry or kinnikinnik, staghorn sumac, fragrant goldenrod; as a source of dyes and paints (25): bristly crowfoot, sweet gale, bloodroot; and for various utilitarian purposes (52): for example, white or paper birch (for bark canoes and house covers, trays and buckets), mountain ash (for snowshoe frames, lacrosse racquets, canoe ribs and thwarts), balsam fir (pitch for sealing canoes and bark containers), larch (roots used to sew canoes), red cedar (bark used for weaving bags, pouches, and mats), black willow (fiber for fish nets, cord, pouches), Indian hemp (fine cordage), and common milkweed (for thread and fishlines).

All of the Hudsonian mammals are present also in the Canadian Biotic Province, only they become progressively more rare southward as ever increasing numbers and varieties of typically more southern, or Carolinian, animals are met. In the province moose are much more widely distributed and common than caribou; deer are now present, being common where deciduous or broad-leaf trees are abundant. The wolverine is now rare, the lynx is increasingly replaced by the smaller bobcat, and the puma or mountain lion appears.

The Carolinian Biotic Province, or Oak–Deer–Maple Biome, occupies parts of southern Wisconsin, the southern half of the lower Michigan peninsula, southern Ontario, and extends southward into Indiana, Ohio, Pennsylvania, and New York in the Great Lakes basin—and far beyond outside the area of the basin. This huge province dominates most of eastern North America south of the Great Lakes and upper St. Lawrence Valley. It is characterized by a much more mature drainage and a great variety of deep, rich soils. Winters are moderate with relatively light snowfall. Long hot summers are typical, although they are significantly moderated along leeward shores.

As already indicated, there is a deep intergradational zone between this province and the Canadian. The most marked feature of the Carolinian Biotic Province is the preponderance of broad-leaf forest which, of course, drops its foliage in the winter. Characteristic trees include oak, hickory, maple, beech, walnut, butternut, elm, tulip, ash, basswood, sycamore, and cottonwood. Cedar and tamarack are fairly common in swampy tracts. White pine and even spruce are locally numerous and healthy where conditions are right, especially in the north reaches of the biome.

The deciduous forest is also rich in animal life. Even with relatively dense Indian populations in much of the Carolinian Biotic Province, game animals were usually supported by the forest in numbers sufficient to reward more often than not the hunter. Indeed, game drives in this and the Canadian province were frequently employed and often netted a bountiful return. With regional abundances varying between an estimated 100 and 840 individuals per 26 km^2, the number one source of red meat throughout the province was the white-tailed deer. Other animals of economic and subsistence importance to people were black bear, turkey (in some sections in numbers of at least 200 per 26 km^2), passenger pigeon (locally in astronomical numbers for the clubbing), opossum, raccoon, cottontail rabbit, gray fox, several species of squirrel, bobcat, cougar or puma, wolf, mink, otter, beaver, muskrat, woodchuck, elk or wapiti and, especially in the western marches where prairies interfingered with the forest, badger and buffalo. Although much more typical of the prairies and plains, buffalos occurred in small herds throughout much of the Carolinian woodlands. As late as 1760 in central Pennsylvania, for instance, an organized hunt over a tract of about 650 km² resulted in the killing of 111 bison, a little over one animal for every two of the colonial hunters. In predators, this same hunt bagged 109 wolves, 41 mountain lions, and 114 bobcats. The rich fish resources of the Great Lakes portion of the Carolinian Biotic Province are those already enumerated for the lakes country generally.

Finally, the last of the four great biotic provinces among which the Great Lakes sprawl is the Illinoian. This might appropriately be labeled the Grass–Oak–Bison Biome. It is much less extensive in the lakes country than the neighboring Canadian and Carolinian provinces and is more on the scale of the Hudsonian. Found mainly west of Lake Michigan and south and west of the Canadian–Carolinian transition zone in southern Wisconsin and Minnesota, the Illinoian extends the great North American grasslands interfingering eastward into the broad-leaf forest. Well developed in central and northern Illinois, it reaches into southern Michigan, central Indiana and, discontinuously, into Ohio. Of course, this is prairie grassland country with organically rich soils. Winters and summers are similar to those of the northern Carolinian Biome.

Characteristic of the Illinoian Biotic Province are open, tall-grass prairies with scattered copses of oak and hickory. Forests occur in stream valleys between low, open plateaus or gently rolling hills. These woods consist largely of oak, sycamore, cottonwood, elm, hackberry, maple, basswood, and beech trees. The usual mammals include skunk, badger, jack rabbit, ground squirrel, gopher, coyote, elk, and most notably, buffalo. For many woodland Indians, familiarity with this last animal constituted an historic invitation to a flamboyant destiny on the western plains; it was accepted along with the fateful triad: firearms, horses, and eviction from ancestral estates.

The Ice Age and the Rise of the Great Lakes

The Great Lakes are children of the Pleistocene Epoch's old age, and the first human beings to set eyes on them witnessed their infancy. The lakes were born between the melting fringes of glacial ice and the higher ground before them or the rubble dams the glaciers left behind to mark their maximum southward thrusts. The ice was still shaping the landscape and the lakes were still aborning when people arrived. This ice was the mobile and sculpting outflow of an enormous accumulation of ice and snow whose center shifted periodically east and west of Hudson Bay; these are called the Labradorean and the Keewatin centers, respectively. Squeezed outward by the sheer weight of ice at the migrating center, the periphery of the Laurentide, or eastern, continental glacier extended at its maximum from the Arctic Ocean south to the Ohio Valley. At maximum, its western margins temporarily abutted and coalesced with the easterly extrusions of the great western, or Cordilleran, continental glacier. These two sprawling ice masses initially appeared perhaps 2 million years ago. Since their inception in early Pleistocene time, they have waxed and waned over hundreds of thousands of years and over millions of square kilometers.

When the eastern and western continental glaciers met and merged near the eastern foothills of the Rocky Mountains, they formed an impenetrable barrier which from time to time sealed off most of the Western Hemisphere from the rest of the world. And repeatedly, as the weather ameliorated and the ice fronts melted and withdrew from their forwardmost positions, corridors opened between north and south; these appeared between the Laurentide and Cordilleran continental glaciers and between the latter and the Pacific Ocean. With the sometime exception of restricted strips of unusually "dirty" fringe ice, the continental glaciers were utterly devoid of plants and animals. Their bitterly cold, windy, sterile surfaces absolutely forbade trespass. So even though the earliest migrants to the New World are thought to have come across the Bering Sea area into Alaska and from there, during an episode of glacial retreat, moved southward along a narrow and extremely rugged strip of Pacific coast and/or skirted the Rocky Mountains between the two glacial systems, once in the continental interior they could have approached the nascent Great Lakes only from the south and southwest.

The continental glaciers expanded and contracted many times throughout the Pleistocene Epoch. The most prolonged and intense periods of glacial expansion are called "glacial stages" or "ages." There were at least four (and probably five or more) of these colossi. The last of these is called, in North America, the Wisconsin or Wisconsinan Glacial Stage. It began in excess of 70,000 years ago and ended in the Great Lakes area roughly 10,000 years ago. It was preceded by a long "interglacial period" during which all but high latitude and mountain glaciers either disappeared or were enormously reduced from their earlier sizes. The pre-Wisconsin interglacial period is called the Sangamon; it followed the earlier Illinoian Glacial Stage. In the standard geological terminology, earlier glacial stages were the Kansan and the Nebraskan. Not including the present, there were three interglacial periods with tenures of tens to hundreds of thousands of years. Recent and still on-going field studies in southern Illinois strongly suggested a more complicated pre-Illinoian glacial chronology than the currently standard one just outlined.

At their peak the Wisconsin continental glaciers of North America, not including the Greenland ice cap, comprised about 35% of the world's glacial cover. Today the same land mass supports only .5% of global glacial ice. The Laurentide ice sheet at the time of the Wisconsin maximum buried more than 12.48 million km². In late Wisconsin time a tongue of ice that covered much of eastern Wisconsin and western Michigan is known from measurements of the lowest and highest places it overrode to have been at least 610 m thick. Northward, of course, the ice was thicker on the average as the Labradorean and Keewatin centers were approached. Between the north shores of Lakes Superior and Huron and the Hudson Bay lowlands, ice depths of up to several miles are probable. Indeed, the Greenland ice cap today is still an impressive 3000 m thick.

Just as the Pleistocene Epoch was marked by massive glacial advances separated one from the next by prolonged episodes of interglacial conditions, so each of the glacial stages was in turn punctuated by smaller scale glacial advances and by retrogressions of shorter duration. The ice boundaries were constantly reacting to fluctuations in temperature and precipitation and to perturbations in prevailing wind directions and velocities, cloud cover, and airborne dust loads. Out of this more or less continuous state of flux certain substage advances and retreats of the ice fronts were much more pronounced and lasting in their impact on the environment than were others. These "stadials" (advances) and "interstadials" (retrogressions) were in themselves long-term phenomena and were small-scale and short-lived only in relation to the spatial and temporal magnitudes of the four or more main glacial stages themselves (i.e., Wisconsin, Illinoian, etc.). The stadials and interstadials spanned hundreds and even thousands of years.

A current classification and chronology of the major advances and retreats of the Wisconsin Glacial Stage in the upper Mississippi Valley and western Great Lakes recognizes three significant substages of glaciation (the Altonian Stadial from before 70,000 to circa 26,000 B.C.; the Woodfordian Stadial from about 20,000 to 10,500 B.C.; and the Valderan Stadial from 9900 to approximately 9000 B.C.—this last depending upon area, with later terminations appropriate at higher latitudes) and three interstadials marked by climatic ameliorations and relatively large withdrawals of ice from formerly glaciated country (the Farmdalian, Two Creekan, and Recent Interstadials). Of greater utility in this book is a classification which subdivides the Woodfordian Stadial into at least two of its component episodes of glacial encrouchment. A proposed fourth, post-Valderan, stadial is the Algonquin Stadial, which dates from 9000 to 8500 B.C. or a little later.

As just intimated, there is an element of arbitrariness about the classifications of Pleistocene glacial activity. The ice fronts were rarely static for more than a few years, and geologists argue among themselves over the magnitude and longevity of ice movement appropriate to recognition as a named event in glacial chronology. Also, differences in latitude, prevailing sources of atmospheric moisture and, especially, topography combined to make the ice front more mobile in some parts of the Great Lakes than in others. Accordingly, fluctuations in the ice margin left more distinct traces where horizontal movement was pronounced than was the case where less moisture was available to feed the glacier, the leading edge was more remote from the centers of snow accumulation and compaction, and where more rugged terrain confined ice movement within more tightly circumscribed arenas. Thus, the last Great Lakes stadial of the Wisconsin Glacial Stage (the Valderan) was a more dramatic event in the western, than in the eastern, Great Lakes. In the west the Valderan ice front appears to have expanded much more rapidly and enveloped much larger areas than it did in the more topographically variable east. As a result, there is less agreement among geologists in the eastern Great Lakes and New England–eastern Ontario–Quebec area about the details of the Valderan advance and retreat. Attempts to demonstrate synchronous events of sub-stage magnitude across so vast a region as the Great Lakes may be partly frustrated by one or more of the factors just cited.

The ice margin was always irregular, its advances being distinguished by the pushing forward of large and small tongues, or "lobes," whose size, shape, and direction were importantly controlled by the terrain over which the ice moved. Almost like a colossal amoeba in slow motion, the glacier probed and overswept some areas while interlobate wedges resisted overriding. In retreat the lobes stagnated and wasted away in place while the main body of the glacier released its grip and contracted rapidly along one front and slowly along another.

When glaciers move they scour the land. They not only bulldoze great heaps and ridges of earth and rock rubble before them and trail similar debris along their flanks, they also pick up and incorporate prodigious quantities of material from the ground over which they progress. In moving over exposed bedrock, the gritty character of glacial ice is attested by the scratches and grooves, or striae, left on the scoured surfaces. With the melting of the glaciers, this load of boulders, pebbles, sand, clay, and silt dropped out of the collapsing ice to mantle the ground (glacial till). Some of this mineral load was heaped up in the form of the ridges of bulldozed rubble that sometimes mark the maximum advance or signal the significant halts or still-stands in the glacier's retreat (terminal moraines). Typically outlining the glacier's flanks are lateral and/or interlobate moraines. Vast gravel, sand, and clay outwash plains resulted from the action of the enormous floods of water the melting ice released. The conical, oval or linear, and elongated sinuous mounds known as kames, drumlins, and eskers, respectively, so common in many parts of the Great Lakes, are combined with the less sculptured glacial till, moraines, glacial outwash, rock striae, and kettles to make up the distinctive topography by means of which ancient glaciations have been reconstructed (kettles are large depressions where the ground collapsed as buried or partly buried remnants of retreating ice lobes gradually melted in place). The famous loess deposits (fine-grained wind-borne silts) of the northern Mississippi Valley were derived by wind action on the fine sediments washed out of the wasting glaciers. The excavating power of the Laurentide glacier is seen in the contours of the Great Lakes themselves. Although it is believed that the lake basins conform in their orientations to the courses of preglacial rivers, they were mainly carved out of the landscape by the repeated episodes of glaciation.

An outstanding feature of the Pleistocene Epoch was a periodically delayed recycling of water between the oceanic basins and the land. With continental precipitation in effective surplus over run-off by virtue of glacier formation, ocean levels fell in phase with glacial advances on the land. In interglacial periods, run-off more nearly approximated precipitation, and sea level rose in response. During glacial maxima, global sea level fell hundreds of meters and exposed broad expanses of the continental shelves. At such times the shallow Bering Sea drained and a 1600-km-wide isthmus connected Siberia and Alaska. The Atlantic and Gulf coasts were correspondingly far seaward of their modern beaches. Oceanographic studies off the coast of New Jersey show that at about 13,000 B.C., when the Wisconsin Stage ice was near its maximum expansion, sea level was about 128 m lower than it is today. Then the New Jersey shore was approximately 200 km east of its present position, and the distance inland to the great bend of the Delaware River just south of Trenton was more than quadrupled. At around 9000 B.C. sea level was about 80 m below its current elevation. It had risen to about 40 m below modern levels by around 6000 B.C., and 2000 years later it was only 20 m lower than today. Well within the time for which we have proof of the presence of man east of the Appalachian Mountains, a broad shelf of what is now sea bottom extended the Atlantic and Gulf coasts far seaward. Because of more abruptly deepening offshore waters, the Pacific littoral was much more modestly extended. And these exposed continental flanks supported vegetation and animal populations. Today commercial fishermen periodically bring up mammoth and mastodon fossils in their nets and shellfish scoops from locations as much as 200 km out at sea off the New Jersey coast. Doubtless many an archaeological site lies out there, too.

With such a volume of water transfered by evaporation and precipitation from the oceans to the land, the earth's crust sank beneath the weight of the continental glaciers. As the Valderan Stadial was coming to an end, the upper St. Lawrence Valley was depressed at least 240 m below its modern elevation. Because sea level rebounded faster than the land could recuperate when the ice melted, the sea invaded far up the valley and may even for a short time have mingled its waters with a portion of those of the Great Lakes. Continuing recovery of the land gradually expelled the marine waters, but the elevated beaches and salt-water fossils remained behind as witnesses of the event. The process of formerly depressed land surfaces slowly rebounding to their preglacial elevations (isostacy) is still going on. Because glacial loading was heaviest north of the Great Lakes, land surfaces were there more dramatically deformed. They have since had a longer way to go in re-establishing their original or preglacial altitudes. In the time since the last glacial maximum, the lands northward to Hudson Bay have rebounded in excess of 900 m, and they are still recovering.

The tilting of many of the fossil beaches of the late and post-glacial Great Lakes is due to these same linked phenomena of glacial loading, crustal depression, and subsequent rebounding following deglaciation. Created in declivities between the ice margin and entrapping higher ground, many small pro-glacial lakes came into being whenever the ice began to withdraw from its utmost positions. As glacial retreat continued, releasing fresh supplies of water, the lakes deepened and expanded to fill their basins. But often the retiring ice unplugged new drainage outlets which were at lower elevations than those through which the lakes had earlier spilled, and lake levels fell to the elevations of the new outlets. Subsequent readvance of the ice front blocked these lower spillways, thus causing water levels to rise again to earlier attained altitudes.

Enormously complicating such ice advance–retreat–readvance–correlated oscillations in lake levels was depression and partial recuperation of the earth's crust in response to ice loading and release. Because even glaciers advance and retrogress faster than the ground can sink and then rebound, these linked phenomena were not strictly synchronous; the latter response always involved a time lag. The north shore of Lake Superior is still rising out of the water at a rate of a few centimeters a century, while the south shore is being inexorably inundated.

A consequence of crustal deformation is seen in many marine beaches at northern latitudes and in the beaches of the premodern Great Lakes. In the lower half of the Lake Michigan basin the earliest post-glacial body of water (Lake Algonquin, or the main Algonquin lake stage) left well-developed beaches which are 8 m higher than the surface of the modern lake and perfectly horizontal. But north of a line drawn between Two Rivers and Kewaunee, Wisconsin, on one side of the lake, and near Manistee, Michigan, on the other, the preserved Algonquin beaches begin to show a progressive increase in elevation. This starting line is the so-called hinge line, or zero isobase, north of which the fossil beaches depart from horizontality and become progressively uplifted above their original elevation. The farther north the Algonquin beaches are traced, the higher their altitude; they provide a convenient register of the amount and rate of crustal rebounding attained since the time of beach abandonment.

The undeformed, horizontal, Algonquin beaches inland of the southern half of Lake Michigan stand at an elevation of 184 m above modern mean sea level. The same beach line near the north end of the mouth of Green

Bay stands at an altitude of 215 m. At its northernmost position just beyond Sault Ste. Marie, Ontario, the Algonquin shoreline reposes at 309 m above sea level, or 125 m above its original level. Successively later lake stages exhibit progressively more northerly positioned hinge lines and less spectacular rates of departure from horizontality. This is accounted for by the shorter time that has elapsed since their beaches were abandoned and by the fact that the rate of post-glacial crustal rebounding has been diminishing toward recent times although it has still not ceased. But even the Lake Nipissing stage of the evolving Great Lakes, with a hinge line across Lake Michigan from near Washington Island, Wisconsin, to just north of Traverse City, Michigan, and which dates almost 7000 years after the time of Lake Algonquin, is recorded at North Bay, Ontario, by fossil beaches that are 29 m higher than those south of the hinge line. The same picture is revealed using data from the Lake Huron basin. Here the zero isobase runs from Greenbush, Michigan (about halfway between Saginaw Bay and Thunder Bay), to near Kincardine, Ontario, on the opposite shore. Rising northward, inclination of the later Algoma stage beaches is conformably less than that of the Nipissing features.

Accompanying the growth and decline of glaciers and the repetitive births, deaths, and rebirths of pro- and post-glacial lakes were fluctuating wind patterns and shifting belts of precipitation. Rather than arctic gales continually blowing off the ice massifs to refrigerate the rest of the continent, paleoclimatological research indicates that often the prevailing winds in the Great Lakes area blew toward the glacier, bringing with them warmer, moisture-laden air. Over the long run this ameliorated the climate and made it less arctic-like than the presence of massive ice sheets would suggest. Nevertheless, conditions along the ice margins and for a considerable distance in their approach must have been harsh in comparison with what is experienced in the same latitudes today. The main differences were not in terms of winter cold but rather in the suppression and abbreviation of summer warmth with the cumulative effect this produced on annual, decade, century and, indeed, millenial temperature averages. How such climatic alterations affected the natural communities of plants and animals may be gauged by the study of whole and fragmentary fossils, including the record of plant pollen trapped and preserved in the bottom sediments of lakes and bogs. During glacial maxima the actual overriding of forests, such as is known to have occured at different times at Two Creeks, Wisconsin, Catfish Creek, Ontario, and some other localities, was but the physical coup de grace administered upon a climatological fait accompli. Actual large-scale changes in vegetation long preceded the arrival of the ice front at any particular place. There was more than a chill in the air before the ice heaved into view.

The overall affect of continental glaciation on vegetation was a far-reaching and long-lasting dislocation. The latitudinal zonation of plant communities was bent, and in many cases broken, as the ice lobes rearranged the landscape and influenced the regional climate. Many arctic species were displaced to the Ohio Valley, and subarctic forests migrated even farther south. There is no question that, along some portions of leading and trailing edges of advancing and retreating ice, true tundra conditions developed with permafrost, or year-round frozen ground. But how extensive such conditions were is a matter of disagreement among students of fossil pollen (palynologists), paleontologists, and geologists. In the Great Lakes country the glacier margin was probably fringed with a 160–320-km-wide zone of quasi- or park-tundra with true, permanently frozen barren-ground tundra limited to especially harsh and isolated stretches. The much more typical park-tundra probably grew right up to the edge of the glacier in many places, except during episodes of glacial retreat. This low-latitude tundra had a very sinuous southern as well as irregular northern boundary, for it certainly interfingered with a more closed coniferous forest in response to local variations in drainage and topography, prevailing temperatures and wind directions, and previous extent and intensity of glaciation. Large open meadows of lichens, herbs, and sedges, as represented by nonarboreal pollen (NAP) were interrupted in sheltered zones by open, parklike stands of mainly spruce and fir trees and also with representatives of dwarf willow, birch, and pine. Such a park-tundra is believed to have had a denser animal population and a higher carrying capacity than is true of modern high-latitude tundras. To early hunters, whose ancestors had had to adapt themselves to ecologically similar and even sometimes inferior conditions in northern Asia, this must have seemed familiar country.

South of the park-tundra there were probably more closed coniferous forests. Of course, park-tundra and relatively more closed boreal forest must have intergraded so often as to defy the mapping of distinct boundaries. This more closed coniferous forest, dominated by spruce and fir, was a less rewarding habitat, sustaining far fewer edible plants and animals than the park-tundra north of it or the more characteristically broad-leaf woodlands to the south. Early hunters probably avoided it as much as possible. But when the glacier withdrew northward, drawing up the park-tundra with it, the boreal forest also moved north and invaded formerly more open country.

As the last Wisconsin glacier melted back from the Great Lakes, the dominance of spruce and fir in the woodlands was increasingly eclipsed and then replaced by pine. This is recorded at multiple pollen-bearing localities from Minnesota to New York. This post-glacial pine maximum in turn gave way to inroads of successively more varied and numerous broad-leaf trees. Within a few thousand years of deglaciation most of the Great Lakes supported a deciduous forest of oak, hickory, birch, beech, and hemlock, with elm, maple, and basswood increasing with time. Then

2. The Inland Seas

as now, boreal species proliferated northward. But except for relatively minor shifts in community composition and species boundaries, there was little alteration in the overall pattern of Great Lakes vegetation from this time until the European discovery.

One of the most interesting but least understood aspects of the transition from late Pleistocene to early Recent times in the Great Lakes and elsewhere in North America was the extinction that truncated the evolutionary careers of a majority of the larger kinds of mammals. Except for range adjustments necessitated by post-glacial climatic and vegetational changes, most of the rabbits, squirrels, shrews, voles, mice, bats, foxes, and other small mammals of the last Ice Age are still with us today. Details of their anatomy are often identical across tens of thousands of years. This fact, and our ability to study their modern habits and environmental preferences and limitations, makes the abundant small mammals ideal indicators of the ancient environments in which their bones have been found. Limestone caves and sinkholes in Pennsylvania, for example, have yielded prodigious numbers of such fossils, and they permit a reconstruction of faunal successions from late glacial to Recent times. From site to site they consistently reveal a shift from species typical of boreal woodlands and woodland–tundra ecotones found in northern Canada to a fauna characteristic of the modern deciduous forest appropriate to their latitude.

In stark contrast to the survival, or sometime displacement, of the small mammals was the inability of a majority of the genera of large mammals to persist beyond the end of the Pleistocene Epoch. Those that did, and they include such "big game" as bear, deer, elk, moose, caribou, and bison, represent an impressive but still much impoverished legacy from the biological richness of the late glacial world. Into the time in which the first Indians are known to have been on the scene, that world harbored an incredibly diverse megafauna. Approaching its close, the lakes country sustained more varieties of large mammals that are now extinct than have survived. These included such beasts as peccaries and woodland and barren-ground caribou which, although vanished from the Great Lakes since the end of the Ice Age, have maintained themselves in habitats hundreds of miles away.

In this same category of regionally-long-extinct animals are the sea mammals which once lived in the Great Lakes. These included seals, walruses, and bowhead, sperm (?), and finback whales. Their bones have been found incorporated in early lake beaches in Michigan. Similar finds, but associated with other marine life forms, have been recovered in Ontario and Quebec. These animals must have entered the Great Lakes sometime between approximately 10,500 and 8200 B.C. during which interval an arm of the sea invaded the depressed St. Lawrence and Ottawa valleys (the Champlain Sea) and met the discharging fresh waters of one or more early high stages of the western Great Lakes. Two Archaic period effigy spear-thrower weights from Kent and Gratiot counties, Michigan, suggest that beluga whales may have to be added to this list. This is much weaker evidence, of course, than the actual bones of the other sea-mammal species, particularly the whale bones incorporated in beach deposits.

Other large mammals with long successful lineages extending far back in the Pleistocene or even earlier epochs failed to survive anywhere and became totally extinct. Among the Great Lakes mammals that were certainly contemporaneous with the earliest people were elephants and cousins of elephants. The former were represented by the impressive Jefferson and Imperial mammoths, some examples of which were half again as large as the largest living African elephants. The latter were mastodons. These are believed to have been more solitary in their habits than mammoths. They were most at home, though not exclusively confined to, park-tundra and boreal forest where they browsed on trees and shrubs. Mammoths were grazers rather than browsers, and they were more common in open country away from the dank coniferous woodlands. Other forms which shared their fate were the woodland musk-ox (a close relative of the surviving musk-ox of Greenland and the Canadian Archipelago), giant moose-elk, giant beaver (up to 183 cm long), native American horse, almost certainly one of the forms of giant ground-sloth, and buffalo, similar to the extinct species *Bison antiquus* and *B. occidentalis*.

Curiously, most of the extinctions occured over little more than 1000 years, ending around 8500 B.C. Extinction was of a magnitude unprecedented in the 70–75 million years of Cenozoic time; it affected only the large mammals; it brought about the total vacating of entire ecological niches; and it was not accompanied by the evolution of competing replacement species. The same kinds of animals had successfully survived earlier periods of comparable climatic and vegetational change with no known reduction in their numbers. The only novel factor associated in time with these puzzling extinctions was the just-recent arrival of man. Although it is difficult to conceive of Stone Age men having such an impact, some biologists and archaeologists believe exactly that. They point to similar extinctions in other parts of the world also coincident with the arrival of fully evolved *Homo sapiens*, noting that in places where man evolved the mammalian faunal extinction record is vastly different. However it came about, the demise of mammoths, mastodons, woodland musk-oxen, and so on marked the end of the Pleistocene Epoch as emphatically as the physical facts of deglaciation, rebounding of the land, recovery of sea levels, and stratified northward expansion of boreal and deciduous forests.

The subject of Early Man's relationship with the Pleistocene fauna will be returned to in the next chapter.

As earlier intimated, the full or partial obliteration by later events of the physical traces of discrete glacial advances and particular lake stages makes the early history of the Great Lakes uneven in reliability and scale of detail from period to period and place to place. Sequences of events in any particular lake basin must be reconstructed with continuing reference to the geological records of the other basins as well. Because the ice front was often much more migratory in some lobes than others and the evidence of pro-glacial lakes was more vigorously erased, the determination of correlative events across basins is often subject to more than one reasonable interpretation. Where lake basins sometimes shared common water planes, as in the cases of Lakes Michigan and Huron and Lakes Huron and Erie, the surviving grounds for determining contemporaneous events may be quite direct and unambiguous. At other times the interposition of an ice lobe and the creation of separate outlets for each lake basin, and then a later drowning of those outlets as ice again withdrew and the land rebounded, may have left very little for detailed comparisons. The late glacial and early Recent history of the Great Lakes is made up of some very strong and some very weak kinds of evidence. The following simplified account begins just before the time man is believed to have entered the lakes country when the area was entirely under ice; it concludes with the establishment of the lakes in their modern form and at their present surface altitudes. Wherever possible the strongest kinds of evidence are relied upon rather than the weakest. In some cases, however, even the strongest kinds are weak indeed. With continuing field studies it is inevitable that any such history faces future alteration in detail, though the main outline is probably less vulnerable to challenge.

The Woodfordian Substage of late Wisconsin time includes several periods of recognizable ice margin fluctuations of more than just local significance. These are recorded in the form of differences in till structure and composition as well as terminal and lateral moraines. In the later career of the Woodfordian ice, but before Port Huron times, at least two successive periods of ice readvance in the western Great Lakes are recorded by the Valparaiso, Tinley, and Defiance moraines, and later by the more complex Lake Border morainic system. The Valparaiso moraine has been extensively mapped in southeastern Wisconsin, northeastern Illinois, northwestern Indiana, and southwestern Michigan. In a terminology now out of favor among Pleistocene stratigraphers, these landforms were ascribed to Cary age. Contemporaneous moraines probably include the Bemis in Iowa and Minnesota, the Union City in Michigan and Indiana, the Powell in Ohio and Pennsylvania, and at least part of the Valley Heads in New York. Radiocarbon dates on wood and other organic material associated with these moraines indicate an age of about 12,000 B.C. or a little earlier. In the eastern Great Lakes some geologists refer to this period as the Port Bruce Stadial. The entire Great Lakes area was beneath the Laurentide glacier at this time.

Sometime after 12,000 B.C. there was a large-scale retrogression of the glacier from the forward positions marked by the Bemis-Valparaiso-Valley

Heads and linking moraines. It was during this retreat that the earliest of the proto-Great Lakes were born. These were the first or Glenwood stage of Glacial Lake Chicago in front of the Lake Michigan lobe, Glacial Lake Maumee in front of the Lake Erie lobe and, a little later, Glacial Lake Saginaw in front of the Saginaw lobe of the Lake Huron ice. The first had a surface elevation of 195 m above modern mean sea level of 18 m above the modern lake and drained into the Mississippi via the Illinois River. Lake Maumee stood successively at 244, 232, and 241 m above sea level and drained, in turn, down the Wabash Valley in Indiana, then northward in front of the Saginaw lobe and across central Michigan to the Grand River valley and into the Glenwood stage of Lake Chicago, and then again via the Wabash River valley. Lake Saginaw emptied across Michigan to Lake Chicago. The multiple moraines of the Lake Border system record more modest readvance and still-stands of the ice during the evolution of these lakes. Glacial Lake Arkona was born when Lakes Maumee and Saginaw merged. Occupying much of the Erie basin and the formerly dry land between the Huron and Saginaw basins in southeastern Michigan, it drained across that state to an expanded Glenwood stage of Lake Chicago. Lake Arkona stood successively at 216, 213, and 212 m.

The succeeding episode of major glacial readvance witnessed a forward movement of the ice front from about 95 to more than 360 km. This new glacial maximum is classically marked by the Port Huron moraine in Michigan, the name of which has been extended to the period during which that and correlative moraines were created. This was the last period of ice advance during the Woodfordian Stadial. Some of the coeval deposits of this well-marked event are the Algona moraine of the Des Moines lobe in Minnesota, the Manitowoc and Shorewood tills in Wisconsin, the Wyoming and Paris moraines in Ontario, and the Hamburg, Auburn, and Fort Covington moraines in New York.

The Port Huron maximum was attained by about 11,000 B.C. At this time a great pro-glacial lake filled the western two-thirds of the Erie basin as well as large adjacent portions of southwestern Ontario, southeastern Michigan, and northwestern Ohio. This was Glacial Lake Whittlesey. It had a surface altitude of 225 m and spilled northward along the ice cliffs to a reborn Lake Saginaw inland of the modern bay. This body of water stood at 212 m and drained across the middle part of the lower Michigan peninsula to Lake Chicago, still at the 195 m Glenwood stage. All of these early lakes must have been extremely cold and infertile bodies. Where especially silt-laden and turbid, they were not as hospitable to fish as the later lakes. With glacial ice collapsing (calving) directly into the lakes, icebergs must have been common. The Lake Superior and Lake Ontario basins, however, were still ice-filled and solidly frozen during the Port Huron period. The end of the Woodfordian Stadial, as measured by the retreat of the Port

2. The Inland Seas

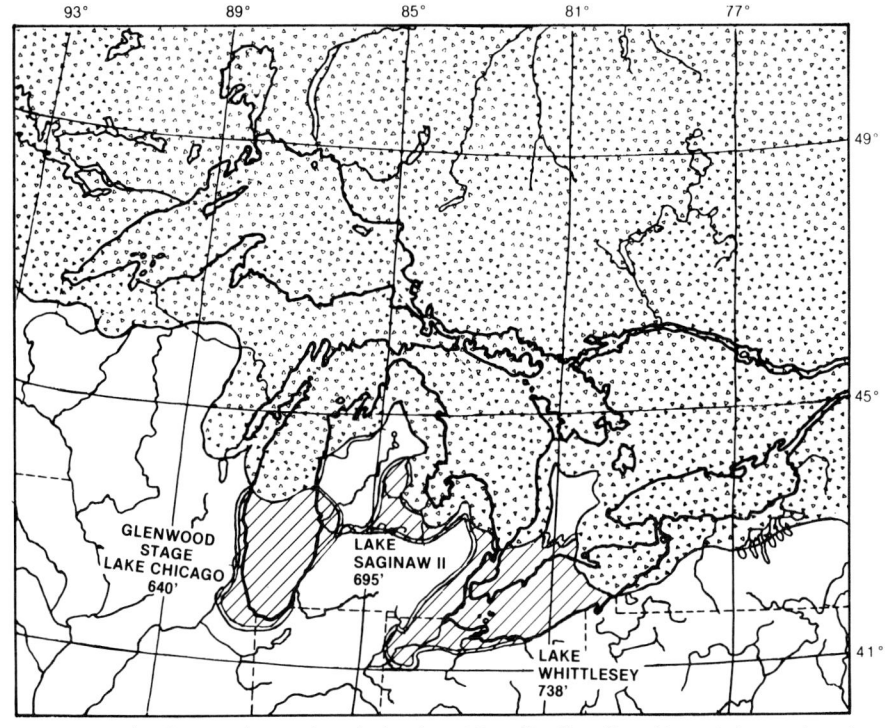

MAP 2.3. *The Great Lakes region during Late Woodfordian (Port Huron) times, showing approximate positions of the ice front and the pro-glacial lakes. Circa 11,000–10,500 B.C. (Modified from Hough 1963 and Prest 1976.)*

Huron ice from its foremost positions is dated between 11,000 and 10,500 B.C.

Major changes took place between the time of the building of the Port Huron moraines, the retreat of the glacier therefrom, and the time of the final Great Lakes ice readvance, variously known as the Valders, Valderan, Two Rivers, or Greatlakean stadial or substage. This episode of ice retreat is the Two Creeks of Twocreekan interval or interstadial. Its end and the maximum ice readvance of the succeeding Valderan Stadial are closely approximated by radiocarbon at around 9900 B.C.

During the Port Huron to Valderan period of glacial retirement and then reassertion, a large pro-glacial lake (Lake Keweenaw) was finally established in the Superior basin as the ice withdrew eastward. Small ice-margin lakes had anticipated Lake Keweenaw in the western part of the basin. The larger lake was evicted when a newly muscled Superior ice lobe reinvaded during the Valderan Stadial. In the Michigan basin the Glenwood stage of Glacial Lake Chicago finally came to an end and was succeeded in turn by the Calumet, Bowmanville, and Tolleston stages at lower levels. The Huron and Erie basins shared a series of lakes with fluctuating shorelines and surface elevations from 210 to 190 m above sea level. These were Lakes Wayne, Warren, Grassmere, and Lundy, and some had multiple beach levels and stages of development. The first two of these lakes drained northward to the Saginaw Bay area and then across the central part of Michigan to the Grand River and the Michigan basin; the later two spilled into the Lake Michigan basin across the northern part of the lower Michigan peninsula. These shifts were produced by a complex interplay of changing lake levels, relative position of the ice margin, and rates of crustal rebounding.

With ice vacating the Lake Ontario basin, Glacial Lake Iroquois was born of the turgid meltwater. Because the Laurentide glacier still filled the St. Lawrence Valley, the new lake drained via an outlet near Rome, New York, thence down the Mohawk Valley to the Hudson lowlands and the sea. For a time its surface was stabilized at about 100 m. A later, short-lived successor stage is sometimes given the separate name Lake Frontenac. Lake Iroquois is believed to have virtually emptied when the Port Huron-age ice blocking a low outlet to the St. Lawrence lowlands withdrew from and unmasked Covey Hill near the New York–Quebec border. Lake Iroquois may have been born as early as about 10,700 B.C. It came to an end at about 9500 B.C. or a bit earlier.

Seeping in as the ice drew back from the deeply depressed St. Lawrence Valley, the Atlantic Ocean invaded as far inland as the eastern end of the Lake Ontario basin and may even for a while have entered it. An arm of this huge marine embayment extended far up the Ottawa Valley. This was probably the route by means of which whales and other sea mammals were able to enter the Algonquin or another early high-water stage in ancestral Lakes Huron–Michigan. Another arm of the so-called Champlain Sea lapped far southward up the Lake Champlain Valley in New York and Vermont. Because the embayment expanded westward and northward with ice withdrawal, and was later expelled as the land rebounded, it had a longer tenure near the Gulf of St. Lawrence than near the Lake Ontario basin. During part of its development the Champlain Sea was coetaneous with Lake Iroquois. Present estimates, based on a number of radiocarbon assays, suggest an age between 10,800 and 8200 B.C. at the outside; during this span there was considerable growth and then contraction of the embayment. At its maximum extent the Champlain Sea inundated at least 53,000 km^2, and the future sites of Montreal and Ottawa lay dark beneath its heaving surface. Many of its beaches are well preserved even today. They and the embayment seabed incorporate not only the remains of salt-water fishes, shellfish, sponges, foraminifera, and bryozoans, but a wide range and abundant representation of seals, porpoises, and whales.

The last generally recognized readvance of the Laurentide ice, the Valders or Valderan, seems to have been somewhat more mobile in the west-

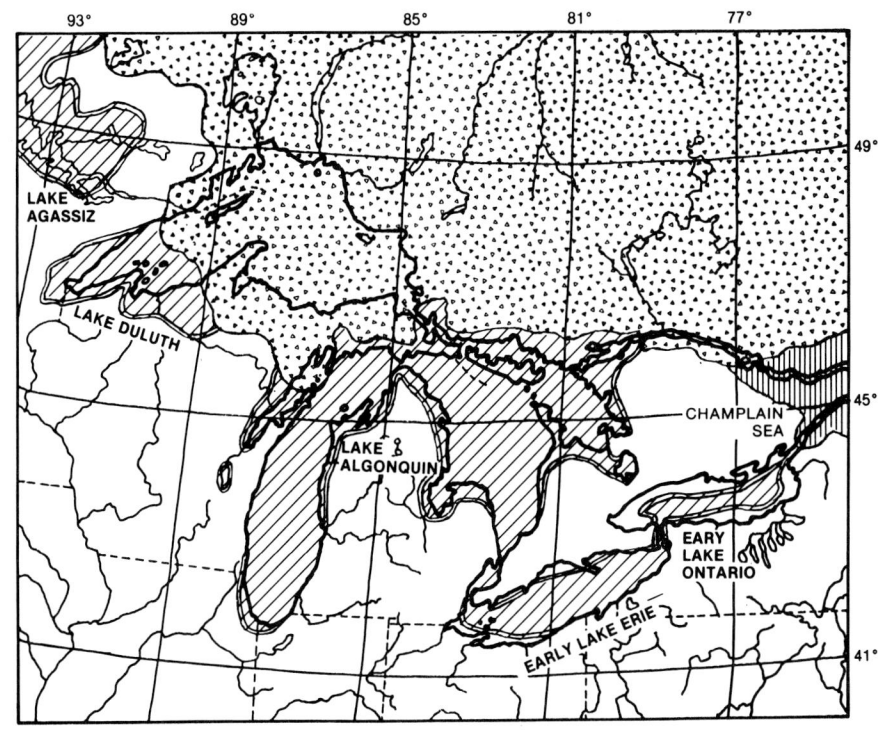

MAP 2.4. *The Great Lakes region during recessional Valderan (Algonquin Stadial) times, showing approximate positions of the ice margin and the lakes, circa 9000–8500 B.C. (Modified from Hough 1963 and Prest 1976.)*

ern than in the eastern Great Lakes. The Lake Simcoe moraine in Ontario, and perhaps the St. Narcisse in Quebec, are definitely post-Port Huron and are probably Valderan in age. The Valderan ice did not override the St. Lawrence Valley but remained north of it.

Following the contraction of the Valderan ice from its southernmost positions, there was an emphatic and wide-spread halt in the upper Michigan peninsula and in Ontario between about 9000 and 8500 B.C. According to some geologists the more recent limit is probably closer to 8100 B.C. Although there was probably no appreciable readvance during this interval, the relative immobility of the hitherto rapidly wasting ice margin was so pronounced that there have been attempts to recognize the still-stand as a distinct post-Valderan stadial: the Algonquin Stadial.

Coincident with the Valderan retreat, including the so-called Algonquin Stadial, a new lake was created in the Superior basin. Its surface varied from 70 to 45 m above that of the modern lake. This was Glacial Lake Duluth. Sometime before 7500 B.C. this was succeeded by the "post-Duluth" and Minong stages. In the Michigan, Huron, and Erie basins Early Lake Algonquin came into being with a surface elevation of 184 m above modern mean sea level. The exact age and duration of this lake are uncertain. However, it was followed by a short-term drop in water level to about 172 m in the Michigan and Huron basins when the ice withdrew from an outlet at that elevation at Kirkfield, Ontario, and the water in those basins drained across Ontario to the Champlain Sea. Lake Erie, at something approaching its modern form, was born about this time. The initiation of overflow from the western lakes eastward via the Trent Valley and later by the Ottawa Valley and the abandonment of the St. Clair outlet made much of southern Ontario for a while an eastern peninsula of Michigan.

A forward pulsation of the ice front or rebounding of the Kirkfield outlet caused the waters in the Michigan and Huron basins to reattain the 184 m level, and the Algonquin lake stage was given a new and longer lease on life; this is the so-called Main Algonquin stage. At various times it drained over the Chicago sill to the Illinois River as well as over the Port Huron outlet into the St. Clair River and on into the basins of the lower lakes and the sea-invaded St. Lawrence Valley. Another spillway may have been along the ice front in Ontario south of the old Kirkfield outlet. For at least a short time, there must have been enough depth of water in the overspill area between Lake Algonquin, or one of its proximate successor stages, and a western arm of the Champlain Sea to allow the entry of sea mammals. Extensive tracts of southwestern Ontario were inundated by Lake Algonquin. Current estimates of the age of the Main Algonquin stage date its inception from 9200 to 8500 B.C., and its demise from 8500 to 8000 B.C. In this account the age of the lake is believed to be bracketed between approximately 9200 and 8400 B.C. During or toward the end of Lake Algonquin, early Lake Ontario was born in the easternmost basin.

At about 7500 B.C. the glacier drew back from North Bay, Ontario, unplugging an outlet so low that it almost emptied the Superior, Michigan, and Huron basins. Between the time of the Main Algonquin stage at 184 m and the unplugging of the very low outlet at North Bay, a series of progressively lower post-Algonquin levels rapidly came and went as the retreating ice sequentially released ever newer and lower spillways. Due to the magnitude of post-glacial uplift along and north of the north shores of the Upper Great Lakes, these early post-Algonquin lake stages are recorded by some of the most dramatically deformed beaches in the world. From earliest to latest these post-Algonquin, pre-North Bay outlet-drained lake stages are named "the Upper Group" (with beaches between 184 and 172 m), Weyebridge (165 m), Penetang (155 m), Cedar Point (150 m), Payette (142 m), Sheguindah (133 m), and Korah (119 m). And even lower levels were yet to come.

When it finally pulled back from the deeply depressed North Bay outlet, the glacier released such a torrent from the already diminished lakes that levels plunged to unprecedented lows throughout the Upper Great Lakes. The Superior basin rapidly drained to the Houghton stage of 110 m. In the

2. The Inland Seas

Michigan and Huron basins the new low-water stages were represented by Lake Chippewa (70 m) and Lake Stanley (55 m), respectively. The existence and surface elevations of these lakes have been established by studies of the bottom topography of the lake basins and of lake bottom cores which show clear evidence of typical shallow-water sediments and shells sandwiched between deep-water deposits. The Houghton-stage lake drained into Lake Stanley via Sault Ste. Marie. Lake Chippewa probably consisted of two interconnected lakes which flowed into Lake Stanley through a now deeply submerged channel in the Straits of Mackinac. During this period of extremely low water, of course, huge areas now beneath Lakes Superior, Michigan, and Huron were dry land and open to plant and animal colonization. Because men had first entered the lakes country long before, it is a virtual certainty that there are many archaeological sites as much as 107 m beneath the surface of Lake Michigan and 122 m beneath Lake Huron. Contemporaneously, Lakes Erie and Ontario were close to their historical levels.

Such extreme low-water levels in the western Great Lakes probably persisted for no more than a few centuries. From their establishment and over the next 5000 years, the lakes slowly refilled their basins as the ice

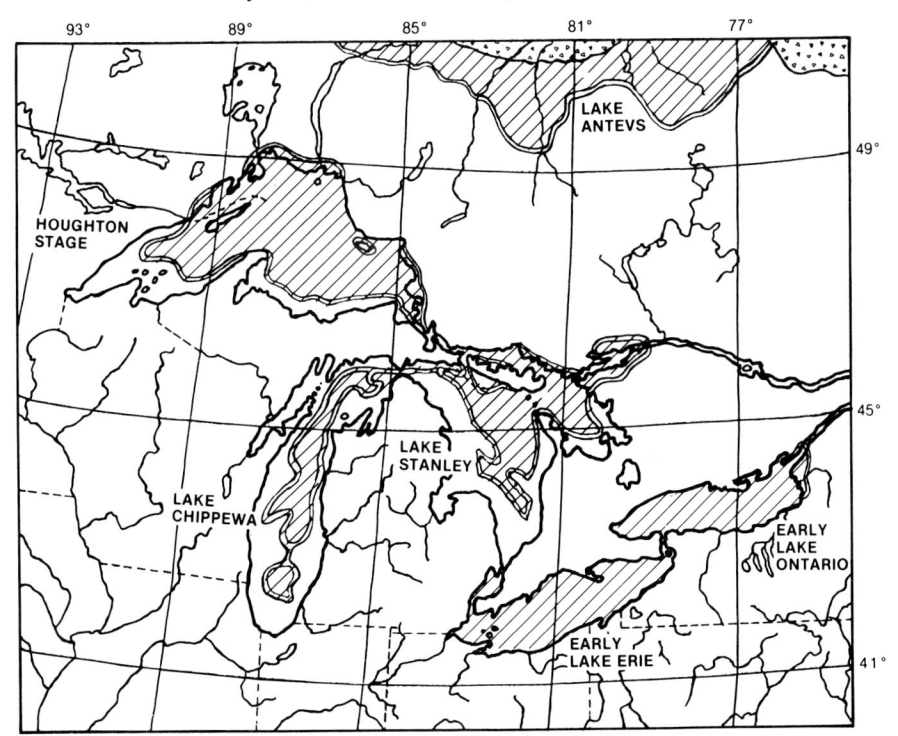

MAP 2.5. *The Great Lakes during the Chippewa–Stanley low-water stage, circa 7500–7000 B.C. (Modified from Hough 1963 and Prest 1976.)*

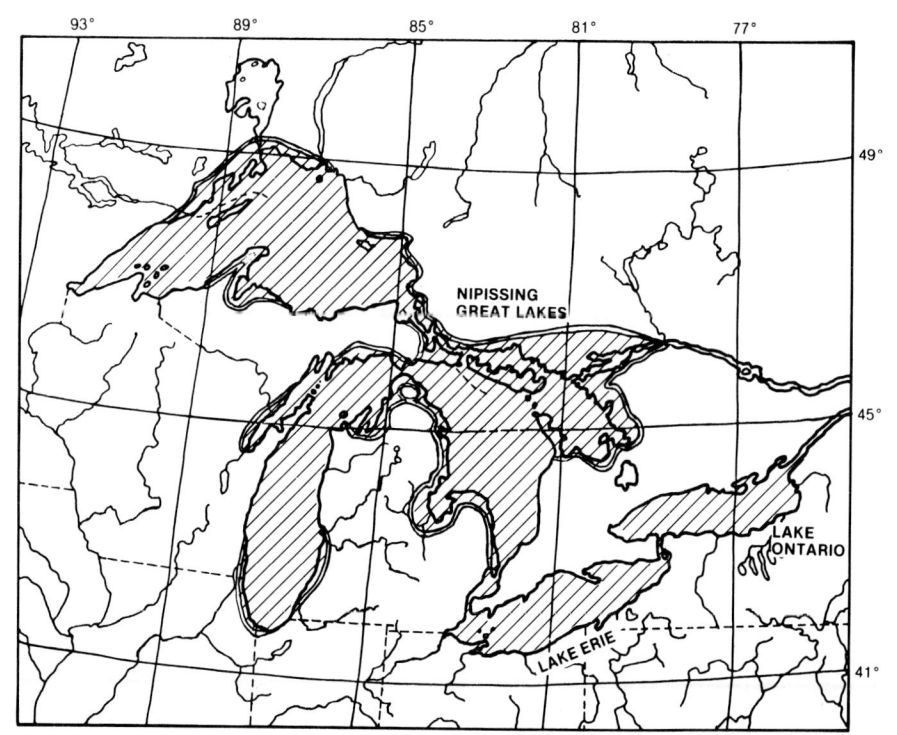

MAP 2.6. *The Great Lakes during the Nipissing high-water stage, circa 2000 B.C. (Modified from Hough 1963 and Prest 1976.)*

continued its contraction far north of the Great Lakes and as crustal recovery sequentially uplifted the low northern outlets above the levels of earlier abandoned higher southern outlets. By about 2000 B.C., or a little earlier, the old Lake Algonquin level of 184 m above sea level was once more, and for the last time, attained. A vast common lake now filled the basins of the three Upper Great Lakes. This was the Nipissing Great Lakes. Its beaches are among the most strongly developed and best preserved of all fossil beaches. Early in its history Lake Nipissing had three outlets: the old North Bay location, now elevated to 184 m by rebounding of the land, the Chicago sill of about the same altitude, and the St. Clair or Port Huron outlet at the southern end of Lake Huron. The latter was cut through glacial gravel deposited thousands of years earlier. Continuing uplift of the northern outlet increased the pressure on the southern. This had little effect on the Chicago outlet, which spilled over bedrock. But the gravel dam at St. Clair offered less resistance. Around 1000 B.C. erosion of this outlet resulted in a 3-m lowering of the enormous lake. This marked the end of Lake Nipissing and the inauguration of the Algoma Great Lakes.

The Algoma Great Lakes still embraced the Superior basin as well as the Michigan and Huron basins with a shared surface elevation of 181 m.

Renewed erosion of the St. Clair spillway eventually dropped the lakes to their modern levels sometime between 500 B.C. and the time of Christ. Because Lake Superior overflows on bedrock at its St. Marys River outlet, it could not drop to the new 177 m level of the other two lakes. Rather than steadily dropping levels from the Algoma to the modern lakes, there seems to have been an interruption in the Superior basin brought about by a temporary halt to this process; an intermediate stage between the Algoma and the modern lake has been called the Sault stage. There is also evidence for a brief post-Algoma high of about 180 m in the Michigan–Huron basins at or within a couple of centuries of the birth of Christ. This still unnamed episode first came to light in archaeological excavations on the Wisconsin Door Peninsula. Except for this as yet unexplained perturbation, the levels of the Great Lakes have remained within their historical vertical ranges for approximately the last two millennia.

References

On the physical geography of the Great Lakes:
Hough 1958.

On the plant and animal communities of the Great Lakes:
Cleland 1966; Hubbs and Lager 1947; Shelford 1963; Yarnell 1964.

On the glacial and post-glacial geological history of the lakes:
Flint 1971; Hough 1958 and 1963; Kelley and Farrand 1967; Mahaney, editor, 1976 (especially Black: "Quaternary Geology of Wisconsin and Contiguous Upper Michigan; Coates: "Quaternary Stratigraphy of New York and Pennsylvania;" Johnson: "Quaternary Stratigraphy in Illinois: Status and Current Problems;" Terasmae and Dreimanis: "Quaternary Stratigraphy of Southern Ontario."); Newman and Salwen, editors, 1977 (especially Dreimanis: "Late Wisconsin Glacial Retreat in the Great Lakes Region, North America;" Edwards and Emery: "Man on the Continental Shelf;" Kirkland and Coates: "The Champlain Sea and Quaternary Deposits in the St. Lawrence Lowland, New York."); Prest 1976; H. E. Wright and Frey, editors, 1965 (especially Frye, Willman, and Black: "Outline of Glacial Geology of Illinois and Wisconsin;" Goldthwait, Dreimanis, Forsyth, Karrow, and White: "Pleistocene Deposits of the Erie Lobe;" Muller: "Quaternary Geology of New York;" Wayne and Zumberge: "Pleistocene Geology of Indiana and Michigan;" H. E. Wright and Ruhe: "Glaciation of Minnesota and Iowa.").

On Great Lakes climatic history and the reconstruction of ancient environments:
Bryson and Wendland 1967; Mahaney, editor, 1976 (especially H. E. Wright: "Ice Retreat and Revegetation in the Western Great Lakes Area"); Newman and Salwen, editors, 1977 (especially Harington: "Marine Mammals in the Champlain Sea and the Great Lakes;" Muller: "Late Glacial and Early Postglacial Environments in Western New York;" Ogden: "The Late Quaternary Paleoenvironmental Record of

Northeastern North America."); H. E. Wright and Frey, editors, 1965 (especially Cushing: "Problems in the Quaternary Phytogeography of the Great Lakes Region").

On the enigma of Late Pleistocene animal extinctions:

Martin and H. E. Wright, editors, 1967 (especially Hester: "The Agency of Man in Animal Extinctions;" Jelinek: "Man's Role in the Extinction of Pleistocene Faunas;" Martin: "Prehistoric Overkill;" Slaughter: "Animal Ranges as a Clue to Late-Pleistocene Extinction").

The Infiltrators
The Paleo-Indians of 9500–8000 B.C.

3

Ice still clutched at the land, and the lactating glacier was nourishing the young, fast-growing lakes when human beings entered the scene. Like the natural order, the later societies and cultures of the descendants of these people underwent profound alterations before the Indian groups known to history made their appearance. But it all started in a Pleistocene landscape.

Because a limited technology buffers the natural environment less thoroughly and more thinly than does a highly developed one, the aborigines of the North American Great Lakes were inevitably and significantly affected by shifting climate and biological resources. But the environment was buffered nonetheless. It was buffered because man always redefines his world into a symbolic order that is not simply the total of any catalog of geological, meterological, botanical, and zoological constituents. As indispensable as adaptations to that changing habitat were, it would be a fundamental error to imagine that, beyond the most elemental level, those adaptations were necessarily immanent in human–natural-order relationships or that by approaching some knowledge of them we have learned most of what there is to know. The archaeological record is a partial one. Human actions in the distant past, as today, were the outcome of more than responses to the flux of externalities. We may be sure that the earliest intruders whose faint traces initiate the Great Lakes archaeological record were in a very large measure what they seem to have been because of the epochal physical and biological changes which they witnessed and of which they were a part. However, we may also be sure that there was more to it than that. A large part of anthropology is testimony that even simple societies to some extent transcend their material settings, finding in them a dynamic tension of enabling and constraining opportunities. Ecological destiny decrees by innuendo rather than iron fiat.

By scholarly convention, the early intruders in the Great Lakes and their contemporaries throughout North America are called Paleo-Indians. Fortunately, some of the stone tools and weapons made by the Paleo-Indians are distinctive, easy to recognize even in broken condition, and not liable to misidentification as the products of later folk. Especially is this true of the projectile points. Unfortunately for ease of discovery, these earliest inhabitants were few in number and lived in such small-scale, widely scattered, nomadic, and lightly equipped societies that they left only a scanty archaeological record. And because they were the first people, erosion has had a longer time to gnaw on their remains.

As if in modest compensation for these latter handicaps, the Paleo-Indians sometimes left their traces at locations that make little sense when compared to the camp and village preferences of later people: at lonely, windswept perches high atop hills or even mountain spurs, or on the relatively slighter elevations of ancient strandlines miles away from the nearest water or any other now recognizable resource. Such locations have only recently come to make some sense as archaeologists have grown to realize how much the environment has changed since men first infiltrated the Great Lakes and the northeast corner of the continent. So while the traces of these ancient folk are rare compared with most later times, here and there they signal like beacons on the raised shores of ancient lakes. They invite correlations among past human actions and the extinguished conditions by which they were partly shaped.

The former presence in an area of these remote inhabitants is most often first signaled by the discovery of one of their tell-tale spearpoints tossed on to the surface by a farmer's plow or a bulldozer's blade, or laid bare in a sand-blow by scouring wind, or dropped from a higher elevation and exposed by slope wash. They most often are found alone, as if lost on some ancient hunt. Occasionally, however, the finding of one Paleo-Indian projectile point leads to the recovery of more, and then of scrapers and gravers and other examples of their chipped-stone products. Such a discovery is something many archaeologists dream about but very few realize. At least today we have a better idea of where to begin looking.

The distinctive spearheads of the earliest Great Lakes people are remarkably similar to those which, when discovered in 1926 and following years in the southwestern United States, established once and for all that men had been in America since at least the end of the Pleistocene Epoch. The Southwestern sites revealed unmistakable and repeated association of artifacts and the butchered skeletons of large Ice Age animals. Such localities as Folsom and Blackwater Draw, New Mexico, Lindenmeier, Colorado, and Lehner, Arizona, have since become among the most famous sites of Early Man in the New World. Mixed with, and in some cases embedded in,

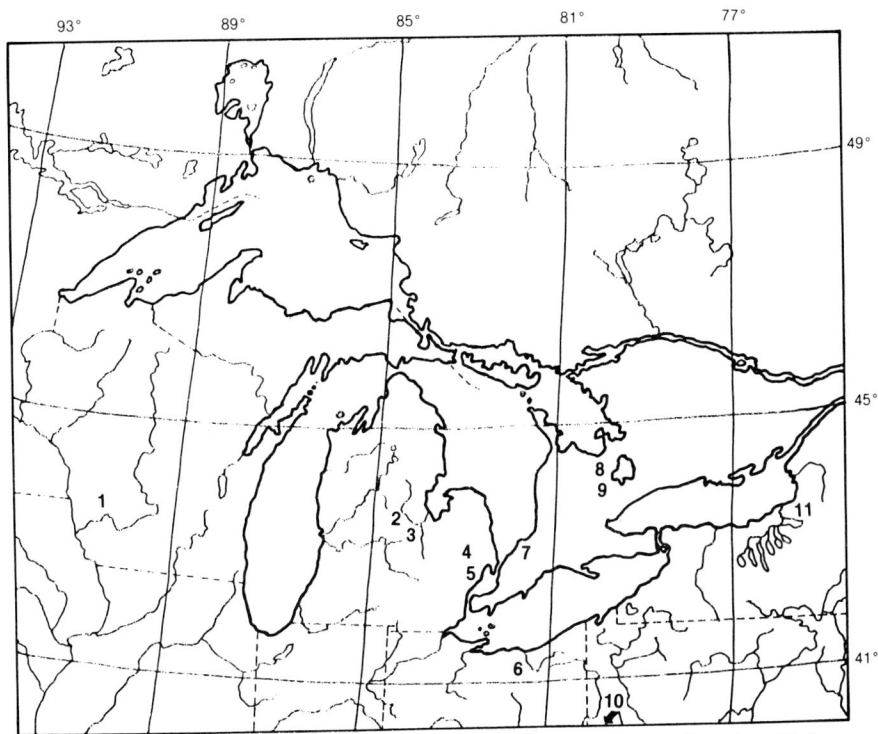

MAP 3.1. *Paleo-Indian sites discussed in the text: (1) Boaz mastodon site; (2) Barnes; (3) Kutsch and Lux sites; (4) Rappuhn mastodon site; (5) Holcombe; (6) Silver Lake; (7) Parkhill; (8) Fisher; (9) Banting and Hussey sites; (10) Meadowcroft (just off map); and (11) Potts.*

the bones of extinct Pleistocene mammals at these and other sites were longitudinally channeled or grooved, lance-shaped, flint spearpoints of extraordinary design and workmanship. They were called fluted points after the longitudinal grooves, their most peculiar and distinctive characteristic. These fluted points have since been proved to have been confined to the end of Pleistocene time and to have been a part of the hunting equipment of the earliest firmly defined and dated prehistoric cultures in America. And they have never been found outside the Western Hemisphere. They appear to have been a New World invention.

In the southwestern United States and on the Great Plains and in the Rocky Mountain foothills, two fluted-point cultures came to be recognized some years after the first realization of the antiquity of the uniquely fashioned spearpoints. Ironically, the most ancient of the two fluted-point cultures was the last to be discovered. It has come to be called the Clovis or Llano Culture, and its signature is the Clovis fluted spearpoint. At a number of sites Clovis points were found in the butchered remains of mammoths. At least over part of their range, then, their makers were elephant hunters. But there is good evidence that they sometimes also hunted other now-extinct animals such as four-pronged antelope, native American horses and camels, and fossil bison.

Folsom was the name bestowed on the later of the two fluted-point cultures. The fluted Folsom point is its most characteristic artifact. Not only have geological evidence and radiocarbon dating shown this culture to be more recent in age than the Clovis or Llano Culture, but the kinds of associated fossil animals are also different. An extinct species of bison was now the major prey, though probably horses and camels were also taken upon occasion. Radiocarbon assays for the Llano Culture fall most consistently within the half millennium between 9500 and 9000 B.C. Dates for the Folsom Culture cluster in the range between 8800 and 8600 B.C., a mere two centuries. However, other Folsom dates stretch the span to about 9000–8000 B.C. While the two-century range is probably too restrictive, a 1000-year tenure for the relatively homogeneous Folsom Culture seems to err in the opposite direction.

Clovis and Folsom spearpoints are fully flaked over both faces. They, the preforms out of which they were sometimes made, and some accompanying knives are usually the only bifaces found on Llano and Folsom sites. Other tools tend to be unifaces (that is, worked on one surface only) or are often flakes simply retouched along one edge. The two very distinctive projectile points differ in a number of ways. Both, however, share the definitive attribute of a hollow ground blade. Commencing at the base and running partly or almost entirely the length of the blade, flutes may occur on one or both faces. Typically, Folsom points tend to have relatively long, wide flutes on both faces. They run almost the full length of the point itself. Clovis points, on the other hand, are frequently fluted on only one face and the fluting scar is relatively narrower and shorter, only rarely exceeding one-third or one-half the length of the artifact. Not uncommonly, the flutes on Clovis points were made by the conjoining and merging of several smaller fluting scars.

Just why Paleo-Indian projectile points were fluted is not known; while fluting would seem to have facilitated hafting, it is not essential, to judge from later projectile points of similar shape which lack it entirely. Both Folsom and Clovis are lanceolate (lance-shaped) points, tending to have parallel opposite edges for at least half their length. They have concave bases. Folsom bases frequently are recurved, having a slight to prominent projection, or "nipple," in the center of the base, a byproduct of the Folsom fluting technique. The concave basal edge of a typical Clovis point lacks this latter feature. Clovis points are generally bigger than Folsom points and much less delicately made. Both types have purposefully dulled lower edges. Many archaeologists think that this minimized the chances of a point's cutting through the sinew bindings which presumably helped secure it in proper alignment in its haft.

In speculating about the purpose of fluting, archaeologists have neglected another important fact about fluted points generally: that such weapons, once embedded in a prey animal, seem to have been designed to stay there until they could be retrieved at butchering. So they were probably not mounted as stabbing spears to be repeatedly thrust in and pulled out. Fluted points always exhibit sharply defined corners, or "ears," where basal and lateral edges meet. These would have functioned as very efficient barbs, and they can only indicate that the projectile points were not intended to be easily pulled out of a wound. Combining this with the presence of fluting—perhaps to help secure alignment on a shaft or foreshaft—as well as heavy edge grinding suggests a functional design of considerable sophistication. Sharp corners acting as barbs, alignment flutes to true and hold the blade for the critical strike, and protective edge dulling to preserve the integrity of bindings, suggest the use of a foreshaft and the expectation that the projectile point, with or without the foreshaft, would disengage from the spearshaft after being struck home—in the manner of a harpoon head, but without the connecting line.

Especially in continental perspective, it is a virtual certainty that in many parts of the Paleo-Indian range tough and resilient straight wood for spearshafts must often have been at a premium. Roving hunters could far more easily carry extra projectile points, or preforms intended for later finishing, than transport additional and far heavier and more cumbersome shafts for spears. This differential would be especially critical if the people had doubts about sources of suitable wood in country they planned to traverse. Far better in such circumstances to risk losing some points in an animal that "got away" than to lose the entire weapon system or to have the vulnerable spearshaft smashed up in the thrashing about of a wounded mammoth or buffalo or caribou. A system designed to allow the spearshaft to disengage and slip out of the wound once the actual armament had been lodged in the quarry, perhaps with the aid of a socketed or beveled foreshaft, would gain a potentially vital economy with no sacrifice in killing efficiency. Indeed, probable bone foreshafts of the appropriate age have already been found at sites in the far west and in Florida. Such a weapon design would not necessarily have been abandoned immediately when early hunters found themselves in better wooded terrain, but may have persisted for some time beyond the necessity—a common enough phenomenon in other human activities. But change did come, of course, because later projectile points are different from their predecessors, fluting specifically was deemphasized or lost entirely, and new weapon designs came into being.

However they were hafted, fluted points were the armament on thrusting or throwing spears energized by the unaided strength of the human arm or they may have tipped javelins which were hurled with the aid of a spear-throwing stick. This device had a hook at one end to engage the proximal end of the javelin. It functioned as an artificial extension of the arm and acted, on the lever principle, to increase measurably the power behind the throw. It was like batting a ball instead of merely throwing one. The spear-thrower was an ingeniously simple and effective launching platform that greatly increased the impact of the projectile with little if any loss in accuracy. It was probably invented in the Old World during the Upper Paleolithic Period; the first migrants may have brought it with them to America. However, the fluted point that armed the spear was native born.

Since the first discoveries of Folsom and Clovis points in the southwestern United States, both types have been found northward into the Canadian plains and eastward across the Mississippi Valley. Folsom points are extremely rare east of the great river, though some have been found near the Great Lakes in Illinois and Wisconsin. Some occur as isolated examples on Paleo-Indian sites as far east as New Jersey. The distribution of Clovis points commonly extends far east of the Mississippi Valley and northward to the Great Lakes. Nevertheless, more typical in these latter regions are other, distinctively eastern fluted varieties. Indeed, it is now apparent that fluted points are much more common east of the Mississippi than west of it and that their range in size, form, and extent and technique of fluting is also greater in the east.

Particularly in eastern North America, fluted points exhibit much more variation than has usually been thought. Some have moderately to markedly constricted edges between the base and some point at or beyond the midpoint of the blade, for example. Some eastern fluted points have a pentagonal outline, some are ovoid, while still others tend to be long quasi-triangles. They also exhibit differences in workmanship and in details of fluting. Holcombe, Barnes, Bull Brook, Reagen, Debert, Cumberland, and Enterline are some of the names of proposed eastern fluted-point varieties. In most cases the appelations are taken from the sites where the points were first found or the largest samples collected. Certain of these variations are probably due to divergenes in age and/or location. To use an analogy from linguistics, some of the variations may be likened to habits of local speech. Certain of the relatively small variations archaeologists observe in fluted points tend to be concentrated in particular regions. Barnes points and Debert points might be thought of as technological and stylistic "dialects" peculiar to the people in two widely separated regions. Enterline and Holcombe points, on the other hand, not only have different geographic distributions but probably differ in age as well, with the former the older. But despite such variations, eastern fluted points are so basically similar to Clovis and Folsom fluted points that a comparable antiquity is a reasonable assumption.

The very limited inventory of other tools of the Paleo-Indian cultures also seem directed at the needs of nomadic hunters. This equipment is restricted in variety and is light, efficient, and remarkably uniform across vast distances. Ovate and lanceolate biface knives and roughed-out blanks

PLATE 3.1. *Fluted points from southeastern Ontario (shown actual size). (Courtesy Peter L. Storck and the Royal Ontario Museum, Toronto, Canada.)*

for the manufacture of spearpoints are normally the only bifaces other than the fluted projectile points themselves. The most common tools are unifacially worked and edge-trimmed flake implements. These take the form of small and precisely fashioned, steeply beveled end-scrapers, many of which must have been mounted in wood, bone, or antler handles. Also common are small to quite large side-scrapers of less uniform shape than the end-scrapers. These would have been indispensable in preparing animal skins for clothing and tent covers. Biface and flake knives were not the only cutting instruments. Fluted points were probably wielded by means of foreshafts as flensing knives following a kill. Some even seem to have been intentionally modified as knives.

Equally common with scrapers on Paleo-Indian sites, although of uncertain function, are so-called gravers. These are flake tools trimmed down at an end or corner to a short, sharp point. They are sometimes exceedingly delicate and needle sharp. Many gravers are equipped with two or more such "spurs." Some authorities speculate that at least the stouter versions may have been employed, chisel-like, to scribe bone and other hard materials in the making and decorating of tool handles, shaft wrenches, foreshafts, awls, needles, and other implements and implement components, only a few of which have managed to survive the ravages of time. Certainly the smaller gravers could have been used to gouge out the eyes in bone needles. They may even have served, in conjunction with powdered red hematite and other pigments, as tattooing needles. That practice was widespread in aboriginal America.

Other ubiquitous Paleo-Indian flints are edge-retouched flake knives and beveled, concave-sided flakes used as drawshaves in thinning and shaping wood, bone, horn, and antler. Especially common on some of the eastern fluted-point sites are wedges or "pièces esquillées." Made on heavy flakes or exhausted cores, they exhibit characteristically battered and worn edges on opposite ends of the tool. It has been suggested that such "wedges" were used to scribe and split bone and other tough material in tool manufacture. Not only are such implements known on Old World archaeological sites, they also persisted in America up to historic times. Indeed, examples from A.D. eighteenth-century Indian sites in the western Great Lakes are essentially identical to those from fluted-point sites. So while they are an important component of many Paleo-Indian tool kits, wedges are not as diagnostic of such contexts as are the other tool types just described. It is interesting that they do not occur on all fluted-point sites where samples are large enough to expect them. This suggests that some tool functions were more specialized than others.

Much less universally distributed on Paleo-Indian stations are burins (transverse-edged chisels widespread in the Eurasian Upper Paleolithic), long parallel-sided flakes or true blades drawn from specially prepared "blade" cores, elongate flint perforators or "twist drills," and heavy percussion-chipped hand-axes or "choppers." Some fluted-point localities more than others produce cores and flakes that are very bladelike and that suggest derivation from an Old World blade industry. On other fluted-point sites it is difficult to see much in the way of such an approach to the fabrication of flints.

A recurring observation about Paleo-Indian sites is how commonly, in dramatic contrast to most sites of later periods, the weapon heads and other artifacts are made of locally or even regionally exotic raw material. Fluted points in eastern and north central Wisconsin, for example, are frequently made of a distinctive quartzite (actually, Hixton silicified sandstone) quarried in the southwestern part of the state. Other specimens from north central Wisconsin are made of Upper Mercer flint from Ohio. The important Shoop site in eastern Pennsylvania contained fluted points and associated tools most of which had been made of a variety of Onondaga chert from western New York. Many New York fluted points are fabricated of jasper from southeastern Pennsylvania or made of Flint Ridge and Upper Mercer flint from Ohio. A number of fluted points in southern New England are chipped out of material quarried in southeastern Pennsylvania and in the Hudson Valley. Some Ontario fluted points are probably of eastern Michigan chert. Although not all fluted-point sites include a high proportion of nonlocal "flints," this pattern is pervasive enough to demonstrate not only a high degree of Paleo-Indian mobility, but in many cases the directions of movement.

The Potts site in Oswego County, New York, is a small, single-component fluted-point station inland of the southeastern corner of Lake Ontario. Located near the terminus of a low promontory overlooking several miles of once marshy lowlands, the site is on a glacial drumlin. It is also well within the area formerly inundated by Glacial Lake Iroquois and thus could not have been occupied until that body of water was drained well down from its maximum elevation. This imposes a maximum possible age of approximately 9500 B.C. for human use of the location. The actual time of first use could have been many centuries after that date, of course. A great many solitary finds of fluted points have also been made on the ancient bed of Lake Iroquois. When occupied, much of the surrounding lowlands must have been relatively wet and boggy.

Less than 100 artifacts were recovered from the Potts site, all of them of Onondaga chert from the western part of the state. Two "Clovis type" fluted points were found in addition to two small narrow side-scrapers shaped like drills as well as a flake scraper-knife. Accompanying these artifacts were simple end-scrapers, some of which look as if they were made from blades, side-scrapers, retouched flake knives, bifacial ovate and lanceolate knives, and a combination drawshave-graver. The few waste flakes recovered indicate that very little chipping was done here other than tool resharpening. The Potts site is a very small and simple Paleo-Indian site compared with other northeastern sites believed to be of approximately the same age, and it has not been directly dated. It is likely that no more than a couple of families of early hunters made camp at the Potts site. And they do not seem to have stayed long or returned often.

A little more imposing than the Potts site is the Barnes site, inland of Saginaw Bay in Midland County in central Michigan. Although this is also a small site, it has yielded approximately 25 whole and fragmentary fluted points and the preforms broken in making them. It is estimated that almost 60% of the fluted points at this locality were broken before they could be finished. A few additional bifaces were found, some of which may also have been preforms. Although between 2000 and 3000 waste flakes were recovered, in addition to 111 channel flakes whose removal produced the flutes on the projectile points, other types of artifacts were rare. These included only a few end- and side-scrapers, a combination scraper-graver, a couple of possible burins, and a small collection of use-modified flakes. About 95% of the waste flakes and most of the finished tools are believed to be of Bayport chert from outcroppings around Saginaw Bay. In view of the conspicuous underrepresentation of scrapers and other tools usually much more common at Paleo-Indian stations, some archaeologists consider Barnes to have been a limited function site where projectile points had been made from highly portable blanks that had been roughed out elsewhere. Presumably spears were re-armed at the Barnes site, also. This may well have been a known and convenient way station for a small group of hunters rather than a usual camp with women and children where a wider range of activities would normally take place.

The Barnes site has been variously reported as having an elevation of 210, 211, and 212 m. Attempts to date it by means of the fossil beach sequence in the region leave considerable leeway. This is because the thought-to-be-associated geological features are mainly uplifted beaches which have not been satisfactorily traced to their zero isobases and thus unequivocally identified with discrete lake stages. Moreover, the suggested lake stages germane to this problem have not been firmly dated themselves. Most archaeologists reasonably maintain that the locality cannot predate the earliest stage of Glacial Lake Warren. This stage had a surface altitude of 210 m as measured elsewhere on undeformed beaches and strandlines. Allowing for some uplift of the Barnes site region since that lake stage was attained offers the virtual certainty that the site location was under water. It was probably still awash when the lake level fell to that of Lake Warren II at 208 m again because of probable upward warping of the beaches, this time of an estimated magnitude 3–5 m at the site. At the earliest, the Barnes site may have been associated with a nearby Lake Warren III beach and a lake elevation of 206 m. Different interpretations of the age of this lake range from 11,000 to 10,500 B.C., 11,000 to 10,000 B.C., and from about 9500 to 9300 B.C. Because the first two age-range estimates include the earlier Warren I and Warren II stages as well as the later Grassmere and Lundy stages, the Warren III stage would presumably fall somewhere near the middle of those outer estimates if the 9500–9300 B.C. range should not be confirmed.

Complicating estimates of the maximum possible age of the Barnes site based on possible beach correlations is the opinion of the archaeologists who have worked with the site material that the major raw material of which the artifacts are made was derived from outcrops around Saginaw Bay that now have a maximum elevation of 195–198 m. These outcrops were under water during the life of Lake Warren III as well as its predecessors. They would also have been submerged during the successor Lake Grassmere whose undeformed beaches stand at 195 m. The outcrops may have emerged from the water for the first time when the lake fell to the Lundy altitude of 189 m. By various correlations, this event took place around 10,500 B.C., 10,000 B.C., or sometime between 9300 and 9000 B.C., but certainly earlier rather than later in this last range.

That the maximum and the intermediate age estimates for the Barnes site are probably too early is suggested by the fact that a particular type of soil called a "podzol," which is believed to have developed over the Paleo-Indian artifacts, is also believed by the site investigators to postdate the establishment of Glacial Lake Algonquin. Actually, no podzol was found over the artifacts at the Barnes site—its onetime presence and later removal by erosion being deduced from observations of staining on the worked flints. Current assays of the career of Lake Algonquin places its main stage somewhere within the span of centuries between 9200 and 8400 B.C. Now it will be recalled that the Barnes site is in Midland County, Michigan. In neighboring Saginaw County, at the Kutsch site, the Lake Algonquin beach overlies the remains of a spruce forest which has been dated by radiocarbon to 9850 B.C., plus or minus 400 years. At that site there is a podzol formed atop the Algonquin beach. The podzol thought to be recorded at the Barnes site by stains on the chert artifacts must postdate their deposition. It cannot have formed before the creation of the Algonquin beach at the Kutsch site or, presumably, an equivalent time at the Barnes site. Unfortunately, no one knows how long a time may have elapsed between the birth of Lake Algonquin and the initiation of podzol formation on its beaches.

The Main Algonquin stage is probably a better candidate for an active lake contemporary with the Barnes site, notwithstanding the closer proximity of the late Warren shore features. The archaeologist most responsible for the detailed analysis of the fluted points and other tools from the Barnes site has later suggested, on the basis of more recent discoveries, that those artifacts are so similar in so many details to others from the Parkhill and other fluted-point sites in Ontario that they may well be the product of the same social group of roaming hunters. The Ontario sites are very convincingly associated with the Lake Algonquin shoreline. The same archaeologist also maintains that the style of fluted point recovered at the Barnes and the thought-to-be contemporaneous Ontario sites is somewhat younger in age than another kind of fluted point which is more like the Clovis type and which has been given the designation "Enterline." Enterline fluted points were first recognized at the Shoop site in eastern Pennsylvania. They have since been found elsewhere. At the Lux site in Michigan, Enterline points have been discovered on a sand ridge only 3 m above the Lake Lundy beach at 189 m. Such a location unequivocally records a time later than any suggested association of the Barnes site and a stage of Lake Warren; it throws into further doubt an age for the Barnes site in excess of the formation of Lake Algonquin. An antiquity no greater than approximately 9200 B.C., the suggested maximum age for Lake Algonquin, seems likely. Of course, the actual time of occupation could have been any time thereafter within the period of fluted-point use.

This somewhat extended and technical discussion of the age and geomorphic associations of the Barnes Paleo-Indian site should demonstrate some of the weaknesses as well as strengths of dating archaeological stations by means of paleogeographical features of the landscape. As has just been seen, the presence of an artifact, or even an entire site, on a raised fossil beach does not of itself date the artifact or the site to the period when the beach was active. People can camp on fossil beaches or raised shorelines long after the extinction of the lake stages which formed them. Such a situation may often simply mean that a particular fossil beach was the only high and dry ground in the vicinity during a rainy spell, that it offered a good lookout, or that more and dryer treefalls were handy there and there were fewer mosquitos in the summer. Such a locality might have provided game animals like caribou or elk with especially good winter forage in a late glacial or early post-glacial tundra–forest edge environment, and thus hunters would naturally be attracted to it. The location of an archaeological site on a fossil beach or a terrace or on or near a glacial moraine can only provide of itself a maximum possible age for the site. Other informatin is needed to ascertain the minimum possible or likely age. The result is a chronological "bracket" within which most chronological indicators converge to indicate probable time of occupation. The confidence that should be placed on such "brackets," or on either end of the range, will necessarily vary from high to low depending on each situation.

Most archaeologists working with early sites have plotted the geographic distribution of certain kinds of artifacts, features, and sites believed likely to be Paleo-Indian. These distributions are then compared with the distribution of other types of artifacts, features, and sites known to be of more recent age. Finally, the distribution of Paleo-Indian remains is compared with geological features, in the Great Lakes with the clues to the last stages of glacial activities and the levels of the early post-glacial lakes. The results do indeed indicate in many cases a close and time-related association. They generally conform with what is known of the age of fluted points elsewhere in North America as determined from geochronology, paleontological associations, and radiocarbon dating.

Some particularly promising work has turned up a number of ancient camp sites of the fluted-point makers along the shoreline of Lake Algonquin in southwestern Ontario from south of Georgian Bay westward to near Lake Huron. Except for a few other camp sites, most previous work in the Great Lakes had been forced to rely on statistical associations of the distribution of individual fluted-point finds and glacial and extinct lake features, as in the pioneering studies in the southern Lake Michigan basin, the lower Michigan peninsula, and New York. There is now an informative and growing collection of actual camp sites situated directly on or very close to (and landward from) shoreline features of Lake Algonquin. In many cases these sites are isolated and remote from extant water sources or any compensating recent or modern resources such as usually attracted Stone Age people to particular localities. Such a pattern of site locations is a powerful argument for the coevality of the ancient lake and the fluted-point makers. While artifacts known from other kinds of information also sometimes occur along the Algonquin shore, unlike the fluted points they also and more commonly occur lakeward of those fossil coasts and are distributed towards more recent shores. This evidence from site and artifact mapping, and the sense it makes when checked against the paleogeography of early post-glacial times, has for some while seemed pretty convincing in view of the independent dating of the similar Llano and Folsom cultures in the West and Southwest. Although none of the Great Lakes Paleo-Indian sites has yet been directly dated by radiocarbon because of failure to find enough firmly associated charcoal or other organic samples, there are now radiocarbon dated fluted-point sites elsewhere in northeastern United States and eastern Canada. And these amply confirm this line of reasoning.

By far the best dated fluted-point site yet excavated anywhere is near the Bay of Fundy in Colchester County, Nova Scotia. This is the multiacre Debert site, and it has yielded one of the richest collections of fluted points and associated tools ever found in a Paleo-Indian site. Like the Bull Brook site in eastern Massachusetts, Debert was a complex encampment of multiple-family living units whose members probably made repeated visits. The average of 14 radiocarbon dates for the Debert site is 8654 B.C. ± 45 years. The chief investigator of the Debert site thinks it was favorably located for the interception of caribou migrations.

In northeastern Pennsylvania at the Shawnee-Minisink site a Paleo-Indian component was found beneath 2 m of deposits, parts of which included later, but still ancient, projectile points and other implements of the Early Archaic Period. The Paleo-Indian component contained a fluted point and more than 70 end-scrapers, side-scrapers, large bifaces, preforms, and cores, in addition to thousands of waste flakes. Radiocarbon dates from the Paleo-Indian occupation are 8640 B.C. ± 300 years and 8800 B.C. ± 600 years. These assays are fully compatible with those from Debert as well as the western fluted-point sites, especially the Folsom ones, and they fall well within the dates presently suggested for Lake Algonquin.

Somewhat anomalous are the radiocarbon dates averaging around 7000 B.C. from the Bull Brook fluted-point site in eastern Massachusetts. This is about 1000 years later than the latest Folsom dates. The assayed material was widely scattered and with no convincing association. Also out of line is the date of 10,580 B.C. ± 370 years from the fluted-point level of the Dutchess Quarry Cave site, Orange County, in southeastern New York. This date is 1000 years older than the oldest best dates for Clovis points in the Southwest.

Most of the Ontario Paleo-Indian sites are very small. Excavation has been minimal or is underway at this writing. Other sites are much larger and more internally complex, suggesting that repeatedly used camps are represented in addition to localities visited only once or twice by small hunting expeditions. Among these sites are the Parkhill, Fisher, Banting, and Hussey sites. The first is on the old Lake Algonquin shore near Parkhill in Middlesex County not far from London. The Fisher site is on a terrace and crest of a knoll immediately overlooking a barrier bar on the fossil coast of Lake Algonquin west of Stayner in Simcoe County. The other two sites are also in Simcoe County. The Hussey site is situated on a small former peninsula which once jutted out into Lake Algonquin, whereas the Banting site is atop a drumlin which was once an island just offshore in a shallow embayment of that same lake.

Both the Parkhill and Fisher sites have provided evidence of discrete and physically separated concentrations of cultural debris suggesting tent locations or other residence or activity areas within the camps. Partly through the clusters thus provided, and partly through an intensive technological and stylistic study of the over 80 fluted points and fragments thereof, the principal site investigator has been able to suggest that at the Parkhill site pairs of men usually worked together in fluting their spearpoints. He believes that fluting was effected by indirect percussion with one individual steadying the weapon head while another delivered a hammer blow to an intervening punch. By fine-scale analysis of small details in workmanship he has also identified "style groups," postulating each as the product of a particular man. Fifteen of these style groups have been isolated at the Parkhill site. As an interesting exercise in trying to estimate the population of the camp, a nuclear family of 3–5 persons has been assumed for each man. An estimate of 45–75 people for the population of the Parkhill site is probably as reasonable an approximation as we are likely to achieve.

Besides fluted points, the Parkhill site has yielded a great many biface

3. The Infiltrators

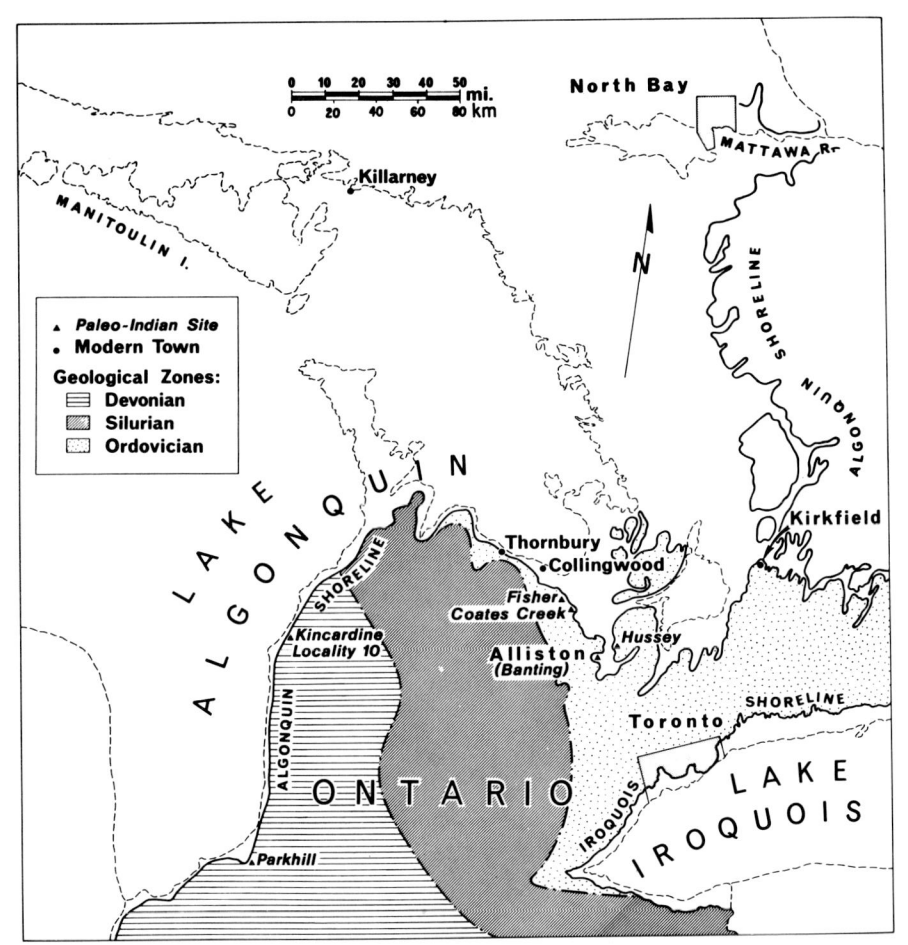

MAP 3.2. *Strandline of Glacial Lake Algonquin in southern Ontario showing locations of Early (Banting, Hussey, Fisher, and Parkhill) and Late (Hussey, Coates Creek) Paleo-Indian sites. (Courtesy Peter L. Storck and the Royal Ontario Museum, Toronto, Canada.)*

and flake knives, scrapers, channel flakes, utilized flakes, preforms, and the waste flakes resulting from finishing preforms into fluted points. Some of the unifacially fluted points show wear perhaps indicative of knife use.

Pollen was recovered from just beneath a hearth containing fluted-point fragments in one section of the Parkhill site. The pollen indicates very high frequencies of pine and spruce in the vicinity. The excavator has noted that the relative types and frequencies of species in the total pollen spectrum are very similar to a pollen spectrum from another locality which has been placed by radiocarbon between 8800 and 7800 B.C. Although hardly convincing evidence, this does, if correct, put a maximum possible age on the archaeological feature. The earlier to middle part of the estimation is com-

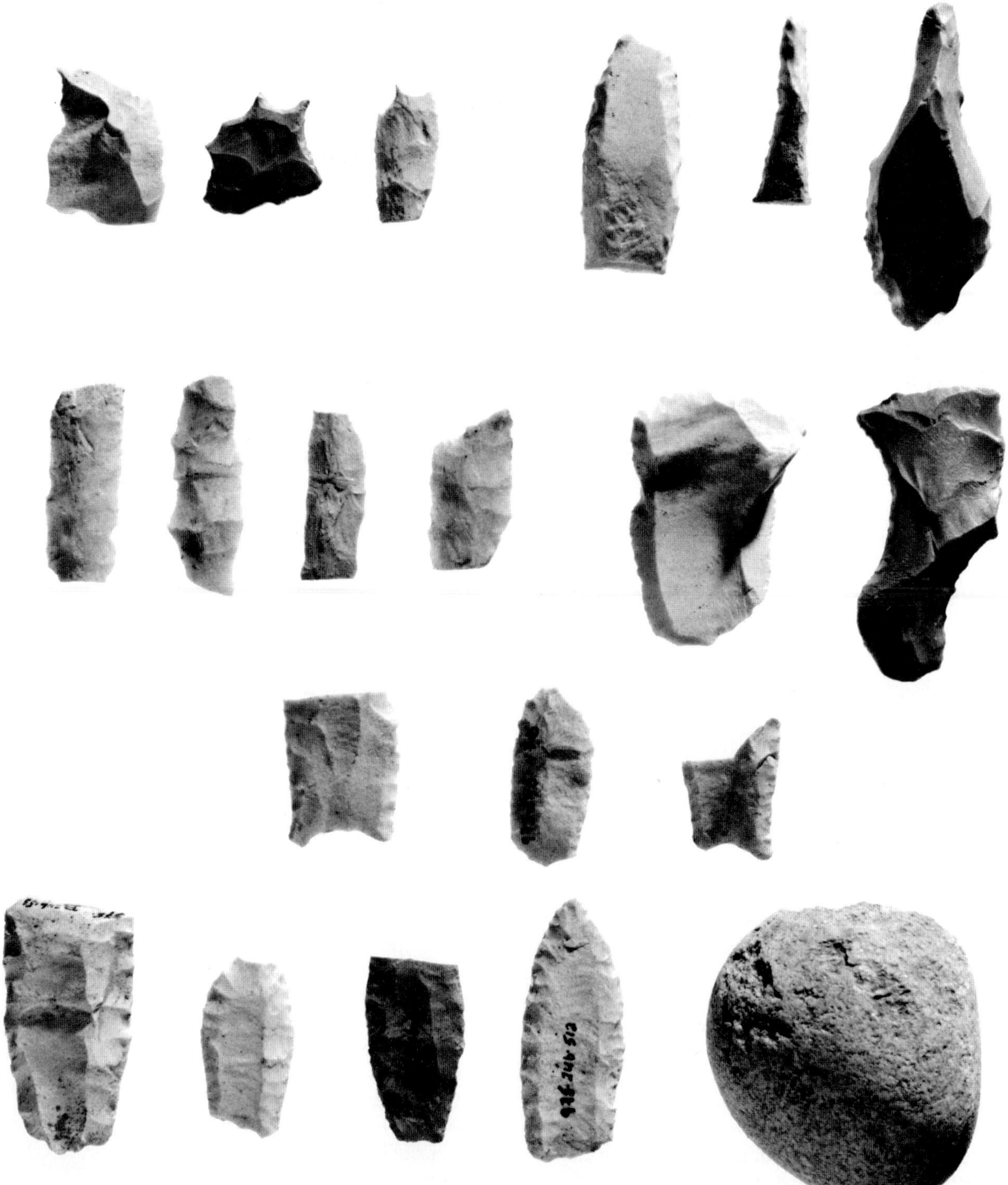

patible with Lake Algonquin age. Although no faunal remains were recovered at the Parkhill site, it has been suggested that, like the Debert site in Nova Scotia and maybe the Holcombe site in Michigan, the location may have been selected in part because it could have been a good place from which to intercept the movements of caribou.

A fascinating and highly controversial question is whether, or to what extent, Early Man in the Great Lakes and elsewhere in eastern North America followed the same habit of big-game hunting as he did on the High Plains and along the Rocky Mountain foothills and in the Southwest. The consistent finding of fluted points in the West with the remains of Pleistocene bison, mammoths, horses, and other long-extinct big-game animals pursuaded some archaeologists that similar artifacts in the East should also have similar paleontological associations. It was likewise assumed that the specialized big-game hunting way of life, so dramatically attested by kill sites in the one part of the continent, would prove to have prevailed in the other as well. However, as eastern fluted point sites were found and investigated, and dramatic kill sites eluded discovery notwithstanding the hundreds of mammoth and mastodon skeletons accidentally unearthed in eastern North America over the last century, enthusiasm for this idea waned. Because most Paleo-Indian sites east of the Mississippi are unaccompanied by preserved bones, it is now a popular notion that big-game hunting was a western specialization not indulged in by the easterners. But just as it is difficult to argue one way in the absence of evidence, so is it difficult to argue the other way. Taken at face value, the reported absence of bones from eastern fluted-point sites can be used neither as reason for nor against the idea that Paleo-Indians in the East hunted now extinct big game, or if, or to what extent, smaller prey were preferred. Fortunately, the absence of bones is no longer total.

The kinds of evidence available on the subsistence practices of eastern North American Paleo-Indians are hardly overwhelming or equally convincing in each case. But there are data bearing on this important question, and they weigh in favor of the initial idea that in the East as well as in the West the makers of fluted points hunted big game now long extinct. This does not mean that only now extinct animals were hunted, nor does it impose the idea that only large beasts were sought after. Indeed, it now seems highly probable that a wide and varying selection of animals large and small, some now totally extinct, some regionally extinct, and others representing genera and species still thriving, were taken when needed

---

PLATE 3.2. *Paleo-Indian artifacts from the the Fisher site, Simcoe County, Ontario. Top row: spurred gravers (left), scraper and two chisels (right); second row: channel flakes from the fluting process (left), scraper and drawshave (right); third row: broken fluted points; bottom row: fluted point broken during manufacture, broken but finished fluted points, hammerstone. (Shown actual size.) (Courtesy Peter L. Storck and the Royal Ontario Museum, Toronto, Canada.)*

and as opportunity permitted. As the ancient hunters entered diverse regions of the New World during their pioneering expansion, they encountered some new kinds of animals and novel ecological situations. We may be sure that they consumed wild plant foods wherever they were familiar and customary components of their diet—much in the manner of historically and ethnographically known hunting people around the world. As opportunity permitted they doubtless varied their fare with small game, birds, and even fish. However, it is important to note that recognizable instruments for the processing of wild plant foods such as nuts and seeds have not been found in fluted-point sites even though they are often abundant in many later archaeological periods. Although berries and certain varieties of tubers and lichens were probably eaten, the lack of vegetable-processing tools is reasonable evidence that plant resources were not as important to the Paleo-Indians as to later people. An expanding role of plants in subsistence is one of the hallmarks of the later Archaic Period cultures, but the shift in that direction was a gradual and halting one. This must have been more a function of the evolving ecosystem than of changing taste.

An initial and necessary hypothesis relevant to this question of Paleo-Indian subsistence in the Great Lakes was that the basic, and in many instances detailed, similarities between western and eastern fluted-point assemblages was a strong case for at least approximate contemporaneity. This has been essentially confirmed as we have seen. Given that fluted-point hunters in the West were taking and eating late Pleistocene big-game animals, further information was provided by the demonstration that eastern fluted-point hunters and many examples of the late Pleistocene megafauna were contemporaries in eastern North America, whether or not in a predator–prey relationship. This certainly suggested that it was reasonable to look for signs of an eastern lifeway comparable to the western. But there was more to it than that.

When the eastern North American localities yielding fluted points and those yielding elements of the late Pleistocene megafauna were mapped and their distributions compared, their several centers of maximum concentration tended to coincide. Furthermore, the sinuous line of northernmost distribution of the one turned out to be also that of the other. This latter phenomenon, dubbed the "Mason-Quimby Line" by one zoogeographer, together with the coextensive maximum density distributions of fluted points and fossil mammals fairly suggest, though they do not prove, that man was attracted for hunting purposes to those places where the now extinct animals were. It is doubtful that the attraction was platonic. Such suggestive mappings of maximum densities have been undertaken in the southeastern as well as the northeastern United States. While an unknown third variable is of course possible for such coincident distributions—such as intensity of farming and other activities which might be expected to increase numbers of reported finds—this fails to explain the congruent lines of northernmost finds. Inasmuch as these latter do not closely coincide in large areas with contemporary ice-front positions (as in Michigan), that consideration may be removed as a possible factor in this relationship. That so many mammoth and, especially, mastodon remains have been found without evidence of the presence of man is most likely due to the fact that most were discovered many years ago by canal diggers, land drainers, and highway builders preoccupied with other concerns in an age when archaeological knowledge was as widely disseminated as archaeologists were rare. Additionally, of course, those extinct mammals had been resident since long before man arrived in the twilight of their evolutionary careers. This further reduces the chances of finding such beasts of the right age to have been encountered and killed by Paleo-Indians.

Direct evidence of what Early Man was killing and eating in and near the Great Lakes is extremely limited but is consistent with the foregoing remarks. Barren Ground caribou (*Rangifer arcticus*), for example, has now been identified among the scanty remnants of bone recovered at the late Paleo-Indian Holcombe site near Detroit. This, of course, is a regionally long-extinct big-game animal limited since late glacial times to the arctic tundra and boreal forest edge in northern Canada and Alaska. Woodland caribou (*Rangifer tarandus*) has been retrieved from the bottom of the lowest of three strata with cultural remains at the Dutchess Quarry Cave site in southeastern New York. This is 485 km south of the known range of caribou in post-glacial time. The bones had been cracked open, probably for extraction of marrow. Also present, though perhaps relating to a separate time horizon, were the remains of deer, elk, and rodents. A fluted point was found near the caribou bones and is almost certainly associated. It is somewhat reminiscent of the so-called Cumberland variety of fluted point, which is much more typical of the southeastern United States. This component at Dutchess Quarry Cave is doubly important because of its unexpectedly early radiocarbon age of 10,580 B.C. ± 370 years, about a millennium before the Llano Culture and Clovis fluted points as presently dated in the West. Regardless of the accuracy of the radiocarbon assay, this is another locality associating fluted points with the late Pleistocene megafauna. It also provides stratigraphic confirmation of the temporal antecedence of fluted points with respect to Archaic Period artifacts, which at this site were found in a higher stratum.

At Silver Lake, Ohio, a broken fluted point has actually been found embedded in a rib of a skeleton of an elk. This big-game animal is one of the Pleistocene forms which has survived into modern times, and when this particular specimen was killed within the period of fluted point use is unknown. Although dating to a later period, numerous remains of a Pleistocene form of extinct bison have been excavated at the Itasca Lake site in northern Minnesota in excellent association with the tools of people who were ultimately descendants of the fluted-point makers themselves.

Although an apparently scavenged, probable mastodon kill, unfortu-

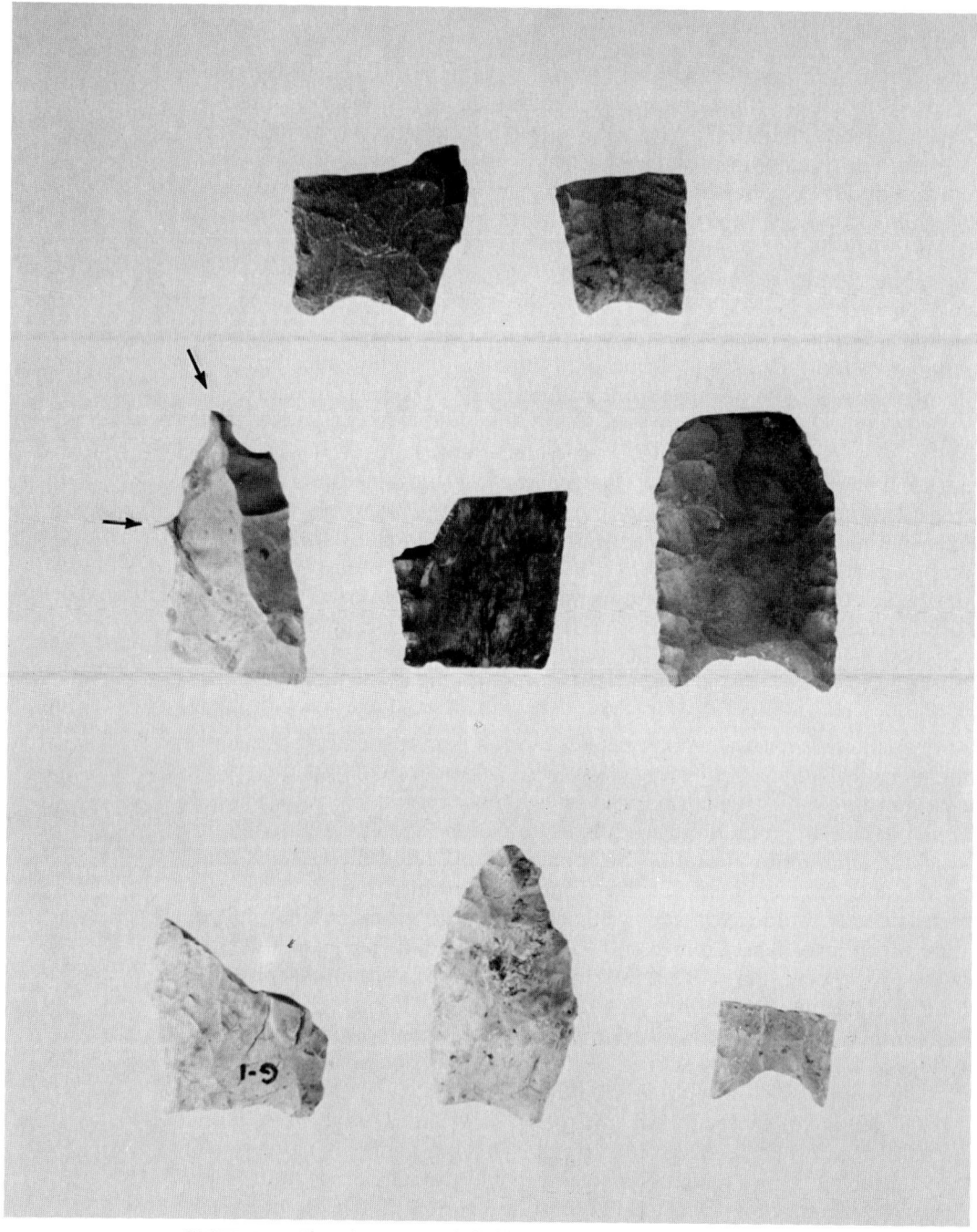

PLATE 3.3. *Fluted points and double-spurred graver from sites in northwestern Ohio and southeastern Michigan (shown actual size). (Courtesy David M. Stothers and the Laboratory of Ethnoarchaeology, University of Toledo, and The Toledo Area Aboriginal Research Society, Inc.)*

nately lacking associated stone tools, has been reported in the lower Michigan peninsula at the Rappuhn site in Lapeer County, the most convincing case for the killing of mastodons in or near the Great Lakes by fluted-point hunters comes from a long-neglected find made many years ago in southwestern Wisconsin. In 1897 some farm boys discovered a mastodon skeleton eroding from a stream bank in Richland County near the town of Boaz. It was subsequently acquired by the state of Wisconsin and has ever since been on exhibit in the geology museum of the University of Wisconsin in Madison. It now appears virtually certain that a projectile point had originally been found in close association with the mastodon bones suggesting, if not a kill, then an attempted one. The significance of this find was overlooked for three-quarters of a century. Painstaking detective work by two University of Wisconsin faculty members, aided and abetted by the longevity and independently confirmed memories of the two surviving discoverers, has at last brought this important find to modern scientific attention. The projectile point believed to have been found so long ago with the Boaz mastodon is a well-made fluted point of Hixton silicified sandstone, or "quartzite," whose source at Silver Mound in Jackson County is 128 km by air north northwest of the Boaz find. This is a common material in the Paleo-Indian Period in Wisconsin. While not "proved," because of the circumstances of discovery, the association of mastodon and fluted point in this case appears highly probable.

Notwithstanding the western Clovis kill sites, no unimpeachable evidence of a mammoth kill has been found in the Great Lakes or, indeed, anywhere else in eastern North America. That Paleo-Indians and mammoths were for some time contemporary in the East is demonstrated by the distributional studies earlier described and by radiocarbon dating. It would certainly be surprising if the eastern mammoths had been immune from attack when their western counterparts were being hunted over a wide area by Clovis people.

Although some prehistorians have wondered about the possibility of hoax, a possibly genuine discovery was the 1864 find near Holly Oak, Delaware, of a whelk shell pendant inscribed with a picture of a woolly mammoth. That Paleo-Indians, if they made such pendants, should have portrayed one of the most impressive of the animals familiar to them is not surprising. The question of authenticity, reasonably raised in view of the uncertainties surrounding the find, has not been settled, although a growing number of archaeologists now accept the artifact as genuine. But it says nothing about the hunting of mammoths. On this question the record remains mute, and the archaeological jury is still out.

Apart from the matter of specific animal associations and their changes over time is the problem of defining the end of the fluted point period in terms of distinct artifact categories. The problem is not as self-evidently resolved as the nomenclature of the period would seem to suggest. The fluting of lanceolate spearpoints did not end abruptly in the Great Lakes region. With little sympathy for the classificatory needs of future archaeologists, the Paleo-Indians gradually reduced the incidence and extent of equipping their projectile points with flutes. So gradual does this process appear to have been in some areas that it becomes an arbitrary judgment where true fluting leaves off and mere basal thinning begins. On most of the early sites there is little difficulty: Fluted points are readily distinguishable from later, nonfluted, points. But at some other sites the fluting is so reduced in frequency and so attenuated in execution that, in one conspicuous instance, two highly reputed and expert archaeologists have been unable to agree whether the projectile points at issue are or are not fluted.

Neither can the end of the fluted point era be defined in a satisfying way by reference to the other kinds of tools usually found with the projectile points. The same basic tool kit found with the fluted points (the characteristic end-scrapers, the side-scrapers, gravers, wedges, ovate bifaces, etc.) survives their demise and occurs with little or no modification into the next period. Although this may be bothersome for those people who prefer neat and mutually exclusive typologies, it is much more importantly an indication of cultural continuity.

A Great Lakes site which thus seems to exhibit the symptoms of fin de siècle status is the Holcombe site in Macomb County in southeastern Michigan. A series of small sites at this locality have produced projectile points and other Paleo-Indian artifacts in considerable numbers along and back of a 184-m beach. The main site also yielded animal-bone fragments, including Barren Ground caribou. The amateur and professional archaeologists who collected and excavated at the Holcombe site identified between five and eight small, discrete clusters of cultural debris arranged around a large central ground. They produced evidence that the small areas were probably tent or individual family locations where, among other activities, chipped stone tools were finished. The much larger and more ill-defined center may have been a "communal area" shared by the individual families. Here butchering and cooking of game took place, and the initial shaping of tool preforms was begun, possibly using communally owned Bayport chert that had been brought from sources 161 km to the north. A very small number of artifacts are of Upper Mercer chert from Ohio. The excavators of the site have estimated a camp population of 20-50 people.

Archaeologists who have worked with the Barnes and Parkhill sites have been so struck by the detailed and minute correspondences in technology and style among their respective groups of artifacts that they have proposed them as the products of a single society moving through a hunting territory. Similarly, the Holcombe site at a later time must have been but one of a number of sites left by other people exploiting country from west of Lake St. Clair to the south shore of Lake Erie. Projectile points indistinguishable from those from the Holcombe site, and likewise of Bayport chert, have been found in northwestern and north central Ohio. They ought to be contemporary with the Michigan specimens.

The age of the Holcombe site has been a matter of some controversy. Some of the projectile points are definitely fluted, some are definitely not, while the great majority are only basally thinned. As a group, they are generally similar to early (but post-Folsom) types widely represented in the West under the catch-all label "Plano." Most of them look very much like the kind of thing one would expect of a site inhabited when the practice of fluting projectile points was on its way out and newer styles were coming into vogue. Probably most prehistorians would place the Holcombe site within the fluted-point tradition but, as in the case of the similar Reagen site high above Lake Champlain in Vermont, as a very late representative.

Attempts to date the site by geochronological means have not met with wide acclaim. A proposed association has been made with "Lake Clinton"—a small, very shallow, and almost closed entrapment behind the Mt. Clemens moraine just inland of Lake St. Clair. This proposed lake would have drained through that moraine via a narrow channel. Lake Clinton has been tentatively connected, because of the 184 m elevation of its beaches, to Lake Algonquin. The site excavators point to the known finds of Holcombe-like points—in northern Ohio especially—on parts of the lake bed of Early Lake Algonquin, and conclude from this that the 184-m Lake Clinton beaches must relate to the later Main Algonquin stage. However, other archaeologists note that Holcombe-like projectile points occur *lakeward* of the Main Algonquin beaches in Ontario. These could only have been deposited after that lake had fallen from its maximum level, thus making the Holcombe site–Main Algonquin correlation more apparent than real.

Equally incompatible with the originally proposed geochronology is the enormously high probability—indeed, virtual certainty—that the dam which maintained the Main Algonquin stage at its 184-m level was the Port Huron sill at the south end of Lake Huron. Because Lake Clinton drained into the Lake St. Clair basin well to the south of this spillway, its surface could not have been in equilibrium and coevality with the Algonquin waters. An alternative argument would be that the Lake Clinton beaches were formed during Early Algonquin times when water in the Lakes Huron and Erie basins shared the same surface elevation, but that the occupants responsible for the Holcombe site did not camp there until much later. Long after Lake Clinton had ebbed from its beaches, its shallow basin probably acted to catch and retain spring melt water and rain; for centuries after its draining from a true lake, it may have been a marsh attractive to waterfowl, its margins periodically traversed by caribou. These considerations would have made the site and its environs attractive to Early Man. The time of actual habitation, and the end of the fluted-point tradition in the Great Lakes, could have been during one of the early post-Main Algonquin lake stages, though there is no direct way to demonstrate this. By such an interpretation, the Holcombe site people were living in the area sometime after 8400 B.C., the current best upper estimate for the age of the Main Algonquin stage, but probably before 7500 B.C., the time at which the ice withdrew from the North Bay outlet in Ontario and the upper lakes drained to their lowest levels. A date of one or two centuries on either side of 8000 B.C. (and probably later rather than earlier) is the likeliest time for the occupation of the Holcombe site.

Such a late date for the end of the period of fluted-point use might seem to be somewhat incompatible with the general pattern of fluted-point distribution in Michigan. Aside from the proposition that Holcombe points are probably the latest fluted points in their area, elsewhere in the lower peninsula by far the greater part of the land where fluted points have been found was ice-free and open for human penetration by about 12,800 B.C. Indeed, one prominent and archaeologically sophisticated geologist has argued that many, if not most, Paleo-Indians were contemporaneous with the ice front of the Port Huron moraine of Late Woodfordian time (about 10,500 B.C. in his reckoning, 11,000 B.C. by most other calibrations). However, caution in accepting such a chronology needs to be exercised. Because there are large stretches of country between the Port Huron and the later Two Rivers (Valderan period) moraines that are virtually devoid of fluted points and because there are many such artifacts south of the Port Huron moraine, it has been maintained that the Port Huron moraine must have been the active ice front when Paleo-Indians pressed to their northernmost limits. But there are equally large tracts of land south of the Port Huron moraines also devoid of fluted points. As suggested before, the limiting factor may have been the distribution of game and its suitable browse rather than the ice front per se.

Similarly, possible associations of isolated fluted points with the post-Port Huron, pre-Valderan Glenwood and Calumet stages of Glacial Lake Chicago, and that between the Barnes site and Lake Warren II beaches, assuming their correctness for purpose of illustration, yield *maximum* limits for the age of the Paleo-Indian remains. Estimates of their *minimum* ages are obtained by the radiocarbon dating of fluted-point sites in the far West and East as well as by the kinds of distributional evidence earlier reviewed. Although much of the land was available for human occupation for approximately 3000 years before about 10,000 B.C., it does not appear that people were available to take advantage of the fact. When the Michigan data are looked at from the vantage point of the whole Great Lakes and beyond, an antiquity on the order of about 9500–8000 B.C. best accounts for the archaeological, geological, biological, and radiocarbon information presently available.

It is now reasonably established by a variety of means that the earliest fluted-point makers were present in the New World south of the continen-

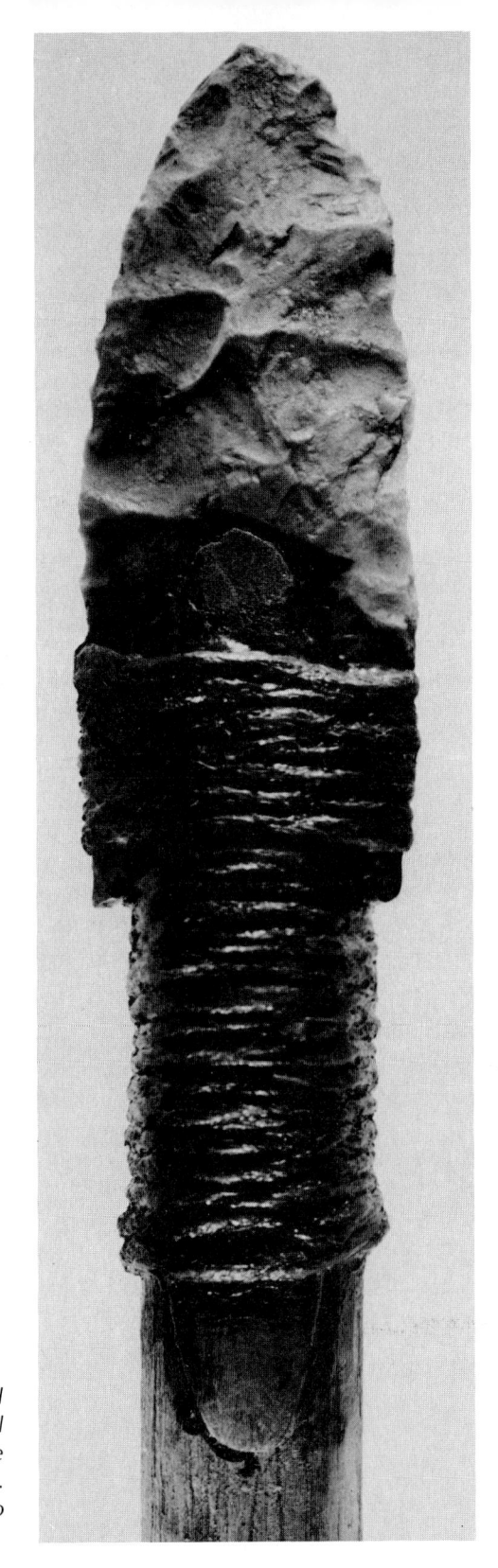

PLATE 3.4. *Fluted point in simulated hafting with foreshaft (twice actual size). This differs from the conjecture offered in the text. (Courtesy Peter L. Storck and the Royal Ontario Museum, Toronto, Canda.)*

tal glaciers by at least 12,000–11,500 years ago. And within a single millennium they had met with such reproductive success as to attain a virtual continental distribution. Their unique artifacts are thinly spread from near the margins of the Valderan ice during an early phase of its retreat, southward into Mexico and Central America, and from the Pacific to the Atlantic coasts. Rare fluted points and associated burins and other tools have also been found in unglaciated parts of Alaska northward to the Brooks Range. Hard on the heels of the earliest dates for fluted points in North America, radiocarbon, geological, and paleontological evidence show man to have been present at the southern tip of South America. There, too, their remains are found with proof of their hunting now long-extinct Pleistocene mammals, though with their own by now unique spearpoints.

All of this suggests at least two things: (*a*) that the fanning out and southward thrusting migrations of the Paleo-Indians from their breakout point between and below the continental glaciers were highly successful and relatively rapid, and (*b*) that the Western Hemisphere south of Alaska was essentially devoid of people until around the time signaled by the earliest dated fluted-point sites. Such hints as there are of possible antecedent populations in the New World are not compelling. They are tantalizing but ambiguous, suggestive enough to promote continued searching, but persistently and puzzlingly "soft." Compared with the empirical record for the fluted-point makers, they have resisted pinning down. Nevertheless, it does appear that it was only *after* people were in America that the signature fluted projectile point was developed; how long after and where that took place are unknown. But this fact is sufficient in itself to establish as a theoretical necessity the existence of a pre-fluted-point cultural period in some part of North America. The so-far unremitting failure of prehistorians to come up with more than isolated dates floating in a cultural limbo, pseudoassemblages, and species of arguments that are vulnerable to alternative logic of equal or greater plausibility has been disappointing. An undoubted pre-Paleo-Indian culture remains to be empirically validated. The search goes on.

There is no pre-fluted-point archaeology in the Great Lakes country. In view of its glacial history, it is unlikely that there ever will be, regardless of whatever the future unfolds elsewhere. The closest nearby possibility of an antecedent cultural stage or, conceivably, an anomalously early Paleo-Indian component, is at the Meadowcroft Rockshelter site in southwestern Pennsylvania. Here very early occupations have been convincingly associated with organic samples yielding radiocarbon ages of around 14,000 B.C. Unfortunately, culturally distinctive artifacts have not been recovered in these most ancient levels; all of the recovered animal bones are of modern forms and of species at home in a post-glacial, rather than a glacial period, environment; associated hardwood plant remains are difficult to reconcile with such an early age; and the possibility of radiocarbon sample contamination by "dead" carbon in this coal-rich region has not been resolved.

Accepting the view that the fluted-point makers were the first people to penetrate most of North America below the ice massifs, their apparent rapidity in moving into and through virgin country must have been due to more than chronic wanderlust and onward beckoning empty space. As previously maintained, a very reasonable case can be made for not only the idea that the fluted-point makers were importantly involved in hunting elements of the late Pleistocene megafauna in eastern North America—including regionally extinct but otherwise surviving forms like caribou and musk ox—but that this was a major reason for their phenomenal dispersion. The key to their remarkable transcontinental distribution was that they had specialized just enough in migratory big-game hunting to allow them to selectively ignore and override ecological differences from region to region that more parochially adapted people would have found insurmountable without more radical changes in their culture than seems to be attested by Paleo-Indian remains. It may be argued that once the primary adaptation had been made to the effective hunting of the Ice Age herbivores, all other adaptations became secondary and derivative. By selective predation man could migrate anywhere the game led, switching from one prey population to another as opportunity suggested or necessity demanded. Smaller game and a restricted variety of wild plant foods supplemented the main diet and buffered episodes between successful hunts. Helpful to this thesis are the mammoth and bison kill sites in the western United States. Also helpful is the knowledge that the probable Asiatic ancestors of the Paleo-Indians were in fact nomadic Upper Paleolithic hunters with an imposing archaeological record of effective big-game hunting.

By 20,000 years ago or before, Upper Paleolithic hunters were deep into Siberia living off mammoths and herds of reindeer and horses. They had already perfected the cold-weather clothing and north-latitude terrestrial hunting techniques prerequisite to passage of the Bering "arctic filter" into the New World. Here they encountered a seemingly limitless extension of the world they already knew. They had in fact, without knowing it, discovered the other side of the moon. And here was naive game—abundant large herbivores whose evolution totally apart from human beings left them, initially at least, ill prepared to cope with this new and lethal predator. As seen in Chapter 2, this picture has so impressed some biologists and archaeologists that, taken in consideration with other data, they have even proposed that it was the arrival of man that precipitated the unprecedentedly large-scale extinctions of large New World mammals at the close of the last Ice Age. While it is by no means necessary to subscribe to so cataclysmic a role for human predatory efficiency, it certainly seems to have been the case that the Asiatic Upper Paleolithic expansion into the Western Hemisphere continued an enormously successful way of life. Their thin tide of widely spaced, small hunting bands, perhaps confined for several centuries to interior unglaciated Alaska, launched southward when conditions permitted.

Only stone and, even rarer, bone tools, hearths, fragments of animal skeletons, and the patterned disposition of debris within sites and of sites on the landscape are all that have survived the 10,000-plus years that have come and gone since the fluted-point makers squinted into the reflections of the aborning Great Lakes. The fur robes and windproof tailored clothes, rawhide containers, skin windbreak and tent covers, twisted sinew thread, braided-hair and bark-fiber cord and carrying straps, wooden sled or toboggan runners and spearshafts and tool handles, and all else fashioned of perishable materials, are gone. And, of course, the people with their language and their social relations and their view of the nature of themselves and the world are gone. Because there is no necessarily close, let alone one-to-one, correspondence between any of these things and the partial and extremely limited cultural refuse people leave behind them, it is hard to get at a sense of the people themselves in their individual and collective complexities. A sovereign cognitive realm inhabited by symbols and reified by practical dreamers expired. Extinct are not only mammoths and mastodons, but equally gone are Progenitor of Mammoth and Sender of Mastodon, and Grandfather and Grandmother of the People. And in all of that ice, on the vast steppe-tundra with the moaning wind, in the dark spruce forests, who now knows what also peopled those places as the Paleo-Indians sought to comprehend and explain themselves and the world. Was Ice Bone-Breaker there? Or Windigo? Or Old Man Coyote's grandfather? If not them, then other things known by other names. But these are not archaeologically recoverable. They dissolve by their nature beyond reconstitution.

The Paleo-Indians doubtless called themselves by a noun signifying "People," "Men," "Original Men," or "Real Men," for that has long and wide been the practice of historically and ethnographically known hunters and gatherers. In what language the name was uttered is forever beyond recapture. Nevertheless, with the perspective of ethnology, the fluted-point people are not unrecognizable despite their distance in time. Small-scale in numbers, social perception, and products, they would have lived in bands or very simple "tribes" structured for mobility and to ensure the cooperation of the males in scouting, hunting, and defense. Their numbers have been hinted at by the camp-size estimates previously summarized. Certainly these were kinship societies, membership being a function of birth or marriage. Probably most archaeologists would back odds that kinship was reckoned, if not patrilaterally, then bilaterally, but with a bias favoring the male line, and that in most instances the preferred place for a newly married couple to reside would have been with the husband's, rather than the wife's, natal band. This is because of a general pattern among hunters and gatherers to reckon descent and maintain living units focused on the father and his kin wherever the male's role is apt to be preponderant or especially critical in food-getting. But the probabilities are somewhat less than 75%. The trouble is, some North American hunting tribes are known to have "been" patrilineal, whereas others were matrilineal or bilateral; some practiced patrilocality, others matrilocality, or neither, or something of both. And these were usually ideal patterns often defied in real life depending on other, more pressing contingencies. Whatever its rules of descent or residence or whether or not preferential cross-cousin marriages were validated by practice, the Paleo-Indians lived out their lives in small societies that were simply extensions on the family. Indeed, they *were* family.

We have no true ethnographic parallels to what often must have been the heady life of the Paleo-Indians. Being the first to hunt the rich big-game of the North American Pleistocene world brought satisfying rewards. That lifeway doubtless entailed episodes of weary tracking followed by explosive periods of high tension and extreme physical exertion, but with the intervention of long stretches of easy living and even indolence, the usual lot of hunters everywhere. The critical times were when the signs of animal movements seemed capricious and events proved unpredictable, or when someone was injured, or the little society was isolated and closed off in blizzard.

Bereft of specifics, we may at least appreciate in a general way the humanity behind the archaeology. Who has knowingly trudged along ancient beach lines and not caught an echo of muffled, lingering thunder where breezes sigh amid grass and trees far from present shores? (And heard another's fainter footfall in a brief respite between successions of breakers). We need not be committed to mysticism to sense ghosts recalled by lonely wind and scudding clouds at a Barnes or a Potts site. We can imagine them wondering with us at the individual's claim on the tenacity of life. The Paleo-Indians opened the trails into the Great Lakes and for 1000 years followed a way of life that to each individual must have seemed eternally fixed.

By 8000 B.C. eternity turned out to be segmented, and the constituent segments finite. The first segment in the history of man in the Great Lakes attained closure. The Ice Age was dissolving and the trumpeting of elephants reverberated into silence. The fluted-point makers were now gone, but they had shared in the final immortality of man and his eternal last hope: They had children.

References

On the Paleo-Indians in continental perspective:
Griffin 1979; Haynes 1964; Jennings 1974; R. J. Mason 1962; Storck 1975; Wormington 1957.

On Great Lakes and neighboring Paleo-Indian artifact and site distributions, their age, and geomorphological associations:
Deller 1979; Farrand 1977; Funk 1972; Funk, Walters, Ehlers, Guilday, and Connally 1969; Garrad 1971; Griffin 1965; R. J. Mason 1958 and 1962; Newman and Salwen, editors, 1977 (especially Griffin: "A Commentary on Early Man Studies in the Northeast;" Adovasio, Gunn, Donahue, and Stuckenrath: "Progress Report on the Meadowcroft Rockshelter—A 16,000 Year Chronicle;" Haynes: "When and From Where Did Man Arrive in Northeastern North America: A Discussion;" McNett, McMillan, and Marshall: "The Shawnee-Minisink Site"); Prufer and Baby 1963; Quimby 1958 and 1960b (especially Chapter 4: "Mastodons and Men"); Ritchie 1957 and 1969; Ritchie and Funk 1973 (especially Funk: "The West Athens Hill Site (Cox 7)," and Ritchie and Funk: "Interpretations—The Paleo-Indian Stage"); Roosa 1965; Stoltman and Workman 1969; Wittry 1965.

On inferring the Paleo-Indian life-way:
Fitting 1970 (especially Chapter III: "The Early Hunters"); Funk 1976 and 1978; MacDonald 1968; R. J. Mason 1962; Williams and Stoltman 1965.

On the Barnes site, Michigan:
H. T. Wright and Roosa 1966.

On the Boaz mastodon site, Wisconsin:
Palmer and Stoltman 1976.

On the Fisher, Banting, and Hussey sites, Ontario:
Storck 1978a and 1979.

On the Holcombe site, Michigan:
Fitting, DeVisscher, and Wahla 1966.

On the Parkhill site, Ontario:
Roosa 1977a and 1977b.

On the Potts site, New York:
Ritchie 1969 (pp. 22–30).

For further references:
Moeller, editor, 1977.

Interregnum
The Late Paleo-Indian or Early Archaic Period

4

Just like children of common parents, cultures descended from the same parent culture have their own individualities. Because contingencies as well as innate properties combine to make up the individual case, the direction and magnitude of uniqueness preclude prediction even though, in the main, legacy assures that the offspring are more similar than different. Biologists, with a somewhat surer understanding of life processes than anthropologists have acquired for cultural processes, express this contrast as between *genotype* (the predisposing genetic inheritance) and *phenotype* (the result of the former acted upon by the total environment—the contingencies). Anthropologists lack such a precise vocabulary. Some archaeologists maintain that, during the first one or two millennia following the Paleo-Indian period, two kinds of cultures, or, at least, projectile-point style traditions, seem to be present in the prehistoric record of the Great Lakes and Northeast, and that they were contemporaries through all or most of this time. As implied in Chapter 3, the paternity of one allows of no doubt, whereas that of the second is perhaps not as clear.

In this perspective, the first culture is such an obvious descendant of the fluted-point makers that it has been called "Late Paleo-Indian." It has been solidly linked to the post-Folsom, but still early, fossil bison-hunting, Plano cultures of the Plains, Rocky Mountain foothills, and Southwest. Aside from its lesser antiquity, the chief difference separating the Late Paleo-Indian cultural pattern from the fluted-point makers—which thus become "Early" Paleo-Indian—is in the matter of projectile-point styles. Otherwise, there is usually little to tell them apart. The limited Paleo-Indian tool kit persists unaltered well into the first half of this next period. And even in the projectile points fundamental continuities persist. Fluting disappears entirely or survives in attenuated forms in one or two varieties of the Late Paleo-Indian point styles. The lanceolate point form survives, however, as does edge dulling where the points were hafted. The development of truly outstanding flint craftsmanship seen in Folsom and some other fluted-point varieties is carried forward and further elaborated in many Late Paleo-Indian projectile points. Although it is known from numerous excavated sites in the West that the Plano groups continued to favor the big-game-hunting way of life of their forebearers, there is no direct evidence bearing on this in the Great Lakes or elsewhere in the East. It seems likely that the same bias would have been indulged wherever conditions permitted. It bears repeating that the archaeologists who have been most impressed by these striking continuities have temporally classified their respective expressions according to an Early Paleo-Indian Period (circa 9500–8000 B.C.) and a Late Paleo-Indian period (circa 8000–6000 B.C.). In the Great Lakes, as elsewhere, the signature artifact of the first period is the fluted point. The second period is signaled by a great increase in projectile-point varieties, but all fundamentally similar to the Plano types in the West.

This neat and unilineal temporal model appears less than adequate, however, when it is remembered that many archaeologists see signs of another post-fluted-point culture more or less contemporaneous with the Plano and Plano-like assemblages of the Late Paleo-Indian period. The hallmarks of this other culture are several varieties of notched projectile points. This attribute of notching never appears on fluted points nor on Plano and related eastern Late Paleo-Indian forms. On the other hand, it is typical of the much better known Archaic cultures which appear in characteristic form thousands of years later. Interestingly, the finest of these early notched points cannot compete with the craftsmanship exhibited by many examples of Plano and Plano-like projectile points. Rarely, the early versions of notched points are associated with flaked and partially ground adzes and celts (grooveless axes) which are clearly prototypic of similar and much more common artifacts in the later Archaic cultures. Because of these forward-looking developmental continuities, many archaeologists classify the truly ancient notched point complexes as "Early Archaic." Sometimes a "Middle Archaic" is proposed to bridge the gap to the much more numerous and far better known Archaic cultures which, in this evolutionary scheme, become "Late Archaic" or "Full Archaic."

There are some prehistorians who feel that the distinctions between the two post-fluted-point cultures are not as sharp or clear as the foregoing description suggests. At some sites Late Paleo-Indian and Early Archaic projectile points have been found directly associated. Some early notched points have a lanceolate shape with concave base and exhibit heavy grinding of the notches and basal edges. The constriction observed on the lower lateral edges of some Late Paleo-Indian point types like "Dalton" and

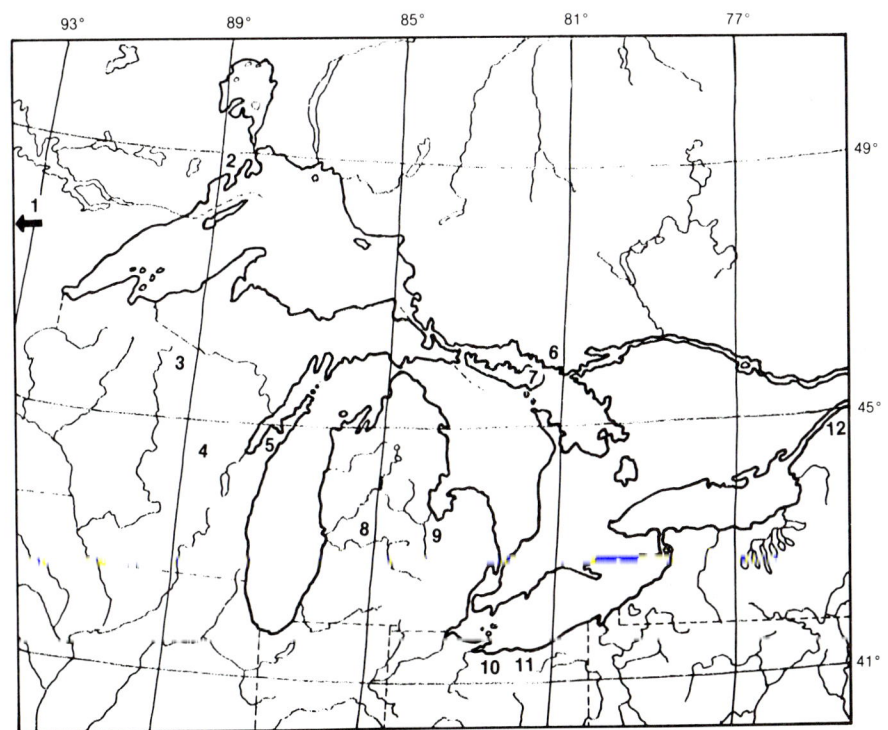

MAP 4.1. *Interregnum (Late Paleo-Indian and Early Archaic) sites discussed in the text: (1) Itasca bison kill (just off map); (2) Brohm and Cummins sites; (3) Robinson and other Flambeau and Minocqua phase sites; (4) Pope; (5) Renier; (6) George Lake 1 and 2 sites; (7) Sheguiandah; (8) Hi-Lo; (9) Satchell; (10) Sawmill; (11) Squaw Rockshelter; and (12) Thompson's Island.*

"Hardaway" sometimes approach notching. Radiocarbon dates from sites of the two cultures significantly overlap. And south of the Great Lakes some of the earliest chipped stone adzes in the world have been found in primary association with the Late Paleo-Indian Dalton type of projectile point. Such considerations have prompted the argument that a single basic culture succeeded the fluted-point makers and that the differences which have been pointed out merely reflect regional ecological adaptations, if not simply inadequate sampling. Those classifiers who are most impressed by the backward-looking continuities of this single or double-cultural period call it Late Paleo-Indian; those most impressed by those attributes anticipating later developments label this same interval Early Archaic. Softening such a contrast of perspectives is the fact that so-called Late Paleo-Indian culture possesses some forward-looking continuities also: The Shield Archaic of a large part of eastern Canada was in great measure derived from it rather than any known Early Archaic complex.

Another view is that the dichotomy is a true one, but that the two kinds of cultures were only partly coeval, with Late Paleo-Indian beginning earlier than the Early Archaic and with the latter persisting later in time. Many Ontario archaeologists believe this is what happened in that province after the (Early) Paleo-Indian period. In Ohio and southern New England stratified sites have revealed just such a sequence. However, south of the Great Lakes, at such famous localities as Graham Cave in Missouri and Modoc Rockshelter in Illinois, Late Paleo-Indian and Early Archaic-style artifacts have been found in no clear-cut sequence, leading some observers to suggest short-term, alternating occupations in zones of overlap between the hunting territories of different people. Indeed, at a number of carefully excavated sites in the southeastern United States, Early Archaic levels have produced radiocarbon age determinations approximately as early as Late Paleo-Indian ones elsewhere. Early Archaic sites are much more common in the Southeast than in the Great Lakes and Northeast, and most students of the earlier cultures have tended to look in that direction for the origins of the Archaic lifeway. It should be noted, however, that while evidences of Early Archaic and Late Paleo-Indian cultures are intermixed on many sites and have been demonstrated to be contemporaneous at some, and at other sites Late Paleo-Indian artifacts underlie Early Archaic style tools and weapons, even if they are apparently associated in higher levels, at no presently known site is this sequence ever reversed.

Another point to be considered in assessing the implications of more or less direct chronological information has to do with spatial distributions. Late Paleo-Indian style projectile points are *relatively* common in the Upper Great Lakes. Although they are also fairly frequent south of Lake Erie in Ohio, especially in the northwestern corner of the state, they are rare around Lake Ontario and eastward where Early Archaic-style points seem to take their place. This contrast is softened if a loosely defined type of projectile point, called Hi-Lo after the type site in Michigan (but also retrieved as surface finds at a number of localities throughout much of the Great Lakes), is considered Late Paleo-Indian rather than Early Archaic. In eastern Ontario a considerable representation of such points has been shown to be present almost to the latitude of the south shore of Georgian Bay. Hi-Lo points are relatively broad and squat and suggest a good deal of resharpening. They vary from lanceolate with slightly constricted lower edges above laterally flaring basal "spurs" to virtually side-notched forms. Basal thinning and concave bases are atavistic reminders of their cultural descent. Throughout the Great Lakes Early Archaic type artifacts are relatively uncommon; their variety and frequency increase dramatically southward to the Ohio Valley and beyond.

In the interpretation favored here, the 4500 years intervening between the (Early) Paleo-Indian and (Late) Archaic periods is viewed as a gradual transition from one dominant culture type to another—as an interregnum. While it is very poorly understood and imperfectly sampled in the Great

Lakes, enough is known to encourage the view that the perception of two partly coetaneous cultural traditions is accurate. Somehow, two related, but in some ways distinctive, cultures emerged with the decline of the fluted-point tradition. Either that tradition underwent an adaptive bifurcation in its translation to this later time period, or peoples with an unrelated ancestry intruded in the form identified as Early Archaic. The former seems the more likely.

With Late Paleo-Indian manifestations distributed over the 2000 years between approximately 8000 and 6000 B.C., and with Early and so-called Middle Archaic occupations variously dating from sometime in that span, but persisting to about 3500 B.C., a full four-and-a-half millennia are represented by just a few excavated Great Lakes sites and a very thin scattering of distinctive projectile points. Doubtless population levels continued low during this long interregnum. Indeed, some scholars have attempted to explain this apparent thinness of numbers to deterioration in the broad-scale, post-glacial carrying capacity of the land, arguing that closed pine forests with their typically impoverished fauna took over much of the Great Lakes region until deciduous trees made significant inroads thousands of years later. This botanical picture has not received much in the way of confirmation from on-going pollen-stratigraphic studies.

But this was also the period of falling water levels from the immediately post-Valderan highs. When the lakes dropped to their lowest known levels—as low as 107 and 122 m below modern surface altitudes in the Lakes Michigan–Huron basins, for example—vast areas were drained and opened up for terrestrial plant and animal colonization and thus, also, human occupation. The extreme low-water period was reached about 7500 B.C. Water levels comparable to those of Lake Algonquin were not again attained until the Nipissing Great Lakes crested at about 2000 B.C. With a majority of campsites undoubtedly established on or near those lower, ancient beaches, the greater part of the archaeological record for this time was destroyed or placed beyond effective recovery due to subsequent reattainment of high water levels.

Components of the Late Paleo-Indian Tradition

Although scattered surface finds of Late Paleo-Indian-style projectile points are relatively unexceptional in the Lake Erie drainage basin of northern Ohio, actual habitation sites are not. A good example of such a Lower Great Lakes site, however, is in Erie County, Ohio. Here the Sawmill site is situated on a small tributary of the west branch of the Huron River, which flows north into Lake Erie.

Even though a few artifacts attributable to later times have also been found, the Sawmill site is mainly a single-component occupation which has been attributed to an eastern expression of the Plano Culture. Approximately 100 projectile points have been collected from the surface of this locality, mainly by amateur prehistorians. The points range from a majority of lanceolate or leaf-shaped ones to a strong minority of weakly shouldered, square-stemmed specimens with lanceolate blade conformation. Members of the first group have straight or moderately convex bases; they most resemble Agate Basin, Angostura, and even Hell Gap points of the western Plano cultures. Some of these show faintly instepped, ground-edge tangs or stems. The points with more distinct, shallowly instepped tangs resemble Scottsbluff and Alberta points, associated in the West with other Plano groups and usually found unmixed with the lanceolate or leaf-shaped forms. While there is a considerable range in the workmanship exhibited on the Sawmill projectile points, some have fine, parallel, so-called ribbon flaking, bespeaking a high level of technical prowess on the part of their makers. They vary from 44 to 112 mm in length. Some of the Scottsbluff points have small lateral projections, called "spurs," on the basal corners. This is a common feature in the Great Lakes area, whereas it is rare west of the Mississippi Valley.

Less frequent than the diagnostic projectile points are large ovate bifaces: some preforms, others probably knives, large perforators or drills with expanded bases, and end-scrapers. An interesting characteristic of this chipped-stone industry is its marked emphasis, as on Early Paleo-Indian stations, on locally exotic raw material. Almost 90% of the Sawmill artifacts are made of Nellie chert from Coshocton County nearly 161 km away.

Unfortunately, the Sawmill site has not been dated by radiocarbon, and its maximum possible age, as established by reference to the geochronology of the Lake Erie basin, is too imprecise to be of much value. Its investigators have been able to show by site location and elevation that its geologically maximum possible age is definitely post-Lake Wayne, and probably also post-Lake Warren III. Because of the suggested possibility of fluted-point association with later Lake Lundy, it has been argued that the Sawmill site most postdate that lake as well. Inasmuch as the latter body of water dates around 10,000 B.C., such maximum estimates of possible site occupation are still far in excess of the probable period of habitation. The age of the Sawmill site is most likely approximated by a radiocarbon date of 7530 B.C. ± 160 years from a stratum containing "Plano" and "Kirk variant" (Early Archaic) projectile points at the Squaw Rock Shelter in Cuyahoga County, Ohio, also near the Lake Erie shore, but further east. Other "Plano" points of unspecified type, again in a common level with Kirk points, have been dated elsewhere in Ohio at around 7160 B.C. at the Aurora Run Rockshelter.

Eastward into Pennsylvania and New York, Late Paleo-Indian type artifacts are rare to virtually nonexistent. Opposite Massena, New York, however, near Cornwall, Ontario, is Thompson's Island. This island in the St. Lawrence River has yielded Agate Basin-like and Eden-like points in a level beneath deposits containing Archaic and later materials. The locality was deep under water at the time of the Champlain Sea. It would not have been available for occupancy until after post-glacial crustal rebound had expelled the embayment sometime just before 8000 B.C. How much later than this time the first occupants arrived has not been ascertained.

Just a few kilometers northeast of the city of Green Bay, Wisconsin, inland about 457 m from the shore of Green Bay, and at an elevation of around 11 m above its surface, remnants of the old Lake Algonquin beach can still be detected in the woodlots and farmlands. Sometime after the lake had fallen from this high stand, a small band of Late Paleo-Indian people carried the body of one of their kinsmen, a mere adolescent, and gently laid it on the crest of the abandoned shoreline. Amid lamentations, men, women, and children scoured the nearby flanks of the sandy ridge for dry wood from old windfalls. Rocks were collected and thrown into a rough pavement either directly on the surface or in a shallow depression scooped out to receive them. These would act to create a draft into the base of the fire they were preparing. A great pile of dry brush and fallen branches was heaped up, and the corpse was placed atop it. However prepared for the journey to the land of the dead, whether with freshly dressed hair or oiled body or painted face, the body was armed with javelins or darts tipped with magnificently crafted blades and was further provided with a kit containing large ovate bifaces with truncated bases, hafted scrapers, possibly additional examples of the superb projectile points, and doubtless other things that did not survive the flames. Some of the ovate bifaces probably served as knives and also, perhaps, as symbols of value and tokens of group solidarity; some may have been unusually finely trimmed preforms. Following preparation, the crematory fire was struck. For a brief while, enormous heat was generated. After the fire had done its awful work, the survivors went away. Decades and centuries would roll on into thousands of years, and drifting sands would bury the place, before the tragedy would come again to human attention.

The archaeologists, in this case my wife and I, were drawn to the Renier site by serendipity. Its existence was unsuspected before our discovery. An awareness of geological history, and the reasonable belief that it should act as a guide in the search for ancient sites, followed a hunch which grew into a compulsion. Again and incessantly again, every time we drove by the place on our way to other archaeological sites our eyes were drawn to it and we were made uneasy, as if we were neglecting some duty in not stopping and investigating. There was something we both sensed, and it was more than an informal reading of topography and an appreciation of lowering the odds on finding something. Indeed, the chances were enormously against finding anything. Nevertheless, without any surface indi-

Plate 4.1. *Eden (two left) and Scottsbluff projectile points from the Renier site, Brown County, Wisconsin. (Collections of the Neville Public Museum, Green Bay, Wisconsin.)*

cations to be guided by, we walked from where we had parked our car up into the meadow and cow pasture on the .4-km-long ridge. When we started test excavations we came down right in the middle of the crematory site. There had been no systematic search strategy, merely a sensitivity to clues of ancient geography—and incredible luck. It seemed that we were literally drawn to that place. Since we are committed to a rationalistic and materialist orientation in archaeology, there is an embarrassment in having to admit to so unscientific a method of discovery. But that is how the Renier site came to light.

Except for one quartz and two chert specimens, the artifacts from the cremation were all fashioned of the very fine pseudoquartzite known as Hixton silicified sandstone derived from across the state in southwestern Wisconsin. This is the same distinctive material of which many Wisconsin fluted points were made earlier. Surprisingly good stone with which to work, experimental studies have shown that carefully heat-treating the

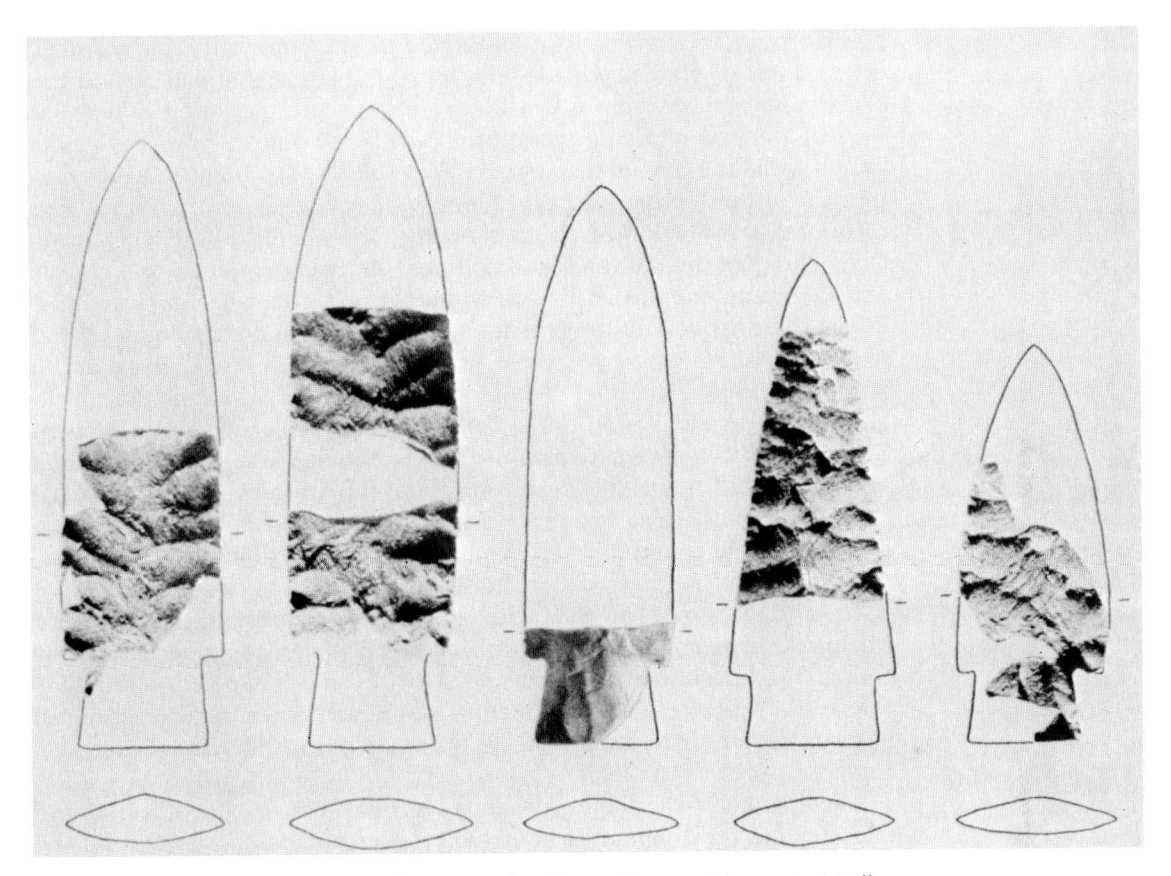

PLATE 4.2. *Scottsbluff points from the Renier site, Brown County, Wisconsin. (Collections of the Neville Public Museum, Green Bay, Wisconsin.)*

"quartzite" further improves its knapping qualities, and it seems likely that the Paleo-Indians did this.

The stylistic and technical excellence of the Renier artifacts is astonishing. Outside of some other Late Paleo-Indian sites, it was rarely equalled and probably never surpassed in the Great Lakes. Clearly, something more than functional utility is reflected in these objects. For the people who made them, the projectile points and some of the other stone tools had to be much more than technologically useful: They had to be superbly crafted. They are mute symbols of a value system as well as of a technology.

With one fascinating exception, the Renier site projectile points represent two intimately related Late Paleo-Indian types. Badly damaged by the intense heat of the makeshift crematorium, some individual specimens had to be painstakingly put together again from over a dozen fragments, and none could be completely reconstructed. A mathematical model derived from observations of metrical ratios and proportions of unbroken similar points from a western site was employed to help inform these reconstructions. A test of predicted blade length using the one complete and unbroken Renier site example was within 1 mm of the measured dimension. Two of the ten partly reconstructed Late Paleo-Indian points are Eden points while the remaining eight are Scottsbluff. Most archaeologists have thought of these projectile point types, which, together with a sometimes associated form of hafted knife, constitute the major artifact types of the Cody complex (one of the Plano cultures), as being confined to Nebraska and Wyoming and Saskatchewan and other western states and provinces. Before the discovery of the Renier site, a few eastern archaeologists recognized that these early types were also represented in the Midwest and in western Ontario. The Renier site drew attention to this fact and also provided the first and, so far, only known instance of a Cody complex burial. Since that discovery a second probable cremation burial linked with Eden and Scottsbluff points has been found, but not scientifically excavated, in Waupaca County in east central Wisconsin (the Pope site). The Cody complex is now demonstrated to have had a major distribution in the Upper Great Lakes.

The thought-to-be-early Satchell complex in a mixed site in the lower Michigan peninsula includes some generally similar projectile points, though manufactured of argillite and other diverse materials. As shown by the Sawmill site in Ohio, Scottsbluff-like points have a distribution which appears to terminate south of Lake Erie. Such artifacts have not been reported north of the lake.

While some of the Plains localities are bison-drives and others are kill sites most often yielding the butchered remains of extinct species of bison, the hunting preferences of the easterners remain to be determined. An eastern regional peculiarity of the projectile points is their large size vis-à-vis the more published western examples. The Renier specimens are from about 95 mm to an estimated 155 mm in length; they average about one-third larger to half again as large as their Plains counterparts. They are likewise appreciably bigger than the Sawmill site points. The reason or reasons for the size differences are not understood, though one archaeologist has hazarded that it may have had something to do with social identification in interaction with Early Archaic peoples.

Eden points are distinctly rarer than Scottsbluff points. Their relative frequency at the Renier site conforms with what is known about their wider representation. They are long, slender lanceolates with relatively thick, diamond-shaped cross-sections and have square bases. They, like the closely related Scottsbluff type, are tanged points; the tang, or stem, tends to be only slightly instepped from the blade edges and is heavily smoothed by grinding of the edges. In some instances, the tang is barely perceptible, being differentiated from the blade proper only by edge grinding. Eden points usually exhibit a median ridge on one or both faces, this being defined by the meeting of the flake scars driven in from the opposing edges of the blade. This impressive style of knapping is called "collateral" flaking and it results in a sequence of regular, almost circular flake scars. The effect is highly symmetrical and pleasing to the eye. It is the work of master craftsmen. This is all the more remarkable when it is remembered that in such simple societies as those in which the Late Paleo-Indians lived the principal divisions of labor were by age and sex, and each man normally made and used all of the weapons and tools he required himself.

Scottsbluff points often are equally well made. They are broader than Eden points and usually have a flatter, lenticular cross-section. Although their tangs are also square-shaped and may be just minimally inset from the blade edges, they are usually much more prominently set off than in Eden points. Instead of the latter's shell-shaped collateral flaking pattern, Scottsbluff points are more variable in the style and precision of flaking. Many of the finest examples, and this would have to include some of the Renier specimens, have long, parallel, flat flake scars which were so carefully produced that they seem to extend entirely across the blade. Such transverse "ribbon" flaking left broad parallel scars in the case of the Renier points. One can only marvel at the delicacy of control attested by such fine products. A feature commonly observed in Great Lakes Eden and Scottsbluff points is a slight widening of the stem towards the base. Eden and Scottsbluff projectile points are linked traits of the Cody complex. Although Scottsbluff points sometimes occur alone in sites, they are frequently accompanied by a smaller representation of Eden points. The latter are not known to occur alone.

Another projectile point that went through the crematory flames at the Renier site is totally divergent from the rest. This is a large side-notched point made of black flint from an unknown source. It shows the same extensive thermal damage as the other artifacts, however. Similar points of regionally different material are characteristic of Archaic contexts and seem incongruous in a Late Paleo-Indian setting. Nevertheless, examples of just such points are known to occur in early levels at a number of Midwestern sites. Smaller versions of such points have been radiocarbon dated to between 6500 and 5000 B.C. in Minnesota and Iowa, and at least that early in Missouri and Illinois. And projectile points similar to the Renier side-notched and Eden–Scottsbluff points have been recovered together at other early sites on the north shore of Lake Huron. In the Renier case particularly, it is hard to believe that the same people made such radically different points of disparate raw materials. But there can be no doubt of their contemporaneity. Somehow, somewhere, Late Paleo-Indian and Early Archaic people were in contact.

Late Paleo-Indian sites have also come to light in north central Wisconsin in the "lakes country." These are small but informative. They suggest small populations, a high degree of mobility, and probably one-time occupancy.

PLATE 4.3. *Scottsbluff (left) and Eden (right) points from eastern Wisconsin (shown actual size). (Collections of the Neville Public Museum, Green Bay, and the Oshkosh Public Museum, Oshkosh, Wisconsin, respectively.)*

Although they are few in number and limited in cultural remains, the sites show a predilection for lakeshore or lake-outlet locations. Common attributes include heavy utilization of regionally exotic raw materials, particularly in the production of the projectile points. Some of these are made of Hixton pseudoquartzite and may have been intentionally heat treated prior to knapping. Two Late Paleo-Indian "phases" have been proposed for this material: Flambeau and Minocqua.

The Flambeau phase, represented by three sites in Price and Oneida counties, Wisconsin, is distinguished by long lanceolate projectile points having somewhat incurvate lower lateral edges with heavy grinding and with slightly convex to slightly concave bases. They resemble Agate Basin points in the West. The Minocqua phase, on the other hand, is based on one of the components at the stratified Robinson site in Oneida County and a few surface finds elsewhere. At Robinson there seems to have been a small work area and temporary camp associated with the Late Paleo-Indian occupation. The projectile points are quite different from those of the other phase and are similar to Scottsbluff points. However, they are more crudely made than those earlier described from the Renier site. Distinctive lateral projections on the base, or "ears," are clearly present—a trait found on many Great Lakes Scottsbluff points, though not found at the Renier site.

Both phases share fairly large bifaces, several not very diagnostic varieties of scrapers, bifacially and/or edge-trimmed flake knives, utilized flake "throw-aways," wedges or pièces esquillées, and bipolar cores. The latter were struck while sitting on a stone anvil; the result was battering and the removal of flakes from opposite ends. Some archaeologists think that this was an attempt to extract the maximum usable material from small cobbles and tabular chunks where bigger sources were unavailable. Bipolar cores are well represented in later archaeological periods in the western Great Lakes.

More of the implements in the Flambeau phase seem to have had scraping functions, and more of the Minocqua phase artifacts (with the significant exception of the projectile points) were manufactured of locally procurable materials. Gravers enter the inventory only in the Flambeau phase, though this may have functional or sampling implications rather than signifying a true cultural difference. Circa 7000 B.C. has been suggested for the Flambeau phase, and 6000–5000 B.C. for the Minocqua. These estimates are only general-order-of-magnitude ones and are predicated on typological cross-ties with the dated projectile-point styles in the West; they are yet to be supported by locally derived radiocarbon samples.

The first in situ discoveries of Late Paleo-Indian points in the Great Lakes were made at the north end of Lake Huron on and near Manitoulin Island, Ontario. Here on uplifted, abandoned beaches dating from the fall from the Lake Algonquin high to the Lake Stanley low water levels, a number of combination hunting–fishing camps and quarry sites have been excavated. The George Lake 1 and George Lake 2 sites are located on the mainland near the village of Killarney in Killarney Provincial Park. George Lake 1 is on one of the so-called "upper group" shorelines at an elevation of 98 m above the modern surface of Lake Huron; the second site is on several strandlines between the Wyebridge and Cedar Point beaches and has a mean elevation 91 m above modern lake level. The Sheguiandah site is near the northeastern end of huge Manitoulin Island, only 40 or 50 km southwest of the George Lake sites as the crow flies. It is between 44 and 34 m above the lake, or between 57 and 46 m lower than the elevations of the first two sites. The beach sequence to which the archaeological finds are tied is still not securely dated; the best available current estimated range is between approximately 8400 and 7500 B.C. Except for their suggestive locations and the presence of a few possibly water-rolled artifacts from the George Lake sites, there is no necessary connection between the human occupations and the several recorded episodes of active beach formation. People could first have arrived centuries after the lake had fallen from any given beach down to the time of the lowest post-glacial lake levels—and perhaps also into the initial centuries of later surface rebounding and the recuperation of earlier, higher water levels. Critical in this last regard is the poorly calibrated time–altitude ratio of surface recovery and rising lake levels.

A major attraction of these localities was not only their presumed nearness to the ancient lake shores, but the availability of high-grade quartzite in easy-to-quarry deposits. Numerous shallow pits have been discovered chiseled and hammered and levered into the bedrock, and enormous quantities of extracted chunks, cores, waste flakes, shatter, broken and unfinished implements, and hammerstones have been found mounded up on and just beneath the surface. Finished artifacts (mainly broken) have also come to light. That some of these are known on firm stylistic grounds to postdate by many thousands of years the formation of the beaches reinforces caution against assuming that the more ancient artifacts must be the same age as the beach or beaches on which they occur.

On very ambiguous grounds which almost all archaeologists have had little difficulty in rejecting, the Sheguiandah site was once touted to be of glacial or even preglacial age. There is not and never was much to support such a claim. A good indication of the likely time of one of the earliest occupations of what is a multicomponent site is given by a radiocarbon date of 7180 B.C. ± 250 years obtained from the bottom of a peat formation overlying an artifact-bearing clay deposit. Because the archaeological assemblage must necessarily predate the superincumbent peat, and because the vicinity would not have been available for occupancy until after falling lake levels had exposed it, antiquity is indicated of sometime between the early stages in the fall from the Lake Algonquin level and the horizon marked by the time of initial peat accumulation. Earlier, the place would have been submerged beneath the pro-glacial lake, and before that it would have been buried under the Laurentide glacier for thousands of years. On these grounds, this part of the Sheguiandah site should date between about 8400 and 7000 B.C., and probably toward the late end of that span. The regional vegetation during this time included forests of spruce and pine with a significant and growing representation of oak, birch, and other deciduous trees.

Archaeologically, the Sheguiandah and George Lake sites are very similar. They undoubtedly reflect the same people utilizing the region over a number of generations. The crudeness of the lithic industry is much more apparent than real and cannot be used to claim any greater antiquity than the lake history will allow. Most of the finds are the products of quarrying as well as the initial roughing out of tools meant to be transported and finished elsewhere. Important finished-tool categories at Sheguiandah and George Lake include projectile points; half-circular or semilunar knives with straight backs and curved blades; a variety of acuminate ovate bifaces, some of which were certainly meant to be knives, others preforms; "choppers" or hand-held axes, some made from cores, still others from massive flakes; quadrangular bifaces of uncertain function (perhaps tool blanks); drills or perforators; scrapers; and multiple retouched flake "throwaways." Overwhelming all of these were cores and waste flakes.

Although very infrequent, among the finished artifacts are some projectile points, and they give away the cultural affiliations and approximate age of the less distinctive associated remains. These are tanged points intermediate in form between the Eden and Scottsluff types, side-notched points like those from the Renier and other early sites to the southwest, and some not very carefully made lanceolate and leaf-shaped specimens, all chipped out of the local quartzite. They should be of about the same age as the Sawmill, Renier, and Flambeau and Minocqua phase sites.

One final Late Paleo-Indian site will serve to close this necessarily Upper Great Lakes-dominated discussion: the Brohm site near Thunder Bay, Ontario, on the northwest coast of Lake Superior. This is not the only known example of such an early cultural level in this region (the Cummins site provides another one), but it is the only one so far to have been fully described. Here have been found magnificently flaked projectile points and a limited variety of other tools made of the locally abundant taconite. Some of the Brohm specimens compare favorably in quality of workmanship with the finest Renier examples, but they relate to an entirely different, though related, Plano point tradition. These are stemless, concave-based lanceolate points shaped by impressively regular and precise transverse "ribbon" flaking, sometimes with carefully thinned bases suggesting vestigial fluting, and with rubbed lower edges. They are essentially eastern examples of Plainview points, though a few more resemble the related Milnesand type. Found with them were ovate bifaces with truncated bases, oval biface knives and/or preforms, end- and side-scrapers, drills, flake knives, choppers, a possible strike-a-light or fireflint, and cores and waste flakes.

The Brohm site lies 69–70 m above Lake Superior on an abandoned, uplifted shoreline believed to equate with the Minong stage of lake history. This post-Duluth, pre-Houghton lake stage is thought to date sometime between 8200 and 7800 B.C. While the site may have been established anytime after the demise of that lake stage, an interval close to the recent end of the suggested age range for the lake would be more compatible with the radiocarbon chronology for virtually identical projectile points from the High Plains. The Brohm site seems to be a single-component one. It was

PLATE 4.4. *Taconite bifaces from the Brohm site near Thunder Bay, Ontario (shown half actual size). (Courtesy Mike McLeod and the Thunder Bay Historical Society Museum, Thunder Bay, Ontario.)*

not occupied very long. In this region caribou probably took the place of the buffalo favored by the westerners. The assemblage is right out of the Paleo-Indian tradition.

Early Archaic Contemporaries and Successors

"Early Archaic" is the term we shall use to refer to the various archaeological assemblages partly coeval with, but not classified as, Late Paleo-Indian. It will also be extended to embrace what many prehistorians call Middle Archaic. In a discussion of the archaeology of the Great Lakes, the distinction between "Early" and "Middle" Archaic periods, pertinent

4. Interregnum

and justified in some other regions of eastern North America, contributes little of substance and merely complicates, without clarifying, a presentation of what is here a scanty cultural record. The interval of time comprehended by this usage is long—from sometime after the end of the Paleo-Indian (fluted point) period up to approximately 3500 B.C. The bulk of the evidence falls in the last half of this interregnum, just as Late Paleo-

PLATE 4.5. *Late Paleo-Indian projectile points (top row); preforms or biface blades (middle row); end-of-blade scraper (lower left); and denticulate tool (lower right) from the Cummins site near Thunder Bay, Ontario. (Shown half actual size.) (Courtesy Mike McLeod and the Department of Anthropology, Lakehead University, Thunder Bay, Ontario, and the Thunder Bay Historical Society Museum.)*

PLATE 4.6. *Tool blanks and other bifaces from the Cummins site near Thunder Bay, Ontario (shown half actual size). (Courtesy Mike McLeod and the Department of Anthropology, Lakehead University, Thunder Bay, Ontario, and the Thunder Bay Historical Society Museum.)*

Indian assemblages dominate the first. This is most clear in the western Great Lakes where Late Paleo-Indian sites appear to be more frequent than in the eastern lakes.

Most of what archaeologists know about Early Archaic cultures comes from outside the drainage basin of the Great Lakes. All that has been found within the region is a very thin and highly discontinuous scatter of typologically suggestive artifacts with only limited and infrequent associations. There are also some isolated radiocarbon dates with a meager accompaniment of diagnostic cultural material. As we have seen, examples of sites with Early Archaic style artifacts in good association with Late Paleo-Indian types of projectile points and other tools are the Squaw Rockshelter, Ohio, Renier, Wisconsin, and George Lake and Sheguiandah, Ontario, sites. A few other such localities exist, but they have not been reported upon.

The most readily identified of the Early Archaic tools are the projectile points. These often have triangular as well as lanceolate blades and are usually moderately broad from edge to edge. Edge grinding and basal thinning, inherited from the preceding period, are frequent attributes. Most arresting are the modifications for hafting involving notching. Big Sandy, Turin, Simonsen, and Otter Creek points are side-notched, Kirk points are corner-removed or stemmed, Eva points are deeply basally notched, the LeCroy and Kanawha types are corner-notched or corner-removed and have indented or bifurcated bases. Hardaway, Hi-Lo, St. Albans, Neville, Palmer, and Stanley are some other Early Archaic projectile-point varieties. Relatively rare throughout the Great Lakes, they are much more common and far better known from excavated as well as surface contexts in the Ohio Valley and southward. Their names were originally taken from the site where the type was either first recognized or found in meaningful contexts. Outside of the Great Lakes drainage basin in New York some of these early projectile point types, though still rare, increase in frequency, as in the lower Hudson Valley and on Staten Island. The poorly known Satchell complex in the lower Michigan peninsula includes material probably coetaneous with some of these point types. Though still uncommon, more Early Archaic finds have been made around the Lake Erie basin in Ohio, southwesternmost Ontario, and southeastern Michigan than anywhere else in the Great Lakes region.

Even though it is not in Great Lakes country proper, the Itasca site in Clearwater County in the northwest quarter of Minnesota is a nearby example of an Early Archaic culture especially adapted to the exploitation of a prairie and prairie–woodland-edge habitat. Here, sometime between 6000 and 5000 B.C., as determined by radiocarbon assay, a small band of people surprised and killed part of a herd of buffalo on the shore of a now-extinct lake. The bones found in the lake marl are those of a no longer living form of long-horn bison, perhaps the species *Bison occidentalis*. Mixed in with the skeletons of the butchered big-game, and likewise preserved in the water-logged marl, were plant remains, mollusk shells, and the bones of many kinds of fish, birds, and turtles, as well as the earliest domesticated dog yet found in or anywhere near the Great Lakes. Analysis of fossil pollen and other plant debris at the site indicates that the hunt took place when the lake was in existence and during a period when the sur-

PLATE 4.7. Early Archaic side-notched projectile points from eastern Wisconsin (shown actual size). (Collections of Department of Anthropology, Lawrence University, Appleton, Wisconsin.)

rounding countryside was an open, pine-dominated woodland giving way to an expanding prairie and then an oak savanna. Contemporaneously, as adduced from pollen-bearing samples procured elsewhere, there seems to have flourished a widespread forest of mixed conifers and broad-leaf trees commencing less than 160 km to the east in the Great Lakes country.

The Itasca buffalo-kill site surrendered to its excavators Early Archaic projectile points and many general and special-purpose stone tools. The former consisted of smallish sublanceolate specimens equipped with broad triangular blades, but parallel lower edges, and having concave bases, and other comparably sized points: broad-bladed for their length, side or corner-notched, with straight to concave bases. Points similar to the side-notched ones have been previously found with butchered remains of *Bison occidentalis* at the Simonsen site in western Iowa radiocarbon dated at around 6500 B.C.

The other implements from the Itasca site were end-scrapers, including some indistinguishable from Paleo-Indian prototypes, side-scrapers, bifacially retouched flake knives, choppers, drills, gravers, flake "throwaways," hammerstones, and grinding stones. The grinding stones are especially important in view of the preserved plant debris; they must have been used to process acorns, hazel nuts, and several varieties of berries. These and other activities such as preparing hides, cooking, and tool manufacture and projectile rearming appear to have been loosely concentrated along the top of a low rise a short distance away from where the bison carcasses were dismembered along the water's edge. The projectile points and other tools were fabricated of locally available materials, materials which Paleo-Indians would typically have scorned. Nevertheless, some of the Itasca projectile points are well made, even if many of the other tools seem to have been hurriedly produced for use on the spot and then discarded. The evidence indicates that it was a small group of people whose activities are recorded at the site—just a few related families whose traces were "fossilized" at this one of the many stops they made in their seasonal rounds. Doubtless other such sites have been destroyed or remain undiscovered where comparable environments once existed in the Great Lakes as far eastward as Ohio. While caribou and moose must have been more important for people in the northern marches of the lakes country, deer was the major "big-game" animal in the areas of significant deciduous forest. In fact, wherever Early Archaic sites are best represented, as in the Ohio Valley and southward, and where preservation of bone permits a statement, deer, bear, raccoon, and other nonextinct animals are exclusively present.

The rarity of Early Archaic sites in the Great Lakes is something of a puzzle. Even when the Late Paleo-Indian components in the western Great Lakes are added, population levels during the 4500 years of the Interregnum do not seem to have risen much, if at all, above those of the pioneering fluted-point period. South of the lakes the Early Archaic population was far higher. Why the difference? After all, the fluted-point makers had earlier penetrated most of the Great Lakes to the northern limits of the known distribution of the Late Pleistocene megafauna and/or the southern fringes of the glacial massif. Why was the successful period of initial exploration and hunting-range expansion not followed up by the increases in numbers of people archaeologically attested by the much more numerous sites in the south-central and southeastern United States? Furthermore, some archaeologists have the impression that population was even lower during the Interregnum than it had been in the Paleo-Indian period, not only in the Great Lakes but throughout the northeastern United States and Canada as well.

It is a virtual certainty that an important part of this picture of puzzling underpopulation, at least in the Great Lakes, must be due to the fact that, throughout most of the Interregnum, lake levels were much lower than they had been earlier, would be again, and are now. Early Archaic hunters would have been attracted to the then existing shorelines and their hinterlands for many of the same reasons later groups of Indians were drawn to more recent shores. These would have included the water itself, amelioration of temperature extremes in winter and summer, ease of travel along shores if not on the water itself, easy accessibility of erosion-exposed chert deposits, increased incidence of treefalls for building materials and easy maintenance of fires, ease of long-distance identification of landmarks, relief from insect pests and, of course, aquatic and shore plant resources and animal protein: fish and waterfowl, and the mosaic of mammalian life naturally associated with lake margins and the lands between. With such large-scale alterations in land–lake relations as are known to have marked the long interval between the fall from the final pro-glacial high water lakes to their virtual draining and then their gradual refilling to the high levels of the Nipissing Great Lakes, a major archaeological record for this same time span must lie deeply submerged beneath the modern lakes. This effect would be much more dramatic in the Upper than the Lower Great Lakes because of their somewhat divergent histories. These hydrologic events must explain some of the quantitative discrepancies in frequencies of Early Archaic sites between the north and the much more geographically stable south.

Nevertheless, great tracts of Great Lakes territory in Wisconsin, Michigan, New York, and Ontario were not directly affected by even these massive lake-level fluctuations, and satisfactory explanation for the rarity, if not absence, of Early Archaic traces must involve other considerations. An attractive path of inquiry, named after the two archaeologists most responsible for pointing it out, is the Ritchie–Fitting Hypothesis. This is based on a generalized model of post-glacial vegetation succession extrapolated from a number of pollen studies of bog and other sediments from Minnesota to New England. These paleobotanical records are incomplete, are clustered in some areas and absent in others, and are subject to differing interpretations among experts. But certain broad trends seem well established. According to this model, the interval 8000–6500 B.C. was predominantly one of edible plant and game-poor, closed coniferous forests in much of the Great Lakes and the Northeast. After about 6500 B.C. there was a slow but accelerating eclipse of the conifer climax as ever more numbers and species of deciduous trees invaded from the south, introducing varieties of nut-bearing trees and increasing populations of deer, bear, raccoon, turkey, and other game. An essentially modern environment was attained by about 3500 B.C., more or less coincident with which the Late Archaic period is ushered in accompanied by an obvious increase in the number and productivity of archaeological sites. The Ritchie–Fitting Hypothesis relates the rise in site frequencies and the changing cultural patterns reflected at those sites to the changes in environment. If the hypothesis is correct, there ought to be a slow but accelerating increase in archaeological site frequencies beginning after about 6500 B.C. Evidence of such a development is slight, however. The proliferation of Late Archaic sites following 3500 B.C. resembles a rapid upsurge rather than the culmination of a steadily steepening curve. Also out of joint with the poor carrying-capacity model for the initial part of the period are the results of some regional studies, such as in western New York, which suggest that the environment was not everywhere as impoverished as assumed in the hypothesis. Especially along the southern approaches to the lakes there was more of a mosaic pattern to vegetational change than has usually been pictured. Nonetheless, in broad-scale perspective, the greater part of the Great Lakes and Northeast must have been less attractive to the hunting and gathering people of the Interregnum than the far longer established and more food-rich broad-leafed forests of the Southeast. Indirectly, this provides another argument for important Paleo-Indian reliance on the Ice Age megafauna: When the regional and total extinctions of the large nomadic herbivores took place, much of the lakes country proved to be a marginal environment. This condition lasted until the establishment of the much later deciduous forests and their accompanying suites of collectible plant foods and the game animals they supported.

During the long interval between the Paleo-Indian Period and about 3500 B.C., the time when the first major population increases began and sites of the Late or Full Archaic pattern seem suddenly to have proliferated, cultural change in the Great Lakes proceeded slowly through internal adjustments to the metamorphosing system of forest, climate, lake levels, and game. But even with the exceedingly low and thinly spread populations indicated by the pauperly archaeological traces of the period, the Great Lakes were not isolated nor unaffected by what was going on in other sectors of the continent. Neither did the lakes simply mirror the cultural achievements gestated elsewhere. That this is so may be observed in the character of the long-lived culture called Shield Archaic.

The Shield Archaic culture is known mainly from north of the Great Lakes. However, its territory included the entire north shores of Lakes Superior and Huron. If not actually classifiable as Shield Archaic, closely related Archaic manifestations occur south of Lake Superior as well, in the upper Michigan peninsula and in north central Wisconsin. An example of the latter is the recently defined, though still poorly sampled, Squirrel River phase. Commencing in the northern portions of the Upper Great Lakes, sites of the Shield Archaic occur northward to the headwaters and middle reaches of the rivers flowing to James Bay and Hudson Bay and from Keewatin District in the northwest to Quebec and the Maritime Provinces in the east. The culture takes its name from the vast geological formation comprising much of its range—the Canadian Shield. Most examples of Shield Archaic sites date to the Late Archaic and even later periods. In fact, in remote interior enclaves, the culture seems to have persisted to the coming of the first white men. However, some sites suggest great enough antiquity that the culture may properly be said to have undergone its formative development during the latter part of the Early Archaic period. In this sense, the Shield Archaic is also a cultural tradition exhibiting in-place continuity over a cultural lifespan of thousands of years. Because it came into being during the Interregnum, even if it is more characteristic of the succeeding period, and because it is the only presently known northern Archaic culture which seems to be traceable to Late Paleo-Indian antecedents rather than representing the intrusion of an Archaic culture or way of

134

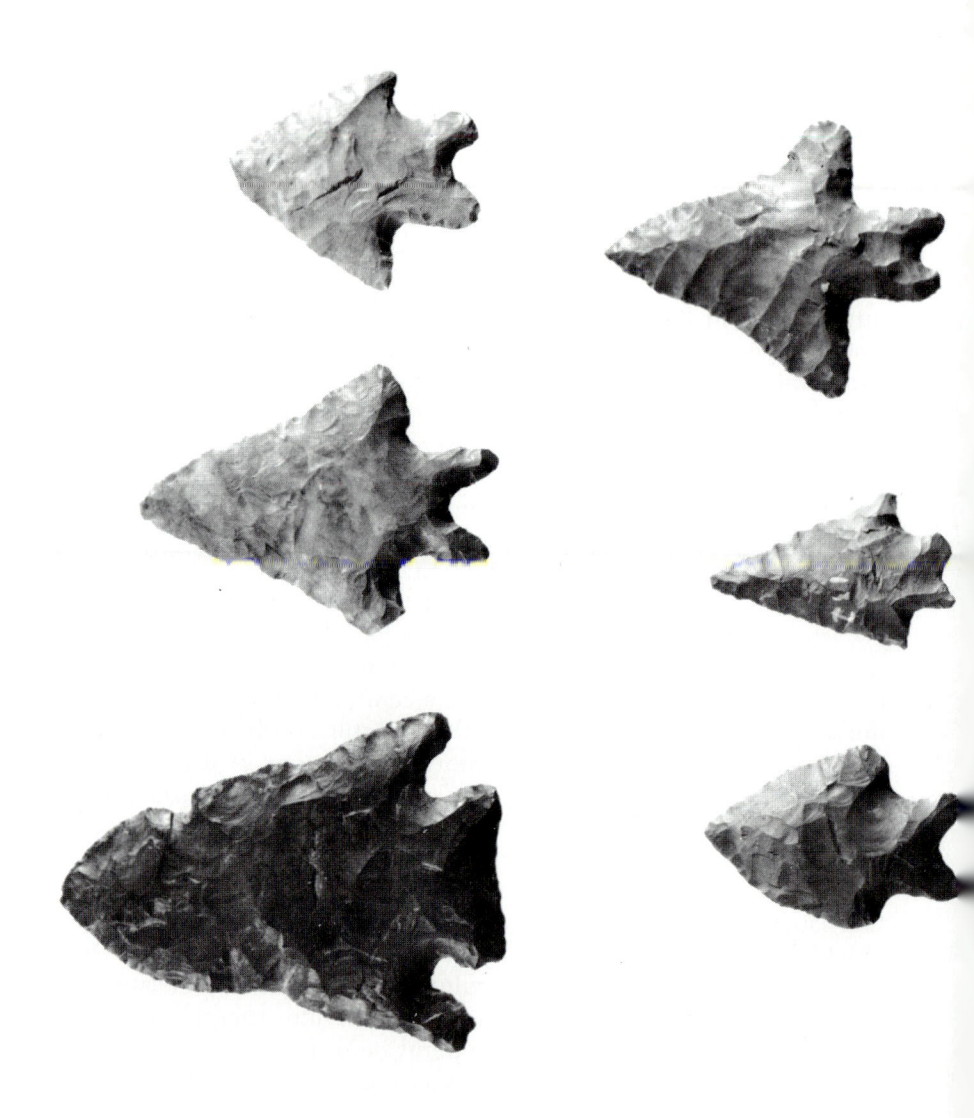

PLATE 4.8. Various styles of bifurcate-stemmed and other early Archaic points from southern Ontario. The right-hand specimen in the third row and the three specimens in the bottom row are Hi-Lo points. (Shown actual size.) (Courtesy Peter L. Storck and the Royal Ontario Museum, Toronto, Canada.)

life previously forged elsewhere, the Shield Archaic is an appropriate part of this chapter.

The lifeway reflected in the Shield Archaic sites appears to have evolved in a gradual succession of individually small-scale accomodations to altered circumstances as Late Paleo-Indian hunters persisted northward into recently deglaciated lands. Their progeny remained to deal with a harsh environment, and in so doing adapted their ancestral culture to their new expectations. This process began perhaps as early as 5000–6000 B.C. The step-by-step transfiguration of the parental to the daughter culture cannot be demonstrated because of the paucity of known sites of the right age in such a huge and barely searched wilderness. Furthermore, most of the known sites were occupied many times, with confusing results. But there is little doubt of the reality of the transformation. The oldest of the projectile-point styles of the Shield Archaic, as well as scraper and biface knife forms, and the inferred way of living itself, are suggestive of a deteriorated Late Paleo-Indian or Plano cultural pattern extended into and forced to come to terms with impoverished prospects. Mainly lacking ground and polished stone tools, the Shield Archaic *looks* ancient. Typologically, it is most similar to cultures of the Early Archaic period in the southeastern United States, radiocarbon dates notwithstanding. The many Shield Archaic stations which in fact date to the Late Archaic or even later periods are proof of the danger of using limited and simple kinds of artifacts, like those predominating on Shield Archaic sites, as straightforward and unambiguous time markers. Stasigenesis is testimony that cultural, like biological, evolution results in the contemporaneity of ancestral and descendant forms where refuge habitats are not as attractive to the latter as the former. The Shield Archaic, confined to a more slowly and only partially changing environment than confronted and stimulated contemporaneous cultures to the south, retained its character long after it had become antique in other climes. Adequate to the needs of its carriers, it witnessed from afar the new fashions whose emergence enriched the lives of Archaic people in much of the rest of the continent.

Not surprisingly, but within a strictly limited cultural inventory, Shield Archaic sites show some diversity, distributed as they are over an enormous country and a great span of time. Doubtless, some of the diversity is masked, and some of the extreme simplicity of material culture is exaggerated by the acid soils and excessive relative moisture typical of much of the Canadian Shield. Bone and antler are rarely preserved, for example, let alone wood and more perishable materials. Thus, to judge from site locations, canoes of some sort must have been in use by this time even though actual remains have not survived. Similarly, snowshoes and toboggans, virtual necessities in this country, must have been present despite lack of direct evidence. Bark and skin-covered shelters, bark containers, and efficient cold-weather clothing may also be inferred.

Still, it is chipped-stone-tool components and an occasional auxillary implement of native copper that are all that have usually been preserved. Even allowing for this caveat, the Shield Archaic has many of the features we would expect of an Early Archaic culture, age considerations suspended. Except for infrequent types of tools like self-hafted semilunar knives of copper, borrowed from Late Archaic folk in neighboring regions, as well as certain distinctive projectile-point styles, the Shield Archaic is a primitive-looking Archaic culture. Put another way, in comparison with Late Archaic cultures elsewhere, with which many Shield Archaic sites are known to have been contemporaries, the culture is remarkably "underdeveloped." In part, this is because of the rigors of the environment to which the Shield Archaic people had had to adapt and, in terms of social interaction, their marginal position vis-à-vis richer and much more numerous populations.

Ground and polished stone tools, which first appear in any number in the Late Archaic Period and are common and elaborate in many regional expressions of cultures of that period, are virtually absent in the Shield Archaic—either in its formative stages in the Early Archaic period proper, or in the Late Archaic or later times into which it survived. And although some native-copper implements like socketed spearpoints and knives, self-hafted semilunar knives, awls, gaffs, and fishhooks occur on some sites—notably along the southern margins of the Shield in or near the Great Lakes—all that usually remains are chipped flint artifacts and the byproducts of their manufacture. The copper tools were obtained from more advanced neighbors, they were not developed independently in the Shield. Projectile points are common and occur in several styles. Some are straight or concave-based lanceolates unmistakably recalling their Plano derivation. Other points, presumably later, are notched, corner-removed, or stemmed, and all relatively broad-bladed. End and side-scrapers are especially conspicuous on Shield Archaic sites, there commonly being two of them for every projectile point. Among the scrapers are more-or-less ovoid, or even circular, cores trimmed along the margins to make large, "heavy duty" planes. Flat-based ovoid bifaces are also common; although many of these were knives, others probably functioned as versatile multiple-purpose implements useful in cutting, scraping, gouging, chopping, and digging. Distinctive, though not numerous, are elongated unifacially worked knives sometimes based on large prismatic blades. These and sometimes other tools are occasionally fabricated of regionally exotic flint. Such information indicates that the Shield Archaic, geographically stamped as it is, did not evolve in the forbidding boreal forest of the Shield country in absolute isolation, though that isolation was impenetrable enough to slow the spread and cripple the acceptance of outside novelties.

Despite the infrequent preservation of bone, the nature of the country and the quantities of projectile points and butchering tools proclaim a major subsistence reliance on hunting. Sites are typically discovered at the narrows of lakes and rivers, places which make for natural caribou crossings. Caribou were probably the single most important game animal in the diet of the Shield Archaic people. Also important, depending on local availability and season, were moose, bear, hare, porcupine, muskrat, and beaver. Fish vied with caribou as the staple. Copper fishhooks have been retrieved at a number of localities, and it is difficult imagining any people living in such country without a heavy and long-term dependence on fishing. In fact, military personnel who may be forced to make emergency landings in this kind of terrain are advised by wilderness experts to put their principal food-getting efforts into fish rather than game. Wild vegetable foods provided a little variety but hardly an equivalent resource to either red meat or fish. The environment of the Shield Archaic people simply did not provide large quantities of acceptable plant foodstuffs. Not surprisingly, tools designed for processing vegetable foods are rare to absent.

Commencing sometime after the emergence of the Shield Archaic, other Archaic cultures developed elsewhere in the Great Lakes under the influence of populations residing in flanking regions. These new cultures will be described in the next chapter. What needs to be reinforced here is the point that people in the Great Lakes during the Interregnum were in contact, however unequally, indirectly, and peripherally, with Early and Middle Archaic groups outside the watershed. While the Shield Archaic exhibits evidence of in situ transformation out of a Late Paleo-Indian cultural base and strong continuity in artifacts and adaptation over thousands of years, there is also unimpeachable evidence of foreign contacts through shared style concepts and the importation of raw materials and finished tools. Thus we find in northern Ontario: Knife River chalcedony from North Dakota, Ramah chert from northern Labrador, and copper from Lake Superior.

The area occupied by people with a Shield Archaic culture was but a small part of the Great Lakes. Although our ignorance is profound, it seems that during at least the last 2000 years of the Interregnum the importation of ideas, materials, and artifacts, and the intrusion of new societies underwent a slow, fateful acceleration. In continental perspective, the Great Lakes had been a social and cultural backwater from the end of the fluted-point period to late in the Interregnum. Exciting and innovating things had been transpiring elsewhere, and they now expanded in their consequences to encompass and partly transform the people of the inland seas. Most of these innovations were incremental, the culmination of accretional improvements in technology and a progressively expanding and deepening involvement with a wider spectrum of environmental resources linked to the creative pressures of an inexorably increasing population. While the developmental sequences and their culminations can be documented in other parts of the continent, especially in the southeastern United States, only the culminations are well represented in the archaeological record of the Great Lakes. A round figure of 3500 B.C. may be employed to mark this change in the archaeological record. Not to be taken too literally in any specific geographic division of the Great Lakes, the figure is a convenient termination for the Interregnum and the beginning of the Late Archaic period.

References

On Great Lakes Late Paleo-Indian complexes:
Deller 1979; Fitting 1970 (especially Chapter III: "The Early Hunters"); Fox 1975; Funk 1972; Jenks 1937; Quimby 1959 and 1960b (especially Chapter 5: "Lanceolate Points and Fossil Beaches"); Steinbring 1974; Storck 1978b; J. V. Wright 1972a (especially Chapter I: "The Palaeo-Indian Period").

On Early Archaic complexes of the Great Lakes and adjoining regions:
Fitting 1970 (especially Chapter IV: "The Return of the People"); Fowler 1959; Funk 1977; Ritchie and Funk 1971 and 1973 (especially pp. 37-51: "The Archaic Stage"); Tuck 1974; J. V. Wright 1972a (especially Chapter II: "The Archaic Period") and 1978.

On the Brohm site, Ontario:
MacNeish 1952a.

On the Flambeau and Minocqua phases of northern Wisconsin:
Salzer 1974.

On the George Lake and Sheguiandah sites, Ontario:
Greenman 1948; Greenman and Stanley 1940 and 1943; Lee 1954 and 1955.

On the Itasca bison-kill site, Minnesota:
Shay 1971.

On the Renier site, Wisconsin:
R. J. Mason and Irwin 1960.

On the Sawmill site, Ohio:
Prufer and Baby 1963.

On the Shield Archaic:
J. V. Wright 1972b.

Transformation Achieved
The Late Archaic Period

5

Although it is true that each dying age is also one aborning, the process is usually so much one of accretional displacements that stipulating the moment of final transition from one to the other is arbitrary. Since many discardings of old ways and accruing of new ones combine to precipitate the transformation, precisely where is the line to be drawn between the dénouement of one age and the inception of the next? This is especially nettlesome when each of the accumulating alterations is hardly revolutionary taken alone. Nevertheless, when we are past the Paleo-Indian–Archaic transition or, as we have called it, the Interregnum, and are into the new age, there is no doubt that both a death and a birth have occurred, or, furthermore, that they are already behind us. The passage was long and archaeologically poorly marked. The new age, the Late Archaic Period, marks something novel.

As something new, the post-transitional, mature Archaic represents an acted-upon reassessment of possibilities for living. The Late or, quintessential, Archaic period coincided in its establishment with the attainment of more or less modern environmental conditions. Thus old ways required new means. New means opened unanticipated possibilities.

By about 3500 B.C. most of the Great Lakes supported the kinds and associations of plants and animals familiar today. Biotic boundaries were approaching those historically known even if the lakes themselves were still in process of adjustment to a post-Pleistocene climatic regime and the crustal reverberations of the one-time tenancy of continental ice. The cultural adjustments of the Interregnum, like the ecosystemic, had entailed millennia. But by the middle to the end of the fourth millennium B.C. that program of readaptation had been successful enough to usher in a long

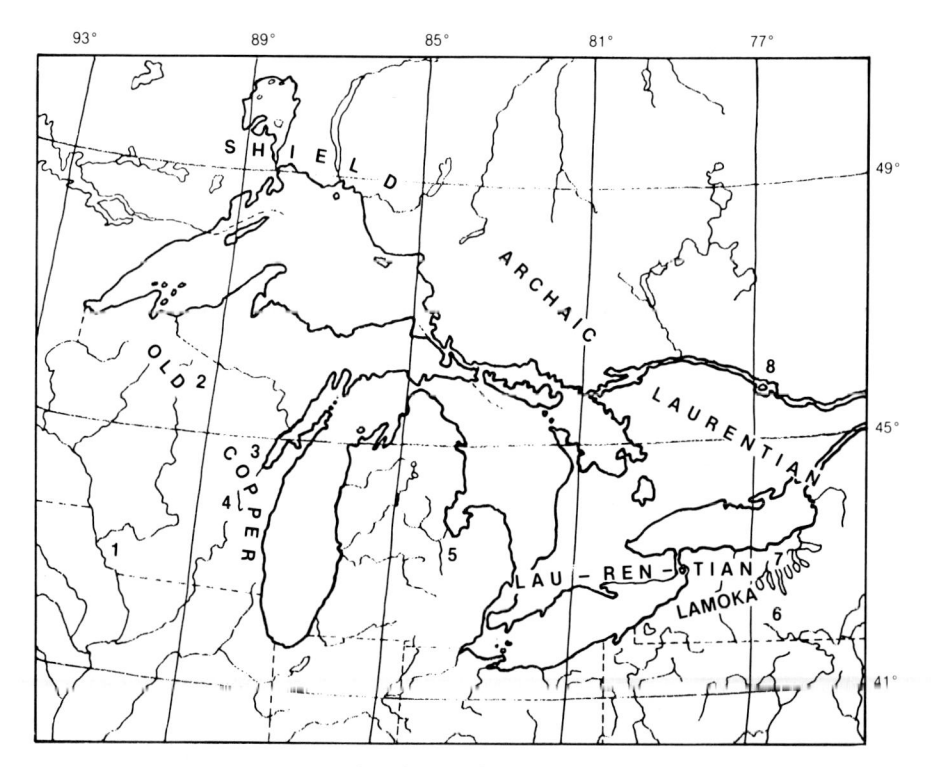

MAP 5.1. *Approximate ranges of Archaic cultures and locations of Archaic sites mentioned in the text: (1) Osceola; (2) Squirrel River phase sites; (3) Oconto; (4) Reigh; (5) Andrews, Feeheley, Hart, and Schmidt sites; (6) Lamoka Lake; (7) Frontenac Island; and (8) Allumette Island-1 and Morrison's Island-6 sites.*

epoch of essential stability. During that period of time, changes, although many and regionally diverse, were accommodated without major dislocations of existing institutions and practices. Most of the experimentation and innovation had been both symptoms and results of the long Interregnum. It was the coming together and the articulation of those results in an essentially modern climatic and biological setting that so much define the new period.

At least in the Great Lakes, if not also in the remainder of northeastern and north central North America, population increases of a hitherto unprecedented magnitude were an apparent accompaniment of the Late Archaic achievement. Late Archaic sites vastly outnumber all known sites representing the enormously longer span of time of the preceding Interregnum and Paleo-Indian period. Furthermore, the increase gives the appearance of having been saltatory rather than simply the culmination of a steady upward trend. Late Archaic sites are also typically larger, deeper, richer in debris, and more complicated in structure than their antecedents. And very likely as a result of population increase, cemeteries suddenly become conspicuous even though they by no means replace the isolated grave within living or abandoned camp ground as accepted burial practice.

The increase in population which helps to mark the Late Archaic period may have been as responsible for bringing into being the innovations and novel practices that serve to describe the period as were the combined effects of changes in the physical enviroment. Once the cultural systems were potentially or effectively able to accomodate the changing physical world to the social and cultural pressures of increasing population, that very success probably rebounded to potentiate, if not stimulate, further supplementing of population. Numbers are hard to resolve out of the time-blurred picture of such demographic events, but there is every indication of major and long-lasting increases in numbers of people, not just in the lakes country but in most of the New World.

A broader, thus more adaptable, subsistence base than that of the Paleo-Indians evolved in the Interregnum to culminate in and characterize life in the Late Archaic period. Not that this was so in every instance; stasigenesis ensured against so monotypic a result. Generally, however, and in most districts, the Late Archaic lifeway was variable, flexible, and supportable because it rested on a multiplicity of prime and secondary food resources. Many contributors to the larder—big game, small game, fish, shellfish, reptiles, waterfowl, ground-running and tree-roosting birds, and vegetable resources—combined to make a broad-spectrum cornucopia. Because these culturally recognized resources were so varied, the food quest was cushioned against the seasonal failure of one or even several of them. It is doubtful that such a broadly cast food-procurement net was the result of free and leisured experimentation, else it should have appeared much earlier than it did. That it constituted a kind of involuntary reimbursement for the antecedent heavy reliance on the fewer, more specialized hunting targets exploited by the Paleo-Indians is indicated by the chronologies of biotic and cultural alterations. The preferred red meat of big game, although peculiarly amenable to supporting the far fewer nomadic intruders of the Late Pleistocene world, could not of itself consistently supply the demands of accelerating rates of human reproduction, especially given the extra debit of large-scale megafaunal extinctions. The consumption of red meat and the hunting of large game seems never to have lost its appeal, however; they remained prestige activities down to and well after the coming of Europeans.

The loss of an assured supply of preferred food must concurrently have forced attention to its replacement or augmentation by the hunting and collecting of food sources earlier known but regarded as less desirable, and ineluctably, to the discovery that some things were edible notwithstanding the prejudices received from one's ancestors. In this wider and richer tap-

PLATE 5.1. *Bannerstone (spear-thrower weight?) from Waupaca County, Wisconsin. (Shown actual size.) (Collections of Department of Anthropology, Lawrence University, Appleton, Wisconsin.)*

ping of nature's munificence, locally, regionally, and seasonally abundant resources tended to dominate the food quest. The roles of caribou and of fish in the Shield Archaic have already been stressed. As known from historical evidence, fish were not simply generally important throughout the Great Lakes, but were the seasonal staple at especially well-endowed locations. Freshwater clams and other shellfish also came to be appropriated, though there was never anything approaching their availability in the rivers of the Mississippi and Atlantic drainages.

In its implications for the future, the most significant of the nutritional reservoirs newly emphasized in the Late Archaic period was vegetable. The new regard for plants is indicated by charred floral remains as well as by the recovery of milling and nutting stones appropriate to their processing. Some sites, such as the Feeheley site near Saginaw Bay in eastern Michigan, a member of a small cluster thought to represent occupations by one or several closely related groups, have unequivocally signaled some regional dependence on the gathering of wild grapes, acorns, walnuts, hickory nuts, and butternuts. Better sampled localities south of the lakes record the garnering of pecans and hazelnuts and such small edible seeds as smartweed, marsh elder, and goosefoot chenopod. Sumpweed, sunflower, Jerusalem artichoke, and maygrass also make their first appearances in Late Archaic middens; the first two may even have been on the threshold of indigenous domestication. Many other plants were doubtless also harvested even though surviving empirical evidence is presently lacking. More than incidental plant use as foods requires more than a passing acquaintance with local plant associations, soils, water courses, microclimates, and all the subtle interacting factors encouraging or inhibiting vigorous vegetal growth. Nomadic hunters have much less need of such information. Its acquisition and its effective utilization favor and are favored by less wandering and more in-settling.

In conjunction, the two processes of growing population and the food-rich deciduous forest's displacement of coniferous forests in large tracts of the Great Lakes must have been responsible in large measure for the new intensification of interest in plants. It has also been suggested that the Late Archaic period, by its contemporaneity with the post-glacial reattainment of high water levels and the consequent reduction of stream gradients and the amelioration of flow velocities, would have coincided with much-enhanced fishing possibilities. Fishing gear at about this time underwent inventive and expansive development, and fish bones in camp middens show an explosive increase. Examples of such sites, in addition to those about to be considered in some detail , include related neighbors of the Feeheley site such as the Hart and Schmidt sites. All of these sites, thought to date around 2000 B.C., are on the fossil shorelines of so-called Shiawassee Bay, a Nipissing and Algoma stage high-water embayment in the Saginaw Valley.

The wider provisioning of the larder, especially by its contribution to the heavy utilization of fish and plants, more than compensated for the loss of the older preterred focus on big-game hunting. The consequence was a more balanced tapping of overlapping food sources with their combined capacities to nourish more people than had been possible under the old regimen. Hunting remained important and the hunter retained his ancient prestige even if the lowlier aquatic and vegetable foodstuffs provided an increasingly bigger, if not in most cases the preponderant, share of Late Archaic nutrition. In this manner the quintessential Archaic way of life was a process of settling in to the challenges and opportunities of the geographic variety of the Holocene world; it was an age of fundamental discoveries in which many things previously seen were looked at again and found to have qualities that rewarded the second look.

Regionally or locally based subsistence patterns did not allow of the same sort of relatively homogeneous pan-North American culture as classically evolved in the Paleo-Indian period. Increasingly, reduced mobility and heightened dependence on locally procurable flora and fauna necessitated the emergence and continuance of more variable cultural complexes. Except in far northerly situations, one of the most far-reaching ramifications of the new mode of life was its eventual value as a kind of preadaptation to the much later development of agriculture. Such a preadaptation to important future events, of course, was neither conscious, planned, nor predetermined in any teleological sense, but was simply a consequence of the more intimate knowledge of local terrain with its various soils and plants. Except for the diffusion of agriculture and its enabling technology from relatively intensive farming societies to simpler ones coming under their cultural dominance, such a precondition was probably everywhere a necessity for the eventual emergence of food production. First things first, and the lowly hunters and gatherers of the Archaic lifeway had unwittingly moved in the direction of a new way of life.

The Late Archaic "second look" took in the mineral as well as vegetable world. Tough, non-flinty rocks like granites, gabbros, basalts, gneisses, and sandstones provided major new sources of raw material for tool production as the techniques of pecking, grinding, and polishing stone rose to a prominence never revealed before in the archaeological record. The new tools made possible by these methods were part of the total cultural response to the evolving ecosystem. Varieties of milling stones to process vegetal foods and heavy wood-working tools to help support the more sedentary manipulation of the evolving Great Lakes forests, as detailed on the following pages, are among the most salient features of the new period. As we shall see, these and other artifacts sometimes took on a regional or local cast, especially in stylistic attributes. Such diversity within uniformity expresses a greater degree of parochialism than obtained in preceding millennia.

PLATE 5.2. *Two examples of Late Archaic three-quarter grooved axes from eastern Wisconsin. The larger axe is 19.5 cm in length. (Collections of Department of Anthropology, Lawrence University, Appleton, Wisconsin.)*

The far-flung and long-lived Shield Archaic of and above the northern reaches of the Upper Great Lakes has already been described. While its formative stages evolved well back in the Interregnum, most actual components are datable to the Late Archaic and even later periods. So even though the northern coasts of Lake Superior and Lake Huron and northward therefrom comprised the homeland of the Shield Archaic people, their culture was atypical of the Late Archaic achievements of the rest, and far larger part, of the lakes country. These other parts were south of the boreal forest and embraced enormously richer and more varied resources in addition to enjoying closer proximity to the more numerous Archaic populations of the Southeast. It is these other cultures that set the tone and have to exemplify the élan of the Late Archaic period in the Great Lakes. The three most famous exemplars are the Lamoka, Laurentian, and Old Copper cultures.

Lamoka

Over a span of several centuries on either side of 2500 B.C., small groups of Indians sharing a common culture settled into the rolling hills of west central New York. Although their names for themselves are beyond recovery, their cultural individuality has at least been partly resurrected by the archaeologist who rescued their traces from oblivion. He rechristened them using the name of one of the places where they have been found: Lamoka.

It was with the remains of the Lamoka culture that the idea of an Archaic stage of culture was first worked out in northeastern North America. But one of many regionally distinct, ancient but post-Interregnum cultures, this one was limited in its occurrence to the Genessee Valley and immediately adjacent areas. Some of its material products, however, like the characteristic projectile points, were fashioned according to precepts shared with other contemporaneous cultures of the Late Archaic period as far away as eastern Michigan, southern New England, and northern Kentucky. Such projectile points are usually small, narrow-bladed, stemmed or shallowly notched—often with minimally finished tangs—and are a far cry fom the craftsmanship of the specimens we have been concerned with so far. These points, the beveled adze, and a group of elongate pendant-like objects of bone, especially when found together (an association exclusive to west central New York), are diagnostic of the Lamoka culture. For some time this was thought to be an "Early" Archaic manifestation. But as subsequent investigations in the Mississippi Valley and the southeastern United States brought to light developmentally and chronologically earlier examples of nascent or proto-Archaic cultures, the Lamoka finds came to

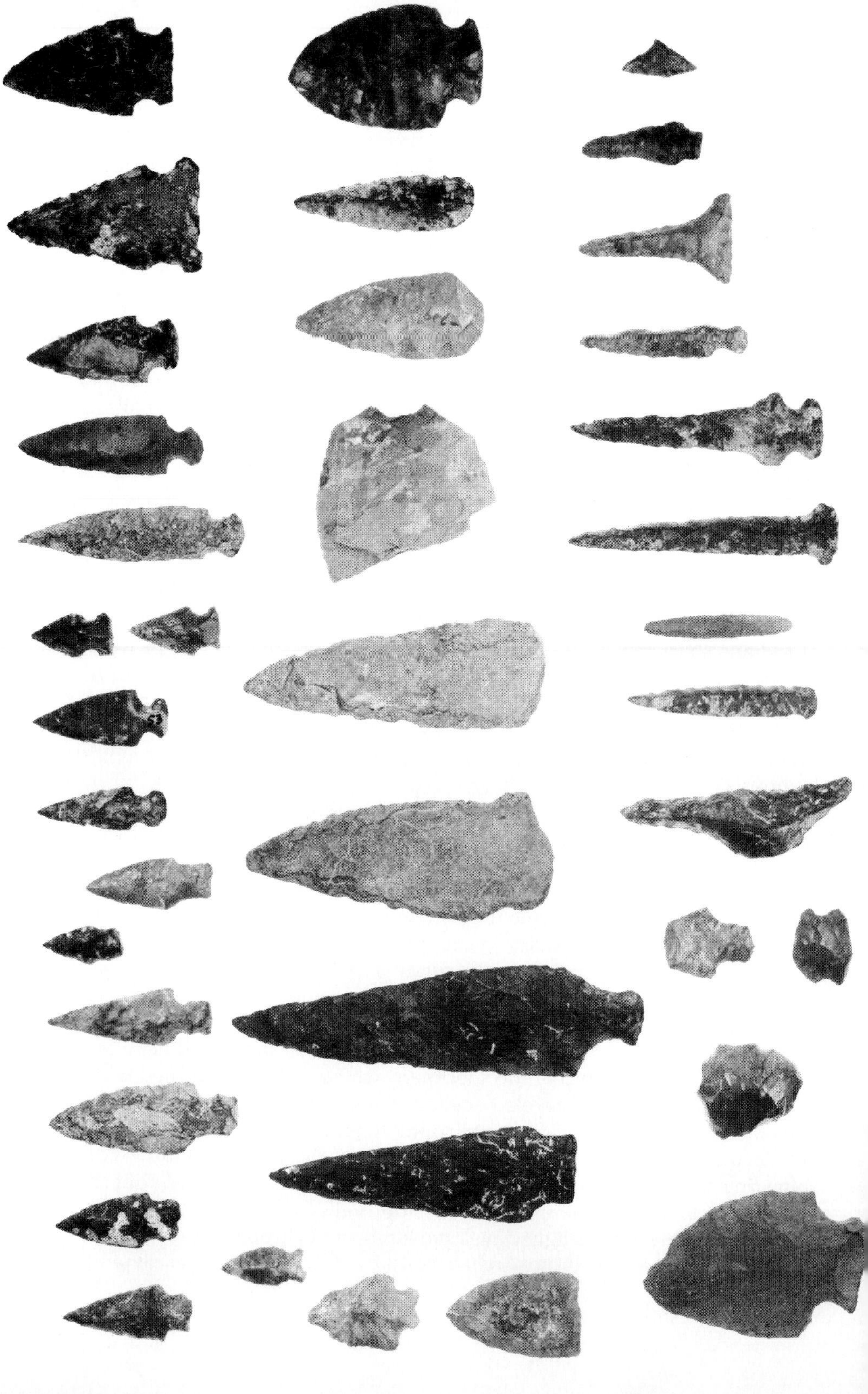

Plate 5.3. Lamoka (mainly) projectile points, knives (top two rows); scrapers, drills (third row); and celts and adzes from the Scottsville, Geneva, and Lamoka Lake sites, New York. Note the beveled adzes just to the right of center in the bottom rows. (Shown half actual size.) (Collection of the Rochester Museum and Science Center. [May not be reprinted without permission of the RMSC.])

be recognized as a fully developed, mature, Late Archaic syndrome. While now known to be neither the earliest nor the most widespread Late Archaic culture in the Great Lakes, it was one of the most important discoveries in the Northeast and bears all of the features its period betokens.

As far as prehistorians have been able to tell, the plants and animals familiar to the Lamoka folk were the same as those that early Europeans found when they discovered the Lower Great Lakes. Possibly temperatures were a little higher on the average than they are now at this latitude. The establishment of the modern type of deciduous forest with its complement of game animals is believed to have been achieved essentially by about 3500 B.C. in the lakes country. These conditions are reflected in the subsistence remains unearthed at Lamoka culture sites.

Hunting, fishing, and the gathering of wild plant foods constituted the tripod underpinnings of the Lamoka way of life. Deer, turkey, and passenger pigeons were the chief food animals, just as they were of the whole Carolinian Biotic Province. The meat they provided was importantly supplemented by the hunting of bear, raccoon, snowshoe hare, fox, squirrel, woodchuck, muskrat, and other animals. They were taken with the spear and the atlatl (spear-thrower)-assisted dart. Although no evidence survives, it is virtually certain that traps and deadfalls were widely used to capture the smaller game. Frogs and, especially, turtles were another important sources of animal protein, as were ducks, geese, and other waterfowl.

Perhaps as important as hunting was fishing. Besides actual fish remains, bone fishhooks, gorges, probable leister prongs, and notched stone net-sinkers attest the crucial part that fishing played in the subsistence base. At least two kinds of fishhooks were in use: the single-piece curved fishhook of bone and the composite kind with a straight and pointed bone hook attached to a wood shank. Both types lacked barbs. Fishhooks in all stages of manufacture have been recovered at Lamoka sites. The gorge was simply a short bipointed splinter of bone but, with a line tied around the middle and wrapped in bait, a gorge turns in a fish's gullet or stomach and is probably as efficient as a hook. The leister, on the other hand, is a fish spear equipped with sharp prongs. It is particularly effective at river narrows during spring runs or used from a boat drifting silently over spawning beds or shallows in lakes. However, for the Lamoka people, netting was probably more productive than line-fishing and fish-spearing combined. Enormous quantities of notched round or oval, flat pebbles, or net-sinkers are good evidence of the employment of nets, as are the recoveries of thin and flat, well-polished bone tools with bluntly pointed ends and drilled holes in the center or near one end or edge. These are very much like ethnographic specimens of net-weaving tools, and it is likely that the archaeological examples served the same function. Most likely all of the species of fish important in western New York's rivers, inland lakes, and marshes were taken for food. Because the Lamoka people mainly lived along southern waterways tributary to Lake Ontario, rather than on the lakeshore itself, it is doubtful that they ever exploited that freshwater sea directly.

The third leg of the Lamoka food base was the heavy and sustained procurement of wild vegetable consumables. With a variety of edible tubers, fruits, nuts, and seeds appropriate to the spring, summer, and fall seasons available to the Lamoka people, it is acorns and hickory nuts that are impressive in the archaeological remains. Particularly abundant were great numbers of charred acorns. Evidently, these were prepared in some of the extensive roasting areas conspicuous in certain excavations. Such treatment would have removed much of the bitter tannic acid present in unprocessed nuts. In addition to the cooked vegetal remains, the importance of wild plant resources in the diet is further signaled by the special stone tools associated with their exploitation. These include pecked cylindrical pestles made of such tough non-flinty stones as granite, graywacke, and sandstone. They were doubtless used in combination with wooden mortars. In this same category, and expressed in the same materials, are milling or grinding stones in the form of bun-shaped mullers and slab mortars. Similar implements first appear in early post-glacial times in the desert West. Rare to nonexistent in Paleo-Indian contexts, their initial appearance in any numbers is usually taken as one of the distinguishing features of Archaic cultures. The techniques of pecking and grinding by which they were fashioned opened up a whole new category of heavy tools based on abundant raw materials not otherwise amenable to shaping. Making their first appearance in the Interregnum, pecked and ground and polished stone tools became common and diversified during the Late Archaic period. Whatever the reason, this appears as an explosive development in the Great Lakes.

Another important application of the newly conspicuous ground and polished stone technology was in heavy woodworking tools. Axes in the form of round cross-sectioned wedges of tough stone had a bit at one end and a rounded poll at the other. Lacking notches or grooves, the Lamoka axes are technically "celts." Mounted on a wooden handle, they were especially effective as hatchets. Experiments have shown that celts and other stone axes are roughly on the order of 75% as efficient in chopping down small trees as a steel axe of comparable weight. However, they lose their keen edges more rapidly and require much more laborious resharpening. Related to celts, and also very abundant, were adzes. Designed for planing and hollowing rather than straight chopping, adzes were hafted differently than celts or axes and had a plano-convex bit. One variety of adze was longitudinally beveled, with its convex back formed of three facets; so characteristic of the Lamoka culture is the beveled type, and so rare is it in any other context, that it has been dubbed "the Lamoka adze." The making

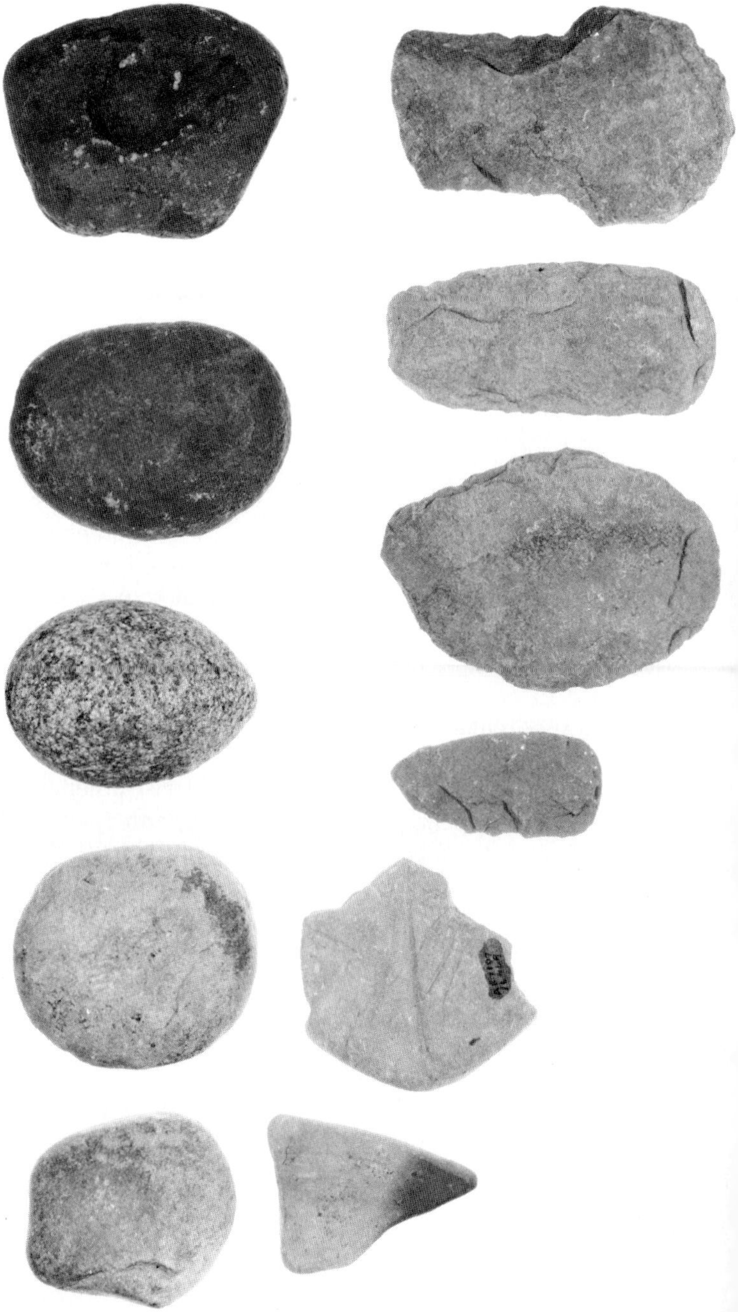

PLATE 5.4. Lamoka hammerstones (top row); abrading stones, choppers, notched sinker, grooved mauls (middle group); and mortar and pestle (lower left) from the Scottsville, Geneva, and Lamoka Lake sites, New York. (Shown two-fifths actual size.) (Collection of the Rochester Museum and Science Center. [May not be reprinted without permission of the RMSC.])

of so many of these carpentry tools hints at the one-time existence of rich wood-craft, probably including the dugout canoe.

Very common on Lamoka sites are heavy stone tools shaped more by use than by design. Typically of quartz, sandstone, granite, or other tough material, these include hammerstones, anvils, and pitted "nutting" stones. These last possibly served a number of shallow-mortar functions as well as holding acorns and other nuts while they were cracked open with a stone or wood hammer. Some milling stones were also only minimally modified, except by use. A final example of tools in this class are whetstones used for sharpening bone utensils and weapons.

Implements and implement components fashioned of chipped flint, the dominant or even exclusive artifact category in times preceding the Late Archaic period, are still highly visible and were of great functional importance notwithstanding the proliferation of ground and polished stone tools. Besides the projectile points described earlier, common Lamoka flaked tools were knives, drills, and choppers. Interestingly, the chipped-stone scraper, so ubiquitous in earlier and many contemporaneous and later cultures, such as the Shield Archaic, is virtually unknown in Lamoka cultural deposits. Its place seems to have been taken by pecked and ground, thin, adze-like tools and by bone implements.

The latter are but one element in a numerous and varied catalog of bone and antler devices which also included the fishing equipment mentioned earlier, projectile points, awls, net-sewing needles, sockets made of deer "knuckle" bones which may have served as bow-drill components, flint-working punches or "drifts," chisels (of split and ground beaver incisor teeth), knives and/or daggers, so-called shaft wrenches to straighten spear and dart shafts, tubular beads and/or hair tubes, and the first undoubted musical instruments: single-stopped whistles and multiple-stopped flutes. Besides these, the Lamoka sites have yielded many examples of long and thin spatulate, trianguloid, and rectangular pendants or pendant-like objects of cut, ground, and polished bone or turtle shell. They are commonly perforated at one end or in a corner. Typically, their edges are almost invariably scored with fine, shallow notches. In many instances they are so shallow that it is difficult to imagine that they were intended as decoration; perhaps they were tallies or some other memory aid. Simple geometric designs were sometimes scratched and/or painted on the surfaces of these curious objects with red paint made from pulverized hematite. These and some other tokens of the bone and antler industry, together with the chipped-flint projectile points, are closely paralleled by finds in the shell heaps of contemporary people in Kentucky who lived very much like the Lamoka folk except for their sometime heavy reliance on the regional mussel shoals, a resource not nearly as extensive nor productive in New York. Because the Lamoka culture cannot be convincingly derived from any known local or regional ancestor, but shares some of its distinquishing features with the Kentucky shell-mound Archaic complex, for which there are regional antecedents, it seems reasonable to postulate some kind of connection with that area. Similarities in detailed skeletal anatomy between the two areas reinforce this contention. Nevertheless, the Lamoka culture is distinct enough to rule out a direct migrational connection with the Southeast. Such conspicuous shell-mound Archaic traits as grooved axes and spear-thrower weights are totally absent in Lamoka sites. In important respects Lamoka has a "home grown" flavor, albeit with a southern accent. The idea of southern connections with or via the Susquehanna Valley of eastern Pennsylvania is being entertained by a growing number of archaeologists.

Most Lamoka sites are quite small, indicating short-term, probably seasonal, occupations by just a few families. The Lamoka country was well endowed by a bountiful nature not only with food-rich deciduous forests, but also with innumerable lakes, ponds, marshes, creeks, and rivers. These were attractive to game animals as well as fish, turtles, and waterfowl. For human beings, the lakes and streams were doubly important for purposes of communication and travel. The streams provided easy trails into and out of the forest-covered hilly country of the Allegheny Plateau immediately south of the Great Lakes Lowlands. Small family bands of Lamoka Indians doubtless moved from high hillside to oak meadow to marsh or lakeside to river narrows in seasonal pursuit of animal and vegetable foodstuffs and raw materials. This was a seminomadic or quasi-sedentary life-style bounded by a distinct range. The people had settled into a definite home territory, tapping a broad spectrum of resources. This reflected and in turn engendered a more intense local awareness than had been the case with their ancestors. And it shows in their surviving products.

Not all Lamoka camps were small or occupied for only one season. Some years living was in some places easy enough that quite sizable communities could be formed and maintained in one place for months on end, if not for several years. The Lamoka Lake site, the type locality of the culture, was such a location. Here the remains of a substantial semisedentary community were uncovered, including some of the earliest traces of houses in the Great Lakes and contiguous surrounding country.

At its maximum likely size the Lamoka Lake settlement consisted of about 27 houses occupying approximately .4 ha. Additional domiciles may have occupied parts of another .61 ha where occupational debris proved to be thinner. The refuse mantle of disturbed soil intermixed with ash beds, charcoal lenses, butchered animal bones, charred nuts, hearths postmolds, pits, graves, and broken, lost, and discarded stone and bone artifacts was from .3 to 1.5 m deep. It indicates a considerable body of people and one or more prolonged episodes of stay, although which played the major role in midden accumulation is impossible to determine. Guided by house sizes and by his knowledge of historic Great Lakes Indi-

156

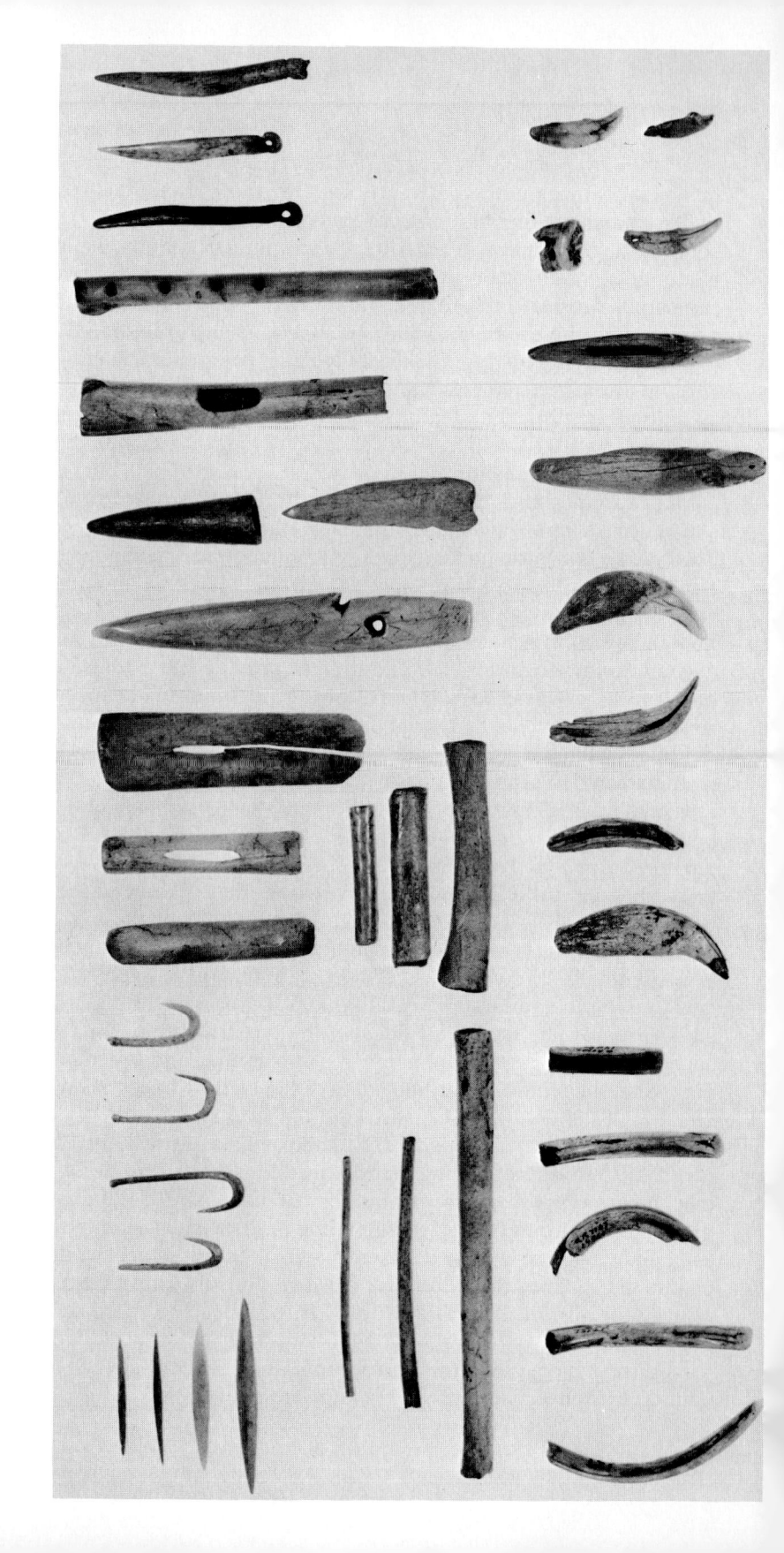

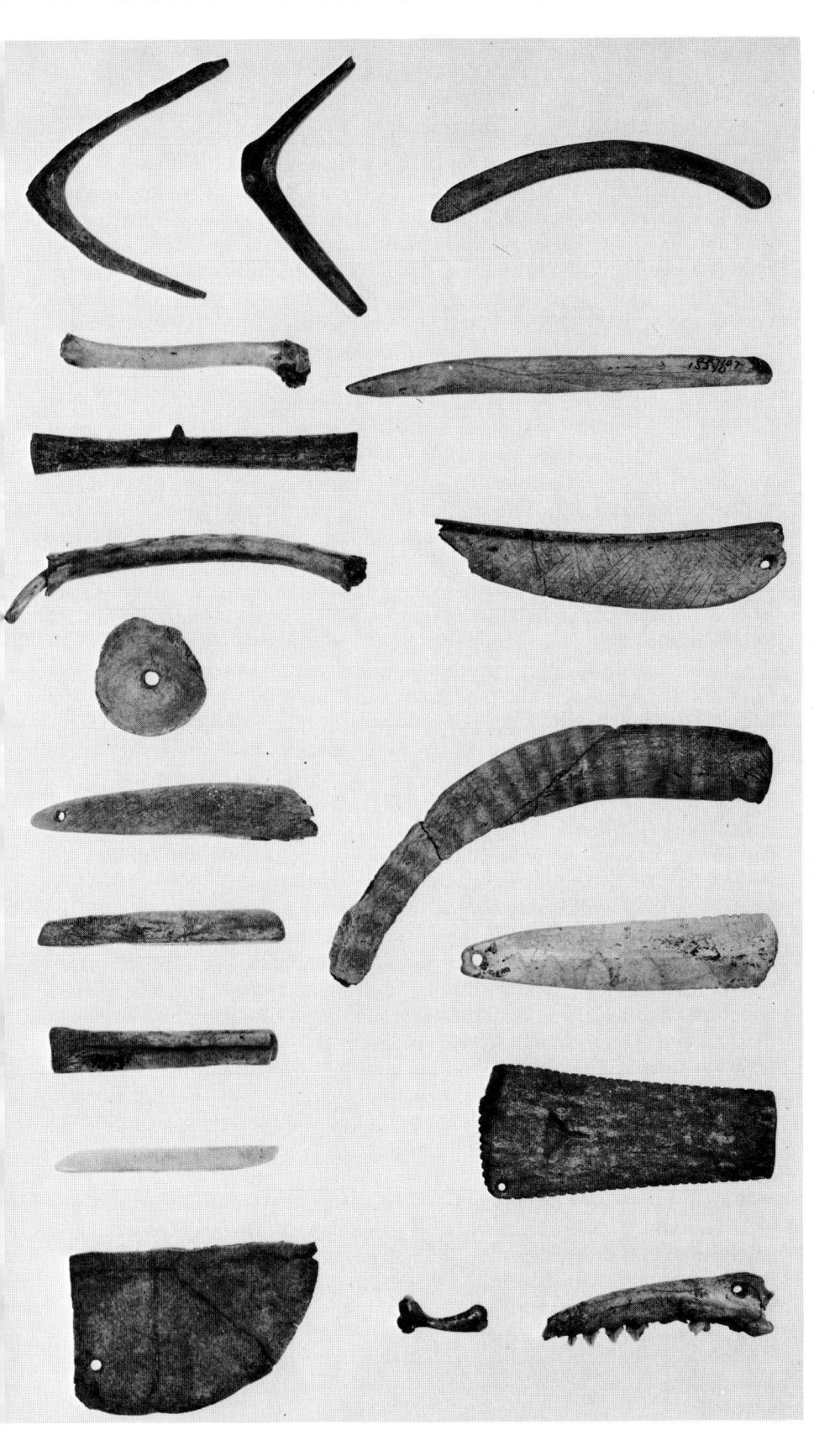

PLATE 5.5. Lamoka bone and antler artifacts: fish gorges and fishhooks, tubes, fishhook blanks, harpoon, conical projectile points, whistles, perforated pins (top row); beaver-incisor knives and chisels, tooth pendants, pendants, and objects of uncertain function (second row); hafted beaver-incisor tool, tool handles, pendants, and objects of uncertain function (bottom two rows) from the Scottsville and Lamoka Lake sites, New York. Note the surviving painted decoration just left of center, bottom row. (Shown half actual size.) (Collection of the Rochester Museum and Science Center. [May not be reprinted without permission of the RMSC.])

ans, the excavator of the Lamoka Lake site believes that the houses probably sheltered six to eight individuals each and that at any one time there may have been between 150 and 200 residents in the village. These people probably used the village as a fixed base from which cooperating groups of men launched hunting expeditions into the nearby hills and family groups set out on fishing and foraging trips. Returning with the fruits of their efforts, they doubtless distributed them to the rest of the community in the time-honored and universal manner of kinship-organized hunters and gatherers. What was lost through gift distribution was made up for in the emotional satisfaction of the provider, the intensification of sense of belonging, and the knowledge that other members of the society would at some future time reciprocate in similar fashion. Under average conditions, hunting, fishing, and gathering parties probably did not have to go too far to meet the community's needs.

Lamoka houses were roughly rectangular in plan and ranged in size from at least as small as 2.6 × 4.3 m (11 m² of floor space) to as large as 4 × 4.9 m (20 m²). There is evidence that some houses, however, were as narrow as 2 m (length unknown). Built like many of the historically known houses in the Great Lakes, they consisted of poles or saplings screwed into the ground to form a framework. It is the organic stains left by these uprights that survive in the postmolds discovered by the hundreds at the Lamoka Lake site. Either the poles were bent over and tied at the top to make an arch or dome, or separate pieces were lashed across the top to form a gable. In either case, the whole would have been covered with bark, animal skins, or woven mats. Probably, cattail or bullrush mats covered parts of the dirt floors. Many foodstuffs, items of skin clothing, bedrolls, and prized belongings would best have been hung from the ceilings. In view of the fact that the Lamoka people had domestic dogs (fox-terrier-like creatures), this would have been a sensible precaution.

Within and outside the postmold patterns outlining the houses were many other postmolds, some of which may mark the locations of former storage racks, meat- or fish-drying frames, and other special-purpose structures. Scattered among these were storage pits, hearths, and immense roasting beds where acorns were cooked and fish and meat smoked. Some of these roasting beds were up to 15 m long. All in all, the signs abound of a prosperous, busy community reasonably secure in its dependence on a diversified, multiresource subsistence economy—dependable over the long run and capable of generating intermittent periods of simple affluence and minimal labor.

Human bones and burials indicate lightly built people of medium stature. The average Lamoka man stood about 168 cm, the average woman a few centimeters shorter. Besides a gracile frame, a characteristic feature of this population is a pronounced dolichocranic, or long-headed, skull form.

The face was relatively long and narrow and lacked prominent cheek bones. Except for very heavy erosion of occlusal surfaces due to the large amount of grit unavoidably added to the diet, the Lamokans enjoyed excellent dental health. Indeed, but for some healed fractures and some cases of mild osteoarthritis, all available signs point to a healthy and well-nourished people.

Most of the skeletons that have come to light were in flexed burials in round or oval graves in the village debris. That is, the deceased had been curled up with the head bent forward, the arms bent at the sides, and the knees drawn up toward the chest. This burial posture, reminiscent of the human fetal position, a resemblance which has stimulated not a few observers to hazard some predictable psychoanalytic interpretations, was probably accomplished by binding the corpse expeditiously after death in order to make a more compact mass for interment. Inasmuch as digging graves is tedious, particularly before the invention of the steel shovel, such a type of inhumation held down the heavy labor with no connotation of lack of respect for the dead. This fact of limited technology helps to explain why flexed burials are so common a feature of early or simple archaeological cultures in most of the world. Much less typical of the Lamoka culture are bundle burials: literally, the stacked bones of disarticulated skeletons. Some archaeologists think that these represent individuals who died alone and away from camp and whose remains were found after decompostition had done its work. They could also represent the final deposition of tree or scaffold burials.

Rarely, one or two simple tools were placed in the graves. Perishable grave goods may also have accompanied them. Such items may have been intended to help the dead in the afterworld. Alternatively, they may simply have been personal belongings of the deceased and, symbolically an extension of the unique human personality, were gotten rid of in order to avoid "contamination." Such notions are widely expressed ethnographically. Finally, the dead were sometimes also dusted or painted with red ocher—pulverized hematite used either as a powder or mixed (with grease?) to create a paint. Again, this is a practice that is both geographically far-flung and, in the Old World especially, ancient. Whether the custom of treating the community's dead and their conjoined grave furniture with red pigment was independently developed more than once or was diffused from a single point in time and space is a matter of debate. Its specific ceremonial or ideological significance, beyond the obvious blood or life connotations of the color red, is likewise unknown. But this custom along with the attention paid to burial flexure or bundling, grave preparation, and deposition of grave goods, scanty as it was, show beyond contention that the Lamoka people invested much more utilitarian interest in disposing of their dead. Simple as these graves seem by contrast with later and far more elaborate types of funerary practices, we can already see that a ritual and ceremony played an imperative role in helping kith and kin survive the emotional crises precipitated by the demise of a loved one.

But in certain Lamoka settlements not all of the people who died had claims on society's love. Fragments of human bone, purposefully cracked open and fire-charred, and mixed with and apparently treated in much the same manner as the remnants of deer and other game, are reasonable evidence of occasional cannibalism. Furthermore, a few skeletons lack heads or hands and feet and exhibit other signs of mutilation. Several have Lamoka-type projectile points imbedded in their bones. Biologically, these individuals are indistinguishable from the other Lamoka skeletons. The conclusion seems inescapable that people both biologically and culturally Lamoka were at war among themselves. This was probably the endless, flickering, low-level feuding occasionally culminating in a moment of terror and one or two killings that is endemic to primitive society generally. Not sustained or intense enough to induce the construction of a stockade around the village and lacking a large and tightly organized population, the violence recorded in the Lamoka remains points to a familiar pattern of hit-and-run raids punctuating lengthy stretches of at least nonovert hostility among the relevant social units, if not peace and tranquillity.

Laurentian

The people in western New York responsible for the Lamoka culture and their cultural relatives in eastern Michigan and elsewhere, were not the sole inhabitants of the country they occupied in the Late Archaic period. Within the Lamoka territory itself, but also extending for a formidable distance beyond it, are the traces of other Late Archaic peoples who did not have a Lamoka culture. Many of these others have come collectively to be called "Laurentian."

In opposition to the tightly drawn, territorially circumscribed Lamoka culture, the Laurentian culture is a much more difficult one to pin down and draw boundaries around. This is in part because there were many variations of this Late Archaic culture and they were distributed over a vastly wider habitat than Lamoka. Also, archaeological sites containing Laurentian cultural attributes variously date over a time range no less than 2000 years. Not surprisingly, early examples of Laurentian sites are in a number of ways, in addition to the distinctions of age, consistently different from late representatives. Many distinct societies seem to have participated in Laurentian culture and to have contributed to it elements from neighboring cultures with which they were also involved. Thus Laurentian on its western and eastern frontiers, or along the southern and northern marches, had enough of a regional cast in each instance to indicate a partly independent history. Such geographic entities reflect separate ecological specializations, the influence of unique neighbors, and differences in the ages of the known sites. Alas, in all too many cases the analytical tools of comparison, and the surviving samples to which they are applied, are insufficient to distinquish the causal from the fortuitous factors.

As originally conceived, Laurentian was *the* Late Archaic culture typical of a major part of northern New York and southern Ontario surrounding Lake Ontario and along both sides of the Upper St. Lawrence River into southern Quebec and Vermont. But it was early recognized that there were many Laurentian attributes and Laurentian-like cultures eastward into the Maritime provinces and the rest of New England, southward into Pennsylvania and New Jersey, and westward into the Upper Great Lakes. This "unity within diversity" proved both a blessing and a curse. It fostered invaluable discoveries of cultural and chronological correlations over great distances lacking intermediate connectives, though often with an unwise extension of the nomenclature to some questionable candidates for comparable status.

The Laurentian culture evinces a full Archaic lifeway exemplified by a broad-spectrum subsistence base of hunting, fishing, and plant collecting. It departs from the Lamoka pattern by its generally heavier emphasis on the hunting of the larger animals, especially deer, and by its seemingly lesser reliance on the gathering of wild vegetable foods. However, at the right localities in the appropriate seasons, temporary emphases were shifted to nut collecting or water fowl trapping or fishing so as to diversify nutritional resources while capitalizing on short-term, but annual, local abundances. Population densities and permanence of occupation thus reflected the calendar as well as the long-term caloric wealth of a given territory. The cultural equipment abandoned at camps and other sites was correspondingly affected. Where sites are small, thin, widely separated, reflective of discrepant purposes, and, more often than not, seriously damaged by recent human activities, recovered assemblages of artifacts typically include in any individual case only an atypical portion of the tools, weapons, features, and faunal and floral remains recoverable from a pooling of all the sites together. While this applies to any archaeological culture, of course, it has especial relevance with respect to such a far-flung one as Laurentian.

Like other people, the Laurentians identified themselves in the things they made. The most conspicuous of these identifying markers were those contrastable with the products of the Lamoka or other Late Archaic non-Laurentian cultures either because they had no counterparts or because their design and execution were unique. Among the prominent artifacts of Laurentian culture, though by no means exclusive to nor necessarily found associated on all Laurentian sites, are numerous chipped-flint dart and

162

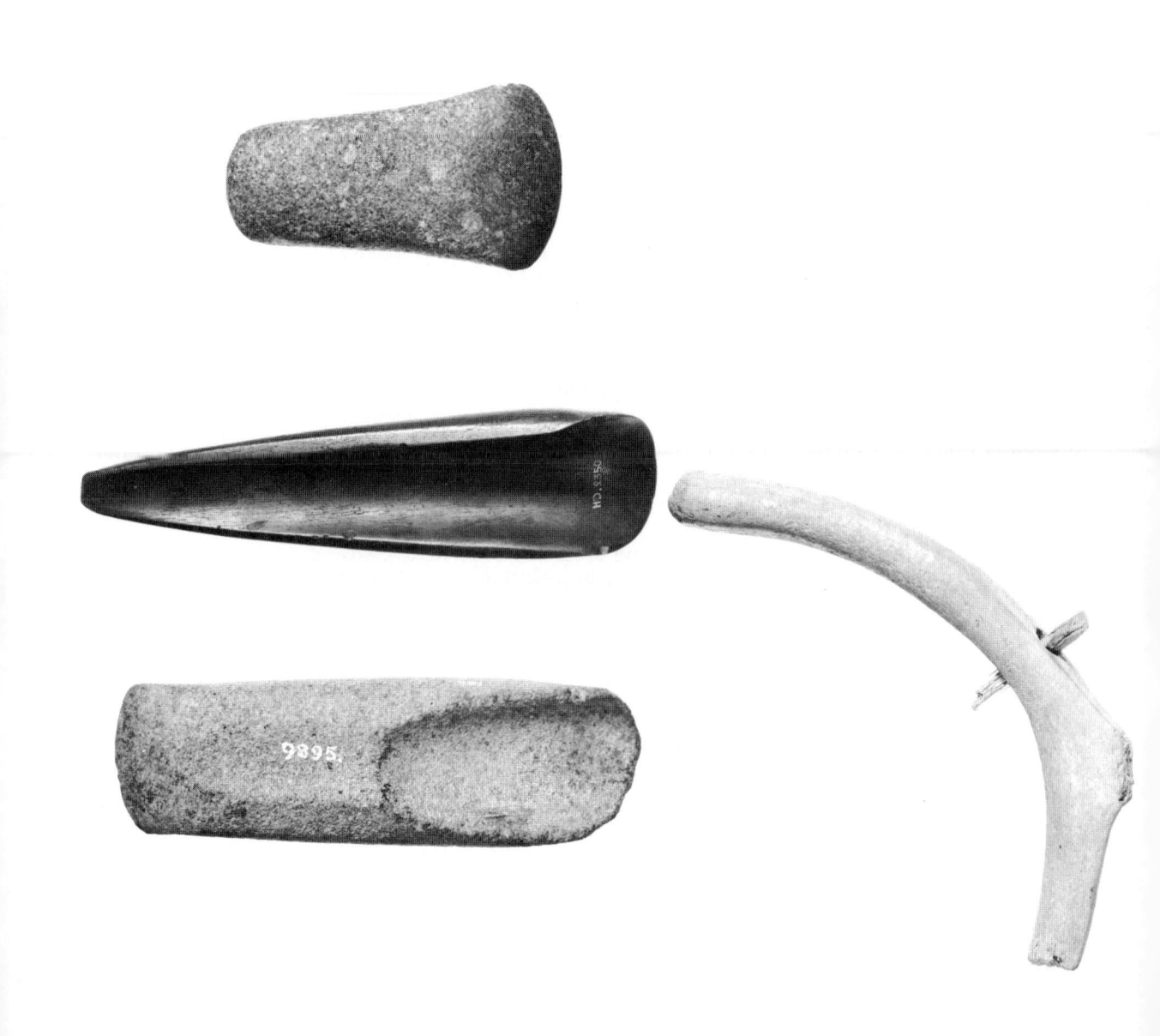

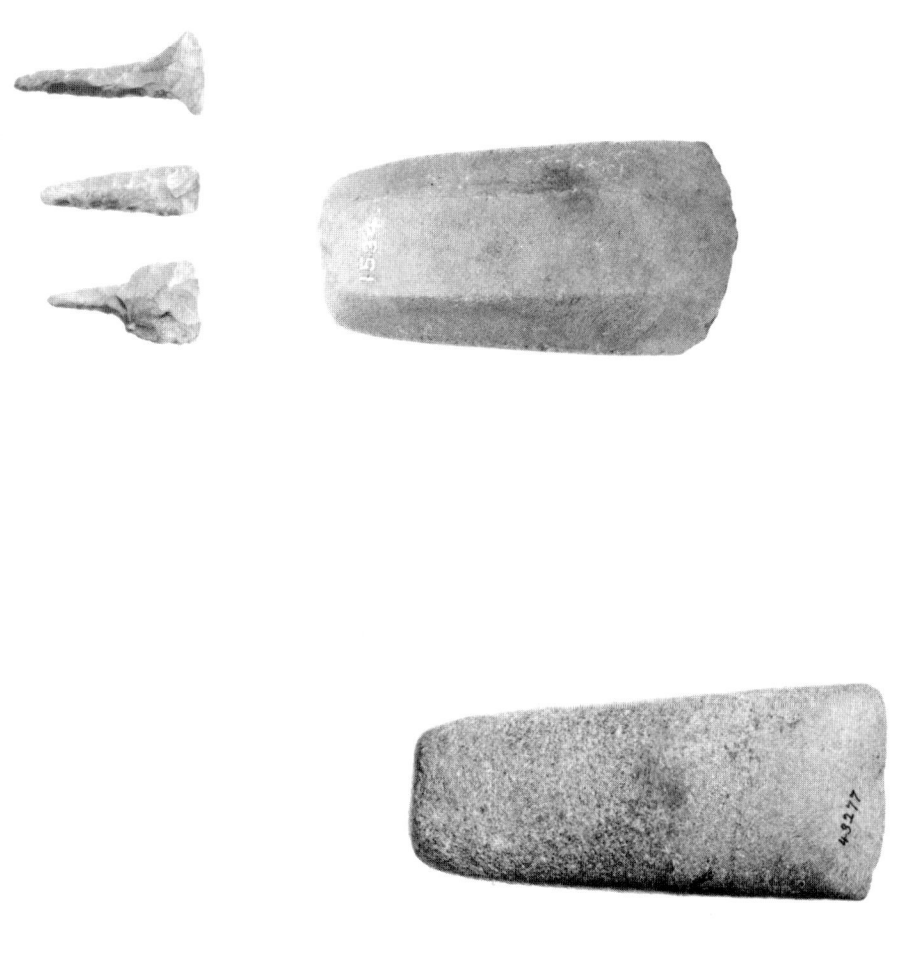

PLATE 5.6. Laurentian hafted beaver-incisor tool, gouges, celt, flint drills, and adze, and a Lamoka-type beveled adze (lower right) from various sites in Ontario. (Shown half actual size.) (Courtesy Peter L. Storck and the Royal Ontario Museum, Toronto, Canada.)

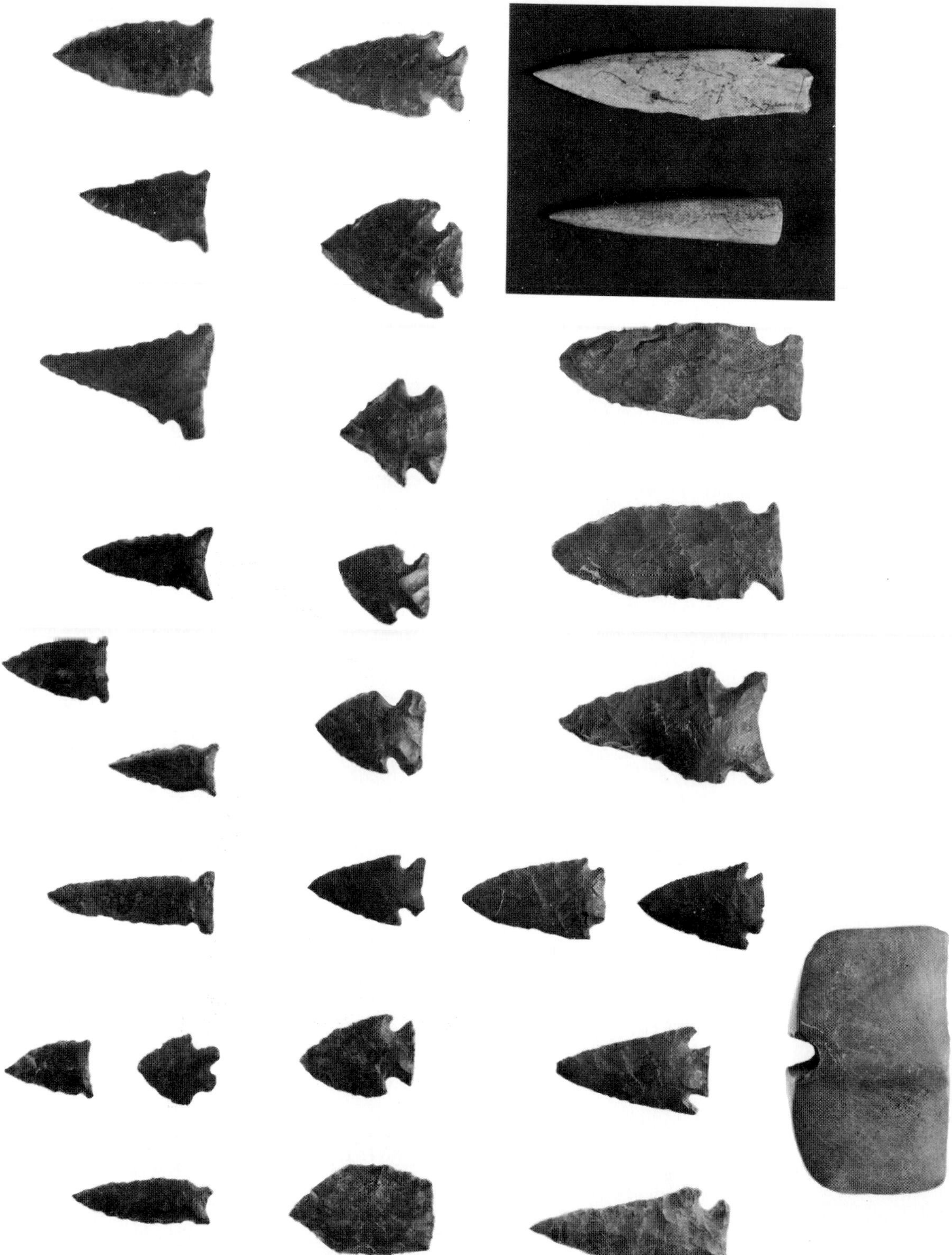

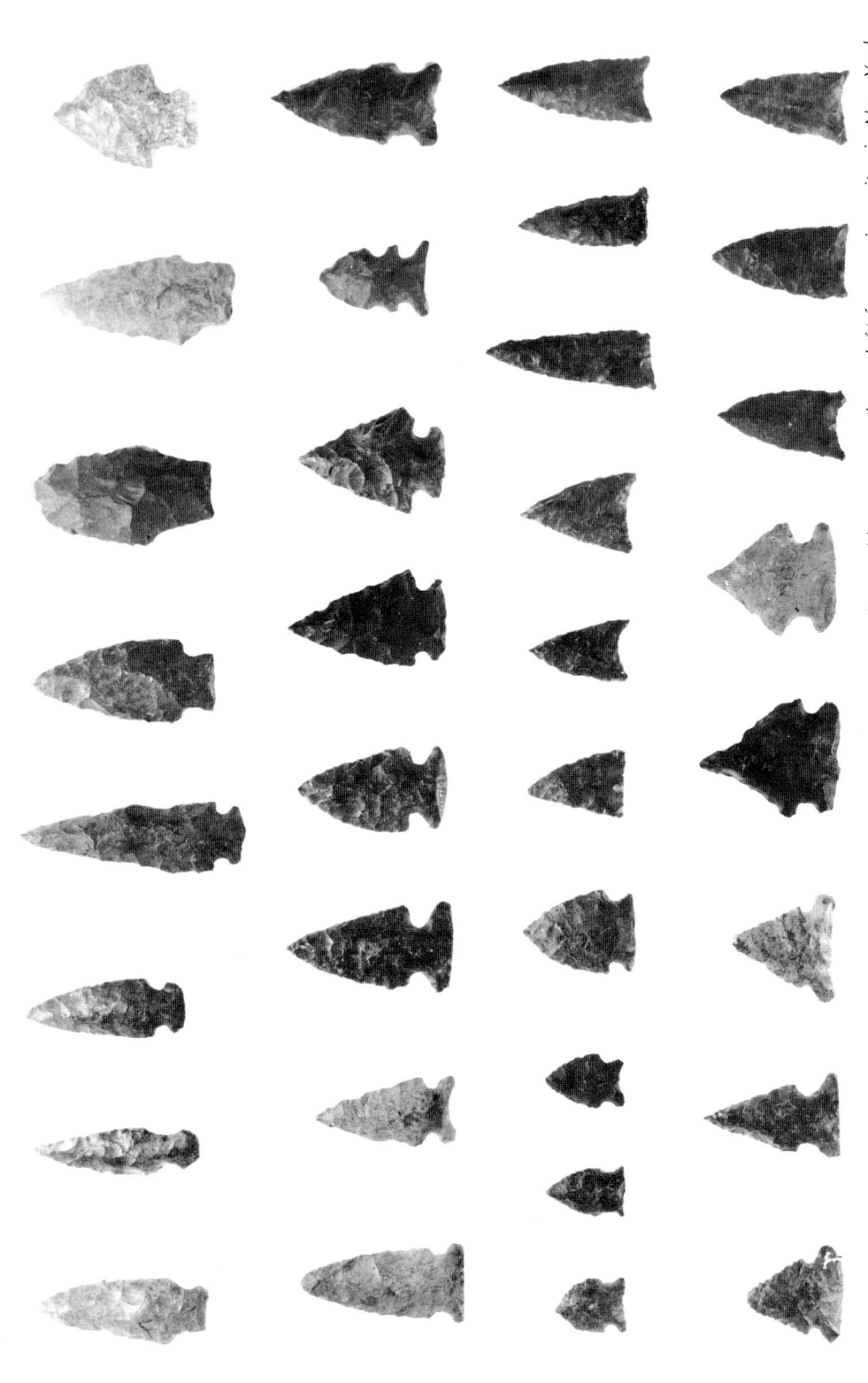

PLATE 5.7. Brewerton Laurentian flint projectile points, bone points (lower right), and bannerstone (lower left) from various sites in New York. (Shown half actual size.) (Courtesy William A. Ritchie and Robert E. Funk, New York State Museum and Science Service, Albany.)

spearpoints with broad blades and side notches; end-scrapers not uncommonly equipped with hafting modifications just like those seen on the projectile points—and most likely made from broken points; simple lobed forms of ground and polished bannerstones, or spear thrower weights; grooved stone plummets; ground and polished bone and antler barbed projectile points and harpoons; ground stone gouges in addition to adzes and celts; occasional awls, celts, and other implements of native copper; and a variety of ground-slate tools and weapons, notably semilunar knives, or ulus, tanged double-edged knives, barbed points with straight or serrated stems, and long slender "bayonets" or spear points. Within the Lower Great Lakes–Upper St. Lawrence Valley where the Laurentian culture was defined and within which most of its sites are located, these are the "diagnostic" artifacts. Of course, many of the artifacts usually recovered— perhaps a majority at most sites—are not so distinctive in cultural ascription. Simple end-scrapers lacking notched stems, flake side-scrapers, some triangular forms of projectile points, ovoid biface knives and preforms, bone whistles, deer-ulna awls, beveled beaver-incisor chisels, conical antler points, bone fish gorges, stone celts, and hammerstones are some of the kinds of remains that are commonly recovered from many non-Laurentian as well as Laurentian sites. Such things tend to be universal in Late Archaic archaeological contexts generally. Some Laurentian sites have yielded abundantly of Laurentian "diagnostics," others only a few. And the particular kinds of examples show discordant distributions bespeaking separate origins and independent histories.

For example, within the geography of Laurentian activity copper tools have a markedly western center of gravity. Indeed, they are infinitely more numerous and varied west of the Laurentian country in the Upper Great Lakes, especially in eastern Wisconsin. Here all of the known Laurentian forms of copper artifacts occur in addition to others either unknown or atypical in Laurentian contexts. These in turn have been ascribed to a poorly defined "Old Copper culture." In this latter area some very Laurentian looking side-notched flint projectile points have been unearthed from Late Archaic graves containing typical copper tools of the so-called Old Copper culture. It should also be noted that "Old Copper" spearpoints, knives, awls, fishhooks, and so on have been found just north of Lakes Superior and Huron in Shield Archaic contexts, and south of the lakes in still others. So just as there is more to Laurentian than was first imagined, there is more to the form and distribution of copper artifacts than an invoked Old Copper culture. There is little doubt that most of the copper found in Laurentian sites, certainly in the form of raw material if not always in finished products, got there though cultural connections with the upper lakes country with its ready accessibility of the high-grade metal.

Conversely, the ground-slate industry is better represented and exhibits greater diversity among the eastern Laurentian sites than among the western. Some of the ground-slate knives and projectile points are very reminiscent of copper forms in the Upper Great Lakes. But ground-slate implements and weapons are far more numerous and diversified in shape and function in New England and the Maritime provinces than in the Laurentian country itself. Indeed, beginning at least as early as 5000 B.C., the lands around the Gulf of St. Lawrence witnessed the rise of a very rich Archaic way of life (the Maritime Archaic) with a spectacular proliferation of ground slates. The same area has also produced evidence of a probably equally ancient evolution of grooved plummets and ground and polished gouges, as well as types of implements unparalleled in Laurentian. Evidently based on the profuse biological resources of the Gulf and northern Atlantic littoral, the antiquity and relative opulence of the Maritime Archaic have come as a surprise to those archaeologists who have been understandably preoccupied with the detailed developmental sequences unearthed in the southeastern United States. It is now clear that a highly significant component of "Laurentian" culture was developed in the greater Gulf of St. Lawrence area and was later introduced to and grafted onto the proto-Laurentian culture to the southwest instead of being independently invented there.

Similarly, bannerstones (atlatl, or spear thrower weights), celts, adzes, and the side-notched and broad-bladed projectile point and scraper forms have earlier and more numerous and elaborated counterparts in the southeastern United States and Lower Mississippi Valley. While the Laurentian articles were overwhelmingly locally produced, they were developed from prototypes in these other regions with their longer and far richer histories of Archaic cultures.

Known skeletons of the people responsible for the Laurentian culture differ markedly from those associated with Lamoka. Indications of disparate origins for the two cultures are accordingly reinforced by biological clues from the people themselves. While they were about the same stature as the Lamokans, Laurentian burials indicate a comparatively stocky, heavily built people. Their faces show prominent cheek bones and their skulls are pronouncedly brachycephalic, or round-headed—in sharp opposition to the long-headed Lamoka folk. Laurentian burials, like the Lamoka, have only been found isolated or in groups in graves dug into or through village and camp middens. Grave offerings are usually sparse to totally absent, and the favored mode of burial was the fully extended body resting on its back. Flexed, bundle, and cremation burials are also known, however. Treating the body with red paint or powder was common but by no means universal.

It was previously remarked that Laurentian culture exhibits regional, as well as temporal, variations. Three widely recognized regional expressions, or "phases," are the Vergennes in northeastern New York and adjacent parts of Vermont and Quebec, the Vosburg in eastern and south-

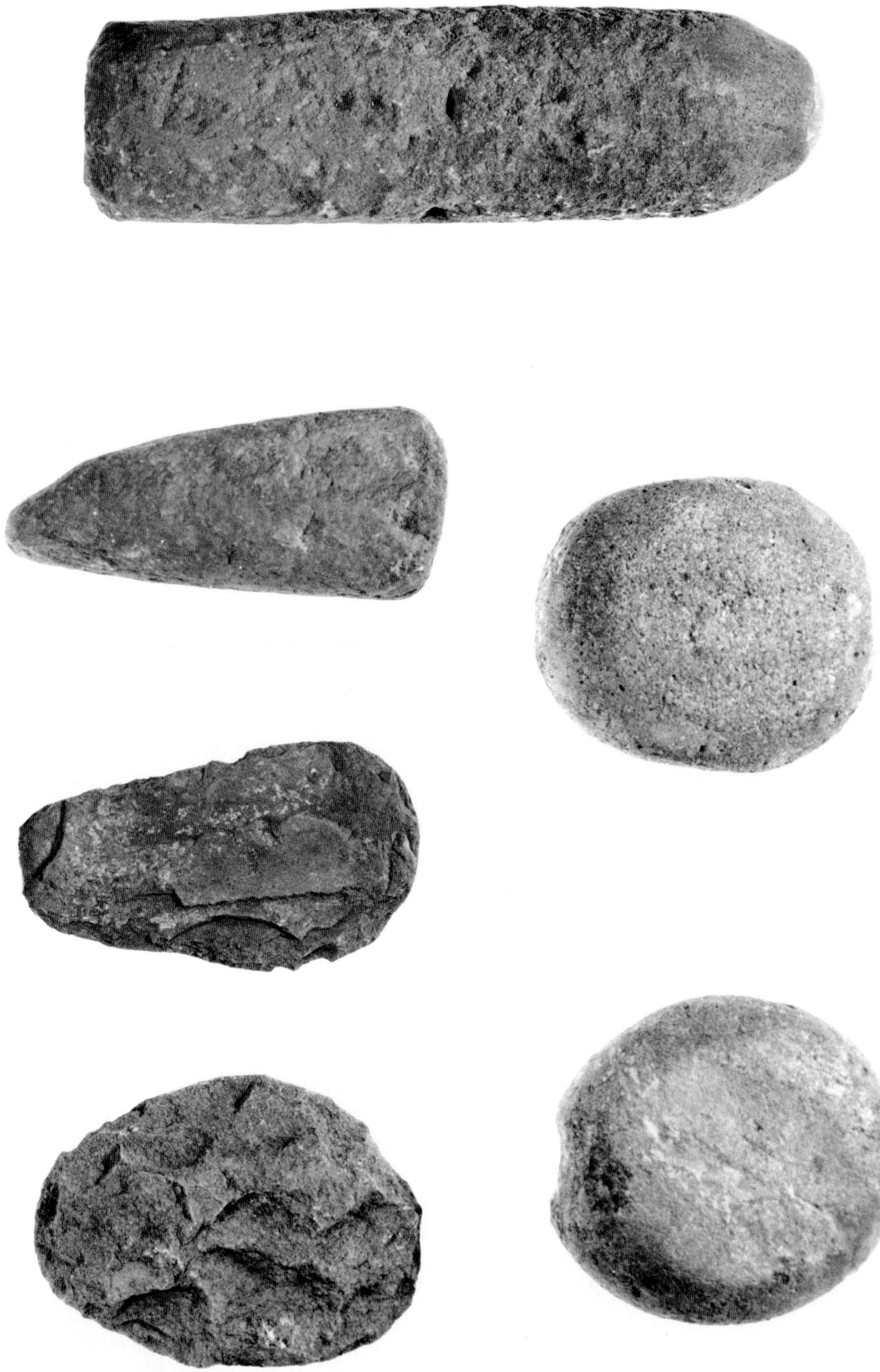

PLATE 5.8. Brewerton Laurentian projectile points, scrapers, knives and drills (top two rows); bone flaking tool? (upper right); biface blades and choppers (third and fourth rows); and rough stone implements (bottom) from New York. (Shown half actual size.) (Courtesy William A. Ritchie and Robert E. Funk, New York State Museum and Science Service, Albany.)

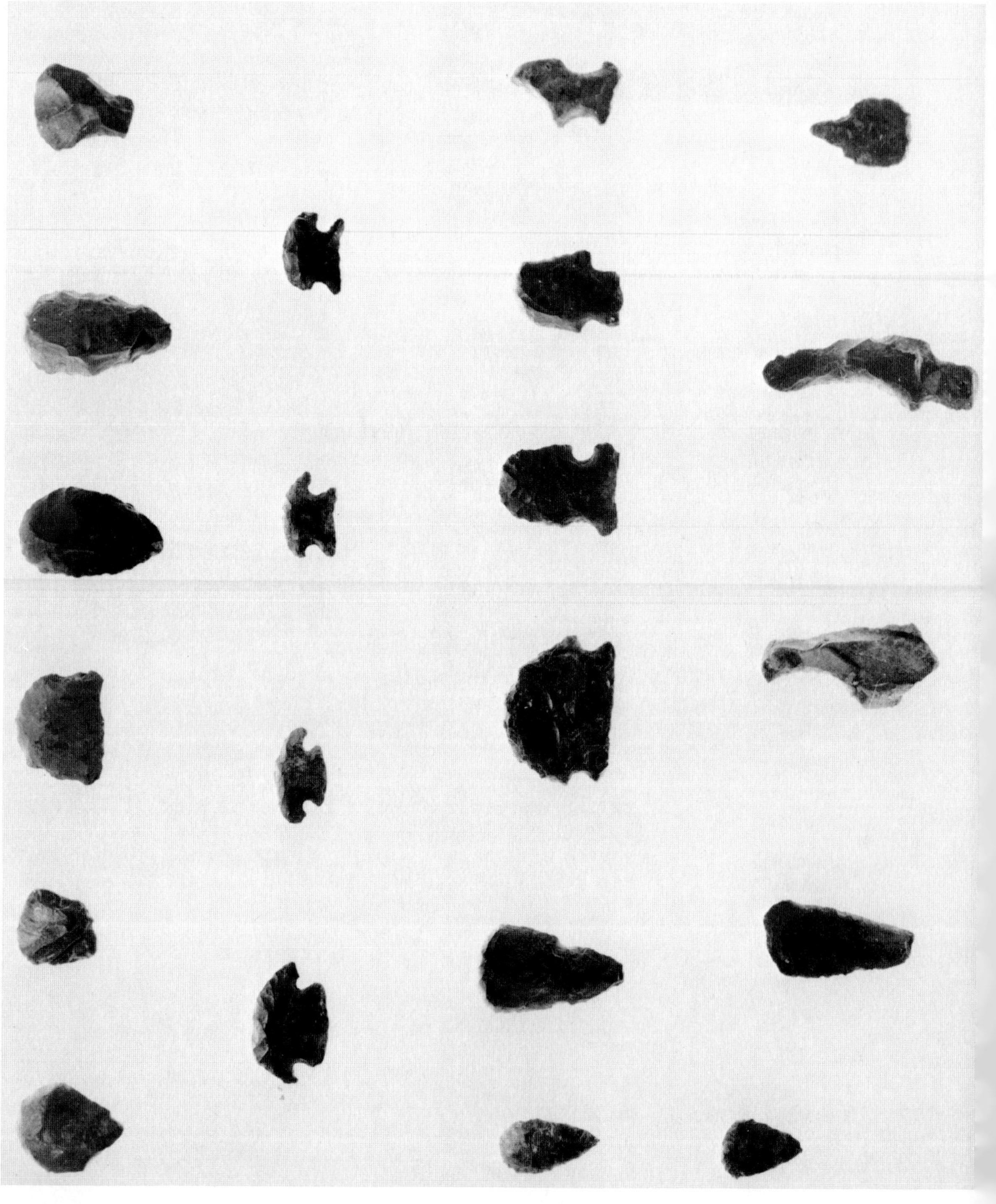

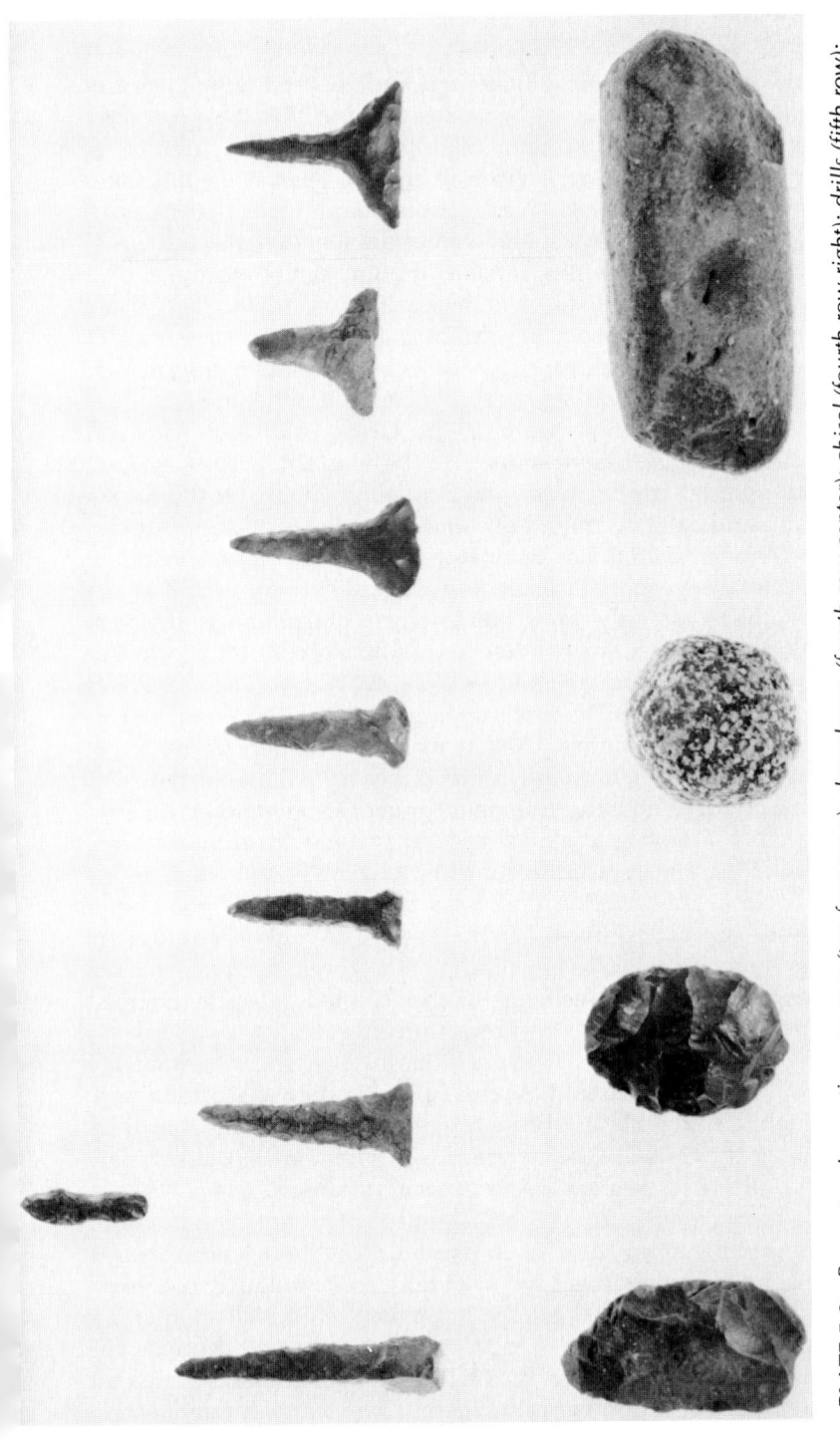

PLATE 5.9. Brewerton Laurentian scrapers (top four rows); drawshaves (fourth row center); chisel (fourth row right); and bifaces and rough stone tools (bottom row) from New York. (Shown half actual size.) (Courtesy William A. Ritchie and Robert E. Funk, New York State Museum and Science Service, Albany.)

ern New York, and the Brewerton in central and western New York and parts of southern Ontario. Radiocarbon dates suggest that the Vergennes variant of Laurentian evolved around 3500–3000 B.C. and persisted for at least five centuries. Vosburg and Brewerton emerged perhaps a little later and lasted until perhaps 1500 B.C. A nascent or formative Laurentian culture, minus gouges, ground slates, and copper implements, has been postulated to precede the Vergennes version, though actual examples of it have eluded detection. So-called Otter Creek points, with lanceolate blade shape and pronounced side notches, were probably a prominent feature of this proto-Laurentian-phase culture, as well as being a salient trait of Vergennes. Such projectile points are very similar to some earlier Archaic types with a wide distribution south of the Great Lakes but with few examples north of them. Ancient models in the western Great Lakes are the specimens associated with Eden and Scottsbluff points at the Renier site, Wisconsin, and at the George Lake and Sheguiandah sites, Ontario.

While Vergennes Laurentian demonstrates all of the elements of "classic" Laurentian, Vosburg lacks copper artifacts entirely as well as any ground slates other than fairly numerous instances of semilunar knives, or ulus. The latter are shared with other Late Archaic cultures in eastern Canada, New England, and the Middle Atlantic states. Their origin is obscure. More characteristic of Vosburg are grooved dart- and spear-shaft sanders and sinewstones. Rather than the Otter Creek type, Vosburg-phase sites yield abundantly of carefully flaked, corner-notched, basally rubbed points. Similarly, the major projectile-point style of Brewerton Laurentian is an ovate to almost triangular one with side notching. Ground slates are rare in Brewerton contexts. Like all known expressions of Laurentian culture, Brewerton possesses bone and antler points and barbed harpoons but no fishhooks. Fishing seems to have been done by harpooning and netting as well as by means of the gorge. Such heavy tools as celts, adzes, gouges, and large ovate to pear-shaped, bifacially chipped "choppers" are well represented on Brewerton sites.

Differences among the regional expressions of Laurentian culture are largely in proportions and quantities, less in kind. They argue for a very successful, highly adaptable culture subsisting mainly in the northern Carolinian and in the Canadian biotic provinces, having more than a single cultural root, and possessing a marked capacity to absorb and assimilate aspects of the technologies of neighboring groups. A potent Southeastern legacy and borrowing from the Upper Great Lakes, the Middle Atlantic seaboard, and, more heavily, the Gulf of St. Lawrence uniquely coalesced in the eastern Lower Great Lakes–Upper St. Lawrence Valley. Increasingly, archaeologists are inclined to view this Late Archaic culture as ancestral to later ones from which the historic Iroquoian peoples are thought to have descended. Certainly, the postulated "formative" Laurentian predated the Lamoka culture, and many manifestations of Laurentian post-

PLATE 5.10. Brewerton Laurentian beaver-incisor tools and celts, adzes, and gouges from sites in New York. The specimen in the upper right and the one to the left of the upper part of the long gouge are of native copper. (Shown half actual size.) (Courtesy William A. Ritchie and Robert E. Funk, New York State Museum and Science Service, Albany.)

date it. An instructive case of the at least partial coevality of Lamoka and, specifically, Brewerton Laurentian cultures is the so-called Frontenac phase.

It was inevitable that within the centuries of Lamoka–Laurentian coexistence people of the two cultures would meet face-to-face. This must have occurred many times and under varying conditions. One such extended occurrence left an unusually detailed record in the thin soils of a .4-ha island in Cayuga Lake, Cayuga County, one of the New York Finger Lakes. Here, sometime between 2500 and 2000 B.C., Lamokans and Brewerton Laurentians met and eventually intermarried. The latter folk seem to have dominated the situation, but their progeny manifested biological as well as cultural legacies from both sides.

The small island is located amid splendid fishing waters. This was most likely what had attracted the people there. As they lived on the island, harvesting the surrounding waters and hunting in the nearby hills, they also came to bury their dead beneath the dirt floors and between family living areas. Extended, flexed, bundle, and cremation burials were placed in the ground, frequently accompanied by ornaments, weapons, and tools. Such grave goods were similar to the debris left behind in the camp refuse. Why one mode of burial was deemed appropriate in one instance and a different one in another seems partly explained by reference to cultural identification: Lamoka burials were flexed, Laurentian, extended on the back. Skull shapes (dolichocranic Lamokan, brachycranic Laurentian) and other skeletal clues of physical type were discovered in conformity with burial fashion. Paralleling these associations, artifacts best ascribable to the Lamoka culture were consistently found with the flexed, long-headed burials, while clearly Brewerton artifacts accompanied the extended inhumations with brachycranic heads. Not all individuals were so neatly classifiable, however. Some graves contained Lamoka and Laurentian traits, as well as others with no clear analogs in either of the parental cultures. And the skeletons in these graves exhibited intermediate, or mesocranic, head forms. These kinds of data on genetic and cultural admixture leave little doubt of intermarriage and cultural fusion at this particular locality.

Judging from range, quantity, and quality of things accoutering the deceased, we find that adult men enjoyed status superior to that of women and children; that this was especially true of brachycranic males is one of the observations supporting the conclusion that the Laurentian was the dominant half in the Frontenac Island liaison. In connection with male status, it should be pointed out that domestic dogs were both common and evidently highly esteemed in the Frontenac culture, both terrier-size and collie-size animals being present. In addition to separate inhumations, they were sometimes buried in common graves with their masters. Overwhelmingly, it was with adult men that dogs were buried. Unusual mortuary features on the island included the burial of a bald eagle and that

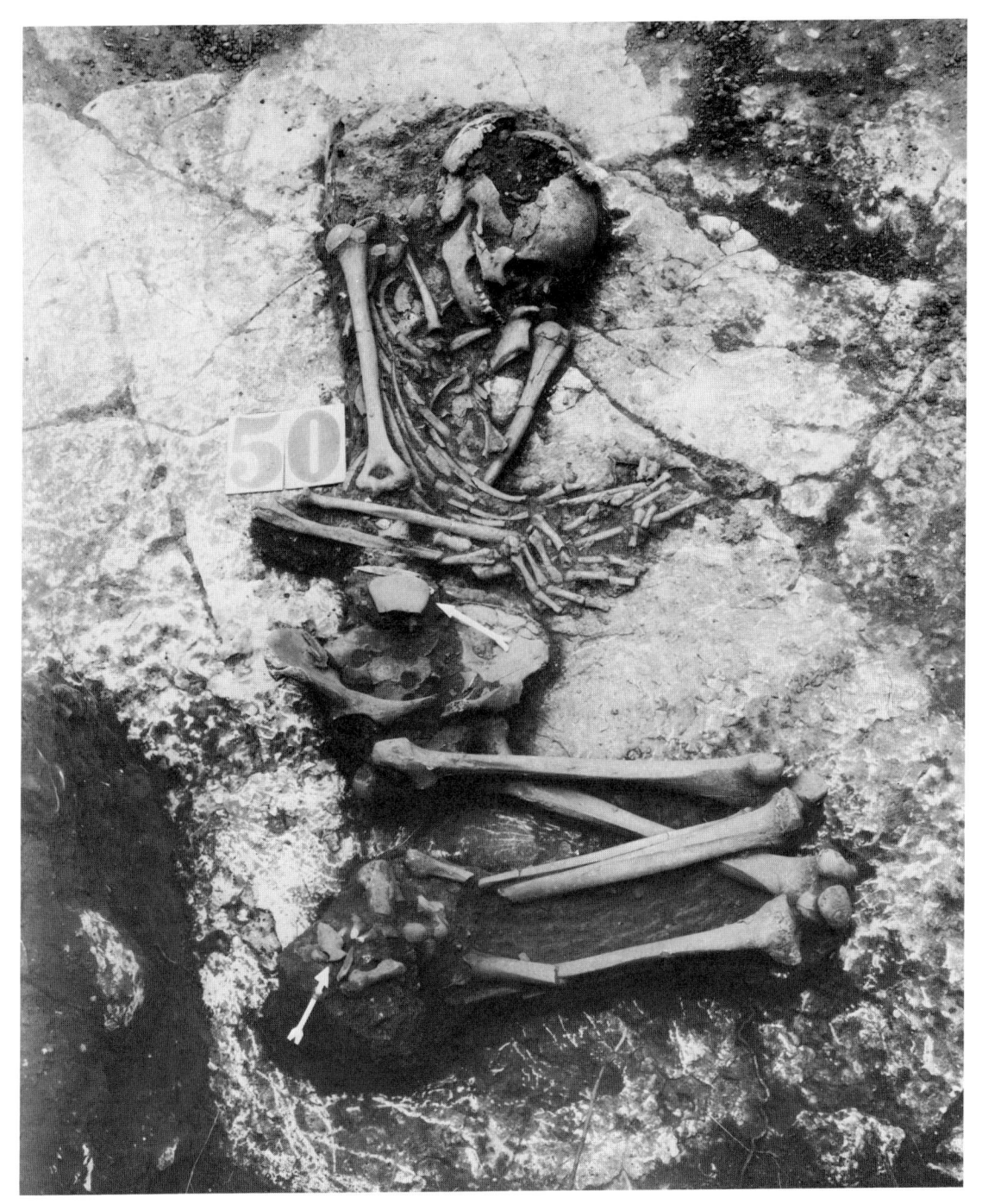

PLATE 5.11 *A Frontenac phase burial (No. 50) at the Frontenca Island site, Cayuga County, New York. (Collection of the Rochester Museum and Science Center. [May not be reprinted without permission of the RMSC.])*

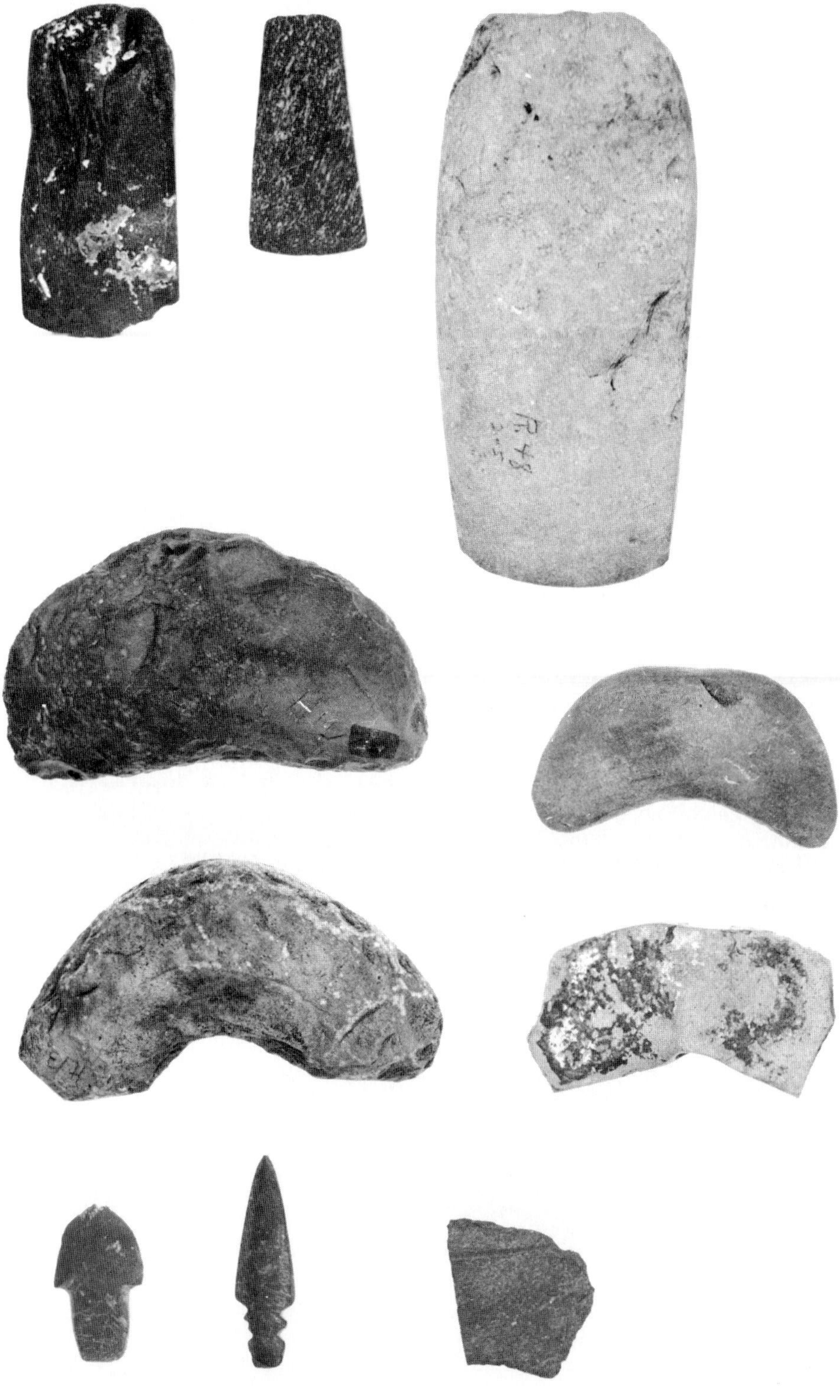

PLATE 5.12. Frontenac phase celts, adzes, and gouges (top); unfinished and finished bannerstones (center left); grooved plummets (center right); ground-slate points and ulu fragment (bottom left); and native copper awls and possible compound-fishhook components (bottom right). From the Frontenac Island site, Cayuga County, New York. (Shown half actual size.) (Collection of the Rochester Museum and Science Center [May not be reprinted without permission of the RMSC.])

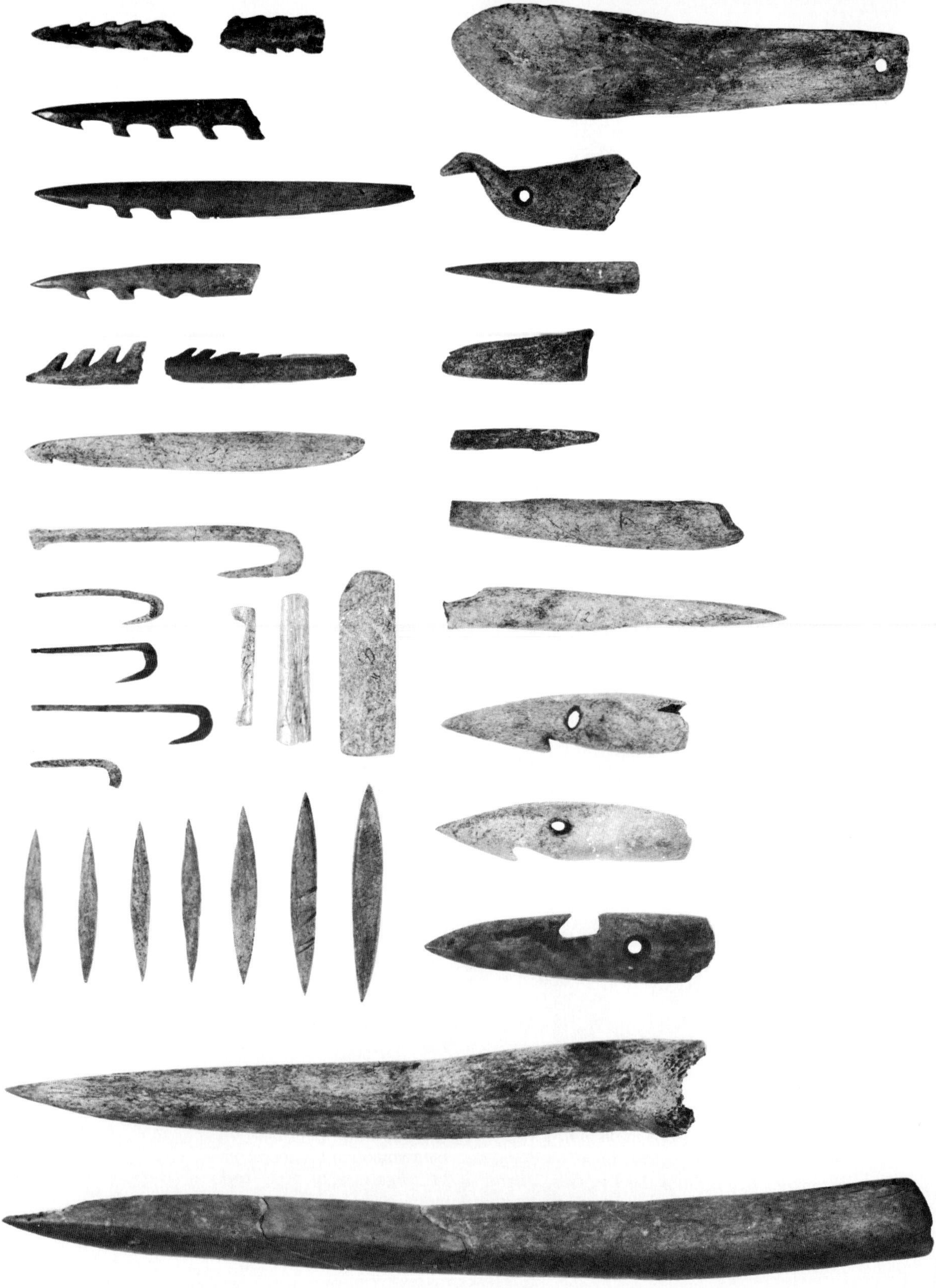

PLATE 5.13. Frontenac bone and antler artifacts from the Frontenac Island site, Cayuga County, New York: daggers, fish gorges, fishhooks, and multi-barbed points (top row); single-barbed harpoons, point tangs, conical projectile points, effigy handle from an antler spoon, and an antler spoon with perforated handle (middle row); and elk-antler cup, whistles or flutes, and tubes (bottom row). (Shown half actual size.) (Collection of the Rochester Museum and Science Center. [May not be reprinted without permission of the RMSC.])

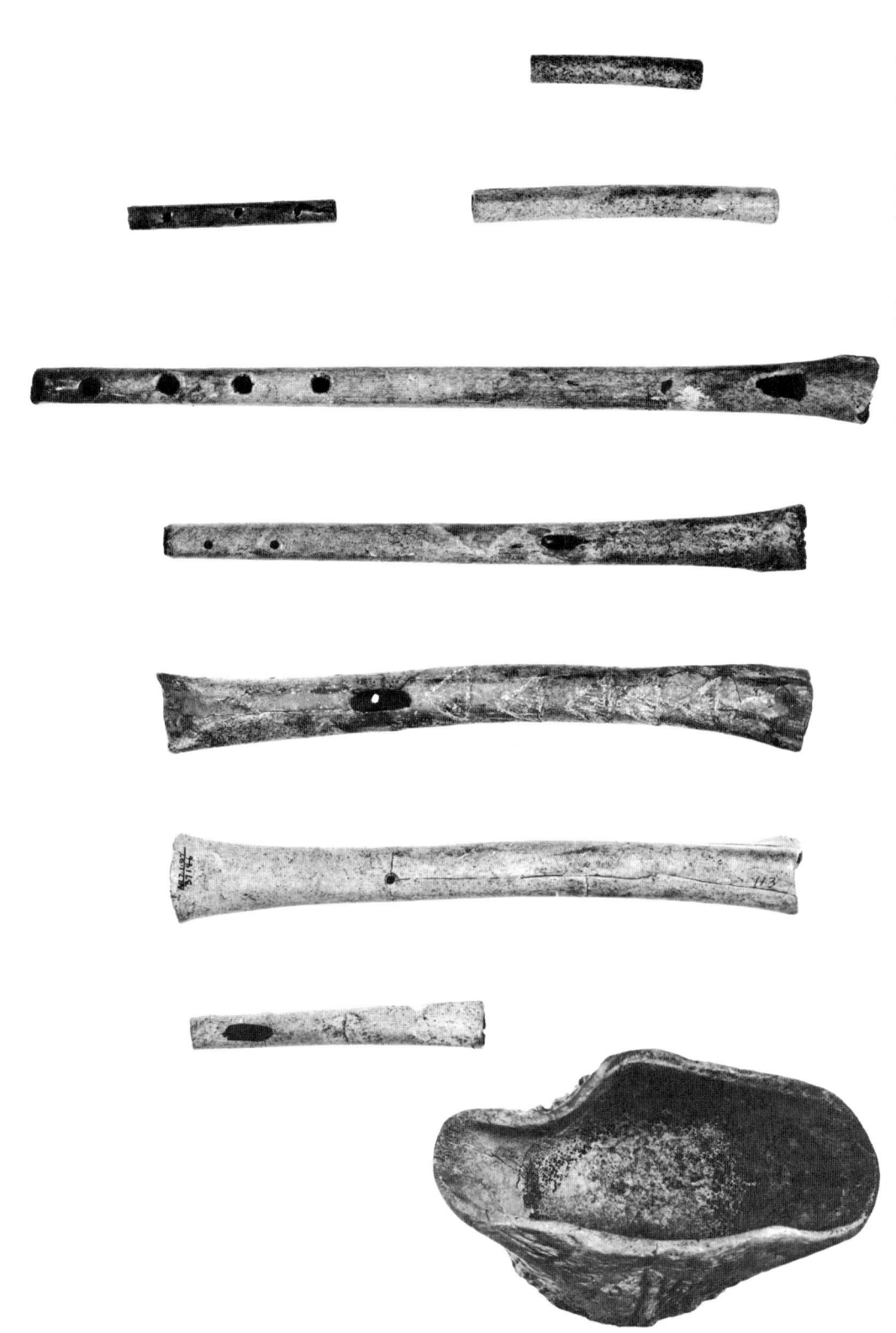

of a small child accompanied by the decapitated head of a young woman (the cervical vertebrae were still in place).

Besides grave offerings, many of the Frontenac Islanders showed that they had gone to their final rest wearing necklaces, bracelets, fancy headdresses or hair decorations, and clothing on which ornaments had once been sewn. Attesting to such decorative functions were ground wolf mandibles embellishing the head; a beautifully carved and incised comb surmounted by facing bird effigies with joined, "kissing" beaks; hawk and bear claws; elk, bear, and wolf teeth suspended on necklaces or sewn sequin-fashion on clothing; and beads and pendants made of Atlantic whelk and other ocean shells. Treatment of the dead with red ocher was common. A shell paint cup containing dried red ocher was even unearthed. Such recoveries are tantalizing clues to a lively symbolic order—a useful reminder that most of the things people think of as vital and meaningful in their lives more often than not leave few material fragments, if any, and then of ambiguous significance, to the frustrated archaeologists seeking to find meaning in them.

Apparently, discrete Lamoka and Brewerton Laurentian societies came into contact at Frontenac Island in the initial years of its occupancy. The former culture is signaled by the tell-tale burials and by such Lamoka hallmarks as the small Lamoka points, beveled adzes, bone fishhooks, and the elongate, pendant-like antler artifacts. The Brewerton presence was evidenced by the equally distinctive graves and living-area refuse containing ground slates, bannerstones, Brewerton Side-Notched points, and barbed bone points and harpoons. Projectile points embedded in bones, skull fractures, and the severed head are evidence of some kind of hostilities during some portion of the contact. Later, more constructive arrangements facilitating accommodation and cultural assimilation brought into being a descendent culture different from both parents but also preserving unmistakable continuities.

Frontenac-phase traits not shared with either ancestor, in addition to the effigy comb and the marine-shell beads and pendants, include antler spoons, turtle-shell bowls, hafted rattles made of turtle shells and with quartz shakers, eyed needles, fire-making kits consisting of iron pyrites and flint strikers, and masses of fire- cracked cobbles used in stone boiling. This latter practice involved heating collected rocks and then dropping them, together with chunks of meat or fish and vegetables, into a water-filled basket, bark bucket, or skin-lined cooking pit. This was an accepted method of cooking among societies lacking pottery or metal containers. Although it unquestionably added grit to the diet and contributed to prematurely heavy wear of the teeth, it is surprising that more evidence of stone boiling has not been found in pre-Frontenac settings. It will also be surprising if some of the other Frontenac attributes do not eventually turn up on other Laurentian, Lamoka, or even less-related sites. Problems of inadequate sampling mask important parts of the archaeological picture.

5. Transformation Achieved

The Old Copper Culture

North American Indians esteemed copper and regarded it as a symbol and as a repository of extraordinary properties. That their prehistoric forebears similarly valued the metal is demonstrated by the repeated presence of copper artifacts far from the sources of the raw material and by the frequency of their recovery from mortuary contexts and caches.

The principal source and major area of copper in prehistoric North America lay in the Lake Superior basin. Here, particularly on the Keweenaw Peninsula and in Isle Royale, Michigan, as well as along the Brule River in northwestern Wisconsin, there are prodigious lodes of virtually pure copper exposed at the surface or so shallowly buried as to be readily detectable and extractable with simple mining implements of wood and stone. Other ore deposits occur on the northern shore of Lake Superior. In overriding such localities, the glaciers pried loose and transported far to the south large and small chunks of the shiny golden, green-weathering material. This "float" copper from the glacial drift was another regionally important source which, probably first tapped because conveniently sized pieces lay directly on the surface, would inevitably have led to the discovery of the far richer bedrock lodes. Due to their own long metallurgical tradition and the fact that metal artifacts of any kind were rare to absent among the tribes encountered by the Europeans, the finding of copper tools when the forests were cleared and the ground plowed aroused great and lasting interest. The heavy weathering seen on many of the copper artifacts suggested considerable antiquity. This, and their exclusion from the lists of things known to have been components of stone-age Indian culture, were even cited as part of the evidence of a lost people (perhaps ancient Norsemen or Egyptians or even remnants of the "Ten Lost Tribes of Israel") who, some suggested, had inhabited America before the Indians. It has since turned out that the would-be historians overestimated the difficulties of primitive metallurgy and underestimated the Indians.

With its heaviest apparent concentration in eastern Wisconsin, but with increasingly spotty representation to and even beyond the confines of the Great Lakes drainage, the "Old Copper culture" was known until quite recent times from accidental surface finds only. Sometimes, however, whole deposits of copper artifacts were unearthed in gravel quarrying or in canal or road building. These "caches" were often graves in which bones were so disintegrated as to have vanished utterly or at least to such an extent that only a trained observer would have noticed their traces. Not uncommonly, only teeth caps will be all that survives of the human skeleton in acidic or poorly drained soils. Certainly many a copper implement has vainly signaled the presence of an otherwise almost vanished grave to persons untrained or insensitive to the signal. Whole cemeteries have been plowed or bulldozed away without any one remarking until too late anything other than the periodic finding of a conspicuous copper tool.

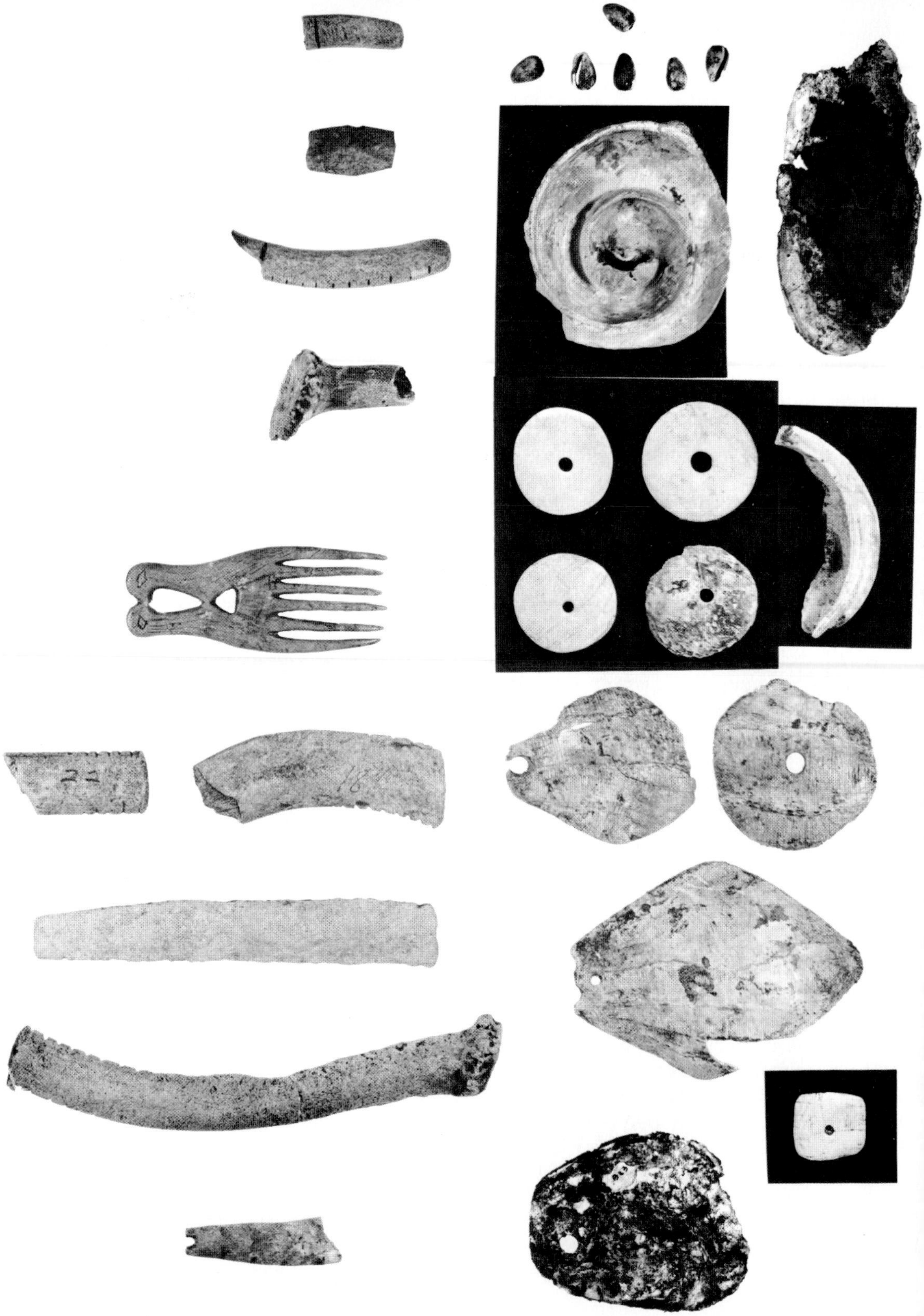

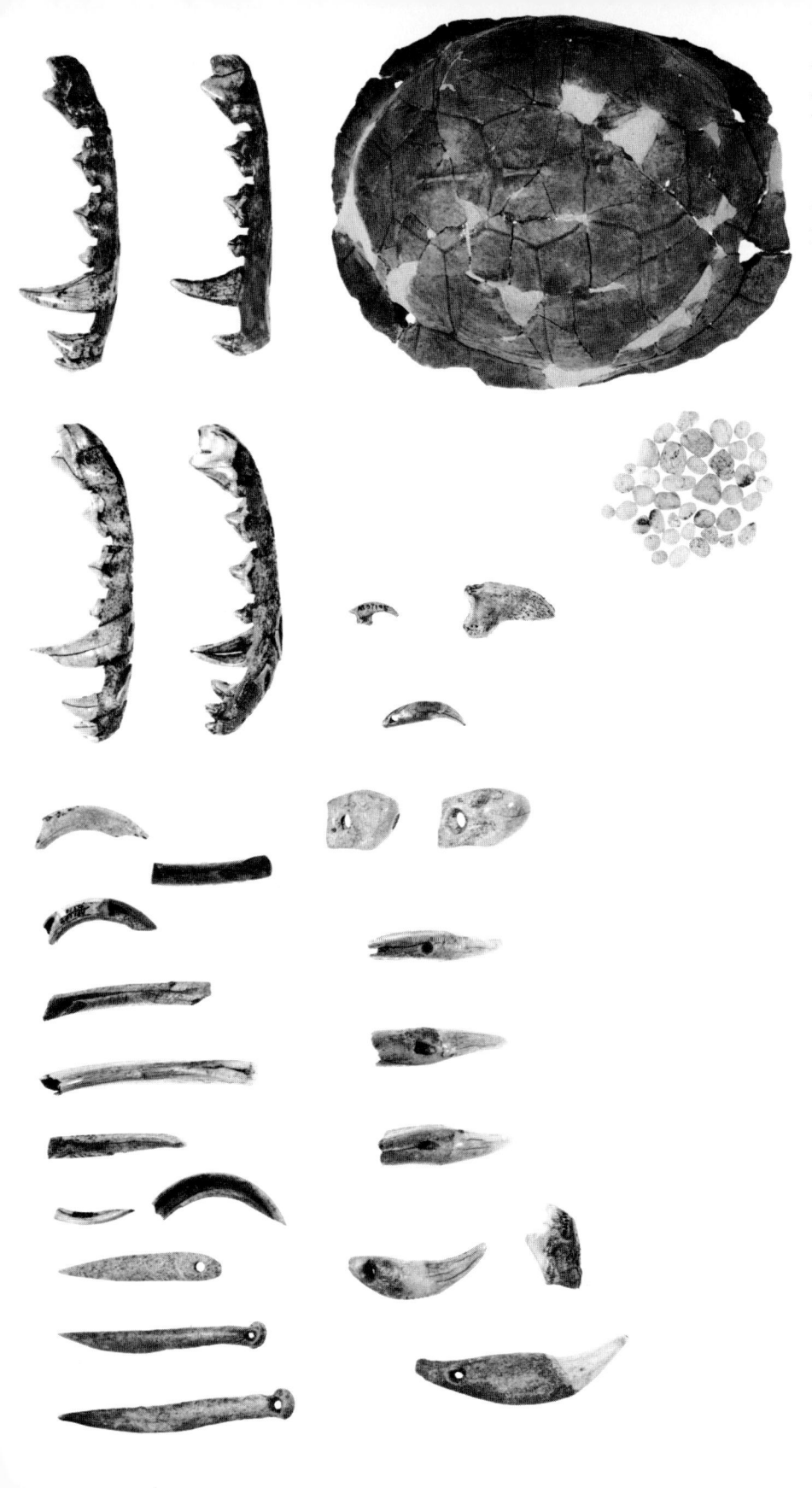

PLATE 5.14. Frontenac bone, antler, and shell artifacts from the Frontenac Island site, Cayuga County, New York: perforated pins possibly for use with feathers in a headdress, beaver-incisor chisels and knives, cut and ground wolf jaws (top row); tooth pendants, split deer tine objects of unknown use, comb, turtle shell rattle with quartz pebble shakers, cut and nocked antler tines (middle rows); marine shell pendants (bottom left and center); conch shell receptacle, fresh water mussel shell filled with dried red paint, and Marginella shell heads (bottom right). (Shown half actual size.) (Collection of the Rochester Museum and Science Center. [May not be reprinted without permission of the RMSC.])

Plate 5.15. Old Copper culture adze (left), gouge, and socketed spearpoints from various sites in eastern Wisconsin. Specimen at lower right is turned over to show ridged back of blade and socketed tang. (Shown two-thirds actual size.) (Collections of Department of Anthropology, Lawrence University, Appleton, Wisconsin.)

Incredible numbers of copper artifacts—tens of thousands in eastern Wisconsin alone—attest to a use of the metal that is at variance with historical and ethnographic descriptions of Indian life. Equally imposing is the range of "Old Copper " tools. The most common copper items are projectile points, semilunar objects referred to as "crescents," awls, tanged knives, and axe or hatchet blades. The points are variable in style and exhibit leaf-shaped, triangular, and lanceolate blade shapes, with many of the finer examples having precisely defined median ridges and beveled ridges and edge facets. They sometimes show enigmatic punch marks on one face. Varieties include simple leaf-shaped points with or without a parallel-sided, tapered, or basally expanded tang or stem; points with notched round or pointed tangs; examples with multiple-notched or serrated tangs, others having basally flared, bifurcated tangs; short, broad-bladed "ace of spades" points; leaf-shaped specimens provided with long, slender, pointed "rat tail" tangs; socketed tanged points with or without perforations and rivets for securing the point to its haft; conical points of rolled sheet copper socketed at one end; and a class of socketed points intermediate between the simple conical variety and the complex socketed forms with their distinct flat blades and their instepped, haft-gripping tangs.

Crescents comprise at least two functional classes of artifacts. On one hand are more-or-less semilunar knives, or ulus, that are doubtless related to the ground-slate versions far to the east but are not infrequently equipped with tangs opposite the cutting edge for insertion in a handle. On the other hand are copper crescents that are simply too thin and fragile to have functioned as tools and which, to judge by sometime placement in graves, probably were intended as ornaments or as talismans. Of course, there are also crescents that are betwixt and between these clearer alternatives.

Awls are the most numerous copper tool. They vary from short to long, thin to massive, and are single- or bi-pointed—all of which hints at a range of tasks. Some copper awls have one spatulate or "screw driver" end; certain of the larger specimens may actually be leister prongs. Tanged knives are single shouldered with either straight or curved blade. Two types of axe or hatchet blades are rectangular or flat-sectioned celts and socketed "spuds." The latter are single-piece axe blades incorporating a large open socket for mounting on a wooden or elk-antler handle; they have flat or keeled blades in back of the bit. Some of them must have been hafted and employed as adzes rather than axes.

Other typical copper artifacts are fishhooks, fish gorges, wedges (like broad-bladed celts but with polls misshapen and flattened by hammering), "punches" (these resemble old-fashioned wrought-iron nails), rivets, pikes (for digging and levering?), gaffs (some of which were actually brought up from the bottom of Lake Superior in commercial fishermen's nets), tanged spatulate objects of unknown use, and a restricted array of ornamental items: C-shaped bracelets, rectangular headdress components, spiraled sheet copper (hair pipes?), and tubular and barrel-shaped beads. Observation and experimentation prove conclusively that all were fabricated without smelting or casting. The very pure and thus malleable copper was cold hammered or, at most, heated in a fire and hammered into the desired shape. Such primitive metallurgy, in which the material is treated as a special and unusual kind of stone, was independently developed in a number of places around the globe. The Great Lakes was one such place.

Some of the copper implements have striking parallels in ground slate in the Laurentian and, especially, Maritime Archaic cultures. These extend not only to semilunar knives, as already remarked, but to celts and adzes and gouges, and even to some of the spear or dart points. The peculiar copper points with multiple-notched tangs, usually subtended to ovoid blades, are precisely duplicated in ground slate in New York, Ontario, Quebec, New England, and the Maritime provinces. Certain bone and antler weapons associated with ground slates, such as straight barbed and toggle-head harpoons, are also, though infrequently, rendered in copper in the Upper Great Lakes. It is difficult to evade an hypothesis of some kind of historical connection among the broad regions displaying these parallels, especially as the cultures represented all bespeak societies of hunters, gatherers, and fishermen, regional subsistence specializations notwithstanding. Moreover, just as the regions are connected by waterways known to have fostered intercourse among later peoples, temporal linkages are assured by overlapping chronologies.

The foregoing should not be taken as an assertion of a discrete "Old Copper culture" in interaction with a "Ground Slate culture." Even as we know that Vosburg is different from Vergennes but that both are Laurentian manifestations and that the Brewerton and, in a critical sense, the Frontenac cultures represent still other versions of the Laurentian culture, we should view "Old Copper" as subsuming a number of societies, each having its own somewhat different culture. These would have shared in varying degree a common metallurgical technology and a set of style concepts regarding those many potential attributes not directly dictated either by the nature of the material or by the specific tasks the tools were meant to perform. The ground slates are analogous in this regard to the copper artifacts. Neither a specific type of ground-slate tool—say, the semilunar knife—nor ground-slate tools collectively betoken a discrete cultural entity in the way that the complex of Lamoka points, beveled adzes, and so on at the Lamoka Lake site signals a Lamoka culture. Particular kinds of ground-slate implements have their own distributions within the more encompassing one of ground slates generally. Ground-slate semilunar knives, for instance, have been found in quite variable Archaic contexts, seemingly independent of their associations, from the Middle Atlantic states to Labrador. This is further complicated by the need to see some of these distributions concurrently as temporal *and* spatial.

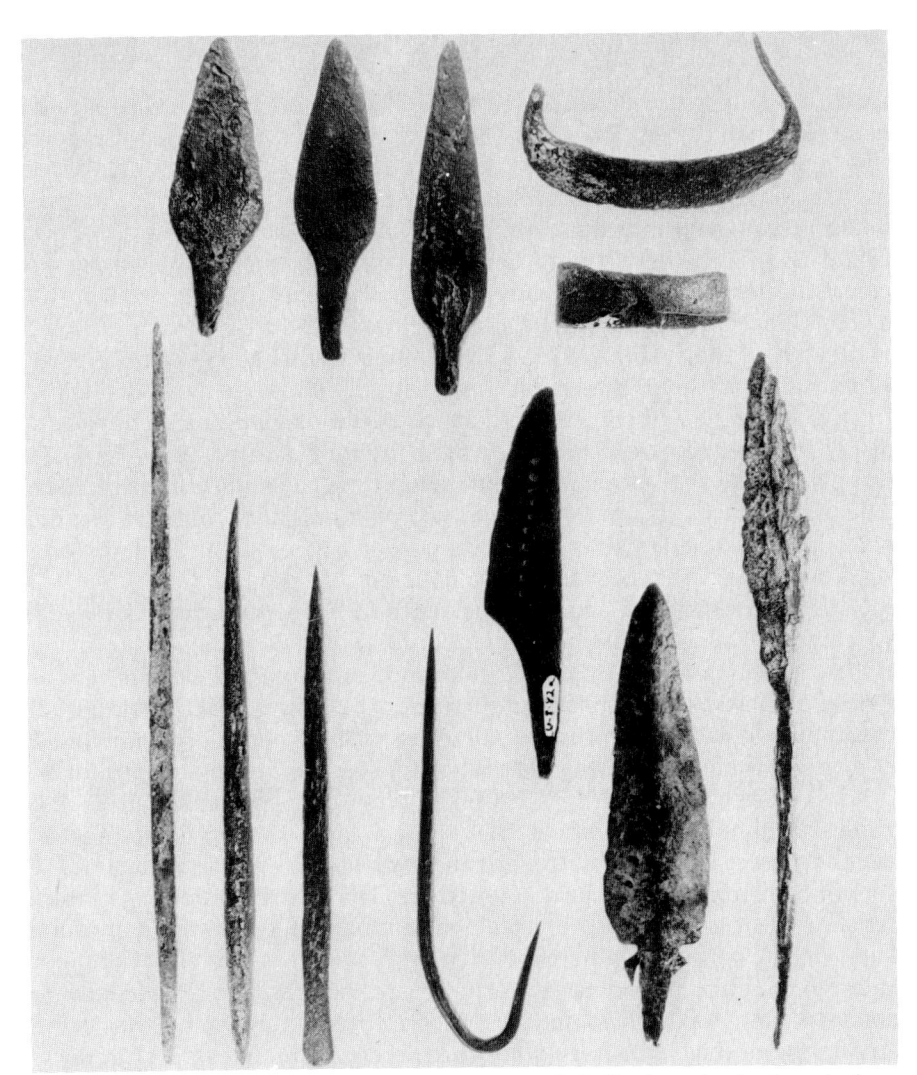

PLATE 5.16. Copper tanged points, ulu or crescentic knife, bracelet (top); awls, large fishhook or gaff, asymmetrical tanged knife exhibiting punch marks of unknown significance, notched tanged point, and "rat-tailed" tanged point. (Shown half actual size.) From various sites in eastern Wisconsin. (Collections of Department of Anthropology, Lawrence University, Appleton, Wisconsin.)

As previously noted, some copper artifacts are a part of the general Laurentian tool kit. They have been cited for some southern components of the Shield Archaic. Archaeologists have also found copper products in divergent styles and combinations in quite different cultural situations within the same regions. In north central Wisconsin the Squirrel River phase, mentioned in Chapter 4, an apparent branch or close relative of the

Shield Archaic and not a culture to which the appelation Old Copper would likely be bestowed, nonetheless reveals the local manufacture of awls, simple conical and socketed projectile points, and a few other varieties of small copper tools. Similar equipment was also present in much later times during parts of the Middle and Late Woodland periods. Native copper fishhooks, awls, bangles or tinklers, and some other forms persisted in use even into the early part of the Historic period, as on Rock Island in the northern Lake Michigan basin. No one knows when the oldest copper artifacts were made, but it is clear enough that the industry had a long and complicated career. Many cultures enjoying ready availability of the metal, and then many others farther afield, came to place a high value on things made of it. A trade gradually developed outside the Upper Great Lakes. By this means Lake Superior copper came to be widely dispersed over the eastern part of the continent, and exotic materials—notably marine shell—came into the region from the middle and southern Atlantic coasts and from the Gulf of Mexico. As distance from the sources of copper lengthened, increasing proportions of ornamental items and small tools seem to reflect rising evaluations.

Yet, notwithstanding abundant evidence of copper utilization by many different cultures far beyond the Upper Great Lakes representing many archaeological periods embracing thousands of years, and despite refutation of earlier speculations about an ancient "culture" responsible for all the copper objects in the upper lakes as well as many of those found elsewhere, there are archeologists who still see merit in the concept of an "Old Copper culture." This is because, when copper beads, awls, celts, gorges, fishhooks, and other artifact types demonstrating wide careers in time and space are removed from consideration, there remains a distinctive core of copper artifacts to be accounted for. This has the following characteristics: (a) it is not found in sites dating much later than the end of the Late Archaic period; (b) where found in undisturbed association with other cultural remains, it is datable by those associations and/or radiocarbon assay to the Late Archaic period; (c) core artifacts are found associated among themselves whether or not the more ubiquitous copper products are also present; and (d) core artifacts are most varied and numerous in a relatively restricted area of the Upper Great Lakes itself. Indeed, even allowing for spectacular caches and sometimes heavy local densities of copper implements, as in part of the Ottawa Valley in Ontario and Quebec and inland from Duluth in Minnesota, there is no doubt that eastern Wisconsin shows by far the greatest concentration. The core copper artifacts include a very distinctive variety of projectile points such as tanged socketed, multiple-notched stemmed, leaf-shaped with "rat tail" tang, and, possibly, "ace of spades" points; tanged socketed asymmetrical knives; the unique socketed axe or adze blades called "spuds"; and the crescents—particularly those that seem to have been designed as semilunar hafted knives.

Plate 5.17. *Old Copper serrated-tanged and split or notched-tanged spearpoints from northeastern Wisconsin. (Shown half actual size.) (Collections of the Neville Public Museum, Green Bay, Wisconsin.)*

Three sites are usually nominated as type stations of the Old Copper culture although, of course, other localities are also known, even though the bulk, by far, of museum and private collections are surface finds. These sites are all in Wisconsin: Osceola in Grant County, Oconto in Oconto County, and Reigh in Winnebago County. The first is in the Mississippi drainage, the latter two in the north eastern part of the state on waterways flowing to Green Bay. While mixed blessings are better than none at all, it is to be stressed that each of these very important sites had been partly destroyed by natural or human erosion and had been dug into by treasure

PLATE 5.18. *Old Copper "rat-tailed" tanged points from northeastern Wisconsin and the upper Michigan peninsula (second from left). (Shown half actual size.) (Collections of the Neville Public Museum, Green Bay, Wisconsin.)*

hunters before archaeologists or serious laymen learned of their existence. These are disturbed sites, and their records are partial. Frequencies or even absences of given traits must be assessed with proper weight accorded that fact. Furthermore, all three stations are cemeteries even though a hint of a one-time village was also detected at Oconto. What were the villages like of people who lay in the cemeteries?

The first to be discovered was the Osceola site. A large bone deposit estimated to have included originally the remains of about 500 people was found weathering out of a stream bank. Excavation showed that two burial modes were present in this phenomenal feature, though they were thoroughly intermixed: bundle and cremation. With and without possible burial association were copper awls, asymmetrical tanged knives, conical points, tanged socketed points, spuds, beads, and a "clasp," a bracelet, and a possible finger ring. Chipped-stone tools present in the unusual mortuary included large, well-made spear or dart points with lanceolate blade form and prominent side notches recalling the Otter Creek points in Vergennes Laurentian. This was the only flint point type present. Also recovered were beveled end-scrapers made from similar broken projectile points and long drills with expanded bases. Hammerstones, grinding stones, galena cubes, clay wads, and lumps of red ocher were scattered throughout the interlocking and superimposed burials. Not excavated by archaeologists but recovered by other people who visited the site were a prismoidal and a winged bannerstone. A radiocarbon date of about 1500 B.C. was obtained. Fragments of aboriginal pottery believed to date to a much later period were found over the burial layer as well as mixed in among the bones. This evidence of disturbance necessarily introduces uncertainty about the reliability of otherwise possible associations among the Osceola copper and stone artifacts. There were at least two cultural horizons represented at the site and, unfortunately, there was little in the way of stratigraphic or areal separation. Although reasonable in the light of archaeological information elsewhere, the apparent association of copper tools, large side-notched chipped-flint points, bannerstones, and other stone artifacts was not empirically established at the Osceola site.

Even though the Oconto site, the next putative Old Copper site to be recognized, had also been destructively intruded upon, this time by sand and gravel quarrying before prehistorians arrived to explore the surviving portions, it afforded the recovery of discrete burials with sometimes unambiguous associations among different classes of artifacts.

Although the remains of 45 individuals were excavated by archaeologists, it is believed that the undisturbed cemetery had originally entombed upward of 200. Besides bundle and cremation burials as at Osceola, the Oconto cemetery yielded flexed and extended burials, including the rather unusual nuance of face-down inhumation. These graves were furnished with some of the same types of copper artifacts found at the former locality but with curious discrepancies in missing and added items. Thus Oconto lacked the Osceola asymmetrical tanged knives, conical points, and the well-represented spuds. And even though both sites yielded socketed tanged projectile points, those from Oconto exhibit circular or rolled sockets and flat blades while the Osceola specimens have sockets with angular profiles and are equipped with ridged blades. An important copper tool type at the Oconto site missing at Osceola is the crescent. Also confined to Oconto were such other copper forms as a long stemmed point with a notched and flared base, a probable "rat tail" tanged point, fishhook, gorge, and a possible twisted or spiraled strip hairpipe.

A startling contrast between the two Old Copper sites proved to be the chipped-flint projectile points. Despite only a few being retrieved at the Oconto site, two were discovered in unassailable contexts in graves and thus in definite association with the copper material at that site. Other examples came to light in the soil around the graves. These are exactly like those unearthed in primary grave association. As at Osceola, here is another Old Copper site where all the flint points are remakably homogeneous. But the type connected with one site is not that found at the other. The Oconto points are all relatively small triangular to ovate-bladed specimens showing very small and shallow notches on the lateral edges *immediately* above the base. Although not the same, they are reminiscent of Brewerton Side-Notched points as previously described for the Brewerton phase of Laurentian. The single scraper from Oconto was not made from a broken point as at Osceola, but is a simple triangular end-scraper without special modification for hafting, though hafted it doubtless once was.

Although no bone implements were present in the Mississippi Valley site, Oconto surrendered an awl, a fine swan-bone whistle with scribed decoration, and three antler tines almost certainly prepared for use. Of uncommon interest because of their intimations of involvement in an extended trade network with the world beyond the Great Lakes were a freshwater clam shell thought to have come from the Mississippi River and a whelk shell from somewhere on the Carolina to Florida Atlantic coast. One burial also exhibited a shell-bead bracelet, though this was fashioned of perforated local pond-snail tests.

The Oconto site has been a controversial one because of anomalous results of attempts at dating it. This began with the publication to two radiocarbon dates, unfortunately mutually irreconcilable by a discrepancy of almost 2000 years, which were measured and calculated when that radiometric method was still very much in its infancy. Although originally accepted by some authorities, the first dates from the site (one of about 3650 B.C., the other 5560 B.C.) were eventually rejected when they could be shown to be incompatible with the radiocarbon chronology being developed with increasing precision at other sites affording better stratigraphic control of organic samples in cultural associations. They also appeared to be disjunctive with the calibration of post-glacial water planes in the Lake Michigan basin. Regardless of radiocarbon dates, the geological history of the lake indicated that the Oconto site, because of its elevation, could not have been established until after the lake had withdrawn from its Nipissing stage level of 184 m above modern mean sea level—unless it could be argued that the cemetery had indeed been inundated by that event. Current estimates for the attainment of the Nipissing level suggest a time around 2000 B.C., or a few centuries earlier. Because of its strongly sculptured beach features, this stage was relatively long lasting. It certainly endured, though perhaps in a gradually falling state, until a number of centuries after 2000 B.C. There is no evidence to suggest that the archaeological site had ever been subjected to inundation, centuries long or any other. Subsequent studies of the accumulation in bone of radioactive salts, using as controls two components from the Andrews site in Michigan—one component known to have been submerged beneath Nipissing level waters, the other known to postdate the lake—seemed to support the abandoning of the early dates. More recently a third radiocarbon assay has been run on material from the Oconto site, this time with results of around 2590 B.C., but with the large margin of error of plus-or-minus four centuries. This brings the radiocarbon age of the site much closer to, but still a little in excess of, the maximum possible age suggested by lake-level studies. Lending credence to the new assay are two other radiocarbon dates associated with some comparable copper implements from sites in the Ottawa River near Pembroke, Ontario, of around 2750 B.C. and 3250 B.C. These three dates, however, are older than that from the Osceola site by 1100–1750 years. Given the apparent cultural differences already observed between Osceola and Oconto, this is not insupportable. But then there is the Reigh site.

Dated by carbon-14 to about 1700 B.C., about the same age as Osceola, the Reigh site provided by far the largest sample of copper artifacts among the three localities. Yet, strangely, awls, easily the single most numerous class of copper implement at the two sites already discussed, were conspicuous by their extreme rarity at Reigh. On the other hand, copper celts were present only at the latter site. In spite of these differences and the seeming disparity in age of the Oconto and Reigh sites, the very distincitve flint projectile points from the last two places are virtually identical. In this regard Osceola stands apart. Similarly, semilunar knives or other crescents were present at Oconto and Reigh but not at Osceola. Conforming to this parallelism in the important matter of flint projectile-point styles and a seeming predilection for copper crescents, the full range of interment modes represented at Oconto was equally expressed among the 43 individuals salvaged by archaeologists and knowledgeable laymen at the Reigh cemetery.

Spuds, a salient feature at Osceola and entirely absent at Oconto, are represented at Reigh by two examples. Unique to the Reigh site are copper "ace of spades" points; a copper-bead necklace with "napkin" trailer; elongate headdress ornaments of strip copper; elk-antler axes (on which spuds were almost certainly hafted); a superb specimen of the "sandal sole" gorget, a marine-shell artifact long taken as the signature of the so-called Glacial Kame culture (marine-shell beads were likewise recovered); an incised deer mandible; and a dog burial.

This tedious listing and comparison of cultural traits among the three principal Old Copper sites is intended to show not only how much is known about Old Copper but, equally importantly, how much is not known. (Another, or fourth, "Old Copper" site listed by some authorities, the Riverside Cemetery site in the Upper Michigan Peninsula, is better classified under another cultural label and is discussed in the next chapter). What should be abundantly clear is how biased by accidents of discovery, preservation, and disturbance these archeological recoveries are. The sites were all subjected to partial destruction before they were investigated by archaeologists. The diagnostic artifact samples were especially limited at the first two sites, though they remain of major significance. Furthermore, all three sites are burial grounds and thus provide a very limited perspective on the people responsible for them. Until much more is known from other sites the possibility must remain high that some of the contrasts among the excavated stations are simply products of partial recovery. The absence of spuds at Oconto or that of crescents at Osceola, or of celts at both, may be explicable in such terms. On the other hand, the similarities between Oconto and Reigh in flint projectile points, and their contrast in this regard to the Osceola site, are expressed in numbers sufficient to make them much more convincing. However, any confidence that here at least is a real, and not simply an apparent, difference among the Old Copper sites has to be limited by the dual-component nature of the Osceola site and the element of uncertainty regarding possible associations of copper and chipped-flint artifacts at that place.

The term Old Copper culture, if it is to be employed at all, should be understood to apply to an incompletely glimpsed Late Archaic mortuary complex. By extension, it may also be used with reference to the as yet poorly perceived wider culture, such as would be recovered at village, camp, and quarry sites of the people whose bones have been found in the cemeteries. Likely as it is that more than one tribal society participated in the species of copper culture envisioned here, it is certain that the metal itself first came into use before the evolution of culture represented at Osceola, Oconto, and Reigh. While the most ancient copper implements predate the rise of the Great Lakes to the Nipissing level by an as yet undetermined number of centuries, the Old Copper culture per se is probably of immediately pre-Nipissing, Nipissing, and post-Nipissing age; a range of between 3000 and 1000 B.C. seems most reasonable. Long after the demise of this culture and the termination of the Late Archaic period, copper tools continued to be made and traded and used in the Great Lakes, though in diminished numbers, until the coming of Europeans. This later usage did not include any of the "core" types, of course, and it involved a gradual shift from an emphasis on utilitarian items to beads and bracelets and other more ornamental goods even though awls and celts and fishhooks continued to enjoy their old popularity.

PLATE 5.19. *Old Copper socketed ax or adze blades ("spuds") from northeastern Wisconsin and the upper Michigan peninsula (bottom center). (Shown half actual size.) (Collections of the Neville Public Museum, Green Bay, Wisconsin.)*

And Morrison's Island-6

Two sites in the Ottawa Valley between Ontario and Quebec have each produced more copper tools than the three excavated Wisconsin Old Copper sites combined. Both sites have been classed as Laurentian components, though they do not belong to the same "phase" of that culture. These are the Morrison's Island-6 site, radiocarbon dated to around 2750 B.C., and the nearby Allumette Island-1 site, dated to approximately 3250 B.C., or half a millennium earlier still. Though in Pontiac County, Quebec, the sites are not far from Pembroke, Ontario. They are important because they dramatically reaffirm the parallels archaeologists have long noted be-

PLATE 5.20 *Old Copper crescentic knives from the upper Michigan peninsula and northeastern Wisconsin (middle left and lower right). (Shown half actual size.) (Collections of the Neville Public Museum, Green Bay, Wisconsin.)*

tween the Laurentian and Old Copper cultures, they make plausible the most recent radiocarbon assay results for the Oconto site and they supply further arguments in refutation of the idea of a single "culture" producing copper implements in Wisconsin and parceling them out to favored clients in the hinterlands. While technically just outside the catchment, these sites in large measure belong culturally to the Great Lakes country and constitute an extension of its history. The Morrison's Island-6 site exemplifies their relevance.

Aligned by its excavator with the Brewerton phase of Laurentian, the Morrison's Island-6 site was a fishing camp and burial ground which yielded 276 copper artifacts and a much larger inventory of chipped-stone, ground-stone, and bone and antler tools. Discounting the possibility of a problematical further example, 18 burials were found. Mostly extended, there were also flexed and bundle inhumations. About half had been sprinkled with powdered red hematite. Lumps of hematite occurred in some graves.

A great many projectile points, mainly of Brewerton side and corner-notched types, dominated the chipped flints, although a few adze-like scrapers and drills were also present. Laurentian ground-stone tools included adzes, gouges, plummets, and some rare examples of ground-slate projectile points and ulus. Very common were hammerstones and whetstones which are believed to have functioned in the fabrication of bone and copper tools.

Bone and antler artifacts at Morrison's Island-6 duplicate the usual Laurentian complement of such products, though harpoons were unusually well represented (not unexpectedly at a fishing station) and there was a more than ordinary tendency for many of the implements to be embellished with simple geometric designs executed by means of short scribed lines, either alone or in conjunction with gouged-out dots, and nonfunctional edge serrations.

Associated copper was astonishing by its variety and quantity. Whereas certain specimens may well have been acquired through trade with the western Great Lakes, there is no doubt that many copper items were locally made by the Morrison Islanders themselves even though radioactive chemical studies of the copper demonstrate a Lake Superior origin of the metal. Chunks and scraps of worked and unworked copper were recovered in addition to finished products. Weapons and tools were represented by stemmed projectile points with beveled blade edges, sometimes equipped with a peculiar "fluke"—or down and outward trailing spur—at the base on one side only, and quite atypical of copper points in the western Great Lakes; a flat lanceolate point with flanged socket midway up the blade, also atypical of "Old Copper"; an asymmetrical, or single-shouldered tanged knife; celts; wedges; a spud like one from the Reigh site in Wisconsin; a harpoon; awls; eyed needles; fishhooks; the impaling points from probable compound fishhooks; gorges; and punches. Copper ornaments embraced beads, pendants, bracelets, arm bands, and a possible finger ring.

This is an impressive list. It points to a sustained and well-accustomed production and comsumption of copper products by a northern Laurentian people well eastward of the sources of the raw material. Most, if not all, of this copper was fashioned into useful and decorative objects by a people who were neither displaced New Yorkers nor eastward trekking Old Copper Indians (nor native easterners on the far receiving end of a trade network). They were representative of a local population in touch with and selectively participating in the technologies and style options current among their neighbors. Despite the conspicuous copper, most of the interaction seems to have been with Laurentian groups. The similarities certainly also hint at social intercourse in more important, but also archaeologically more fragile, matters.

This discussion of the Late Archaic period opened with the observation that copper was widely regarded as an extraordinary substance by native peoples. Archaeologically, it must have played roles supernumerary to that of "something to make tools out of." Its wide trading and its translation into burial and cache goods suggest something more. There is historical record of its prestige value. Even though most copper implements appear to have been manufactured for prosaic utilitarian purposes, and most examples show the breakage and nicking and wear of actual use, the items probably also rendered an additional margin of satisfaction to the user. Copper, after all, was not uniformly available to everybody. It was restricted by nature and by the incompleteness of outwardly groping social interaction. It had that strange and wonderful property of malleability and repairability, and things made of it were instantly and permanently recognizable. They just did not look like the stone and bone and wood and antler tools available to everybody and seen everywhere. They fostered in some others a desire for possession. That copper must accordingly have taken on certain social and ideological functions is suggested by later developments which will be reviewed in subsequent chapters.

Assuredly, copper was an important item in intertribal relations in the Late Achaic period. This would have been not only for purposes of trade, in the purely economic sense of quid pro quo for received or anticipated salt-water shells or whatever, but as signal of social identification and family prestige. Like the Indians seen by Europeans, who opened almost all their dealings among themselves and with foreigners by exchanges of gifts, the Old Copper Indians doubtless effected as wide a knowledge and demand for copper through the network and rationale of social relations as through commodity trading. Similar social exchange with the land of the dead, concurrently with the survivors' reaffirmation of societal endurance, is part of the credentialing of the deceased through the medium of grave offerings. As has been witnessed, this idea was vastly older than the Old Copper culture. The latter, along with other Late Archaic cultures, promulgated and pushed the idea further in their camp-midden graves and in their cemeteries. In so doing, they contributed to the emergence of practices better known in the succeeding period.

But with regard to the technology of metal-working itself, this product of the Great Lakes was arrested from the start. While the tradition of crafting copper ornaments and tools long survived the Old Copper culture, and was even later expressed in a few novel styles, it was never thereafter enriched nor augmented by further technological innovation. Copperworking had been a limited accomplishment. Not carried beyond the initial steps, the experiment became routinized and stuttered down to the time of French contact, its products diminishing in variety and volume. Copper had remained what it had always been: a magical stone. Until introduced by others, the age of metals lay beyond the horizon. The Stone Age endured.

References

On the Late Archaic cultural stage and its Great Lakes manifestations:
Fitting 1970 (especially Chapter IV: "The Return of the People"); Quimby 1960b (especially Chapter 6: "Boreal Archaic Culture From 5000 to 500 B.C., and Chapter 7: "The Changing World of the Old Copper Indians"); Ritchie 1932 and 1969 (especially Chapter II: "The Archaic or Hunting, Fishing Gathering Stage (c. 3500–1300 B.C.)"); Ritchie and Funk 1973 (especially pp. 37–51); Willey and Phillips 1958 (pp. 104–143).

On the Lamoka culture:
Ritchie 1932, 1944 (pp. 292–310), 1961, 1969 (especially pp. 36–79).

On the Laurentian culture (including Frontenac):
Ritchie 1940, 1944 (pp. 235–292), 1945, 1961; 1969 (especially pp. 79–124); Tuck 1977.

On the Morrison's Island-6 site, Quebec:
Kennedy 1966.

For overviews and distributional studies of the Old Copper culture:
Fogel 1963; Griffin, editor, 1961; Mason and Mason 1961 and 1967; Penman 1977; Popham and Emerson 1954; Quimby 1962; Ritzenthaler 1946; Ritzenthaler, editor, 1957; Wittry 1951; Wittry and Ritzenthaler 1956.

On the social, ideological, and technological functions of copper artifacts:
Binford 1962b; McHugh 1973; Penman 1977.

On the Oconto site, Wisconsin:
Binford 1962; Mason and Mason 1961; Ritzenthaler and Wittry 1952.

On the Osceola site, Wisconsin:
Ritzenthaler 1946

On the Reigh site, Wisconsin:
Baerreis, Daifuku, and Lundsted 1954; Ritzenthaler *et al.* 1957.

A Quickening Pace:
The Archaic–Woodland Transition of 1500–100 B.C.

6

Endurance does not presuppose immutability. The opposite more often assures survival. This may be seen in the new interregnum, here called the Transitional period, that encompassed the eclipse of the Archaic way of life and the complementary rise of the Woodland. Once more change and continuity compel attention.

Unequally intense in their manifestations from area to area in the Great Lakes country, but widely enough expressed to indicate far more than just a local trend, changes in a number of matters concerning both the living and the dead quickened in the second millennium B.C. By the last couple of centuries remaining to the next millennium, accelerating accommodations to change had metamorphosed important aspects of the native societies. Some of the catalysts were external, though the results they stimulated were in crucial ways regionally determined.

How to describe, let alone explain, this next period has especially troubled archaeologists since the development of the radiocarbon dating method. The approximation of a calendrical chronology in parts of the Great Lakes and contiguous regions has produced a hitherto undreamed of complexity, one yielding to clarity only infrequently. This is advertised by the multitudinous labels proposed for the period, or important segments of it: "Terminal Archaic," "Early Woodland," "Proto-Woodland," "Transitional," "Initial Woodland," and still others. Proponents of each of these designations have tended to agree, notwithstanding the individual stress on this or that particular set of features, that the time appropriated for the proposed period was one which harkened back to the past but also presaged the future.

In many ways the sites of the Transitional period exhibit profound and unmistakable continuity with regional ancestors both biologically and culturally. The basic Archaic lifeway proved persistent. There are few signs of intruding populations. Patterns and trends conceived in preceding centuries and millennia continued: the accelerating-upward population curve; the increasing complexity and variety of the things people made; a renewed investment in interregional trade in exotic materials and even products; an underlining of the growing emphasis on the elaboration of rituals for the dead—so much so in fact that some archaeologists have attempted to characterize the period in terms of "cults of the dead"; and innumerable continuities, often regionally or locally specific, in underlying technology and even in many matters of style or taste.

But true innovation occurred in the last 1500 years B.C. There were developments not wholly conformable with expectations based on internal factors alone. That is, things happened that would not have been predictable from a detailed familiarity with the Late Archaic cultures and their native haunts. Human events are never entirely foreseeable, of course, so novelty and innovation are neither so surprising in themselves nor so unsettling of our notions about how customs or institutions change that it automatically becomes necessary to invoke such special causes as migrations bringing in cultural innovators. The question becomes one of determining or, rather, trying to determine, if the enabling potentials of indigenous Great Lakes societies or their neighbors were sufficient to support the thesis of independent innovation unaided by some variety of outside help. Our appraisal of those enabling potentials—whether or not they were sufficient in themselves—must depend upon the kinds of innovations, the nature of the archaeological evidence germane to each case, and the theoretical bias of the evaluator. Here reasonable people may honestly disagree.

There appear to have been four kinds of material innovations that help to mark this period of cultural transition, and some of them, at least, must have accompanied more important developments in sociology and ideology. These material innovations were (*a*) the beginnings of undisputed plant domestication and agriculture; (*b*) the invention or introduction of earthenware pottery; (*c*) the appearance of burial mounds; and (*d*) an interrelated series of new artifacts and style shifts in old ones. These four did not make their first appearances at the same places or at the same time. The first good evidence of agriculture, for example, predates by centuries the initial appearance of pottery in the south central United States, but in the lakes country and elsewhere the priority is emphatically reversed. The distribution of burial mounds overlaps significantly that of native American agriculture, but it is not coextensive. Some parts of the Great Lakes were profoundly affected by the changes, others only superficially or not at all.

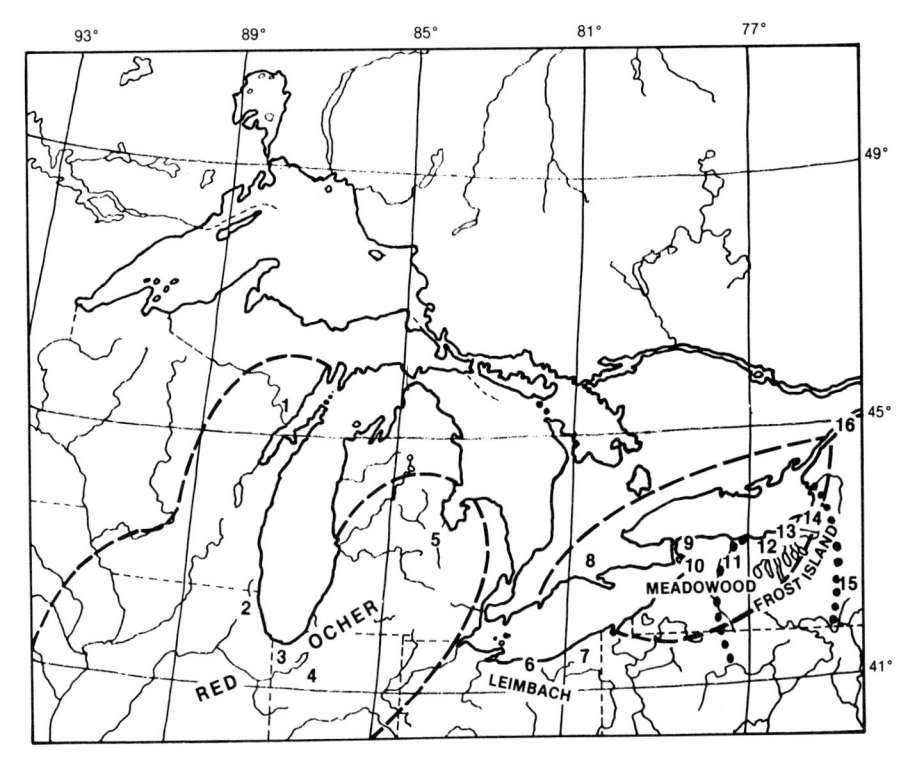

MAP 6.1. Principal distributions of the Frost Island, Leimbach, Meadowood, and Red Ocher cultures, and locations of Transitional Period (Archaic–Woodland transition) sites mentioned in the text: (1) Riverside Cemetery; (2) Beake and Doetsch; (3) Dyer; (4) Peterson; (5) Schultz; (6) Leimbach; (7) Girdled Road; (8) Bruce Boyd; (9) Riverhaven No. 2 and Spicer Creed; (10) Sinking Ponds; (11) Scaccia; (12) Frontenac Island; (13) O'Neil and Hickory Hill Marsh; (14) Oberlander No. 2; (15) Nahrwold No. 2; (16) Long Sault Island. The cultural distribution boundaries are only static approximations of what surely were fluctuating and interpenetrating cultural frontiers.

Of all the novel elements none was as potentially important as agriculture, although contemporary observers of its early career would hardly have guessed it. The cultivation of plants was slow to arrive and incremental in development. Once the potential of deliberate human interference in native plant reproduction was archaeologically expressed in tell-tale modifications in plant size or morphology or in suspicious shifts in distribution, clearly domesticated foreign plants had already supplied their own refuse to the archaeological record.

In eastern North America squash (*Cucurbita pepo*) and gourd (*Lagenaria siceraria*) had been introduced by at least 2300 B.C. from Mexico, where they had been domesticated much earlier. On present evidence this is earlier than the first traces of indigenously domesticated plants. Other Mexican cultigens seem to have arrived much later. Although corn, or maize (*Zea mays*), had been introduced into the southwestern United States by 1800 B.C., its first known appearance east of the Mississippi was delayed until the third or fourth century B.C. Tobacco (*Nicotiana rustica* L.) may not have been brought into the East much before A.D. 500. Beans (*Phaseolus vulgaris*) seem to have arrived later still, undoubted examples not predating approximately A.D. 1000. All of these dates are subject to revision, of course, as the presently available limited samples of intrinsically perishable materials are added to by future discoveries. Corn, for instance, while definitely present in the Hocking Valley in Ohio by 300 B.C., does not appear in any appreciable quantities until after about A.D. 800. However, linguistic analysis of the expressions for corn among eastern North American Indian languages suggests that, at least in the early centuries following its introduction, this crop was usually consumed in its immature, or "green corn," stage. If true, this practice would have operated to substantially reduce the incidence of corn preservation in archaeological deposits. Corn may have been more important in times earlier than present limited examples and radiocarbon assays suggest.

Curiously, the gourds and the kind of squash found in the most ancient sites in eastern North America were probably cultivated not for their dietary value but to provide tough, portable, lightweight containers and ladles. The translation of squash to food status came much later. In the Great Lakes squash is again the earliest cultigen known. It has been recovered at the Leimbach site in northern Ohio from contexts radiocarbon dated to around 500 B.C. At the Schultz site in eastern Michigan squash and gourd first appeared at about the same time or a trifle earlier. Both sites are excellent exemplars of the later phase of the Transitional period, designated Early Woodland by their excavators.

As mentioned in the last chapter, there is evidence of the indigenous domestication of some of the native vegetation of the eastern United States and Canada. The Archaic lifeway itself, coupled with the post-glacial spread of deciduous forest and meadow at the expense of boreal elements, in addition to the need to secure additional sources of food to maintain a growing population, would have sensitized people to some appreciation of the dietary value of a range of wild plants. It would not have been surprising if this in turn resulted in the inauguration of unintended domestication through the differential harvesting of the plants with the biggest edible seeds, the inevitable loss and subsequent generation of some of those seeds in the chemically enriched soils of the disturbed clearings used by the Indians as campsites, and then the later focusing of gathering activities at these same localities due to their higher productivity of the more desirable plants. This may well have taken place more than once. Nevertheless, it now appears from the latest information that the process may have been stimulated by the introduction of squash and other non-native plants previously brought under cultivation elsewhere.

The prehistoric Indians of eastern North America did domesticate and bring under cultivation at least two native plants: marsh elder, or sumpweed (*Iva annua* L.), and sunflower (*Helianthus annuus* L.)—the former by the middle of the first millennium B.C., the latter perhaps by 1000 B.C. or a little before. Four other plant species native to the Carolinian biotic province in the East and known from solid archaeological and ethnographic data to have been harvested wild, may also have experienced incipient domestication, although the available evidence is not yet convincing. These are goosefoot (*Chenopodium* sp.), amaranth (*Amaranthus* sp.), Maygrass (*Phalaris caroliniana* Walt.), and knotweed (*Polygonum* sp.).

Agriculture was not greeted with open arms by practitioners of the new domestic art within or beyond the Great Lakes. Early signs of farming are spotty; intensification of the novel practices was long in coming and was variable in its impact on the indigenous societies. In most of the lakes country 3000 years were to pass following agriculture's modest first appearance elsewhere in the East and the emergence of subsistence economies predominantly dependent on its success. Over vast areas the older Archaic patterns of hunting and the gathering of a plethora of naturally propogated vegetable foods, with local and seasonal shifts of emphasis to particularly abundant or dependable resources, long withstood any detectable alteration in the direction of food production. For a long while, agriculture was at most a marginal enterprise, a supplement to the ancient dependence on a usually sufficient nature. By far the greater number of Transitional period societies in the lakes country appear to have been wholly nonagricultural. Nevertheless, an event of transcendental significance had taken place. The pattern of autochthonous cultural change had been only slightly nudged, though the effects of that nudge accumulated down the succeeding centuries to redirect radically the direction of future adaptations. Slight as it was, the initial impetus was supplied by diffusion.

Diffusion was important, too, in the generation of the other innovations by means of which the Transitional period is importantly defined. Not that Great Lakes peoples were passive recipients of other peoples' richer inventiveness. It was the stimulus of widening contacts and the opening up of environmental and social potentials brought about by previous achievements that are together reflected in the unfolding Transitional period. These other innovations are best recounted in the contexts of the individual cultures in which they initially emerge, and are best documented or are most illuminated by associated events.

The Frost Island Culture

"Late Late Archaic" or "Transitional" culture, however it seems best categorized, the Frost Island culture, or "phase," was the product of a group of people who intruded into the lakes country, albeit mainly south of Lake Ontario, and made a new home in what is now central New York. This is one regional manifestation, among others peculiar to the Hudson Valley, Long Island, and other areas east of the lakes, of a cultural pattern that had earlier developed along the Middle Atlantic fall line out of a proposed "Coastal Archaic" with sites distributed along the Coastal Plain from northern Florida to southern New England. The immediate ancestor of the Frost Island culture, and doubtless also its contemporary for several hundred years, was the Susquehanna Soapstone culture of eastern Pennsylvania, itself with strong ties into the Chesapeake tidewater country southward into the Carolinas.

Best represented at such sites as O'Neil and Hickory Hill Marsh on the Lake Ontario-bound Seneca River, and at the previously described Frontenac Island in levels above those yielding Lamoka, Brewerton, and Frontenac cultural materials, the Frost Island culture has been radiocarbon dated to approximately 1250 B.C. Beyond doubt, components of the culture existed for at least a century or two both before and after this date. Frost Island appears to mark a strong but geographically limited intrusion into the easternmost part of the Lower Great Lakes by people from the Susquehanna Valley. They probably intermarried with some of the local folk, though they retained their foreign flavor and their original, essentially riverine, way of life. The culture disappeared as a distinctive entity not many centuries after its initial appearance, and it left no known descendents.

The mortuary customs of the Frost Islanders remain unknown. Indirect evidence via the study of culturally related groups suggests the practice of cremation, heavy use of red ocher, and deposition of caches of projectile points in graves. Such practices show a wide distribution in the Great Lakes on this general time level and through following centuries.

Most characteristic of the Frost Island culture, and shared with the Susquehanna Soapstone culture to the south, are very distinctive projectile points (and equally distinctive end-scrapers, knives, drills, and fire-flints or strike-a-lights made from them or in conformity with their style) and cooking vessels literally carved out of stone ("soapstone," or steatite). Because there were no local sources of soapstone, that material—or, more likely, the carved bowls themselves—had to be imported, probably from the important quarries located near Christiana, Lancaster County, in southeastern Pennsylvania. Whereas most projectile points, scrapers, choppers, and other flaked-stone artifacts were fashioned out of local or at least reginally available flints, some were made of rhyolite, a material exotic in New York, ubiquitous in the Susquehanna Soapstone culture, and obtained from deposits near Gettysburg, Pennsylvania, not far from the steatite sources. The rhyolite points and other tools were probably the original equipment of the Susquehanna Valley intruders into central New York.

Unable to secure a steady supply of that stone, they and their descendents apparently turned to the use of the regional flints, retaining, however, the traditional forms. Evidence of soapstone bowls in the Frost Island Culture is scanty compared with Pennsylvania, Maryland, and farther south. The vessels and their fragments which have come to light suggest that they were brought into New York by the pioneering Frost Island immigrants or that, at most, there was a short-lived, diminishing supply coming up the Susquehanna Valley.

Typical projectile points, whether of Pennsylvania rhyolite or New York flints, are of the so-called Susquehanna Broad Spearpoint style. They look like wide-based isosceles triangles with their bottom corners cut away. Such points have sloping shoulders rather than barbs, and the stems are relatively narrow where they meet the blade and expand toward the base; the latter is straight or faintly concave. Tell-tale portions of this configuration have survived on many of the end-scrapers and other implements made from broken projectile points. Other than some of the chipped-flint artifacts, additional Frost Island stone tools are much less culturally diagnostic: flaked and ground-and-polished chert celts, notched net-sinkers, pebble hammerstones, anvilstones, grinding stones, whetstones. Rarely preserved are bone tools. Those which have escaped destruction must be a shadow of what once existed: a few bone awls and some bilaterally multibarbed points and unilaterally barbed harpoons.

The soapstone bowls signal the first innovation in the making of cooking vessels since the ancient discoveries of the uses of hide, wood, and bark. While widespread eastward and southward to the Atlantic coast, in the Great Lakes the innovation was extremely restricted in geographical distribution, being virtually confined to the region immediately south of Lake Ontario. It was also short-lived in this northern salient. Developed elsewhere, then introduced into this corner of the lakes country, the stone bowls were whittled out of one of the softest rocks known to man. In addition to a softness conductive to easy carving with flint knives or chisels, steatite is also very heavy. It is thus doubtful that the raw material or the vessels carved from it were disseminated by overland travel. Their distribution, along with that of the Susquehanna Broad points and the complex of artifacts associated with them, tends to be confined to major river courses, implying a heavy reliance on dugout or bark canoes.

Apparently most common in the Frost Island culture were stone vessels in the shape of lidless rectangular boxes with vertical or slightly outward sloping sides. Another style, probably more frequent to the south and east, was shaped like a watermelon sliced lengthwise; such vessels exhibit flat to somewhat rounded bottoms, vertical to slightly everted walls, and rounded ends. A solid projection, or lug, typically occurs at each end on both styles. Decoration, if it occurs at all, is confined to nicking the ends of the lugs or the lip of the orifice. These cumbersome pots have smoothly

PLATE 6.1. *Rare carved soapstone bowl from southern Ontario. (Shown approximately two-thirds actual size.) (Courtesy Peter L. Storck and the Royal Ontario Museum, Toronto, Canada.)*

ground interiors, but whittled exteriors which preserve the marks of the tools by means of which they had been sculpted.

Late in the aborted career of the Frost Island culture stone vessels were replaced by the earliest known earthenware pottery to appear anywhere in the Great Lakes. Not abundant in its initial appearances, this pottery was first introduced near the end of the second millennium B.C. or very early in the first. Called "Vinette 1," it bears no resemblance to the soapstone vessels it superceded and was assuredly not an invention of the Frost Islanders. This Vinette 1 pottery will be described later in the context of the Meadowwood culture in which it is much more typical. But the Frost Island people may not have been wholly uninvolved with its genesis.

Southward from the Great Lakes in Pennsylvania, New Jersey, Delaware, Maryland, and Virginia the first pottery is exactly modeled after the carved soapstone containers, sometimes even to the extent of simulating on the exterior clay surfaces the tuncated and overlapping chisel and knife scars seen on the stone prototypes. This pottery is even tempered by the heavy admixture with the clay of fragments of soapstone, thus giving the ware an appropriately soapy feel like that of the stone vessels themselves. Indeed, in many instances the pottery tempering was acquired by cutting up and breaking apart preexisting stone vessels. Either the potters were positively ecstatic over the novel technology and were anxious to get rid of the "old fashioned" stone pots or, far more likely, they simply used the old and worn out stone utensils as a handy and familiar source of tempering material. Enormously reinforcing the latter view is the existence of so many slavish ceramic copies of the stone originals. Called by a number of regional names such as Marcey Creek Plain and Koens-Crispin Ware, such steatite-tempered earthenware is the most ancient pottery yet discovered in the regions of its occurrence and is very likely as old as and older than Vinette 1 and related potteries to the north and west.

An even more antique fiber-tempered pottery in the southeastern United States, again with shapes and embellishments unique to its area, goes back to at least 2500 B.C. It thus appears that the earliest ceramics originated far south of the Great Lakes. Rather than actual earthenware pots being introduced by direct contact or by trade through third parties, it now seems that neighboring groups of people progressively picked up information about the infant technology from their southerly acquaintances, applying their own notions about how pots ought to look. As we have seen, the Frost Island culture excepted, where stone vessels were in use, the first pottery was modeled after them. In the Great Lakes the earliest ceramics may have been fashioned after basket shapes. Interestingly, the Frost Island culture seems to represent an instance of the actual, physical introduction of pottery instead of just the idea. The most logical at hand source for the injection of Vinette 1 pottery into the late Frost Island culture is the Meadowood culture.

Meadowood and Middlesex

Information from Meadowood sites reveals a sectional enterprise concurrently involved in practices widely dispersed in and beyond the Great Lakes. Loosely aggregated in a circum-Lake Ontario distribution, though with the Bruce Boyd and a few other stations as far removed as the north central shore of Lake Erie, Meadowood sites are believed to date between as early as 1200 B.C. and as late as sometime after 500 B.C. The persistence of the Archaic lifeway, inherited from Laurentian forebears, of hunting, fishing, and plant collecting, as well as the basic technologies, is shown by excavations at the Riverhaven No. 2, Nahrwold No. 2, Scaccia—all in New York—and some other known camp and village sites. These are fairly small, intimating perhaps 25–150 inhabitants, and they seem to reveal a preference for locations along major streams or large lakes and marshes. That some degree of seasonal sedentariness was more than a rare luxury is indicated by the presence of large round to rectangular storage pits which, when last emptied of their charges, saw final reuse as trash pits and graves.

In a detailed analysis of Meadowood stations in the Niagara Frontier region on or near the New York–Ontario border between Lakes Erie and Ontario, particularly the Sinking Ponds, Riverhaven No. 2, and Spicer Creek sites, the application of interpretive models drawn from ethnography and anthropological theory has permitted some fleshing out of the social organization that had once generated the material evidence now remaining. This theoretical reconstruction of Meadowood society, in some of its proposals testable against the empirical record derived from excavation, roughly approximates the now extinct way of life while plausibly accounting for such things as site locations with reference to natural resources, some of the variability in artifact segregation or clustering within and among sites, kinds and proportions of associated floral and faunal remains, the distributions of the several stages of flint tool manufacture, and such clues as there are to community and society size.

The kind of society social anthropologists call "band" has been proposed as best fitted to account for the details of the archaeology. Encompassing the simplest known human societies anywhere, bands were for a long time the dominant type of society. With the evolution of tribes and other more advanced kinds of societies, bands diminished greatly in number and contracted enormously in their control of living space. They had survived into historically recent times, however, in the northern reaches of the Great Lakes and in the boreal forest and Arctic wastes. The proto-Ojibwas, Crees, and Eskimos are relevant examples. Old World representatives include such peoples as the South African Bushman, the Indian Ocean Andamanese, and the Australian Aborigines. The essential nature of band society has been presented in Chapter 1 with the descriptions of the Algonkins, Nipissings, Ottawas, and Ojibwas. What is similar among all of these otherwise disparate peoples, Old World and New World, is what defines "band."

Combined archaeological and ethnographic information suggests that the Meadowood people lived out their lives as members, simultaneously, of two "levels" of band society. On one hand, people belonged with their immediate and extended families to a "local band." This was for many purposes the optimum and, indeed, the maximum one, being largely autonomous and economically self-sufficient. A local band numbered perhaps 150 persons according to this model and habitually resided in and roamed over a territory of something on the order of 1000 km^2. Considerable departures from these approximations doubtless occurred from place to place and time to time. They should be understood as being no more than order of magnitude estimates. Within the larger Niagara Frontier itself, it is likely that there were several such local bands of Meadowood folk and that they interacted among themselves in the bigger and more amorphous entity designated the "regional band." A gross estimate of about 500 persons has been hazarded for the population of this larger collectivity. Presumably its dimensions were isomorphic with the maximum social distance within which most people married—it being assumed that local bands were exogamous. Not surprisingly, the existence of regional bands is much more difficult to verify archaeologically than the local band.

Four kinds of Meadowood sites have been tentatively identified in New York's Niagara Frontier. They are functionally defined as "base settlements," "extractive settlements," "chert resource sites," and "mortuary activity sites." The first, the so-called base settlements, were semisedentary communities occupied by all or a great many of the local bandsmen during the autumn, winter, and early spring. A wide spectrum of activities transpired in the base settlement as attested by multiple hearths, storage pits, remnants of dwelling floors, and evidence of bone and hide processing, preparation of wild vegetable foods, and the making and refurbishing of stone tools and weapons. Such sites are typically larger and have more midden than "extractive settlements." The latter are thought to have been spring-through-summer camps, and among several of these camps the members of the larger settlement divided, probably along kinship lines, into special purpose task groups. Such camps may have been inhabited by 20–50 people. Fishing camps and temporary havens convenient to good plant-collecting grounds are examples. A special kind of site is that situated where material for making flint (chert) tools could be procured. These places might be visited only by men on and off for generations and yield little beyond artificially fractured raw material, broken roughed-out tool blanks, and hammerstones. The "mortuary activity sites" are usually isolated from the others and may have been shared by several local bands.

Formerly known as Point Peninsula I, the Meadowood culture owes its distinctiveness to a select group of material traits either unique to it or especially typical in form or numbers even if shared by contemporaries. On any particular site, of course, these may account for only a minority of the items recovered, the greater number being much less peculiarly confined in space and time and accordingly of less taxonomic value.

Most numerous of the diagnostic Meadowood artifacts are the thin, very well-made projectile points and the hafted end-scrapers, knives, and drills either deliberately made with the same style hafting provisions or made on the broken armament. Meadowood points mark an obvious change in the areas where they appear; on the whole, they are thinner and lighter when compared with their predecessors. They exhibit triangular to truncated ovate-trianguloid blades, straight bases, and very small, precise side notches set close to the basal corners. Some examples closely resemble the side-notched points from the Oconto and Reigh Old Copper sites far to the west in Wisconsin. Nevertheless, a few archaeologists have speculated that the general stylistic shift represented by Meadowood points, taken in conjunction with an apparent decrease in weight, may relate to the spread of the use of the bow-and-arrow which may have been introduced from the eastern Arctic at about this very time. But this is a problem where the classic phrase, "more work needs to be done," is doubly applicable.

Caches of thin biface blades, ovate to tear-shaped and excellently made, are characteristic, especially as grave accompaniments in the small cemeteries. These, like the projectile points, are usually chipped out of a western New York variety of Onondaga chert—even at locations distantly removed from the sources. Hoards of up to 1500 of these blades have been recovered from single Meadowood graves! Representing, as they do, especially in such quantities, conspicuous investment of labor in fabrication and transportation, they are reminiscent of both tool preforms intended for later functional translation as weaponry, knives, or other useful articles, and of visible repositories of wealth or status. This latter—their symbolic load—in some cases clearly superceded any mundane or utilitarian destiny they might ever have had. The blade must have been meant to be nonspecific with respect to utility and thus to harbor a range of possibilities so as better to forearm the dead as they faced the unknown contingencies of another world. They who gave to so equip the dead simultaneously gave witness to their primary allegiance to the living. It is an anthropologically familiar pattern.

Though less exclusive in their provenience, other Meadowood traits are the earliest pottery in the Great Lakes (Vinette 1 pottery, described p. 217); cigar-shaped smoking pipes made of the same kind of clay as the pottery; occasional sherds from steatite vessels; two-holed trapezoidal and rectangular gorgets, sometimes medially keeled on one face; double-ended flaked scrapers; tubular and barrel-shaped copper beads; disc-shaped shell beads; copper adzes; numerous ground-stone adzes and celts; and small, highly stylized, vaguely bird-like stone sculptures appropriately dubbed "birdstones" which seem to replace bannerstones and may similarly have sometimes served as atlatl weights. Unique, but important for cross-tying Meadowood with the Red Ocher culture of the western Great Lakes, is a "turkey-tail" blade of southern Indiana flint discovered at the Oberlander No. 2 site.

Besides the evidence of the Indiana flint blade and the western New York Onondaga chert points and cache blades in eastern New York and in Ontario, the involvement of Meadowood people in some sort of exchange network by means of which access to regionally exotic articles and materials was at least once in a while facilitated is indicated by the presence of salt-water shell from the Atlantic Ocean, smoky chalcedony from northern Quebec or Labrador, jasper and soapstone from southeastern Pennsylvania, slate gorgets and birdstones from southern Ohio, and copper from Lake Superior.

Most of the best known Meadowood sites are cemeteries. They express an intensification of mortuary rituals anticipated in the Late Archaic period. Cremation was the usual treatment of the deceased even though flexed and bundle burials are also known; indeed, cremations and bundle or flexed burials have been found in common graves. Dogs as well as people were cremated and then ceremoniously buried. In most instances

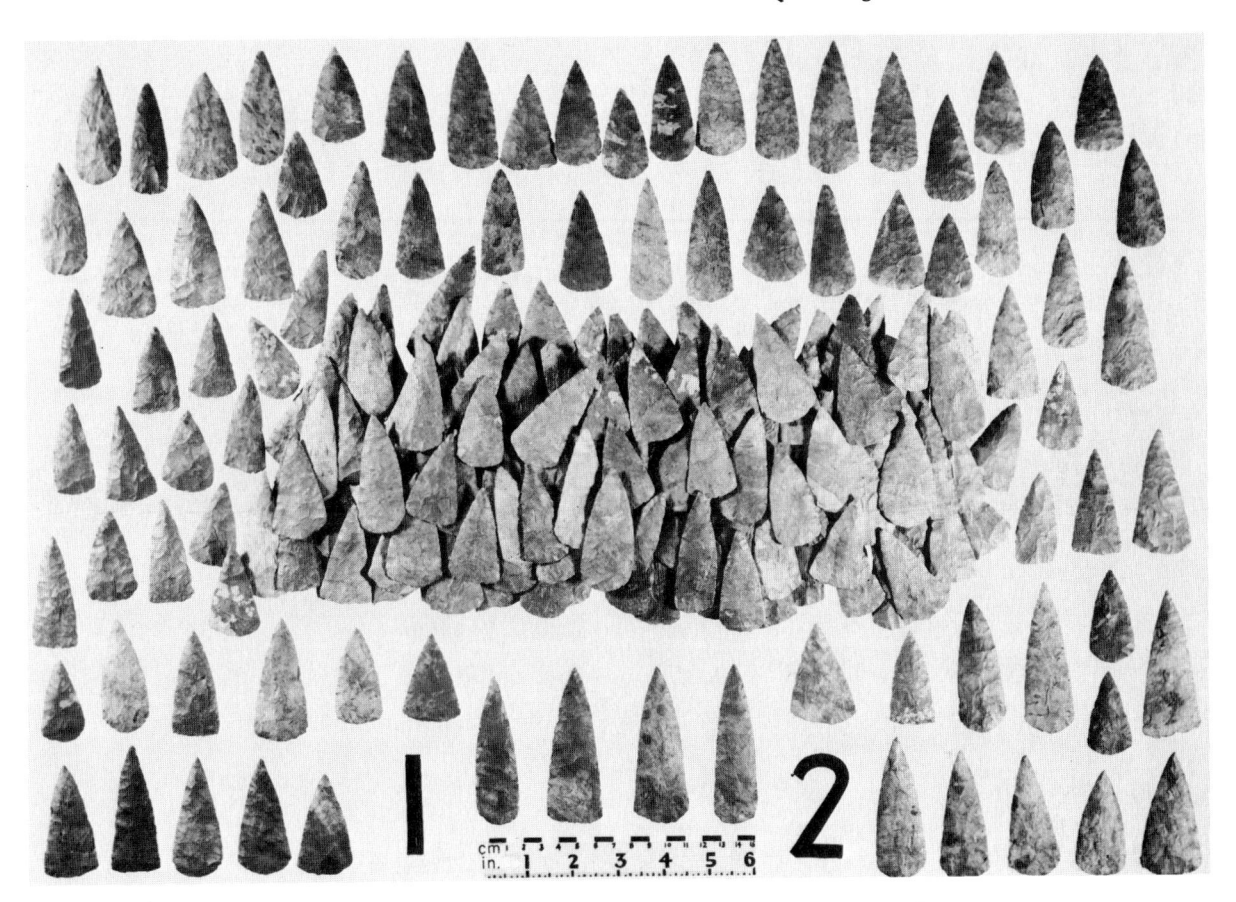

PLATE 6.2. *Cache of 243 mortuary blades (Feature 1) from the Meadowood site at Red Lake, Jefferson County, New York. (Courtesy William A. Ritchie and Robert E. Funk, New York State Museum and Science Service, Albany.)*

the burning took place in small rock crematoria within the cemeteries. These were sited on east-facing flanks of sandy knolls where they would be bathed in the light of the mounting sun. This preference for knoll or hillock burial, shared with other Transitional period cultures, presages the later popularity of artificial mound construction and may have been prototypic. It is well to remember the rare burial mounds of the Maritime Archaic in the Gulf of St. Lawrence, however, which long predate the Meadowood and other knoll inhumations. But they may not be unconnected.

Laboratory studies of the physical effects of burning bone point to the probability that the cremation of defleshed corpses—not bodies still in the flesh nor, on the other hand, dried skeletons—explains the particular kinds of thermal alterations characteristic of the Meadowood cremations. This hints at deliberate exposure of the dead or temporary scaffold or other

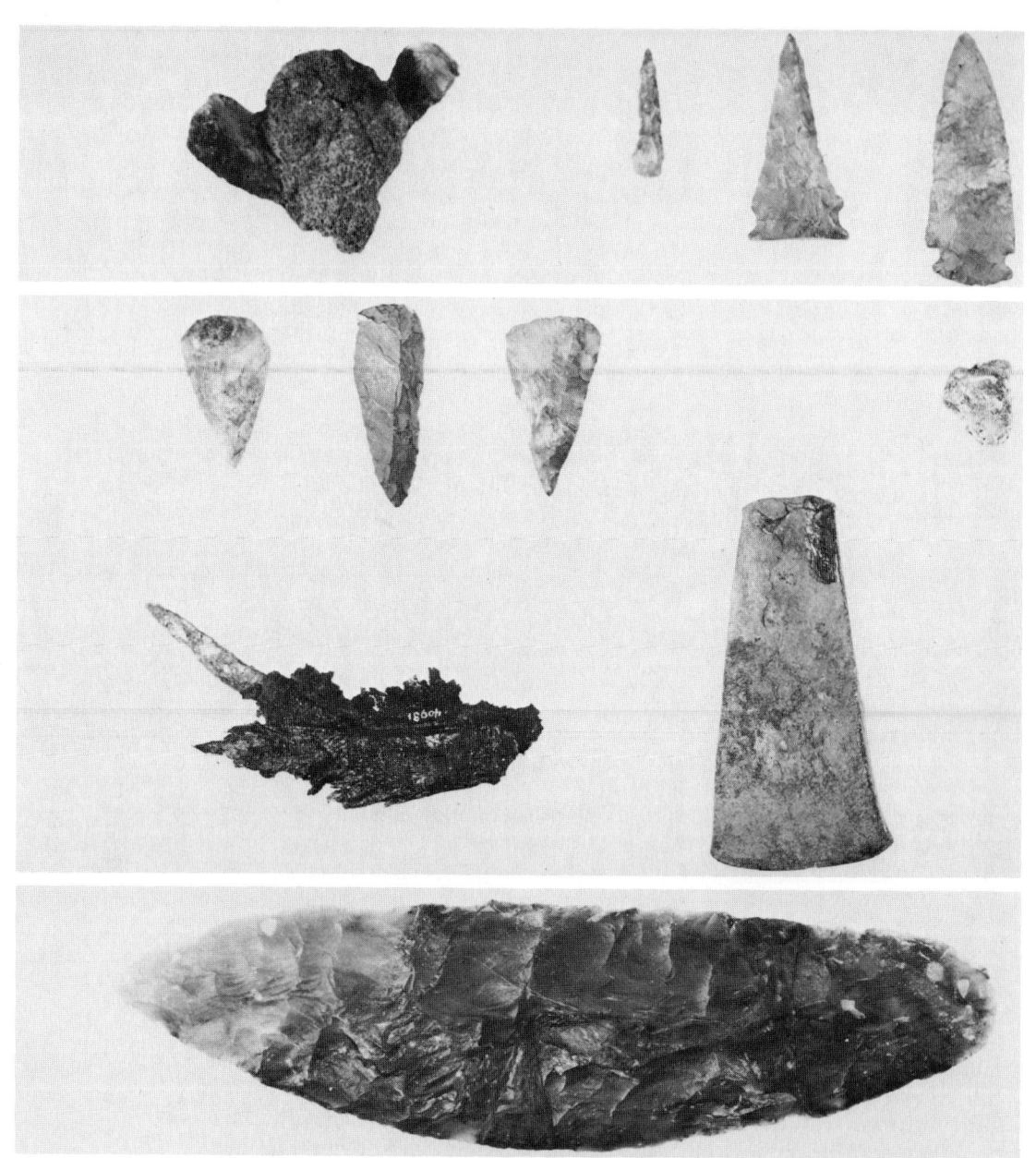

PLATE 6.3. Meadowood grave goods from the Muskalonge Lake and Red Lake sites, Jefferson County, New York: fire-making set of nodule of iron pyrites and two flint strikers or fireflints (upper left); drill (second from upper left); projectile points (rest of upper row); end-scraper and two fireflints (second row left); galena nodules (second row center); copper flaking tool mounted in a carved wooden handle and partly encased in bark grave lining (third row left); native-copper adzes (third row center); restored "killed" chalcedony knife (lower left); adze (lower center); and ground and polished slate gorgets (right hand column). (Shown half actual size.) (Courtesy William A. Ritchie and Robert E. Funk, New York State Museum and Science Service, Albany.)

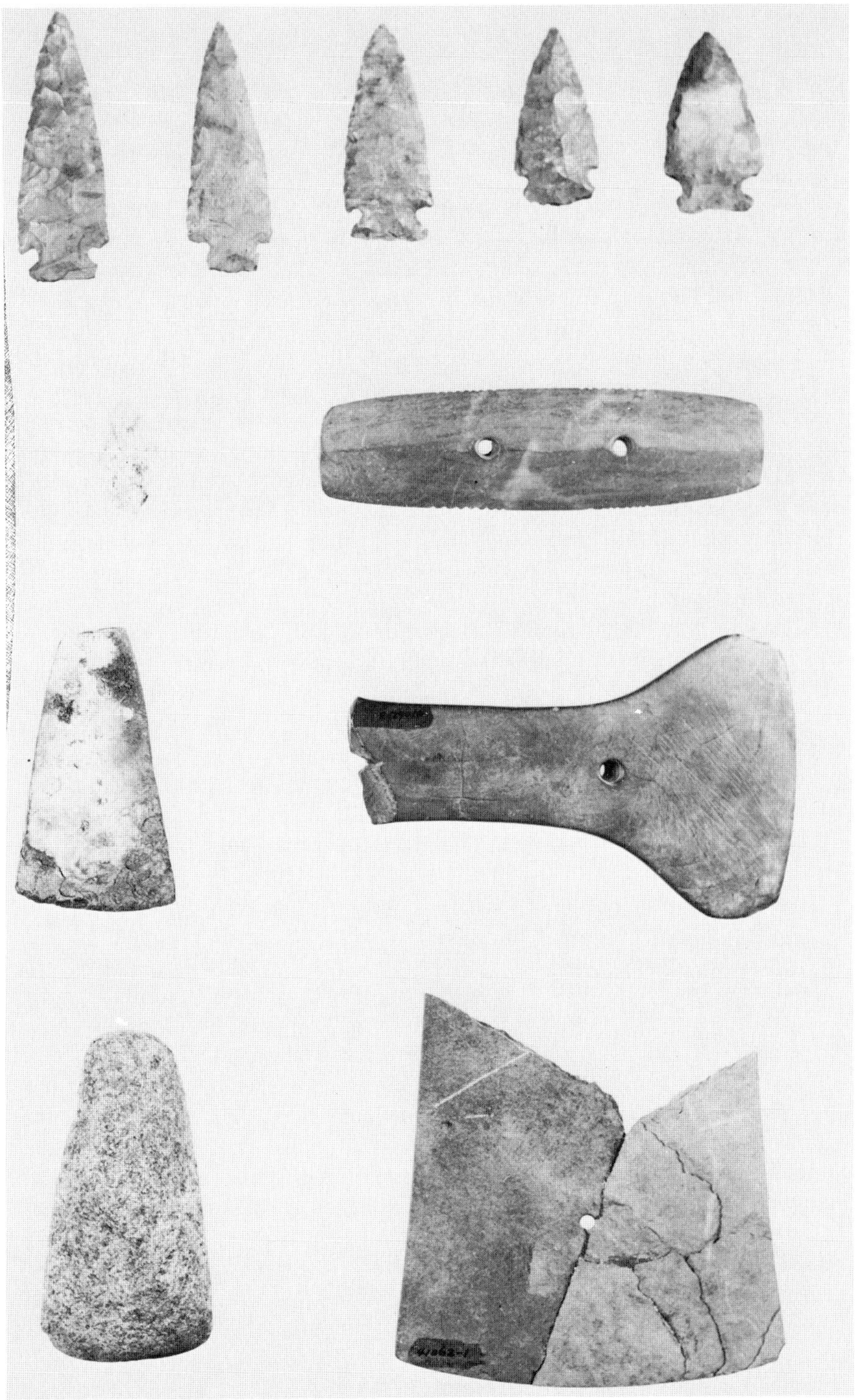

preliminary treatment before consignment to the flames. Some of the artifacts placed in the graves had also undergone preparatory rituals: they had been intentionally broken, or "killed," before being placed in their ultimate abode.

Typical grave accouterments are groups of the thin cache blades, sometimes in astonishing numbers, and commonly heavily sprinkled with red ocher. Many graves have also revealed clay tubular pipes, birdstones, gorgets, and copper beads and celts. More interesting is the incorporation in grave bundles of fossils. A recurring theme is the fire-making kit, each consisting of iron pyrites (since decayed to limonite) and a fireflint originally rolled up together in birchbark and/or placed in an animal skin or woven pouch. As is characteristic of the earliest pottery-making cultures throughout the Great Lakes, no ceramics were placed in graves. Some burials were lavishly equipped, others hardly at all. Adult males seem to have been favored in this regard. There is obvious intimation here of proliferating social distinctions which help to bridge the contrasts between the more and the less egalitarian societies of the Archaic and the post-Transitional periods.

As has already been noted, a little pottery of the type known as Vinette 1 was introduced into the Frost Island culture late in its history, probably near the conclusion of the second millennium B.C. This earthenware, the most ancient known wherever it has been found, has been recovered in much greater quantity in Meadowood habitation sites. It is this culture that is the most reasonable donor of pottery to the relatively short-lived one intrusive from the Susquehanna Valley. Whether its development may be similarly credited is not known. Vinette 1 pottery is not only the oldest earthenware in the Lower Great Lakes and elswhere in the Northeast, but it has unmistakable connections with a number of other similar, but by no means identical, potteries, each likewise the oldest in its respective territory. Included among these are Half-Moon Cordmarked in the Upper Ohio Valley, Fayette Thick in West Virginia and Ohio, some versions of Leimbach ware in northern Ohio, Schultz Thick in Michigan, and Marion Thick in Indiana, Illinois, and parts of Wisconsin and Minnesota.

It has already been noted how progressively more remote in time are the first known appearances of ceramics with increasing distance southwards from the Great Lakes. Conversely, northward or westward from the lakes the oldest pottery is of lesser antiquity. Whereas the forms in which the first ceramics are expressed indicate some degree of regional and even local interpretation of how earthenware pots ought to look, the radiocarbon chronology is supportive of the theory that pottery making was invented elsewhere—probably originally in South America—and, once introduced into eastern North America, the idea rather than the product traveled northward, each successive group adopting the idea and placing its own distinctive stamp upon the technique.

Vinette 1 pottery was hand coiled and tempered by the addition of crushed gabbro, gneiss, granite, or other rock to the clay. The temper particles are often coarse. They were added as a binder and to help retard, if not prevent, cracking during the critical drying and firing. Vessels were shaped by building up loops of clay and then by compressing and thinning the walls. The potter's wheel, of course, was unknown. Supporting one side of the vessel wall with the hand, the opposite face was malleated with the other hand or with a wooden paddle. Hand or paddle, whichever it was, was wrapped with a cord or a coarsely constructed fabric, for the vessel surfaces are characteristically covered both inside and out with their impressions. Such a surface finish superficially resembles bark or other fibrous substance and could again, as in the case of the soapstone-tempered pottery described previously, be an attempt to simulate the appearance of an older and comfortably familiar type of container. Resembling a bag or basket with pointed bottom, Vinette 1 vessels were conoidal-based and had more or less straight sides with wide mouths. For cooking they would have had to have been set into a small pit around which firewood or coals would be built up, or they would have required propping up with rocks in the fireplace. Marion Thick and the other closely related wares in and south of the Great Lakes often have flat bottoms and reconstructed pots will stand by themselves.

Partly overlapping in the beginning with the tenure of the Meadowood culture but surviving its demise by several centuries, another culture or, more properly, mortuary complex, also overlapped with that entity in space and in ideas concerning the dead. Known exclusively from burial sites—and from not too many of these—the Middlesex "culture," to a far greater extent than its antecedent, is apt to conjure up migrations as responsible for certain of its features. Especially is this so because its few discovered sites, located in central and eastern New York and in western New England but with at least one important component (the Long Sault Island site) in the St. Lawrence River southwest of Montreal, contain some exotic objects which could only have come from the central Ohio Valley. In fact, close to a third of the known types of Middlesex artifacts are of form and/or material indisputably derived from that quarter, and there most closely identified with the Adena culture.

Within the high proportion of exotic paraphernalia recovered from Middlesex sites are fireclay or pipestone from sources located near Portsmouth in Scioto County in southern Ohio; a unique kinds of flint or chalcedony from Flint Ridge, Licking County, in central Ohio; banded slate from several possible outcroppings in southern Ohio; and limestone and nodular chert ("hornstone") from Harrison County in southern Indiana. Copper from the Lake Superior basin indicates trade connections with the Upper Great Lakes as well.

Finished artifacts particularly characteristic of Adena found in Middlesex graves include blocked-end tabular pipes of stone or fireclay, Ohio-slate pendants and gorgets as well as bar amulets and boat-shaped stones (perhaps atlatl weights), and broad-bladed projectile points with lobate and squared stems similar to "Adena" and "Cresap" points. Not as distinctively Adena, but shared with it as well as with contemporaneous Transitional cultures in much of the lakes country, are large and ellipsoidal "knives" with flat bases, triangular and ovate-trianguloid cache blades, so-called bust-type birdstones, copper beads and awls and celts, and other tools. Such burial practices as an emphasis on cremation, rich provisioning of graves, and use of red ocher were similarly widely shared. Middlesex is one of the cultural entities associated with Vinette 1 pottery, presumably adopting it from Meadowood. Vinette 1 pottery is not found in Adena country, though closely related pottery is.

Middlesex stations are at the end of a thin and broken trail of Adena and Adena-like archaeological sites extended eastward from the central Ohio Valley and the Kanawha River in West Virginia to Maryland and Chesapeake Bay, thence northward with connecting sites in Delaware and New Jersey. These sites are few in number and widely spaced, similar enough to guarantee that they belong together, linked as if by a trail, yet so unequally and distantly separated as to draw attention to the individuality of each. There are hints of a retrogression in Adena attributes as the sites are traced to the loose cluster of their northern members. But there are also contradictory shifts in some other features. On a thesis of some sort of south to north movement as demanded by the material origins of some of the Middlesex artifacts, it would hardly be surprising if many typically Adena traits diminished in frequency or disappeared altogether the farther the distance to be traveled, and that the sites at the end of the series would exhibit more features indigenous to their locale. In fact, this is the case. In dramatic and curious opposition, however, is the observation that the Long Sault Island site on the New York–Ontario–Quebec frontier at the northern extremity of the Adena–Middlesex range is the only Middlesex site with burial mounds. And burial mounds and other earthworks are a prominent emblem of the Adena culture and the greater Ohio Valley generally. There are other mounds in New York and Ontario and western New England, but only the Long Sault Island mounds have been linked to the Middlesex mortuary complex.

Archaeologists have avoided unanimity in putting forth explanations for the patent Adena similarities and unambiguous Ohio Valley artifacts in Middlesex sites—explanations which must concurrently account for the indigenous non-Adena constituents as well. Any idea of correspondence due to accidental independent convergences in artifact styles can be ruled out for reasons already given. The migration theory holds that Middlesex is the product of remnant communities of Adena people who relocated themselves on this far northern frontier, leaving as testimony of their trek the tell-tale graves at such intermediate locations as the Rosencrans site on the Delaware River in New Jersey and the Felton site in Delaware. These sites, like those classified as Middlesex in the north, are so conspicuous because of their yielding up blocked-end tubular pipes and other rare items foreign to the characteristic products of the local cultures. By this theory, the Adena immigrants were at last forced to die out from want of numbers or to intermarry with the local people among whom they found themselves. This latter they presumably did, the result being a short-lived cultural hybrid. Why some groups of Adena people should have left their original homeland and traveled to so distant and different a place, one already inhabited by others, has been unconvincingly blamed on population displacement attendant on an invasion of southern Ohio by Hopewell migrants from an assumed sally port in Illinois. The cause of this precipitating migration is unexplained.

Opposed to the migration theory is a simpler scenario positing diffusion as a more likely mechanism. Trade and other social interaction via the Hudson, Delaware, and other natural avenues of movement inevitably exposed far-separated peoples to some of the practices and products of others. The denser population and somewhat more complex and materially productive culture of the Adena folk would likely have made for the kind of relational imbalance archaeologically uncovered with the main axis of novelty anchored in the south. Developing notions of social inequalities, indicated by high-status mound inhumations in Adena, may have been faintly echoed along the northern trade networks, thus fostering some demand for the physical symbols of such status differentiation. Or maybe the Adena objects were simply divorced from whatever social symbolism they may have had when they entered the outbound channels of societal interaction. Passing through the hands of who knows how many middlemen, their final significance for the persons responsible for the Middlesex interments could easily have been unrecognizable to their original creators. They could have been gifts or momentos collected by those few individuals who, over several generations, journeyed far enough south to come by them, perhaps incidentally to the purposes of the trips. Others were traveling too.

Red Ocher and Some Thematic Variations

Many years have come and gone since an amateur prehistorian dug up a skeleton on the Dyer Farm in Lake County, Indiana, unearthing in the process accompanying artifacts of arresting craftsmanship. This was not the first such find in the area, nor was it to be the last. A farmer and his young son uncovered much more fragmentary human remains years later on another northwestern Indiana farm (their own, the Peterson Farm), this time in Pulaski County. Although the three discoverers were unaware of each other's finds, later archaeologists, when they learned about them, recognized a familiar pattern. Similar burials similarly equipped had been found and mainly forgotten from the time of the first ground-breaking in northern Indiana down to the present. Today, because such finds are much more rare and people tend to place a higher valuation on things historical, comparable accidental discoveries receive wider publicity, and professional prehistorians are sometimes able to complete the job of recovery.

The finds at the Dyer and Peterson sites have been virtually duplicated in northern Illinois and in the southern halves of Michigan and Wisconsin. Given the unfortunate name Red Ocher, from the lavish use of that readily and widely available pigment, other sites of the "culture"—all single burials or small cemeteries—came to be recognized farther afield in Iowa and even near Chillicothe in southern Ohio and at the top of Lake Huron in the Manitoulin District of Ontario. But it was in the contiguous portions of Michigan, Indiana, Illinois, and Wisconsin that the sites proved to be most concentrated.

The Dyer and Peterson sites, similar as they are, have their individual characters. At the first, the flexed skeleton of a man was found in a deep grave intruded into a sand ridge. The grave had probably been dug during the period when Lake Michigan stood at the Algoma stage 4.6 m above its present surface or when it was falling from that level. At this time the site was a high point on the shore of a shallow lake, embayment, or swamp. Found with the human bones were three so-called turkey-tail points or biface blades of distinctive dark flint, a magnificent "ceremonial" biface blade of white flint, a broken flint projectile point, a necklace consisting of 45 thick barrel-shaped to spheroidal copper beads, a square cross-sectioned copper awl, three copper hatchet blades or celts, a faceted lump of galena (lead ore), and an incredibly fine 16 cm (6½ in.) bar amulet of ground slate. The latter object is of uncertain purpose, though it may have been an atlatl weight; it looks like a dowel split lengthwise or a piece of half-round molding, carefully thinned between the center and both ends, and it exhibits a perforation at each end angled through the flat side or base to permit attachment.

It is the turkey-tail blades and the single white-flint ceremonial blade that are the unequivocal clues to the cultural affinities of the Dyer burial. Almost always made of a distinctive bluish-gray nodular chert, an exceptionally fine material sometimes called hornstone, from Harrison County in far southern Indiana, sets of 3 or 4 to even 20 or more turkey-tails are a recurring, though not universal, feature of Red Ocher graves wherever they have been encountered. These are big bifaces with peculiarly broad ellipsoidal blades having remarkably thin and flat cross-sections; the undersized side-notched stem with sides converging to a point resembles the

PLATE 6.4. *Red Ocher Culture white-flint mortuary knife from the Dyer Farm site, Lake County, Indiana. (Shown one-third actual size; measures 48 cm.) (Courtesy James W. VanStone and the Field Museum of Natural History, Chicago.)*

tail of a plucked turkey, hence the name. The Dyer specimens are between 11 cm (4½ in.) and 13.5 cm (5½ in.) long. These readily identifiable artifacts are superbly crafted. Many are so finely executed, in fact, that they were too fragile to have acted as ordinary weapons or implements. This fact, plus their usual recovery from mortuary contexts, must signal a paramount ritual function resolving itself into servicing otherworldly needs. In view of their high workmanship, narrow stylish variation, and the restricted source of the raw material from which they were crafted, similarly restricted authorship is a persuasive conclusion. Notwithstanding the impressive geographical distribution of the finished product, it seems likely that completed artifacts, and not just quarry blanks, were introduced into a distribution network at only one or two places. The latter is implied by occasional recoveries of southern Illinois flint similar to the predominant Harrison County, Indiana, material. Widely dispersed, the turkey-tails eventually exited the distributive network in intimate association with other kinds of things which, in turn, could only have arrived at their final destinations after travel through still other distributive channels converging on the same end points.

The white-flint ceremonial blade discovered at the Dyer site was fully 48 cm (19 in.) long, a masterpiece of flint knapping. Pointed at one end, this long, thick-sectioned, dagger-like blade is tapered to a straight base at the other. Comparable objects, if not so large, have been found at other Red Ocher stations, similarly accompanying caches of turkey-tail blades. As at Dyer, these ceremonial blades usually occur singly and are invariably fashioned out of white flint. At some sites they have been "killed" by breaking.

At the Peterson site, disturbed by cultivation, another form of prominent Red Ocher emblem was emphatically expressed in the presence of at least 320 cache blades. At this and other sites these are typically small (2.5–7.6 cm [1–3 in.] long), broad, ovate-trianguloid, frequently asymmetrical bifaces, pointed at one end and flat to round at the opposite. They are usually thicker and less well made than their Meadowood counterparts. Commonly produced out of a different kind of flint than either the turkey-tails or the white ceremonial blades, the ovate-trianguloid blades have also been found at sites with no known inhumations. In such situations they may have been hoarded as tool blanks intended for future retrieval and finishing. Something like this may also have been intended for those placed in graves, though incorporeal hands in an afterworld similar enough to this to warrant such provisioning would have to do the work.

While no turkey-tails and no white ceremonial blade were found at the Peterson Farm, seven "modified" turkey-tails of the bluish-gray Harrison County hornstone were. These are broad-bladed, barbed, short-stemmed bifaces with rounded bases. Indeed, grouping such artifacts from many Red Ocher sites, it can be seen that they range from almost perfect turkey-

PLATE 6.5. *Red Ocher Culture turkey-tail (left) and stemmed blades of southern Indiana or southern Illinois flint from sites in eastern Wisconsin. (Shown actual size.) (Collections of Department of Anthropology, Lawrence University, Appleton, Wisconsin.)*

tails at one extreme to lobate-stemmed "projectile points" at the other. As at Dyer, the Peterson find included thick rolled copper beads, this time at least 50 in number.

The archaeologists who have been most familiar with the core area of Red Ocher sites around the south half of Lake Michigan eastward to southern Lake Huron have characterized the mortuary complex as comprised of certain major features, several of which are variously combined on most stations, and less distinctive minor traits having spatial representation and associations common to some other cultural groupings as well. The major Red Ocher characteristics are (*a*) flexed (but sometimes cremated and bundled) burials intruded into sandy natural prominences; (*b*) liberal application of red ocher; (*c*) turkey-tails and/or "modified" turkey-tails—usually in groups; (*d*) white ceremonial blades—usually singly; (*e*) caches of up to 400 small ovate-trianguloid blades; (*f*) tubular beads of marine shell from the Atlantic Ocean or Gulf of Mexico; and (*g*) copper in the form of beads (usually) or awls, celts, knives, or projectile points. The less exclusive associations include circular and ovate marine-shell gorgets, birdstones, unworked galena cubes, bar amulets, celts, grooved axes, three-hole rectangular gorgets, and tubular pipes. To this last group may be added rare possible associations of Marion Thick (Vinette 1-like) "Early Woodland" pottery and occasional interments of human remains in burial mounds.

Almost imperceptibly, Red Ocher, including a regional variant in the putative Pomranky complex around Saginaw Bay in eastern Michigan, emerged out of a Late Archaic patrimony sometime around 1500 B.C. or a little after. The latest sites in any way attributable to it fall in the first or second centuries B.C. In the interim other regional and even spatially overlapping Transitional cultures with equally heavy commitments to mortuary ceremonialism came into being. Because they shared many features and appear to intergrade along their frontiers, they are difficult to segregate on other than a few differences in this or that artifact style. The discriminations are real, however, for slight as they are they do show tendencies to sort themselves out in terms of geography, associations, and in a few cases, age. The cultural reality behind these differences is obscure. The so-called Glacial Kame culture, for example, rests its claim to uniqueness mainly on the three-hold sandal-sole gorget of marine shell and the fact that the small cemeteries in which they have been discovered have an overlapping but not coextensive distribution with Red Ocher sites. Additionally, as the name intimates, Glacial Kame burials usually occur in glacial gravel hillocks. Red Ocher in the western Great Lakes and Meadowood in the eastern are similar enough that they must not only have shared some common cultural ancestors, but continuously participated in a diffusional network even wider than the Great Lakes.

Exemplifying the overlapping or interdigitating quality of the Red Ocher and Glacial Kame ranges are the Beake and Doetsch sites, both in Lake

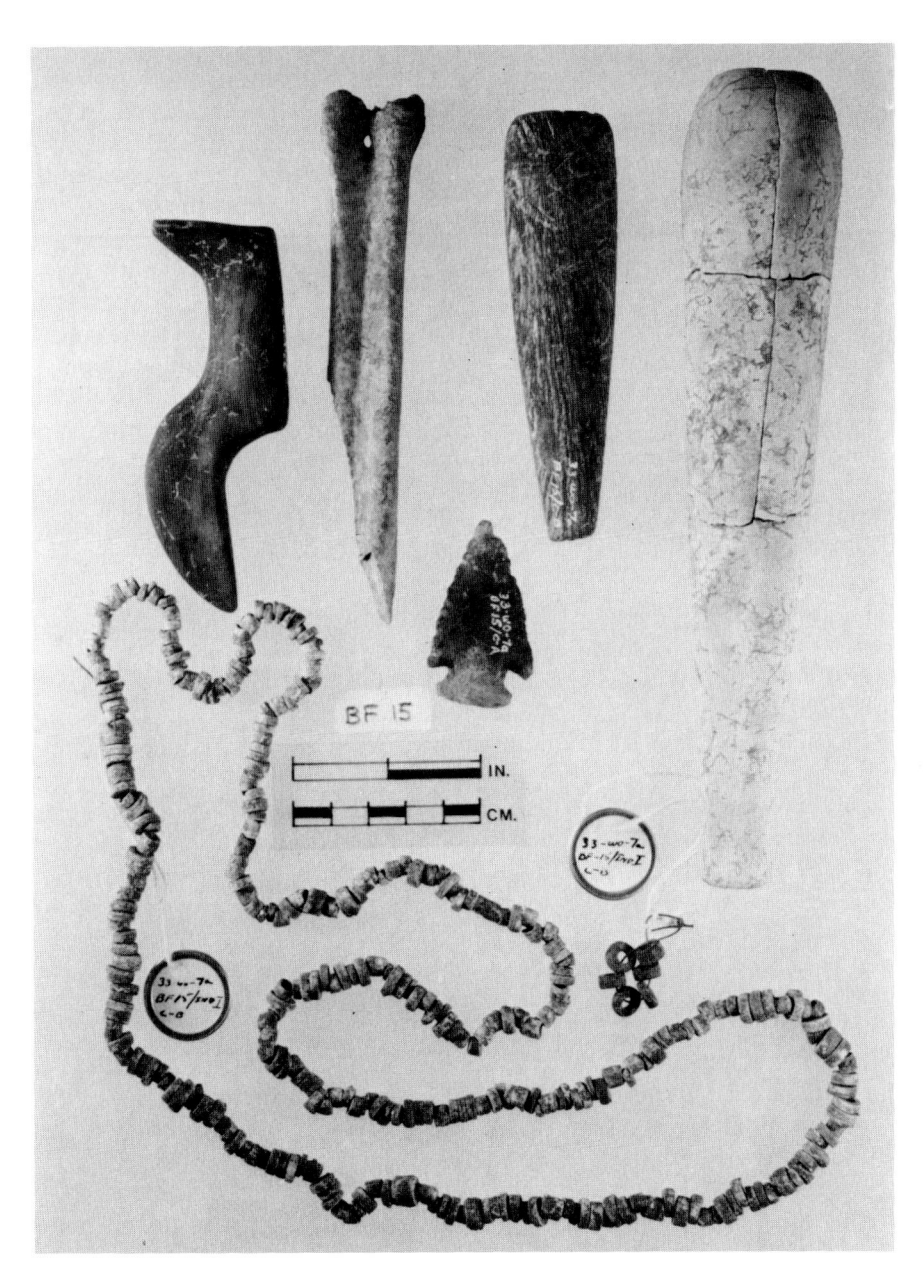

PLATE 6.6. *Artifacts from the Transitional period Williams cremation burial site, Wood County, Ohio: birdstone, bone implement, two tubular stone pipes (top row), flint projectile point (center), and conch-shell beads. (Shown half actual size.) (Courtesy David M. Stothers and the Laboratory of Ethnoarchaeology, University of Toledo, and The Toledo Area Aboriginal Research Society, Inc.)*

Country, Illinois. In the all-too-usual pattern, both sites were discovered by accident and were extensively disturbed by the time archaeologists arrived on the scene. The former locality, on the Des Plaines River, revealed the presence of at least six graves. The cultural signature was provided by the recovery of 23 turkey-tail blades stained with red ocher and a long cream-colored quartzite blade (the familiar solitary white ceremonial blade). The Doetsch site, a commercial gravel pit just a few miles to the south of the Red Ocher site, also yielded evidence of multiple burials, only this time accompanied by two marine-shell sandal-sole gorgets and a handful of beads made from fossil crinoid stems or from native copper.

A site within the northernmost range of Red Ocher, but exhibiting enough attributes not reported in Red Ocher sites to exclude it from such identification, provided another example of the phenomenon of social variation on an underlying cultural theme. The Riverside Cemetery site on the Menominee River a few miles from its mouth on Green Bay, Menominee County, in the upper Michigan peninsula, revealed deep, straight-sided graves intruded into a stabilized sand dune. Many of these showed evidence of poles, probably used in conjunction with sheets of bark, to support tomb walls or roofing. Some of these poles had been burned in place.

The artifacts from a village midden also found at Riverside were overwhelmingly of later types than were found in the cemetery. The latter were associated with flexed, bundle, and partial-cremation burials. Sometimes more than one mode of inhumation occurred in a single grave and often with surviving remnants of bark shrouds. Red-ocher treatment of graves and their contents was invariable. Grave goods were numerous. They included small to big stacks of cache blades of southern Indiana flint as well as long, lobate-stemmed points of the same material. The blades are not like typical Red Ocher cache blades, but are long, beautifully fashioned, and bipointed. One cache made up of 110 blades was radically divergent, however, the constituent blades being short and broad and ovate to tearshaped. Many of the blades in funerary caches had been "killed." While no turkey-tail blades turned up at Riverside, some projectile points resemble the "modified" turkey-tails from Red Ocher sites farther south. Still other projectile points resemble Adena "beaver-tails." There are also a few corner-notched and side-notched points and some tanged points having wide, barbed blades.

Objects of copper were common in the Riverside Cemetery graves, not in itself surprising in view of age considerations and nearness to the sources of that metal. They embraced tubular, barrel-shaped, and globular beads worn as necklaces and sewn on garments; awls; celts; tanged socketed, tanged with spurred base, and "ace of spades" projectile points; and crescents. One of the latter bore traces of having been mounted on a "slingshot," or Y-shaped handle. In a number of instances copper salts had impregnated and helped preserve fragments of bark, woven fabrics, and wooden tool handles. Some of the graves also contained beaver-teeth chisels and knives, ear ornaments of moose teeth, and marine-shell beads. Unusual grave accompaniments were a perforated "shaft straightener" made of caribou antler and what must be the most ancient example of obsidian in eastern North America. The big block of dark volcanic glass was somehow imported from northwestern Wyoming!

Although one grave was radiocarbon dated to approximately 1100 B.C. and may in face represent an Old Copper culture feature later surrounded by the interments of a descendent population, a battery of dates from the other graves testifies that the cemetery had been mainly in use between 500 B.C. and the end of the first century B.C. These dates fall within the late portion of the Transitional period. Because of its attenuated Red Ocher and Old Copper appearance, the idiosyncratic qualities of the Riverside Cemetery site are eloquent testimony to the somewhat arbitrary nature of some of the "cultures" of the period. An enriching interpenetration of regional groups is without question shown by these few but cogent signs.

The Leimbach Culture

As the Frost Island, Meadowood, and Leimbach cultures witness, not all sites of the Transitional period are burial sites nor all the "cultures" mortuary complexes.

Just east of Cleveland, on the bank of Big Creek in Lake County, Ohio, a tributary of the Lake Erie-bound Grand River, is the Girdled Road site. This modest fragment of prehistory is of little intrinsic consequence. Consisting of a thin, discontinuous spread of unimpressive cultural residue beneath 30–60 m of loam, and revealed within an area only 4.6 × 6 m, the site had once been somewhat larger before the creek and rain and modern land use had cut into and carried away its flank and eroded and reburied its face. The Girdled Road site hardly deserves notice except that it is a representative of the great majority of surviving Great Lakes sites: small, inconspicuous, badly reduced by natural and cultural agencies, seemingly reflective of short-term limited purpose—the kind of archaeological shadow that it is tempting to ignore when there are other richer, more internally informative sites still awaiting excavation. In just the lake counties of Ohio alone there are uncounted numbers of such sites as yet undiscovered or largely surviving in farmers' and antiquity collectors' cigar boxes or in financially undernourished county or municipal historical-society museums. Too infrequently, such unprepossessing collections are cataloged or are otherwise accompanied by accurate provenience information. Yet such sites sometimes yield insights into prehistoric behavior not derivable from the larger or more famous ones. And taken

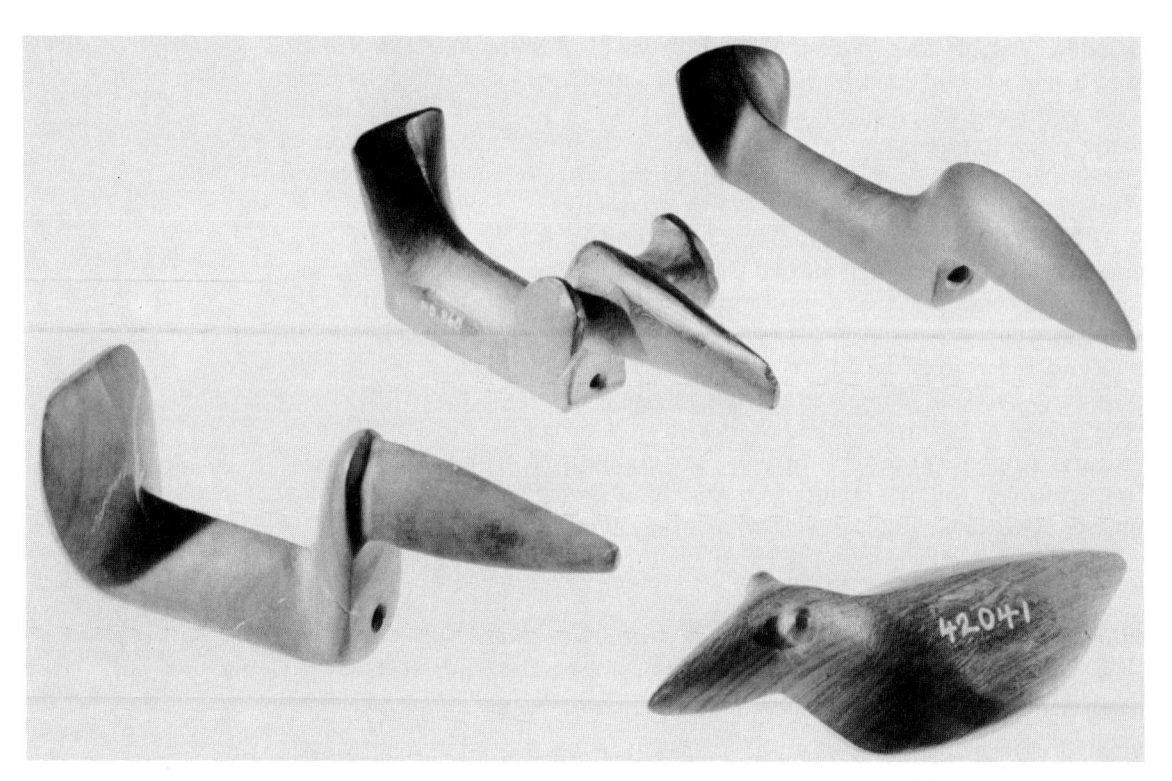

PLATE 6.7. *Ground-slate birdstones from Transitional period sites in southern Ontario. (Shown approximately two-thirds actual size.) (Courtesy Peter L. Storck and the Royal Ontario Museum, Toronto, Canada.)*

together they take on an informational value difficult to anticipate from knowledge of just one or a few.

All that the Girdled Road site produced were two handfuls of waste flakes left over from the finishing or resharpening of tools (they had been made elsewhere), three stemmed projectile points, two bifacial knives, a big bifacial side-scraper, a slate or shale celt, and two rolled copper beads. No graves or pits or other features were recovered. Only the projectile points proved especially distinctive, pointing unequivocally to sometime in the middle to late first millennium B.C. These are broad-bladed specimens with slightly to moderately instepped stems tapering to a straight, truncated base; they are like Cresap points from farther south and in West Virginia. Such projectile points are common at sites of the Adena culture in the Ohio Valley and, closer to home, in so-called Leimbach "phase" sites in northern Ohio. These are the regional expressions of "Early Woodland" Transitional culture in their respective areas.

The two bifacial knives, one ovate, the other pear-shaped, resemble some of the "Adena leaf-shaped" blades also common on Adena and

Leimbach sites. These and the side-scraper, celt, and copper beads are much less distinctively "Early Woodland" than the projectile points, though they are fully if not exclusively compatible with such ascription. The interpretation of the Girdled Road site as a short-term single-occupancy one belonging to the Leimbach culture is a reasonable one. It may have been a hunting camp, though its eroded state must preclude certainty. When compared with the longer term occupancy and multiple functioning of the Leimbach site itself, type locality of the culture or "phase," the Girdled Road site is particularly valuable in revealing how different in size, complexity, structure, and content two approximately coetaneous sites assignable to a common culture can be.

The Leimbach site lies on the other side of Cleveland on the Vermilion River in Lorain County, Ohio. This is a multiple-hectare site extending over a spur in the steep-sided river valley. Portions of relatively undisturbed village midden were detected here, replete with pits, hearths, scatters of fire-cracked rocks, house-floor outlines, and special-purpose activity areas indicating prolonged use by sizable groups of families, probably in the summer and fall. Defensive earthworks and log palisades attributed to the Leimbach culture occupation more likely belong much later in time and should probably be ascribed to a Late Woodland component also present at the site.

In addition to everything found at the Girdled Road site, Leimbach yielded far more in variety as well as in quantity. At Leimbach and similar sites more variable stemmed points were retrieved in addition to stemmed scrapers and stemmed and expanded-base drills, bifaced knives, and edge-trimmed flakes. Ground and polished stone artifacts were well represented by small celts, three-quarter-grooved axes, polished hematite cones, perforated sandstone discs, blocked-end tubular smoking pipes of Ohio fireclay or pipestone, and polished tubes of Ohio pipestone which may have been employed as medicine-man's sucking pipes or, as some archaeologists have suggested, as atlatl grips. A great deal of pottery was found. Some of this is similar to that found on the earliest pottery-bearing sites elsewhere in northeastern North America, though there is more of it than is typical on such sites, and there is also somewhat greater variety. In fact, four kinds of pottery have been unearthed at this and some other sites of the Leimbach culture. But the differences are hardly great.

"Leimbach Thick" is the name given a variety of earthenware survived by potsherds having thick cross-sections, incorporating many large pieces of grit temper, and exhibiting coarse cordmaking, sometimes partly smoothed, on exterior surfaces. Fashioned by coiling a rope of clay into the desired shape and then paddling the surfaces to obliterate and bind the conjoined coils, the resulting pots were bowl-shaped with rounded to semicoidal bases and with slightly inverted to moderately outsloping rims, or were shaped somewhat like flower pots and had flat bottoms; some

PLATE 6.8. *Rimsherds of the pottery type Leimbach Thick from the Leimbach site, Lorain County, Ohio. (Shown actual size.) (Courtesy Orrin C. Shane III, The Science Museum of Minnesota, St. Paul.)*

were provided with lugs. Excepting an absence of interior cordmarking, Leimbach Thick resembles Marion Thick, Fayette Thick, Vinette 1, and the other sectional versions of the most ancient pottery in the Northeast. In fact, small quantities of true Fayette Thick sherds were also present, constituting a second variety. A third type of Leimbach culture pottery, Leimbach Cordmarked, is much finer than the first and second, being only half as thick. It is tempered with finer grit particles or with sand, and is altogether a more carefully made, better fired, and harder ware. Nevertheless, it was clearly associated with the cruder-looking pottery and was contemporaneous. Likewise recovered was a fourth, unnamed, thin, sand-tempered, plain pottery similar to "Adena Plain" ceramics found in many Adena sites in southern Ohio, West Virginia, and Kentucky.

As mentioned earlier, the Leimbach site is one of the most ancient localities in the Great Lakes which has preserved evidence of agriculture, albeit of probably the most marginal type. The presence of squash seeds at this place and also at the Schultz site in Michigan has been independently dated by radiocarbon assay to the sixth century B.C. Such evidence is so sparce and so susceptible of escaping recovery, if it survives at all, that prehistorians are well advised to consider that Transitional period farming was probably more widespread and perhaps more important than present meager evidence has suggested. Even so, it doubtless was supplemental rather than equally reliable compared with the nutritional returns from

PLATE 6.9. *Stemmed Leimbach Phase projectile points from the Leimbach site, Lorain County, Ohio. (Shown actual size.) (Courtesy Orrin C. Shane III, The Science Museum of Minnesota, St. Paul.)*

hunting, fishing, and the collecting of wild vegetable foods. The latter enterprise is amply confirmed by recoveries of the seeds of raspberries, strawberries, goosefoot, grape, and ragweed, and the remains of hazelnuts, acorns, and hickory, butternut, and walnut shells. Perhaps the overriding significance of the apparently intrusive beginnings of food production in the Great Lakes was not its subsistence potential, which initially could only have been marginal, but that it signals the insinuation of foreign influence, ultimately of Mesoamerican origin. And though a testable answer will prove illusive, the question must be posed: What other things, customs, practices, or ideas diffused along with early agriculture? A small door had been opened on a larger world. What else came through that door?

While the Leimbach site, and with it the Leimbach culture or "phase," has been dubbed the Adena culture of northern Ohio, it seems best to avoid extending that already overburdened name in this way and to simply regard the Leimbach culture as one of the regional manifestations of the far-flung, though interrelated, cultural phenomena differentially expressed in the other cultures considered in this chapter. Certainly, like Middlesex, Leimbach lacks many of the specific attributes of its Adena relative.

The other most convincing evidence of nascent farming communities in the Great Lakes is the aforementioned Schultz, or Green Point, site southwest of Saginaw Bay in Saginaw County, Michigan. In this stratified multicomponent station, the remains of an occupation very similar to that just described for the Leimbach site was uncovered and radiocarbon dated to around 530 B.C. Squash seeds were recovered among much more numerous fragments of butternuts, walnuts, hickory nuts, and other indications of plant collecting. Bone refuse attests the importance of hunting and fishing. The site was located in the old Shiawassee Bay region which had been largely drained when Lake Huron fell from its Algoma stage level. But vast tracts of swampy lowlands interfingering with higher ground associated with the relic shorelines made for a rich biotic zone. Attempts to relate the Schultz and some other Saginaw County sites to a single community sequentially occupying seasonally advantageous locations in a multiple resource subsistence round, while plausible, have fallen far short of demonstration. Schultz has been nominated as the winter camp in this schedule, so the squash seeds were presumably the product of the same people at one of the other sites. Significantly, all of the abundant nuts would have been gathered in the autumn; if not consumed as gathered, they would have constituted a welcome store for winter use.

The Schultz site, like Leimbach, has provided archaeologists with one of the best samples of early pottery in the lakes country. Much of this Schultz pottery is very similar to the Ohio material. Some flat-bottomed vessels, however, typically bear cordmarking on interior as well as exterior sur-

PLATE 6.10. Schultz Thick interior-exterior cordmarked potsherds from the Schultz site, Saginaw County, Michigan. Note lugs *C* and *D*. (Shown two-thirds actual size.) (Courtesy Richard I. Ford and the Museum of Anthropology, University of Michigan, Ann Arbor.)

faces, this latter attribute, though not the former, more closely recalling Vinette 1 ceramics to the east.

Similarly, many of the stone tools at Schultz are similar to Leimbach examples and supply further evidence of not simply contemporaneity, but of relatedness. Most of the projectile points are broad-bladed and stemmed and have a tendency to rounded shoulders; some are lobate stemmed. Common are drills fabricated on broken projectile points; round-based, pointed, ovate bifaces; end-scrapers; utilized flake knives and side-scrapers; and a variety of cores and flakes indicative of on-site tool manufacture and not just trimming and resharpening. Bone artifacts were rare, being virtually confined to a few conical points, awls, flaking tools, long side-scrapers or beamers, and some animal-teeth chisels. Many of these tools were discovered concentrated with waste flakes, bone refuse, and fire-cracked rocks around several loci, each consisting of a large postmold and associated pits. These probably record the one-time presence of tents, wickiups, or lean-tos.

Again, but for the recovery of a few squash seeds, the presence of potsherds, and the projectile-point styles, the Schultz site is not markedly different from many a Late Archaic station. Obviously, important changes were taking place—but they were taking place slowly and with less than profound impact on the daily life of the average person. It was the accumulation of change that mattered in the end, and the lowly inhabitants of the Schultz site or the Leimbach site could hardly have speculated how, had they ever been disposed to make the attempt.

Red Ocher, Glacial Kame, Meadowood, Leimbach, and so on should probably be thought of as reflecting in their respective domains the traditional interactions of innumerable small societies sharing a fundamental heritage and mutually influencing neighboring societies more obviously than remoter ones. Certain themes, especially ritual ones, presumably because they were satisfying and proved adaptive, came to be interwoven among these societies. They have partially escaped oblivion because of their cultural shreds and tatters. Once recognized in one locale, the others have a kindred look.

While archaeologists have understandably been preoccupied with the burial practices as reflective of religious ideas, it is the ethnographically generated proposition that ritual and ceremony minister to the needs of the living, whatever their efficacy in the concerns of the dead, that promises some understanding. Providing for the deceased is a time-honored way of pulling together the survivors—and not just with reference to psychological support in time of need. Usually involving the presentation of gifts, especially ones of nonlocal origin or material which could only be procured through dealings with other societies, elaborating mortuary ritual can also be a subtle and, perhaps for that reason, a more efficient means for the extension or reinforcement of alliances among people who otherwise have it in their power to hurt one another. This was certainly a latent function of the celebrated Feast of the Dead among the historically known Hurons and northern Algonquians. Given the likelihood of increasing populations and growing preoccupation with locally or regionally bounded resources, trends bequeathed by their Late Archaic progenitors, and unknown additional factors possibly connected with the introduction of food production and pottery making, a not unexpected consequence would be the fostering of mutually beneficial relations among select Transitional period societies. Need of such relations is further implied by the defensive arrangements revealed at some of the sites of the Leimbach culture. Because outsiders are potential enemies, undertakings in their direction must be structured in unalarming ways, that is, by indirection. It is thus likely that the cache blades and other paraphernalia of obvious funerary ritual were also components of more imperative social relations, the former, ironically, merely being what has by its very nature proved less susceptible of destruction with the passage of time.

Some Transitional period societies held aloof from innovation and clung to the Archaic pattern of living, thus carrying it forward into times uncharacteristic of it. Particularly was this so along the northern reaches of the Upper Great Lakes. Other Transitional societies were transitional in fact as well as in time; they were the foreshadowings of later and larger, more complex things. For the former societies the period was a bridge to a later time, for the others, to a new age.

References

On the introduction and development of plant domestication:
Asch and Asch 1977; Chomko and Crawford 1978; Munson 1973; Struever and Vickery 1973; Watson, editor, 1974; Yarnell 1976.

On the Archaic–Woodland transition in and near the Great Lakes:
Fitting and Brose 1970; Griffin 1952; Ritchie 1955; Ritchie and Funk 1973 (especially "The Transitional Stage" and "The Early Woodland Stage"); Stoltman 1978; Tuck 1978a.

On the Frost Island culture:
Ritchie 1969 (especially Chapter III: "The Transitional Stage—From Stone Pots to Early Ceramics (c. 1300–1000 B.C.)"); Ritchie and Funk 1973 (especially "The O'Neil Site (Wpt. 11-4)").

On the Meadowood and Middlesex cultures:
Granger 1978; Ritchie 1944 (pp. 186–201), 1955, 1969 (especially Chapter IV: "The Woodland Stage—Development of Ceramics, Agriculture and Village Life (c. 1000 B.C.–A.D. 1600)," particularly "The Meadowood Phase," pp. 178–200, and the

"Middlesex Phase," pp. 200–203); Ritchie and Dragoo 1960; Ritchie and Funk 1973 (especially "The Scaccia Site (Cda 17-3)"); Spence, Williamson, and Dawkins 1978.

On the Red Ocher and Glacial Kame cultures:
Cunningham 1948; Faulkner 1960; Quimby 1960a and 1960b (especially Chapter 6: "Boreal Archaic Culture from 5000 to 500 B.C.," and Chapter 8: "Burial Mounds and Pottery, 500 to 100 B.C."); Ritzenthaler and Quimby 1962; Young, Wenner, and Bluhm 1961.

On the Riverside Cemetery site, Michigan:
Hruska 1967.

On the Leimbach culture and the Leimbach site, Ohio:
Brose 1971; Shane 1967.

On the Girdled Road Site, Ohio:
Brose 1971.

On the Schultz site, Michigan:
Fitting, editor, 1972; H. T. Wright 1964.

The Middle Woodland Period
Circa 200 B.C.–A.D. 500

7

It is a characteristic of myths that they are apt to hang on long after their useful lives are over. One such myth was born on the trail when frontiersmen from the English colonies climbed the Appalachian barrier and descended into the Ohio Valley. Here in the continental interior below the Great Lakes they discovered amazing circular and serpentine earthworks and enormous artificial mounds. Impressive notwithstanding the obscuring forest growing over them, and thus evidently of appreciable age, the mysterious structures stood in mute testimony to a level of cultural attainment the European visitors could not discern in the trading post and fort-hangers-on Indians they were familiar with on the Atlantic side of the mountains. And the tribes encountered in the Ohio country seemed to have little interest in such antiquities and less knowledge. None of their members built such things and neither had their remembered ancestors. The number and colossal size of many of the earthworks, and the surveying and engineering skills they must have demanded for their construction, fired the imaginations of the more philosophically inclined newcomers. The "Mound Builder" myth was born. Among the myth's several permutations, the earthworks were ascribed to an unknown and disappeared race whose members were wiped out or who lost their genius through intermarriage with the later Indians. Or the earthworks had been constructed by ancient Egyptians, Phoenicians, or wandering Israelites. Or, as the most recent revisions proclaim, they were the work of pre-Columbian Irish monks or Basques or Libyans or even ancient astronauts on a civilizing visit from another planet—almost anybody but Indians.

Thomas Jefferson, in overseeing the first systematic excavation of a mound in Virginia, believed that it had probably been built by prehistoric Indians, though he thought that there might be something to the idea that one of the Lost Tribes of Israel might have wandered for a while in America. He instructed Meriwether Lewis and William Clark on their historic expedition to be alert to any linguistic, social, or other clues which might bear on this romantic possibility as they made their way up the Missouri River into the lands of the remoter Indian tribes. The explorer captains, it may be assumed, had their hopes, too, but they proved to be keen and honest observers.

As archaeologists and other adherents to the canons of historical and scientific evidence have now long known, the Ohio Valley burial mounds and other ceremonial earthworks were, indeed, the creations of prehistoric American Indians. The most important of these topographic sculptors were the people identified with the Adena and, particularly, the Hopewell, cultures. The latter and the much later Mississippian culture are fairly regarded as marking the most materially elaborate, socially intricate, and ideologically complex of any of the indigenous cultures of eastern North America. So impressive was the Hopewell cultural achievement and so far-flung its influence that it has come to symbolize for many people the Middle Woodland period to which it is dated. In fact, before the advent of radiocarbon dating, which places the Middle Woodland period between approximately 200 B.C. and A.D. 500, the degree of similarity of non-Hopewell cultures to the Hopewell culture itself was the litmus test of Middle Woodland status. This is still one of the best tests though it is now evident that there was more to the Middle Woodland period than Hopewell and that there were contemporaneous cultures whose remains exhibit little or no evidence of contact with that famous period archetype. While it is not a Great Lakes culture, some understanding of Hopewell is indispensable to any appreciation of the distribution and significance of related or influenced groups in the lakes country.

Besides the celebrated earthworks, Hopewell has become known for many of its distinctive products which had their nexus in other than mundane activities: sometimes superlative ceramic vessels of a technical competence never achieved before or later; superbly crafted stone effigy platform pipes with a curious conjunction of naturalistic anatomical fidelity and conventionalization—owls, frogs, dogs, a magnificent black beaver with inlaid mother-of-pearl eyes and real beaver incisor teeth, an otter holding a fish in its lethal mouth, a raven with inset pearls as eyes—the finest such pipes being among the most splendid artistic accomplishments of pre-civilized peoples anywhere in the world; raptorial bird feet or talons or geometric cut-out figures of mica or sheet copper; work in copper, meteoric iron, and even (rarely) silver and gold; the importation of exotic materials from far-off places such as marine shells, sharks' teeth, and barricuda jaws from the Atlantic Ocean or Gulf of Mexico, mica from the Carolinas, galena from Illinois and Missouri, fossiliferous flint from North Dakota and Manitoba, copper from Wisconsin and Michigan, and obsidian from Wyoming; cymbal-shaped ear ornaments; copper and silver covered panpipes; ceramic human figurines; pearl beads; incredibly cut and polished upper and lower jaws of humans, wolves, bears, bobcats, and other animals; finely knapped flint blades struck from specially prepared cores; magnificent ceremonial biface blades; sets of exquisitely matched flint projectile points; perforated bear canines and other animal teeth inlaid with pearls. These and other items are best known from tomb burials of high-status persons in the mounds, though examples have also been found in village sites. On the later sites, however, less aesthetically arresting artifacts predominate, things made in the household for everyday use rather than for show or ceremony. Because the fine Hopewell "ceremonial" artifacts are often virtually identical over wide areas, whereas the usual things recovered from living sites much more strongly express local materials, styles, and traditions, and because the latter far outnumber the former, it appears that the quintessentially Hopewell products in some sense represent something extrinsic and special: a cultural overlay on several otherwise different local and regional "folk" cultures.

The principal centers of Hopewell development were outside the Great Lakes in southern Ohio and in the central and lower Illinois River valley in Illinois. In Ohio the "base culture" associated with the Hopewell material has been called Scioto after the Ohio River tributary on whose banks are located many of the great Middle Woodland sites. Havana is used with reference to the quite different Illinois Valley "base" or "folk" culture. Away from these areas archaeologists have located local or regional contemporaneous cultures, important aspects of which resemble the archetypal Ohio and Illinois discoveries. These are generally referred to as Hopewellian, their similarities to Hopewell being ascribed to not simply trade but in some sense an identification with or participation in the affairs of the Hopewell culture. The precise nature of those affairs is a matter of considerable debate among prehistorians. It is characteristic of the Hopewellian groups that they exhibit fewer varieties and lesser amounts of Hopewell-style artifacts and that they sometimes yield their own homemade copies of the prestigious originals. They often also reveal parochial interpretations of the Scioto or Havana styles. Typically, the Hopewellian cultures bear the unmistakable imprints of in-place developmental continuity with local forebears, the Hopewellian attributes being adopted directly or in round-about ways from the Ohio or Illinois country. In some cases it is also possible that certain correspondences were as much indigenous to the Hopewellian cultures as to Hopewell, their Hopewell identification being due to more complex development in that milieu.

The Great Lakes Hopewellian cultures are the so-called Waukesha

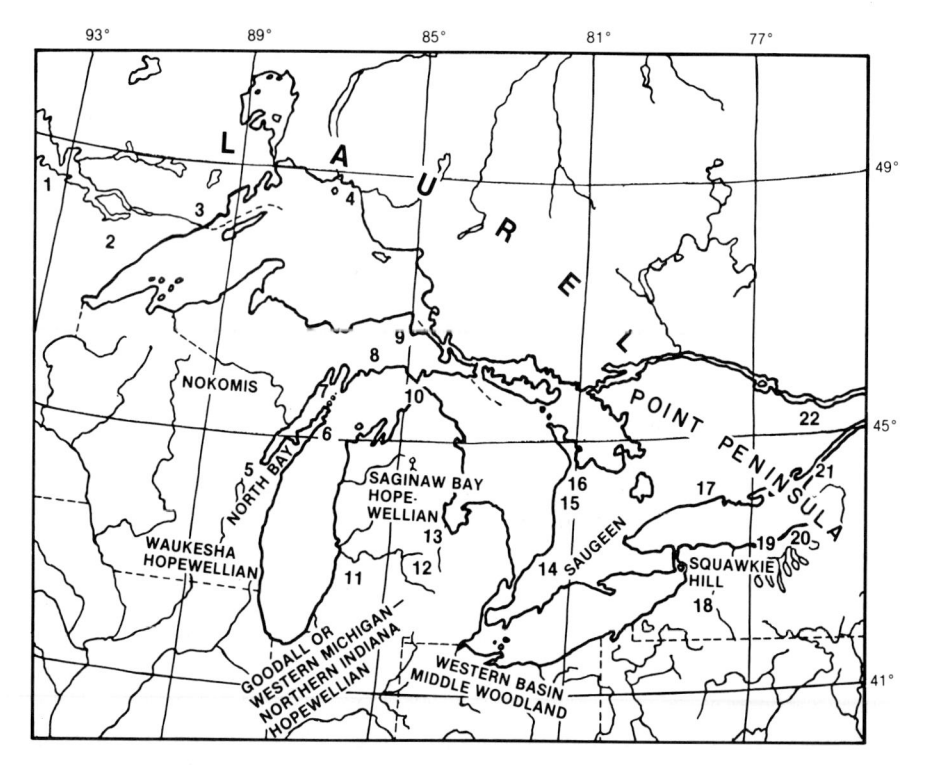

MAP 7.1. *Middle Woodland cultures and sites (numbered) mentioned in the text: (1) McKinstry and Smith Mounds sites; (2) Pike Bay; (3) Macgillvray and McCluskey; (4) Heron Bay; (5) Lawton; (6) Mero, Porte des Morts, Richter, and Rock Island II; (7) Summer Island; (8) Ekdahl–Goudreau; (9) Naomikong Point; (10) Fort Michilimackinac; (11) Norton Mound Group; (12) Bussinger and Schultz; (13) Kantzler; (14) Burley; (15) Inverhuron–Lucas; (16) Donaldson and Thede; (17) LeVesconte Mound and Serpent Mounds (Rice Lake); (18) Squawkie Hill; (19) Kipp Island; (20) Vinette; (21) Canoe Point; and (22) Constance Bay No. 1.*

"focus" in southeastern Wisconsin, the northwestern Indiana and Michigan phase or phases, and the western New York Squawkie Hill phase. Individual Hopewellian artifacts and examples of Hopewellian-style aesthetic concepts are somewhat more broadly distributed, sometimes occurring in quite foreign contexts. The Great Lakes Hopewellian manifestations appear to reflect in their site distributions rather clear-cut ecological adaptations, those at the south end of Lake Michigan and eastward to Lake Huron's Saginaw Bay being in the Illinoian and Carolinian biotic provinces or their ecotones, those south of western Lake Ontario being in the Carolinian. This generous east–west apportionment constitutes the "southern tier" of Great Lakes Middle Woodland cultures. In the case of the Hopewellian communities of southwestern Michigan and northwestern

Indiana, it is likely that there was an actual migration of Hopewell culture-bearers from Illinois, that they intermarried with the local natives with whom they had probably traded previously and had established reciprocally advantageous social relations, and that it was their immediate descendents who produced the Hopewellian culture peculiar to that locale.

The cause or causes of the Hopewell efflorescence are not understood, nor is the nature of the social institutions signified by the physical trappings that have survived their denouement. Some authorities have argued that a productive agriculture generated the economic wherewithal to underwrite the impressive cultural accomplishments, and they point to the recovery of corn in a number of Hopewell sites and the known presence of squash in some earlier ones. Such retrievals are few and far between,

PLATE 7.1. *Hopewellian vessel from western Michigan. (Shown approximately one-half actual size.) (Courtesy James W. VanStone and the Field Museum of Natural History, Chicago.)*

PLATE 7.2. *Hopewellian vessel from Western Michigan. (Shown approximately one-half actual size.) (Courtesy James W. VanStone and the Field Museum of Natural History, Chicago.)*

however. They are much less noteworthy than in the succeeding period. The intensive harvesting of wild or quasi-domesticated crops in riverine mud flats has also been put forward as a significant enabling factor and likewise has received only modest support from field investigations. The notion that Hopewell represents simply the culmination of a long and slowly increasing efficiency in exploiting the natural resources of the environment has been championed by those prehistorians least impressed with the available evidences of Hopewell farming. As pointed out in the last chapter, however, marginal agriculture by its very nature may be difficult to detect in archaeological deposits. It may be that Hopewell agriculture was somewhat more extensive and important than the surviving empirical records suggest and that, coupled with hunting and gathering in a richly productive biological environment, it helped make possible the other achievements which so impress us today. At any rate, it seems significant that across so expansive a front none of the Hopewellian cultures adopted an abode in the Canadian, let alone the Hudsonian, Biotic Province. The Lake Forest Middle Woodland cultures to be described in the following pages cannot be classified as Hopewellian.

Apart from the problem of the subsistence base is that of the meaning of the panpipes, earspools, platform pipes. mica cut-outs, the fine "ceremonial" ware, and the other Hopewell paraphernalia. Hopewell has been envisioned as a dominant society whose broad cultural, if not political, hegemony is mirrored in the scatter of the distinctive artifacts. Hopewell has also been thought of as a great religious movement, the climax of the religious and mortuary ceremonialism developing since the Late Archaic period, with the mound building and esoteric things being ecclesiastical symbols ("high church" trappings according to one wag). Like Islam or Christianity, Hopewell might have been a proselytizing movement. Such an interpretation, however, overstresses the occurrence of Hopewell artifacts in burial contexts, underestimates their occurrence in village middens where they are not as apt to be well preserved, and fails to account for the extensive exchange network in exotic goods and materials oftentimes translated into vernacular objects. Another suggestion is that Hopewell was a vast trading enterprise controlled by Illinois or Ohio entrepreneurs, a sort of prototype North American multinational corporation.

More anthropologically sound is the proposal that within the Hopewell "heartland," and in conformity with long-term trends, more complex forms of social integration had evolved by Middle Woodland times and that petty chiefdoms and a hierarchically organized society of ascriptively high- and low-ranked persons had by now eclipsed the more ancient and more egalitarian tribes. Monumental architecture (in this case mounds and geometric earth embankments) is a frequent accompaniment of chiefdoms. Similarly, and accredited to the Hopewell culture through excavation, are such other criteria as fairly large-scale labor mobilization for communal projects; increased craft specialization; economic diversification of community functions, perhaps overseen and coordinated by a paramount leader who "finances" all of this through the redistribution of resources via an interlocking mechanism of gift exchanges, feasts, and public ceremonies; increased demand for rare and unusual things from afar; ritual exchange among chiefs representing widely separated districts of high-prestige items (including sons and daughters and sisters in marriage); and disparities among persons in social rank—signified in life by differences in dress, codes of etiquette, deferential or subordinate behavior, and other contrivances, and in death by status-reflecting divergences in burial mode and location and in quantities, qualities, and varieties of associated grave offerings.

Certain aspects of some or all of the proffered interpretations of the essential nature of Hopewell culture have been brought together under the covering title "Hopewellian Interaction Sphere." While each archaeologist seems to have his own idea of what that institution was, it is generally agreed that it does relate to a higher and more complicated kind of society in Illinois and Ohio than had existed there before, that the social order was doubtless supported by ceremonial rationalization, and that the fancy ways of the Hopewell people and their expanding interest in and demand for new and exotic things drew many outside ethnic groups into interaction with them. In some instances this interaction may well have taken the form of political alliances, in others of the growth of sharing in a common value system, in still others of trade relations facilitated by diplomacy and ceremonial gift giving among proudly independent societies with significantly autonomous cultural inheritances. As in the case of the earlier acquisition of Adena products by the people of the Middlesex culture, it is highly probable that major reinterpretations of the symbolic freight and the social role of some of the diagnostic Hopewell artifacts accompanied their insertion into the Hopewellian provinces. A particular casualty in the Great Lakes societies must have been whatever precise status-grading functions they may once have served in the more elaborate conditions of their genesis. External forms may have been mimicked in naive emulation of the far-off but prestigious southerners. A coronet on a bumpkin's head is a hat.

The Great Lakes Southern Tier: Hopewellian Middle Woodland Cultures

WESTERN MICHIGAN HOPEWELLIAN

The two most important Hopewellian precincts in Michigan are on streams tributary to Lake Michigan in the southwest part of the state south of the Muskegon River, and across the central part of the lower peninsula in the Saginaw basin. A major site in the former territory, and the one best reported, is the Norton Mound Group. Its component structures were raised sometime during the first two centuries A.D. Located near Grand Rapids in Kent County, the group consists of 17 more or less conical burial mounds constructed on a slight rise of ground in the valley of the Grand River. The 3 largest mounds are in a line parallel to the river's course while the 14 somewhat smaller mounds are aligned in a rough arc behind them. Although most of the Norton mounds are between 10.5 and 18 m in diameter and vary in height from 1.2 to not quite 3 m, the smallest is under .6 m high; the largest mound, on the other hand, is 4.8 m high and is 30.5 m in diameter. By Ohio Valley standards these are unremarkable, if not picayune. Nevertheless, they are the result of a lot of work.

Excavation revealed different colored soils making up much of the internal structure of the mounds. That is, distinct splotches or lenses of soils preserved the original character of individual loads of dirt that had been dumped in the process of raising the mounds. Careful dissection of these splotches indicated that each consisted on the average of about 11 kg of dirt, or one basketload. The archaeologists who directed the excavations of the Norton mounds were able to calculate that the biggest mound contained approximately a half-million basketloads. Given the compatible soil characteristics in the immediate vicinity of the mounds and the likelihood that people would naturally have preferred to minimize brute labor, it was assumed that the tumuli had been built up of loads garnered within about 270 m of construction. Assuming also that it had taken a full 7 months to build (the minimum figure for frost-free ground conditions), 120 people, each scraping together and bringing in a moderate average of 23 kg of soil daily (20 full basketloads), could easily have done the job. This estimate makes no allowance for the mound floor preparation or for the actual ceremonies surrounding the interments, of course, and it takes for granted that there were supporting personnel to hunt and otherwise tend the community's logistics. Obviously, fewer hands or a more leisurely pace would have required a longer time; more people or greater compulsion would have hurried things up. But the estimate does provide a reasonable idea of the magnitude of the task and of its importance to the people who labored to perform it.

Where a mound was to be erected, the sod, topsoil, and some of the underlying ground were scraped away, presenting a fresh base or floor for the construction. In most cases a rectangular subfloor pit was dug as a burial crypt. In the largest mound a prepared rectangular floor of yellow silt substituted for the pit. Usually an earth ramp was heaped up encircling the mortuary area, with slabs of bark used as facing. After the burials and tomb offerings had been put in place, the mortuary was covered with bark, woven rush mats, or animal skins, which were secured in place by large pins fashioned from the lower limb bones (specialized elongated toe bones) of deer and elk; and the building up of the mound commenced.

It is evident that the people placed in the mounds had died long enough before their final deposition to have undergone some kind of preliminary and temporary treatment. Bundle burials were most frequent. Articulated as well as re-articulated skeletons in extended position on the back were also well represented. Many exhibited signs of disarticulation or dismemberment and, in the case of some of the extended skeletons, attempts to rearrange the bones in approximate anatomical order. Bones of hands and feet and of the torso were commonly totally missing. Bodies of the de-

PLATE 7.3. *Mound H at the Hopewellian Norton Mound Group, Kent County, Michigan, before excavation. (Courtesy Richard I. Ford and the Museum of Anthropology, University of Michigan, Ann Arbor.)*

ceased must have been intentionally exposed to the elements, temporarily buried, placed on a scaffold, or otherwise "stored" until the time appropriate for permanent interment. Perhaps family, lineage, or community dead who had succumbed during the long winter months were somehow kept until spring or summer and then disposed of in a collective ritual. Discounting plundered mounds for which accurate information is lacking, the number of individuals interred in the Norton mounds ranged from 5 to 18. In several mounds one of the skeletons would be in a more complete or otherwise better condition than any of the others. The excavators suggested that these individuals were the most recently deceased of all the burials in any particular mound and that it had been their demise and funeral which had stimulated the burials of the other dead and the construction of the associated mounds.

That men and children were more commonly represented among the Norton mound burials than were women suggests sex-linked prestige differences. Obviously, many more people must have been buried elsewhere without benefit of mound interment. It is hard to avoid the conclusion that some kind of social ranking is implicit in such differences and that it was in some sense senior kin-group members (of patrilineages?), together with their favorite children, who were placed in the mounds. Artificial cranial deformation was also common among this segment of the population and may be another sign of exalted status. Another important feature of these crania is the presence of a deliberate postmortem perforation, invariably on the left side toward the back. It has been suggested that this may have related to ideas about releasing the soul. A particularly interesting burial of a child in one of the Norton mounds showed a type of bone pathology strongly suggestive of congenital syphilis. Many other skeletons show arthritic conditions, healed fractures, or other more "normal" abnormalities.

The Norton mounds had been generously to even lavishly provided with grave offerings. Among the most numerous of these were containers, some of which presumably had been filled with ritual food and drink. These containers were made from large conch shells from the Gulf of Mexico or southern Atlantic coast, from turtle shells, or they were earthenware pottery. There were also mussel-shell spoons with and without carved handles. Many of the turtle-shell plates and bowls bore handsome incised designs consisting of abstract symbols with emphasis on curvilinear lines, or they bore depictions of elk and bear. The pottery is a far cry from the simple varieties of the previous period.

Clearly inspired by Illinois Hopewell society, the Norton pottery shows many and detailed similarities with both the fine Hopewell Ware and the ruder Havana Ware of everyday village life. Indeed, a few vessels had been brought in from the Illinois Valley or had been so faithfully copied from Illinois models that it is difficult to distinguish them from the former. Nevertheless, by far the greater number of earthenware vessels found in the Norton mounds had been made by local potters. Most seem to have been produced for tomb placement. In a regionally peculiar style they sometimes combine on the same pots attributes that in Illinois would have been discretely separated on Hopewell and Havana vessels. In diffusing to the Great Lakes country, the segregation of aesthetic and functional signals so vital to the parental style was lost sight of as reinterpretation adapted it to a more provincial setting.

Tempered with crushed granitic rock with or without the admixture of sand, the Norton ceramics took the form of wide-mouthed jars with straight or (more usually) slightly everted rims. They reveal a moderate degree of neck constriction above rounded shoulders and a round or egg-shaped base. Some vessels are round or flat-bottomed and have a rim cambered to simulate a collar. Also present is a Hopewell Ware vessel in which the round mouth contrasts with a shoulder circumference which has been pressed sufficiently out of round to describe a rounded-cornered square. Similarly reminiscent of Hopewell Ware is a vessel form in which the body wall has been distended in two pairs of opposing lobes, with a fifth lobe forming the bottom. The most unusual pot is olla-shaped but

PLATE 7.4. *The central burial area in Norton Mound M of the Norton Mound Group, Kent County, Michigan. (Courtesy Richard I. Ford and the Museum of Anthropology, University of Michigan, Ann Arbor.)*

with a straight wide-mouthed neck almost half the height of the entire vessel. Interiorly-beveled lips, a Havana Ware trait, are common on the Norton pots.

Vessel surfaces were carefully smoothed before decoration was added. The techniques of decoration were incising and trailing (broad, shallow incising), punctating, and stamping, usually in combination. Hemi-conical punctates were created by pushing a dowel into the clay at an acute angle, sometimes in pairs to produce a "rabbit track" effect; ring-like or annular punctates were made with a hollow reed or similar instrument. Stamping included dentate stamping, cordwrapped-stick impressing, and cord im-

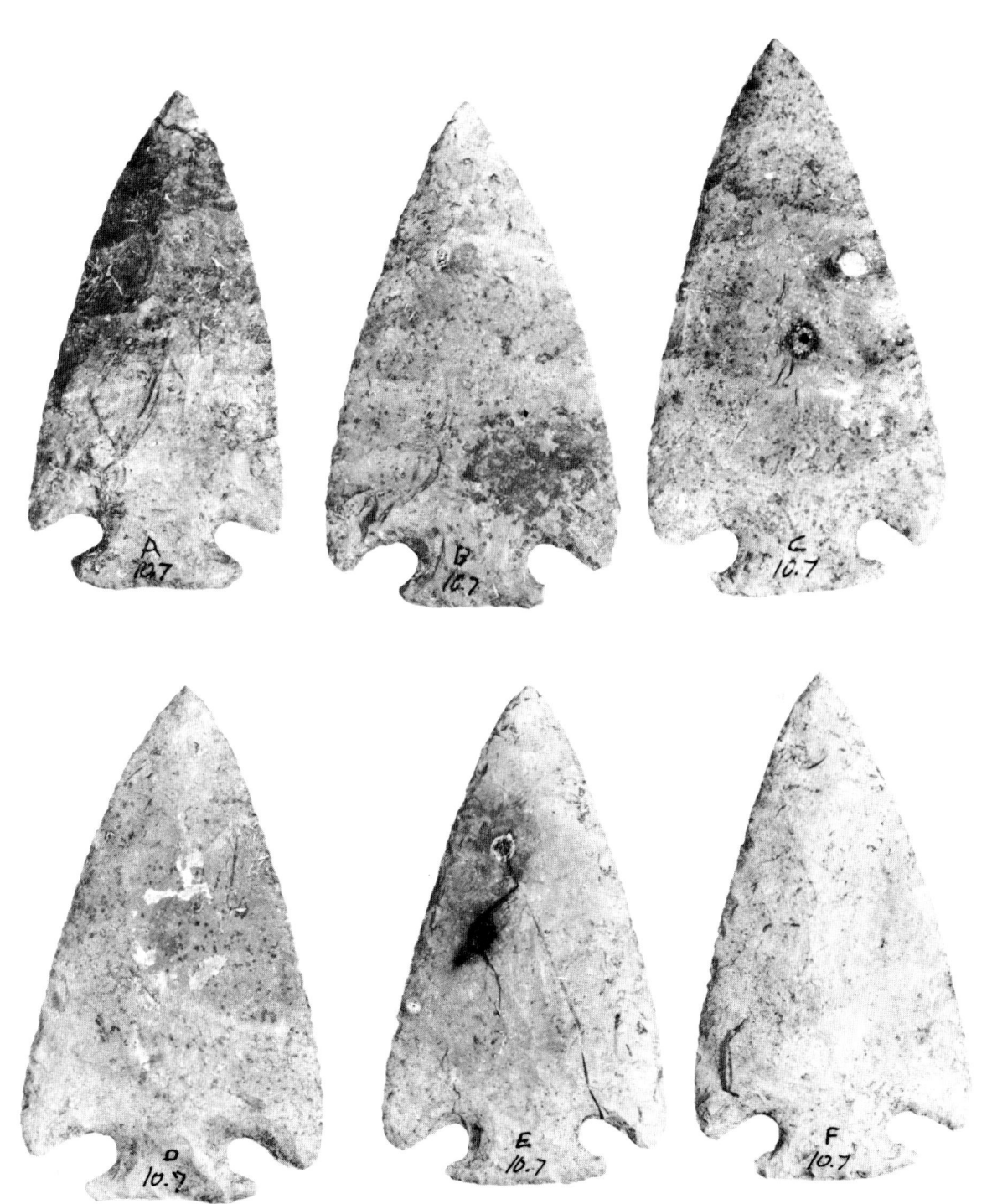

PLATE 7.5. *Set of corner-notched projectile points found with Burial 3 in Norton Mound M. (Shown actual size.) (Courtesy Richard I. Ford and the Museum of Anthropology, University of Michigan, Ann Arbor.)*

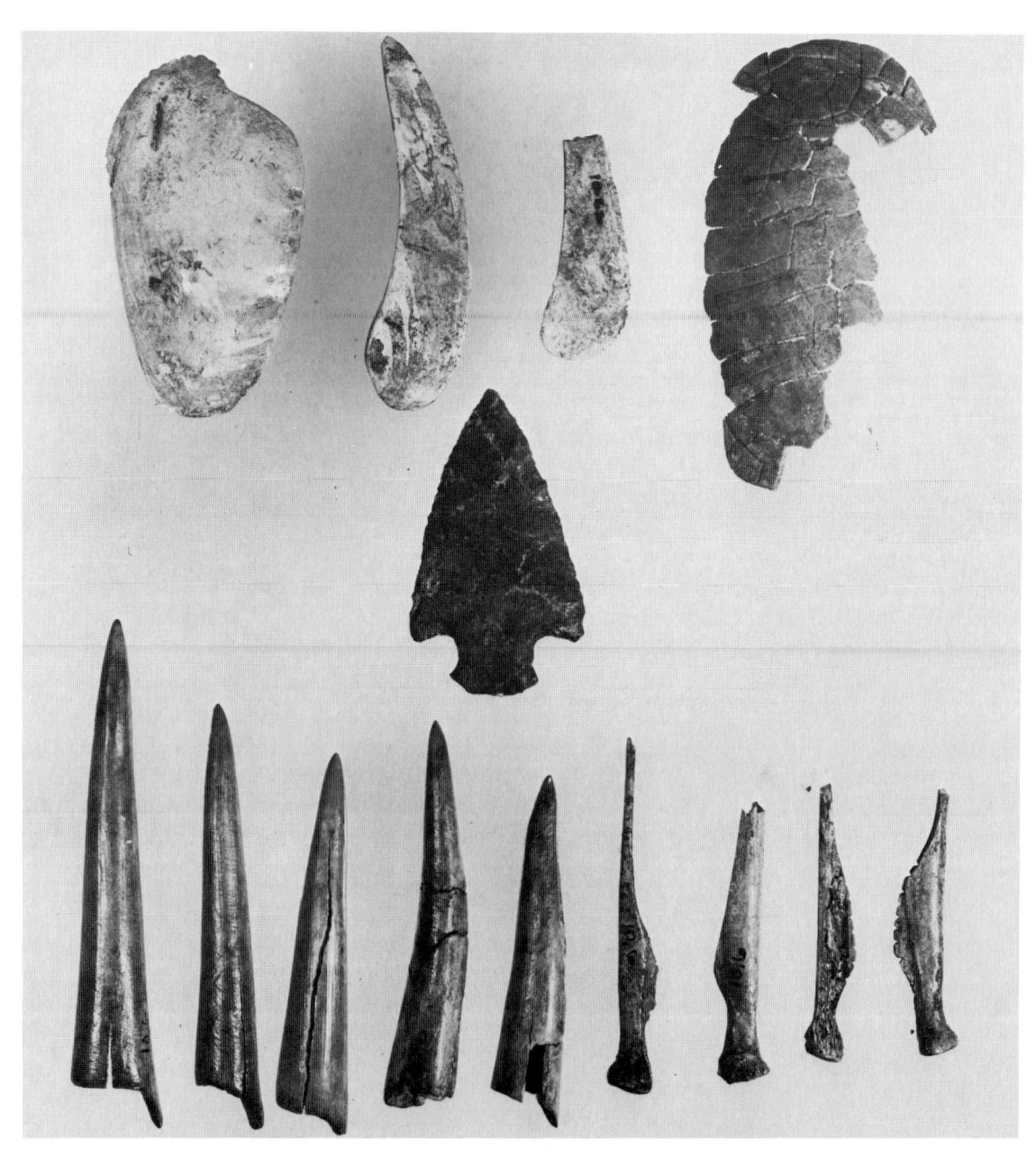

PLATE 7.6. *Grave goods from Burial 3 in Norton Mount M: mussel shell spoon, two mussel shell claw effigies, turtle shell dish (top row); corner-notched projectile point (center); antler tine points and notched turkey bone awls (bottom row). (Shown two-thirds actual size.) (Courtesy Richard I. Ford and the Museum of Anthropology, University of Michigan, Ann Arbor.)*

pressing. The first involved use of a comb-like implement having square or rectangular teeth which left regular, close-set, segmented depressions. Cordwrapped-stick stamping simulates dentate stamping but is affected by means of a string or cord tightly or loosely spiraled over a paddle edge or around a dowel. Lines of convoluted depressions were executed by pressing a length of twisted cord onto the vessel surface.

Embellishment was typically restricted to the upper half or two-thirds of the vessels. Characteristic are vertical stamps or cross-hatched lines on the rim, often set off by an underlining scribed line or a row of punctations. The neck was frequently left unadorned. The most common body decoration emphasized horizontal or diagonal rows of stamps, usually outlined with incised or trailed lines; semicircular or lobate horizontal zones filled with dentate stamps or cordwrapped-stick impressions set off by incised or trailed lines and contrasting with alternating plain lands; solidly banked punctates or dentate stamps below the rim or below a plain neck zone outlined by incised lines below the rim; or incised nested triangles alternating with similar inverted triangles. The use of incising and trailing to zone off and separate stamped from plain areas is especially marked in this and other regional Hopewellian potteries. Types of decorated vessels, such as Norton Zoned Dentate Stamped, Norton Incised, Norton Zoned Corded, and Norton Zoned Cordwrapped Stick, were identified and named after their chief techniques of decoration.

Other numerically important grave goods were split turkey-bone awls or pins, often in sets; cut deer- and elk-antler sections; ground beaver-incisor teeth; flake knives, frequently of blue-grey Dongola chert, from Union County in far southwestern Illinois, or of a white flint, probably also of southern Illinois origin; a range of hammerstones, grinding stones, and whetstones; marine-shell beads; conical antler projectile points; and clusters of six or seven Norton Corner Notched projectile points. To judge from how they had been stacked in the various grave lots, some instances of the latter artifacts suggest hafted points, others not. These are very broad-bladed, ovate-trianguloid, thin, deeply corner-notched, barbed weapon tips having straight to moderately convex bases. Superbly crafted in matched homogeneous sets, they are similar to what are called Snyders and Gibson style points in Illinois Havana-Hopewell sites.

The Norton mounds also yielded burial-associated awls, beads, and flat celts hammered out of native copper. Some of the celts had been deposited in their final resting place in woven bags or wrapped in a bast-fiber cloth, for fragments of the highly perishable material were preserved by contact with the metal. Large sheets of cut mica, probably from North Carolina, had made their way via the Hopewellian Interaction Sphere to the Norton mounds and the end of their journey. Three splended examples of Hopewellian platform pipes had been carved out of local raw material while a fourth is of southern Ohio pipestone. Two of the pipe bowls are

PLATE 7.7. *Pottery vessel of the type Norton Zoned Dentate Stamped from Burial 17, Norton Mound C. (Shown half actual size.) (Courtesy Richard I. Ford and the Museum of Anthropology, University of Michigan, Ann Arbor.)*

plain, one is carved to suggest the head of a turtle, and the last represents an elk's head. Besides these arresting artifacts were other riches: freshwater shell beads, pearl beads, bear canine teeth with and without drilled suspension holes, models of bear claws carved out of mussel shell, tear-shaped and discoidal chert blanks, incredibly cut and polished bear and wolf jaws. Undoubted medicine bundles had also accompanied the Norton dead. Among their surviving contents were the skulls, beaks, talons, and other parts of the snowy owl, peregrine falcon, and golden eagle. This fascination with raptorial birds united the Hopewellian with many other earlier and later North American cultures.

EASTERN MICHIGAN HOPEWELLIAN

Across the state and just inland of Saginaw Bay are sites of another regionally distinctive Hopewellian culture. Here at Green Point where the Tittabawassee and Shiawassee rivers come together and the Saginaw River commences its short course to the bay, is the multicomponent

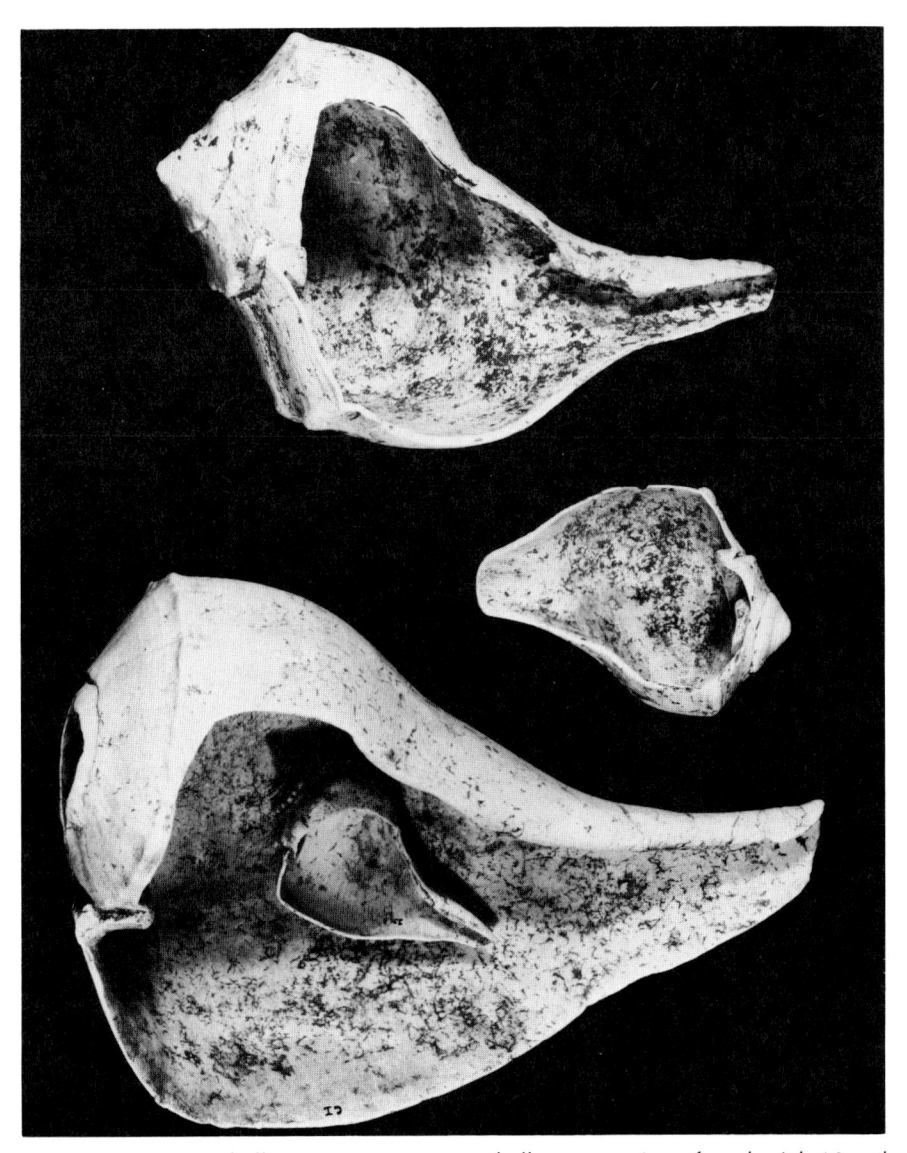

PLATE 7.8. *Marine shell (Busycon contrarium) ladles or containers from burials 16 and 17, Norton Mound C. (Shown one-third actual size.) (Courtesy Richard I. Ford and the Museum of Anthropology, University of Michigan, Ann Arbor.)*

Schultz site whose Transitional period, or Early Woodland, occupation was described in the last chapter. This same locality was reoccupied in later times, impressively during the Middle Woodland period. Not just geographically distinct, the Hopewellian remains at the Schultz site are mainly the detritus of a true settlement, not a burial ground as at the Norton site. This fundamental disparity in site function must be borne in mind when comparing the two localities. At least three burial mounds, largely destroyed before archaeologists worked there, were present at the Schultz site, but they contributed relatively little to information regarding the Hopewellian occupations.

Stratigraphic, distributional, and radiocarbon data show that there had been two main settlements of Hopewellian people or, rather, two extended episodes during which the place had been repeatedly occupied by such folk. It is differences in pottery that show the clearest division. The earliest, or Tittabawassee Hopewellian phase, is dated between the time of Christ and A.D. 300. It is marked by a dominance of Havana-like Tittabawassee Ware. The latest, or Green Point Hopewellian phase, has both Tittabawassee Ware and (mainly) Green Point Ware, the last with affinities to Hopewell and late Hopewell Baehr Ware in Illinois. Dates for this occupation are believed to fall somewhere between A.D. 300 and 400. This postdates the time of maximum popularity of the Illinois wares in their homeland and indicates a slight time lag in the demise of analogous ceramics in the northern hinterlands.

Among the differences between the pottery vessels in the Norton mounds and at the Schultz village site is the clear development of two quite separate classes of pottery at the latter site as well as a strongly contrasting interest in the use of interior punctates which result in the production of small projections, called bosses or nodes, on the vessel exteriors, and the technique of walking plain-edged and dentate stamps across vessel surfaces (rocker stamping). These traits are absent at Norton. Although not nearly as common as plain surface finishing, there are examples of cordmarked surfaces at the Schultz site in the earlier of the two Middle Woodland occupations.

Tittabawassee Ware vessels were big, heavy, and wide-mouthed with only slight neck contraction and round to almost pointed bottoms. They exhibit a heavy emphasis on adorning the rim with closely spaced vertical or slightly oblique columns of dentate or cordwrapped-stick stamps, often set off by a vessel-encircling trailed line or row of bosses. A recurring arrangement has a horizontal line of bosses in the middle of the rim where an upper bank of vertical stamps joins a lower. Curvilinear zoned-stamped body decoration is typical. One type, Tittabawassee Plain Noded, lacks any embellishment other than a row of nodes on the rim.

Vessels of Green Point Ware are smaller and have thinner walls than the predominantly earlier ware. They have much more pronounced necks and

PLATE 7.9. Hopewellian (Tittabawassee Ware) rimsherds from the Schultz site, Saginaw County, Michigan. (Shown two-thirds actual size.) (Courtesy Richard I. Ford and the Museum of Anthropology, University of Michigan, Ann Arbor.)

have rounder bases. Also characteristic are thickened and cambered rims. A distinct minority were miniature quadrilobate pots. Rocker stamping using plain-edged and dentate stamps was very popular, as was liberal employment of nodes and punctates and curvilinear zoned body decoration. Most rims bore vertical, diagonal, horizontal, or crosshatched incising or plain or dentate rocker stamping. In some cases surfaces were wiped or brushed with coarse grass or a bundle of twigs in sloppy imitation of multiple incised lines. Still other Green Point pots were plain or carried only a row of punctates on or just below the rim.

Not surprisingly, considering site function, the projectile points are much more heterogeneous than at Norton and reveal less careful attention to fine craftsmanship. They are of local flints. Numerous corner-removed and expanding-stemmed examples were recovered. Among the many chipped-stone tools, those shaped or trimmed on one face only outnumber the fully or bifacially flaked tools. This, it has been suggested, is positively correlated with a preponderance of fishing and gathering as opposed to hunting. Faunal remains at the Schultz site appear to support this contention.

As in the Norton mounds, the Schultz village site produced conspicuous numbers of containers made out of the carapaces or shells of turtles. Many were likewise engraved with geometric or abstract figures. Of interest because of implied connections with more northerly and non-Hopewellian Middle Woodland cultures and not present in the southwestern Michigan material, are antler-tine toggle-head harpoons. Such weapons are subsequently described in the context of the Middle Tier Middle Woodland where they are much more at home.

Within the time span represented by the Schultz site, Hopewellian components' change was by no means confined to shifting fashions in pottery or other manufactures. There appears to have developed an increasing reliance on a diminishing variety of game animals for food with a heavier taking of deer, elk, beaver, and bear. Accompanying this was growing reliance on plant collecting, fishing, clamming, and the taking of birds. No evidence of agriculture has been found despite its earlier presence in the same locality. Some 13 species of snails and mussels were being collected, and they increased in importance over time. Certain of these shifts must have been related to changes in the site environs. And it was during the Green Point phase that the Schultz site took on some purposes over and above the domestic ones which had hitherto dominated the locality. At least three burial mounds and a ceremonial circular stockade 45 m in diameter were built in or alongside the village. The latter structure was too slight for any defensive usefulness, and the enclosed ground had been cleared of the usual debris associated with living precincts. As a likely "sacred enclosure" it suggests a back-country version of the more numerous and substantial ones in the Ohio Valley with their earth embankments.

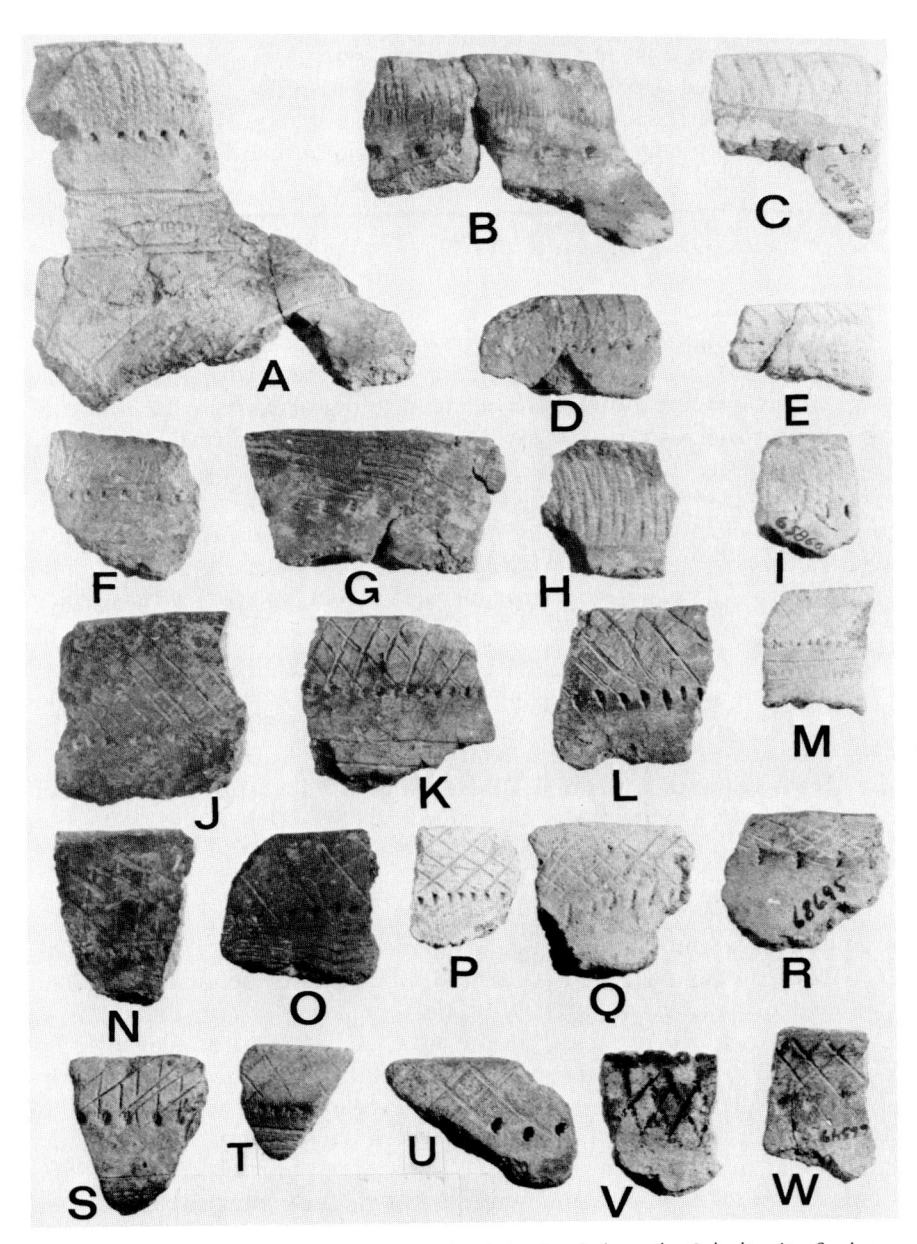

PLATE 7.10. *Hopewellian (Green Point Ware) rimsherds from the Schultz site, Saginaw County, Michigan. Sherds **A–I** have rocker stamped rims, **J–W** have incised or trailed cross-hatchings. (Shown two-thirds actual size.) (Courtesy Richard I. Ford and the Museum of Anthropology, University of Michigan, Ann Arbor.)*

With regard to diet and people's health, one of the more remarkable recoveries was of coprolites, preserved fecal material, of human and/or canine origin. Dissection and miscroscopic examination revealed the presence of tapeworm eggs, thereby establishing the probability that the parasite was established in and had exacted its toll of the human population. People could have contracted tapeworm by close contact with infected dogs or by ingesting undercooked fish, a common carrier of the parasite.

There is interesting geological evidence of a prolonged episode of extensive flooding sometime between the two main periods of Middle Woodland occupation. It argues for a rise of at least 1.8 m in the surface level of Lake Huron. Conformable evidence of such a rise had been previously reported from stratigraphic data at archaeological sites in the interconnected Lake Michigan basin on the Door Peninsula of Wisconsin. Relatively cooler and wetter climatic conditions are believed to have been responsible. Whether the wetter conditions were owing to increased precipitation or to increased cloud cover and lower rates of evaporation is not known. It appears that by the time of majority Green Point Ware use lake level had dropped again, local flooding was much less severe, and somewhat warmer and drier weather prevailed.

Other sites in the Saginaw basin, such as Kantzler and Bussinger, have been found to contain the remnants of lesser Hopewellian occupations. These were probably outliers of the Schultz site during a part of its history. The archaeologists who have investigated these sites have reasoned that they were some of the small winter camps of the spring–summer–fall communities present at the richer, more complex Schultz site.

SQUAWKIE HILL

A quite different kind of regional Hopewellian culture is that of western New York: the Squawkie Hill phase. Not well understood, distributed over a relatively small area and probably a short time span, the phase looks to be the cultural expression of local people who had been very selectively influenced by ideas and products emanating from the Ohio Valley, probably by way of the Allegheney River, in the first or second century A.D.; nevertheless they retained most of their native inheritance, a variety of the widespread and non-Hopewellian Point Peninsula culture. Unlike most Point Peninsula peoples, who did not erect burial mounds, the people responsible for the Squawkie Hill Phase did.

In addition to the practice of mound building, the Squawkie Hill folk also had access to some of the exotic Hopewell paraphernalia. Such foreign manufactures included platform pipes of Ohio fireclay, copper disc-shaped ("cymbal") earspools, flake knives of the Ohio flint from Flint Ridge, sheets of mica, pearl beads, the distinctive cut and polished animal jaws, copper and silver panpipes, and large corner-notched and straight-stemmed "ceremonial" spearheads. It is noteworthy that none of the Hopewell Ware or Hopewellian concepts of pottery design—so salient an identifier of Hopewellian status in Wisconsin and in Indiana and Michigan—accompanied the intrusion of the Hopewell contributions to western New York. What associated pottery is present is from the Point Peninsula ceramic tradition. Why so different an Hopewellian manifestation should have emerged in this area and just what the mechanisms of the process were are further puzzles. The camp and village sites of the mound builders, which might throw some much-needed light on the problem, have not been found.

Beyond the range of the Squawkie Hill phase, occasional discoveries have been made of Hopewellian materials in other cultural contexts. Sometimes these are of surprising quantity and quality. A superb and enigmatic example has been supplied by excavations at the LeVesconte Mound on the Trent River in Northumberland County, Ontario. Among the Hopewellian items found with the burials at this Point Peninsula-ascribed site were an incredible nine panpipe covers—four of copper, five of silver. Notwithstanding the southern stamp of these diagnostic Hopewellian artifacts, the silver of which some had been fashioned has been traced by chemical analysis to the Cobalt district of northern Ontario. In most Hopewell and Hopewellian sites no panpipes are found, or at most only one or two. They seem to have been placed with the bodies of unusually respected individuals. How did nine of these rare artifacts come to repose in the LeVesconte Mound? Clearly, the phenomenon called the Hopewellian Interaction Sphere entailed more than has been deciphered in the earth monuments and the lithic, ceramic, and metal creations ascribed to that sociologically obscure but very real entity.

Middle Tier Middle Woodland Cultures

Among the Middle Woodland period manifestations of the Great Lakes, archaeologists have discerned a great east–west spread of cultures, together occupying by far the larger part of the lakes country, which reveal a far less intensive involvement in the Hopewellian Interaction Sphere than those just discussed. Mainly distributed within the Canadian Biotic Province and the Lake Forest forest formation, but with some representatives present in bordering reaches of the Hudsonian and Carolinian biotic provinces, these culture have a collective identity that sets them apart from the Hopewellian cultures and that intimates a significantly independent history. Hopewellian artifacts have from time to time been found in certain of these sites, and Hopewellian stylistic influences have sometimes been perceived in at least attenuated and heavily reinterpreted form. Such evidence documents diffusion and perhaps even trade, and has proven useful for purposes of cross-dating. But it is assuredly of a much lesser magnitude than among the Southern Tier cultures and it speaks to a different order of social relations. East–west interaction now seems of greater importance than north–south. Clearly, an enabling mechanism was joint adaptation to the latitudinally disposed Lake Forest environment. Originally it was proposed to label this phenomenon Northern Tier Middle Woodland. Because the north central and northwesternmost of these non-Hopewellian culture, the Laurel culture of western Ontario, northern Michigan and Minnesota, and parts of Manitoba, is itself of unusually definitive character vis à vis the other Northern Tier members, a recent suggestion has been to reclassify the others and make Laurel the sole exemplar of the "Northern Tier" Middle Woodland cultural pattern. By this proposal, accepted here, the Great Lakes area in the Middle Woodland period was occupied by many different Indian societies, each sharing with the others one of three broad kinds of historically connected cultural patterns. These three great patterns show a latitudinal stratification. In the southern parts of the lakes country were the mainly Hopewellian cultures of the Southern Tier pattern. In the north central and northwestern Great Lakes was the Laurel culture of the Northern Tier pattern. And in the broad intervening Middle Tier were the Nokomis, North Bay, Saugeen, and Point Peninsula cultures.

Complicating such a neat geographical layer-cake is the certainty that other local and regional Middle Woodland cultures remain undiscovered or unrecognized. An example is provided by evidence of a vaguely perceived non-Hopewellian group of sites around the western end and south shore of Lake Erie. The north–south symmetry is also unbalanced by major Point Peninsula occupations in New York on the same latitude with sites of the Squawkie Hill phase and by the fact that many components of the Saugeen and Point Peninsula cultures in Ontario are actually south of the latitude of the Saginaw Bay Hopewellian representatives in Michigan. Nevertheless, the tripartite north–south "stacking" of broadly similar cultures identifiable over an imposing east–west axis has considerable utility; it does seem to derive from the nature of the archaeological remains.

A final caveat needs to be stressed. Whereas the three tiers are conceptualized as three geographical–historical *groups* of cultures, the constituent cultures should not be equated with an equal number of aboriginal societies. While it may be that the Saginaw Bay Hopewellian culture at any one point in time was the product of a single society (crudely, "tribe"), it is most unlikely that only a single society is signaled by the cultural debris called Point Peninsula. The first is far more localized than the second, the second more variable in the spatial expressions and associations of its defining characteristics. Defining cultural and sociological entities on archaeological evidence are two different and separate problems, and the latter is intrinsically more difficult than the former.

7. The Middle Woodland Period

THE SAUGEEN CULTURE

Occupying portions of the Canadian and Carolinian biotic provinces, the Saugeen culture is known from sites distributed between the southwestern shore of Georgian Bay to the west end of Lake Ontario and the north shore of Lake Erie, and from the eastern coast of Lake Huron to about the middle of the Ontario Niagara Peninsula. Within this southwestern Ontario range the Saugeen culture seems to have been divided into a number of regions, each manifested by a small concentration of sites located along or near a major river. Three of these "local groups" or "localities" are on the Saugeen, Grand, and Thames rivers. The most fully reported of these is the Saugeen group south of the Bruce Peninsula in Bruce County, Ontario. Here, in the "Bruce locality" are the rich Donaldson and Thede sites, both situated at stretches of rapids in the Saugeen River, and the Inverhuron-Lucas site on the shore of Lake Huron. They are opposite and a little north of the Saginaw Bay Hopewellian stations on the Michigan side of the lake, but the cultural distance is far greater than the geographic.

With the assumption that each of the Saugeen culture "localities" marks the physical remnants of a separate society, two settlement types have been put forward to account for the differences observed among the constituent sites within each locality. Among the Bruce locality sites, Donaldson and, perhaps, Thede are believed to have been spring–early–summer "macroband settlements" occupied when most members of the local group resided together in the same village. The Inverhuron-Lucas site is envisioned as a late–summer–fall "microband settlement," the product of just a few families come together in order to exploit the special resources of that place. The dichotomy rests upon interpretations of site locations, varieties and quantities of tools, habitation features, and the analysis of floral and faunal debris. It is similar to the distinction between "base settlements" and "extractive settlements" independently proferred for the earlier Meadowood culture on the New York Niagara Frontier. The Saugeen "local groups" would generally correspond to the Meadowood "local bands." Although they have yet to be identified, there may also have been many smaller camps to which the constituent Saugeen family groups repaired for winter hunting.

The seasonality and special purpose of the Inverhuron-Lucas occupation is insinuated by its location on the Lake Huron shore and the evidence of fishing in the shallows by means of line, as attested by copper fishhooks, and by nets, as indicated by the recovery of notched stone net-sinkers. Hunting seems to have been locally focused on the taking of abundant small animals like rabbits, woodchucks, and beavers. Large numbers of rabbits could easily have been procured in the late fall and early winter. Despite the relatively small size of the Inverhuron-Lucas site, impressive quantities of the remains of raspberries, elderberries, cherries, dogwood berries, beech nuts, and butternuts were found. These would have been collected between July and November. The far larger Donaldson site, only about 32 km away on the Saugeen River, yielded a much smaller quantity of these important foodstuffs. At none of the Saugeen culture sites has any evidence been recovered of domesticated plants.

At the Donaldson site plant collecting appears to have been incidental to other subsistence activities. No fall-ripening nuts or fruits were recovered at all. Riverine fishing was the main activity, particularly the taking of spring-spawning species. Most abundant were sturgeon, freshwater drum, pickerel, sucker, channel catfish, and bass. While there is evidence of the use of nets, the larger fish were sometimes captured using antlertine toggle-head harpoons. This simple but ingenious weapon was an elongated cone, usually with a spur or barb at its base; it was socketed to accept a shaft and equipped with a line hole above the apex of the socket. When driven home, the harpoon head detached from the shaft and tension on the connecting line caused the head to turn, or "toggle," in the quarry to an angle 90° from the axis of insertion. Thus firmly gripped, the fish could be hauled in with the attached line. Toggle-head harpoons are

PLATE 7.11. *Saugeen Culture burials (GB-GF) at the Donaldson site, Bruce County, Ontario, showing extended, flexed, and bundle styles of inhumation. The latter is represented by the remains of the deliberately defleshed and dismembered body at the feet of the extended individual. The two flexed burials at the head of the extended individual are of small children. (Courtesy William D. Finlayson and the Archaeological Survey of Canada, National Museum of Man, Ottawa.)*

PLATE 7.12. *Grave offerings from directly beneath the bundle burial in the group GB-GF at the Donaldson site, Bruce County, Ontario (approximately one-third actual size). Note the four-barrel copper panpipe (lower left); sheets of cut mica (left center); cut wolf jaws (upper left); and antler-hafted beaver-incisor tool (right). The other grave goods include bone toggle head harpoons, bone awls, antler club spike, beaver-incisor tools, a stone earspool, and other objects of uncertain function. (Courtesy William D. Finlayson and the Archaeological Survey of Canada, National Museum of Man, Ottawa.)*

characteristic of many of the Middle and Northern Tier Middle Woodland cultures. Such hunting as was pursued from the Donaldson site concentrated on large game such as deer, elk, and bear. Bones of smaller animals were uncovered also, though their numbers indicate only a slight contribution to the larder.

The stone tools from the Saugeen sites have struck many observers as undistinguished, difficult to characterize in neat, crisp terms, and as "poorly developed." Indeed, it is an unenviable task to attempt to sort them from mixed collections also containing lithic material from the Inverhuron Archaic, the regional Late Archaic culture. This fact has stimulated the belief that the Saugeen culture evolved in southwestern Ontario from Inverhuron Archaic ancestors and that, through stasigenesis, many old types of stone implements continued with little or no modification into association with a widely and fully evolved ceramic industry.

The most numerous Saugeen chipped-flint tools are scrapers. Even though end-scrapers dominate the category, it also includes large circular

PLATE 7.13. *Cache of biface blades at the Donaldson site. (Shown one-third actual size.) (Courtesy William D. Finlayson and the Archaeological Survey of Canada, National Museum of Man, Ottawa.)*

and oval examples made on big spalls struck off cobble cores. Biface knives and preforms and edge-trimmed or utilized flake knives are well represented. Wedges (pièces esquillées), bipolar cores, and flaked choppers are somewhat less frequent. Projectile points are variable in form and of unimposing workmanship. They are mainly broad, side-notched, corner-notched, and straight stemmed. Many celts have been found, but they are flaked and/or pecked rather than ground and polished. A full range of domestic rough-stone implements has been recovered: pitted and faceted hammerstones, sharpening stones, anvilstones, abraders, net-sinkers. Copper is represented by just a few fishhooks and a patch on a highly atypical earspool found in a grave at the Donaldson site. From similar contexts has come most of what is known about Saugeen bone products, these otherwise being poorly preserved at the other sites. By combining the sites it is clear that knives and chisels fashioned out of split and ground beaver-incisor teeth were very important in the Saugeen domestic tool kit. Likewise awls, pins, tool handles, chisels, flaking tools or drifts, and beamers (split animal leg bones with long scraping edges). Bone and antler weapons included the previously described toggle-head harpoons as well as straight barbed harpoons, conical projectile points, and antler spikes for mounting at the business end of a club. Some of the Saugeen bone awls may actually have been prongs from leisters or fish spears, since it is hard to believe that the Saugeen folk did not know of or refused to make and use so ancient, widespread, and basic a food-catcher. That the Saugeen bone industry is so poorly sampled severely limits its usefulness as a criterion of cultural connections with other groups having far better bone preservation.

Fortunately, the Saugeen sites have given up very respectable collections

PLATE 7.14. *Saugeen vessel from the Donaldson site with pseudo-scallop-shell stamping above a rocker stamped body. (Shown half actual size.) (Courtesy William D. Finlayson and the Archaeological Survey of Canada, National Museum of Man, Ottawa.)*

of potsherds. The pottery so salvaged for posterity is a coarse, thick-walled, very heavily grit-tempered, crumbly ware. The original pots were semiglobular and possessed conoidal bases; they had slight neck constriction and vertical or slightly outcurved rims. This is a heavily decorated, not to say baroque, pottery which was hurredly and sloppily embellished from top to bottom. Even the lips and the upper portions of the vessel interiors were usually decorated. The instruments used in such aesthetic exercise were those already detailed for Hopewellian pottery but with the addition of linear and pseudo-scallop-shell stamping—all applied, of course, in a most non-Hopewellian manner. The first is simply a thin straight-edged tool which was cleanly applied to the clay, usually in banks. The second was a thin-edged tool alternately notched on opposite sides so as to produce a sinuous or serpentine impression. Together with dentate stamps and cordwrapped sticks, these same devices were often deliberately dragged from one application point to the next. This more complicated effect is called "push-pull," "stab-and-drag," or "complex stamped." It is tantamount to a constantly interrupted trailing with a linear, dentate, pseudo-scallop-shell, or cordwrapped-stick stamp, and the result can be quite bizarre. Very frequently the stamping tool was walked or "rocked" so as to create continuous zig-zag patterns on the clay.

The Saugeen potter seems to have suffered from a horror of unfilled spaces. The balanced, imaginative use of plain versus decorated bands and lands seen in much Hopewellian pottery was unappealing, if it was known, to the former. Similarly, care and restraint are replaced by hurrying and extravagance. It is difficult to imagine that the two kinds of ceramics are related in such a way whereby one may be derived from the other. They must have been separate developments, presumably ultimately sharing a common ancestor in the Vinette 1 and related Early Woodland pottery of the preceding Transitional period. Such developments, reasonable as they are in theory, remain to be demonstrated.

The principal design of Saugeen pottery stressed multiple bands encircling the upper part of the vessel while the lower part would be covered with ornamentations applied in contiguous or even overlapping columns. Individual stamped imprints were oriented obliquely or vertically and parallel to each other to form bands, or they were set end to end in parallel lines—in either case effectively dividing the surface among horizontal parallel rows. A favorite combination was to mass individual, discrete stamps on the rim, neck, and upper body, and to cover the lower body with rocker stamping using the same implement. Incised or trailed lines were sometimes superimposed.

Many postmolds, pits, hearths, and scattered lenses of charcoal were located in the excavations of the Donaldson site. Among these were traces of pole-frame dwellings which had doubtless been covered with sheets of bark or woven mats. One of the houses was rectangular and measured

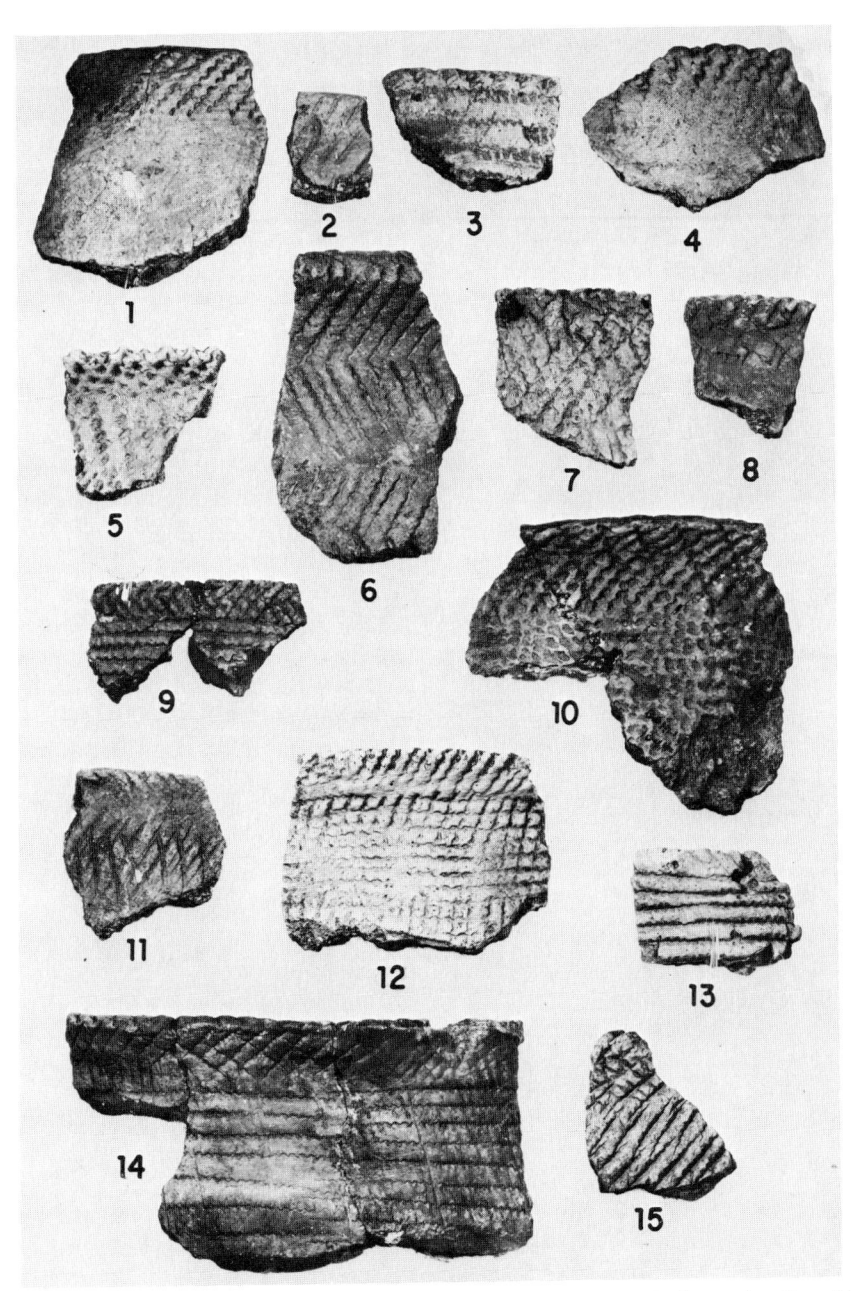

PLATE 7.15. *Saugeen pseudo-scallop-shell-stamped rimsherds from the Donaldson site. (Shown approximately two-thirds actual size.) (Courtesy James V. Wright and the Archaeological Survey of Canada, National Museum of Man, Ottawa.)*

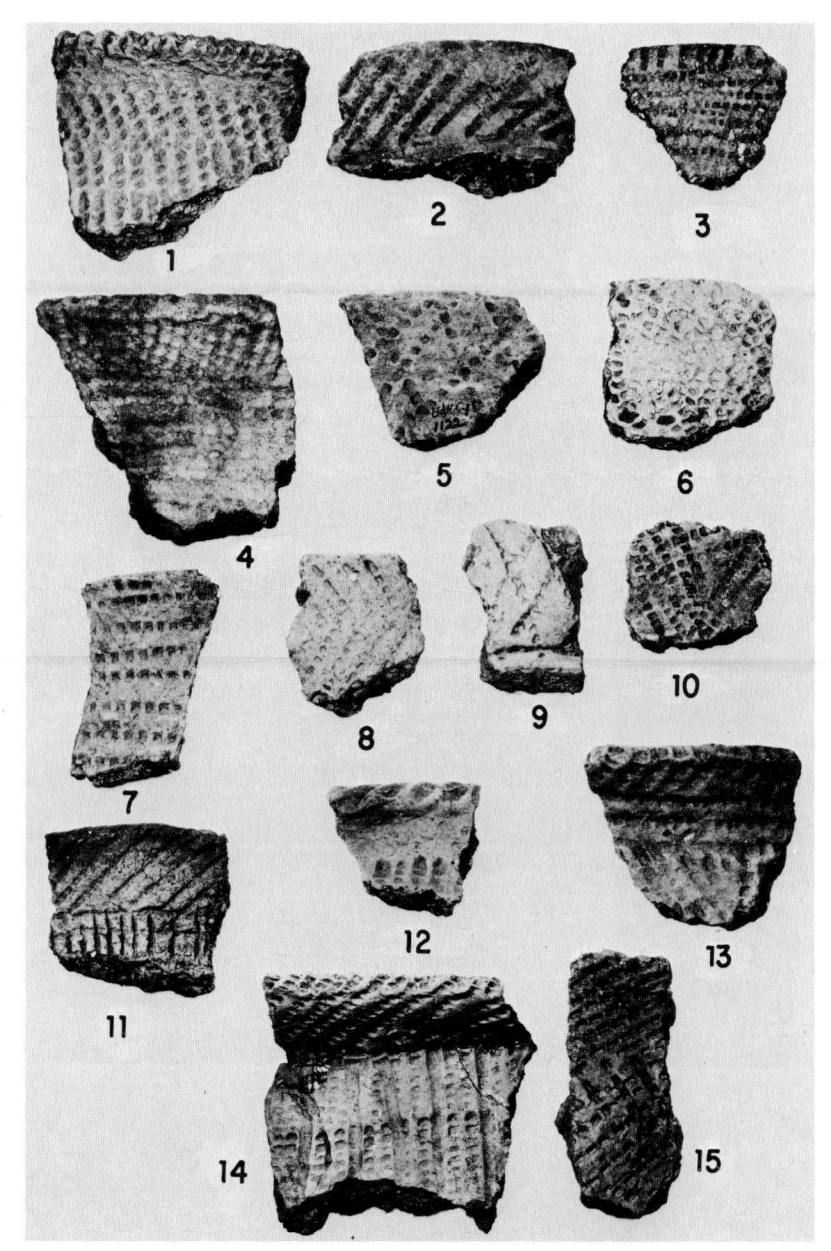

PLATE 7.16. *Saugeen dentate-stamped rimsherds from the Donaldson site. (Shown approximately two-thirds actual size.) (Courtesy James V. Wright and the Archaeological Survey of Canada, National Museum of Man, Ottawa.)*

approximately 5 × 7 m. With a door at one end, it seems to have had a peaked or gabled roof, for indications of centerline roof support posts could be discerned in the welter of other postmolds in the dirt floor. Probably several periods of rebuilding are indicated. Another smaller house was 3 × 5 m and had rounded corners. These suggest from their size extended family domiciles.

Another important discovery at the Donaldson site was of two small cemeteries. One consisted of three graves in which 11 people had been interred. The other had six graves containing the remains of 12 individuals. Extended, flexed, bundle, and partial-cremation burials were present, some unaccompanied by grave goods, others well provided.

One of the bundle burials was extraordinary. It was of particular value because of its indications of foreign contacts and for their implications for cross-dating. Cut marks on the bones indicate that this particular individual had been both dismembered and defleshed before interment. An instructive assortment of artifacts had been deposited with the bones. These, but not the bones, had been painted with red ocher. Among a collection of things at home in the Saugeen culture were some others of Hopewellian stamp: a copper panpipe, a stone earspool (incorporating the previously mentioned copper patch), a cut and polished upper jaw of a wolf, and three sheets of cut mica. This unusual burial was radiocarbon dated to around the time of Christ, a date in close agreement with the known antiquity of similar artifacts in Hopewellian sites in the Michigan, Ohio, and Illinois country.

Unfortunately, few Saugeen radiocarbon dates are as internally consistent with their cultural associations as the one from the bundle burial with its clear Hopewellian time markers. The available radiocarbon assays purporting to date the Saugeen culture are bewilderingly inconsistent. They are spread over a time range that is simply incompatible with the relative homogeneity of those manifestations and their indications of contemporaneity with related and much more tightly dated cultures elsewhere. The Saugeen dates exhibit a range from the eighth century B.C. to the thirteen century A.D. Ruling out the latest date as probably attributable to a brief later occupation by Proto-Iroquoian peoples, the proposal has been made to divide Saugeen into two temporal phases. Early Saugeen would incorporate those radiocarbon age determinations between about 700 B.C. and A.D. 100; Late Saugeen would encompass the years A.D. 100–800. If real, this is a total span of 1500 years. To judge from comparable assemblages in neighboring regions, the upper end of this time range is very likely too late by two or three centuries. At the other extreme the very early dates appear even more out of line. Radiocarbon samples from the early, or Canoe Point phase, of the Point Peninsula culture in New York, which most authorities regard as closely related to Saugeen, fall in the second and third centuries A.D. Because there was evidence of a possible Meadowood

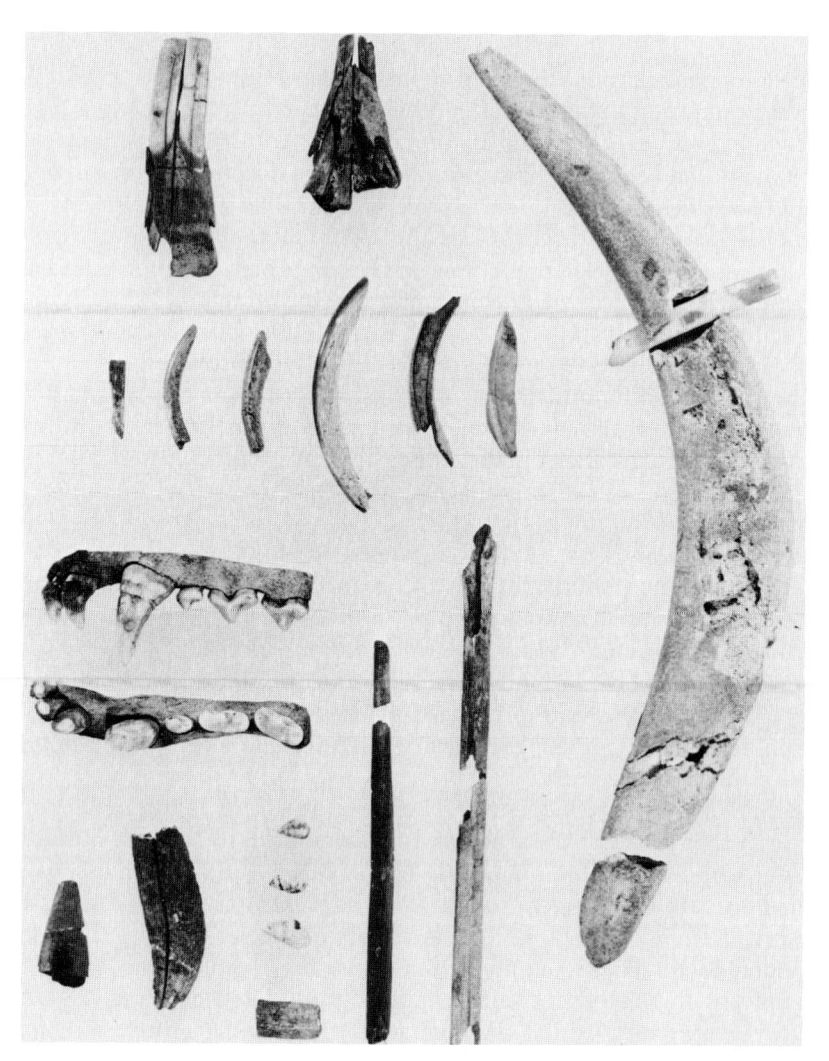

PLATE 7.17. *Artifacts of bone and teeth from the Donaldson site. The cut wolf jaws and the antler-hafted beaver-incisor tool may be seen in situ in Plate 7.12. The other artifacts are beaver-incisor chisels and knives, a modified bear canine tooth, snail-shell beads, and two bone pins. (Shown half actual size.) (Courtesy William D. Finlayson and the Archaeological Survey of Canada, National Museum of Man, Ottawa.)*

component at the Donaldson site and a definite Late Archaic occupation at the Burley site—both localities that have produced the oldest Saugeen dates—there is the possibility of the admixture of older and more recent carbon samples in the Saugeen features.

Opposed to this line of reasoning is the earliest age determination from the Thede site. This date is about 290 B.C., and only Saugeen cultural remains have been identified at that place. This is appreciably later than the earliest Saugeen dates, of course, but even it seems a century or two too early. Furthermore, other Thede site dates run as late as A.D. 770. Compatible with the very early age estimates for beginning of Saugeen are radiocarbon dates of about the same magnitude from the ought-to-be contemporary Constance Bay Site No. 1 just west of Ottawa in the Ottawa Valley (about 490 B.C.), and from sites of the North Bay culture on Rock and Washington islands off the northern tip of Wisconsin's Door Peninsula in northern Lake Michigan. But these, too, are themselves inconsistent with other North Bay assays. These radiocarbon dates pose a major unresolved dilemma. If for one or more reasons, such as inadvertent sample admixture, introduction of natural ancient carbon from groundwater, or other agents of contamination, the earlier dates should eventually be proved untrustworthy, the beginning phases of the Saugeen and North Bay cultures can then be more tightly and satisfactorily integrated into the emerging picture of Middle Woodland development in the Great Lakes and eastern North America generally. On the other hand, if the dates should be sustained, then components of these two reginal cultures will disjunctively stand apart as conspicuous anomalies, temporally and developmentally isolated from their cultural relatives elsewhere. They would constitute the most ancient and chronologically incongruous "Middle Woodland" cultures yet discovered, and thus would represent the potential, if surprising, ancestors of the Lake Forest or Middle Tier Middle Woodland cultural pattern. Only the results of future field investigations will tell.

POINT PENINSULA

A very similar and certainly in large part contemporaneous cultural development in eastern Ontario, southwestern Quebec, and New York has been named Point Peninsula. This culture, or attenuated versions of it, was also present in northern Pennsylvania and New Jersey and in New England and the Maritime provinces. Not only do the Saugeen and Point Peninsula distributions in Ontario overlap, but it is sometimes extremely difficult to separate artifacts of the one from the other.

Because Point Peninsula has been shown to have persisted over many centuries during which its identity was expressed most directly in ceramics, it is sometimes called a "tradition." Four developmental phases have been proposed for this tradition. The earliest is the poorly known Early Point Peninsula or Canoe Point phase, radiocarbon dated to the second and third centuries A.D. It has often been maintained that Saugeen belongs in this archaeological phase. With its removal, due to recognition of its partly independent history, the Canoe Point phase was much reduced in content and meaning. A second Point Peninsula phase is that connected with Hopewellian trappings in the previously described

Squawkie Hill phase in western New York between approximately A.D. 100 and 300. This overlaps with the now somewhat amorphous Canoe Point, of course, and hints at strains in the taxonomy. By far the most substantial and best known is the Kipp Island Phase dated A.D. 300–ca. 650. The final Point Peninsula phase, Hunter's Home, while undoubtedly an outgrowth of the Point Peninsula tradition, is not a Middle Woodland but a Late Woodland manifestation. As such, it is treated in the next chapter.

Kipp Island phase burial practices, though still sometimes impressive, were less elaborate than those of the Squawkie Hill phase. They clearly signal a decline in the far-flung complex of mortuary ceremonialism. Except for several examples in southern Ontario and, of course, the Hopewellian-inspired Squawkie Hill sites in western New York, the construction of burial mounds was not an activity characteristic of the Point Peninsula folk. But among the exceptions is the mound group on Rice Lake near Peterborough, Ontario, which includes the impressive 59-m-long Serpent Mound.

From first to last, as far as is known, the subsistence underpinnings of the Point Peninsula continuum were, as in the case of Saugeen, hunting, fishing, and wild plant collecting. Not a suggestion of agriculture has been recovered. It is likely that harvesting of wild rice was locally important. Little is known regarding the size or structure of Point Peninsula villages. In sites of the Kipp Island phase both circular and rectangular house-post outlines have been revealed in addition to numerous hearth structures and storage pits—all proclaiming a fair degree of prolonged settlement.

As intimated earlier, the most diagnostic attributes of Point Peninsula adhere to the pottery. Named after the second stratigraphic level at the multicomponent Vinette site in north central New York, the pottery was called Vinette 2 to mark its separate status vis-à-vis the earlier Vinette 1 pottery. This Vinette 2, or Point Peninsula, pottery is so different from its predecessor that it cannot be stylistically derived from Vinette 1 except by positing an as-yet-undiscovered intermediate form. Indeed, late examples of Vinette 1 have been found in apparent association with Point Peninsula sherds at a number of sites without evidence of merging of the two styles. Although the precise origins of Point Peninsula pottery are unknown at this time, it does not appear that the technology was added to a resident Laurentian Archaic base culture just as Saugeen ceramics were grafted onto the regional Inverhuron Archaic farther north and west. The new ceramic style is shared by the Canoe Point, Squawkie Hill, Kipp Island and, in attenuated fashion, Hunter's Home phases. It is very similar to Saugeen pottery, though more carefully made, with dentate stamping, pseudo-scallop-shell stamping, rocker stamping with both plain and toothed implements, heavy use of the dragged stamp or push–pull technique, cordwrapped-stick impressing, punctating, and incising. With the passage of time certain trends established themselves. Thus the generally early great popularity of rocker stamping declined dramatically late in the history of the tradition and dentate stamping was gradually replaced by use of the cordwrapped stick. From early to late there was a tendency for pots to become bigger and more globular in shape, bases underwent progressive modification from conoidal to subconoidal to round, and overall decoration gave way to increasing use of plain surfaces as the area of decoration retracted toward the upper portions of the vessels. And early in Point Peninsula times surface finishing (before garnishment) tended to be plain or smooth; cordmaking grew in popularity at its expense. The fact that these and other alterations show coetaneous parallels in other sectors of the Great Lakes and that they are conformable with the emergence of early Late Woodland techniques and styles over so broad a domain, allows of little question regarding the historical roots of the later potteries.

In the Kipp Island phase smoking pipes underwent an increase in quantity and variety. Noneffigy versions of the Hopewellian-style platform pipe and even the more antique straight tubular pipe continued in use but were gradually supplanted by obtuse-angle and right-angle elbow pipes. Projectile points were stemmed, side-notched, and corner-notched, with the types Jack's Reef Corner-notched and Jack's Reef Pentagonal being especially characteristic. There were also the first few appearances of the triangular Levanna points, which may have tipped arrows. A conspicuous exotic import in the Kipp Island phase was fossil sharks' teeth. These similarly may have been hafted on arrows. Particularly well known as burial accompaniments are whole shells strung as necklaces or bracelets or sewn on clothing, carefully crafted pendants pecked and ground out of banded slate and then given a high polish, and beautiful large hair combs made from moose antler. The slate pendants are shaped like truncated isosceles triangles, like two conjoined hexagons having rounded corners, like the tongue of a short necktie, or they are rectanguloid. Unlike gorgets, they are provided with but a single suspension hole. The hair combs have from four to eight teeth and a prominent crown, the latter part invariably enriched with incised devices. Line-filled triangles are common. A guess would be that, in addition to their presumed grooming function, these interesting artifacts were sometimes worn in a bun or other hair arrangement as an ornament.

The moose-antler combs are but one example of the rich and multifaceted Point Peninsula bone and antler industry. Other of its productions are straight-tanged harpoons with multiple barbs carved along one side of the blade, toggle-head harpoons like those detailed for the Saugeen culture, projectile points (probably spearpoints) with multiple barbs on one or on both blade edges, conical antler-tine arrowheads, dagger-like knives, serrated-ended bird-humerus tools of unknown purpose, awls, pins, and tool and weapon hafts and handles. An especially characteristic implement is the antler-hafted beaver-incisor tool. Although end-mounted beaver in-

VERA ACHEN

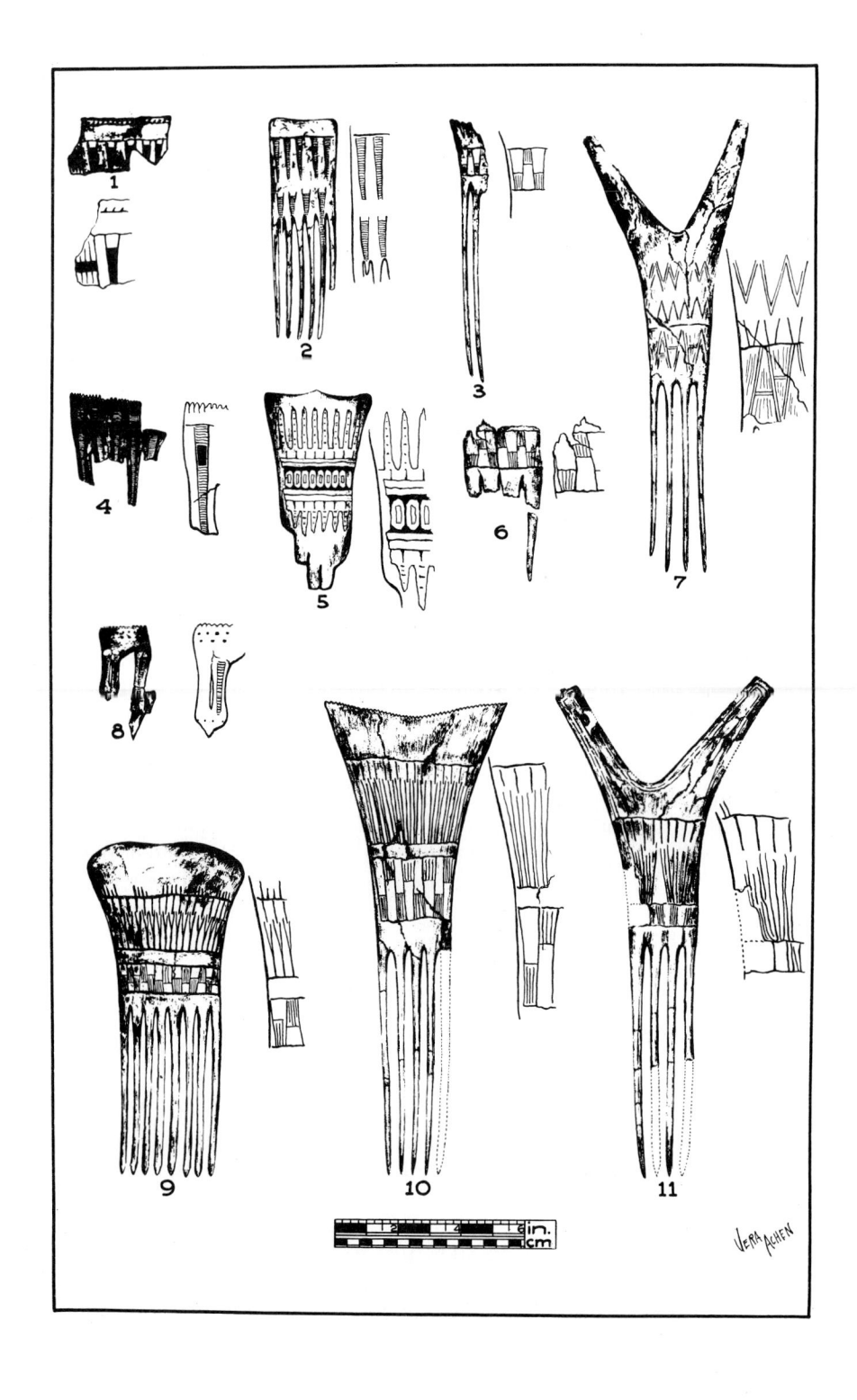

PLATE 7.19. Point Peninsula artifacts from various sites in southeastern Ontario: conch-shell pendant, shark-tooth pendant, notched bone points, bone awls and dagger (top row); shell cup filled with pigment from mines near Cobalt, Ontario, lump of silver ore from the Cobalt area (middle row); quartzite knife, antler toggle-head harpoon, piece of Cobalt silver, and fragment of worked copper (bottom row). (Shown one-third actual size.) (Courtesy Peter L. Storck and the Royal Ontario Museum, Toronto, Canada.)

cisor chisels and draw-knives have been found, the typical design has the tooth inserted at a right angle to the handle, wedged in a socket or slot and secured with a resinous glue.

Hundreds of kilometers westward many correspondences in bone and antler, chipped flint, and pottery have been found combined in unique ways in the camp and village refuse of other hunting, fishing, and gathering peoples. The same age of Saugeen and Point Peninsula and the Hopewellian cultures is geographically reiterated in a partly separate his-

PLATE 7.18. Point Peninsula antler combs from the Jack's Reef (1, 4, 8), Avon or Durkee (2), and Kipp Island (3, 6, 7) sites, New York, and from the Bay of Quinté (5) and Port Maitland (9), Ontario. The similar combs, Nos. 10 and 11, are from Rockingham County, Virginia. (Collection of the Rochester Museum and Science Center. [May not be reprinted without permission of the RMSC.])

tory. Here in northern Wisconsin are the sites of the North Bay and Nokomis Middle Woodland cultures of the same Middle Tier.

NORTH BAY AND NOKOMIS

Even allowing for incomplete mapping, the Wisconsin Middle Tier Middle Woodland cultures occupied more tightly circumscribed ranges than did Saugeen in Ontario. But like that manifestation they, too, were the nearest of kin and the legatees of the Late Archaic lifeways native to their respective habitats. Nokomis and North Bay were the first pottery-making cultures in northern Wisconsin. No ceramic Transitional, or Early Woodland, cultures have been detected here. Instead, as with an important part of the Saugeen area, the Late Archaic period survived longer than in the south and surrendered its tenure to Middle Woodland successors.

As with Saugeen, in contrast with Hopewellian and Point Peninsula and even the Northern Tier Laurel culture, Nokomis and North Bay are parochial expressions. They bespeak conservative adaptations notwithstanding their adoption of pottery, were of slight diffusional weight, but were generative of regional heirs. Both were influenced to some degree by the activities of the Hopewellian Interaction Sphere, though their remote locations isolated them from any sustained or intimate role. In ceramics some general similarities to Havana Ware and, at two of the North Bay sites, actual Havana and Hopewell trade vessels from the Illinois Valley, provide tangible evidence of this southern connection. But neither Nokomis nor North Bay can be called Hopewellian cultures or phases. They were involved with technologies and fashions and social concerns experiencing wide currency in the Great Lakes to the north of the tier of regional Hopewellian cultures. It was not a matter of Nokomis and North Bay people designing everything they made and did out of things preferred them by their neighbors (that such diffusion was operating is testified by the Havana ceramic traits, the Hopewell pots, and a few other considerations), but that they worked out their own preferred ways of doing things through a creative combination of their unique experiences and what they picked up or rejected in their leisurely interactions with all those other folk beyond the four horizons.

Sites of the North Bay culture appear to be confined to the Door Peninsula and the last few kilometers of the Fox River valley below Green Bay. All known locations are shore sites, mainly on Lake Michigan or on Green Bay or the lower Fox River. It is at a site in the river valley in modern day DePere (the Lawton site) that undoubted Havana tradition pottery was discovered as part of a North Bay assemblage. Examples of North Bay pottery, of course, have been recovered much farther afield than the distribution of North Bay settlements. The Nokomis culture, on the other hand, is reconstituted from sites on the small inland lakes, bogs, and streams of north central Wisconsin. Only a portion of this territory is in the Great Lakes drainage, draining either into Lake Superior or Green Bay or to the Mississippi River. This more terrestrially insular position is underscored by the nature of borrowed items: North Bay and Hopewellian pots were carried into Nokomis haunts to influence local design habits whereas a corresponding opposite influence is less apparent.

By the nature of their habitats the people of the two northern Wisconsin cultures must have relied heavily on water travel. Dugouts and bark canoes were doubtless made by the Nokomis folk. On the Door Peninsula dugouts would have been useful only in the back bays and on the inland lakes and swamps; for coastal travel the speedier and more buoyant and capacious bark canoes were vastly superior. Presumably with such versatile craft the North Bay people occupied the islands at the stormy mouth of Green Bay as well as the sandy, sheltered coves along the rocky coast of the mainland. Overland travel between many of these mainland villages and camps would have been extremely difficult, especially for whole families and encampments, due to intervening rough terrain, dense tangled forest, and mucky bogs. But certainly more than ease of transportation lay behind the selection of these shore stations. Rich fishing and the taking of water birds were prime benefits of such situations. In the north central lake country of Iron, Vilas, Oneida, Lincoln, Price, and Forest counties, the surveyed area within which the Nokomis sites were discovered, wild rice was probably an additional major equatic resource. Whatever the precise local combinations of hunting and fishing and gathering, that measure of success known as population was significantly higher than it had ever been before in these regions.

Whereas the regional Archaic forebears of the Nokomis culture have been provisionally identified in the Burnt-Rollways phase, those of the North Bay people remain to be isolated. It is the pottery that in both cases is the innovative harbinger of altered status. Both are coarse wares with heavy tempering and thick walls. North Bay vessels were bigger than their Nokomis counterparts. Many must have been close to 61 cm high and only a little less than 46 cm wide at the mouth and at the shoulder. Plain and cordmarked surfaces are present in the two ceramic assemblages with cordmarking much more common in Nokomis. The most characteristic Nokomis type, Lake Nokomis Trailed, bears broad finger-trailed lines drawn across a cordmarked surface. Incised-over-cordmarked sherds (so-called Dane Incised) have also been found as they have in several of the North Bay sites; such sherds have an enormous distribution extending far beyond the territories of the two Middle Woodland cultures, and they are specific to neither. Besides the finger-trailed and these ubiquitous sherds, Nokomis sites also reveal the presence of North Bay and Havana-Hopewellian trade vessels or vessels influenced in their design by those styles. Dentate stamping, cordwrapped-stick impressing, corded stamping (short cordwrapped-stick imprints simulating a dentate stamp), pseudo-scallop-shell stamping, finger pinching, cord impressing, and round, fingernail, end-of-cordwrapped-stick, and annular punctates are all present, if with unequal representation. Much more dentate stamping, cordwrapped-stick impressing, and pseudo-scallop-shell stamping are present in North Bay. Linear stamping, important in North Bay, is absent in Nokomis. Apparently also confined to the Door Peninsula-style constellation are such minority treatments as simple and complex stab-and-drag and plain and dentate rocker stamping.

In some North Bay sites periodic abandonment and reoccupation over several generations allowed wind-drifted sand or, in two clear instances, lake-deposited sand and gravel to cover and separate earlier from later habitation surfaces. Thus at the key Mero site on North Bay, a prominent embayment on the Lake Michigan coast, two sequent phases of North Bay cultural occupation were isolated by such stratification. This was the first site in the Upper Great Lakes where evidence of a post-Algoma high-lake stage was found—beach deposits, replete with water-rolled potsherds, sandwiched between Middle Woodland camp middens. The earlier, or North Bay I, stratum contained higher relative frequencies of plain unadorned pots than the later, or North Bay II, stratum. Between the two periods dentate stamping increased in popularity, punctating declined, one minority pottery type (Becker Punctated) vanished while another (Dane Incised) appeared for the first time, and there were a few alterations in details of paste, surface finish, and temper. These empirically established technical and style shifts in the North Bay ceramic tradition reflect, of course, the activities of the successive groups coming to live at this site. It has still to be determined if these were general long-term shifts or merely local perturbations. Because such splendid vertical segregation of successive phases within a single Middle Woodland culture is often searched for but not usually so unambiguously found, it is a strong temptation to unjustifiably extrapolate the observed particular trends onto a general model of culture change. For example, in part of the Mero site, clean wind-blown sand separated two episodes of occupation *within* the North Bay II period (North Bay IIa and IIb). The remains of two, possibly three, Dane Incised vessels were wholly restricted to the earlier episode. But finds from many other sites show the same kind of pottery associated with some later components as well. This local disparity records events that were not necessarily reflective of trends in the larger domain.

At the Porte des Morts site 16 km in a straight line north of the Mero site, middens probably best correlated with the North Bay II occupation at Mero have been radiocarbon dated to the middle of the second century A.D. Compatible with this assay is a superb example of a limestone-tempered (leached) plain rocker-stamped Hopewell pot found in a North Bay midden at the Porte des Morts site. This locality, too, yielded evidence of lake

PLATE 7.20. *North Bay Linear Stamped vessel from Rock Island Site II, Door County, Wisconsin. (Shown half actual size.) (Collections of Department of Anthropology, Lawrence University, Appleton, Wisconsin.)*

PLATE 7.21. *North Bay projectile points from the Mero site, Door County, Wisconsin. (Shown actual size.) (Collections of the Neville Public Museum, Green Bay, Wisconsin.)*

PLATE 7.22. *North Bay cordwrapped-stick decorated and plain (top row) and dentate-stamped (bottom row) pottery from the Mero and Porte des Morts sites, Door County, Wisconsin. (Shown about two-thirds actual size.) (Collections of the Neville Public Museum, Green Bay, Wisconsin.)*

transgression on a North Bay village or camp. The major occupation, however, is thought to postdate the transgression.

In dramatic contrast with Nokomis, the North Bay sites have revealed excellent bone preservation because of faster draining soils and more benign soil chemistry. Among the remains of deer, elk, beaver, bear, turtles, ducks, sturgeon, drum, channel catfish, smallmouth bass, and other meaty consumables was evidence of occasional cannibalism. Bone and antler weapons and tools were likewise well preserved. Especially prominent are awls and toggle-head harpoons just like those previously described for the Saugeen culture. Because such harpoons have also been recovered from Laurel culture sites to the north of the mapped Nokomis habitat, it would be justifiable to maintain that they were similarly a part of the weaponry of the latter folk as well.

Light copper tools are unexceptional in both cultures, though in this industry Nokomis is more imposing in variety and quantity. Typical are awls, punches, chisels, compound fishhook components, socketed conical projectile points, tanged points having flat blades and beveled edges, and

PLATE 7.23. *North Bay linear stamped (left), corded stamped and stab-and-drag (upper right); annular punctated (right center); incised-over-cordmarked (lower center); and pseudo-scallop-shell stamped (lower right) sherds from the Porte des Morts and Mero sites, Door County, Wisconsin. (Shown about two-thirds actual size.) (Collections of the Neville Public Museum, Green Bay, Wisconsin.)*

beads. Nokomis sites have even preserved copper workshop areas with stone-lined annealing hearths, copper scraps, and stone hammers, anvils, and abraders used in working the metal. Pieces of raw copper, if not finished articles, must sometimes have departed these precincts in reciprocation of the traded pottery and whatever else may have escorted it. This is a likely source of some of the North Bay copper tools.

Other signs of Nokomis involvement in trade are the presence of exotic materials in the chipped-stone industry: Dongola chert from southern Illinois, Knife River chalcedony from North Dakota, red chert from Barron County, Wisconsin, and even some rare flakes of obsidian from an ultimate provenience in Wyoming. It is more than likely that such attractive minerals passed through many hands on an indirect passage. North Bay lithics are much more provincial, being derived almost exclusively from chert pried out of the local Niagaran dolomitic limestone or selected out of the glacial gravels. In both cultures there is a considerable range in the forms of associated projectile points. Stemmed, side-notched, corner-notched, and corner-removed points have been found together with intergradational examples. Their fashioning was not guided by the same compulsion to achieve closely similar and aesthetically pleasing results as characterized many earlier flint knappers. In this regard, not surprisingly, they resemble Saugeen and Point Peninsula rather than, say, Meadowood or Red Ocher. However, these are strictly utilitarian creations. If more were known about what went into the graves of these peoples, it is possible that our evaluation of their flint-working prowess might be raised somewhat.

Wedges, scrapers of several ill-defined varieties, tanged knives, flake knives, ovate bifaces, preforms, and utilized flakes are common in both cultures. Typical of Nokomis are multiple-use plano-convex bifaces, while some North Bay sites have produced crude transverse and acuminate choppers. The latter are an instructive example of how deceptive mere appearance can be with regard to such essentially simple artifacts. Even

PLATE 7.24. *Hopewell (Baehr) rimsherd, three Laurel or Laurel-like rimsherds, four water-rolled North Bay sherds (top row), and a plain and two cordmarked North Bay body sherds from the Porte des Morts and Mero sites. (Shown about two-thirds actual size.) (Collections of the Neville Public Museum, Green Bay, Wisconsin.)*

though some resemble certain Old World Lower Paleolithic hand axes and chopper tools of an antiquity of hundreds of thousands of years, they all date to a few centuries around the time of Christ. They were heavy-purpose tools used without hafting for chopping, hacking, cutting, butchering, and other rough functions. They usually have sinuous edges produced by percussion flaking and retain sections of original cobble cortex, or weathered surface. In both North Bay and Nokomis, ground and polished stone tools are conspicuously rare if not altogether absent.

The problem of dating the North Bay culture was discussed earlier in the context of Saugeen problems. Nokomis sites have not been chronometrically dated. Samples of charred food incrustations scraped off of North Bay potsherds from Rock Island Site II, just north of Washington Island off the tip of the Door Peninsula, have produced divergent radiocarbon dates of about 65 B.C., which is not incompatible with the Porte des Morts date, and 590 B.C. The Richter site, a North Bay village on Washington Island, has a date of 520 B.C.

The Northern Tier: Laurel

Societies sharing geographical and temporal versions of the Laurel culture were to be found over a huge belt, or tier, at the top of and northward from the Upper Great Lakes. These were the northernmost of the Middle Woodlanders, and they cherished and retained their customs into times when people with Late Woodland types of cultures were coming on the scene in more southerly climes. The spatial range extended all the way from east central Saskatchewan to west central Quebec. In Ontario, where most of the Laurel sites have been recorded, they occur as far north as Big Trout Lake in the west and Lake Abitibi in the east. The southern frontier passes through northern Minnesota, at least the eastern half of the upper Michigan peninsula (with a southward salient out onto the islands at the entrance to Green Bay on Lake Michigan), the northern shores of the lower Michigan peninsula, and through eastern Ontario at about the latitude of the French River and Lake Nipissing. Laurel trade pottery has been found somewhat farther afield, of course. Specimens have been found at several points on the Wisconsin Door Peninsula in association with North Bay remains and, rarely, as far away as Lake Winnebago. The so-called Anderson and Nutimik "foci" in southern Manitoba are representative of local interpretations of the Laurel cultural pattern in that area. In eastern Ontario Laurel and Saugeen and Point Peninsula territories overlap and there is often considerable blurring of their individualities.

Although, as remarked, the greater number of Laurel sites have been found in Ontario, they are predominantly very small and unprepossessing campsites yielding sparce cultural detritus; they constitute scant impressions of seasonal rhythms, of one or two families temporarily encamped at a good hunting or fishing spot, which was perhaps visited over a period of several seasons. In particularly favorable haunts larger transient groups made repeated stopovers down the decades or even centuries. Most of these sites are in the boreal forest. But the largest, most complex, and richest have been found along the lower marches of the cultural range in northern Minnesota and Michigan. This intergrades with and is in the ecologically richer Canadian or Lake Forest environment rather than the Hudsonian Biotic Province. Moose and caribou in the north, deer and bear in the south, combined with smaller game such as beaver and porcupine, when joined to the abundant fisheries and seasonal vegetal pickings, made possible the support of sizable spring and summer aggregations at better-endowed places. Such places were simply fewer and farther apart in the boreal forest, and they were separated and surrounded by more thinly inhabited hinterlands.

Like the cultures just described, Laurel Middle Woodland deposits directly overlay Late Archaic and show sufficient correspondences in bone and, especially, stone weapons and tools (acidic soils have frequently obliterated all traces of organic remains) to indicate beyond much doubt that a major component of the former culture is the direct descendant of the latter. The pottery, of course, is an utter novelty without known regional forebears.

Among the common flint artifacts are a variety of usually smallish notched projectile points, edge-trimmed flakes, wedges, and strikingly high frequencies of scrapers—typically far higher than in other Middle

PLATE 7.25. *Laurel Culture platform pipe of polished stone from western Ontario. (Shown actual size.) (Courtesy Peter L. Storck and the Royal Ontario Museum, Toronto, Canada.)*

Woodland cultures. Notched net-sinkers are plentiful, but there is an extreme paucity of axes, adzes, pendants, or other ground and polished stone forms. Most of the kinds of small copper tools catalogued for the Nokomis culture occur in some, though by no means all, Laurel stations. Flat spiral-form beads seem to be an exception. Toggle-head harpoons join awls, "snowshoe" netting needles, and beaver-incisor knives as the most frequently encountered bone tools wherever preservation permits identification.

The first and, in most cases, last burial mounds in most of the country occupied by Laurel people were built by them. The great majority have been found along the Pigeon and Rainy rivers on the Minnesota—western Ontario border. Others have been discovered around Lake Nipigon. Over the greater part of the Laurel range, mounds were never thrown up. Because pottery-making and almost all mound-building were more ancient and widely honored practices to the south, it seems likely that they were borrowed by these northerners and immediately adapted to their native endowment. Although the ceramic innovation came to enjoy a much wider popularity than mound-building, there is no reason to suppose that it was everywhere accepted. There is a high probability that there were some people in the Laurel country who did not manufacture or use earthenware but who were fully contemporaneous with those who did and that the only empirical difference between their respective sites would be the presence or absence of sherds. That some aceramic sites are functionally explainable as transient hunting or other limited-use camps to which such a relatively fragile product would not ordinarily be transported is hardly to be doubted, but neither is the thesis that, on this remote frontier of the eastern North American ceramic culture area, there were coetaneous ceramic and aceramic cultures. Pollen studies based on Minnesota lake and bog sediments dating to the first millennium B.C. have produced hints of climatic amelioration which may have encouraged a northward expansion of wild rice and with it some southern cultural practices. These same pollen profiles appear to indicate that, from about the beginning of our era, climate and environment along the Rainy River have been essentially as they are now. If such paleoenvironmental indicators are at all applicable to more than just the few sampled local pollen catchments, they help make intelligible the northward expansion of pottery-making and mound-building, although they are not in themselves an explication. Why burial mounds should have been adopted by western Laurel groups, but not central or eastern ones, if not merely owing to differential propinquity to the Upper Mississippi Valley, one of the continent's major mound-building provinces, is difficult to fathom.

Laurel pottery is the most tell-tale marker of the culture. Ironically, given its geographically marginal position, many examples are among the finer technical accomplishments of North American prehistory. Granting that

PLATE 7.26. *Laurel rimsherds from northern Minnesota: incised, plain bossed, dentate stamped (top row), pseudo-scallop-shell stamped with bosses and punctates, banked complex stab-and-drag, pseudo-scallop-shell stamped, and simple stab-and-drag stamped (bottom row). (Shown two-thirds actual size.) (Courtesy Elden Johnson, Department of Anthropology, University of Minnesota, Minneapolis.)*

some Laurel potters were less skilled or simply took less care than others, most Laurel pottery is superior to most of the Middle Tier wares and is at least as good as the best of the Great Lakes Hopewellian. Hard, thin-walled, symmetrically crafted vessels, usually with conoidal to subconoidal bases and straight to moderately excurvate rims, are often provided with flat lips which meet the rim at so precise a right angle as to counterfeit planing. This sometimes superb, if simple, pottery is also much more crisply and precisely decorated than is Nokomis or North Bay or Saugeen or Point Peninsula pottery. Because decoration tends to be restricted to the upper half or third or less of a vessel's surface, great numbers of plain sherds typify Laurel sites. Furthermore, some vessels were without any trace of adornment or bore only one or two rows of rim-encircling bosses and/or punctates. There was no eschewing plain surfaces here.

The decorated vessels bear one or several circumferential bands of dentate stamping, pseudo-scallop-shell stamping, linear stamping, or stab-and-drag imprints—the last two subsumed under the type name

PLATE 7.27. *Laurel artifacts from various sites in western Ontario: rimsherds (top row); projectile points (second row); scrapers and a hafted scraper (third row); bone harpoon (lower left); and copper projectile points, awl, coil, and bead. (Shown half actual size.) (Courtesy Mike McLeod and the Department of Anthropology, Lakehead University, Thunder Bay, Ontario.)*

Laurel Oblique. Incising crosshatches was also employed. Except for the addition of bosses and/or punctates and, sometimes, incised lines, a single technique of embellishment was normally the preferred pattern. And such embellishment is remarkably neat and metrically regular in application. The type Laurel Bossed bears only bossing with or without alternating punctates. Rocker stamping, so conspicuous an element of Saugeen, Point Peninsula, and much Hopewellian pottery, is totally absent. Also absent are cordmarked surfaces and the use of cords or the cordwrapped stick in decoration. That the various types of Laurel pottery exhibit statistically significant variations in relative frequencies among the sampled sites has important implications for the study of Laurel culture history.

Disparities in type frequencies, orderings based on those disparities and on assumptions of regularity in the direction and pace of the rise and fall in type popularities (seriation analysis), some stratification, and all-too-sporadic attempts at chronometric control have generated a provisional sequence in the northern Minnesota sector of the Laurel range. While based on data from Minnesota sites, some broad correspondences with trends among far-removed sites lend credence to the sequence. According to the Minnesota chronology the Laurel culture, or at least its ceramic expression in northern Minnesota, divides into three temporal phases, each named after a key site. From earliest to latest these are: Pike Bay, McKinstry, Smith. In the earliest phase the ceramic profile shows that fully half of the pots belong to the type Laurel Oblique (with linear and stab-and-drag stamping), that there are only low percentages of dentate, pseudo-scallop-shell, bossed, or plain vessels, and that punctated rims are almost absent. By the time represented by the McKinstry phase, Laurel Oblique was in eclipse, dentate stamped and plain vessels had not improved their low popularities, but there had been a great increase in the incidence of pseudo-scallop-shell stamping. In this same phase Laurel Bossed doubled its popularity and there was a signal advance in the frequency of punctated rims. Finally, the late, or Smith, phase ushered in an impressive upswing in dentate stamping and in the use of punctating on all kinds of vessels; there was a corresponding decline in pseudo-scallop-shell stamping and in the making of plain vessels, and there was a resurgence of the type Laurel Oblique.

The changes in ceramic habits accompanying the passage of time are also to some extent congruent with the geographic disposition of the sampling stations. Laurel Oblique, for example, is the main pottery type at the southernmost Laurel sites but is a minor type at the northernmost. Laurel Pseudo-scallop Shell, on the other hand, is represented in reverse order, as in Laurel Dentate and the frequencies of bosses and punctates. In conjunction with the Minnesota sequence, the geographical plotting of type frequencies would seem to argue that the earliest Laurel sites occur in the southern frontier of that culture's range, that there had been a northward spread of Laurel population, and that the northernmost Laurel sites should be on the average the most recent in age. Available radiocarbon dates, while far from definitive in this regard, lend some modest support to the thesis of a south-north time gradient. The southernmost dated site of the Laurel tradition, Summer Island, in the Grand Traverse island group in Delta County, Michigan, in the entrance to Green Bay, has been dated to A.D. 50–250, whereas the Heron Bay site on the north central shore of Lake Superior appears to fall somewhere in the range A.D. 400–800. Geographically intermediate Laurel components are conformable chronometrically: Naomikong Point on the south shore of Lake Superior in Michigan, and the richest Laurel site ever dug (circa A.D. 430); the Laurel level at the Ekdahl-Goudreau site, also in the upper Michigan peninsula, in Schoolcraft County (circa A.D. 660); pertinent levels underlying the main occupations at Fort Michilimackinac at the Straits of Mackinac (between about A.D. 450 and 650). On the other hand, the McKinstry site in north central Minnesota, which is as far north as the Heron Bay site in Ontario, has produced a range of dates from about the time of Christ to approximately A.D. 560. The mound from which the radiocarbon samples were extracted showed evidence of several building stages, which fact seems reflected in the range of dates. The nearby Smith Mounds site has a radiocarbon age determination of circa A.D. 565. The McCluskey and Macgillvray sites on Whitefish Lake in western Ontario at about this same latitude have Laurel components dated cira 40 B.C. and A.D. 20, respectively.

The type locus of the Smith phase is the Smith Mounds site located on the Rainy River, Koochiching County, in far north central Minnesota. At least four burial mounds had been built at this place. The biggest measured 42 × 30 m and stood an impressive 14 m high. The two smallest mounds, which were the only ones ever to be scientifically excavated, were 12–15 m in diameter and 1–1.5 m high. Smith Mound 4, the smallest, contained the remains of 109 people, not including four intrusive burials probably ascribable to the descendent Late Woodland Blackduck culture. Overwhelmingly, these were bundle inhumations. There had been four different episodes of such group burials as attested by physically distinct and stratigraphically discrete clusters of bone bundles. Additional interments made at other times are reflected in smaller deposits of osseous material away from the principal concentrations.

The typical burial in Smith Mound 4 was a neat stack of arm and leg bones, often with the mandible inverted on top, and with the skull placed alongside or at one end. As with the bundle burials in the Hopewellian Norton mounds, all bones of the torso and of the hands and feet were usually lacking. Dusting or painting with red ocher was common. Surviving grave offerings were rare. All of the skulls bore witness to decapitation and revealed intentionally removed or shattered occiputs (the large bone at the lower back and bottom of the cranium). The great majority of femurs,

PLATE 7.28. *Laurel vessel from site EaJf-1 on the Wabinosh River, Lake Nipigon, Ontario. (Shown half actual size.) (Courtesy Mike McLeod and the Department of Anthropology, Lakehead University, Thunder Bay, Ontario.)*

tibias, ulnas, and other long bones also showed the nicking, cutting, and scraping scars of dismemberment and defleshing as well as deliberate perforation of the bone wall at one or both ends. Children's bodies were less subject to this curious kind of treatment. The breaking out of the occipital bones and the perforation of long bones may represent incredibly sloppy attempts at releasing the souls of the departed, the belief being widely entertained by many historic Indian people that the true seat of the soul is within the skeleton. Alternatively or additionally, the violence done to the bones may signify what the damage suggests: means of getting out the brains and extraction of bone marrow, respectively. This is the usual fate of the bones of game animals.

Because many Indian societies visited by early European explorers defleshed the skeletons of their dead preparatory to burial, the defleshing marks on the Laurel human bones are not necessarily signs of cannibalism. If the Laurel people did engage in such practices, a recurring phenomenon among other prehistoric as well as historic Indians, the evident ceremony with which the bones had been interred in the mound and anointed with the sacred red ocher, doubtless amid suitable lamentations, suggests the type called endocannibalism, the eating of one's kinsmen. This has been rationalized as the binder of generations, the transformation and rebirth of the ancestors in their descendants. The bones of enemies wind up in the midden or in the trash pits along with the offal from other animals. The bones of ancestors, their flesh eaten or not, receive honorable disposition. If not endocannibalism, the bones would seem to indicate prior exposure on a funerary scaffold or temporary burial and then ceremonial cleaning and soul release.

It is certainly not fortuitous that such arresting parallels in mortuary features as group interments, perforated crania, bundle burials, and mound construction occur in Laurel and in Hopewellian. The connection was previously hinted at with regard to the geographically expressed ambivalence toward mound building. While some archaeologists have looked as far afield as Siberia for the origin of the Laurel culture, others find a more parsimonious and convincing derivation by looking southward and much closer to home. Just as Laurel was the first Middle Woodland manifestation in the northernmost Great Lakes and beyond, so was it the last. Its most ancient known successor is best classified as Late Woodland. There were no Middle Woodland cultures north of Laurel; it truly constituted the sole exemplar of the Northern Tier. Even if Laurel may have persisted a trifle longer than the Middle Woodland cultures to the south, it is all the more testimony to the pervasiveness of now unfolding changes that the disappearance and replacement of Laurel was paralleled in many ways by what the archaeological record seems to reveal elsewhere in the lakes country.

References

On the Middle Woodland concept and its application in the Great Lakes:
Caldwell 1958; Fitting 1970 (especially Chapter V: "Burials and Fisherman"); Griffin 1952; R. J. Mason 1970; Ritchie 1969 (especially Chapter IV: "The Woodland Stage—Development of Ceramics, Agriculture and Village Life [c. 1000 B.C.–A.D. 1600]"); Ritchie and Funk 1973 (especially "The Middle Woodland Stage"); Stoltman 1978; Struever 1964 and 1965; J. V. Wright 1972a (especially Chapter III: "The Woodland Period"—particularly pp. 38-55 and 59-63).

On Southern Tier Middle Woodland—western Michigan Hopewellian:
Brown 1964; Flanders 1977; Griffin, Flanders, and Titterington 1970; Quimby 1941 and 1960b (especially Chapter 9: "The Hopewell Indians and the Beginnings of Agriculture in the Region").

On Southern Tier Middle Woodland—eastern Michigan Hopewellian:
Fitting, editor, 1972.

On Southern Tier Middle Woodland—Squawkie Hill:
Ritchie 1944 (pp. 202-226) and 1969 (pp. 213-228: "The Squawkie Hill Phase").

On Middle Tier Middle Woodland—Saugeen:
Finlayson 1977; Kenyon 1959; Watson 1972; J. V. Wright and Anderson 1963.

On Middle Tier Middle Woodland—Point Peninsula:
Emerson 1955; Johnston 1968; Ritchie 1944 (pp. 115-186) and 1969 (pp. 203-213: "The Early Point Peninsula Culture," pp. 228-232: "The Middle and Late Point Peninsula Cultures," and pp. 232-253: "The Kipp Island Phase"); Ritchie and Funk 1973 (especially "The Kipp Island Site (Aub. 12-1, 13-1)"), Ritchie and MacNeish 1949.

On Middle Tier Middle Woodland—North Bay and Nokomis:
R. J. Mason 1966 and 1967; Salzer 1974.

On Northern Tier Middle Woodland—Laurel:
Brose 1970a; Dawson 1974 and 1976a; Janzen 1968; Stoltman 1973; Wilford, 1955; J. V. Wright 1967.

Farmers without Plows, Warriors without Swords
The Last Act of Prehistory

8

Before the last Laurel bone bundles had been committed to earth, the northern marches were reverberating to summonses of change which earlier and more emphatically had been declared in the south. New things were astir. As always, old ways were refurbished to confront the challenge of novel situations. And also as always, the result was compromise. In retrospect, enough of the old persisted for archaeologists to later recognize continuity in change; enough of the new prevailed to force the recognition that another age had dawned. The familiar and the fresh had been accommodated in a regional modus vivendi. A similar pattern, different in detail, is to be seen in the North Bay country. It is also discernible in the concluding expressions of Point Peninsula and the other regional Middle Woodland cultures. The most apparent disjuncture between Middle and Late Woodland is in the Hopewellian Southern Tier and here mainly because of the disintegration of the system which had introduced and for a while sustained the circulation and copying of the imported ceramic wares, platform pipes, repoussé copper work, mica cutouts, and other exotica. So there were processes at work which crosscut cultural frontiers even if they were expressed in local idiom.

The early part of the Late Woodland period, which for convenience will be called Late Woodland I, is archaeologically recognized in different parts of the Great Lakes by the replacement of the Laurel culture by the Blackduck, of Nokomis by the Lakes phase, North Bay by the Heins Creek complex, Saugeen by Princess Point, Point Peninsula by Princess Point and Owasco, and the far-flung Hopewellian manifestations by the Effigy

Mound culture in Wisconsin and by a multiplicity of successor and more localized cultures elsewhere. In other areas where these particular cultural terms are overextended or inappropriate because of inadequate field work and scanty sampling or other considerations as, for example, in parts of the upper Michigan peninsula, northwestern Wisconsin, and sections of northern Ohio and Indiana, there is usually some evidence of analogous developments. In certain of these transitions, the Point Peninsula—Owasco being the best one, the almost step-by-step evolution of the successor culture from its antecedent can be traced in satisfying detail and with fine chronological control. In others much less is known of precisely what took place or of how or when or where, and the telescoping effect of insufficiently finely dated and too spatially separated sites presents an unrealistically flat or featureless succession. Even so, most sectors of the Great Lakes reveal a proliferation of contemporary and sequent cultures. There is no doubt that the reality was more complicated than our understanding of it.

For one thing, population continued its accelerating growth. For another, the Late Woodlanders were the beneficiaries of the earlier limited achievements in agriculture. There were simply more possibilities for combinations of elements of the demographic and cultural patrimony under the stimulus of local contingencies. The later Late Woodland times, here called Late Woodland II, are characterized by increased evidence of greater numbers or more localized cultures. Certainly part of this is only apparent, due to better preservation of the later components. But in part for reasons just adduced, it is also real. Through the early and late stages of Late Woodland, the three-tier latitudinal stratification described for the preceding period is still discernible even if it is less marked.

The Late Woodland period has been defined as much by the disappearance of specifically Middle Woodland, especially Hopewellian, traits as by the emergence and dissemination of new ones. In line with the previous observations regarding continuities between the two periods, it should be stressed that most of the differences, apart from the subtraction of the classic Middle Woodland attributes, have to do with variations and the deemphasis or the intensification of inherited institutions and technologies. But these were at least as important in themselves as were the relatively few true innovations that mark the period.

In general, the Late Woodland cultures demonstrate a lessened attention to elaborate mortuary ritual, at least as they were expressed in lavish grave furnishings. The contrast between high-status burials with abundant and often exotic appurtenances and the simple graves of the great majority, itself largely restricted to the Hopewellian cultures, virtually vanishes in the Late Woodland sites. Instead, a more approximately equal apportionment of fewer and simpler artifacts reduces the graves to a much more homogeneous and duller range. This fact strongly implies the triumphant resurgence in the Great Lakes of the ancient egalitarian folk ethic and the abandonment of the Hopewellian-inspired experiments with an hierarchical social order. Paradoxically, however, the construction of burial mounds did not come to a halt. Indeed, more mounds were built in Wisconsin and Minnesota during the Late Woodland period, for example, than in all previous time. The first burial mounds to be erected in the northern lakes country of Wisconsin date from the Late Woodland period. Nevertheless, this sometimes prolific mound-building activity had more to do with funerary duties owing all manner of kinship or residence groups than with the honoring of a minority elite. While the earthworks are often of impressive dimensions and shapes, as in many of the productions of the Effigy Mound Culture west of Lake Michigan, the people who were interred in them were but simply and relatively uniformly equipped. Many mound inhumations yield nothing in the way of associated grave offerings. And the western Great Lakes even increased its enormous preponderance of mounds over the eastern. In fact, mound building east of Michigan virtually ceased.

The increase in the number of Late Woodland burials, cemeteries, and camp and village locations was due to a growing population, as already asserted, and not just to better preservation as a function of relative recency of abandonment vis-à-vis Middle Woodland sites. This greater and growing population depended much more than ever before on agricultural crops. Especially after about A.D. 1000 native agriculture's contribution to the subsistence base attained its maximum development and had probably spread as far north as it ever would. Whereas northern Great Lakes tribes continued throughout Late Woodland times to practice little or absolutely no farming, relying instead on the ages-old triad of hunting–fishing–gathering, some of the southern societies had come to a dependence on large-scale agriculture as great as that of the historic Iroquoian peoples of the eastern Great Lakes. Even many of the wilderness-harvesting northerners traded for agricultural produce and thus came to be influenced by the results of practices they did not themselves engage in. Abundant remains of corn, beans, squash, and sunflower seeds are now unexceptional in the archaeological record. Of course, hunting and fishing and the collecting of wild plant foods continued as valued activities even among the most committed of the farmers. Even at its very productive peak, Great Lake native agriculture remained a primitive rather than wholly sufficient subsistence system. Technically, it was horticulture, its tools confined to digging sticks and hoes. Nothing even remotely resembling a peasantry ever arose among these societies.

In favored northern locales a quasi-agriculture evolved around the annual harvesting of abundant wild rice. Undoubted ricing pits (for threshing the grain) in northwestern Wisconsin and Minnesota Late Woodland sites attest its significance. Sites with such features tend to fall late in the period.

An unpleasant concomitant of population increase and the much enhanced value of cultivated vegetable foodstuffs and the tracts of land best adapted to food production was a dramatic upswing in the frequency and scale of warfare. Walled villages, indeed towns, multiplied, many with double or even triple defensive stockade lines. In some areas, as in New York and parts of Ontario, settlements were removed from intrinsically hard-to-defend riverbank locations and relocated inland atop natural rises, thus reducing chances of surprise and maximizing defensive fields of fire. This convenience-transcending concern with settlement consolidation and fortification was vastly more widespread than in any antecedent period. Accompanying it was a correspondingly great increase in the importance and practice of the war-captive torture-and-cannibalism syndrome that was such a shocking aspect of the Indian scene as recorded by early European visitors. Such evidence of cannibalism as knife-scarred and cracked and charred human bones in roasting pits or scattered in general village trash along with deer and other game animal bones identically treated and disposed of is abundant in many, though by no means all, sites.

The single most characteristic flint artifact of the Late Woodland period is the simple triangular projectile point. The bulk of these ubiquitous flints was certainly arrowheads. Notwithstanding the fact that the bow and arrow had been known in eastern North America long before, its widespread use was for some reason delayed until Late Woodland times. This observation suggests that it was the mounting intensity of warfare that bestowed on this weapon a value not perceived earlier. While sometimes side-notched, the vast majority of triangular points were made without notching. At different times among different groups they were beautifully finished with bifacial flaking, were only unifacially finished, or were simply edge-trimmed flakes. Some components yield examples of all three varieties, perhaps the results of the personal preferences of abilities of their makers. Occasionally, small-stemmed points were made. Imported flints became the exception rather than the rule. Inasmuch as arrows tend to be expended in greater numbers and more of them are apt to be lost than darts and spears, the virtually universal conversion to the easily produced simple triangular point made sense in terms of labor expenditure as against the odds of projectile losses.

Because potsherds are usually the most numerous artifacts after flint-chipping debris and there are almost always at least one or two diagnostic rims or decorated body pieces in any handful of sherds, it is usually pottery fragments that first proclaim the period of occupation and the cultural affinities of the site's former inhabitants. Even though there is a bewildering range of stylistic variation in Late Woodland ceramics from area to area, doubtless reflective of the sociological complexity giving rise to it, sufficient cross-cutting style concepts and technical attributes were shared by so many even widely separated societies that their approximate coevality is readily suggested by inspection. In the Late Woodland period the demise of pseudo-scallop-shell stamping and rocker stamping and the great reduction in the popularity of dentate stamping, for example, were generally compensated for by a mushrooming employment of varieties of cordwrapped-stick and linear cord impressing as well as incising and trailing. The incidence and extent of cordmarking as a surface finish changes; round-bottomed globular vessel shapes become common; particularly later in the period the free use of shell tempering appears for the first time; and collars, rim peaks, castellations, and even handles now appear, even if they are not universal. The major ceramic innovation in the western Great Lakes, however, was linked to the introduction and dissemination of Mississippian peoples, products, and ideas. In the east it was the gradual evolution of the distinct pottery traditions associated with the Iroquoian peoples. Another Late Woodland development was the proliferation and further elaboration of the smoking-pipe complex. This was most intense, not surprisingly, in those areas where tobacco could most successfully be grown and along major trade routes.

Besides the sharply divergent new pottery styles introduced by the Mississippians, their culture was the inspiration for the adoption of lightning symbols and snake designs and the strikingly stylized "weeping eye" motif—all usually rendered in cut-out sheet copper or as shell figures or inscribed on marine-shell pendants and gorgets. These and other traits, when they make their appearance in the Great Lakes, are most familiarly connected with what archaeologists call the Upper Mississippian cultures rather than the more celebrated Middle Mississippian. The latter type of culture is known from stunningly big and internally complex sites from south central Wisconsin to the Gulf of Mexico and located in the sprawling river valley after which the culture was designated. These impressive sites, having monumental ceremonial centers with plazas and flat-topped pyramids supporting traces of temples and the residences of a ruling elite, signal an attenuated salient of the Mexican or more general Mesoamerican cultural pattern of hierarchically organized, theocratic, fully sedentary, farming societies. Second only to corn and the other introduced domesticated crops, Middle Mississippian offers the clearest instance of Mesoamerican diffusion into eastern North America. But even though the great fortified site of Aztalan on the Crawfish River does represent a definitive Middle Mississippian presence as far north as southern Wisconsin, it remains in the Mississippi drainage and had slight discernible influence on the people of the Great Lakes. The Mississippian cultures of the lakes country were representatives of the Upper, not the Middle Mississippian, group. Undeniably related to the latter, though just how remains unclear, the Upper Mississippians had a much simpler way of life and shared many characteristics with the non-Mississippian Woodland groups. It should be clear from the foregoing that the terms "Upper" and "Middle" refer to geographic displacement, not temporal or stratigraphic position.

Upper Mississippian culture itself has been divided into two grand regional groupings: Oneota in the western Great Lakes and northern Mississippi Valley, and Fort Ancient in southern Ohio and Indiana and contiguous portions of Kentucky and West Virginia. While Fort Ancient trade vessels and social influence made their way into the Great Lakes, especially along the south shore of Lake Erie, it is Oneota that is the preponderant version of Upper Mississippian in the lakes country. This cultural pattern arose several centuries after the beginning of the Late Woodland period, perhaps first appearing a little before A.D. 900 even though it was not widely disseminated nor represented by numerous sites until after the year 1100.

Late Woodland I

As previously suggested, a general overview of the whole Great Lakes is facilitated by the adoption of a useful, if crude, division of the Late Woodland period into two parts. The first occupied the time between the end of the Middle Woodland period and, in the west, the intrusion and adaptation of Mississippian cultural groups and, in the east, the emergence of proto-Iroquoian cultures. In the northern reaches of the lakes country these later developments were much retarded in their initial appearance or they did not manifest themselves at all. Here there was much less change, and the divisions early and late, while still meaningful, are not nearly as contrastive as elsewhere. In some sections the advent of Mississippian culture was abrupt and unequivocal, marking a sharp break in the continuity of local cultural evolution; elsewhere its arrival is only hinted at by the adoption of shell tempering in pottery or the addition of a scroll or other curvilinear style motif where it had never been known before. Of course, trade amplified the Mississippian and Iroquoian innovations far beyond their familiar domains. Calendrically, then, the end of the early stage varies from area to area. In northeastern Illinois and southeastern Wisconsin the first Mississippian cultural influences (Oneota, Fisher, Huber) date after A.D. 900; in the southern Ontario the earliest cultures that can be called proto-Iroquoian (Glen Meyer and Pickering) are dated no earlier than about A.D. 900; New York proto-Iroquois (Oak Hill) evolution was under way by approximately A.D. 1300; but along the north shore of Lake Superior the Blackduck culture enjoyed a tenure with relatively little modification in life-style or material products from the end of Laurel times to the coming of the Europeans.

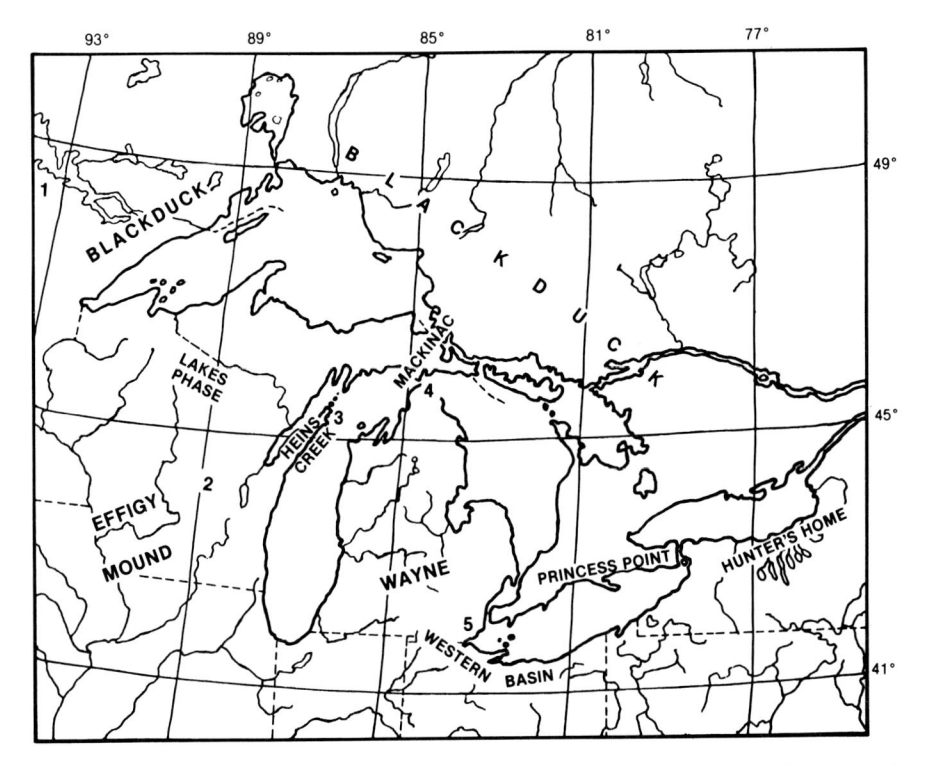

MAP 8.1. *Major cultural groupings in the Late Woodland I period and archaeological sites mentioned in the text: (1) Smith Mounds; (2) Sanders I; (3) Heins Creek and Mero; (4) Juntunen; and (5) Sissung.*

An excellent example of this widespread early Late Woodland, or Late Woodland I, cultural stage is the Heins Creek complex of northeastern Wisconsin. The type site is on Lake Michigan on the Door Peninsula not quite 16 km south of the Mero site. Here at the Heins Creek site, buried in an old occupation layer by a stabilized sand dune, the complex was first recognized and was radiocarbon dated to approximately A.D. 720. The same culture was also represented at the Mero site where, intermixed with later material, it overlay a culturally sterile aeolian or wind-blown sand deposit atop the strata containing the remains of the North Bay culture. Like many of the other Late Woodland I cultures, the Heins Creek complex looks like a home-grown successor of the antecedent regionally defined Middle Woodland culture. Although the transitional sites remain to be discovered, there is little doubt regarding the Heins Creek ancestry.

Mingled with the butchered and cooked remains of mammals from the size and heft of deer and bear to mink and muskrat, of turtles, of birds (especially waterfowl like ducks, loons, and grebes), and of a variety of fish

Plate 8.1. *Heins Creek Ware rimsherds from the Heins Creek site, Door County, Wisconsin. (Shown half actual size.) (Collections of the Neville Public Museum, Green Bay, Wisconsin.)*

were broken grit-tempered earthenware pots, chipped-stone weapons and household tools made out of local Niagaran chert, bone and antler implements, and the lesser detritus of flint chippage, fire-cracked rocks, and flecks of charcoal from long-dead fires. Among the stone artifacts, the projectile points afforded the sharpest contrast with what had gone before. These were now all simple triangular arrowheads. Only 22 mm (⅞ in.) to 45 mm (1¾ in.) long, they are much smaller and lighter than their predecessors. Just a third had been bifacially finished. The rest retained large unmodified surfaces of the original flakes on which they had been made. While a few had been carefully produced, the majority displayed little regard for strict symmetry or precise edge conformation. The other chert artifacts displayed the same level of craftsmanship: a straightforward functional approach little inclined to entertain aesthetic considerations. Large ovate to triangular knives, hurredly fabricated beveled scrapers, a drill, and a few tool fragments of unascertainable function complete the chipped-stone inventory.

Needles, awls, pins, socketed conical arrowheads made from antler tines, a bipointed grooved splinter which may have been a net-weaving instrument, harpoons, and unidentifiable fragments comprised the bone and antler tools. The harpoons are not the toggle heads favored by North Bay people but are a straight-tanged type equipped with multiple barbs aligned along one edge.

Virtually all of the Heins Creek pottery was heavily cordmarked. The few exceptions were secondarily smoothed cordmarked sherds from basal sections of the original vessels and some sherds bearing the impressions of a coarse mat-like fabric. Some of the cordmarked sherds were also brushed, that is, after a pot had received the cordmarked surface finish, parts of its surface were wiped with a handful of rough vegetable matter which left parallel scratches or striations obscuring but not oliberating the texture of the cordmarking. While a preponderant majority of the sherds bore no decoration over the surface finish, hypothetical reconstruction of the numbers and kinds of the whole pots originally present, based on correlated details of curves of rim sections, sherd thickness, decoration patterns, slight but consistent divergences in temper, and similar criteria, revealed that most of the original vessels had been decorated. But because decoration was mainly confined to the upper third or less of vessel surfaces, and there were in fact some plain vessels, a majority of sherds were without embellishment.

This well-made pottery was left plain or was decorated by means of the cordwrapped stick. In one fashion, short oblique or vertical imprints were made on the rim and lip or on the vessel neck. Such sherds were assigned the type name Heins Creek Corded-stamped. A minority of vessels also bore rows of corded stamping in chevron pattern on the body below the neck. A second fashion, Heins Creek cordwrapped-stick, employed the full length of the implement laid end to end to effect a band of multiple rows encircling the vessel on the neck. This band was usually bordered above and/or below by a row of hemiconical punctates produced by stabbing the clay at an angle with the end of the cordwrapped stick. Corded stamped imprints frequently occur on lips, at rim-lip juncture, and on the upper rim interior on both of these types. Besides a few examples of pots decorated almost exclusively with punctations, about a fifth of the vessels

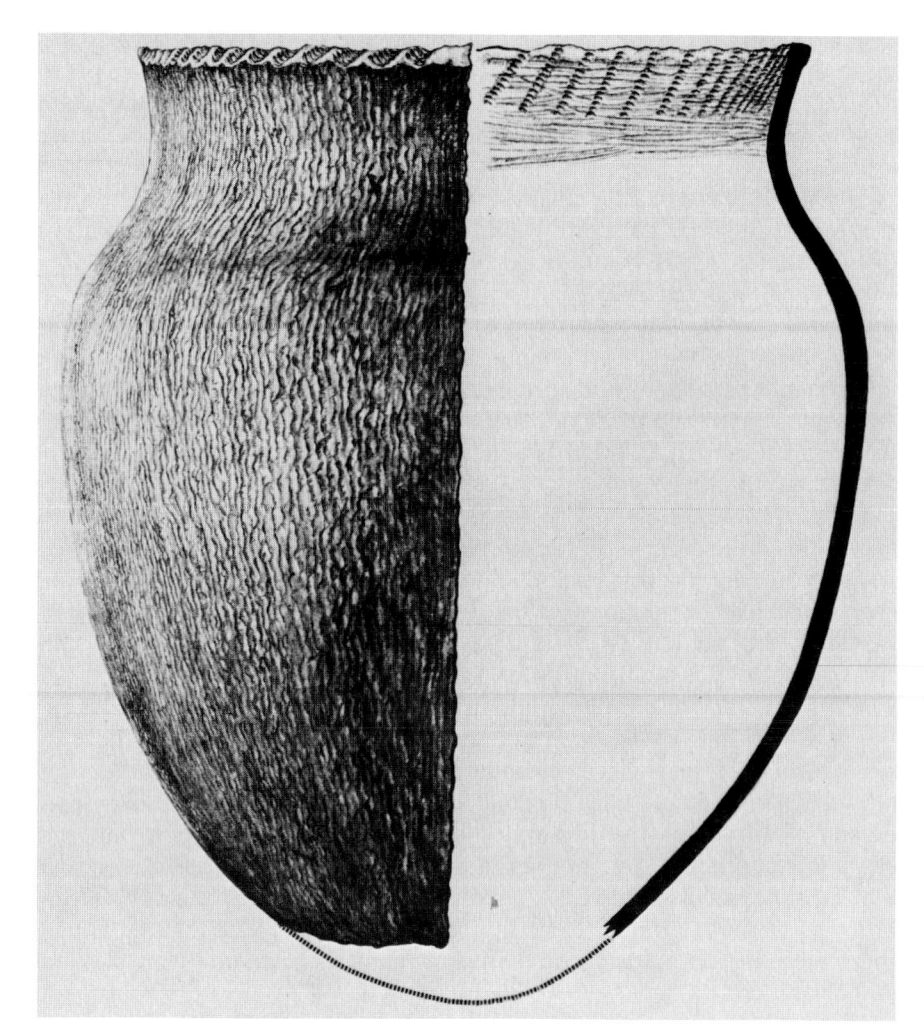

PLATE 8.2. *Reconstructed Madison Ware cordmarked vessel from the Effigy Mound culture Sanders site, Waupaca County, Wisconsin. The interior rim decoration has been sketched in at right. (Shown approximately one-third actual size.) (Courtesy William M. Hurley, University of Toronto, and the Museum of Anthropology, University of Michigan, Ann Arbor.)*

associated in the Heins Creek complex represent trade or the intrusion of new ceramic styles by visiting friends or relations from a society having a somewhat different cultural tradition.

The imported pottery types at the Heins Creek site are Madison Cord Impressed and Point Sauble Collared. These are varieties of Madison Ware, a Late Woodland class of pottery typical of the Effigy Mound culture. These types, like Heins Creek Ware, are virtually always entirely cordmarked. Madison Cord Impressed decoration may be similar to Heins Creek Cordwrapped-stick, though it frequently includes more complex geometric designs often running to triangular plats of opposed diagonal, horizontal, or vertical lines, to chevron and criss-crossed zones, and to parallel bands beneath upper rim-lip obliques and above pendant looped cord punctations. Such embellishment is usually restricted to rim and neck. A major difference is in the means whereby decoration was applied. In Madison Cord Impressed and Point Sauble Collared, the cordwrapped stick was rolled across selected portions of the vessel surface to produce multiple parallel lines of twisted cord impressions, or else single strands of twisted or even braided cord were repeatedly impressed in the clay. This mirror impression of cordage is often so detailed and well preserved that its study has thrown much light on aspects of ancient technology that otherwise could hardly have escaped total erasure. The makers of the pottery were skilled at fabricating cords and weaving nets and fabrics. They were doubtless also good at basketry.

One patient study of cord casts made from their impressions in pottery revealed unsuspected complexity. In a common type of cord, two simpler cords could be seen to be wrapped around each other. Because a length of twisted cord will tend to become unraveled, it must be combined with another identically twisted cord and then twisted in the direction opposite to that of its constituent cords. By this ingenious use of opposing forces cords can be made to maintain their desired form. In the example of the cord just given, two cords each twisted in a clockwise fashion will necessarily be twisted together in a counterclockwise direction; if the consituent cords are themselves twisted counterclockwise, they must be twisted around themselves clockwise. A cord showing a clockwise twist is called an S-cord, one with a counterclockwise twist a Z-cord, the downslope of the letter conforming with the orientation of the cord segmentation resulting from the particular twist. Thus the first cord described in the foregoing would be designated a Zss-cord, signifying that it consists of a counterclockwise-twisted strand of two clockwise-twisted cords. The reverse of this would be an Szz-cord. Examination of cordmarked and cord-decorated pottery has demonstrated that the Effigy Mound and other people were rarely content with so simple a cordage. Simple cords like two S-twist cords would be combined to produce a Z-twist cord which would be combined with another compound Z-twist cord to make a more complex S-cord. Such a cord would be designated an S/Zss/Zss cord. And this was only the beginning of a whole series of combinations and permutations. Seventy-eight different cord combinations have been identified to date! In this study of an ancient technology, the ceramic, impressively detailed "hard" information was produced relative to another seemingly unrelated technology whose original products long ago fell to dust. Work is now going forward to determine how and at what rate these cords changed over space and time and to what extent they will provide another source of information on cultural identifications, affiliations, and interactions.

The important pottery type Point Sauble Collared differs from Madison Cord Impressed in a number of details, but most conspicuously in the presence of a distinct, if low and narrow, collar or "braced rim" produced either by modeling excess clay purposefully extruded from the lip–upper-rim area or by the addition of a thin strip of clay to the rim. Closely spaced twisted-cord impressions cover this collar as well as the lower rim and vessel neck and upper shoulders. Massed simple geometric arrangements of contrasting verticals, obliques, opposed obliques, and horizontals prevail. Subcollar punctates, often made with a knotted loop of cord, frequently border the collar or serve as a fringe to the zone of neck decoration. An unusual feature of some of the Point Sauble Collared vessels associated with the Heins Creek complex are very deep, perfectly round subcollar or neck punctates which have produced corresponding bosses on the interior. Coexisting with Madison Cord Impressed for a long time, Point Sauble Collared attained its peak of popularity after the other type had reached and passed its own. But both types survived well into Late Woodland II times.

As indicated in the foregoing, Madison Cord Impressed and Point Sauble Collared are two important types of what has been designated Madison Ware. Pottery types such as Madison Plain, Madison Fabric Impressed, and Aztalan Collared are other divisions of Madison Ware, though not all sharing exactly the same spatial range or being entirely coetaneous. Aztalan Collared, to take one example, is more numerous in the southern than in the northern half of its distribution. There is evidence that it developed as a style category somewhat later than, say, Madison Cord Impressed. It differs from Point Sauble Collared in possessing a usually more pronounced collar, a high incidence of out-of-round or angular vessel mouths, sometimes large rim peaks and castellations, a strong tendency for the collars to have a smooth surface finish with the rest of the vessel surface cordmarked, and a restriction of decoration, if present at all, to the collar itself and to a row of subtended punctates. Many Aztalan Collared vessels were quite plain; others bore splendidly adorned collars. The type takes its name from its popularity at the Woodland–Mississippian Aztalan town site in south central Wisconsin. Here, it and other Madison Ware ceramic types have been recovered in repeated association with Middle Mississippian pottery identical to that typical of the Cahokia site opposite St. Louis in western Illinois.

PLATE 8.3. *Point Sauble Collared rimsherds from the Heins Creek, Mero, and Porte des Morts sites, Door County, Wisconsin. (Shown actual size.) (Collections of the Neville Public Museum, Green Bay, Wisconsin.)*

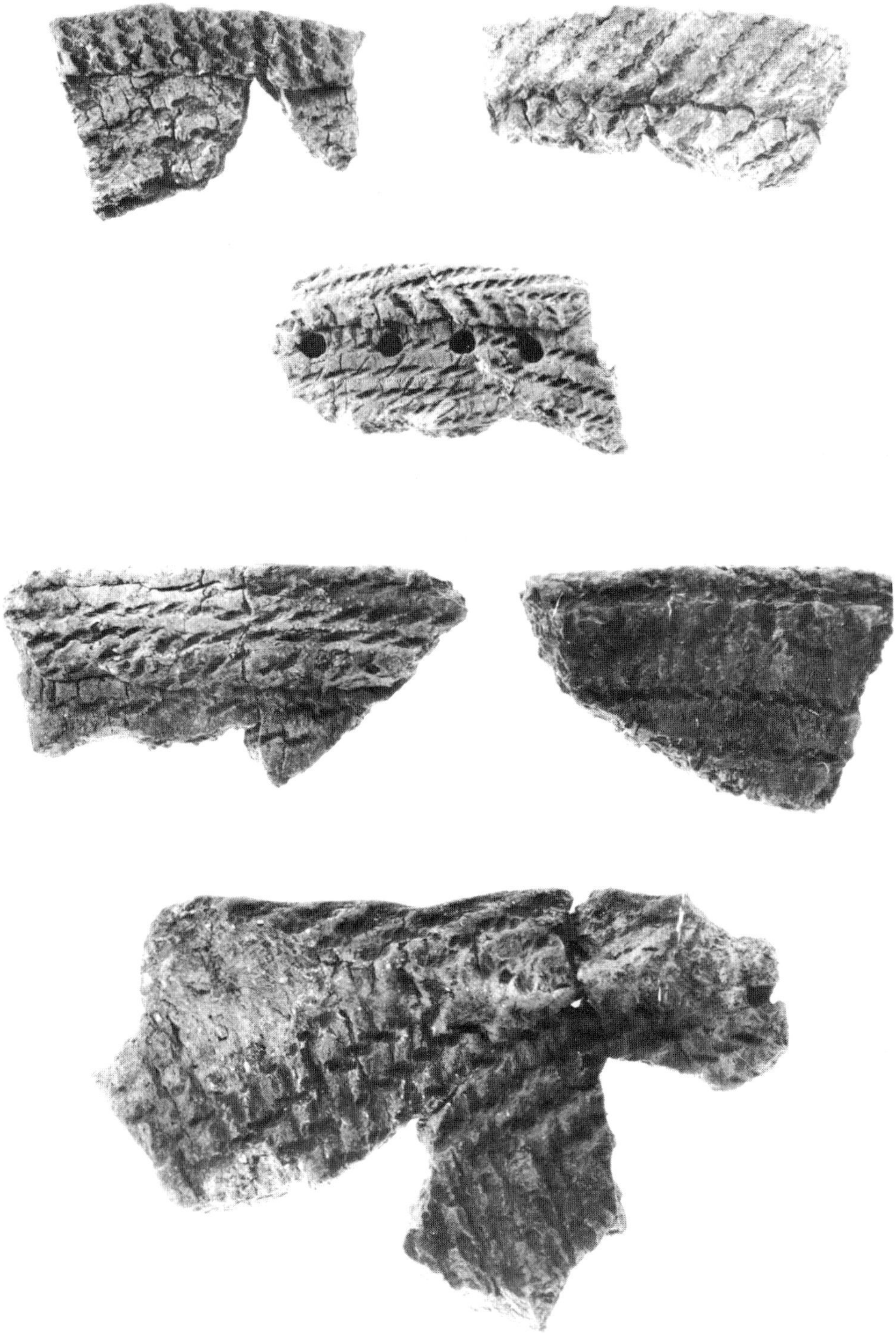

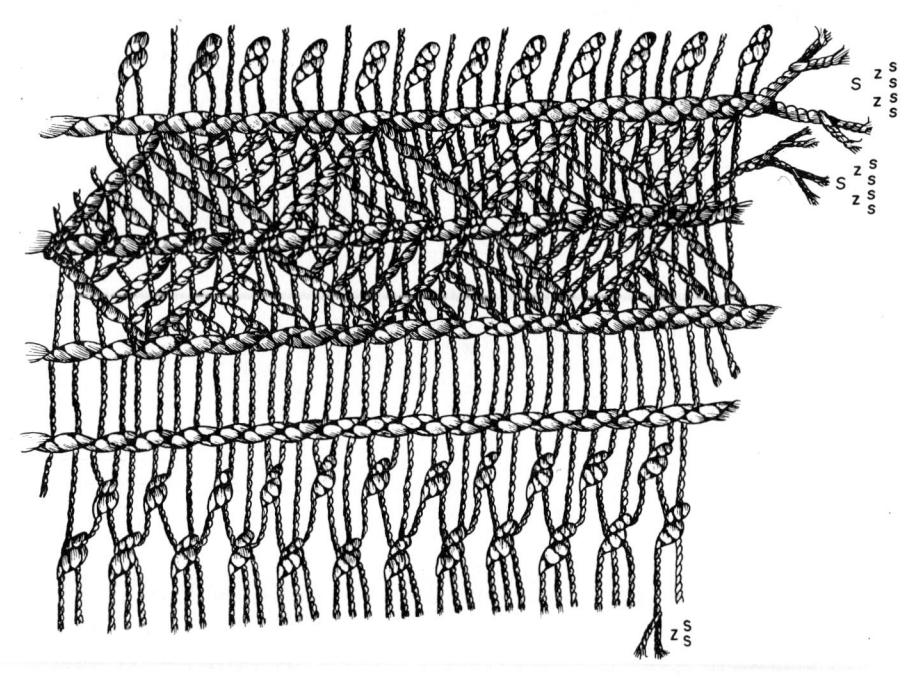

PLATE 8.4. *Cord and fabric reconstructed from impressions on a Point Sauble Collared rimsherd from the Effigy Mound Sanders site, Waupaca County, Wisconsin. The pattern is one of spaced horizontal and oblique weft-twining with spaced warps and fixed knotted loops. (Courtesy William M. Hurley, University of Toronto, and the Museum of Anthropology, University of Michigan, Ann Arbor.)*

Although its mapped distribution exceeds that of the Effigy Mound culture, Madison Ware was the pottery complex of the people responsible for the thousands of simple to zoomorphic burial mounds of that Late Woodland development. These earth monuments are usually very low, being only a meter or less in maximum height. But they are sometimes of enormous linear proportions, often 100 m or more. In ground plan most Effigy Mound culture mounds are round, oval, conical, rectilinear, or tapered rectilinear (the so-called catfish mounds). The more famous tumuli, of course, are the many animal-shaped ones. These were modeled in the silhouettes of flying birds with great outstretched wings, stubby-legged deer or elk, bears, panthers, dog or other canines, turtles, and other perhaps mythological creatures. They typically contain relatively little in the way of grave offerings, though the labor that went into them was no mean offering in itself. The symbolism the mounds have fossilized in earthen form is obscure despite the shapes they took. One idea is that some, if not all, signify the burial places of people who in life organized themselves in totemic clans or band societies. Notwithstanding some claims to authorship, effigy mounds were not the creations of the Winnebago Indians.

In Effigy Mound culture graves flexed, bundle, and cremation burials occur, sometimes associated with a stone or clay hearth feature called an "altar." As pointed out before, most bones are unaccompanied by grave offerings. Most of the artifacts that have been recovered from effigy mounds have come from the mound fill, that is, they represent debris that was already in the ground when the mound builders went to work. Fortunately, the Effigy Mound people sometimes erected their funerary monuments beside or even in their villages. In these cases the artifacts from the mound fill can be connected with the people who were responsible for the mound construction. While solitary Effigy Mound culture mounds are known, they are probably rare. In by far the greater number of instances Effigy Mound culture sites consist of at least half a dozen mounds to 40, 65, 80, and even more such structures. Although they occur in all kinds of topographical situations, most mounds and mound groups have been discovered arrayed along ridge tops or in other elevated environments. Because they are characteristically only .5–1 m in height, unknown but certainly large numbers of effigy mounds have been unintentionally or unfeelingly leveled and plowed into oblivion wherever they were built on what later came to be regarded as desirable agricultural land or home sites.

PLATE 8.5. *The Madison Ware type Aztalan Collared as represented by rimsherds from the Aztalan site, Jefferson County, Wisconsin (bottom), and from sites on the Wisconsin Door Peninsula (top). (Shown half actual size.) (Collections of Department of Anthropology, Lawrence University, Appleton, Wisconsin, and the Neville Public Museum, Green Bay, Wisconsin.)*

PLATE 8.6. *Madison Cord Impressed (B, E, F, J) and the closely related Madison Fabric Impressed (A, C, D, G-I, K-N) rimsherds from the Sanders site, Waupaca County, Wisconsin. (Shown half actual size.) (Courtesy William M. Hurley, University of Toronto, and the Museum of Anthropology, University of Michigan, Ann Arbor.)*

Knowing, deliberate destruction of such prehistoric monuments was for many years much more common practice than preserving them.

The Effigy Mound culture had a long career. Concentrated in the southern two-thirds of Wisconsin, but with sites also in northern Illinois, northeastern Iowa, and southeastern Minnesota, the culture was a recognized

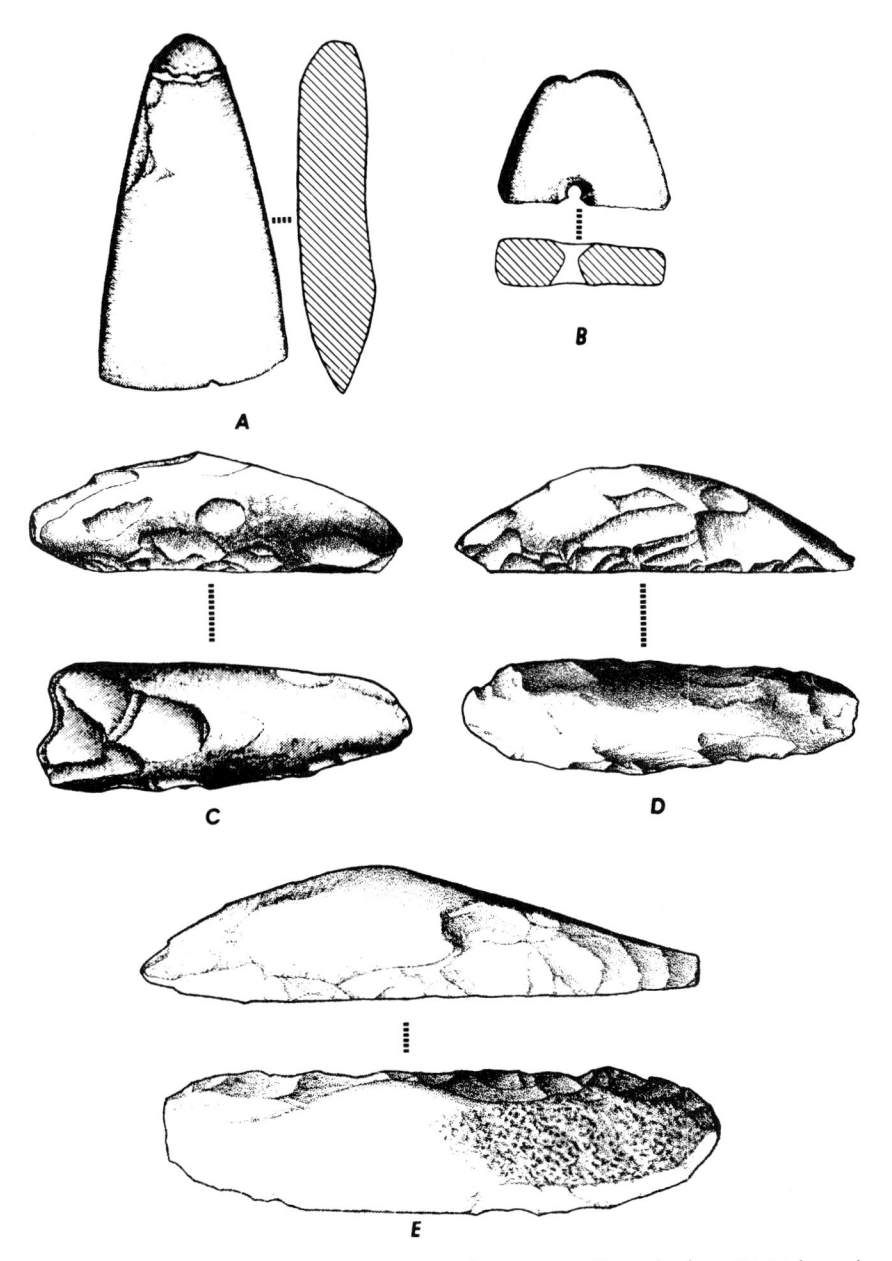

PLATE 8.7. *Effigy Mount Culture celt (**A**), broken gorget (**B**), and adzes (**C–E**) from the Sanders site, Waupaca County, Wisconsin. (Courtesy William M. Hurley, University of Toronto, and the Museum of Anthropology, University of Michigan, Ann Arbor.)*

entity by at least the sixth century A.D. Its terminal expressions were late enough to show contemporaneity with Middle Mississippian and Oneota peoples. It appears, nevertheless, that most mound building, and probably all effigy mound building, had gone out of favor by the time of the arrival of the first French explorers.

Very little evidence of agriculture has been linked to the Effigy Mound culture. That hunting, fishing, and gathering appear to have been the economic foundation (the bulk of the known sites are in the naturally highly productive Carolinian Biotic Province) does not preclude the possibility that corn and other agricultural resources may have been procured through trade, especially following the northward spread and multiplication of Oneota farming communities after A.D. 900–1000. Meat, animal skins, and other forest products surely sometimes accompanied the Effigy Mound pottery that frequently found its way into Oneota villages.

Evidence of farming is also lacking for the Heins Creek complex and for the partly contemporary Lakes phase. This latter is a collective name for the eight or nine centuries of Late Woodland occupations in north central Wisconsin following the Nokomis Middle Woodland culture and ending by perhaps 1400. Stratigraphic evidence from some Lakes phase sites indicates an internal sequence conformable with what has already been presented. Cordwrapped-stick and twisted-cord-impressed pottery predominates, with the promulgation of the practice of putting collars on vessels following an early period characterized by styles reminiscent of Heins Creek Ware and Madison Cord Impressed. Aztalan Collared-like and Point Sauble Collared-like vessels are more typical of the later components in Lakes phase sites. In some places they appear to be associated with Oneota pottery—probably the result of trade and perhaps some intermarriage rather than the refuse of a separate resident population.

Chipped-stone tools comparable to Heins Creek and Effigy Mound types dominate the lithic assemblage except that locally collected quartz was the pedestrian raw material. Wedges are common and are indistinguishable from examples many thousands of years older from the Flambeau and Minocqua Late Paleo-Indian phases. The use of copper shows a definite decline, though small simple-tanged projectile points, tanged single-edged "butterknife" knives, flat spiral beads, awls, and fishhooks were occasionally turned out. As indicated, the first burial mounds in this remote area have proved to be of Late Woodland age and have been assigned to the Lakes phase. Ossuaries have been found beneath some of them. Bone is poorly preserved. Except for the pottery, the burial mounds, and what they were able to receive in trade, the people of the Lakes phase during all of Late Woodland I and II times adhered to a way of life not profoundly different from that adduced for their Archaic ancestors. This country then, as today, was far more of a cul-de-sac than a crossroads, and it seems likewise to have encouraged a conservative tenacity which helped secure life even if at a pace behind those of some other areas.

In many ways similar was the Blackduck culture, though its sites are distributed over an enormously vaster territory. With a range from northern Lake Huron to Manitoba, it is not surprising that Blackduck exhibits many localized versions. Yet throughout there is a Blackduck identity that rarely allows confusion with the Lakes phase or Effigy Mound or any other Late Woodland culture. That this is so, and that its constituent sites virtually span the Late Woodland I and II sequence, makes it possible to speak of a Blackduck "tradition."

The best-studied large samples have come from Minnesota. Here the most typical reconstructed vessel form is distinctly round-bottomed and globular with round shoulders, moderately constricted neck, and moderately to but slightly excurvate rim; especially noteworthy is a marked tendency to very broad, splayed lips. Large storage pots, smaller cooking pots, and small vessels made as grave furniture have been found. Most Blackduck pots are cordmarked from top to bottom. In some instances, however, net or fabric impressing was substituted. Smooth surface finishing or brushed ("combed") surfaces, when present, are restricted to the neck and rim of otherwise cordmarked or fabric-marked vessels. These alternatives were acted upon by time so that they have some chronological significance.

Decoration is so dominated by cordwrapped-stick impressing and by punctating that for most purposes optional techniques may be ignored. Twisted-cord impressing, for example, is virtually absent from the Blackduck repertoire. Placed on the rim and/or neck, horizontality of design is emphasized by very tightly spaced vessel-encircling rows of cordwrapped-stick impressing either alone or in combinations with a single row of punctates or, rarely, bosses. The punctates may be round or rectilinear or they may be the hemiconical results of the high-angled application of the end of the cordwrapped stick. Other Blackduck vessels were embellished solely by short vertical or diagonal imprints of a cordwrapped stick on the upper rim. A favorite combination was oblique lines on the upper rim and a band of horizontal lines below, sometimes with subtended punctates or with punctates placed between two of the upper rows of lines in the band. This stamping and punctating typically has a deep crisp execution that sets it apart from all other wares. The characteristic thickened and often beveled lip is also adorned with cordwrapped-stick impressions oriented obliquely, in criss-cross or chevron fashion, or placed centrally and running parallel to the vessel wall.

As already pointed out, Blackduck pottery was made over a long time. Stratigraphic excavation in northern Minnesota has produced information relative to some of the changes time impressed on that pottery. Excavation

PLATE 8.8. *Rimsherds of the Blackduck Culture from sites in northern Minnesota. (Shown half actual size.) (Courtesy Elden Johnson, Department of Anthropology, University of Minnesota, Minneapolis.)*

at the multicomponent Smith Mound site on the Rainy River resulted in the identification of an "early" and a "late" phase of Blackduck in northern Minnesota. Among the distinctions, cordmarking was the dominant early surface finish whereas fabric-impressing dominated the late phase. Interior rim decoration was much more frequent in early than in late Blackduck. Nodes or bosses were confined to the early phase. Undecorated rims or the mutually exclusive use of cordwrapped-stick impressions or punctations are characteristic of the late period. Other statistically significant shifts were discovered with respect to types of punctations, relation of the punctations to the overall design, preferred design combinations, lip modifications, and the specific types of cordwrapped sticks used in marking the pottery.

Perhaps most of this variation through time, and the Minnesota excavations have intercepted it only toward the ends of the continuum and in but one, albeit a major one, of the culture's territories, is the slow cumulative affect of miniscule changes. Handmade things are inherently and inescapably subject to small deviations notwithstanding unconscious cultural pressures to conform to generally accepted ways of doing things. The changes any individual potter might initiate are normally constrained by group expectations and are not copied or further amplified if they result in unfavorable reactions. Most are not repeated but unconsciously eliminated from replication by other potters. But individuals make mistakes, some are sloppy or have poor hand-eye coordination while others are deliberate and skilled, and some element of play or experimentation inevitably comes into action, particularly where outside influences provide additional models. And time as well as space is the great deviation-amplifying agency. Even though not obvious over one or two generations, deviations are added to earlier ones so that over several generations very detectable changes may come about. Directions of change, style trajectories, come quite innocently into being in small-scale, relatively isolated societies. Once underway, they may accelerate or quickly come to an end. They rarely reverse themselves in any given cultural tradition. Time-honored analytical techniques such as seriation dating rest squarely on this fact.

Some Blackduck populations, again prominently along the Minnesota-Ontario border, continued the old practice of constructing burial mounds, only there was a shift to the adoption of flexed inhumations. Likewise the custom of making holes in the skulls of the deceased continued. Some Blackduck skulls also had clay packed in the eye orbits, and sometimes these in turn were inset with shell "pupils." Dogs were on occasion buried with or near the human remains.

Triangular arrowheads and most of the same kinds of chipped-flint and bone and antler tools reported from the Heins Creek complex, the Lakes phase, and the Effigy Mound culture are also found in Blackduck or have close correlatives. Blackduck small copper tools such as awls, fishhook components, single-edged knives, and beads reflect the proximity of the metal's sources. Stone smoking pipes (these have not yet been found in Heins Creek or Lakes phase sites; if present in Effigy Mound they are rare) tend to exhibit a flange or spur fore and aft of the bowl suggesting a degenerated version of the old platform pipe.

Many Blackduck sites, particularly the later ones, reveal the presence of one or even several vessels belonging to a foreign ceramic tradition. Sometimes, as in a number of sites on the north shore of Lake Superior, these are Selkirk culture vessels, fabric-marked and undecorated or adorned only with a single row of punctates on the rim. Such ceramics are most common north and west of the major Blackduck areas. Selkirk pottery is known to have been made by the Cree Indians in early historic times and was presumably made by their ancestors in late prehistory. Plain, grit-tempered Oneota-like pots with outflaring rims and crenelated lips have been recovered in clear association with some of the Blackduck material. This pottery is much more at home in the upper Michigan peninsula and in northern Wisconsin. Ontario Iroquois-like pottery, believed to have been copied by

PLATE 8.9. *Blackduck culture vessel from the Martin Bird site (DbJm-5), Whitefish Lake, Ontario. (Shown half actual size.) (Courtesy Mike McLeod and the Department of Anthropology, Lakehead University, Thunder Bay, Ontario.)*

the Algonquian-speaking Indians of the north shore of Lake Huron and the Georgian Bay region, has also been discovered in Blackduck sites. Because of the great importance of hunting to these northern peoples in this sparsely inhabited country, which put a premium on each community retaining the cooperative hunting bonds of related men intimately familiar with the complex of game trials and resources in their own band territories, and because of the exogamous nature of most bands and the known proclivity of historic Indian groups in this same country to recruit wives from sometimes far-distant places, these foreign vessels must in many instances be the result of wide-ranging marital ties. The nature of women's tasks made them more ready candidates for relocation at marriage than men. They brought with them, of course, the traditional ceramic styles they had acquired in growing up in their natal communities. In this way certain pottery styles came to have a far-flung if spotty representation beyond their more typical ranges. A sometime product of the practice was the periodic and atypical combination of some of the characteristics of regional and imported styles on quite localized, short-lived ceramic creations. This phenomenon is well illustrated, for example, on a vessel from late-prehistoric contexts at Rock Island Site II in the northern Lake Michigan basin off the tip of the Door Peninsula. On this one vessel is a well integrated if unusual juxtaposition of surface finishing. rim form, and decorative attributes which, taken singly, are peculiarly suggestive of Blackduck, Madison, and even Selkirk wares. This particular comingling seems to have inspired no copiers.

Somewhat south of the main distribution of Blackduck, in the eastern part of the upper Michigan peninsula and in the northern part of the lower

PLATE 8.10. *Artifacts from the McCluskey and other western Ontario Blackduck sites: pottery fragments (top row); projectile points, end scrapers, biface knife or preform (second row); side scrapers, perforator, wedge (third row); copper knife and awl, stone smoking pipe (fourth row); and unilaterally multibarbed bone harpoon (bottom). (Shown half actual size.) (Courtesy Mike McLeod and the Department of Anthropology, Lakehead University, Thunder Bay, Ontario.)*

Michigan peninsula, archaeologists have found sites pertaining to a much more spatially and temporally circumscribed cultural complex. This complex was first uncovered at the Juntunen site on Bois Blanc Island, the largest of the islands in the Straits of Mackinac. Bois Blanc Island sits astride the eastern approaches to the waterway connecting Lakes Huron and Michigan. Besides affording superb opportunities for subsistence fishing, the island was ideally poised to intercept the traffic of people and ideas at this crossroads of the Upper Great Lakes. It acted as a kind of cultural sieve, sampling what was about. A thin scatter of Late Archaic material has been found on the place. However, the main activities took place during the Late Woodland period.

At the very productive and stratified Juntunen site three sequent phases of Late Woodland activity were identified, named, and radiocarbon dated. Each being accompanied by a distinctive suite of pottery and the ware of each given the same nomenclature as the phase, these are the Mackinac (A.D. 800–1000), Bois Blanc (1000–1200), and Juntunen (1200–1400) phases and wares. The three spans of two centuries each are rounded-off approximations, of course, and should not be taken as sign of metabolic-like periodicity in the prehistoric life of the Straits of Mackinac. The same sequence of phases has also been uncovered along the St. Marys River near Sault Ste. Marie, Ontario.

It is the earliest of the three Juntunen site phases, the Mackinac, that is the regional representative of the Late Woodland I stage. Like the two later phases, the first reflects a heavy commitment to fishing. Inasmuch as floral and faunal analyses support what such lacustrine fishing activity implies, the Juntunen site and Bois Blanc Island itself preserve only a part of the archaeological record of the people responsible for the phases. Some portions of the warm months in addition to the winter were spent on the mainlands north and south of the straits. Undoubtedly affiliated sites, for example, have been discovered southward along the eastern shore of Lake Michigan to Grand Traverse Bay and even beyond. So while corn has been identified among the charred vegetable debris, this does not necessarily mean that it had been grown on the island. It may well have been planted somewhere on the mainland by the people before their summer removal to the island for the fishing. It could also have been received in trade. However that may be, it is important to note the availability of cultivated foodstuffs by A.D. 800–1000 this far north. In this connection, the ameliorating "lake effect" here extends the growing season beyond 140 frost-free days, more than ample for the growing of corn. But fishing was a major consideration, if it was not *the* consideration, in bringing people to the island—fishing for immediate consumption and also to produce dried and smoked stores for the coming lean months.

The tools and weaponry of the Mackinac phase are the ubiquitous ones of the period. Wedges, sometimes called "'gouged-end' artifacts" in the report on the Juntunen site, were an important tool at this locality. Flint sources were available for tapping on the island, but better flint required a good 2 days of travel for its procurement; sometimes excellent flint could be had in local deposits of glacial gravel. To extract maximum utility out of pebbles of such material, the bipolar core technique was extensively employed. In this approach, the use of stone anvil and hammer sheared off flakes from opposite ends of the pebble core, minimizing waste. There is sometimes great difficulty in differentiating exhausted bipolar cores from wedges. In fact, some wedges were made from salvaged exhausted bipolar cores. Surprisingly, there was little evidence of native copper.

Mackinac Ware, the diagnostic product of the phase, is characterized by cordmarked and fabric-marked vessel surfaces, a relatively squat vessel shape with subconoidal to round bases, pronounced shoulders, moderately constricted necks, and excurvature rims. Thickened "splayed" lips are a prominent feature of this pottery. Decoration involved cordwrapped-stick and cord impressing and the use of punctations in horizontal geometric patterns on rim and neck. Within these limits practically every pot was different. This means more than that because these were handmade, each was in some sense unique. It is in comparison with the Bois Blanc and Juntunen phase ceramics that the Mackinac examples show a high degree of vessel-to-vessel variability. The provocative suggestion has been made that this difference between the phases was brought about by a shift from patrilocal residence patterns, with wives introducing variety in the community's ceramic inventory commensurate with the range of their natal villages, to matrilocal ones reducing ceramic variety to greater homogeneity. Such a shift, if it took place, would also have been in keeping with other evidence to be cited later of a cultural change in the straits area in the direction of early Iroquois developments in Ontario.

Mackinac phase pottery is unmistakably Late Woodland I in character. It shows strong correspondences with the widespread Wayne Ware of southern Michigan, Canton Ware in northern Illinois, Princess Point in southwestern Ontario, some of the Kipp Island phase of Point Peninsula pottery and more of the Hunter's Home and Carpenter Brook Owasco in New York, and Blackduck north and mainly west of the Straits of Mackinac. At least equally compelling are the similarities in overall configuration, in *gestalt*, and in many details of technique and motif that Mackinac pottery shares with Heins Creek and Madison wares in Wisconsin. They are not the same, but they are often so similar that it is clear that they are closely related phenomena. In the succeeding Bois Blanc phase this western connection is equally marked if not stronger.

On the same general time level with the Heins Creek complex, early Effigy Mound, early Blackduck, the Mackinac phase, and other Late Woodland I local and regional manifestations is the Hunter's Home phase in New York and the related Princess Point complex in eastern Ontario. De-

PLATE 8.11. Mackinac Banded vessel, Mackinac phase, Juntunen site, Bois Blanc Island in the Straits of Mackinac, Michigan. (Shown approximately half actual size.) (Courtesy Richard I. Ford and the Museum of Anthropology, University of Michigan, Ann Arbor.)

velopmentally and chronologically, Hunter's Home is intermediate between the Point Peninsula Kipp Island phase, earlier described, and the Owasco Carpenter Brook phase. It provides such a smooth, continuous transition from the one to the other that clear lines of demarkation are hard to come by. There is no question that Hunter's Home is a direct outgrowth and successor of the Point Peninsula tradition via the Kipp Island phase. It is usually considered to be the terminal manifestation of Point Peninsula and of the Middle Woodland period in New York. Without in any way denying the first contention, the Hunter's Home phase in this discussion is allocated to the Late Woodland period and specifically to Late Woodland I. In the wider perspective of the Great Lakes that is where it properly belongs by virtue of radiocarbon dates and similarities in form and content with the aforementioned cultures. Although both Kipp Island and Hunter's Home require further radiocarbon dating before their beginning and ending dates can be specified with confidence, and there is the definitional problem of when one gives way to the other, the latter must belong somewhere in the interval A.D. 650–1000. The few available radiometric assays fall in the last half of this range. Earlier dates will doubtless be forthcoming.

Inasmuch as Point Peninsula has been, and Owasco will be, described in some detail, little need be said by way of close description of the transitional culture except to emphasize the multifarious continuities. In moving from the Kipp Island phase to Hunter's Home, Point Peninsula ceramic elements such as dentate stamping, rocker stamping, stab-and-drag, and interior surface "channeling" (brushing) persist even if in dwindling frequencies. Pottery concepts foreshadowing those of the Owasco culture, such as overall or nearly overall surface cordmarking and decoration by means of cordwrapped-stick impressing and end-of-stick punctating, become dominant. Styles of notched projectile points common in Kipp Island are much less popular in Hunter's Home; there is a corresponding increase in numbers of the broad, equilateral triangular Levanna arrowheads that later were to be so commonplace in the Carpenter Brook phase of the Owasco culture. Platform pipes are rare in Hunter's Home contexts—they seem to have been treated as heirlooms—whereas there is an upsurge in the frequency of straight or obtuse-angle elbow pipes. These are usually without adornment. The Kipp Island penchant for wearing shark's-tooth pendants became much less fashionable in Hunter's Home times. On the other hand, the elaborated multigrooved sinewstones, so favored by the Owasco folk, began their careers in this bridging culture. No signs of agriculture have yet been recovered from Hunter's Home sites, available evidence pointing to the continuation of hunting, fishing, and gathering. However, the discovery of carbonized corn in the contemporary, neighboring, and related Princess Point complex, and in the somewhat more removed but still partly coeval Western Basin complex, hints that it is only a matter of time before that cultigen, and perhaps others, is found in Hunter's Home contexts.

So far divided into three geographical clusters with slight cultural distinctions, the details of which need not detain us, and occupying a time span comparably divided, the Princess Point complex is known from a great many sites in southern Ontario. The three spatial divisions have been termed "foci." In the extreme southwest from the Lake Erie shore to the Detroit River and Lake St. Clair, is the Point Pelee focus. On the southeast coast of Lake Huron is the Ausable focus. The largest, the Grand River focus, extends from the Niagara Frontier and the western and northwestern shore of Lake Ontario to the north central shore of Lake Erie. The Grand River focus extends into westernmost New York. Thus, the Princess Point complex, like Hunter's Home, lies almost entirely in the Carolinian Biotic Province. Radiocarbon dates and some guessing place the periods "Early," "Middle," and "Late" between circa A.D. 600–750, 750–850, and 850–900, respectively.

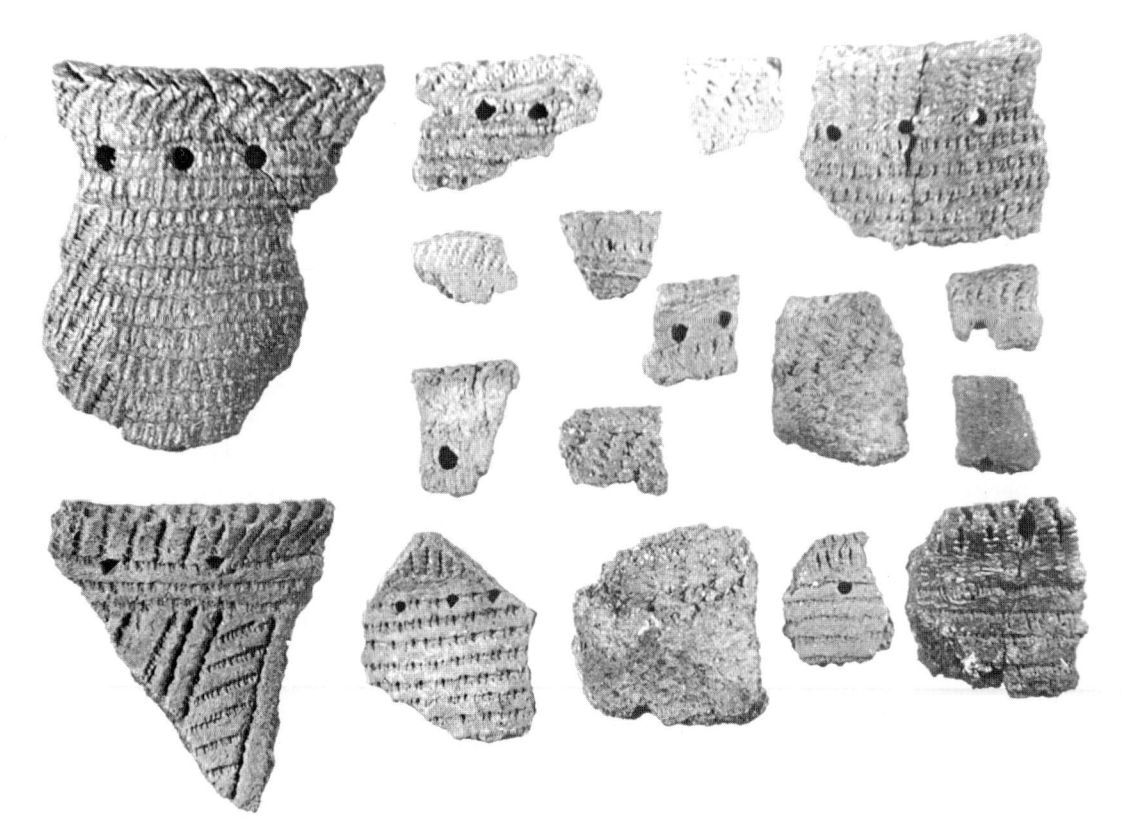

PLATE 8.12. *Princess Point complex pottery from the Middleport site, Haldimand County, Ontario. (Shown half actual size.) (Courtesy David M. Stothers and the Archaeological Survey of Canada, National Museum of Man, Ottawa.)*

Unlike its New York contemporary, Princess Point cannot with entire conviction be derived from a resident, well-defined Middle Woodland precursor, though Saugeen or a still amorphous Ontario Point Peninsula must have played an important part. Some late and attenuated Hopewellian traits, such as the vestiges of a blade industry, very rare platform pipes, some vaguely Havana-like ceramic features, possible burial-mound associations, and also some resemblances to post-Hopewell Weaver Ware pottery in Illinois, have suggested to some archaeologists a stronger western affiliation than anything seen in Hunter's Home. This is still a very unclear situation. Continuing research on the recent end of the Middle Woodland period in southern Ontario may dispel some of the current attractiveness of an intrusive origin of Princess Point.

During the late period ("phase") Princess Point developed into the Glen Meyer culture. This and the similar Pickering culture, the latter with somewhat more suggestive Point Peninsula continuities, constitute the most ancient crystallizations of proto-Iroquois culture in Ontario. In fact, the two together have been jointly baptized "Early Ontario Iroquois." By approximately A.D. 850 there was an apparent turning to increased reliance on agriculture by the Princess Point people (though corn has been found in the early history of the culture as well). There was a general shift in settlements from lakeshore and riverine floodplain, seasonally occupied, to the establishment of more permanent communities on interior sandy uplands bordering or just back of river valleys. A rise in population and, with it, an increase in warfare accompanied this adjustment. And coincidentally, there is evidence from the paleoclimatic record of northeastern North America of a warming trend associated with an increase in summer rainfall. This has been labeled the Neo-Atlantic climatic episode. How much this affected the Princess Point territories remains to be established. Al-

PLATE 8.13. *Stratification of Princess Point complex occupations at the Cayuga Bridge site, Haldimand County, Ontario. The three right-hand markers (2A, 2C, 4) indicate the cultural levels (note pit outline at left in 4). (Courtesy David M. Stothers and the Archaeological Survey of Canada, National Museum of Man, Ottawa.)*

though there is an attractive correspondence in these developments, more work needs to be done before the causal arrow may be confidently pointed from the somewhat general environmental model to the somewhat more specific cultural record. Whatever the precise mechanisms, the first Glen Meyer communities are recognizable by A.D. 950. These, however, belong in the second half of the Late Woodland period where, as will be seen, they had a lot of company.

Late Woodland II: Lower Lakes

As indicated in the foregoing, Princess Point and Hunter's Home gave rise to daughter cultures which are archaeologically clearly defined and solidly dated. These daughter cultures made their debuts in their respective areas by around the turn of the first millennium A.D. They are convenient markers for the inception of Late Woodland II times in much of the Lower Great Lakes. Perhaps most importantly, the similar Glen Meyer and Pickering cultures in eastern Ontario and the Owasco culture in New York initiated or forwarded an interrelated series of settlement and subsistence practices, social arrangements, and style predispositions anticipating those of the historic Iroquoian tribes of the Northeast and which profoundly influenced many neighboring Algonquian peoples as well. As we have seen, the Glen Meyer–Pickering manifestations have even been identified as Early Ontario Iroquois. Although the earliest entity to be unambiguously and universally termed Iroquois in New York is the Oak Hill phase of circa 1300–1400, there is little doubt about the Iroquoian debt to the Owasco heritage.

The Owasco culture in New York was spatially largely restricted to the central and eastern counties and temporally to the eleventh, twelfth, and thirteenth centuries. The culture has been subdivided into three sequent phases, each of approximately a century's duration. These are, beginning around the year 1000, Carpenter Brook, Canandaigua, and Castle Creek. Their most conspicuous differences among themselves are in types and relative frequencies of ceramics. In these and other regards, and in conformity with chronology, Carpenter Brook Owasco is most similar to Hunter's Home, while Castle Creek Owasco shows close and intimate affinities with the Oak Hill phase of the New York Iroquois tradition.

Aside from temporary sojourns in prime fishing spots, hunting or collecting camps, or at places where good flint or some other desired resource could be procured, Owasco folk were inclined to settle in large year-round villages occupying from one to several acres. These tended to be away from main waterways and situated atop a natural rise. Many such villages were surrounded by a stockade or by ditch-and-embankment earthworks sup-

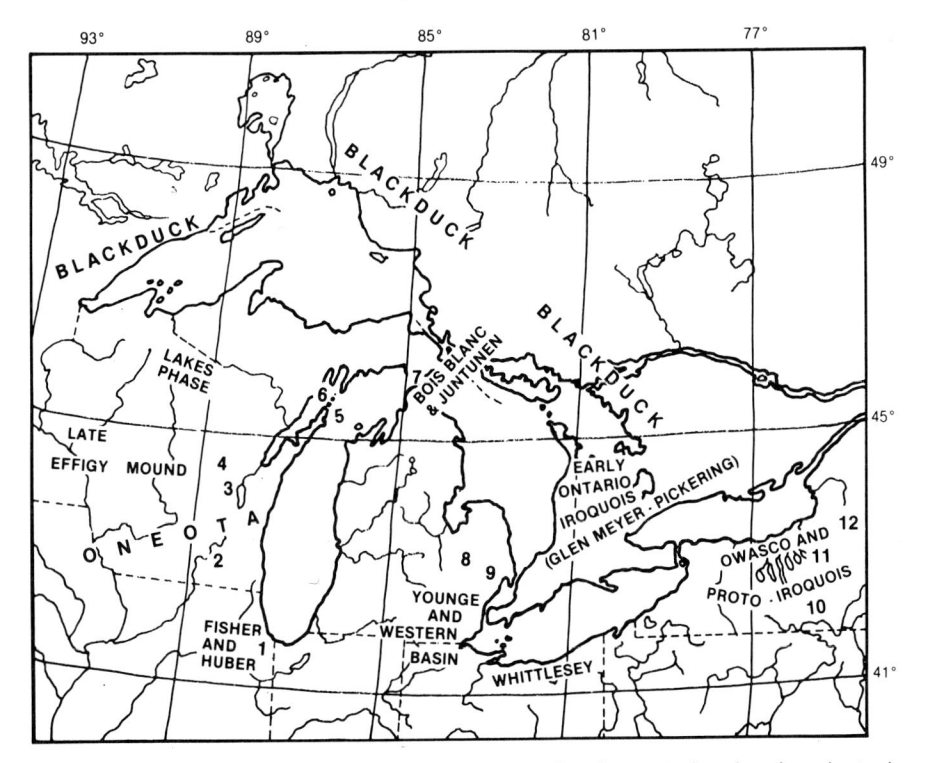

MAP 8.2. *Major cultural groupings in the Late Woodland II period and archaeological sites mentioned in the text: (1) Anker; (2) Aztalan; (3) Lasleys Point; (4) Sanders I; (5) Mero; (6) Rock Island II; (7) Juntunen; (8) Younge; (9) Rivière au Vase; (10) Castle Creek; (11) Howlett Hill; (12) Garoga and El Rancho.*

porting a stockade. Single to multiple lines of stockade posts have been traced out, typically describing a simple circular to ovoid plan. In some cases of multiple stockade lines, expanding community size seems to have been what precipitated enlargement of the protected precincts. The defensive walls were composed of upright poles or logs forced into the ground and probably interlaced with vines, branches, and strips of bark. In the case of earthworks, a shallow borrow ditch was dug around the village periphery with the banked spoil used to secure the bases of the posts. The practice of fortifying settlements increased over time as hostilities grew ever more demanding in their exactions. Violent conflict had earlier existed, as we have seen, but in Late Woodland II times it erupted with unprecedented magnitude and frequency. Doubtless connected with the fact of significant population increases and the transforming role of a much heavier reliance on plant husbandry, which necessarily would have realigned man–land attitudes and their supporting institutions, war itself stimulated further its own proliferation in ways not unfamiliar to readers of other histories. Unceremoniously mutilated and arrow-ridden skeletons reinforce the architectural and topographic evidence of more frequent and more sustained episodes of violence. One of the results of such warfare with its accompanying terrorism and thus perhaps one of its causes, as suggested in Chapter 1, was to space communities with respect to available arable terrain as well as hunting and foraging resources so that the environmental carrying-capacity transformation that agriculture implies was in fact realized. A related speculation bearing on the increased population-intensified agriculture-heightened warfare correlation cites the erosion of the traditional male role in food-getting and its redirection in armed conflict as a causal relationship. By the time of first historic accounts this facet of the masculine role was embedded in the ideologies of the native populations.

Within the stockaded walls, Owasco towns were composed of four kinds of bark or mat-covered pole-frame houses: small circular ones, square ones having rounded corners, oblong quasi-longhouses, and true longhouses. Traces of attached shed-like structures are also known. These probably had a number of functions, including that of keeping firewood dry. The multifamily longhouse gradually became the favorite domicile type. These must have been very similar to historic Iroquoian longhouses as described in the first chapter. They, too, sometimes preserve traces of centerline roof supports, bench-bed frames aligned along the walls, multiple cooking hearths, storage pits, partitions, and even clues to the sometime construction of a storage vestibule at one end. Owasco longhouses were also entered and exited by means of doors at each end. Within and between houses investigators have found many cylindrical and bell-shaped storage and trash pits and circular rock-filled roasting pits. There are residues of bark or grass lining in some of the storage receptacles. Analysis of pit and general midden contents has resulted in the repeated identification of corn, beans, and squash in addition to the remnants of nuts and berries and other foraged plants and, of course, fish, bird, and mammal bones typical of the historic period in the same regions.

Owasco burials were mainly flexed-in-the-flesh inhumations deposited either in scattered graves or in cemetery groups of clustered individual and small group graves. Abandoned storage pits were on occasion resorted to as graves. Little ceremony is reflected in the individual burial pits or cemeteries. Few artifacts accompanied the dead. On the other hand, there are signs that ceremonialism centered around the bear, a recurring Iroquois interest, had already come into being at least as early as the Carpenter Brook phase.

PLATE 8.14. *Pottery vessel of the Owasco Canandaigua phase from the Bates site, Chenango County, New York. (Shown half actual size.) (Courtesy William A. Ritchie and Robert E. Funk, New York State Museum and Science Service, Albany.)*

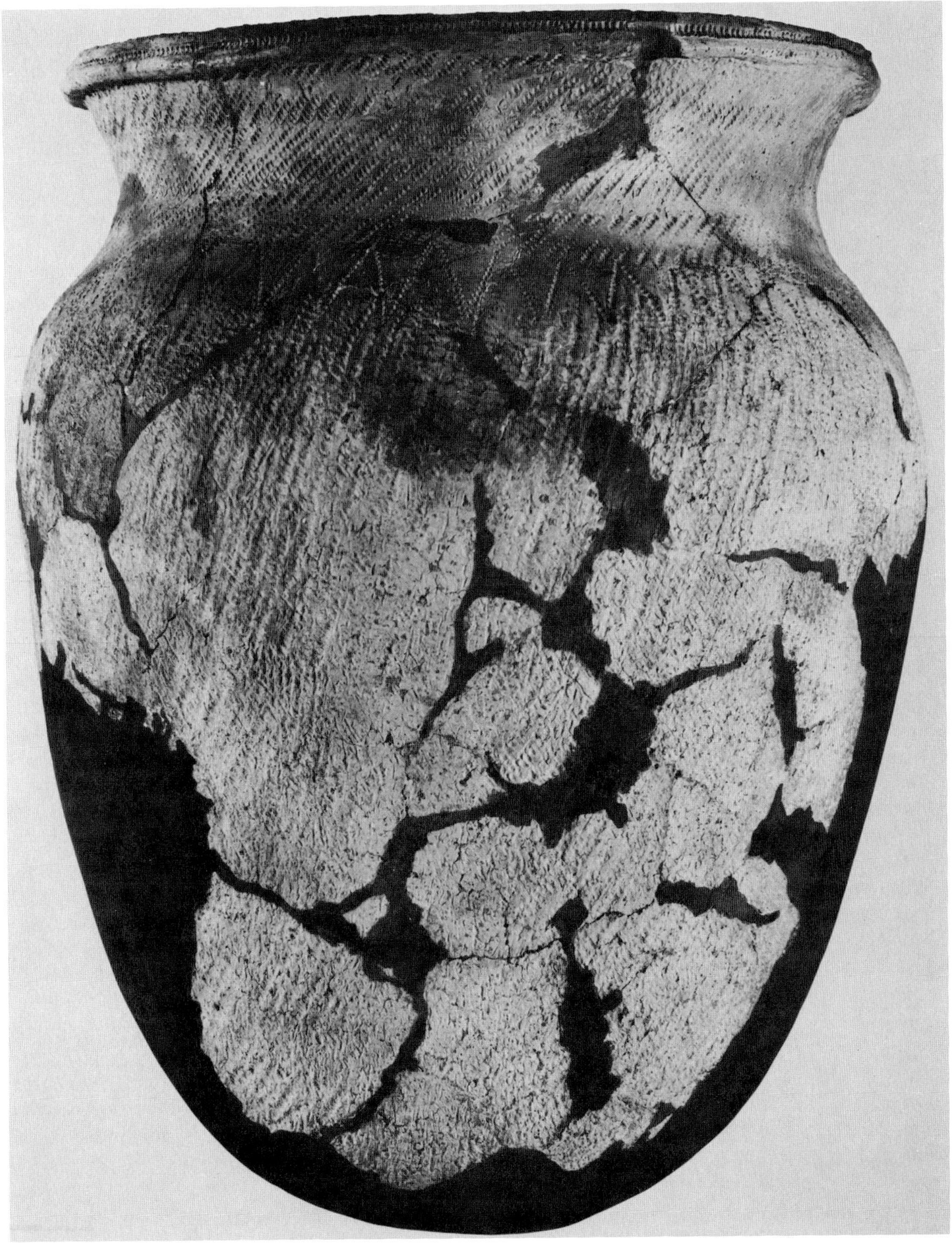

PLATE 8.15. *Owasco Canandaigua phase rimsherds from the Bates site, Chenango County, New York. (Shown half actual size.) (Courtesy William A. Ritchie and Robert E. Funk, New York State Museum and Science Service, Albany.)*

The nascent Iroquois character of Owasco is seen with increasing clarity in the pottery and many of the stone and other material products as they are followed in their evolution from Carpenter Brook to Castle Creek. The pottery is especially sensitive in this regard. Vessels were often quite large, some having a capacity of 38 or 45 l. In early Owasco these were most often tall and lobate, having conoidal bottoms and modestly everted rims. Later Owasco pots were more globular in shape with broader, round bases. They exhibit more rim flare. Many vessels by now have collars.

Heavy cordmarking is characteristic of Owasco pottery, overall corded surface treatment being the rule during the Carpenter Brook phase, whereas by Castle Creek time vessel rims and necks were frequently smoothed. Another surface finish popular in late Owasco was check stamping as a substitute for cordmarking. This was accomplished by use of a paddle scribed with a checkerboard pattern. The imposition of design motifs was initially overwhelmingly by cordwrapped stick; this was subsequently under intensifying competitive pressure from incising and linear stamping. Even at the end of the Owasco sequence, however, many vessels were still being treated with cordwrapped-stick impressing. Decoration was bestowed on outer and inner rim, lip, neck, and on vessel shoulders. Geometric motifs, simple in conception but complicated by repetition and conjunction, monopolized the style repertoire: horizontal bands; perpendicular or diagonal lines, frequently on rims, with horizontals on necks and shoulders; opposed rows or columns of banked obliques resulting in herringbone patterns; vertical or diagonal plats on vessel necks and/or shoulders; end-of-cordwrapped-stick punctates alone or in combination with one of the foregoing. Incipient Iroquoian stylistic themes, particularly when expressed in incising on squat, high-collared pots, anticipate many of the classic creations of the New York Iroquois.

Owasco ceramics extended to the fashioning of smoking pipes. Straight or tubular pipes in early Owasco were gradually discarded in favor of an obtuse-angle, elbow configuration. Preferred manners of adornment likewise underwent change. Although punctated and cord-decorated examples are known, most Carpenter Brook pipes were left plain. Canandiagua pipes tended to greater elaboration with animal effigies sometimes added to the bowls. Castle Creek pipes were the most fanciful with frequent resort to stylized depictions of the human face, sculpted animal forms, incisions, and precisely punctated and very finely cord imprinted designs. A repeated device was a filleted and bossed addition to the bowl which seems to be a conventionalized symbol of an ear of corn.

In chipped flint the simple triangular arrowhead had become virtually the universal style by Carpenter Brook time. The majority of such points were the fairly large (but diminishing in size over the centuries), Levanna-type equilateral-triangular arrowhead, often with a concave base. These almost imperceptibly evolved into the usually smaller isosceles triangles called Madison points, a common weapon tip on Castle Creek sites. Especially distinctive among Owasco lithics are lozenge-shaped strike-a-lights or fireflints, the active component of fire-making kits. Also indicative of cultural lineage are multigrooved, convoluted sinewstones and enigmatic, thin, edge-trimmed, square, circular, or oval sandstone discs. Some prehistorians have suggested that the discs may once have been hafted as blades on hoes. At least as common, if not as diagnostic of Owasco culture, are T-shaped and spall-based drills, triangular biface knives, edge-trimmed flake knives and scrapers, polished celts or grooveless axes, very shallow biconcave mortars, notched pebble net-sinkers, pebble hammerstones, anvilstones, and whetstones.

The full complement of Owasco bone and antler products reveals on one hand the hallmarks of ancient legacies and, on the other, the proximate ancestry of prehistoric and early historic Iroquoian artifact conventions. Included are awls and needles, mat-sewing needles, chisels, both barbed and barbless simple fishhooks equipped with either straight or knobbed shanks, unilaterally and bilaterally multiple-barbed projectile points and harpoon heads, flaking implements, leister prongs, beaver-incisor knives and drawshave chisels, and pendants and drinking cups fashioned of turtle carapace. A fortuitous find at the type site of the Castle Creek phase, and suggestive of the technical ingenuity and craft attainments once expressed in perishable media, is a finely woven fishing trot-line to which a series of still-preserved thorn hooks is attached.

As within the Owasco sequence, each of the following phases of prehistoric New York Iroquois culture are discriminated and recognized as having some degree of separate identity on the basis of small quantitative, rather than qualitative changes, by shifts in emphasis, by style elaboration, by nuance. The named phases each bespeaks developmental continuity, of time between times, of a transmission of a core, a "deep structure," a common identity binding past, the transient present, and future. No migrations of outsiders nor any signs of disruptive foreign influence have been detected in the archaeological record. No marked incongruities isolate one phase from its temporal neighbors. These are important observations, for until the recent past the Iroquoian peoples had been regarded by most scholars as intruders in their historic homeland. Migration from the St. Lawrence Valley or from somewhere in the Ohio or Mississippi valleys was invoked. The alternative point of view, that the Iroquois of New York and Ontario were the lineal descendants of the ancient inhabitants of these

---

PLATE 8.16. *Representative Owasco bone and antler artifacts from New York: fishhook and fishhook blanks, harpoons, awls, tubes, hollowed deer phalanges, antler tool sockets (upper rows); combs, plates or spoons, beaver-incisor tools, pins, pendants, beads, and worked antler (lower rows). (Collection of the Rochester Museum and Science Center. [May not be reprinted without permission of the RMSC.])*

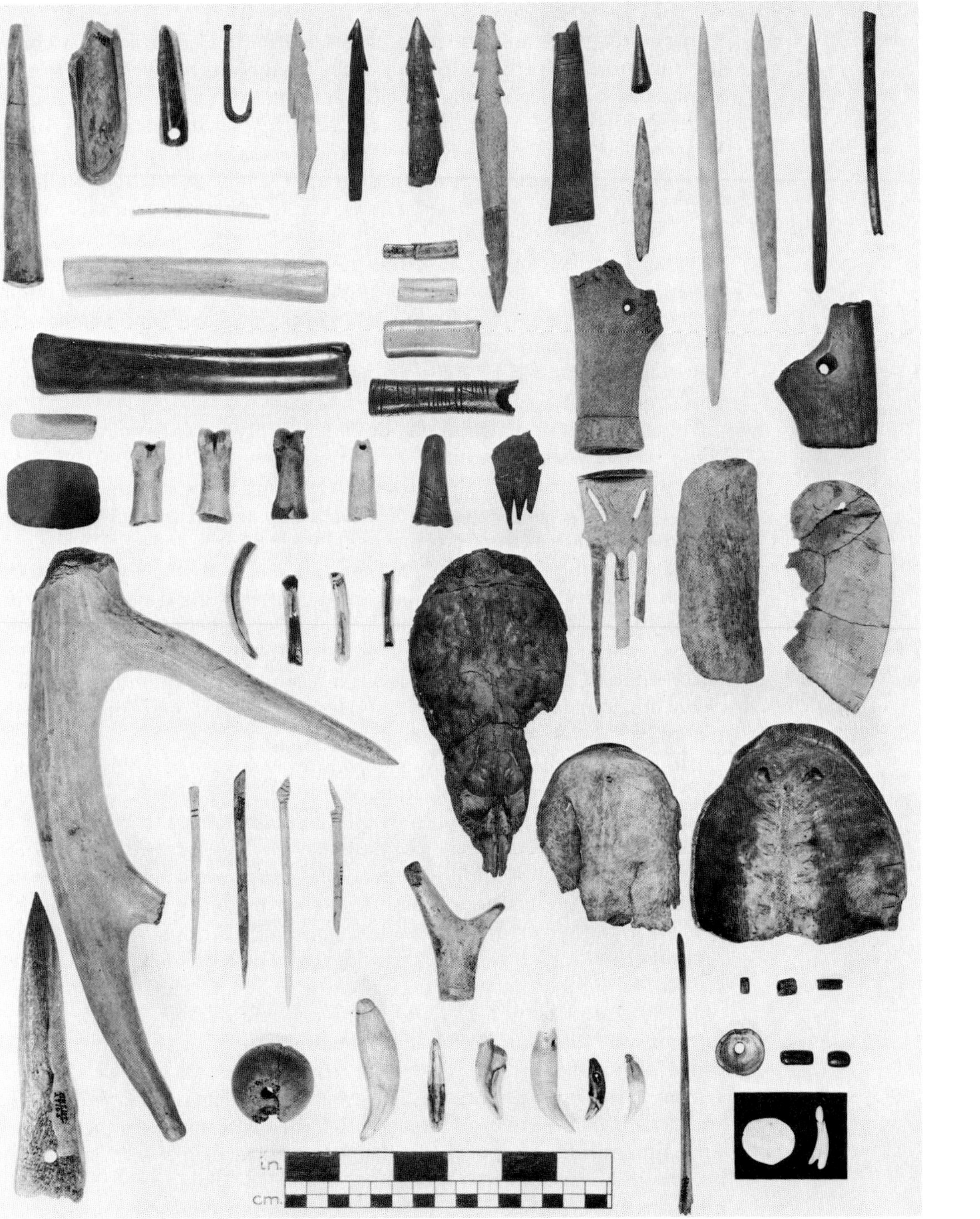
in.
cm.

same lands—the "in situ" hypothesis of Iroquois origins—has come to prevail among all serious students of the Iroquois as recent, numerous, and sometimes large-scale archaeological excavations have produced abundant and repeated evidence in its favor. Evidence that the New York Iroquois had evolved their culture in New York and that Ontario Iroquois peoples had followed a parallel course in their area is now overwhelming in magnitude and variety. The Owasco antecedents of historic Iroquois culture in New York are linked to it by the stage-by-stage succession Oak Hill, Chance, Garoga, and finally, the historical tribes of the League themselves. Because, as just indicated, the intermediate stages reflect comparatively slight, though amplifying, alterations and not fundamental transformations, detailed accounting of these changes will not be attempted. A few examples, however, will serve as illustrations in underlining the essential fact of in situ continuity.

The early New York Iroquois, or Oak Hill phase, dated circa 1300–1400, could just as well be classified as terminal Owasco, with Castle Creek the penultimate expression. Even though revealing somewhat reduced variety in its pottery vessels than its predecessor and ancestor, most Oak Hill pots bore collars and decoration imposed by cord-wrapped-stick impressing. Check stamping attained its highest popularity in the Owasco-Iroquois tradition, hereafter falling away. Castle Creek-style clay smoking pipes persisted into Oak Hill times but in diminishing representation amid enhanced variety that embraced pipes with straight vasiform, bulging barrel-shaped, conical, square-mouthed, and flaring-mouthed bowls. Incising and punctating and appliqued animal effigies are common on these pipes.

Although smaller ovoid houses continued in use, longhouses increasingly foreshadow the classic Iroquois model. The Oak Hill examples include houses well over 30 m in length, typically longer than any ever built before. Indeed, one atypical longhouse at the Howlett Hill site near Syracuse was 102 m long. Midline hearths and postmold clues of interior space partitioning are sometimes combined with evidence of attached aboveground storage structures. Palisade construction during the Oak Hill phase replicated what had been earlier achieved. Their builders, of course were already committed by cultural legacy to a heavy dependence on farming.

By Chance phase times, roughly the century 1400–1500, many community consolidations and intervillage alliances appear to have been well advanced, presumably as an adaptive consequence of chronic internecine warfare. At a number of sites, bear ceremonialism, war-captive torture, and cannibalism have been linked with large bathtub-shaped hollows filled with fire-cracked rocks, charcoal, beds and lenses of ash, and burned human and bear bones. Functionally, from all available appearances, there must have been powerful pressures at work on the existing social institutions to integrate more effectively the emerging structures that would be

PLATE 8.17. *An Oak Hill Phase proto-Iroquois vessel of the type Oak Hill Corded from the Clark site, Broome County, New York. (Shown one-third actual size.) (Collection of the Rochester Museum and Science Center. [May not be reprinted without permission of the RMSC.])*

realized in named tribal forms in the early historic period. The famous False Face Society, for example, as well as other medico-religious sodalities were probably operating by Chance times. In this connection, some False Face mask designs seem to be prefigured in Chance phase figurines or pottery maskettes. In fact, an arresting sculptured human face on an earlier Oak Hill pipe bowl from a site (El Rancho) in Montgomery County, New York, lacks only a twist in the lip and a dropping of an eye to be plausible prototype.

It is now possible to perceive, here with greater clarity, there only obscurely, the emergent individualities of the historically known tribes. In their traditional homeland, for example, it has recently been possible for archaeologists, using area surveys, subsurface testing, selective large-scale excavation, and minute village site to village site comparisons, to trace the establishment of the Onondaga tribal settlement pattern of dual villages—upon first coming together and subsequently through the shifting locations of coeval paired village sites. Onondaga archaeology has provided an uncommonly detailed confirmation of the in situ developmental hypothesis of Iroquois origins. It has convincingly been traced back into late Owasco.

Madison isosceles-triangular arrowheads, conforming with established trends, now almost entirely superceded the older Levanna points. In pottery, a preference for smooth surface finishing had by now largely replaced cordmarking and check stamping. Highly competent incised versions of pottery embellishment challenged the cordwrapped stick for preeminence with both expressed on some of the finest (some say *the* finest) pottery ever produced in the Iroquoian tradition. Some of the Chance pottery features human faces modeled or incised on the rim castellations. Pipes are by this time very common, of course, and they incorporate anthropomorphic and zoomorphic bowls as well as a new stress on the classical Iroquois trumpet shape. These continued and underwent further proliferation in the succeeding period.

With the ill-named Garoga phase (ill-named because it is apt to be equated with a specific Mohawk site of that name), circa 1500–1575, prehistory closed as the historical New York Iroquois tribes stepped into the freshly expanded orbit of European cognizance. The mature development of Iroquois culture was by now attained, lacking only those additions and modifications ascribable to the arrival of the ocean-crossers. Globular, round-bottomed pots with prominent collars boldly notched along the lower margin, with renewed attention to the use of rim peaks and castellations, with decoration almost entirely by incising, and with the retentive honoring of many favorite Chance designs, Garoga phase pottery stands at the end of a grand cultural tradition. In company with many another ancient technology it rapidly degenerated following on the dawn of a new age, and was replaced by iron and copper kettles and, later, by china. What had long been a household production, a mute hallmark of the self-sufficiency of the old order, was rendered an anachronism and was obliterated, replaced by monotonous but far more practical metal containers, themselves blunt symbols of a new order in human relations and not simply optional replacements in technology. The new technology proved to be the nose of the camel's head, tolerated to enter the Arab's tent.

As previously pointed out, the Princess Point complex offers the first glimmerings of the Ontario Iroquois tradition. In this sense, and timewise too, it is comparable to the proto-Owasco Hunter's Home and Carpenter

PLATE 8.18. Early Ontario Iroquois (Glen Meyer culture) pottery of the types Ontario Oblique (1–7) and Glen Meyer Oblique (8–14) from sites in southern Ontario. (Shown approximately two-thirds actual size.) (Courtesy James V. Wright and the Archaeological Survey of Canada, National Museum of Man, Ottawa.)

Brock Owasco south of Lake Ontario. However, formative Ontario Iroquois ("Early Ontario Iroquois") usually signifies the aforementioned Glen Meyer and coeval Pickering cultures which together span the years 900–1300. With their appearance, Late Woodland II commenced in eastern Ontario.

Glen Meyer sites occupy a northwest–southeast-trending corridor across the Ontario peninsula between Lakes Huron and Erie. A center line drawn through the length of this corridor would begin in Ipperwash Provincial Park on the Lake Huron coast and terminate at Long Point, the most prominent peninsula on Lake Erie. The corridor would be roughly 48 km wide on the Lake Huron shore and about twice that on the Erie. The Pickering culture occupied an enormously larger L-shaped tract extending the entire length of Lake Ontario and from Hamilton to the southern end of Georgian Bay, thence sporadically up the east coast to the northeast corner of the great embayment and then along the French River to Lake Nipissing.

Glen Meyer, certainly a lineal descendant of Princess Point, and Pickering, thought by some archaeologists to show somewhat more of a debt to Point Peninsula, were very similar cultures aside from their occupation of separate territories, both having much in common with Owasco developments in New York. Most of the differences separating the two branches of Early Ontario Iroquois were relatively trivial. They shared the same kind of life and made much the same kinds of things. Importantly agricultural, living in multifamily longhouses doubtless ordered on lineage principles, with residences nucleated within stockaded walls, wary enough of the outside world to undertake the labor of such fortifications and to locate their villages on rises of ground away from major streams, evolving an elaborate smoking-pipe complex, eating dogs and probably using them in certain medico-religious rituals, the Glen Meyer and Pickering cultures represent a by now familiar pattern. Their material products are unmistakably kin to those of the Owasco folk to the east and south. Such differences as the continued use of dentate stamping, the high incidence of rim bosses, and a few other practices are enough to obviate claims of common identity, however. Between Glen Meyer and Pickering the great majority of ceramic attributes were shared, but their particular combinations and frequencies were somewhat divergent. Exclusive differences were few. For example, check stamping and simple stamping (impressions produced by a ribbed paddle) are Pickering traits, whereas brushing ("scarifying") is confined to Glen Meyer.

Sometime around 1300 the Pickering people were able to enlarge their ancestral estate. They curled around the western end of Lake Ontario and pushed eastward over the Niagara Peninsula into western New York, exerting influence into northwestern Pennsylvania. Some other groups may have migrated northeastward, perhaps becoming the ancestors of the enigmatic St. Lawrence Iroquois. A major change was a thrust southwest-

PLATE 8.19. *Early Ontario Iroquois (Glen Meyer culture) vessel from southern Ontario. (Shown one-third actual size.) (Courtesy Peter L. Storck and the Royal Ontario Museum, Toronto, Canada.)*

ward into the territory occupied by the Glen Meyer people. This seems to have caused the absorption of some of the victims of the expanding Pickering culture and the dispersal of others with removals into eastern Michigan and northwestern Ohio. By this scenario, Pickering continued as the sole cultural entity north of Lake Ontario. Southwestward Glen Meyer had now ceased to exist as an integral complex. But enough of it had become incorporated in the westerly extruded Pickering communities to distinguish them thereafter from their eastern brethren. If this was in part a

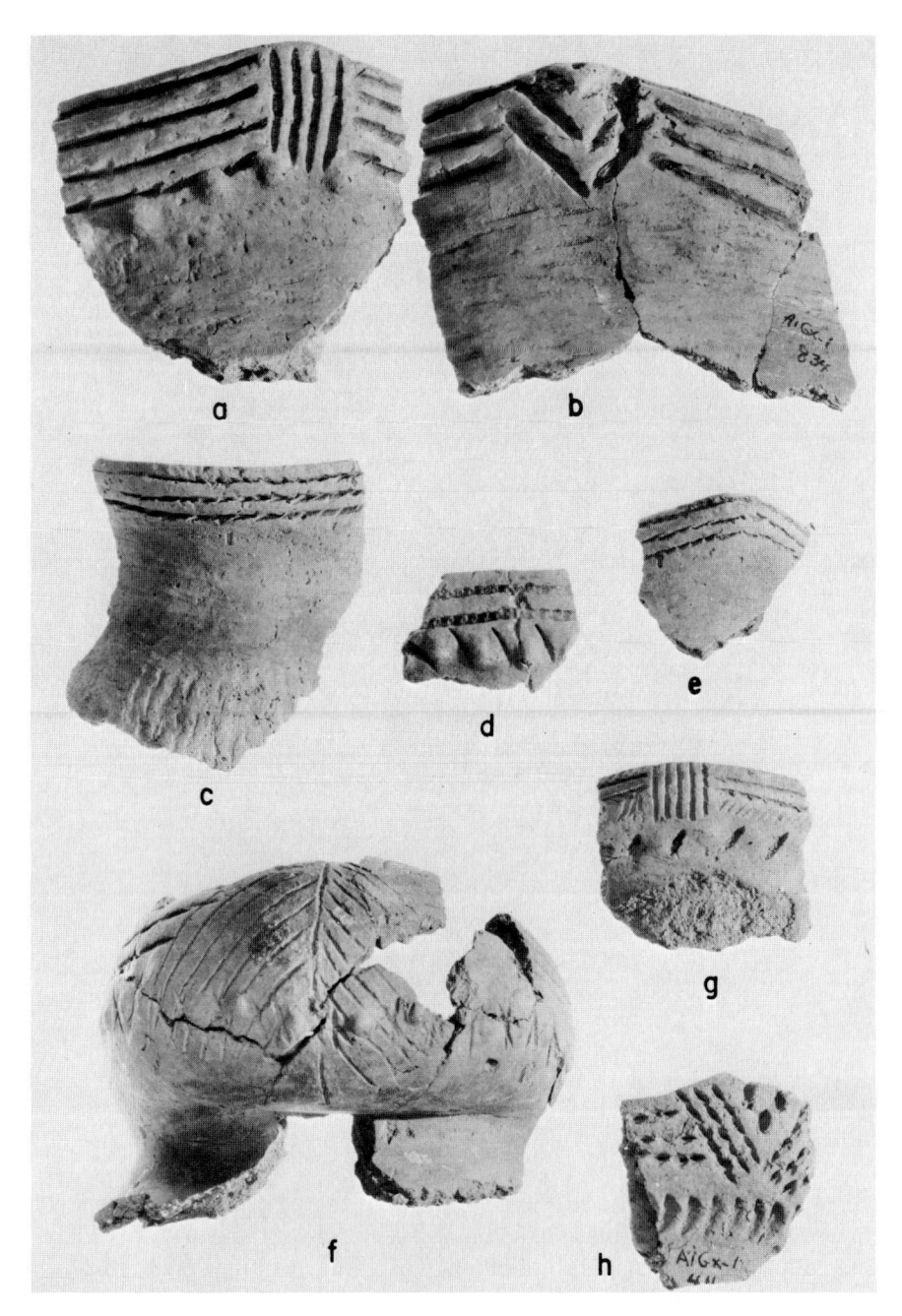

PLATE 8.20. *Early Ontario Iroquois (Pickering culture) pottery from the Bennett site near Hamilton, Ontario. (Shown approximately two-thirds actual size.) (Courtesy James V. Wright and the Archaeological Survey of Canada, National Museum of Man, Ottawa.)*

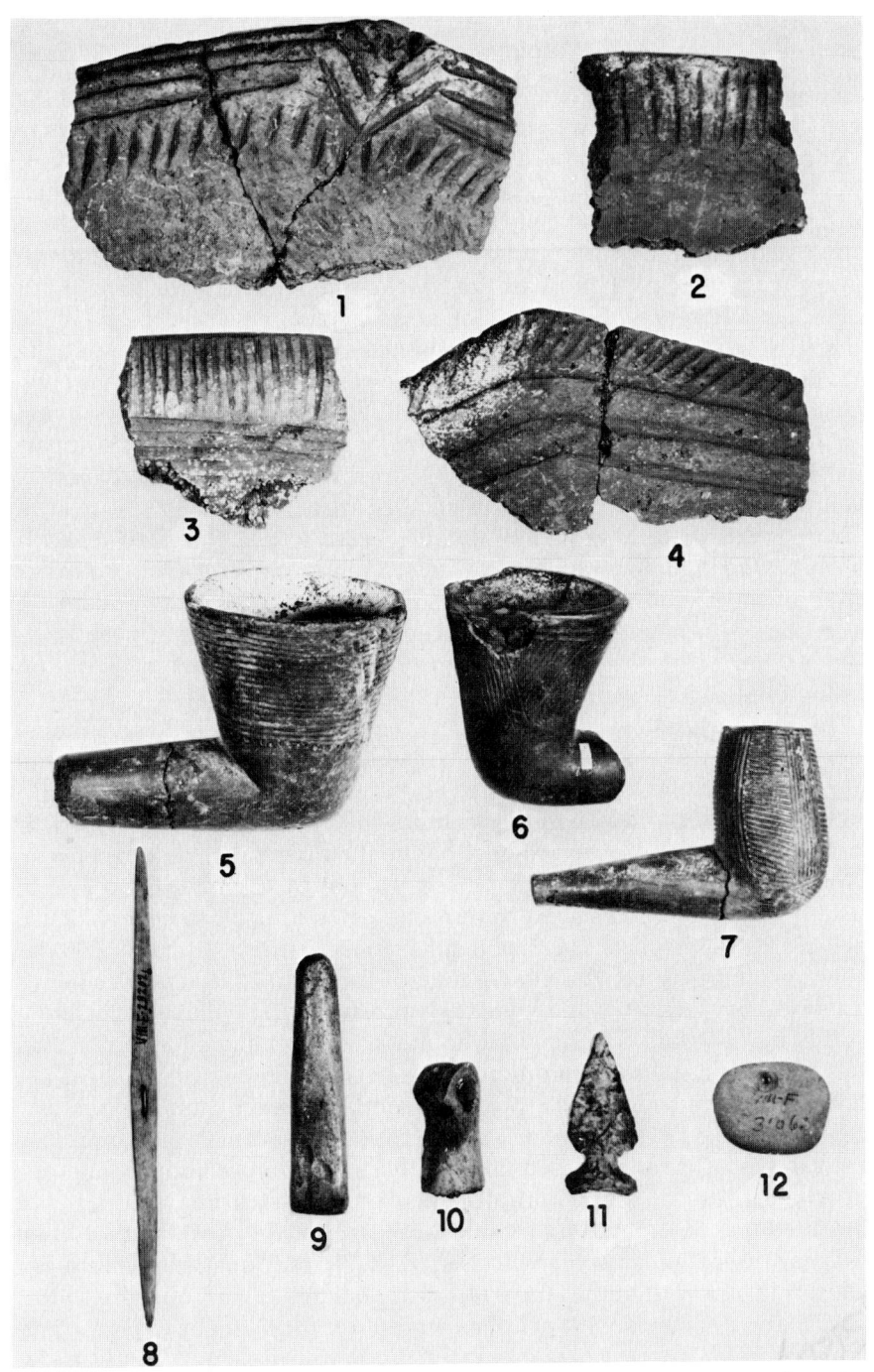

PLATE 8.21. *Middle Ontario Iroquois (Middleport) artifacts from sites in southern Ontario: rimsherds (1–4); smoking pipes (5–7); net-making bone needle (8); flaking tool of antler (9); worked deer toe bone possibly used in "cup-and-pin" game (10); flint projectile point (11); and pebble pendant (12). (Shown approximately two-thirds actual size.) (Courtesy James V. Wright and the Archaeological Survey of Canada, National Museum of Man, Ottawa.)*

result of the adoption of Glen Meyer people into the family structure of the newly paramount Pickering society, one of the most dramatic practices of Iroquois culture had been born. With these developments the Middle Ontario Iroquois stage came into being.

The Middle Ontario Iroquois stage occupied a century, give or take a couple of decades, between approximately 1300 and 1400 and was contemporary with the Oak Hill phase in New York. With relatively small but tenacious differences between east and west, a nevertheless basically homogeneous culture was now established over the eastern part of the province south of Georgian Bay. This stage has itself been divided into two substages: Uren and the slightly later Middleport. Ignoring this internal division (some scholars dispute the reality of a Uren substage), it is apparent that it was out of the Middle Ontario Iroquois that the historical Wenro–Neutral–Erie–Huron–Petun peoples arose.

During this cultural gestation period, the prototypic northern Iroquois ossuary came into general use. Previously, single or very small groups of flexed or bundle burials had been the rule. Now the bundled remains of many individuals were interred in a common pit alongside or near a settlement. For some reason the custom of ossuary burial never caught on among the League Iroquois.

The first archaeological recoveries in the province of sunflower, beans, and squash date to the Middle Ontario Iroquois stage where they were integrated with the long established and highly successful raising of corn and probably tobacco. These agricultural innovations must have experienced a long history in the province before their demonstrated presence in Middle Ontario Iroquois. With squash present in northern Ohio and in eastern Michigan by the sixth century B.C., it is difficult to believe that it took almost 2000 years for that crop to make it into southern Ontario. However that may be, the archaeology of the Uren–Middleport stage reveals a level of agricultural success in advance of anything that went before.

Although warfare continued bitter and chronic, many small unfortified sites have been found in addition to the larger palisaded ones. These are thought to have been special-purpose, short-term occupations when and where perceived risks of attack were slight. Cannibalism and probably war-captive torture increased in frequency, assuming proportions approaching those of the historically documented syndrome. Perhaps not unrelated was the adoption of central and eastern New York Iroquois pipe designs, indicative of some direct traffic with that quarter. From other quarters, again with implications of substantial military actions, the southern Ontario peninsula west of Lake Ontario was receiving as well as expelling people.

As indicated earlier in this chapter, archaeologists working around the western end of the Lake Erie basin have postulated a "Western Basin Tradition" to accommodate a lengthy series of sites and components

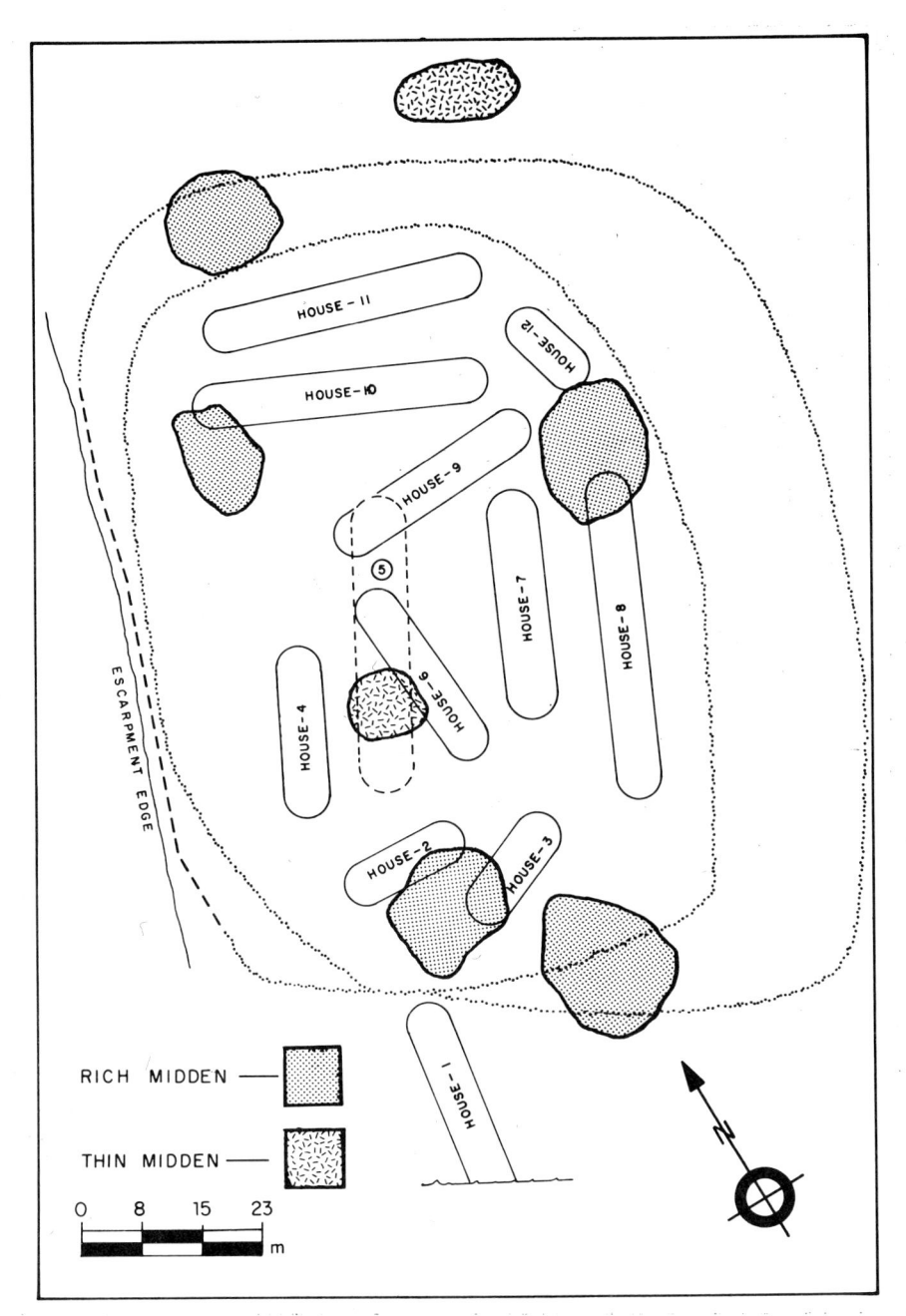

Plate 8.22. Site plan of the Middleport substage Nodwell site at Port Elgin, Bruce County, Ontario, showing longhouse outlines, concentrations of midden, and the encircling palisades. (Courtesy James V. Wright and the Archaeological Survey of Canada, National Museum of Man, Ottawa.)

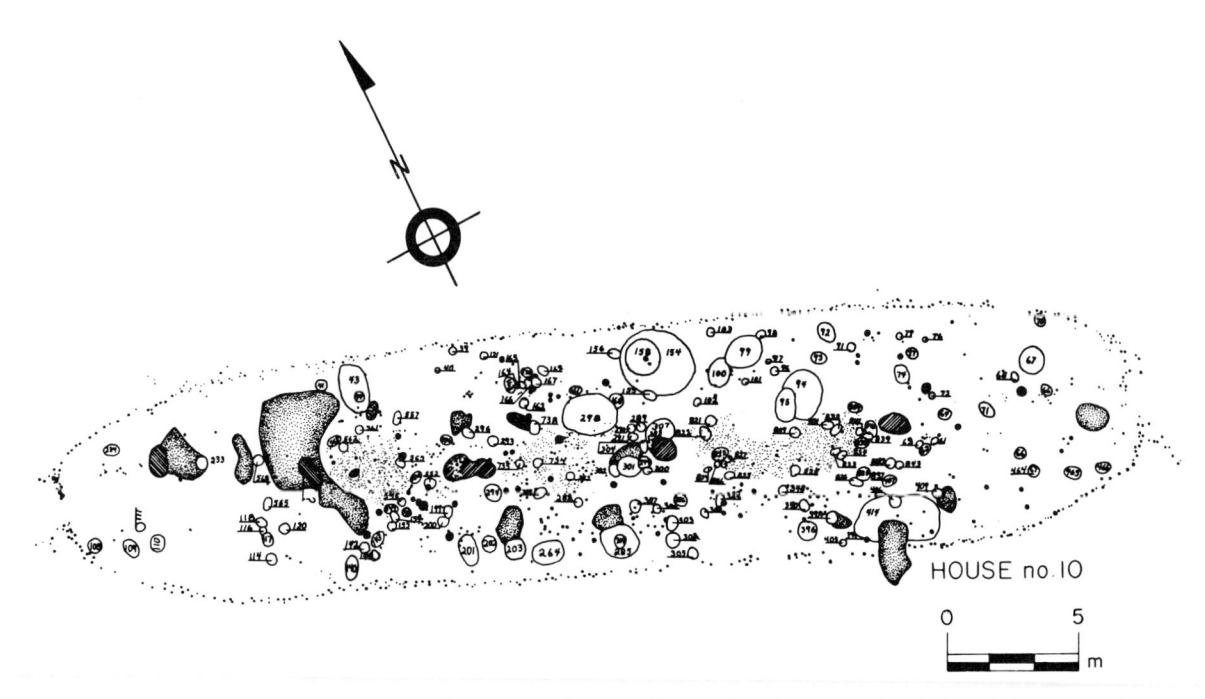

PLATE 8.23. *Plan of one of the Middleport longhouses at the Nodwell site at Port Elgin, Bruce County, Ontario, showing postmolds, pits, and other features of the house floor. (Courtesy James V. Wright and the Archaeological Survey of Canada, National Museum of Man, Ottawa.)*

within sites that seem to reflect a considerable degree of regional in situ growth and elaboration beginning, some have claimed, as early as Late Archaic times. Unfortunately, most of the recent investigations contributing to the Western Basin concept are as yet unpublished, and there are controversies over exactly what the concept includes and just what it excludes. In the Late Woodland period the Western Basin tradition has been defined to include all or a large part of what has up to now been known as the Younge tradition, a thread of stylistic and temporal continuity uniting a large assortment of sites in southeastern Michigan and contiguous portions of Ohio and Ontario. A particularly controversial proposal has been to identify this Western Basin tradition as having been promulgated by Iroquoian speakers and to grant it coequal taxonomic and historical status with the Ontario and New York Iroquois traditions. According to some current interpretations of the later history of this cultural tradition, it became extinct as a separate entity sometime shortly after 1450, having been ejected from its immemorial homeland and forced eastward into hitherto foreign reaches of southern Ontario where its remnants were absorbed by the Ontario Iroquois on the late or just post-Middleport hori-

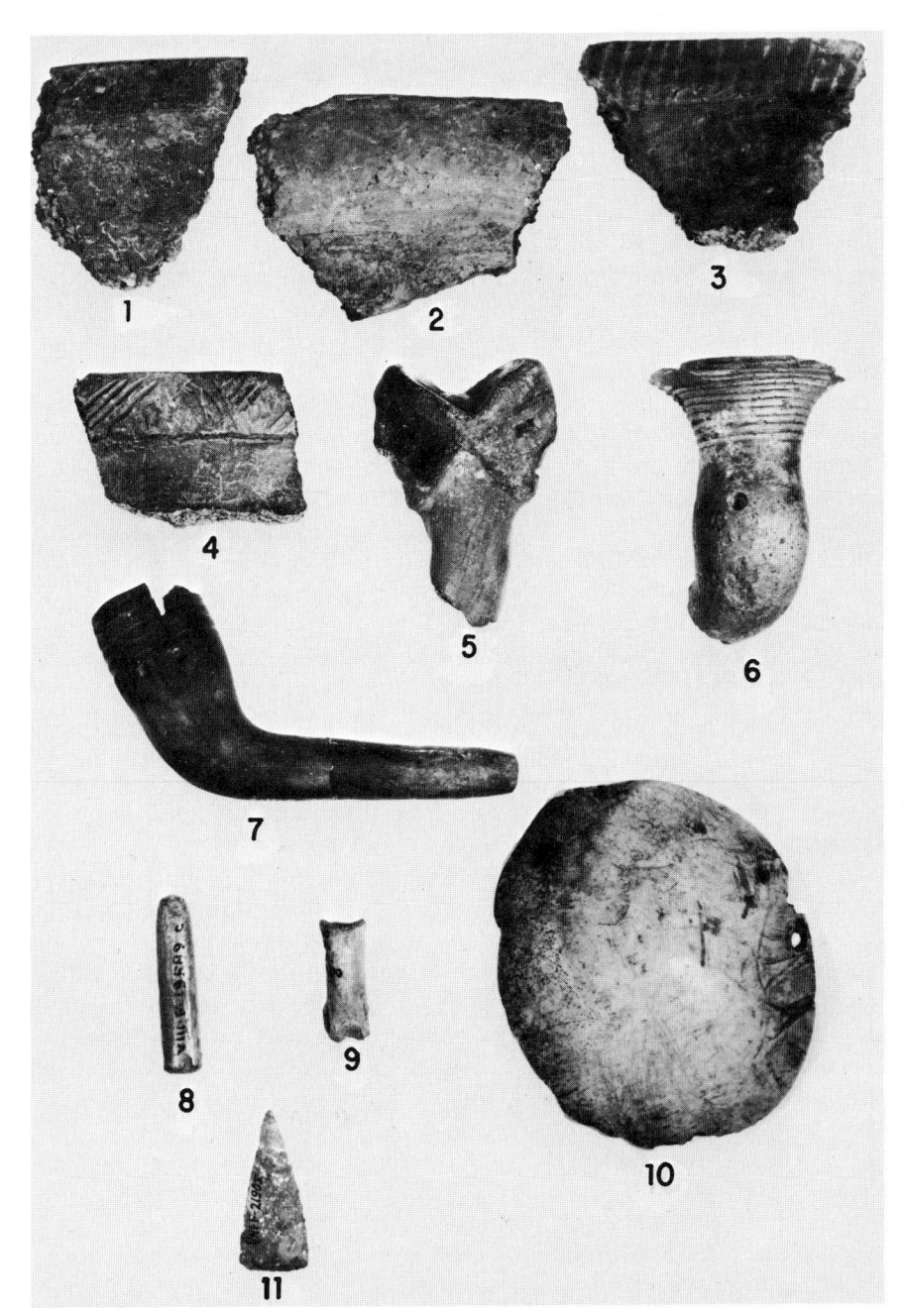

PLATE 8.24. Late prehistoric Neutral or Nuetral-Erie artifacts from the Lawson and other sites in southern Ontario: pottery (1–4); clay pipes (5–7); antler flaking tool (8); worked deer toe bone for possible use in the "cup-and-pin" game (9); circular gorget made from section of a human skull (10); and triangular point (11). (Shown approximately two-thirds actual size.) (Courtesy James V. Wright and the Archaeological Survey of Canada, National Museum of Man, Ottawa.)

zon. The initial displacement is attributed to intrusions of Upper Mississippian peoples at a time when their influence was being exerted elsewhere as well. While there is at least as much speculation as hard evidence in this, it is by now reasonably clear that site assemblages in many ways comparable to those just reviewed for developmental Ontario Iroquois are present well west and south from the Windsor–Detroit area and that they too can be shown to have been in major part the products of regional evolution with a substantial degree of residential integrity. Whether all of the people involved were also Iroquoian-speakers is going to be difficult to test.

Late Ontario Iroquois, commencing by scholarly convention just after 1400, witnessed the emergence of the known Iroquoian tribal societies of Ontario and westernmost New York. From the southern branch sprang the Eries, Neutrals, and Wenros. A merger of Late Ontario Iroquoians withdrawing from along the northern shore of Lake Ontario with others already resident in the historical estate of the Hurons between Lake Simcoe and Georgian Bay gave rise to the Huron–Petun peoples. More of the original Pickering legacy was preserved in this latter branch of the great Ontario family than in the other, more of Glen Meyer in the former. Longhouses, villages, palisaded enclosures, and ossuaries, indicative of population growth and the sureness of the economy, grew in numbers and size to about their maximum attainments. They were flourishing and warlike peoples, these Ontario Iroquoians, when the doors of written history opened upon them. And in New York there were cultural–linguistic kinsmen to take their measure.

In the country between the Lower Great Lakes and the Upper, from the western end of Lake Erie to the southern tip of Lake Huron, the division Late Woodland I and Late Woodland II is reflected, as previously intimated, by the partly sequential, partly coeval, Wayne and Younge "traditions." These are largely defined in terms of pottery and both exhibit close similarities with previously described cultures. Though not all archaeologists agree, all or a major part of the Younge tradition has been subsumed, as we have seen, in the recently and tentatively formulated concept of a Western Basin tradition.

The Wayne tradition coexisted in its dotage with the earliest and unnamed developmental phase of the Younge tradition sometime between A.D. 700 and 900, although various locally defined descendants of the Wayne Tradition are thought to have persisted in western and central Michigan until well after this latter date. At the Sissung site in eastern Monroe County, just south of Detroit, radiocarbon dated at around A.D. 700, pottery fragments from both the Wayne and Younge traditions were recovered in seeming association—sometimes in the very same refuse pits. In fact, some sherds seem to show the commingling of style attributes from both sources. These data have been variously interpreted to mean that the later tradition was an outgrowth of the earlier, that the site had been

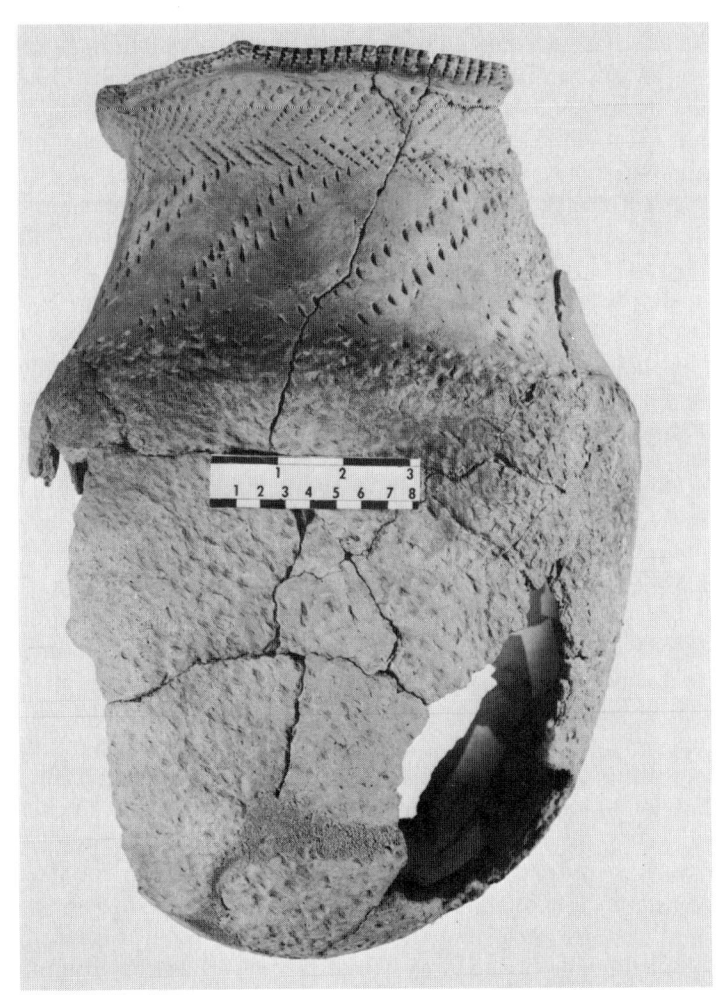

PLATE 8.25. *Rivière au Vase* type vessel of the Younge (Western Basin) tradition from the MacNichol site, Wood County, Ohio. (Courtesy David M. Stothers and the Laboratory of Ethnoarchaeology, University of Toledo, and The Toledo Area Aboriginal Research Society, Inc.)

alternately inhabited over a short period by members of two unaffiliated groups, or that there had been interaction resulting in acculturation. The second suggestion least accords with the style juxtapositions and provenience information. The Sissung site is doubly important because of the finding of corn in a feature which produced a radiocarbon assay of circa A.D. 700.

Whatever the precise ontogeny of the Sissung site itself, the Younge tradition was inextricably involved in many of the events just reviewed in the rise of the Early Ontario tradition. Where manifestations of one begin and the other end are currently matters of lively debate. Sustained social interaction and considerable population movement across the Detroit and St. Clair rivers is abundantly clear even if the nature and facilitating circumstances of those interactions and movements are but dimly understood. The Younge tradition has even been attributed to the influence, if not the actual arrival, of Glen Meyer folk removing westward. Reversing poles, all or a part of the Glen Meyer culture has been proposed as a Michigan derivative. Movement in both directions with more or less continuous social intercourse in this ecologically rich, geographically strategic, and populous crossroads seem much more likely theoretical options than either unidirectional alternatives. Those archaeologists who find in the current viability of these counterclaims justification for assigning the label "Iroquois" to the Younge or the Western Basin Tradition, and it certainly has an appeal, need to reflect on the archaeological correspondences between the New York Iroquois and some of their known-to-have-been Algonquian-speaking neighbors.

The majority of Younge tradition ceramics are varieties of what is called Rivière Ware. The name was taken from a key site of the tradition, the Rivière au Vase site just west of Lake St. Clair in Macomb County, Michigan. This pottery has been influential in suggesting a strong phylogenetic connection between the tradition and Early Ontario Iroquois, as has been seen. Supporting indications of interaction and some kind of affinity are such nonpottery traits as intensive agricultural commitment, construction of longhouses in palisaded precincts, and sometime resort to ossuary burial.

The Younge tradition has been apportioned among four successive periods with strongly overlapping representative components. Suffice it to note that these are, including the initial and unnamed phase, a Younge phase, a Springwells phase, and a final or Wolf phase. By the time of the Younge phase, circa 900–1100, Rivière Ware had completely overtaken and replaced Wayne Ware ceramics, at least locally. A longhouse (perhaps, it has been suggested, a specialized charnel house) at the Younge site, an incredible 178 m in length, was put up at this time. The Younge phase was approximately coetaneous with the beginnings of the Whittlesey culture, a regional Late Woodland manifestation on and inland of the southeast shore of Lake Erie in eastern Ohio. In northern Michigan the late Mackinac and Bois Blanc phases were other contemporaries. Trade vessels and style convergences tie these widely separated locales together on a common time plane by their indications of contact and communication.

By the time of the Wolf phase, between about 1300 and 1450, Upper Mississippian influences, if not actual incursions, were being felt in the Younge–Western Basin territory. Notwithstanding this fact, efforts to classify the Wolf phase as Mississippian are unconvincing. The Wolf phase

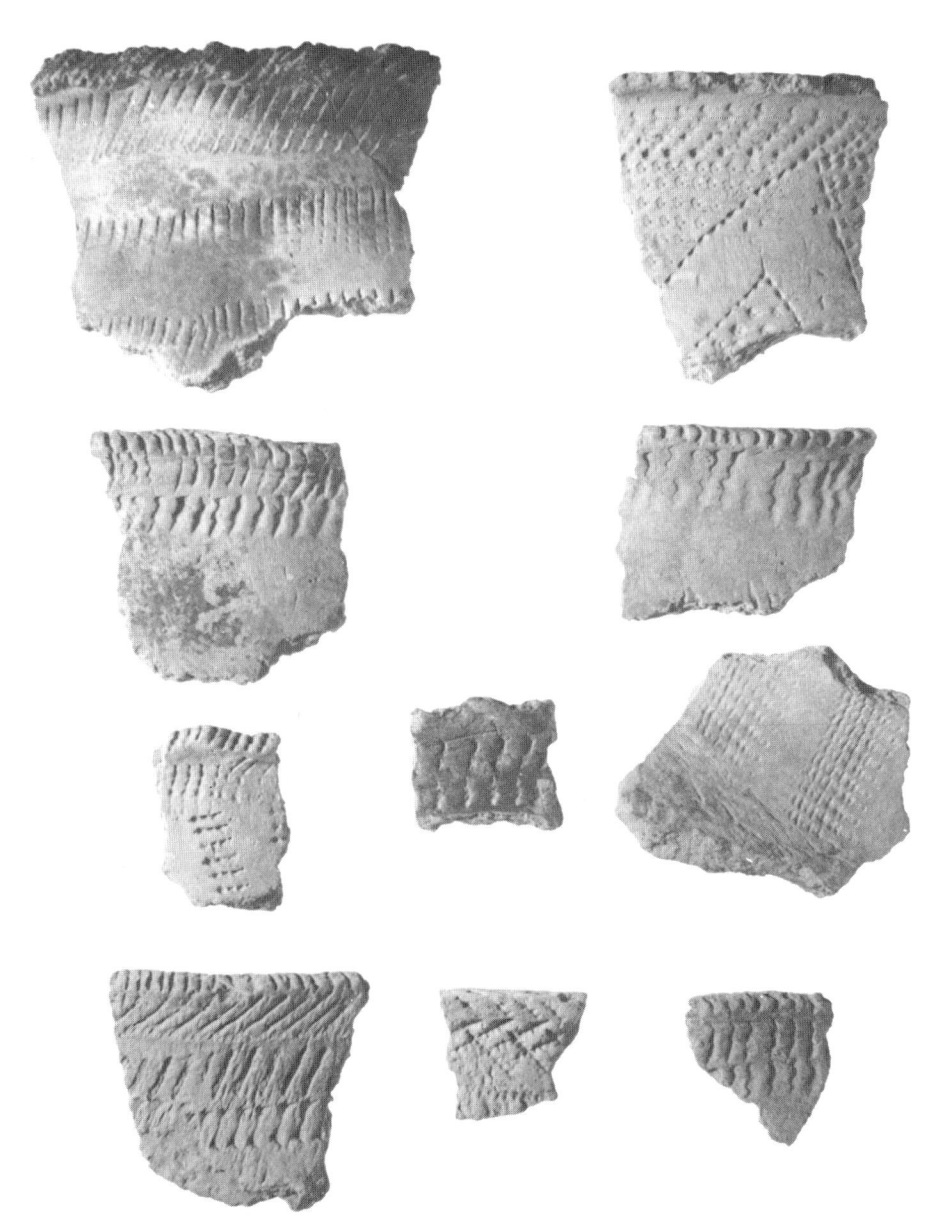

PLATE 8.26. *Younge phase Western Basin pottery from the Petrie site, Lucas County (Toledo), Ohio. (Shown half actual size.) (Courtesy David M. Stothers and the Laboratory of Ethnoarchaeology, University of Toledo, and The Toledo Area Aboriginal Research Society, Inc.)*

PLATE 8.27. Upper Mississippian-related Late Woodland II pottery from the Fort Meigs site, Wood County, Ohio. (Shown about half actual size.) (Courtesy David M. Stothers and the Laboratory of Ethnoarchaeology, University of Toledo, and The Toledo Area Aboriginal Research Society, Inc.)

TABLE 8.1. Correlations of Ontario and New York Proto-Iroquoian Cultures with the Western Basin or Younge tradition[a]

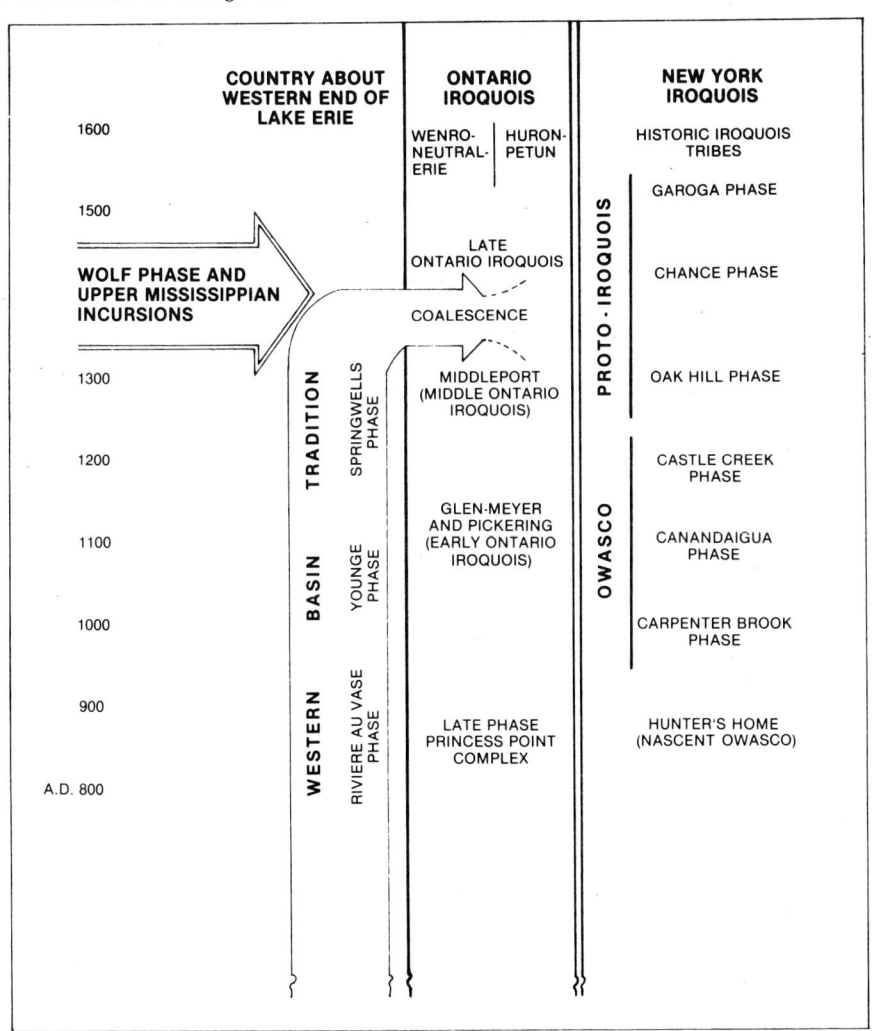

Year	Country about Western end of Lake Erie	Western Basin Tradition	Ontario Iroquois	Proto-Iroquois / Owasco	New York Iroquois
1600			Wenro-Neutral-Erie / Huron-Petun		Historic Iroquois Tribes
1500					Garoga Phase
	Wolf Phase and Upper Mississippian Incursions		Late Ontario Iroquois	Proto-Iroquois	Chance Phase
		Springwells Phase	Coalescence		
1300			Middleport (Middle Ontario Iroquois)		Oak Hill Phase
1200					Castle Creek Phase
		Younge Phase	Glen-Meyer and Pickering (Early Ontario Iroquois)	Owasco	
1100					Canandaigua Phase
1000					Carpenter Brook Phase
900		Rivière au Vase Phase	Late Phase Princess Point Complex		Hunter's Home (Nascent Owasco)
A.D. 800					

[a] This model departs from the text in removing the Wolf phase from the Western Basin tradition and in linking it with the Upper Mississippian intrusions, and in identifying the "initial and unnamed phase" of the tradition as the Rivière au Vase Phase. Although the eventual coalescence of the Springwells phase and the Ontario Iroquois tradition implies common linguistic affiliations, such implication is not necessary to satisfy the model even if it would be helpful. (Modified from Stothers 1979.)

pottery type, Parker Festooned, with sometimes bizarre appliqué decoration can no more be derived from such a source than can the remainder of the pottery. And in this particular region, at least, it is pottery that constitutes the sine qua non for identification as Mississippian. As already pointed out, the Younge, or Western Basin, Tradition is believed to have been extinguished as a separate identifiable entity by around 1450, the responsible society or societies perhaps having been driven eastward into the absorbing embrace of the Ontario Iroquois by the mounting pressure of Mississippian peoples to the south and west. Following the Wolf phase there appears to have been a near abandonment of extensive tracts of southeastern Michigan and adjoining Ohio. None of the historical tribes can be tied to a specific sequence of prehistoric sites in this region.

Late Woodland II: Upper Lakes

A return to the Straits of Mackinac to look again at the stratified Juntunen site rewards the effort. By around the year 1000 the earlier Late Woodland inhabitants identified with the already described Mackinac phase had either given way to new people or they had modified their traditional manufactures in such directions that they now possess a new archaeological identity in the Bois Blanc phase. This and its successor, the Juntunen phase, are the exemplars of the Late Woodland II stage in their area. Despite their differences the interlacing continuities are such that the phases may well have been the products of descending generations of a long resident population as they reacted to the stirrings of the wider world.

There is some floral and faunal evidence of slight climatic change coincident with the tenure of the Bois Blanc phase, a shift to a somewhat warmer and drier regime. Nevertheless, fishing continued to be the principal pursuit of the islanders during their seasonal encampments. Access to a supply of corn also continued and evidence persists of an important role for hunting and collecting. Bois Blanc phase ceramics abandoned the splayed lips of the earlier styles, adopting instead the sometime addition of small collars produced by modeling or cambering and by the application of extra clay to upper rims. Castellations, or prominent upwellings in the line of rim and lip constitute another novelty. These paralleled more or less contemporary realignments in ceramic design elsewhere, especially in Wisconsin where the type Point Sauble Collared constitutes a reasonable analog of the Bois Blanc "braced rim" vessels.

Internal and external factors during the following Juntunen phase, dated by radiocarbon to sometime between 1200 and 1400, brought into being a number of significant departures from past practices. One external factor of debatable importance was a probable reversion to the slightly cooler and

PLATE 8.28. *Ossuary (Feature 11) of the Juntunen phase occupation at the Juntunen site in the Straits of Machinac, Michigan. The remains of 35 individuals were recovered from this mortuary. (Courtesy Richard I. Ford and the Museum of Anthropology, University of Michigan, Ann Arbor.)*

wetter climate which seems to have preceded the Bois Blanc phase. With regard to social change, a reduction and tightening up of between-vessel-variability contrasts especially with the more heterogeneous Mackinac Ware. As discussed earlier, this has been offered as possibly linked to sociological rearrangements in postmarital forms of residence from patrilocality to matrilocality. Such a suggestion is not incompatible with other data having skewed geographic, hence cultural, leanings. Now collared vessels with rim peaks and castellations became common. Designs reveal the use of linear stamping or punctating and the technique of stab-and-drag. Cord-impressed decoration persisted even though much reduced in

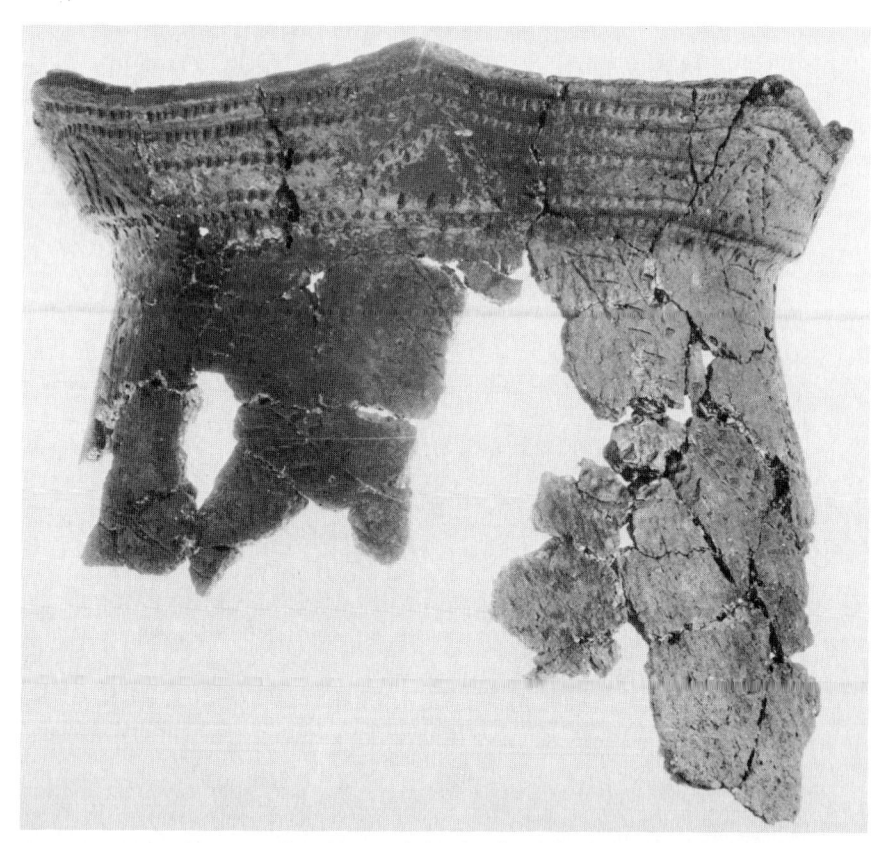

PLATE 8.29. *Partly restored Juntunen phase pot from the Juntunen site in the Straits of Mackinac, Michigan. (Shown one-third actual size.) (Courtesy Richard I. Ford and the Museum of Anthropology, University of Michigan, Ann Arbor.)*

popularity. Besides heavily adorned rims and collars habitually underscored with punctates, vessel lips and interior rims were more often than not decorated as well. Juntunen phase pottery betrays an apparent tilt in the direction from which style cues were being courted, a reorientation of attention from west to east. Strong correspondences are manifested with the contemporary emergence of the Uren–Middleport Middle Ontario Iroquois cultural pattern in southern Ontario. Nevertheless, lingering contacts with Blackduck may still be detected and, for the first time, Mississippian pottery is present in the form of trade vessels. While most of this trade pottery is grit-tempered Oneota ware indistinguishable from the Mero I complex of northeastern Wisconsin, a trace of Middle Mississippian pottery of the type known as Ramey Incised has also been recovered from the same deposits yielding Juntunen Ware.

Among the nonceramic characteristics of the Juntunen phase occupation was the local establishment of copper tool manufacture. The limited products of this new enterprise were small awls, knives, and beads. And for the first time the use of the locality as a fishery was soberly augmented by a mortuary role. The community's dead were buried in a number of ossuaries over which low mounds of earth were finally heaped. The inhumations, ranging from 5 to 35 individuals in each ossuary, were the bundled remains of corpses which had undergone preliminary burial or other preparatory treatment elsewhere. Evidence was preserved of bark shrouds and pit lining. Many of the skulls showed the post-mortem removal of bone plaques. Very few artifacts had been placed in the pits, at least of types that would survive. An interesting exception to the paucity of grave offerings was in the case of the articulated skeleton of a man who seems to have confronted the hereafter armed with a "medicine kit" containing fire-making equipment and some other handy precautions. While the Juntunen ossuaries have been cited by some prehistorians as examples of the possible forerunner of the famous Huron Feast of the Dead, no ethnic nor linguistic affiliations are necessarily thereby implied. Furthermore, as the chapter on the Middle Woodland period demonstrated, the origins of ossuaries long predate the Juntunen or other Late Woodland models.

To the west, the shallow-soil (exposed bedrock), myriad-shallow-lakes country of north central Wisconsin and adjoining tracts of the upper Michigan peninsula has always been at the end of secondary routes of Great Lakes–Mississippi Valley communication rather than constituting the crossover point of primary ones. That such a quarter should harbor archaeological sites that recapitulate in general ways, locally rendered, something of the same sequence of artifact forms as has just been reviewed for the busy Straits of Mackinac, minus the late eastern attraction, is impressive testimony of the role of diffusion in moderating the centrifugal tendencies of cultural change among innumerable small societies, each constantly adapting itself to the unique opportunities and limitations of its own peculiar niche. The Late Woodland Lakes phase of this region, like its local predecessors, remained in touch with the world outside its own quieter bailiwick. At different times the direction shifted from which the greatest influences were being felt. As already shown in a previous section, Heins Creek, Effigy Mound, and Oneota groups interacted at intervals with the Lakes phase, the first early in its ontogeny, the second virtually throughout, and the third last of all and only intermittently.

Spanning the two divisions of Late Woodland time, but with the sites so far discovered most abundant in the late half, the Lakes phase evolved over some 800 or even 900 years. Considerable stylistic change, at least, must have occurred during this time as already intimated in the preceding paragraph. Unfortunately, field work in this still heavily forested country has been so recent and limited, considering the time depth and space involved, that most of this change is as yet masked by limited sampling and analysis.

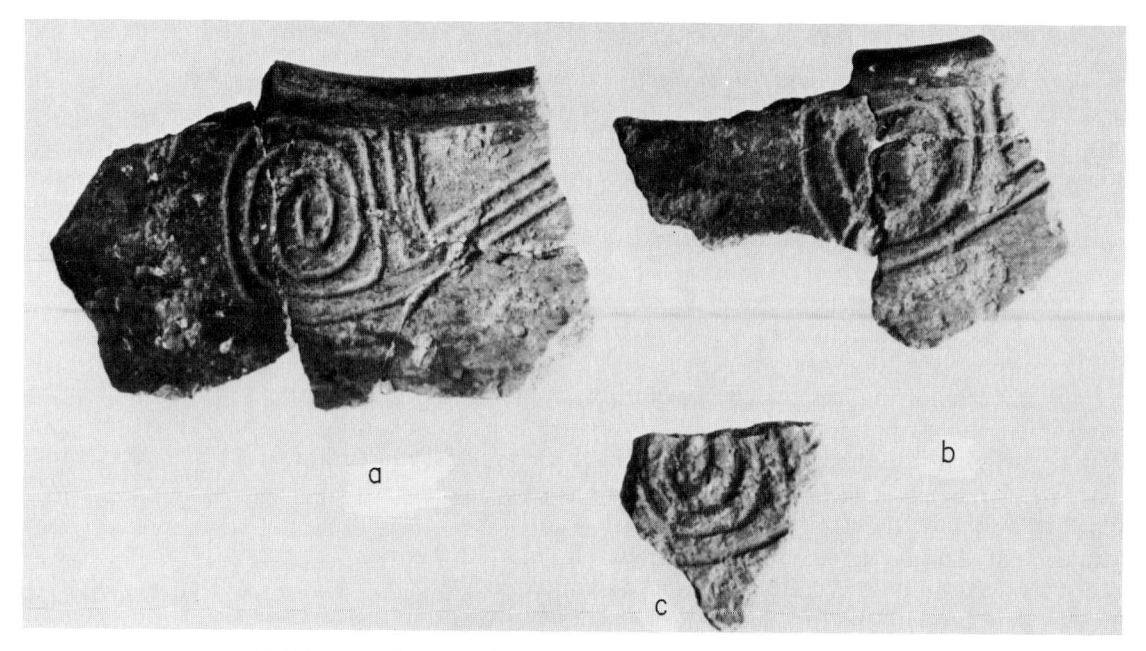

PLATE 8.30. *Rare Middle Mississippian (Ramey Incised-like) pottery from the Juntunen site in the Straits of Mackinac, Michigan. (Shown half actual size.) (Courtesy Richard I. Ford and the Museum of Anthropology, University of Michigan, Ann Arbor.)*

Certain things are clear nevertheless. The salient features of this change have been previously outlined in the context of comparisons with the Heins Creek and Effigy Mound cultures. As was suggested there, and is of special relevance here, the discovery of minimally decorated grit- and shell-tempered Oneota pottery in Lakes phase middens is good evidence of that interaction with the outside world that has just been invoked. There is neither enough of this pottery nor signs of any degree of exclusive spatial distributions to support the hypothesis that there had ever been a separate occupation by Upper Mississippian folk in the Lakes phase habitat. Exchange relations with the south were probably analogous with those proposed for the partly coeval Effigy Mound culture and Oneota, though less frequent or important to the parties concerned.

By virtue having a preponderance of sites dating after A.D. 1100, the Upper Mississippian culture called Oneota is the prime example of Late Woodland II stage culture west of Lake Michigan. Of course, it coexisted with Woodland groups, notably the Effigy Mound culture and, far to the north, Blackduck, both having come by their essential configurations during the Late Woodland I stage, as well as the Lakes phase and other as yet undefined cultural entities. It is important to remember, furthermore, that some Oneota sites may be older than this date and that certain of the features that are most frequently cited as typical of the culture, such as shell tempering and triangular arrowheads, have individually an enormously greater spatial distribution and a higher order of antiquity than their association in the Oneota culture. Viewed as a constellation of settlement types, artifact styles, and so on, displaced over a wide landscape, Oneota may be thought of as a broad cultural pattern comparable to, say, that of the prehistoric New York and Ontario Iroquois—an archaeological classification of a core, and even many sections of the veneer, of cultural similarity shared among a number of territorially distinct, autonomous societies. And again, as with the Iroquois example, many of these societies were very probably linguistic relatives as well, only this time the languages were Siouan. Such known tribal heirs of Oneota as the Iowas and Otos, and such presumptive heirs as the Winnebagos, spoke languages of the Chiwere branch of the Siouan stock. Other likely descendants of Oneota ancestors such as the Omahas also spoke Siouan, only of the Dhegiha branch. It would be a mistake, however, to assume a necessary correspondence between language and culture even though the linkage is certainly a strong one in the present instance. On the margins of Oneota distribution, at least, Algonquian speakers were sometimes making some remarkably Oneota-like pottery. While Oneota sites have been found throughout a large part of Wisconsin, northern Illinois, eastern Iowa, southern Minnesota, and even farther afield, this discussion must confine itself to those manifestations within the Great Lakes drainage and aspects of those others germane to their understanding.

Another useful way of looking at Oneota is as a tradition, as a cultural continuity descending the generations of its bearers, changing in details but retaining its identity. As a tradition, Oneota seems to have emerged in Late Woodland I times even though it is much more characteristic of later centuries. It had possibly come into existence by A.D. 900. There are provocative though inconclusive signs of Oneota pottery associated with site features of the Effigy Mound culture dating back to the late seventh or the eighth century A.D. at the Sanders I site in Waupaca County, Wisconsin. Such atypically early dates involve extremely small sherd samples and they still await corroboration. On the other hand, the Oneota tradition crossed the historic threshold in the ethnic personalities of the aforementioned Siouan tribes and perhaps in some other guises as well.

Certain traits, some intrinsically weighty, others bordering on the trivial, mainly taken from the later rather than the earlier portions of the culture's lifetime, are usually called upon to give an image to the name. A well-developed and dependable agricultural way of life with a corresponding access to sedentariness was modulated by considerable hunting and collecting. Where the environment was as well endowed with inland lakes, marshes, and streams as on the western side of Lake Winnebago and in parts of the Fox and Rock River catchments of eastern Wisconsin, Oneota communities made extensive exploitation of virtually inexhaustible resources of fish, mussels, waterfowl, and wild rice. Early French explorers ascending the lower Fox River from Green Bay and the upper Fox from the chain of large lakes and marshes draining into Lake Winnebago were awed by the horizon-obliterating marsh grasses and the teeming wildlife they encountered, conditions which must also have prevailed for centuries earlier.

Although surprisingly little is known of the styles of dwellings the Great Lakes Oneota people favored, domed circular wigwams and arched or gabled-roofed small rectangular houses have actually been determined from excavations, and many of their villages were stockaded for defense. Around some of them, agricultural fields were cleared by intentional burning, sometimes taking advantage of small prairies, oak meadows, or other natural openings in the forest. In these fields hoes were used to scrape out long shallow trenches and to heap up the loose soil in parallel ridges between them. Even today, acres of such ditch-and-ridge "garden beds," geometrically arranged in plats and sometimes associated with scattered rock and village refuse "dumps," are still discernible alongside of or surrounding some Oneota sites, especially of that regional variety of Oneota called the Lake Winnebago phase. They are best seen in early winter when the leaves are down in the woodlots and a light dusting of blown snow has been captured in the long hollows, throwing into enhanced relief the modest ridges. As described in Chapter 1, somewhat similar practices by the Iroquois are thought to have had as one of their purposes the trapping of early frosts and thus the protection of the crops. Perhaps the Oneota farmers were similarly motivated in preparing their furrowed garden beds. It is clear that they are to be correlated with a high concentration on plant husbandry, not simply the ancillary gardening of people who were primarily food collectors.

In their treatment of the dead considerable variety in preparation and inhumation was accompanied by a new preference for the fully extended on-the-back posture in village cemeteries. The construction of burial mounds seems to have been restricted to just one geographical-temporal segment within the Oneota cultural pattern and tradition: the Grand River phase (not to be confused with the other two identically named phases of the Saugeen and Princess Point cultures), though by no means do all Grand River Oneota sites boast mounds. Oneota pots have been found as inclusive grave objects in a few effigy burial mounds. But the pottery was not an intrinsic property of Effigy Mound culture, and the mounds had not been thrown up by the same hands that had shaped the pots. Some contemporaneity and trade or gift exchange were the facilitating contingencies. Small quantities of Oneota pottery have also been recovered from Effigy Mound village middens and trash pits. Effigy Mound pottery is not unusual at Oneota sites. The high frequency of localities exhibiting the association of at least a few Oneota sherds in Effigy Mound contexts, or vice versa, argues for a long-lived, low-level social intercourse of beneficial reciprocity across boundaries of some ecological specialization, probably not involving extensive intermarriage. The ceramic attributes of the two traditions remained discrete, notwithstanding contact and interaction, and have only rarely been found juxtaposed. There is no evidence of any kind of derivative relationship in spite of attempts to posit one.

Aside from the new intensification of agricultural practices, it is the pottery that sets Oneota apart. It represents something fresh, something different from most of what had been done earlier or was being done contemporaneously in Effigy Mound or other Woodland ceramic design. Different though it also is from Middle Mississippian pottery, in this case there are sufficient similarities to indicate the sharing of a common phylogeny. Oneota pottery as a whole exhibits a seemingly quite-sudden near-universality of plain, smooth surface finishing. There are infrequent instances of cordmarking on Oneota pots, however, and the custom of wholly or partly smoothing vessel surfaces had appeared long before its latest burst of popularity. But the Middle Woodland examples had been eclipsed and largely replaced by the predominantly cord-roughened surfaces of the Late Woodland I stage. The reappearance of plain surfaces as overall vessel surface treatment in Middle and Upper Mississippian seems to have been saltatory rather than the gradual culmination of a demonstrable evolutionary trend.

Equally impressive for contrastive purposes was the wholesale adoption of shell tempering. Again, more ancient examples of this practice have been found, as in certain Middle Woodland contexts, though they are far too restricted in numbers, time, and space to have been likely sources for the later proliferation of the trait. An additional qualification is that some Oneota communities, in blithe disregard of the needs of future archaeologists, retained the use of crushed rock as their tempering material. In the Oneota occupations unearthed at the Mero site on the Wisconsin Door Peninsula (the Mero complex), 38% of the original pots had been tempered with grit. Nevertheless, shell tempering in most sectors of the Oneota realm appears to have been extremely popular from early to late in the tradition. The use of crushed shell as the tempering agent in place of grit had several results. For one thing, being relatively light itself, it reduced the weight of the finished vessel. For another, the excellent binding qualities of shell and the fact that vessel shaping and surface smoothing tend to align the platelet-shaped temper particles parallel with the vessel walls made possible thinner walls than had been practicable heretofore, another reduction in weight. As an example of this result, a not unusual vessel of the type called "Lake Winnebago Trailed" from the Lasleys Point site in Winnebago County, Wisconsin, with the considerable diameter at the shoulder of 41.5 cm (16¼ in.), has a wall thickness on the upper shoulder of only 2 mm (3/32 in.). This reflects a high order of craftsmanship from the aesthetic as well as the technical viewpoint.

There is a tricky problem in using shell to temper pottery, however. When shell-tempered pottery is fired, there is the danger that the calcium carbonate ($CaCO_3$) will break down. One of the products of such thermal alteration, calcium oxide (CaO), has the unhappy property of combining with water vapor in the clay. This combination may expand beyond the volume of the original shell-temper particles, thus fracturing the embedding clay and ruining the pot. Experiments have shown that the admixture of a little salt solves this problem before it can develop, and microscopic thin-section examination of shell-tempered sherds has revealed readily identifiable cube-shaped casts, often with a yellowish stained reaction halo where the now long-dissolved crystals had been. Not only, then, did potters have to master some applied chemistry before the seemingly simple option of shell tempering could be widely adopted, the uneven availability of salt sources necessitated procurement of that commodity via trade.

Other peculiarities of Oneota pottery include a greater range in vessel shapes than that seen in Woodland ceramics. Even though cups, straight-sided bowls, and occasional almost platelike shallow open bowls have been retrieved from some Oneota sites, and these are reminiscent of the much greater diversity to be experienced in a Middle Mississippian milieu such as Aztalan, the typical vessel shape is a wide-bodied, round, yawning-mouthed jar with relatively short outflared rim recovering part of the widest diameter of the pot above a short neck constriction. Rim eversion is sometimes so pronounced in some of the eastern Wisconsin material as to reach the horizontal. Many Oneota pots were equipped with handles, usually an opposed pair, in the form of straplike or ropelike loops of clay connecting rim and upper shoulder. The time-honored decorative resort to stamping was abolished entirely to be replaced by incising, trailing with finger or blunt tool, punctating, and sometimes the modeling of large shoulder bosses or circular depressions in the same place. There are no collars on such vessels, nor are there rim peaks or castellations. Although the statistics have never been pulled together and collated in a systematic way, Oneota folk appear to have been prolific potters. Throughout most of the sprawling range where their sites have been found, always excluding Middle Mississippian town sites, their per capita production of pottery seems to have been appreciably greater than that inferred for antecedent periods or for coeval Woodland folk in the western Great Lakes. To the east, Iroquoian sites show a parallel increase in relative quantities of ceramics. In both areas the upward flux correlates with the maximization of agricultural dependence and the densest, sustained population aggregations in the Great Lakes.

Aside from the distinctive pottery vessels, there are only a few artifact types that are peculiarly characteristic of Oneota, either by virtue of unique

8. Farmers without Plows, Warriors without Swords

design or special abundance. Relatively numerous circular discs made from potsherds by grinding their edges, often with a drilled central hole, have been found at many Oneota stations. Perforated specimens are thought by some archaeologists to have been spindle whorls or flywheels for bow drills. Imperforate discs may have served as surface-smoothing tools in pot making. Gaming pieces has been another popular interpretation. Nobody really knows. In the chipped-flint tool inventory high proportions of endscrapers, by no means unique to or even characteristic of, all or even most Oneota components, nevertheless are a recurring phenomenon. More apt to signal "Oneota," though many such sites fail to yield them up, are paired oblong, grooved, "arrowshaft straighteners" of sandstone or other abrasive rock; ground and polished pendants and so-called Siouan disc-shaped smoking pipes, usually of the very pleasing red "sacred" mineral called catlinite (but even more typical of the historic period); and hafted hoe blades made of deer, elk, or bison scapulae—the latter increasingly represented toward and west of the Mississippi River. Finally, and obviously restricted to those locations where they could be counted an important ancillary food resource, the heaviest harvesting of shellfish by any Great Lakes society is linked to the occupation of certain Lake Winnebago phase Oneota sites in east central Wisconsin. Tools as well as food were obtained from these invertebrates. Perforated shells probably utilized as hoe blades are quite common as are shell spoons, pendants, beads, and small ground pieces which may have been fishing lures.

The many qualifications prefacing or appended to some of the foregoing descriptions are functions of observed discrepancies about whose meaning scholars are wont to quarrel. Time and space considerations reduce simplicity but they bring us a little closer to what the Oneota world was really like. To take the last aspect first, the clusters of Oneota sites in one area often differ in consistent, albeit seemingly minor, ways from Oneota sites in other places, even when site function can be held more or less constant. In or adjacent to the Great Lakes drainage in Wisconsin there are at least five such areas, each having its own idiosyncrasies within the more pervasive commonality making them all Oneota as opposed to something else. These named geographical "phases" (formerly "foci") are the Koshkonong phase in south central Wisconsin, the Lake Winnebago phase just west of the big lake of the same name, the Grand River phase (again!) between the first two, the Green Bay phase (Mero complex) in the lower Fox Valley and the Door Peninsula, and the Orr phase in western Wisconsin and on into Iowa. Some of the diagnostic features of these phases are far more widely distributed than this geography specifies—Orr or Grand River or Green Bay ceramic styles, for instance—but it minimally has the usefulness of indicating the approximate districts which yield the most intense representations of the five generally recognized divisions. At the south end of Lake Michigan in northeastern Illinois and northwestern

PLATE 8.31. *Ocean-shell gorget with face and "weeping eye" motif from the Anker site, Cook County, Illinois. (Shown approximately actual size.) (Courtesy James W. Van-Stone and the Field Museum of Natural History, Chicago.)*

Indiana are the poorly understood remains of the Oneota-like Fisher and Huber (Blue Island) cultures. These sometimes show some unusually strong Middle Mississippian influences, probably through trade. The Anker site in Cook County, Illinois, immediately south of the city of Chicago, is a rich, if now destroyed, exemplar of the Oneota-like Huber or Blue Island culture. This village and cemetery site produced startling evidence of trade and other connections with the Arkansas region, most dramatically in the form of painted and effigy pots unlike anything ever found before in the Great Lakes.

A few examples will serve to illustrate the kinds of distinctions apparent

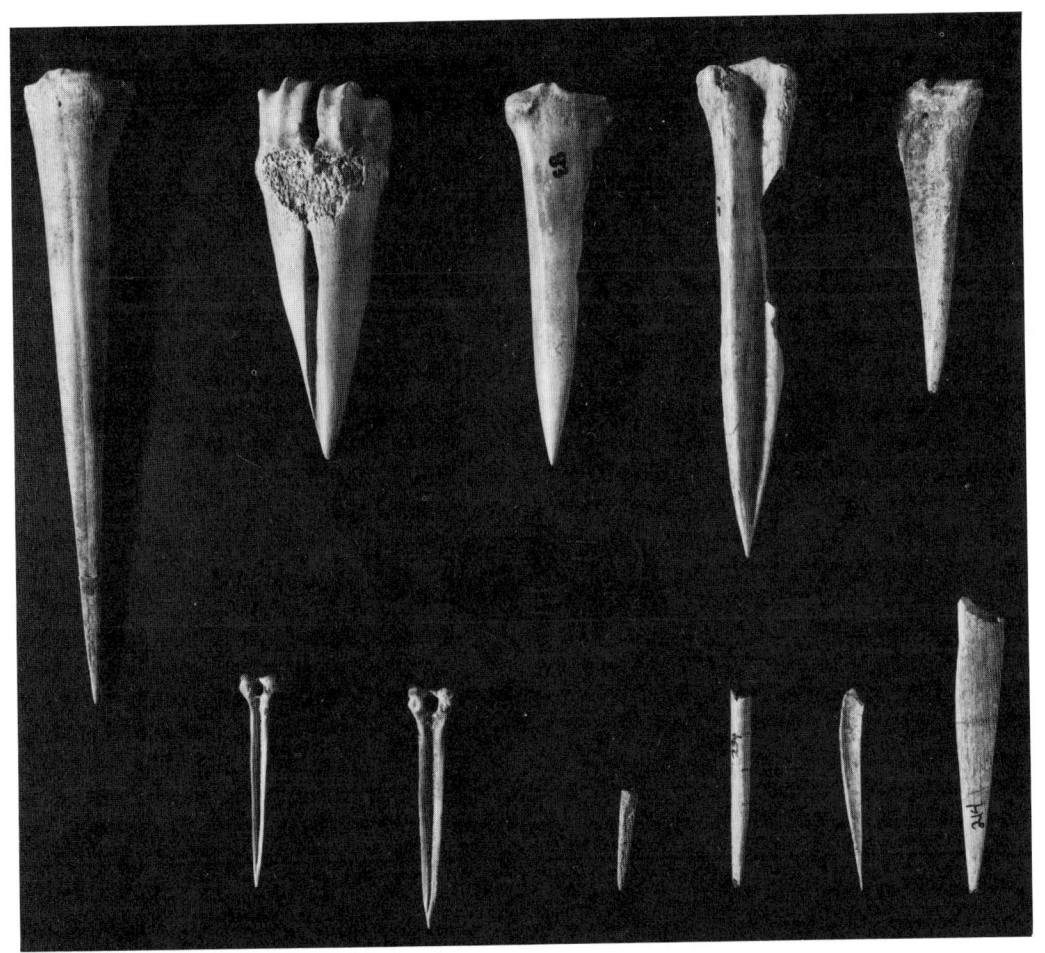

PLATE 8.32. *Oneota bone awls, pins, and needles from the Pipe site, Fond du Lac County, Wisconsin. (Shown half actual size.) (Courtesy David F. Overstreet, Great Lakes Archaeological Research Center, Inc.)*

among the Oneota phases, distinctions overwhelmingly concerned with pottery. To what degree these correspond to or are independent of other less tangible differences no one at present really knows. Some may be more important to archaeologists than they were to the original people. Grand River pots were only rarely decorated aside from lip crimpimg whereas Orr pots were hardly ever left unadorned. A salient feature of Koshkonong ceramic decoration is the use of curvilinear motifs, including Middle Mississippian-like interlocking scrolls, whereas Lake Winnebago phase pots are more solidly embellished on the shoulders with strictly standardized designs emphasizing plats of straight lines. Orr phase rims tend to be relatively high and moderate in their eversion, Lake Winnebago, short and extreme. Handles are common in the former, rare in the latter. Orr ceramics are shell tempered, Green Bay Phase pottery is noteworthy for its unusually common resort to grit tempering and for having the least development of vessel decoration. Some other bases for segregation have been previously alluded to with regard to associations of burial mounds, ditch-and-ridge garden beds, bison-scapula hoes, and so on. Certain of these are also symptomatic of age.

The Oneota tradition is known by a persistence of cultural identity through four successive periods or "horizons." These and their approximate dates are: Emergent (circa A.D. 900–1000), Developmental (1000–1300), Classic (1300–1634), Historic (post-1634). The first, as intimated by its

PLATE 8.33. *Oneota disc-shaped catlinite pipes. The larger specimen is from Outagamie County, Wisconsin, the smaller from an unknown locality but probably also Wisconsin. (Shown actual size.) (Collections of Department of Anthropology, Lawrence University, Appleton, Wisconsin.)*

PLATE 8.34. *Green Bay phase (Mero complex) Oneota rimsherds from the Mero site, Door County, Wisconsin. The upper five specimens are shell tempered, the lowe four are grit tempered. (Shown half actual size.) (Collections of the Neville Public Museum, Green Bay, Wisconsin.)*

name, is conceived of as the interval during which Oneota culture came into being as a recognizable entity. Components are few and equivocal and our knowledge slight. By the Developmental horizon, Oneota sites are numerous and exhibit a generous appropriation of space. Many sites of the Koshkonong, Grand River, and Green Bay phases date to this time. The Classic horizon is most familiarly characterized by the Orr and Lake Winnebago phases, though communities whose archaeological debris would be classified as belonging to one or another of the antecedent phases continued into this horizon. The most intensive farming is attributed to the Classic horizon as is a tendency for settlements to grow in size and permanence even while some areas of settlement apparently contracted. The Lake Winnebago phase, for instance, occupied a much smaller territory than that within which Grand River settlements were established. On the other hand, the geography of the Orr phase is quantitatively more impressive than the Koshkonong.

The Historic horizon is surprisingly underrepresented by archaeological sites. Late components of Orr and Lake Winnebago have often been cited as examplars of historic-period Oneota. Only Orr, however, has actually been shown to cross the historical threshold, producing a few sites in which early European trade artifacts are unequivocally associated with native. Notwithstanding the belief by many scholars and interested laymen, there is as yet no good archaeological evidence that Lake Winnebago Oneota had an historic extension, let alone one that can be demonstrated to have been the culture of the Winnebago Indians. The only Oneota material which archaeologists have so far brought to light in or near

PLATE 8.35 *Oneota vessel from Rock Island Site II, Door County, Wisconsin. (Shown one-third actual size.) (Collections of Department of Anthropology, Lawrence University, Appleton, Wisconsin.)*

PLATE 8.36 *Lake Winnebago phase Oneota pottery from the Lasleys Point site, Winnebago County, Wisconsin. (Shown half actual size.) (Collections of Department of Anthropology, Lawrence University, Appleton, Wisconsin.)*

the historic homeland of the Winnebagos that can be empirically tied to the historic period by European trade-goods associations in undisturbed stratigraphic contexts (or in any context for that matter) has come from Rock Island Site II at the mouth of Green Bay. This pottery is of Orr and Green Bay (Mero Complex) phase styles and not Lake Winnebago.

As unsatisfactory as our knowledge regarding the destiny of eastern Oneota on the threshold of history, or of the prehistoric culture of the Winnebago Indians, is the current state of ideas respecting the origins of Oneota. These are variations of migrationist and partial diffusionist–evolutionary hypotheses. The first, capitalizing on the undisputed (though sometimes ignored) similarities of certain Oneota cultural traits, preemi-

PLATE 8.37. *Lake Winnebago phase Oneota pottery from the Lasleys Point site, Winnebago County, Wisconsin. The three right-hand specimens in lower row are handles. (Shown half actual size.) (Collections of Department of Anthropology, Lawrence University, Appleton, Wisconsin.)*

nently ceramic, with Middle Mississippian, would derive the former from the latter. In this view, a northward-removing community budded off from a demographically successful Middle Mississippian society, perhaps a colony of emigrants from the burgeoning town and ceremonial center of Cahokia in Illinois, and established itself at the Aztalan site in south central Wisconsin and at perhaps a few other less conspicuous places as well. For some reason, possibly involving climatic deterioration and the accordingly stressed marginal capacity of corn agriculture as yet unadapted to so northerly a habitat, the intruding population found itself with a now less than adequate customary food base to support their elaborate culture. Forced to diversify and intensify their subsistence efforts, that is, to relapse into a more primitive economic regimen, they were unable to maintain the preferred nonsubsistence practices which had marked them as a people apart when they had first arrived. The culture known as Oneota was the impoverished heir of reduced Mississippian fortunes in the hinterlands. With early Oneota radiocarbon dates signaling times fully contemporary

8. Farmers without Plows, Warriors without Swords

with and even antecedent to the Middle Mississippian establishments at Cahokia and Aztalan (circa 1100–1300 for the latter), this model of Oneota beginnings has had to be abandoned in its original form.

A proposed alternative approach has been to combine the *fact* of the diffusion of maize agriculture into the northern Mississippi Valley–western

PLATE 8.38. *Lake Winnebago phase Oneota rough stone tools from the Lasleys Point site, Winnebago County, Wisconsin: hammerstones (left column); grooved "shaft-smoother" (upper right); and disc-shaped objects of unknown but common use. (Shown half actual size.) (Collections of Department of Anthropology, Lawrence University, Appleton, Wisconsin.)*

PLATE 8.39. Lake Winnebago phase Oneota triangular arrowheads from the Lasleys Point site, Winnebago County, Wisconsin. (Shown actual size.) (Collections of Department of Anthropology, Lawrence University, Appleton, Wisconsin.)

PLATE 8.40. Lake Winnebago phase Oneota end-scrapers from the Lasleys Point site, Winnebago County, Wisconsin. (Shown actual size.) (Collections of Department of Anthropology, Lawrence University, Appleton, Wisconsin.)

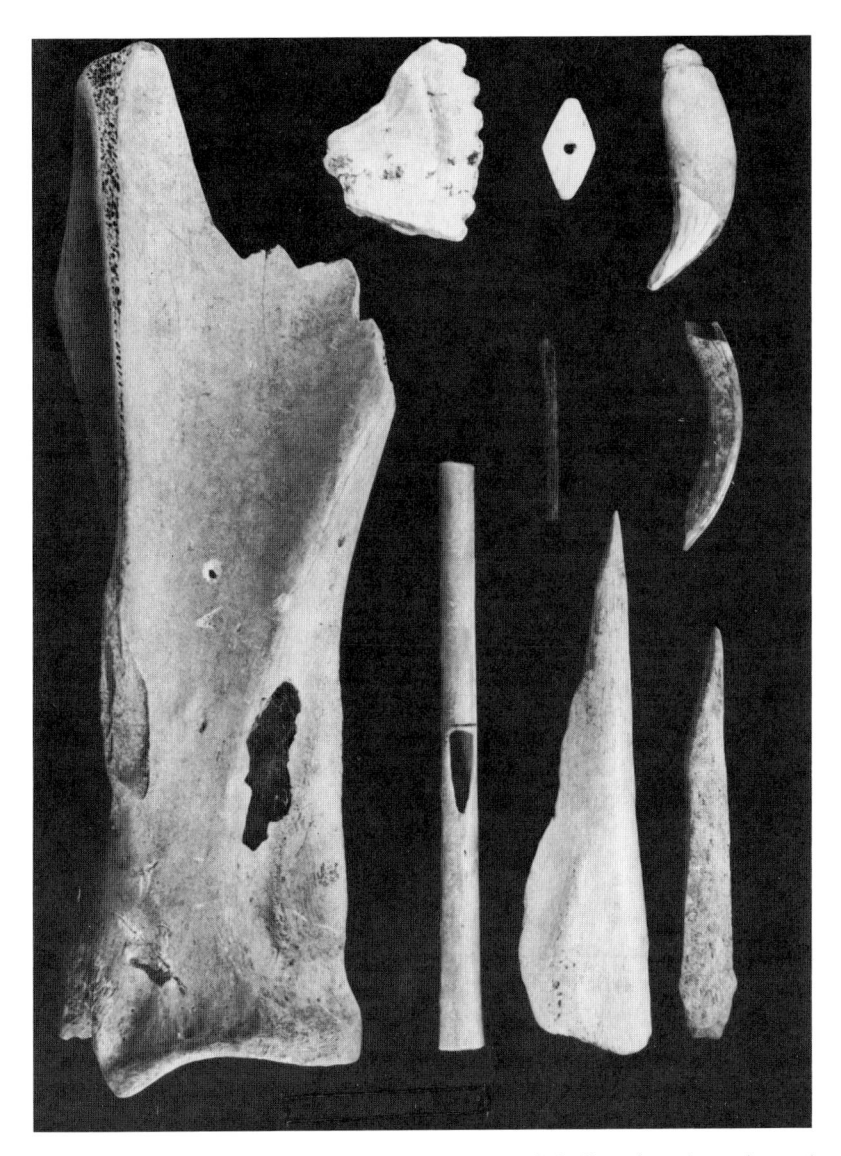

PLATE 8.41. *Lake Winnebago phase Oneota bone and shell artifacts from the Lasleys Point site, Winnebago County, Wisconsin: bison-scapula hoe (left); shell pottery maker (?), shell pendant, bear-incisor pendant (top row); bone needle and beaver-incisor chisel (middle row); and bone whistle and awls (bottom). (Shown half actual size.) (Collections of Department of Anthropology, Lawrence University, Appleton, Wisconsin.)*

Great Lakes with the assumption of its *adoption* by people of the Effigy Mound culture who are known to have been the resident population in many areas later inhabited by people possessing an Oneota culture. The impact of reliable food production on societies previously dependent on wild food gathering was presumably sufficient to precipitate a cultural transformation affecting much more than access to consumables, with Oneota emerging from the metamorphosis. This partly diffusionist, partly in-situ developmental hypothesis unfortunately ignores the fundamentally Mississippian character of Oneota ceramics, a character that cannot be independently distilled out of any presently known Woodland base. However Oneota came about, it was a cultural relative of Middle Mississippian at least in the sense that the two shared a common ancestor. An in situ evolution of Oneota out of Effigy Mound cannot account for the fact that the former is clearly a Mississippian culture, however impoverished it may look when compared with its more illustrious relative. An Effigy Mound pupa giving rise to an Oneota imago is empirically untenable also by virtue of radiocarbon dates and artifact associations at stations of the two cultures. They coexisted from the Emergent horizon of the latter to late prehistoric time. As earlier noted, typical wares of one culture occur repeatedly, but not invariantly, in sites of the other with no breakdown in discreteness. The minority vessels in each case appear to represent trade or the gifts of separate people engaged in sporadic exchange or the establishment of peaceful relations if not alliances. Neither was in the process of growing out of or turning into the other.

Because Oneota culture was a manifestation of a much broader phenomenon which in turn was more highly developed, dominant, and regionally intensive in the middle Mississippi Valley and the southeastern United States, an indispensable part of its cultural heredity must necessarily be credited in that direction. That Oneota had the range it did, that developmental stages have been plausibly suggested for it and backed up by a range of data, and that spatial clustering of variability can be shown to have come about are persuasive observations in support of a considerable degree of regional in-place evolution. Who the genetic ancestors of the Oneota culture-bearers were, nobody knows. But that they owed something of their essential culture to Mississippian folk on their southern flank cannot be gainsaid. Neither can the amply supportable picture of a lot of residential continuity following the introduction of those Mississippian elements. It is these last, of course, that are so fascinating in their implications for cultural theory as well as history: remote, indirect, reinterpreted and passed on by intermediaries, there was a Mexican connection without which Mississippian culture, and thus Oneota laterally, could not have come into existence and without which the late prehistory of the Great Lakes would show a different face. The self-sufficiency of even great territories in accounting for their internal histories is never absolute. Oneota interlocked more than trailed scrolls on pottery. It had connections now only dimly seen. These in turn are like a tap on the shoulder of regional archaeologists reminding them of a larger universe their theories must take into account.

And in still later years, an eon's leap for those involved, that larger universe closed in on the Oneota folk and their neighbors. It must have happened many times, mediated or not by rumors or by messengers: an early morning, perhaps, a lazy stroll to the golden water's edge, a stretch shrugging off sleep, and then a yawn aborted in the throat as a bark canoe intrudes upon the brightening field of vision, and between unfamiliar but doubtless friendly intentioned paddlers another man with a strange pallor and with hair growing out of his face.

References

Overviews of the Late Woodland period and site studies not listed below:
Bettarel and Smith 1973; Bluhm and Liss 1961; Brose 1978; Brose, editor, 1976; Fitting 1970 (especially Chapter VI: "Crops and Cooperation") and 1978; Griffin 1943; Quimby 1960b (especially Chapter 10: "Cultural Diversity in Late Woodland Times, A.D. 800–1600"); Ritchie and Funk 1973 (especially the sections on "The Late Woodland Period").

On paleoclimatology, cord twists, and the chemistry of shell tempering pottery:
Baerreis and Bryson 1965; Baerreis, Bryson, and Kutzbach 1976; Hurley 1979; Stimmell 1978.

On the Late Woodland I period—the Heins Creek site, Wisconsin:
R. J. Mason 1966.

Late Woodland I—the Effigy Mound culture:
Hurley 1975; Rowe 1956.

Late Woodland I—the Black Duck culture:
Dawson 1974 and 1977; Evans 1961; Lugenbeal 1978; Wilford 1955.

Late Woodland I—the Juntunen site, Michigan (Mackinac phase):
McPherron 1967.

Late Woodland I—Hunter's Home:
Ritchie 1969 (pp. 253–265: "The Hunter's Home Phase").

Late Woodland I—the Princess Point complex:
Stothers 1977.

On the Late Woodland II Period—Owasco:
Ritchie 1944 (pp. 29–101) and 1969 (pp. 271–300: "The Owasco Culture").

Late Woodland II—prehistoric New York Iroquois:
Griffin 1944; Lenig 1965; MacNeish 1952b and 1976; Ritchie 1952 and 1969 (pp. 300–323); Tuck 1971 and 1978b; White 1961.

Late Woodland II—the Ontario Iroquois tradition:
Emerson 1966; Kenyon 1968; MacNeish 1952b and 1976; Noble 1975; Smith 1979; Tuck 1978b; J. V. Wright 1966b, 1969, 1972a (especially Chapter III, pp. 64–107: "The Terminal Woodland Period"), and 1974.

Late Woodland II—the Western Basin tradition:
Fitting 1965; Stothers 1979.

Late Woodland II—the Juntunen site, Michigan (Bois Blanc and Juntunen phases):
McPherron 1967.

Late Woodland II—Lakes phase:
Salzer 1974.

Late Woodland II—Oneota and its cultural setting:
Faulkner 1972; Gibbon 1972a and 1972b; Griffin 1943 and 1960; Hall 1962; C. Mason 1970 and 1976; R. J. Mason 1966; McKern 1945; Overstreet 1978.

After the End
Historic Indian Archaeology to the Close of the Eighteenth Century

9

From a very early time, possibly even antedating by a few years Columbus's discoveries in the Caribbean, Breton, Norman, English, and other commercial fishermen from Atlantic Europe had been exploiting the fabulous fisheries of the Grand Banks. By 1500 or soon thereafter, ships manned by crews from many nations were whaling and sealing in the Gulf of St. Lawrence in addition to hauling in enormous stores of fish. So important had Portuguese fishing in Newfoundland waters become by 1506 that a 10% import tax was imposed on the catch that year when the fleet returned home. As aptly noted by one historian, this was the first European protective tariff raised against American imports.

Early on, many of the boat crews made landfalls to dry the catch for the home market. They were also enticed ashore to collect birds' eggs, shoot game, taste fresh water, or simply indulge curiosity. Ineluctably, as the numbers of fishermen increased, so did chance encounters with the natives, and bartering naturally ensued when each side saw what could be procured from the other. By the time of Jacques Cartier's voyages into the Gulf of St. Lawrence and the St. Lawrence River in 1534 and 1535, there were Indians already accustomed to exchanging their beaver, otter, marten, and other furs with the ocean-crossers for beads, knives, cloth, and other "trifles." Successively encountered aboriginal communities, as we saw in Chapter 1, were usually astute enough to attempt immediately the control of further commercial operations with upriver or more inland groups by offering service as middlemen. The fur trade, ironically shortly destined to fix the absorbing interest of kings, cardinals, ministers, and governors, grew out of

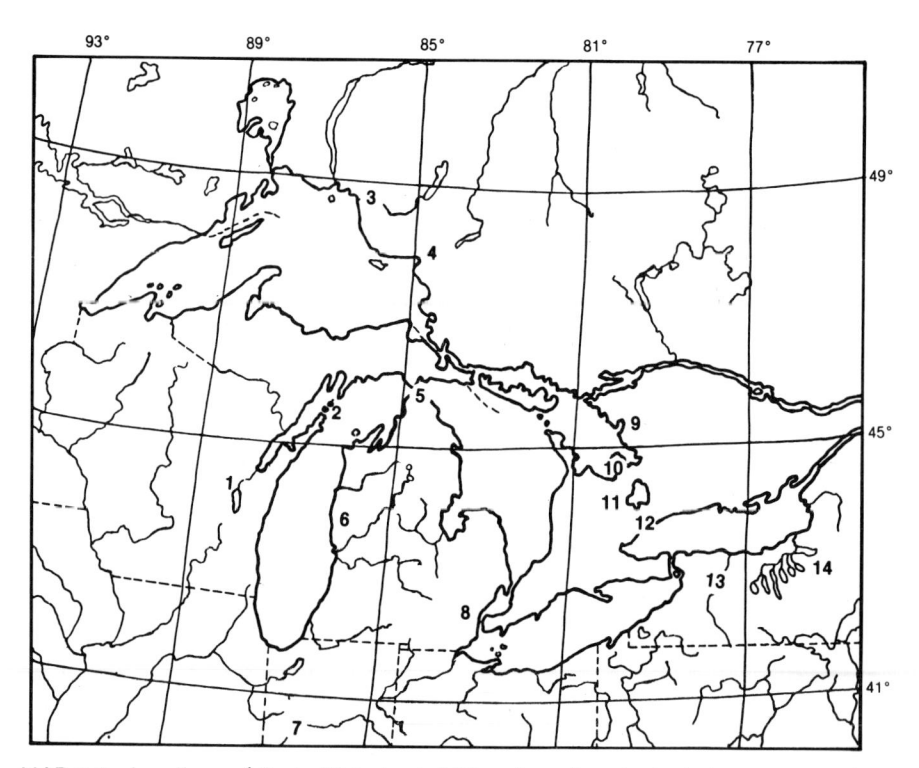

MAP 9.1. *Locations of Proto-Historic and Historic archaeological sites mentioned in the text: (1) Bell; (2) Rock Island II; (3) Pic River; (4) Nyman and Michipicoten; (5) Lasanen, Fort de Buade, Fort Michilimackinac, and Juntunen; (6) Dumaw Creek; (7) Fort Ouiatenon; (8) Fort Ponchartrain; (9) Shebishikong; (10) Ossossane; (11) Sidey-Mackay; (12) Draper and Parsons; (13) Dutch Hollow; and (14) Beecher, Marshall, and Thurston.*

the fortuitous side-ventures of the overseas European fishing industry. And it now appears that archaeologists have underestimated its preprofessionalized volume, geographical penetration, and its pervasive appeal.

Recognition has long been tendered the fact of considerable long-distance prehistoric trade in the Great Lakes and eastern North America generally. The institutions of indigenous trade proved remarkably responsive to the new opportunities presenting themselves in the far northeast. There can be no doubt that the injection of European goods moved rapidly along preexisting trade networks to interior tribes far in advance of the actual arrival of the ocean-crossers themselves in those remoter parts. The new cargoes seem to have energized those networks to a level beyond past ordinary experience. The haste with which most later Great Lakes societies accommodated themselves to the requirements of the carriers of the trade and their own perceptions of self-interest in their acculturating embrace are fairly well known even if sometimes oversimplified and sentimentalized. Whatever the details of transmission and interaction, the affects of trade with Europeans were more immediate and far reaching than previously believed.

Inland a few kilometers from the northwest shore of Lake Ontario in present-day Toronto lie the remains of the palisaded Parsons site, a Huron community estimated to date around 1500–1550. Not many kilometers east in Pickering Township is the Draper site, another fortified Huron settlement of about the same age. Both sites can tentatively be assigned to the historic period despite their early dates and the remoteness of the European presence at this time. In site assemblages which are in most respects conformable to strictly late-prehistoric Huron ascription, a handful of controversial metal goods—a knife blade, a finger ring, some rolled "brass" beads some of which seem to reflect European ideas if not, as has been alleged, manufacture)—may be the first glimmerings within the Great Lakes of the vigorous new epoch already sorting out its priorities in the Gulf of St. Lawrence and on the lower river. But even aside from these meager traces, there are certain other qualities that separate these sites from other coeval and antecedent sites of the Huron tradition. Both are larger than the other known sites (Draper covers about 37 ha, Parsons about half that); both appear to incorporate within their stockaded enclosures several residential precincts whose pottery and other products strongly suggest the coming together, but incomplete consolidation, of originally separate communities; both show hints of craft specializations (such as the production of stone adze blades) unusual at other sites; and bones in both middens tell of a marked increase in the mutilation and eating of war captives. Both sites are also placed on the plain above the Lake Ontario shore, and they are so situated with regard to the Humber and Rouge rivers, respectively, that they would have commanded easy access to the north and the waterways leading to the Upper Great Lakes. Concurrently, the two towns occupied potential facilitating and blocking positions in any trade traversing their districts.

Although the proposition will require ingenious testing, it does not seem likely that the unusual properties of the Parsons and Draper sites had nothing more than a coincidental connection with the possible arrival of the first low quantities of the high-demand European goods. Indeed, some of the archaeologists working in the western Lake Ontario basin view these two sites, and perhaps a few others nearby, as providing not simply the first traces of the westward movement of European trade goods into the Great Lakes, but more importantly as signaling a realignment in settlement patterns and intertribal relations aimed at taking maximum advantage of the now suddenly revitalized trade that was introducing marvels which, once seen, could not lightly be done without.

It is hard for us at this distance removed from the events to appreciate

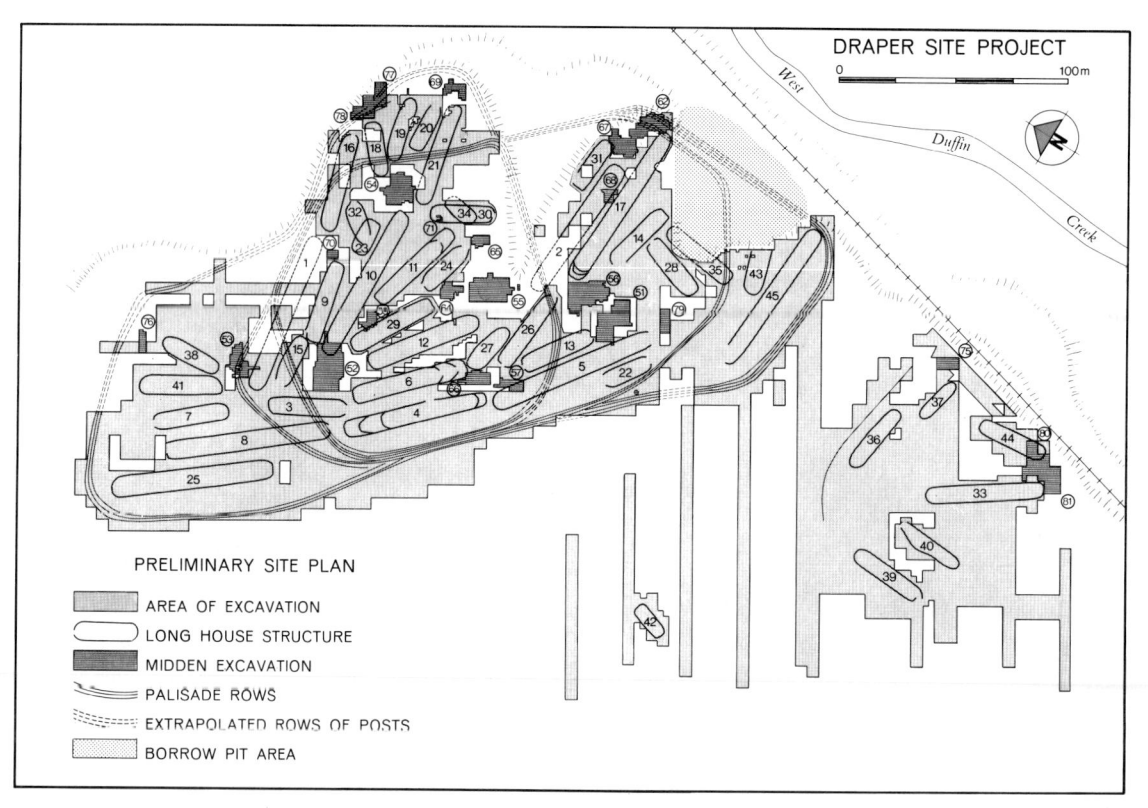

PLATE 9.1. *Plan of the Draper site near Pickering, Ontario. An artist's reconstruction of this community is reproduced as Plate 1.5. (Courtesy William D. Finlayson and the Museum of Indian Archaeology, University of Western Ontario, London.)*

properly what must have been the seductive appeal that the ocean-crossers' wares held for people whose own technology they themselves almost instantly and universally concluded to be inferior. And permanent proved to be the fascination with the awesome powers of firearms, the keenness of iron axes and knife blades, the miracle of glass (like clear ice immune to melting), the fantastic color of trade beads, the labor-saving addition of the firesteel to flint, the luxury and latent indispensibility of wool clothing and blankets, the terrible mystery of alcohol.

Consider the brass kettle. Until sullied by the cooking fire it could catch the sun and throw it back in the faces of all who peered into it. When struck, it uttered a cry. As it aged it assumed the venerable color of old copper. Moreover, it was light and would stand up to abuse. Its sides seemed so thin that thumb and finger could almost feel each other when the vessel was picked up by the rim rather than the bail. Compare that with the thickness and weight of a clay pot of equivalent capacity! Brass kettles

PLATE 9.2. Early historic-period artifacts from southern Ontario Iroquois (Huron, Petun, Neutral) sites: small catlinite and large marine-shell zoomorphic pendants (left); iron sheath knife and ax (right); and glass trade beads and marine-shell beads. (Shown half actual size.) (Courtesy James V. Wright and the Archaeological Survey of Canada, National Museum of Man, Ottawa.)

cooked faster, traveled easier, and much more often bounced than broke when dropped. When they did crack or wear through after hard use, the handle and the circular rim support served as neck ornaments and the bottom and sides could be scribed with a flint chisel and bent back and forth until they yielded the shapes of desired derivative things. Scraps of kettle brass were turned into finger rings, bracelets, triangular or cruciform pendants for suspension on necklaces or earrings, conical bangles or tinklers for jacket or legging fringes, cylindrical beads and hair-tubes, simple triangular or stemmed and barbed arrowheads, circular "gaming" pieces, diamond-shaped objects of now unknown use, and even miniature harpoons for the amusement of children.

Brass kettles were marvelous things indeed. Once introduced into a community, their superiority over the traditional clay cooking pots ensured that there was no voluntary turning back from their use. Furthermore, the ocean-crossers seemed naive regarding their worth—or so it seemed for awhile. They would accept commonplace items for them, even beaver pelts which had been trapped the year previous and had been worn as clothing, fur against oily skin. Such "pretreatment," however, was highly desirable from the traders' point of view because it got rid of all the loose hairs and conditioned the pelt. Perceptions of naiveté were bound to alter with increased familiarity, and there were to be substantial future grounds for complaints about rising prices and stingy traders. But by then what had been a luxury had become a virtual necessity. The same was true of needles, firearms, and a hundred other marvels of the new technology.

In token of individual ownership, or of condolence ceremonies in which families and friends acknowledged their ties to deceased and survivor alike by helping to furnish the grave, many kettles and knives and other trade items eventually made their way into Indian graves, at first in addition to, then ultimately replacing entirely, objects of native manufacture. The high valuation of brass kettles finds its supreme testimony in the looting of graves by the Indians themselves, an activity which did not disturb any earthenware pots or other traditional accompaniments of graves. Evidence of such plundering during the first half of the seventeenth century among the Oneida Iroquois, for example, has come from the Beecher, Thurston, and Marshall sites, all located in Madison County, New York. Within their own territories members of the Seneca, Cayuga, and other tribes were also sometimes implicated in "recycling" the highly regarded kettles as long as they were serviceable for more than incorporeal needs.

Representative of a period later than that of the Parsons and Draper sites, but still very early in the historic period, is Dutch Hollow across Lake Ontario in Avon Township, Livingston County, New York. This complex village and cemetery of the Senecas was mainly in use sometime during the years 1590–1615. Like the antecedent sites, Dutch Hollow exhibits the full range of the intact aboriginal industries, including a vigorous pottery and

PLATE 9.3. *Early historic Seneca burial (No. 61) at the Dutch Hollow site, Livingston County, New York. (Collection of the Rochester Museum and Science Center. [May not be reprinted without permission of the RMSC.])*

smoking-pipe complex with strong indications of trade, particularly in this case with other Iroquoian peoples to the west. The Dutch Hollow Seneca were even supplied with many ancient styles of flint projectile points which they must have picked up themselves from archaeological sites in their country, perhaps regarding them as good luck pieces or hunting charms. Their own arrows, of course, were tipped with the ubiquitous Madison triangular points. But by now the inventory of European goods had swollen far beyond that seen at Parsons or Draper or at the earliest presently known historic period communities of Onondaga, Mohawk, or other Great Lakes tribes. The Dutch Hollow list includes glass and brass beads; brass kettles, "hawk" bells, awls, tinkling cones, discoidal pendants, and even a pipe-bowl liner; iron knives, axes, wire bracelets, and scrapers and chisels jerry-built of iron scraps; and a two-sided ivory "louse" comb. Some of the fine bone work at Dutch Hollow, especially the native-made hair combs, suggest the use of iron implements in their fashioning.

While the possibility cannot be dismissed that an itinerant French trader, a *coureur de bois*, may have visited the Seneca cantons, such an adventure

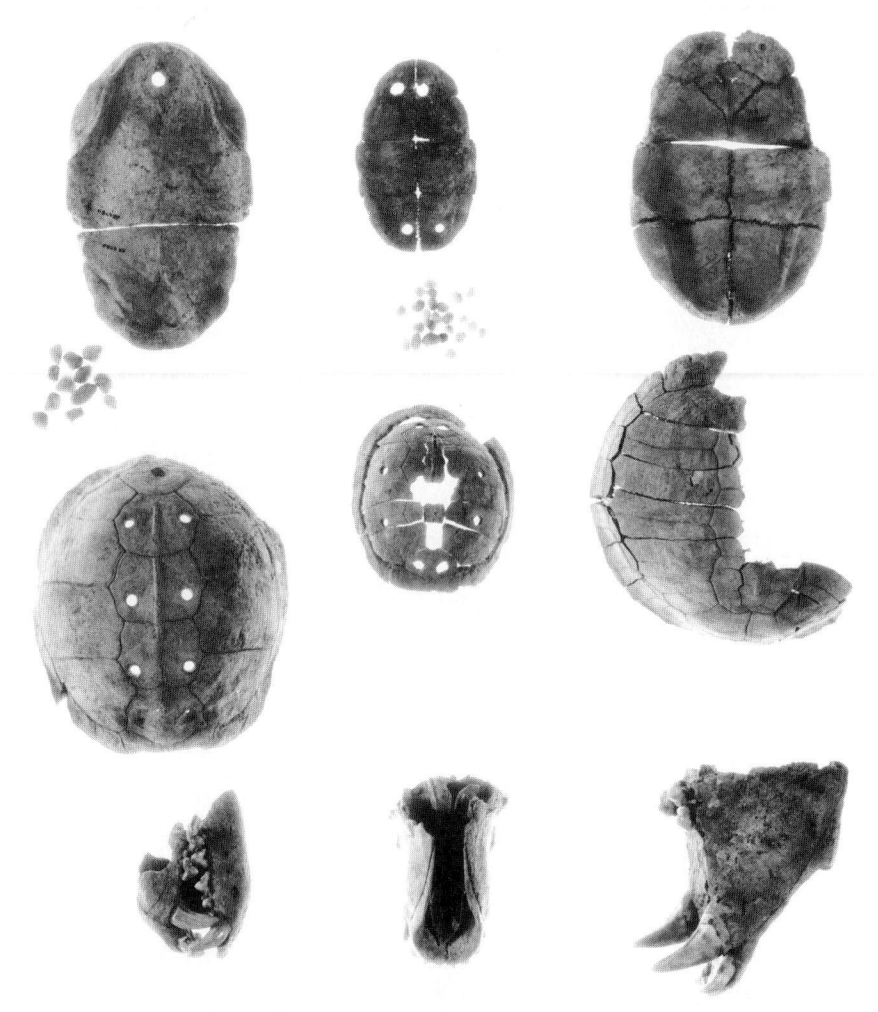

PLATE 9.4. *Turtle-shell rattles and cut animal jaws from the Dutch Hollow site, Livingston County, New York. (Shown one-third actual size.) (Collection of the Rochester Museum and Science Center. [May not be reprinted without permission of the RMSC.])*

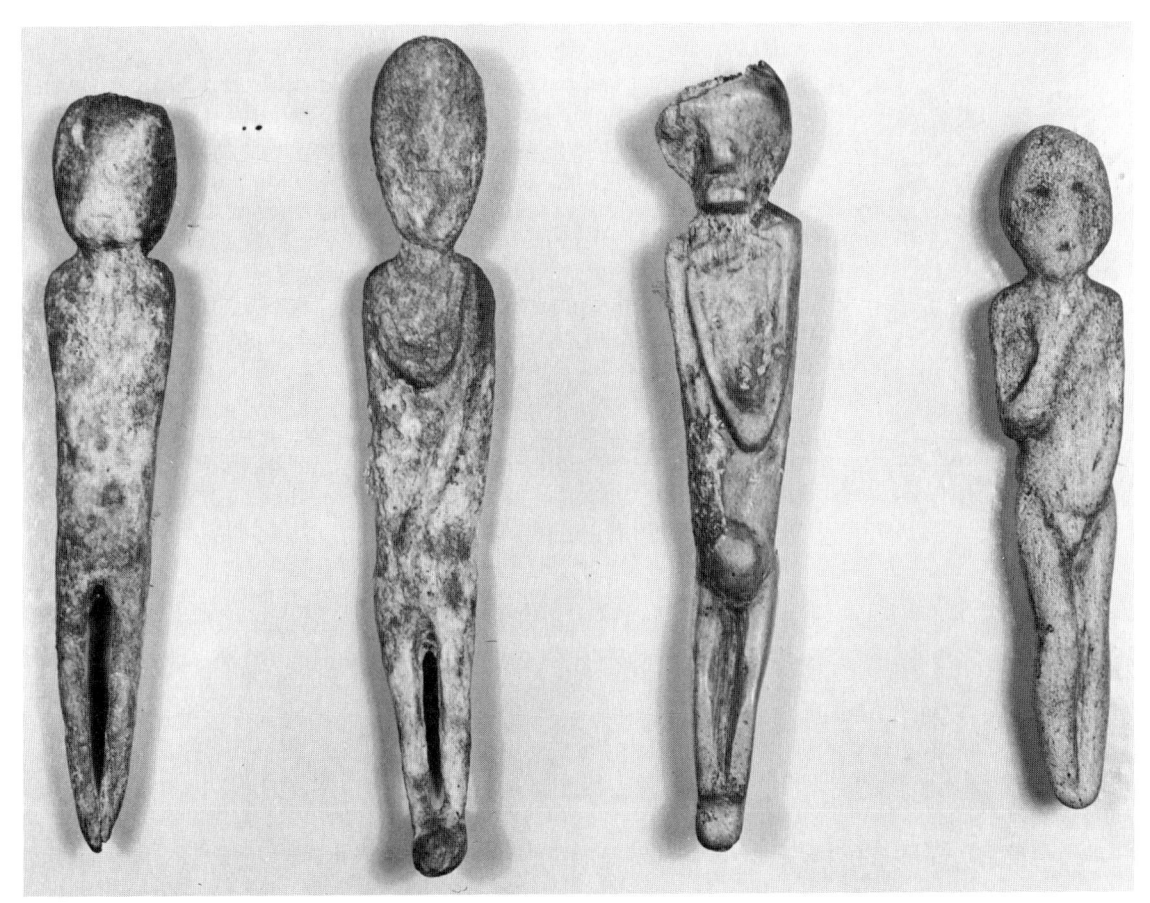

PLATE 9.5. *Carved antler anthropomorphic figurines from the Dutch Hollow site, Livingston County, New York. (Shown approximately actual size.) (Collection of the Rochester Museum and Science Center. [May not be reprinted without permission of the RMSC.])*

to so remote a corner at such an early date is improbable. It was a long, arduous trip from the sources of supply. Furthermore, the trip would have necessitated safe passage through lands inhabited by people with a passionate interest in keeping the trade in their own hands, as later would-be traders found out. More likely, the European commodities at the Dutch Hollow site arrived there circuitously from the west, courtesy of the Neutrals. Imported Indian pottery and diffused smoking-pipe styles support such a contention. These latter folk came by their stock through and at the pleasure of the Hurons who, in turn, were probably at this time still encumbered by their need to consider Algonkin sensibilities in approaching the French. By indirect passage, then, their products insinuated themselves well in advance of the French themselves.

Some archaeologists, cognizant of the precedence of trade goods over their suppliers, interpose between prehistory and history another demarkation of time to accommodate the fact. This twilight zone between the prehistoric and historic periods, the time during which European goods first became available to the indigenous societies via native middlemen, but before the first recorded face-to-face contact of Indian and European, is sometimes called the "protohistoric" period. By this terminology, the sites just described are strictly protohistoric. Because the twilight trade and trailing actual exploration advanced more swiftly and penetrated more deeply in some areas than in others, the dates assigned the beginning and ending of the protohistoric period necessarily vary from place to place. It may be questioned whether the simple arrival of a transient European into a new country thereafter immediately abandoned until a later time, even though the event was fortunate enough to be noted in an isolated surviving document, should be taken as terminating the protohistoric period in that country. The distinguishing attribute of history, after all, is the recording of a series of events in written form so that there exists a narrative or commentary on past human experience. In a sense, prehistory in many parts of America was followed by a brief episode of history only to be succeeded by a resurrection of prehistory before its final demise with the inception of the *continuing* accumulation of documents which the term "history" usually implies. In protohistory, as just defined, the archaeologist is still almost exclusively dependent on the same kinds and sources of information that are the prehistoric archaeologist's stock-in-trade. With the accession of a surviving written record, an expanded and independent reservoir of insights becomes available, permitting the combination a picture of the past far richer than either archaeological or historical sources alone can provide.

PLATE 9.6. Early historic Seneca pottery of the type Seneca Barbed from the Dutch Hollow site, Livingston County, New York. (Collection of the Rochester Museum and Science Center. [May not be reprinted without permission of the RMSC.])

9. After the End

In May of 1636 the Jesuit missionary Jean de Brebeuf, destined for horrible martyrdom at the hands of the Iroquois and eventual sainthood, was eye-witness to a celebration of the most important communal ceremony of the Huron Indians. This was the Feast of the Dead, usually held only once every 10 or 12 years. The particular staging Brebeuf observed with mixed wonder, pity, amusement, and disgust was held near the Huron town of Ossossane, which was acting as sponsor. The location of this town was just inland of the eastern shore of Nottawasaga Bay, Ontario, at the south end of Georgian Bay. Fortunately for posterity, Brebeuf left a detailed account of what he saw. Similar ceremonies at other places had been earlier recorded by Gabriel Sagard and even by the illustrious Samuel de Champlain himself.

What Brebeuf reported near Ossossane was the great coming together of many of the Huron communities and their allies in other tribes in order to rebury in a common pit all of the people who had died since the previous Feast of the Dead a decade or longer ago. People arrived in throngs, many carrying bundles of kinsmen's bones and even the still putrifying corpses of the recently deceased. Upon their arrival the grisly burdens were unwrapped, lamented over afresh, and honored with presents, food, and speeches. On their trek to Ossossane the bearers of the precious dead had been sheltered and fed by villagers along the way. Gifts had been given and received. Honor owing the ancestors had been freely bestowed and redoubled in extending it to the survivors.

At the place selected for the climax of the Feast, a large circular pit had been dug to receive the remains. A scaffolding surrounded the ossuary. Bodies were suspended from this structure while disarticulated bundles of the longer dead were placed on and near it, all the time being talked to as though alive. Before being carried on the back to the scaffold for temporary placement, any adhering flesh was stripped from the skeletons and burned in a fire. The Christian priest was struck by the easy familiarity of the living with the handling of even worm-infested cadavers, his own feelings of repugnance being quite foreign to the participants. With some of the funerary activities prolonged far into the night, the eerie illumination of flickering torches in such a setting seared his memory. The impact of that scene is transmitted to the reader of Brebeuf's description published in *The Jesuit Relations and Allied Documents*, the compilation of missionary reports to the ecclesiastical authorities and now, centuries later, an unparalleled source of information on Indian life in the early historic period.

At last the burial pit was lined with rich beaver-skin robes and the dead, often individually wrapped in separate beaver furs, were lowered or even thrown to their final resting place. A few people stood in the pit to arrange the bundles. Many of the skeletons were adorned with shell, stone, or glass trade beads sewn on apparel or strung on necklaces. Some had bracelets or finger rings. Many gifts were offered the dead although a good number of these were reclaimed and distributed among the living. Included were iron knives, brass kettles, necklaces of glass beads, and other valued things of European manufacture as well as beaver robes, tobacco, and additional indigenous products including offerings of food and drink. Finally, the ossuary was covered with woven mats and more beaver pelts and was then filled in.

While much speculation has accrued concerning the social function of the Huron Feast of the Dead, it does seem that it occasioned the reinforcement of internal and even intertribal feelings of friendship and support and thus that it served a useful integrative role in a society lacking strong central governance. It is also apparent from the accounts of Brebeuf and others that a lot of goods and services were moved around and exchanged, a not inconsiderable function in a society lacking internal markets. The Feast has been compared in this regard to the famous potlatches of the Indians of the Northwest Coast. But how necessary the Feast of the Dead was to the fulfilling of the functions theorists have suggested for it may be open to debate on the observation of its absence in many nearby societies having similar problems in the maintenance of social cohesion and economic distribution. Not that the Feast of the Dead was uniquely Huron. Some of the Algonquian tribes also participated in their own versions. The Feast of the Dead as historically known was doubtless a native initiative though it may have been elaborated or intensified under the novel stresses and strains European contact placed on it. Certainly ossuaries, as seen in preceding chapters, if not the Feast of the Dead itself, have a hoary antiquity in the Great Lakes and elsewhere in eastern North America. The two are not necessarily coextensive, nonetheless. But in the instance of the Ossossane ossuary and the 1636 Feast of the Dead held in western Huronia, the two were fused in the ceremony vividly recounted by Father Brebeuf. Comparison of site-survey results, archaeological excavation, and careful attention to geographical details mentioned in the surviving Jesuit missionary records indicate just short of absolute proof that the bone-filled circular pit located on the Daoust farm in Concession 7, Tiny Township, Simcoe County, Ontario, and the site of the Ossossane drama are one and the same.

Intermixed with the jumbled bones of close to 100 human beings, both native- and European-made articles which had come there either as personal belongings and adornment or as grave offerings to the community of the dead were recovered by archaeologists. Included in the category of native-made articles are shell beads, both polished red slate and catlinite beads, chipped-flint triangular arrowheads, smoking pipes, a conch-shell vessel, imitation elk teeth carved out of shell, a shell pendant, a small bone carving of a human face, deposits of red ocher, and occasional fragments of birchbark containers, native cords and textiles, and beaver fur. Among the original offerings of foodstuffs, only the remains of beech nuts survived.

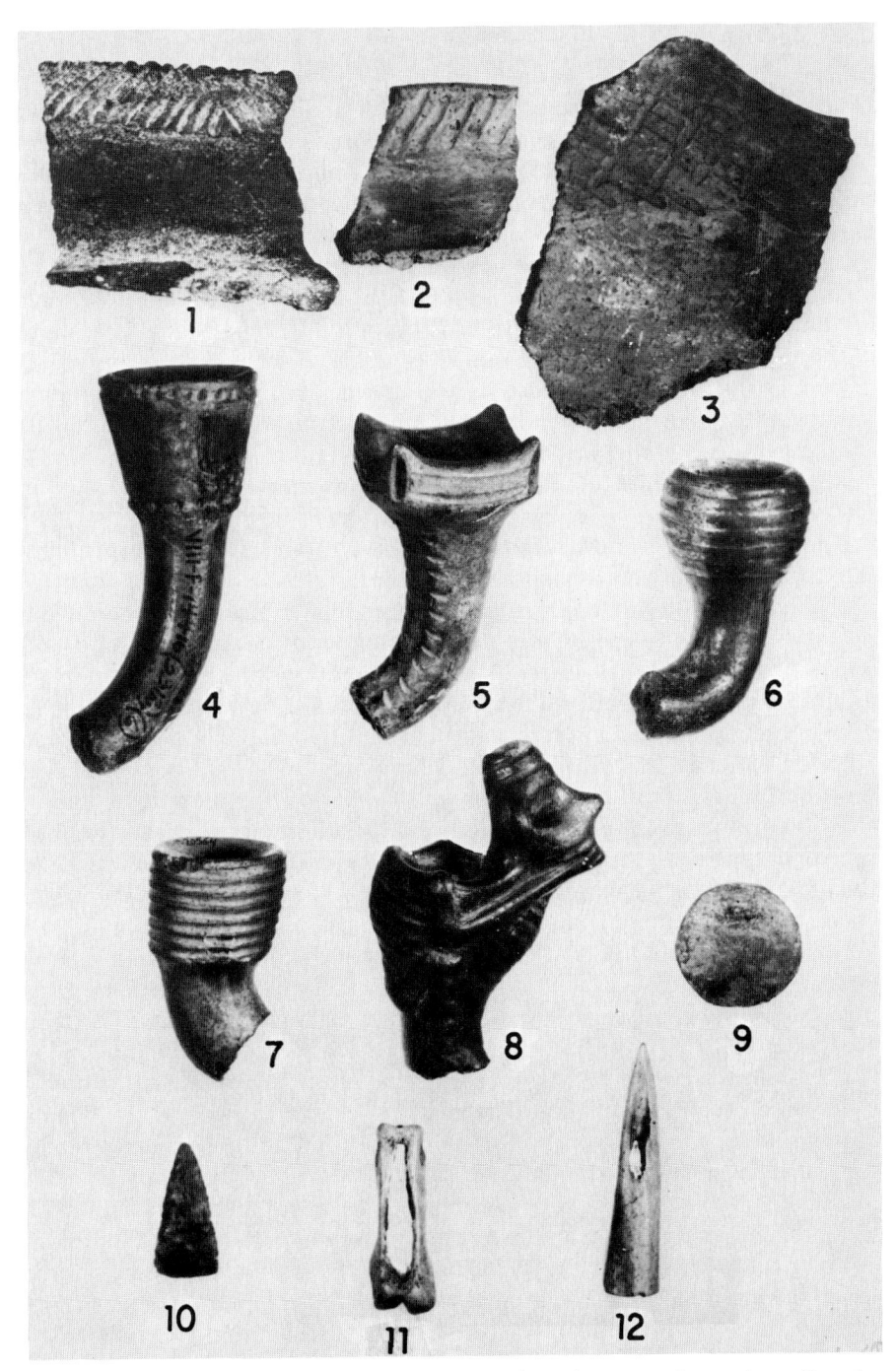

PLATE 9.7. *Protohistoric and historic Huron artifacts from sites in southern Ontario: pottery fragments (1–3); smoking pipes (4–8); pottery gaming piece (9); flint arrowhead (10); toggle of dear toe bone (11); and socketed bone arrowhead (12). (Shown approximately two-thirds actual size.) (Courtesy James V. Wright and the Archaeological Survey of Canada, National Museum of Man, Ottawa.)*

Objects of European origin were many glass trade beads of several types, the remnants of two or three brass kettles, beads and tinklers made from cut-up kettles, iron bracelets, brass finger rings, iron knives and awls, unidentifiable corroded pieces of iron, a burning glass, an iron hook, a pair of scissors, part of a possible wine glass, and an iron key.

The Ossossane burial site, tied as it is to a specific historical event and to behavior recorded in some detail, is a superb source of information bearing on the beliefs and sociology of the Hurons of the 1636 period and on some of the types of European trade goods available to them. Such sites are of enormous aid to the identification and dating of approximately contemporaneous sites which did not find their way into written accounts. In comparison with earlier and later sites they yield data indispensable to the study of cultural change among the Hurons and neighboring peoples as well.

Another burial ground across Georgian Bay and Lake Huron at the Straits of Mackinac records a time well after the Huron dispersal, was very probably the result of Ottawa activity—though by this juncture there were many Hurons living among and intermarried with the Ottawas—and was apparently observed in its ceremonious operations by another eminent Frenchman of his age, the then post commander at nearby Fort de Buade, Lamonthe Cadillac. This fort had been established at St. Ignace sometime between 1679 and 1683 and was later abandoned in 1698. Afterwards Fort Ponchartrain was built at Detroit as part of a major effort to shift the Indian allies southward in support of overextended French power as it tried to control the fur trade, overawe the Iroquois, and counter British influence in the Ohio Valley while simultaneously excluding the British from the upper lakes. While still at St. Ignace, Cadillac had occasion to see one of the last known performances of the Feast of the Dead, this time involving mainly Ottawas. Inasmuch as the ceremony took place when Cadillac was commandant of the garrison at Fort de Buade, the date was sometime between 1694 and 1697.

Although the case is less tight than in the historical identification of the Ossossane ossuary, archaeologists have been able to make a reasonable argument that the Feast of the Dead reported by Cadillac left the remains they have excavated at the Lasanen site at St. Ignace, Mackinaw County, Michigan. That ceremony left a number of features in the ground which suggest some derivation from the prehistoric burial pattern at the Juntunen site on nearby Bois Blanc Island, indicative of the strong likelihood that the Feast had not evolved as the exclusive property of the Hurons, and that its presence among Algonquian speakers was not attributable only to borrowing. Whether the fact that by this time the Feast was reportedly being held every 3 years reflects one of the differences between Huron and Ottawa practices or was perhaps due to changes underway since the Ossossane

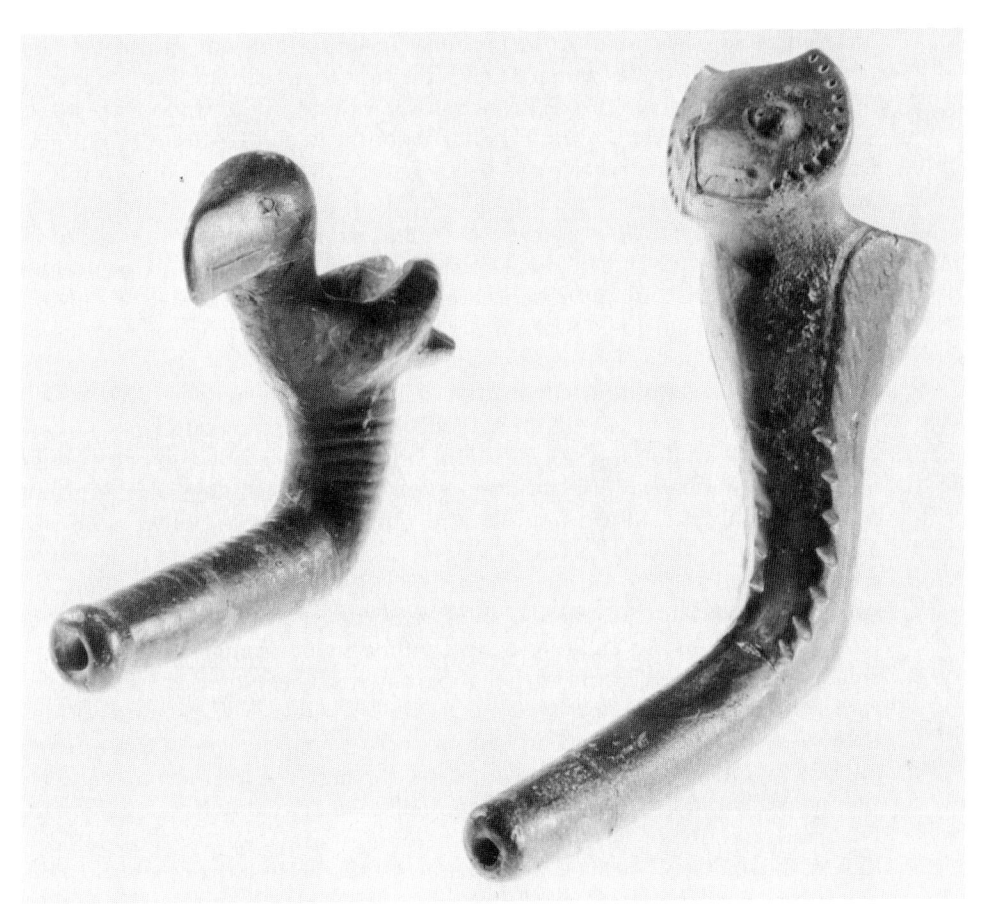

PLATE 9.8. *Ontario Iroquois bird-effigy smoking pipes. (Shown approximately two-thirds actual size.) (Courtesy Peter L. Storck and the Royal Ontario Museum, Toronto, Canada.)*

and earlier Huron ossuaries were constructed is not known. Another intriguing difference is the substitution of many small pits, each entombing the bones of only a few individuals, for the large communal repository reported earlier. Furthermore, close inspection of the skeletal remains, particularly with respect to genetically determined anomalies, supports the idea that the most closely related people were buried in the same pit, more distant relatives being interred with their closest kin in other graves. Again, it is hard to tell if this contrast was tribal in nature or if it had come about with the passage of time, possibly reflecting growing Christian influence as the old integration of traditional society dissolved. The first interpretation is strongly supported by the separate pits and small ossuaries of undoubted prehistoric age at the Juntunen site. Certainly the many differences in associated artifacts reflect in important ways the later temporal position of the Lasanen site and its strategic geographical stance at the operational center of the French-Indian trade in the upper lakes.

A variety of European trade goods came from the Lasanen burial pits. Especially numerous were glass beads (over 7000), shell wampum manufactured for the Indian trade (over 14,000), ivory and bone rosary beads, iron awls and knives, preserved swatches of wool blankets or clothing, wire bracelets and finger rings, bells, and buttons from apparel. More parsimonious in their representation were gunflints, firesteels, "Jesuit" rings (finger rings having plaques or bezels bearing religious symbols), religious medallions, and some other items. Also found were triangular arrowheads and tinkling cones that the Indians themselves had locally fabricated out of scrap sheet brass, probably obtained by cutting up worn-out kettles. Traditional tools were still being produced by the people who interred their dead at the Lasanen site, though doubtless in dwindling numbers. Chipped-flint triangular and tanged projectile points were present in addition to flint knives, scrapers, and wedges. Work in other materials embraced socketed antler-tine arrowheads, an antler harpoon (an iron specimen was also recovered); shell beads, pendants, gorgets, and fish effigies; and polished catlinite beads, pendants in a range of shapes, and small beaver effigies. Some of the latter may have been made by Europeans for fur trade purposes or by Indians using iron tools. The catlinite artifacts that are so frequently found on historic Indian sites such as Lasanen reflect an enrichment of an indigenous industry through the peculiar demands of the fur trade and the introduction of metal tools. Notably missing from the historical account of the St. Ignace ceremony and likewise not detected during the archaeological excavations, notwithstanding the recovery of bits of leather, cordage, and woven fabrics, were the beaver-fur coverings so conspicuous at Ossossane.

The number of persons interred in any single burial pit at Lasanen ranged from 1 to 13. Twenty-four pits were excavated. It is known that only a part of the burial ground has been sampled; house construction in the vicinity of the excavated burial pits has from time to time uncovered more human bones. From a skeletal population of 76 individuals whose approximate age at death was ascertainable, 12% were small children less than 2 years old, 22% died between the ages of 2 and 12 years, 12% between 12 and 18 ,42% between 18 and 40, and 22% were older than 40.

That only two infants were found among so large a collection of skeletons must mean that most infants' deaths prompted a divergent treatment than was habitually accorded even slightly older children and their elders. Studies from other sites show that infant mortality at this time was typically far higher than the Lasanen figures would indicate. At the other end of the scale one old man (older than age 65) was buried in the cemetery. A disproportion of older men indicates that significantly more men than women enjoyed lives in excess of 40 years. Twice as many women as men died between the ages of 12 and 40, if the burial pit figures are to be taken at face value. That there may be something to this is rendered more plausible by the observation that these are close to the outer limits of childbearing and that many women must have succumbed to associated complications. The far lower representation of men in this age group, however, is most likely artificial. Many men would have been lost far from home on war or trading expeditions or have been the victims of hunting accidents.

In terms of that segment of the population receiving its ultimate disposition at Lasanen, the average adult male stature was 170 cm. Women, on the average, were about 5 cm shorter. Pathologies that register on the bones affected only a minority. These were visible in seven individuals afflicted with osteoarthritis; one person with rheumatoid arthritis; one case each of suspected syphilis, mastoiditis, and benign bone tumor; two bone fractures in addition to three cases of vertebral compression fractures; five instances of periostitis; and three cases of violent injuries to the head, two of which were doubtless lethal. Smallpox and influenza and other European-introduced epidemic diseases ravaged the Great Lakes tribes from time to time, culling appalling numbers. These scourges would not be detectable from just the bones, of course. All in all there were 19 dental caries in the population and 25 abscesses, many of which were associated with the same skulls. Most of the Lasanen Ottawas enjoyed excellent dental health. Similarly, there were few signs of malnutrition.

With few exceptions, one of which is the Lasanen site itself, early historic sites in the Upper Great Lakes have proved much less amenable to tribal identification than those appertaining to the somewhat more tightly integrated and sedentary Iroquoian societies of the lower lakes. There is little dispute about the ethnic designations appropriate to the Dutch Hollow, Beecher, Ossossane, or even the extremely early Parsons and Draper sites. Indeed, imposing lists now exist of sites specifically creditable to the Mohawk, Onondaga, Petun, Neutral, and other Iroquoian tribes at various intervals in their respective histories. The upper lakes have proved more intractable. As seen in the preceding chapter, even the alledgedly numerous and relatively settled Winnebagos have proved elusive when it devolves on the archaeologist to pin them to specific sites of the early historic and late prehistoric periods. The myriad Algonquian-speaking groups of historical record have been the despair of everyone in this regard. Fortunately, the qualifying phrase opening this paragraph is true: there are some exceptions to the dismal generalization.

At a number of archaeological sites Blackduck ceramics, invariably accompanied by some other wares, persisted in use into times late enough to permit association with early European trade goods. Prominent examples of such places are the Shebishikong (stratum I), Nyman (strata II and III), and Pic River (stratum I) sites, Ontario. The first site is on the east central coast of Georgian Bay, the Nyman site near the mouth of the Michipicoten River on the northeastern shore of Lake Superior, Pic River on the north central shore of the same lake. The latter station, specifically its historic component, stratum I, is believed to have been deposited sometime between 1700 and 1750. The other components should date between the late seventeenth and middle eighteenth centuries also.

Pic River stratum I yielded large numbers of glass trade beads, pieces of lead shot, brass and iron bangles for decorating clothing, and cut-up brass-kettle fragments in addition to small quantities of gunflints, kaolin pipe fragments, metal triangular pendants, and other items of European authorship. Intermingled were sherds of aboriginal pottery and tools made of stone, bone, and native copper. Chipped flint included plain triangular and small notched arrowheads, a variety of scrapers, wedges, some small cutting and gouging tools, and biface blades.

Three different kinds of native pottery occurred in stratum I at Pic River. More than half of the pottery was classified as "Michigan" ware by the analyst. This is similar to certain varieties of Late Woodland II pottery from the Straits of Mackinac and adjoining parts of the two Michigan peninsulas, as well as a so-called Peninsular Woodland complex from the Lake Superior and northern Lake Michigan shore of Wisconsin. A little less common were sherds of Blackduck pottery. A third and last kind of pottery was a single vessel of Selkirk ware. In the two lower, and strictly prehistoric, strata of the Pic River site there were no "Michigan" or Selkirk sherds at all; Blackduck accounted for all of the sherds in stratum II and almost all in stratum III. A few sherds from the bottom stratum belong to the Pickering branch of Early Ontario Iroquois. A reclassification of the Pic River pottery by another archaeologist has subtracted from the relative frequency of Blackduck ceramics and further broken down "Michigan" ware into "Mackinac," "Peninsular Woodland," and "Push-Pull" wares. This has altered the details, but not the substance, of the original reports. Stratum III has been radiocarbon dated at around A.D. 950. By contrast with the pottery, the chipped-stone artifacts exhibit strong stylistic continuity throughout the 700- or 800-year history of the locality.

Snatches of early travel accounts record congeries of names by which the Europeans variously identified greater or lesser geographical bands of Indians along the northern coasts of the Upper Great Lakes. These encompass such appelations as Nopeming, Gens de Terre, O'pimittish Ininiwac, Marameg, and Men of the Land. In Chapter 1 it was seen that these are among the names by which some of the bands of the proto-Ojibwas (or proto-Chippewas) were known. The historical sources indicate that Ojibwas under one or more of the foregoing designations resided at the mouth of the Pic River in the early historic period. References to such people are especially numerous along and inland of the northeastern margin of the lake. Except for occasional visits by Crees and Ottawas and others essentially transient to the region, the broad ethnicity "Ojibwa" clearly dominated this sector of the Great Lakes from the time of the first written records. This label is the most reasonable one to put on the archaeological component in stratum I at the Pic River site. It is also fitting for the historic Indian components at the Shebishikong and Nyman sites. But how far can Ojibwa identity be traced in space and how far pushed back beyond the European incursions into prehistory? In their responses, archaeologists, ethnohistorians, linguists, ethnologists, and others have experienced less than full agreement.

Another stratified site with an historic component reasonably assigned to the Ojibwa, and also on the north shore of Lake Superior, is the Michipicoten site. This is opposite the Nyman site, likewise near the mouth of the Michipicoten River. There are actually two historic-period strata at the Michipicoten site. Because stratum I belongs to a time after the cessation of aboriginal pottery making and fabrication of stone tools, it is the earlier historic occupation, stratum II, that is germane here. Beneath this level there were seven successively anterior prehistoric levels.

Associated with native ceramics and flints, Michipicoten stratum II surrendered a small but significant collection of glass beads; articles made from brass-kettle scrap such as strips crimped over buckskin thongs to simulate beads, an unfinished tinkling cone or triangular pendant, and awls formed by rolling strips of the metal; gunflints; a lead pendant; and an iron knife. Almost half of the pottery from stratum II has been attributed to the Huron–Petun ceramic tradition. More than half would be so attributed if a minority sherd category called "Stamped" had not been ascribed, arguably and probably erroneously, to a cultural tradition other than Huron–Petun. In this connection, and despite the hyphenated ethnic nomenclature, at least some of the "Huron-Petun" clay pots are thought by the analyst to have been the outcome of Algonquian potters—presumably Ojibwa women—copying the Iroquoian fashions. No such pottery, it will be recalled, was recovered from the historic period level of the Pic River site. But half of the pottery from Shebishikong stratum I belongs in the Huron-Petun category. While Blackduck ware is a major component of the historic assemblages at all of the aforementioned sites, no examples were found at Michipicoten. Once again, however, so-called Peninsular Woodland pottery was retrieved from historic and prehistoric contexts, signaling a strong connection with the Michigan–Wisconsin region.

There are major discontinuities in types and proportions of ceramics among the historic-period components ascribed to Ojibwa occupation. There are also important differences between hsitoric and prehistoric strata *within* the same archaeological sites. The stone-implement assemblages, on the other hand, are seen to be less variable as they are followed over space and through time. The recurrence of a basically similar stone tool kit from site to site and stratum to stratum, with due allowance for divergences believed to reflect community size, site function, sampling error, and so on, is suggestive of population continuity. A part of this relative uniformity, however, is owed to the fact of a simple utilitarian stone industry. The observed variations in pottery, a generally more sensitive barometer of cultural affiliation and change, seem to contradict the lithic evidence. One way around the dilemma was broached in the last chapter. It is known from ethnohistorical studies that the Ojibwas favored a patrilocal bias in a settlement pattern typified by a relatively high degree of mobility. On the fairly safe assumption that pottery-making was the province of women and on the much less comfortable assumption that stone tools were invariably the domain of men (it would be surprising if women did not from time to time make their own household knives and scrapers and other frequently used implements), the introduction of women at marriage into regional, exogamous, patrilocal bands should have resulted in greater variety in any community's pottery than would be apparent in its stone products. The correspondence of empirical record and theoretical expectation, supported by ethnohistorical insights into early Ojibwa sociology, offers a highly plausible, if not wholly satisfying, explanation.

Another attempt to account for the contradictory behavior of ceramic and lithic artifacts also makes the foregoing assumptions. Much heavier stress is laid on long-range *community* mobility, however, and on the proposition that that mobility made it possible for different communities to introduce exotic wares to others and even for the same community to participate in multiple ceramic traditions. In either explanation, the observed time-depth of the stone-tool assemblages from the historic strata well back into prehistory is hard to reconcile with the movements of populations as reconstructed by many ethnologists and ethnohistorians. Most such reconstructions have confined the Ojibwa peoples to the eastern end of the Lake Superior basin and eastward therefrom, their great western and southwestern distribution being initiated in the historic period and attributed to the impact of Iroquoian and other disorders in the east and to the new opportunities the fur trade opened in the west.

Some archaeologists who are convinced that Blackduck pottery like that at the aforementioned sites was made by the ancestors of the modern Ojibwas have extended the equation *Blackduck = Ojibwa* or, at least, *Blackduck = Algonquian-speakers* (but excluding the Cree), to the far western end of Lake Superior and beyond the watershed to wherever Blackduck pottery has been found. This would mean that Algonquian-speakers, if not the proto-Ojibwas themselves, were already resident in central and northern Minnesota by the second half of the first millennium A.D. Yet in that state, where the Blackduck culture is heavily represented and was first defined, archaeologists, impressed by suggestive parallels in ethnographic and ethnohistoric reconstructions of tribal territories and archaeological site distributions, argued equating Blackduck with the Assiniboins, a Siouan-speaking tribe. Similarly in southeastern Manitoba where archaeologists more recently have unearthed a regional variant of Blackduck culture called the "Manitoba Focus," it, too, has been plausibly identified with the early historic and late prehistoric Assiniboins. In western Ontario there are historical accounts placing some Assiniboins at the time of initial European contacts within the tract of land running from Lake of the Woods to Lac Seul to the mouth of the Kaministikwia River on the northwestern coast of Lake Superior at Thunder Bay. This area is prolific of Blackduck sites. Locations of former Cree occupation, usually linked to the finding of Selkirk pottery, tend to lie north of Assiniboin and Ojibwa ranges, however drawn. In one reconstruction the Assiniboins are credited with the manufacture of Blackduck ware and the Ojibwas with "Michigan Ware," the sometimes associated wares being assigned a trade origin. Furthermore, the early historic range of the Ojibwas is drawn eastward from the Michipicoten site. The historic stratum at Pic River is ascribed to a westward movement of those people whereas the prehistoric strata are assigned to the Assiniboins. In this assessment the argument is advanced that previous claims of lithic continuity among alledged Ojibwa components are overdrawn and not supportable by the evidence and, further, that due weight has not been accorded the full cultural implications of the ceramics. Thus, by diverse interpretations Blackduck is connected with the Siouan-speaking Assiniboins exclusively, with Algonquian-speakers (if not strictly Ojibwas) exclusively, or with both. Correspondingly, trade, indigenous manufacture, or acquisition via wide-ranging marital ties have been invoked to account for the Blackduck ceramics found in Ojibwa sites.

Still other information pertinent to the problem of Blackduck authorship has been forthcoming from physical anthropological research. In an attempt to determine how and to what extent variations in the physical characteristics of human populations correspond to cultural differences collections of archaeological crania from Minnesota, North Dakota, southern Manitoba, and western Ontario were compared with others drawn from historical populations of known tribal affiliations. Estimates of closeness of genetic relationship were derived from observations of 26 independently inherited discrete traits of the skull. These are all features that are either present or absent on a skull, whose presence or absence is genetically determined, which are not sex-linked, are not known to be affected by nutritional or other environmental factors, and for which the expression of any one is not causally linked to any other. Examples of such traits are trochlear spur (an anomalous bony projection within the eye socket), accessory optic canal (an anomalous extra opening in the back of the eye socket), and clinoid bridging (a joining of the usually separate anterior and middle clinoid processes of the sphenoid bone). Mapping the spatial distributions and relative frequencies of these morphological details has demonstrated distinctly nonrandom behavior with regard to both archaeological cultures and ethnographic tribal units. Because of the preliminary nature of important parts of the study, merely a small segment of which is relevant to the present problem, it should be understood that only tentative conclusions should be drawn vis-à-vis the cultural identity of the people responsible for the Blackduck culture. It appears that things are even more complicated than the preceding discussion has intimated.

The pertinent results of the physical anthropological study indicate among other things that the skulls from northern Blackduck sites are most similar, and thus probably most closely related, to known Ojibwa populations. Southern Blackduck sites, on the other hand, have produced a series of skulls that measure closest in biological distance to Dakota (Sioux) groups. It is with crania from western Blackduck ("Manitoba Focus") that the known Assiniboin sample most tightly aligns itself. These assessments, tentative as they are, are in agreement with the views of those archaeologists who have maintained that Blackduck ceramics and linguistic or ethnic units were not coextensive. Like "Iroquoian" pottery in the east, Blackduck pottery seems to have been produced by more than one people. Which particular people—Ojibwa, Assiniboin, or some other—must be determined in each case by ethnohistoric or other independent lines of evidence.

In much of the same country which has produced the northern historic Ojibwa sites there are other less tangible manifestations of cultural behavior as well. These are pictograph, or rock-art, sites. In the Great Lakes rock-art sites are virtually restricted to the northern Lake Superior and Huron littoral and hinterland, though they are much more common between Lake Superior and Lake of the Woods. On the assumption that most were painted within historical time, they are almost certainly the work of Algonquian-speakers. Many, in fact, are startlingly reminiscent of figures on Ojibwa medico-religious bark scrolls.

Most often arranged on sheer rock faces along waterways, usually at a height appropriate to a man standing in a canoe, the paintings are almost invariably done with red pigment. Exhibiting little in the way of a decipherable pattern, the pictographs seem to have been painted with the finger. Animals (moose, caribou, bison, bears, dogs or wolves, turtles, birds, etc.), anthropomorphic figures, hands, "sea-serpent" and other mythological creatures, man-made contrivances (boats, huts, possible mortuary scaffolds, flagpoles), and a miscellany of abstract symbols (meandering trials, dots, crosses, sets of lines) were painted singly or in various combinations. Depictions of men shooting guns, of horsemen, and of fort-like buildings equipped with flagpoles attest to the historicity of certain, if not all, of the paintings. Human figures are drawn in stick form or with solid colored bodies. Some are drawn with horns, rabbit ears, or a lightning-like line entering or emerging from the head. Still others are rendered holding what appears to be a beaver pelt or an animal-skin pouch and are accompanied by a dog or wolf or even a porcupine-like creature. While a majority of the figures are stiff, sketchy, and sloppy in execution, there are a few carefully composed, well-proportioned animals containing a dynamic tension between realism and conventionalized exaggeration. Certain of these could hold their own in the company of the much more famous and enormously older Upper Paleolithic cave drawings of France and Spain.

Whatever meaning the pictographs were meant to convey is now largely lost. Probably each had a personal significance that died with its creator even though many of the symbols must have been widely shared among the people wherever the rock art found expression. Manifestations of the vision quest, hunting magic, attempts at pictorial capturing or control of underwater and other supernatural beings, and just the elemental desire of passersby to leave a mark of their journey are among the interpretations observers have hazarded. Plausible attempts at identifying certain of the symbols with astronomical phenomena have also been put forward, the historic Ojibwa being known to see some of the same kinds of figures in neighboring star clusters as Europeans. Thus the depiction of a hunter may have been intended as a symbol for the constellation Orion; the often accompanying wolf or dog, the constellation Canis Major (which incorporates Sirius, the "Dog Star," brightest of all the stars) similarly accompanying Orion; and the beaver pelt or animal skin pouch would be equatable with Gemini. By their very nature, however, such "readings" are notoriously difficult, if not impossible, to verify. The same symbol could have borne a quite different semantic weight in diverse places or times. Idiosyncratic variations are so much the rule that a correct understanding of a particular painting would not necessarily be of help in trying to interpret the others.

Students of the rock art have had a hard time getting more than an impressionistic idea of its antiquity. Obviously, the paintings showing the use of horses and guns and flags have to be of post-contact inspiration. But that observation hardly constitutes precise dating. Most authorities believe that the more numerous pictographs lacking signs of European-introduced elements are probably not much older than those that do. That no great gulf of time separates them is indicated by basic similarities in style, the concentration of rock-art localities within districts, the placement of the designs on the rock faces, and on the degree of preservation. Nevertheless, only hasty judgment would categorically consign all of the known specimens to historic age. Too much is unknown. The bulk of the paintings may be vestiges of an old tradition, one conceivably extending back into the Late Woodland period. Attempts are currently underway to extract a relative chronology using measures of the thickness of mineral deposition over painted lines, extent of lichen invasion of decorated surfaces, and searching for instances of overpainting or of symbols on exfoliated faces the scars of which impinge upon antecedent figures. The ideal of somehow connecting a rock painting with a datable habitation site has so far eluded consummation. Except for their undoubted parallels with Ojibwa Midewiwin scrolls, and the fact that some modern as well as earlier historic-period Ojibwas have been known to acknowledge a spiritual connection with certain of the pictograph sites by leaving offerings of tobacco or other things, the rock-art syndrome continues to stand somewhat apart from the principal body of information about Great Lakes archaeology.

No anthropologist ever saw a Great Lakes pictograph being composed. No contemporary documents exist describing the people who lived at the Parsons or the Draper or the Dutch Hollow or the overwhelming majority of other Indian sites which were occupied after the European discovery notwithstanding their technical status as historic or protohistoric. But Father Brebeuf was in personal attendance at the Ossossane Feast of the Dead. His narrative of that occasion is rich in information that would otherwise have been lost. His account explicitly supplies intelligence relevant to questions about who, what, when, and where. The Cadillac-Lasanen site connection, a little less reliable, is nevertheless not much inferior in value for the light it throws on activities otherwise dependent for their interpretation on the manifold strengths and weaknesses of archaeological data alone or by reasoning by analogy from later ethnographies of other people. Not less important, the personal observations of individuals whose names are already familiar to the reader have a peculiar force; they are a bit like rare opportunities to peek through a keyhole into a scene of opulently variegated colors and textures and of having an exhilarating sense of shared experience in doing it.

On the southern shore of one of the loveliest islands in northern Lake Michigan, at the mouth of Green Bay between the Garden Peninsula of Upper Michigan and the Door Peninsula of Wisconsin, two very different but equally outstanding men parlayed on the mutual obligations and rewards of alliance. In mid-September, 1679, René-Robert Cavelier, Sieur de la Salle, arrived at Rock Island aboard the *Griffon*. This phenomenon, a vessel 11–12 m long and of approximately 50 t burden, was the first sailing ship to breast the waves of the Great Lakes. La Salle had built her above Niagara Falls that very year, had brought her through a perilous storm on Lake Huron, shown his few countrymen and their more numerous Indian allies at Michilimackinac in the Straits of Mackinac an astonishing sight, and wowed the natives on Rock Island when the cannon-carrying floating fort hove into view out of the northeast.

Though doubtless impressed, there was at least one man in the Potawatomi village, other than several French voyageurs who were there awaiting the ships's arrival anxious to load their stock of prime furs, who was not at all astonished. This was the "okama," or "leader," of the Rock

PLATE 9.9. *Soil profile at Rock Island Site II, Door County, Wisconsin, showing the physical stratification of old humus zones, living surfaces, and wind-blown sand. The pit outline intrusive from stratum V on the left is a part of the stockade trench dug by refugee Hurons, Petuns, and Ottawas sometime in the period 1650–1653. (Negative in Department of Anthroplogy, Lawrence University, Appleton, Wisconsin.)*

Island Potawatomis: one called Onangizes, "the Shimmering Light of the Sun." Not only had this man traveled with the canoe flotillas to Montreal and Quebec and there seen French sailing vessels with his own eyes, he had also met and impressed Governor Frontenac. With the self-assurance of one accustomed to the company and high regard of other important men, Onangizes paddled out to greet the *Griffon,* despite rough seas.

Then, very likely reminding his guests of his friendship with the renowned Frontenac, and perhaps also recalling his role in escorting the highly regarded Nicolas Perrot to Green Bay 11 years earlier, the "okama" accompanied the Frenchman La Salle ashore, extending the hospitality of his village. It is indeed fortunate that La Salle's party included another whose name was also destined to survive: the Recollect priest Louis Hennepin, the first European to have seen the Niagara Falls and a man much given to writing memoirs. Hennepin's description of the "Island of the Poutouatamis," Perrot's recollection of events on "Huron Island," together with the observations of a few later writers, when combined with the results of recent archaeological investigations have made possible the identification of the island where the *Griffon* anchored and La Salle came ashore.

This relatively small island, having the agricultural and hunting potential of the far larger Washington Island just under a kilometer away, however, was a widely known place. It was a trading station and a strategically located stopping-off point in the irregular chain of islands in the straits between la Baye des Puants and le Lac des Illinois, as those bodies of water were then known by the French. The island had earlier served for a brief time as one of the refuges of the allied Hurons, Petuns, and Ottawas after they had been driven from their Ontario homelands by the Iroquois in 1649–1650. It was probably to this island and those people that the explorer brothers-in-law Pierre-Esprit Radisson and Médart Chouart, Sieur de Grossilliers came on their second western voyage in 1658. The occupants, nascent Wyandots, threw up a pentagonal palisade as a redoubt in case of surprise, island or no. A part of this was evidently still serviceable when the Potawatomis moved onto the island sometime following its abandonment by the Huron–Petun–Ottawa refugees, or future Wyandots. Prior to 1641 the Potawatomis had resided in the western half of the lower Michigan peninsula. Exhausting wars with the Neutrals and other Iroquoian-speaking tribes finally impelled them to yield those parts and to take up residence in the country around Sault Ste. Marie and on the Door Peninsula. They soon established themselves as the dominant people in northeastern Wisconsin, allied to the French, but competing with the Ottawas, another French ally, for control of the fur trade. In their new habitat the Potawatomis flourished, gradually expanding their territorial claims southward and westward at the expense of resident tribes. Before the middle of the eighteenth century, the center of gravity of their interests having shifted permanently between those compass points, the Potawatomis retired from the Green Bay area never to return as occupants.

On September 18, 1679, La Salle, having been feted and accorded a successful trade with the Rock Island Potawatomis, launched the *Griffon* with a crew of six men on her return trip. The ship fired one of her five cannons in jaunty salute. The next day La Salle himself set out with the rest

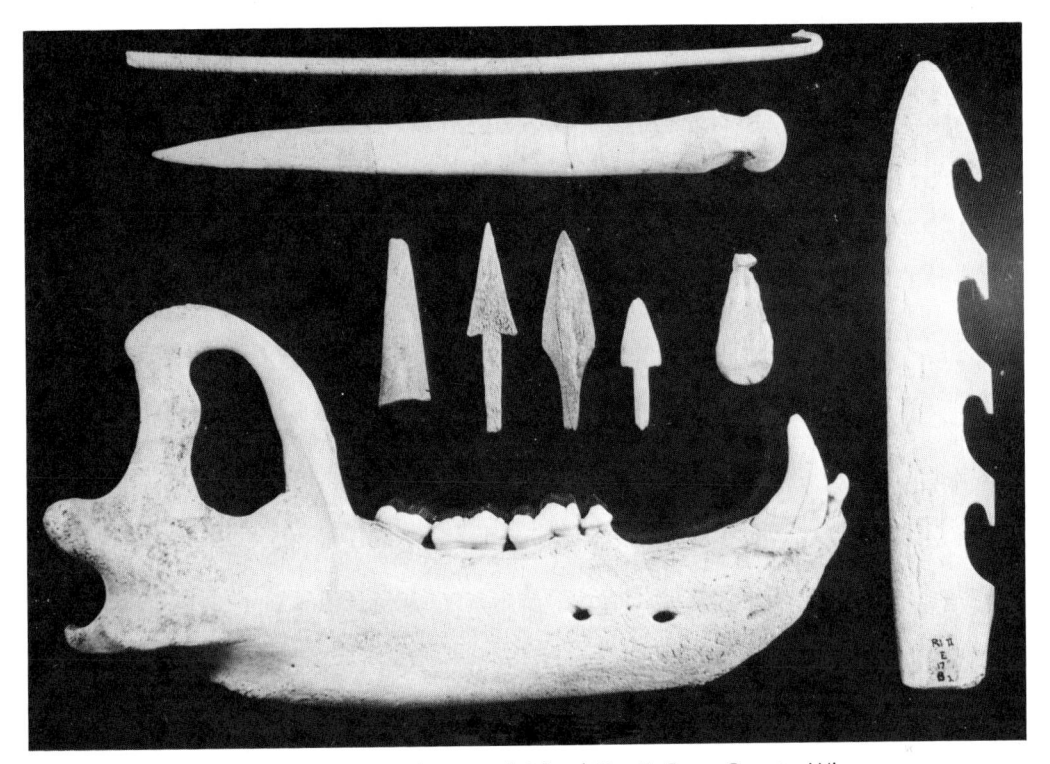

PLATE 9.10. *Bone and antler artifacts from Rock Island Site II, Door County, Wisconsin: animal-headed hair pin and heavy awl or "dagger" (top); socketed arrowhead, tanged arrowheads, and unfinished pendant (middle); bear-mandible tool (bottom); and unilaterally miltibarbed harpoon (right). (Shown half actual size.) (Collections of Department of Anthropology, Lawrence University, Appleton, Wisconsin.)*

of his party in four bark canoes for the nearby mainland and the long journey to the southern end of the giant lake. Almost immediately, however, and with little warning, a ferocious autumnal storm forced them ashore near the Porte des Morts straits, enforcing a 4-day halt in their trip. But far worse overtook the *Griffon* on the return leg of her maiden voyage. She was never seen nor heard from again. The ship, her crew, and La Salle's fortune in furs must have foundered and sunk in the maelstrom. No word was ever received of her having passed the Indian settlements or the French establishment at Michilimackinac. It is therefore highly likely that the *Griffon* met her onrushing fate somewhere between a day or a day-and-a-half's blustery sail out of Rock Island (at which time the storm was building up) and the westerly approaches to the straits. That she went down well west of Michilimackinac is suggested by the fact that no flotsam or jetsam from the wreck were ever found, or at least reported, by the inhabitants of the straits.

The Rock Island site—there are actually several sites on the island, though this discussion must be confined to that occupied by Indians in the historic period (Rock Island Site II)—was intermittently inhabited over a radiocarbon-assayed span of some 2500 years. Its extraordinary attraction was because of: its nearly central position among the chain of islands whose circuit had to be made by any and all travelers between Michilimackinac and Green Bay or anywhere else on the entire western shore of Lake Michigan southward therefrom; its flanking post at one of the widest of the straits between the main body of the lake and its great western arm; its splendid sandy shore, especially inviting among the much more typical gravel beaches and limestone bluffs of the archipelago; its easy accessibility to, yet readily defensible separation from, the much larger Washington Island; and its excellent potential as a fishery. As has been seen, the island was a known place by the time of French expansion into the upper lakes.

The fact of sandy beach and a complex of low sand dunes immediately landward proved of enormous usefulness to archaeologists trying to unravel the several discrete occupations where many people had come and gone over a long time. Here and there drifting sand had buried part of a recently abandoned camp surface. This migrating mantle was sometimes anchored at last by the encroachment of vegetation, in effect offering a fresh living floor for the next people. A few areas were found where alternating cultural and natural deposition permitted the empirical establishment of a sequence of tool types and artifact styles, importantly augmented by associations of cultural and environmental data relatively sealed in architectural features, cooking pits, graves, or other discrete loci of activity. These permitted an uncommonly detailed reconstruction of the sequence of Indian occupation of the island during the early historic period, thus facilitating a more accurate correlation with those associated comings and goings of named individuals and ethnic groups which made their way onto the pages of recorded history.

The historical documents relating to the extension of European interests into the northern Lake Michigan–Green Bay area, particularly those relating to "Huron Island," "the Island of the Poutouatamis," and the "islands at the mouth of Green Bay," point to a sequence of Indian occupations on Rock Island punctuated by increasing intercourse with the agents of those interests. Documentary sources can be found in support of five periods of Indian habitation *within* historic times:

1. A short-term occupation by Potawatomis inaugurated the historic period on the island, an occupation presumably postdating 1641 when the main body of the tribe withdrew from the lower Michigan peninsula to establish new homes on the Door Peninsula and at Sault Ste. Marie, and predating approximately 1650–1653 when the next community ensconced itself on the just recently vacated island. Un-

PLATE 9.11. *Trade goods and associated artifacts from Rock Island Site II, Door County, Wisconsin: bangle and stemmed arrowhead or brass kettle scrap, glass trade beads, French gunflints (left-hand specimen was used as a fireflint), and strike-a-light or firesteel (first row); piece of worked brass kettle scrap, Iroquois clay pipe, and stone "Micmac" pipes (middle row); ax, and French clasp knives. (Shown half actual size.) (Collections of Department of Anthropology, Lawrence University, Appleton, Wisconsin.)*

fortunately, there is only an editor's comment on an historical document in support of such an occurrence, but that editor's scholarly authority in other matters commands respect; his unsupported assertion became an hypothesis to be archaeologically tested.

2. Sometime between 1650 and 1653 an amalgam of Hurons, Petuns, and Ottawas, refugees from their native lands and the immediate precursors of the aborning Wyandot tribe, built a fortified village on the island, only to forsake it after a brief time because of the renewed threat of Iroquois depredations. Apparently, a handful of the Petuns later returned to Rock Island, remaining until 1658–1660.

3. The Potawatomis again claimed tenancy, refurbishing the stockade sometime before La Salle visited in 1679, and intermittently occupied the settlement until after 1728 when this particular Potawatomi com-

munity was last accorded mention in the surviving written sources; in round figures this episode of recurrent Potawatomi occupations may be bounded by the dates 1670–1730.
4. An Ottawa village on adjacent Washington Island was reported by an English traveler in 1766, and a smaller village and cemetery on Rock Island were probably also used by these same people, probably within the decade 1760–1770.
5. There is record of a mid-nineteenth-century occupation by Chippewas (Ojibwas).

The archaeological record, that is, the actual physical segregation of components as determined by stratigraphy and spatial clustering and artifact correlations with palisade and building-wall trenches, postmolds, house floors, hearths, graves, and other features, has preserved traces of four cultural occupations dating to the historic period and pertaining to Indian tenancy. While the detailed report on the Rock Island excavation program is still being written, and has not yet been submitted to the necessary scrutiny and evaluations of other scholars, it does appear that the first four of the five episodes of Indian habitation alluded to in the documentary sources are matched by the four historic-period components on Rock Island as established by archaeology. No certain traces of the latest episode recorded in the written accounts were found. Presumably, this last Indian community had its dwellings elsewhere on the island.

The first of the historic period episodes is represented only by scanty remains. However, these were recovered in excellent cultural and stratigraphic contexts. The most culturally sensitive artifacts of this initial habitation are fragments of pottery. These are absolutely foreign to the known prehistory of the region whereas, significantly, they are duplicated in a minority pottery type at the early historic Bell site, a fortified village in Winnebago County, Wisconsin. At that place this pottery has been called "Type II." The majority ware at the same site (Bell Site Type I), convincingly credited to the Fox Indians, has also been found at Rock Island, only in deposits assigned to the third period of historic occupation and then as a rarity. Another locality where pottery suggestively similar to Bell Site Type II and the earliest historic pottery on Rock Island has been reported is the Dumaw Creek site in Oceana County in the lower Michigan peninsula. The Dumaw Creek site belongs on the very threshold of the historic period and is the best candidate of its age for attribution to the Potawatomis in their ancestral estate. Similar pottery constitutes the dominant ware of the third and largest of the Rock Island historic occupations. Because the earliest historic ceramics on the island are indistinguishable from the majority ware of the third occupation and there are no significant criteria for differentiating them on the basis of other associated artifacts, the two components have been identified as probable Potawatomi encampments. The latter

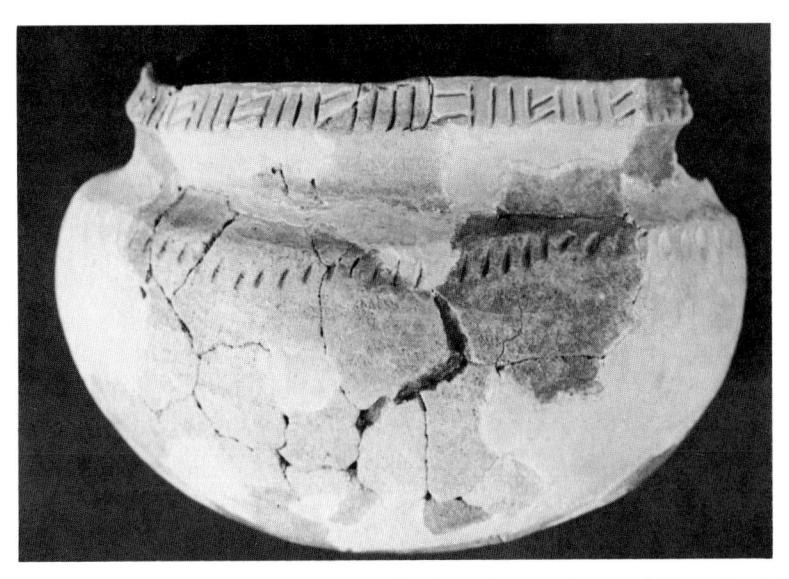

PLATE 9.12. *Huron-style vessel from Rock Island Site II, Door County, Wisconsin. (Shown half actual size.) (Collections of Department of Anthropology, Lawrence University, Appleton, Wisconsin.)*

example incorporates rich and varied remains many of which are compatible with the age of the voyage of the *Griffon*.

Between the two Potawatomi occupations were the scanty middens but impressive features attributed to the Hurons, Petuns, and Ottawas. The defensive stockade they constructed survived in the form of postmolds and, in some sectors, a filled-in ditch with postmolds in the bottom and with wedging rocks in place. In one especially informative stratigraphic profile the palisade trench could be seen to cut through midden of the initial Potawatomi period, and the sterile subsoil thrown out in digging the trench was spread out atop that earlier cultural horizon. Here and in other excavation units the trash of the second Potawatomi settlement (third historic period) extended undisturbed over the line of the palisade. Particularly distinctive of the second period was pottery, in some instances like that from the Sidey-Mackay and other Huron and Petun sites in Ontario and, in other instances, like the "Huron–Petun Branch" ceramics from the Michipicoten and other Ojibwa sites on the north shores of Lakes Superior and Huron. Probably introduced at this time, though more popular in the second Potawatomi sojourn, were enigmatic implements made of the lower jaws of black bears. Incorporating large perforations in the ascending ramus which were worn in irregular patterns through heavy use, such artifacts are otherwise known only from historic Huron and Petun villages in Ontario. The only known exceptions to this rule are a solitary specimen possibly from a New York Iroquois site and another example from Wea or Ottawa occupation at Fort Ouiatenon, a French (later British) post established in 1717 in Tippecanoe County in western Indiana. At Rock Island, as we have seen, this interesting tool type was adopted by the Potawatomis.

French trade goods were present in low frequencies in the initial Potawatomi and in the Huron–Petun–Ottawa middens on Rock Island. They became numerous in the second Potawatomi and in the Ottawa levels. A few British trade goods were also present in association with the latter, especially diagnostic being a couple of Bristol-made white kaolin smoking pipes stamped with the name R. Tippet and a flintlock musket bearing the date 1762, the maker's name (Wilson), and the mark of the Hudson's Bay Company. Glass beads (almost 40,000) occurred in the last two components in company with shell wampum beads, brass kettles, a wide assortment of tools and jewelry made from brass scrap, iron sheath and clasp knives, iron axes and awls, gunflints, "Jesuit" rings, crosses and crucifixes, metal brooches, earrings, brass and iron triggerguards and other gun parts, glass mirror and bottle sherds, firesteels, and many other things. Silver armbands and brooches appeared in the Ottawa occupation. Limestone and catlinite pipes of the "Micmac" style, either made for the trade or crafted by the Indians, were common. So were catlinite beads, pendants, and beaver effigies. It is noteworthy that as the native manufactures gave way to the substitution of European commodities, pottery making disappeared before flint knapping ceased to be practiced, work in catlinite flourished, and bone and antler craftsmanship experienced a temporary renaissance, presumably in part because of the technical advances metal tools afforded.

The Rock Island site is one of an illustrious, if now sadly depleted, company. The earliest Lake Ontario Huron trade centers, a not much younger Seneca village and cemetery, Huron and Ottawa ossuaries, Ojibwa camps, genetic anomalies and problems of tribal identifications, pictograph sites, the ill-fated voyage of the *Griffon,* refugees and aborning Wyandots, Potawatomi withdrawal and rebirth, French and British trade—all exemplify the challenges confronting the archaeologist of historic-period Indians in the Great Lakes. The described examples are but a sampling of the period's complexity and its potential for providing insights into the workings of Native American societies in their migration from prehistory to the age of European dominion. It has been clear from this discussion and from information derived from antecedent periods that Great Lakes Indian societies were active and perceptive participants in a cultural evolutionary course importantly involving at one or more points subcontinental, continental, hemispheric, and even global dimensions. The people of the inland seas were at all times intelligent users of their natural and cultural environments, fully capable of adapting themselves to challenging exigencies and, in turn and at the end, of exacting not inconsiderable concessions of the ocean-crossing interlopers themselves. That they were overwhelmed was an inevitability cascading out of the quantum imbalance between their own numbers and those upwelling from across the ocean; between the virulence of new diseases and their inadequate immunities; between their inferior weaponry and tool-making, when it came to competition with the technology of the ocean-crossers; between a finitely accommodating and an endlessly jealous ideology; and between a type of social system intrinsically geared to small populations organized on principles of kinship obligations and the impersonal musterings and coercive combinations of the nation-state. That the native peoples were not extinguished is testimony to a tenacity, a resilience, a toughness at the core of people long accustomed to internecine hostilities and the recurrent problems of wrestling a livelihood from a sometimes capricious nature. And, of course, the amply documented but often overlooked fact remains that their extirpation was never attempted.

This account of Great Lakes archaeology closes with the end of the eighteenth century. By about this time even the most remote of Great Lakes aboriginal communities had been so basically affected by the massive incursions of European culture that their overriding adaptational imperatives had to do with accommodating themselves to that reality. Although still important, relations among Indian groups were simply no longer as independently determined as they once had been. And of course, by this time almost all of the traditional inventory of material things was but a memory. The manufactured tools and weapons that had replaced the indigenous products, the pots and pans, the door hinges and harness furniture, the glass bottles and iron nails, and all the spewed out debris of abandoned Indian homes and ended lives were the same as those to be found on the farms and in the villages of the new majority. By the century's conclusion, indeed, well before in most instances, the trajectory of indigenous Great Lakes cultural change had been forever deflected from largely internal determination to one inescapably responding to preponderating external factors.

By closing the narrative at the selected time in no way means to imply that the later histories of Great Lakes Indian societies are either somehow less interesting or that they are of intrinsically less value for the study of history or anthropology. The exercise of historic archaeology, informed by general anthropological theory, has already produced useful and interesting results in the analysis of more modern sites. Nor is our neglect of the archaeology of European and Colonial settlement meant to convey that that study is in any way unworthy of mention. These latter subjects require no defense and are enormously important and endlessly fascinating in their own right. It must simply be admitted that they are postscripts, however prominent, to the course of autochthonous Native American life in the Great Lakes which this book has endeavored to follow.

References

On early European explorations and accounts of Indian customs (also consult list in references at end of Chapter 1):
Biggar, editor, 1922–1936; Morison 1971; Quimby 1966a; Thwaites, editor, 1896–1901, and 1903; Wrong, editor, 1939.

On the Draper and Parsons sites, Ontario:
Hayden, editor, 1979; Ramsden 1978.

On the Dutch Hollow site, New York:
Ritchie 1954; Wray and Schoff 1953.

On the Ossossane site, Ontario:
Kidd 1953.

On the Lasanen site, Michigan:
Cleland, editor, 1971.

On the Shebishikong, Nyman, Pic River, and Michipicoten sites, Ontario:
Dawson 1976a, 1976b, and 1977; Quimby 1961; J. V. Wright 1965, 1966a, 1968a, and 1968b.

On Blackduck–Ojibwa–Assiniboin relationships:
Bishop and Smith 1975; Dawson 1974 and 1977; Ossenberg 1974; J. V. Wright 1965 and 1968b.

On the rock art:
Dewdney and Kidd 1967.

On Rock Island Site II, Wisconsin:
Clifton 1977; R. J. Mason 1974.

On other sites or special studies of relevance to one or more of the described sites:
Brose 1970a and 1970b; Garrad 1969; C. Mason 1976; Pendergast and Trigger 1972; Pratt 1976; Quimby 1966b; Ridley 1954; Wittry 1963.

References

Asch, Donald L., and Nancy B. Asch
   1977   Chenopod as cultigen: A re-evaluation of some prehistoric collections from eastern North America. *Midcontinental Journal of Archaeology* 2(1):3–45.

Baerreis, David A., and Reid A. Bryson
   1965   Climatic episodes and the dating of Mississippian cultures. *The Wisconsin Archeologist* 47(3):101–131.

Baerreis, David A., Reid A. Bryson, and John E. Kutzback
   1976   Climate and culture in the western Great Lakes region. *Midcontinental Journal of Archaeology* 1(1):39–57.

Baerreis, David A., Hiroshi Daifuku, and James E. Lundsted
   1954   The burial complex of the Reigh Site, Winnebago County, Wisconsin. *The Wisconsin Archeologist* 35:1–36. (Reprinted in Ritzenthaler, editor, 1957, pp. 244–278.)

Bettarel, Robert Louis, and Hale G. Smith
   1973   The Moccasin Bluff Site and the Woodland cultures of southwestern Michigan. *Anthropological Papers, Museum of Anthropology, University of Michigan,* No. 49.

Biggar, H. P. (editor)
   1922–1936   *The works of Samuel de Champlain.* 6 vols. Toronto: The Champlain Society.

Binford, Lewis R.
   1962a   Radiometric analysis of bone material from the Oconto Site. *The Wisconsin Archeologist* 43(2):31–41.
   1962b   Archaeology as anthropology. *American Antiquity* 28(2):217–225.

Bishop, Charles A., and M. Estellie Smith
   1975   Early historic populations in northwestern Ontario: Archaeological and ethnohistorical interpretations. *American Antiquity* 40(1):54–63.

Blair, Emma Helen (editor)
   1911–1922   *The Indian tribes of the Upper Mississippi Valley and regions of the Great Lakes, as described by Nicolas Perrot, French commandant in the Northwest; Bacqueville de la Potherie, French royal commissioner to Canada; Morrell Marston, American army officer; and Thomas Forsyth, United States agent at Fort Armstrong.* Vols. 1 and 2. Cleveland, Ohio: Arthur H. Clark Co.

References

Bluhm, Elaine A. (editor)
    1959   Illinois archaeology. *Illinois Archaeological Survey, Bulletin* 1. Urbana, Illinois: University of Illinois.

Bluhm, Elaine A., and Allen Liss
    1961   The Anker site. In *Chicago area archaeology*, edited by Elaine A. Bluhm. Illinois Archaeological Survey Bulletin, No. 3. Urbana, Illinois: University of Illinois. Pp. 89–137.

Bonvillain, Nancy (editor)
    1979   Studies on Iroquoian culture. *Occasional Publications in Northeastern Anthropology*, No. 6, *Man in the Northeast*.

Brose, David S.
    1970a   The archaeology of Summer Island: Changing settlement systems in northern Lake Michigan. *Anthropological Papers, Museum of Anthropology, University of Michigan*, No. 41.
    1970b   Summer Island III: An Early Historic Site in the Upper Great Lakes. *Historical Archaeology* 4:3–33.
    1971   The Girdled Road site, an Early Woodland hunting station in Lake County, Ohio. *Kirtlandia*, No. 13. The Cleveland Museum of Natural History.
    1978   Late prehistory of the Upper Great Lakes area. In *Northeast*, vol. 15, edited by Bruce G. Trigger, in *Handbook of North American Indians*, edited by William C. Sturtevant. Washington, D.C.: Smithsonian Institution. Pp. 569–582.

Brose, David S. (editor)
    1976   *The Late Prehistory of the Lake Erie Drainage Basin: A 1972 symposium revised*. Cleveland, Ohio: Scientific Publications of the Cleveland Museum of Natural History.

Brown, James A.
    1964   The northeastern extension of the Havana tradition. In *Hopewellian Studies*, edited by Joseph R. Caldwell and Robert L. Hall. *Illinois State Museum Scientific Papers* 12:107–122.

Bryson, Reid A., and Wayne M. Wendland
    1967   Tentative climatic patterns for some Late Glacial and Post-Glacial Episodes in Central North America. In *Life, land and water*, Proceedings of the 1966 Conference on Environmental Studies of the Glacial Lake Agassiz Region, edited by William J. Mayer-Oakes. *Occasional Papers, Department of Anthropology, University of Manitoba*, No. 1.

Caldwell, Joseph R.
    1958   Trend and tradition in the prehistory of the eastern United States. *American Anthropological Association, Memoir* 88.

Callender, Charles
    1962   Social organization of the Central Algonkian Indians. *Milwaukee Public Museum Publications in Anthropology*, No. 7.
    1978   Great Lakes—Riverine sociopolitical organization. In *Northeast*, vol. 15, edited by Bruce G. Trigger, in *Handbook of North American Indians*, edited by William C. Sturtevant. Washington, D.C.: Smithsonian Institution. Pp. 610–621.

Castile, George Pierre
    1979   *North American Indians, an introduction to the Chichimeca*. New York: McGraw-Hill.

Chomko, Stephen A., and Gary W. Crawford
    1978   Plant husbandry in prehistoric eastern North America: New evidence for its development. *American Antiquity* 43(3):405–408.

Cleland, Charles E.
    1966   The prehistoric animal ecology and ethnozoology of the Upper Great Lakes region. *Anthropological Papers, Museum of Anthropology, University of Michigan*, No. 29.

Cleland, Charles E. (editor)
    1971   The Lasanen site, an historic burial locality in Mackinac County, Michigan. *Publications of the Museum, Michigan State University, Anthropological Series* 1(1).

Clifton, James A.
- 1977 *The prairie people, continuity and change in Potawatomi Indian culture 1665-1965.* Lawrence, Kansas: The Regents Press of Kansas.
- 1978 Potawatomi. In *Northeast*, vol. 15, edited by Bruce G. Trigger, in *Handbook of North American Indians*, edited by William C. Sturtevant. Washington, D.C.: Smithsonian Institution. Pp. 725-742.

Cunningham, Wilbur M.
- 1948 A study of the Glacial Kame culture in Michigan, Ohio, and Indiana. *Occasional Contributions from the Museum of Anthropology of the University of Michigan*, No. 12.

Dawson, K. C. A.
- 1974 The McCluskey site. *National Museum of Man, Mercury Series, Archaeological Survey of Canada,* Paper 25.
- 1976a Algonkians of Lake Nipigon: An archaeological survey. *National Museum of Man, Mercury Series, Archaeological Survey of Canada, Paper* 48.
- 1976b The Nyman site, a seventeenth century Algonkian camp on the north shore of Lake Superior. *Canadian Archaeological Association, Bulletin 8*:1-56.
- 1977 An application of the direct historical approach to the Algonkians of northern Ontario. *Canadian Journal of Archaeology 1*:151-181.

Deale, Valentine B.
- 1958 The history of the Potawatomis before 1772. *Ethnohistory 5*:305-360.

Deller, D. Brian
- 1979 Paleo-Indian reconnaissance in the counties of Lambton and Middlesex, Ontario. *Ontario Archaeology 32*:3-20.

Dewdney, Selwyn, and Kenneth E. Kidd
- 1967 *Indian rock paintings of the Great Lakes* (Second edition). Toronto: University of Toronto Press.

Emerson, J. Norman
- 1955 The Kant site: A Point Peninsula manifestation in Renfrew County, Ontario. *Transactions of the Royal Canadian Institute 31*(1):24-66.
- 1966 The Payne site: An Iroquoian manifestation in Prince Edward County, Ontario. *National Museum of Canada, Bulletin 206*:126-257.

Evans, G. Edward
- 1961 Ceramic analysis of the Blackduck Ware and its general cultural relationships. *Proceedings of the Minnesota Academy of Science 29*(4):33-54.

Farrand, William R.
- 1977 Revision of the Two Rivers "Valders" drift border and the age of fluted points in Michigan. In *For the director: Research essays in honor of James B. Griffin,* edited by Charles E. Cleland. *Anthropological Papers, Museum of Anthropology, University of Michigan 61*:74-84.

Faulkner, Charles H.
- 1960 The Red Ochre culture: An early burial complex in northern Indiana. *The Wisconsin Archaeologist 41*(2):35-49.
- 1972 The Late Prehistoric occupation of northwestern Indiana—a study of the Upper Mississippi cultures of the Kankakee Valley. *Prehistory Research Series 5*(1). Indianapolis, Indiana: Indiana Historical Society.

Fenton, William N.
- 1940 Problems arising from the historic northeastern position of the Iroquois. *Smithsonian Institution, Miscellaneous Collections, 100*:159-252.
- 1971 The Iroquois in history. In *North American Indians in Historical Perspective,* edited by Eleanor Burke Leacock and Nancy Oestreich Lurie. New York: Random House.
- 1978 Northern Iroquoian culture patterns. In *Northeast*, vol. 15, edited by Bruce G. Trigger, in *Handbook of North American Indians*, edited by William C. Sturtevant. Washington, D.C.: Smithsonian Institution. Pp. 296-321.

Finlayson, William D.
   1977   The Saugeen culture: A Middle Woodland manifestation in southwestern Ontario. *National Museum of Man, Mercury Series, Archaeological Survey of Canada, Paper* 61.
Fitting, James E.
   1965   Late Woodland cultures of southeastern Michigan. *Anthropological Papers, Museum of Anthropology, University of Michigan,* No. 24.
   1970   *The archaeology of Michigan.* Garden City, New York: Natural History Press. (Revised edition, 1975, Cranbrook Institute, Bloomfield, Michigan.)
   1978   Regional cultural development, 300 B.C. to A.D. 1000. In *Northeast,* vol. 15, edited by Bruce G. Trigger, in *Handbook of North American Indians,* edited by William C. Sturtevant. Washington, D.C.: Smithsonian Institution. Pp. 44-57.
Fitting, James E. (editor)
   1972   The Schultz site at Green Point: A stratified occupation area in the Saginaw Valley of Michigan. *Memoirs of the Museum of Anthropology, University of Michigan,* No. 4.
Fitting, James E., and David S. Brose
   1970   The northern periphery of Adena. In *Adena: The seeking of an identity,* (edited by B. K. Swartz, Jr.) A symposium held at the Kitselman Conference Center, Ball State University, Muncie. Pp. 29-55.
Fitting, James E., Jerry DeVisscher, and Edward J. Wahla
   1966   The Paleo-Indian occupation of the Holcombe Beach. *Anthropological Papers, Museum of Anthropology, University of Michigan,* No. 27.
Flanders, Richard E.
   1977   Some observations of the Goodall focus. *For the director: Research essays in honor of James B. Griffin,* edited by Charles E. Cleland. *Anthropological Papers, Museum of Anthropology, University of Michigan* 61:141-151.
Flint, Richard Foster
   1971   *Glacial and Quaternary geology.* New York: John Wiley.
Fogel, Ira L.
   1963   The dispersal of copper artifacts in the Late Archaic period of prehistoric North America. *The Wisconsin Archeologist* 44(3):129-180.
Fowler, Melvin L.
   1959   Summary report of Modoc Rock Shelter. *Illinois State Museum Investigations, Report* No. 8.
Fox, W. A.
   1975   The Paleo-Indian Lakehead complex. *Canadian Archaeological Association, Collected Papers, March, 1975,* edited by P. Nunn. Research Report No. 6, Historical Sites Branch, Ontario Ministry of Natural Resources. Pp. 29-53.
Funk, Robert E.
   1972   Early man in the Northeast and the Late Glacial environment. *Man in the Northeast* 4:7-39.
   1976   Recent contributions to Hudson Valley prehistory. *New York State Museum, Memoir* 22.
   1977   Early to Middle Archaic occupations in upstate New York. *Current perspectives in northeastern Archeology, essays in honor of William A. Ritchie,* edited by Robert E. Funk and Charles F. Hayes III. *Researches and Transactions of New York State Archeological Association* XVII(1):21-29.
   1978   Post-Pleistocene adaptations. In *Northeast,* vol. 15, edited by Bruce G. Trigger, in *Handbook of North American Indians,* edited by William C. Sturtevant. Washington, D.C.: Smithsonian Institution. Pp. 16-27.
Funk, Robert E., G. Walters, W. F. Ehlers, Jr., J. E. Guilday, and G. G. Connally
   1969   The archaeology of Dutchess Quarry Cave, Orange County, New York. *Pennsylvania Archaeologist* 39(1-4):7-22.

Garrad, Charles
  1969 Bear jaw tools from Petun sites. *Ontario Archaeology* 13:54-60.
  1971 Ontario fluted point survey. *Ontario Archaeology* 16:3-18.

Gibbon, Guy E.
  1972a The Walker-Hooper site, a Grand River phase Oneota site in Green Lake County. *The Wisconsin Archeologist* 53(4):149-290.
  1972b Cultural dynamics and the development of the Oneota life-way in Wisconsin. *American Antiquity* 37(2):146-185.

Goddard, Ives
  1978 Central Algonquian languages. In *Northeast,* vol. 15, edited by Bruce G. Trigger, in *Handbook of North American Indians,* edited by William C. Sturtevant. Washington, D.C.: Smithsonian Institution. Pp. 583-587.

Granger, Joseph E., Jr.
  1978 Meadowood phase settlement pattern in the Niagara frontier region of western New York state. *Anthropological Papers, Museum of Anthropology, University of Michigan,* No. 65.

Greenman, Emerson F.
  1948 The Killarney sequence and its Old World connections. *Papers of the Michigan Academy of Science, Arts and Letters* 32:313-332.
  1961 *The Indians of Michigan.* John M. Munson Michigan History Fund, Pamphlet No. 3. Lansing: Michigan Historical Commission.

Greenman, Emerson F., and George M. Stanley
  1940 A geologically dated camp site, Georgian Bay, Ontario. *American Antiquity* 8(3):260-265.
  1943 The archaeology and geology of two early sites near Killarney, Ontario. *Papers of the Michigan Academy of Science, Arts and Letters* 28:505-531.

Griffin, James B.
  1943 *The Fort Ancient aspect.* Ann Arbor: The University of Michigan Press. (Reprinted in 1966 as *Anthropological Papers, Museum of Anthropology, University of Michigan,* No. 28.)
  1944 The Iroquois in American prehistory. *Papers of the Michigan Academy of Science, Arts and Letters* 29:357-375.
  1952 Culture periods in eastern United States archeology. In *Archeology of eastern United States,* edited by James B. Griffin. Chicago: University of Chicago Press. Pp. 352-364.
  1960 A hypothesis for the prehistory of the Winnebago. In *Culture in History: Essays in Honor of Paul Radin,* edited by Stanley Diamond. New York: Columbia University Press. Pp. 809-865.
  1965 Late Quaternary prehistory in the northeastern Woodlands. In *The Quaternary of the United States,* edited by H. E. Wright, Jr., and David G. Frey. A Review Volume for the VII Congress of the International Association for Quaternary Research. Princeton, New Jersey: Princeton University Press. Pp. 655-667.
  1979 The origin and dispersion of American Indians in North America. In *The first Americans: Origins, affinities, and adaptations,* edited by William S. Laughlin and Susan T. Wolf. New York: Gustav Fischer.

Griffin, James B. (editor)
  1961 Lake Superior copper and the Indians: Miscellaneous studies of Great Lakes prehistory. *Anthropological Papers, Museum of Anthropology, University of Michigan,* No. 17.

Griffin, James B., Richard E. Flanders, and Paul F. Titterington
  1970 The burial complexes of the Knight and Norton Mounds in Illinois and Michigan. *Memoirs of the Museum of Anthropology, University of Michigan,* No. 2.

Hall, Robert L.
  1962 *The archaeology of Carcajou Point.* Madison, Wisconsin: University of Wisconsin Press.

References

Hayden, Brian (editor)
    1979 *Settlement patterns of the Draper and White sites, 1973 excavations.* Publication No. 6, Department of Archaeology. Burnaby, British Columbia: (Simon Fraser University.)

Haynes, C. Vance, Jr.
    1964 Fluted projectile points: Their age and dispersion. *Science* 145(3639):1408–1413.

Heidenreich, Conrad
    1971 *Huronia, a history and geography of the Huron Indians, 1600–1650.* Toronto: McClelland and Stewart.

Hickerson, Harold
    1962 The southwestern Chippewa, an ethnohistorical study. *American Anthropological Association, Memoir* 92.
    1970 *The Chippewa and their neighbors: A study in ethnohistory.* New York: Holt, Rinehart and Winston.
    1971 The Chippewa of the Upper Great Lakes: A study in sociopolitical change. In *North American Indians in Historical Perspective,* edited by Eleanor Burke Leacock and Nancy Oestreich Lurie. New York: Random House.

Hodge, Frederick W. (editor)
    1907–1910 Handbook of American Indians North of Mexico (vols. 1 and 2). *Bureau of American Ethnology, Bulletin* 30.

Hough, Jack L.
    1958 *Geology of the Great Lakes.* Urbana, Illinois: University of Illinois Press.
    1963 The prehistoric Great Lakes of North America. *American Scientist* 51(1):84–109.

Hruska, Robert
    1967 The Riverside site: A Late Archaic manifestation in Michigan. *The Wisconsin Archaeologist* 48(3):145–260.

Hubbs, Carl L., and Karl F. Lager
    1947 Fishes of the Great Lakes region. *Cranbrook Institute of Science Bulletin* No. 26.

Hunt, George T.
    1940 *The wars of the Iroquois.* Madison, Wisconsin: University of Wisconsin Press.

Hurley, William M.
    1975 An analysis of effigy mound complexes in Wisconsin. *Anthropological Papers, Museum of Anthropology, University of Michigan,* No. 59.
    1979 *Prehistoric cordage: Identification of impressions on pottery.* Aldine Manuals on Archeology, No. 3. Washington, D.C.: Taraxacum Inc.

Janzen, Donald R.
    1968 The Naomikong Point site and the dimensions of Laurel in the Lake Superior region. *Anthropological Papers, Museum of Anthropology, University of Michigan,* No. 36.

Jenks, Albert E.
    1937 Minnesota's Browns Valley man and associated burial artifacts. *American Anthropological Association, Memoir* 49.

Jennings, Jesse D.
    1974 *Prehistory of North America* (second edition). New York: McGraw-Hill.

Johnson, Elden
    1969 *The prehistoric peoples of Minnesota.* Minnesota Prehistoric Archaeology Series No. 8. St. Paul, Minnesota: Minnesota Historical Society.

Johnston, Richard B.
    1968 The archaeology of the Serpent Mound site. *Royal Ontario Museum, Division of Art and Archaeology, Occasional Paper* No. 10.

Kellar, James H.
    1973 *An introduction to the prehistory of Indiana.* Indianapolis, Indiana: Indiana Historical Society.

Kelley, R. W., and William R. Farrand
    1967 The glacial lakes around Michigan. *Michigan Geological Survey, Bulletin* No. 4.

Kellogg, Louise Phelps (editor)
   1917   *Early narratives of the Northwest, 1634–1699.* New York: Scribner's.
Kennedy, Clyde C.
   1966   Preliminary report on the Morrison's Island-6 site. *National Museum of Canada, Bulletin* No. 206.
Kent, Barry C., Ira F. Smith III, and Catherine McCann (editors)
   1971   Foundations of Pennsylvania prehistory. *Pennsylvania Historical and Museum Commission, Anthropological Series* No. 1.
Kenyon, Walter A.
   1959   The Inverhuron site. *Royal Ontario Museum, Art and Archaeology Division, Occasional Paper* 1.
   1968   The Miller site. *Royal Ontario Museum, Art and Archaeology Division, Occasional Paper* 14.
Kidd, Kenneth E.
   1953   The excavation and historical identification of a Huron ossuary. *American Antiquity* 18(4):359–379.
Kinietz, W. Vernon
   1965   *The Indians of the western Great Lakes, 1615–1760.* Ann Arbor, Michigan: University of Michigan Press. (First published in 1940 as *Occasional Contributions, Museum of Anthropology, University of Michigan,* No. 10.)
Kroeber, A. L.
   1953   *Cultural and natural areas of native North America.* Berkeley and Los Angeles, California: University of California Press.
Leacock, Eleanor Burke, and Nancy Oestreich Lurie (editors)
   1971   *North American Indians in historical perspective.* New York: Random House.
Lee, Thomas E.
   1954   The first Sheguiandah expedition, Manitoulin Island, Ontario. *American Antiquity* 20(2):101–111.
   1955   The second Sheguiandah expedition, Manitoulin Island, Ontario. *American Antiquity* 21(1):63–71.
Lenig, Donald
   1965   The Oak Hill horizon and its relation to the development of Five Nations Iroquois. *Researches and Transactions of the New York State Archaeological Association* 15(1).
Lounsbury, Floyd G.
   1978   Iroquoian languages. In *Northeast,* vol. 15, edited by Bruce G. Trigger, in *Handbook of North American Indians,* edited by William C. Sturtevant. Washington, D.C.: Smithsonian Institution. Pp. 334–343.
Lugenbeal, Edward
   1978   The Blackduck ceramics of the Smith site (21KC3) and their implications for the history of the Blackduck ceramics and culture in northern minnesota. *Midcontinental Journal of Archaeology* 3(1):45–68
MacDonald, George F.
   1968   Debert: A Paleo-Indian site in Central Nova Scotia. *National Museum of Canada, Anthropology Papers,* No. 16.
MacNeish, Richard S.
   1952a   A possible early site in the Thunder Bay district, Ontario. *National Museum of Canada Bulletin* 126:23–47.
   1952b   Iroquois pottery types. *National Museum of Canada, Bulletin* No. 124.
   1976   The in situ Iroquois revisited and rethought. In *Cultural change and continuity: Essays in honor of James Bennett Griffin,* edited by Charles E. Cleland. New York: Academic Press. Pp. 79–98.
Mahaney, W. C. (editor)
   1976   *Quaternary stratigraphy of North America.* Stroudsburg, Pennsylvania: Dowden, Hutchinson and Ross.

Martin, P. S., and H. E. Wright, Jr. (editors)
- 1967 *Pleistocene extinctions, the search for a cause.* Proceedings of the VII Congress of the International Association for Quaternary Research, vol. 6. New Haven and London: Yale University Press.

Mason, Carol I.
- 1970 The Oneota component at the Porte des Morts Site, Door County, Wisconsin. *The Wisconsin Archeologist* 51(4):191-227.
- 1976 Historic identification and Lake Winnebago focus Oneota. *Cultural change and continuity: Essays in honor of James Bennett Griffin,* edited by Charles E. Cleland. New York: Academic Press. Pp. 335-348.

Mason, Carol I., and Ronald J. Mason
- 1961 The Age of the Old Copper culture. *The Wisconsin Archeologist* 42(4):143-155.
- 1967 A catalogue of Old Copper artifacts in the Neville Public Museum. *The Wisconsin Archeologist* 48(2):81-128.

Mason, Ronald J.
- 1958 Late Pleistocene geochronology and the Paleo-Indian penetration of the Lower Michigan Peninsula. *Anthropological Papers, Museum of Anthropology, University of Michigan,* No. 11. (Reprinted by Demand Reprints, University Microfilms International, No. OP23275, Ann Arbor, and High Wycombe, Bucks, England.)
- 1962 The Paleo-Indian tradition in eastern North America. *Current Anthropology* 3(3):227-278. (Reprinted in the *Bobbs-Merrill Reprint Series in the Social Sciences,* No. A-439, Indianapolis.)
- 1966 Two stratified sites on the Door Peninsula of Wisconsin. *Anthropological Papers, Museum of Anthropology, University of Michigan,* No. 26.
- 1967 The North Bay component at the Porte des Morts Site, Door County, Wisconsin. *The Wisconsin Archaeologist* 48(4):267-345.
- 1970 Hopewell, Middle Woodland, and the Laurel culture: A problem in archaeological classification. *American Anthropologist* 72(4):802-815.
- 1974 Huron Island and the Island of the Poutouatamis. In *Aspects of Upper Great Lakes anthropology, papers in honor of Lloyd A. Wilford,* edited by Elden Johnson. Minnesota Prehistoric Archaeology Series, No. 11. St. Paul, Minnesota: Minnesota Historical Society, Pp. 149-156.
- 1976 Ethnicity and archaeology in the Upper Great Lakes. In *Cultural change and continuity: Essays in honor of James Bennett Griffin,* edited by Charles E. Cleland. New York: Academic Press. Pp. 349-361.

Mason, Ronald J., and Carol Irwin
- 1960 An Eden-Scottsbluff burial in northeastern Wisconsin. *American Antiquity* 26(1):43-57.

McHugh, William P.
- 1973 "New Archaeology" and the Old Copper culture. *The Wisconsin Archeologist* 54(2):70-83.

McKern, Will C.
- 1945 Preliminary report on the Upper Mississippian phase in Wisconsin. *Bulletin of the Public Museum of the City of Milwaukee* 16(3):109-285.

McPherron, Alan
- 1967 The Juntunen site and the Late Woodland prehistory of the Upper Great Lakes area. *Anthropological Papers, Museum of Anthropology, University of Michigan,* No. 30.

Moeller, Roger W. (editor)
- 1977 *Archaeological bibliography for eastern North America.* Eastern States Archaeological Federation and American Indian Archaeological Institute.

Morison, Samuel Eliot
- 1971 *The European discovery of America: The northern voyages, A.D. 500-1600.* London and New York: Oxford University Press.

Munson, Patrick J.
- 1973 The origins and antiquity of maize-beans-squash agriculture in eastern North America: Some linguistic implications. In *Variation in anthropology: Essays in honor of John C. McGregor,* edited by Donald W. Lathrap and Jody Douglas. Urbana, Illinois: Illinois Archaeological Survey. Pp. 107-135.

Murdock, George Peter, and Timothy J. O'Leary (editors)
- 1975 *Ethnographic bibliography of North America* (fourth edition). 5 vols. New Haven, Connecticut: Human Relations Area Files Press.

Newman, Walter S., and Bert Salwen (editors)
- 1977 Amerinds and their paleoenvironments in northeastern North America. *Annals of the New York Academy of Sciences 288.*

Noble, William C.
- 1975 Van Besien (AfHd-2); a study in Glen Meyer development. *Ontario Archaeology* 24:3-95.

Ossenberg, Nancy S.
- 1974 Origins and relationships of Woodland peoples: The evidence of cranial morphology. In *Aspects of Upper Great Lakes anthropology, papers in honor of Lloyd A. Wilford,* edited by Elden Johnson. *Minnesota Prehistoric Archaeology Series,* No. 11. St. Paul, Minnesota: Minnesota Historical Society. Pp. 15-39.

Oswalt, Wendell H.
- 1973 *This land was theirs, a study of the North American Indian* (second edition). New York: John Wiley.

Overstreet, David F.
- 1978 Oneota settlement patterns in eastern Wisconsin: Some considerations of time and space. In *Mississippian Settlement Patterns,* edited by Bruce D. Smith. New York: Academic Press. Pp. 21-52.

Palmer, Harris A., and James B. Stoltman
- 1976 The Boaz mastodon: A possible association of man and mastodon in Wisconsin. *Midcontinental Journal of Archaeology* 1(2): 163-177.

Pendergast, James F., and Bruce G. Trigger
- 1972 *Cartier's Hochelaga and the Dawson site.* Montreal: McGill-Queen's University Press.

Penman, John T.
- 1977 The Old Copper culture: An analysis of Old Copper artifacts. *The Wisconsin Archeologist* 58(1):3-23.

Popham, R. E., and J. Norman Emerson
- 1954 Manifestations of the Old Copper industry in Ontario. *Pennsylvania Archaeologist* 24(1):3-19.

Potter, Martha A.
- 1968 *Ohio's prehistoric peoples.* Columbus, Ohio: Ohio Historical Society.

Pratt, Peter P.
- 1976 Archaeology of the Oneida Iroquois (vol. 1). *Occasional Publications in Northeastern Anthropology,* No. 1. George's Mills, New Hampshire: Man in the Northeast, Inc.

Prest, V. K.
- 1976 Quaternary geology of Canada. In *Geology and economic minerals of Canada,* edited by R. J. W. Douglas. Geological Survey of Canada, Economic Geology Report No. 1, Part B, Ottawa. Pp. 675-764.

Prufer, Olaf H., and Raymond S. Baby
- 1963 *Palaeo-Indians of Ohio.* Columbus, Ohio: Ohio State Historical Society.

Quimby, George I.
- 1941 The Goodall focus: An analysis of ten Hopewellian components in Michigan and Indiana. *Indiana Historical Society Prehistory Research Series* 2(2):63-161.
- 1958 Fluted points and geochronology of the Lake Michigan Basin. *American Antiquity* 23(3):247-254.

1959 Lanceolate points and fossil beaches in the Upper Great Lakes region. *American Antiquity*, 24(4):424-426.

1960a Burial yields clews to Red Ocher culture. *Chicago Natural History Museum Bulletin* 31(2):5.

1960b *Indian life in the Upper Great Lakes.* Chicago: University of Chicago Press.

1961 The Pic River site. In *Lake Superior copper and the Indians: Miscellaneous studies of Great Lakes prehistory. Anthropological Papers, Museum of Anthropology, University of Michigan* 17:83-89.

1962 The age of the Oconto site. *The Wisconsin Archeologist* 43(1):16-19.

1966a *Indian culture and European trade goods.* Madison, Wisconsin: University of Wisconsin Press.

1966b The Dumaw Creek site, a seventeenth century prehistoric Indian village and cemetery in Oceania County, Michigan. *Fieldiana* 56(1).

Ramsden, Peter G.

1978 Two views on Late Prehistoric Iroquois trade and settlement I: An hypothesis concerning the effects of early European trade among some Ontario Iroquois. *Canadian Journal of Archaeology* 2(101-106).

Ridley, Frank

1954 The Frank Bay site, Lake Nipissing, Ontario. *American Antiquity* 20:40-50.

Ritchie, William A.

1932 The Lamoka Lake site. *Researches and Transactions of the New York State Archeological Association* 7(4).

1940 Two prehistoric village sites at Brewerton, New York. *Research Records of the Rochester Museum of Arts and Sciences*, No. 5.

1944 The Pre-Iroquoian occupations of New York state. *Rochester Museum of Arts and Sciences, Memoir* No. 1.

1945 An early site in Cayuga County, New York. *Research Records of the Rochester Museum of Arts and Sciences*, No. 7.

1952 The Chance horizon, an early state of Mohawk Iroquois cultural development. *New York State Museum, Circular* 29.

1954 Dutch Hollow, an early Historic period Seneca site in Livingston County, New York. *Research Records of the Rochester Museum of Arts and Sciences*, No. 10.

1955 Recent discoveries suggesting an Early Woodland burial cult in the Northeast. *New York State Museum and Science Service, Circular* 40.

1957 Traces of early man in the Northeast. *New York State Museum and Science Service, Bulletin* 358.

1961 A typology and nomenclature for New York projectile points. *New York State Museum and Science Service, Bulletin* 384.

1969 *The archaeology of New York state* (revised second edition). Garden City, New York: Natural History Press.

Ritchie, William A., and Don W. Dragoo

1960 The eastern dispersal of Adena. *New York State Museum and Science Service, Bulletin* 379.

Ritchie, William A., and Robert E. Funk

1971 Evidence for Early Archaic occupations on Staten Island. *Pennsylvania Archaeologist* 41(3):45-59.

1973 Aboriginal settlement patterns in the Northeast. *New York State Museum and Science Service, Memoir* 20.

Ritchie, William A., and Richard S. MacNeish

1949 The Pre-Iroquoian pottery of New York state. *American Antiquity* 15(2):97-124.

Ritzenthaler, Robert

1946 The Osceola site, an "Old Copper" site near Potosi, Wisconsin. *The Wisconsin Archeologist* 27:53-70. (Reprinted in Ritzenthaler, editor, 1957, pp. 186-203.)

Ritzenthaler, Robert (editor)
   1957   The Old Copper Culture of Wisconsin. *The Wisconsin Archeologist* 38(4):185-329.

Ritzenthaler, Robert, et al.
   1957   Reigh site report—number 3. *The Wisconsin Archeologist* 38(4):278-310.

Ritzenthaler, Robert E., and George I. Quimby
   1962   The Red Ocher culture of the Upper Great Lakes and adjacent areas. *Fieldiana: Anthropology* 36(11):243-275.

Ritzenthaler, Robert E., and Pat Ritzenthaler
   1970   *The Woodland Indians of the Western Great Lakes.* Garden City, New York: Natural History Press.

Ritzenthaler, Robert, and Warren L. Wittey
   1952   The Oconto site—an Old Copper manifestation. *The Wisconsin Archeologist* 33(4):199-223. (Reprinted in Ritzenthaler, editor, 1957, pp. 222-224.)

Roosa, William B.
   1965   Some Great Lakes fluted point types and sites. *The Michigan Archaeologist* 11(3-4):89-102.
   1977a   Great Lakes Paleoindian: The Parkhill site, Ontario. In *Amerinds and their paleoenvironments in northeastern North America*, edited by Walter S. Newman and Bert Salwen. *Annals of the New York Academy of Sciences,* 288:349-354.
   1977b   Fluted points from the Parkhill, Ontario site. In *For the director: Research essays in honor of James B. Griffin,* edited by Charles E. Cleland. *Anthropological Papers, Museum of Anthropology, University of Michigan* 61:87-122.

Rowe, Chandler W.
   1956   The Effigy Mound culture of Wisconsin. *Milwaukee Public Museum Publications in Anthropology,* No. 3.

Salzer, Robert J.
   1974   The Wisconsin North Lakes project: A preliminary report. In *Aspects of Upper Great Lakes anthropology, papers in honor of Lloyd A. Wilford,* edited by Elden Johnson. *Minnesota Prehistoric Archaeology Series* 11:40-54.

Shane, Orrin C., III
   1967   The Leimbach site, an Early Woodland village in Lorain County, Ohio. In *Studies in Ohio archaeology,* edited by Olaf H. Prufer and Douglas H. McKenzie. Cleveland, Ohio: Western Reserve University Press. Pp. 98-120.

Shay, C. Thomas
   1971   *The Itasca bison kill site, an ecological analysis.* St. Paul, Minnesota: Minnesota Historical Society.

Shelford, Victor E.
   1963   *The ecology of North America.* Urbana, Illinois: University of Illinois Press.

Smith, Sheryl A.
   1979   The Methodist Point site: A Middle Ontario Iroquois camp on Georgian Bay. *Ontario Ministry of Culture and Recreation, Historical Planning and Research Branch, Archaeological Research Reports,* No. 11.

Spence, Michael W., Ronald F. Williamson, and John H. Dawkins
   1978   The Bruce Boyd site: An Early Woodland component in southwestern Ontario. *Ontario Archaeology* 29:33-46.

Spencer, Robert F., Jesse D. Jennings, et al.
   1965   *The native Americans: Prehistory and ethnology of the North American Indians.* New York: Harper and Row.

Steinbring, Jack
   1974   The preceramic archaeology of northern Minnesota. *Aspects of Upper Great Lakes anthropology, papers in honor of Lloyd A. Wilford,* edited by Elden Johnson. *Minnesota Prehistoric Archaeology Series* 11:64-73.

References

Stewart, T. D.
- 1973 *The people of America.* New York: Scribner's.

Stimmell, Carole
- 1978 A preliminary report on the use of salt in shell tempered pottery of the Upper Mississippi Valley. *The Wisconsin Archeologist* 59(2):266-274.

Stoltman, James B.
- 1973 *The Laurel culture in Minnesota.* Minnesota Prehistoric Archaeology Series, No. 8. St. Paul, Minnesota: Minnesota Historical Society.
- 1978 Temporal models in prehistory: An example from eastern North America. *Current Anthropology* 19(4):703-746.

Stoltman, James B., and Karen Workman
- 1969 A preliminary study of Wisconsin fluted points. *The Wisconsin Archeologist* 50(4):189-214.

Storck, Peter L.
- 1975 A preliminary bibliography of early man in eastern North America. Archaeology, Monograph 4. Toronto: Royal Ontario Museum.
- 1978a Some recent developments in the search for early man in Ontario. *Ontario Archaeology* 29:3-16.
- 1978b The Coates Creek site: A possible Late Paleo-Indian–Early Archaic site in Simcoe County, Ontario. *Ontario Archaeology* 30:25-46.
- 1979 A report on the Banting and Hussey sites: Two Paleo-Indian campsites in Simcoe County, southern Ontario. *National Museum of Man, Mercury Series, Archaeological Survey of Canada, Paper* 93.

Stothers, David M.
- 1977 The Princess Point complex. *National Museum of Man, Mercury Series, Archaeological Survey of Canada, Paper* 58.
- 1979 The western basin tradition: Algonquin or Iroquois? *Pennsylvania Archaeologist* 49(3):13-30.

Struever, Stuart
- 1964 The Hopewell Interaction Sphere in riverine-western Great Lakes culture history. In *Hopewellian studies*, edited by Joseph R. Caldwell and Robert L. Hall. *Illinois State Museum Scientific Papers* 12:85-106.
- 1965 Middle Woodland culture history in the Great Lakes riverine area. *American Antiquity* 31(2):211-223.

Struever, Stuart, and K. D. Vickery
- 1973 The beginnings of cultivation in the Midwest-riverine area of the United States. *American Anthropologist,* 75:1197-1220.

Sturtevant, William C., and Bruce G. Trigger (editors)
- 1978 *Handbook of North American Indians,* edited by William C. Sturtevant; Vol. 15, *Northeast,* edited by Bruce G. Trigger. Washington, D.C.: Smithsonian Institution.

Swanton, John R.
- 1953 The Indian tribes of North America. *Bureau of American Ethnology, Bulletin* 145.

Thwaites, Reuben Gold (editor)
- 1869-1901 *The Jesuit relations and allied documents: Travels and explorations of the Jesuit missionaries in New France, 1610-1791.* 73 vols. Cleveland, Ohio: Burrows Brothers.
- 1902 The French regime in Wisconsin—I: 1634-1727. In *Collections of the State Historical Society of Wisconsin* 16. Madison, Wisconsin: Wisconsin State Historical Society.
- 1903 *A new discovery of a vast country in America* (vol. 1). By Father Louis Hennepin. (Reprinted from the second London edition of 1698.) Chicago, Illinois: A. C. McClurg.

Tooker, Elisabeth
- 1964 An ethnography of the Huron Indians, 1615-1649. *Bureau of American Ethnology, Bulletin* 190. (Reprinted by The Huronia Historical Development Council and The Ontario Department of Education.)

Trigger, Bruce G.
- 1969 *The Huron, farmers of the North.* New York: Holt, Rinehart and Winston.
- 1976 *The children of Aataentsic, a history of the Huron People to 1660.* 2 vols. Montreal and London: McGill–Queen's University Press.
- 1978 Early Iroquoian contacts with Europeans. In *Northeast,* vol. 15, edited by Bruce G. Trigger, in *Handbook of North American Indians,* edited by William C. Sturtevant. Washington, D.C.: Smithsonian Institution. Pp. 344–356.

Tuck, James A.
- 1971 *Onondaga Iroquois prehistory, a study in settlement archaeology.* Syracuse, New York: Syracuse University Press.
- 1974 Early Archaic horizons in eastern North America. *Archaeology In Eastern North America* 2 (1). Ann Arbor, Michigan: Eastern States Archaeological Federation.
- 1977 A look at Laurentian. In *Current perspectives in northeastern archeology, essays in honor of William A. Ritchie,* edited by Robert E. Funk and Charles F. Hayes III. *Researches and Transactions of New York State Archeological Association XVII*(1):31–40.
- 1978a Regional cultural development, 3000 to 300 B.C. In *Northeast,* vol. 15, edited by Bruce G. Trigger, in *Handbook of North American Indians,* edited by William C. Sturtevant. Washington, D.C.: Smithsonian Institution. Pp. 28–43.
- 1978b Northern Iroquois prehistory. In *Northeast,* vol. 15, edited by Bruce G. Trigger. in *Handbook of North American Indians,* edited by William C. Sturtevant. Washington, D.C.: Smithsonian Institution. Pp. 322–333.

Tucker, Sara Jones (compiler)
- 1942 *Indian villages of the Illinois Country.* Scientific Papers, vol. 2, part 1, *Atlas.* Springfield, Illinois: Illinois State Museum.

Washburn, Wilcomb E. (editor)
- 1964 *The Indian and the white man.* Garden City, New York: Doubleday.

Watson, G. D.
- 1972 A Woodland Indian site at Constance Bay, Ontario. *Ontario Archaeology* 18:1–24.

Watson, Patty Jo (editor)
- 1974 *Archaeology of the Mammoth Cave area.* New York: Academic Press.

White, Marian E.
- 1961 Iroquois culture history in the Niagara frontier area of New York state. *Anthropological Papers, Museum of Anthropology, University of Michigan,* No. 16.

Wilford, Lloyd A.
- 1955 A revised classification of the prehistoric cultures of Minnesota. *American Antiquity* 21(2):130–142.

Willey, Gordon R., and Philip Phillips
- 1958 *Method and theory in American archaeology.* Chicago, Illinois: The University of Chicago Press.

Williams, Stephen, and James B. Stoltman
- 1965 An outline of southeastern United States prehistory with particular emphasis on the Paleo-Indian era. In *The Quaternary of the United States,* edited by H. E. Wright, Jr., and David G. Frey. A Review Volume for the VII Congress of the International Association for Quaternary Research. Princeton, New Jersey: Princeton University Press. Pp. 669–683.

Wittry, Warren L.
- 1951 A preliminary study of the Old Copper culture. *The Wisconsin Archaeologist* 32(1):311–329. (Reprinted in Ritzenthaler, editor, 1957, pp. 204–221.)
- 1963 The Bell site, Wn9, an Early Historic Fox village. *Wisconsin Archaeologist* 44:1–57.
- 1965 The Institute digs a mastodon. *Cranbrook Institute of Science Newsletter* 35(2):14–18.

Wittry, Warren L., and Robert E. Ritzenthaler
- 1956 The Old Copper complex: An Archaic manifestation in Wisconsin. *American Antiquity* XXI(3):244–254. (Reprinted in Ritzenthaler, editor, 1957, pp. 311–329.)

Wormington, H. M.
  1957 *Ancient man in North America* (fourth edition). Denver Museum of Natural History, Popular Series No. 4.

Wray, Charles F., and Harry L. Schoff
  1953 A preliminary report on the Seneca sequence in western New York, *Pennsylvania Archaeologist* 23(2):53-63.

Wright, H. E., Jr., and David G. Frey (editors)
  1965 *The Quaternary of the United States*. A Review Volume for the VII Congress of the International Association for Quaternary Research. Princeton, New Jersey: Princeton University Press.

Wright, Henry T.
  1964 A transitional Archaic campsite at Greenpoint (20 Sa 1). *Michigan Archaeologist* 10:17-22.

Wright, Henry T., and William B. Roosa
  1966 The Barnes Site: A Fluted Point Assemblage from the Great Lakes Region. *American Antiquity* 31:850-860.

Wright, James V.
  1965 A regional examination of Ojibwa culture history. *Anthropologica* (New Series) 7(2):189-227.
  1966a The Pic River site. *National Museum of Canada Bulletin* 206:54-99.
  1966b The Ontario Iroquois tradition. *National Museum of Canada, Bulletin* 210.
  1967 The Laurel tradition and the Middle Woodland period. *National Museum of Canada, Bulletin* 217.
  1968a The Michipicoten site, Ontario. *National Museum of Canada Bulletin* (Contributions to Anthropology VI) 244:1-85.
  1968b The application of the direct historical approach to the Iroquois and the Ojibwa. *Ethnohistory* 15(1):96-109.
  1969 The Bennett site. *National Museum of Canada, Bulletin* 229.
  1972a *Ontario prehistory, an eleven-thousand-year archaeological outline*. Ottawa: National Museums of Canada.
  1972b The Shield Archaic. *National Museums of Canada Publications in Archaeology*, No. 3.
  1974 The Nodwell site. *National Museum of Man, Mercury Series, Archaeological Survey of Canada, Paper* 22.
  1978 The implications of probably Early and Middle Archaic projectile points from southern Ontario. *Canadian Journal of Archaeology* 2:59-78.

Wright, James V., and James E. Anderson
  1963 The Donaldson site. *National Museum of Canada, Bulletin* 184.

Wrong, G. M. (editor)
  1939 *Father Gabriel Sagard: The long journey to the country of the Hurons*. Toronto: The Champlain Society.

Yarnell, Richard Asa
  1964 Aboriginal relationships between culture and plant life in the Upper Great Lakes region. *Anthropological Papers, Museum of Anthropology, University of Michigan*, No. 23.
  1976 Early plant husbandry in eastern North America. In *Cultural change and continuity: Essays in honor of James Bennett Griffin*, edited by Charles E. Cleland. New York: Academic Press. Pp. 265-273.

Young, Philip D., David J. Wenner, Jr., and Elaine Bluhm
  1961 Two early burial sites in Lake County. In *Chicago area archaeology*, edited by Elaine A. Bluhm. *Illinois Archaeological Survey Bulletin* 3:21-28.

Index

A
Adena culture, 217-218, 219, 228, 232, 238, 244
Adena Plain pottery, 230
Adena points, 218, 226
Agate Basin points, 116, 122
Agriculture, 17, 37-40, 144-145
 origins, 203-205, 230-232, 297, 340
Alberta points, 116
Algoma Great Lakes, 67, 78-79, 145, 220
Algonkian, *see* Algonquian languages
Algonkins (tribe), 5, 7-8, 210, 381
Algonquian languages, 5, 6
Allumette Island-1 site, 195
Amikwas, 9, 31
Anderson focus, 284
Andrews site, 193
Angostura points, 116
Anker site, 361
Arendarhonon, 6
Assiniboins, 12, 393, 394
Ataronchronon, 6
Attignawantan, 6, 45
Attigneenongnahac, 6
Aurora Run Rockshelter, 116
Ausable focus, 321
Aztalan Collared pottery, 306, 312
Aztalan site, 299, 306, 358, 366, 367

B
Baehr Ware, 254
Bands, 8-10, 27-32, 210-211
Banting site, 94
Barnes site, 90-92, 102, 104
Beake site, 224-226
Becker Punctated, 278
Beecher site, 378, 389
Bell site, 402
Big Sandy points, 129
Biotic provinces, 56-61
 Canadian, 58-60, 243, 259, 285
 Carolinian, 60-61, 150, 205, 240, 259
 Hudsonian, 57-58, 243, 285
 Illinoian, 61
Blackduck culture, 295, 300, 313-317, 319, 352, 354, 389-394
Blue Island culture, *see* Huber culture
Boaz mastodon site, 101
Bois Blanc phase, 318, 319, 346, 350, 351
Brebeuf, Jean de, 383-384, 396
Brewerton Corner-Notched points, 196-197
Brewerton phase, 172, 174, 180, 196, 206
Brewerton Side-Notched points, 180, 192, 196-197
Brohm site, 125-126
Bruce Boyd site, 209
Bull Brook site, 93, 94
Burley site, 270
Burnt-Rollways phase, 277
Bussinger site, 258

C
Cadillac, Lamonthe, 386, 396
Cahokias, 12

Index

Cahokia site, 306, 366, 367
Canandaigua phase, 324, 329
Canoe Point phase, 269, 271, 272
Canton Ware, 319
Carpenter Brook phase, 319, 320, 321, 324, 326, 329, 334–336
Cartier, Jacques, 373
Castle Creek phase, 324, 329, 330, 332
Cat Nation, *see* Eries
Cayugas, 5
Champlain, Samuel de, 12, 383
Champlain Sea, 69, 74, 76, 117
Chance phase, 332–333, 334
Chippewas, *see* Ojibwas
Climate, 56–57, 59–61, 132–133
Clovis culture, 83–84, 86
Coastal Archaic, 206
Cody complex, 120, 121
Constance Bay Site No. 1, 271
Cord twist studies, 305–306
Crees, 210, 315, 390, 392, 393
Cresap points, 218, 228
Cummins site, 125

D

Dakota, *see* Sioux
Dalton points, 112, 113
Dane Incised, 277, 278
Daoust Farm site, *see* Ossossane site
Debert site, 93
Doetsch site, 224–226
Donaldson site, 261–263, 265, 266–269, 270
Draper site, 375, 379, 389, 396
Dumaw Creek site, 402
Dutchess Quarry Cave site, 94, 99
Dutch Hollow site, 378–381, 389, 396
Dyer Farm site, 219–222, 224

E

Early Archaic, 112–115, 126–139
Early Ontario Iroquois, 319, 323, 324, 332, 336–340, 346, 390
Early Point Peninsula culture, *see* Canoe Point phase
Early Woodland period, *see* Transitional period
Eastern Michigan Hopewellian, 253–258
Eden points, 120–121, 125
Effigy Mound culture, 295–296, 297, 304, 305, 308–312, 315, 319, 353, 354, 355, 356, 357, 370
Ekdahl–Goudreau site, 290

El Rancho site, 333
Eries, 6, 344
European contact, 1–5, 373–405
Eva points, 129
Exploration, *see* European contact
Extinction, post-Pleistocene faunal, 69–70

F

False Face Society, 26, 333
Fayette Thick pottery, 216, 230
Feast of the Dead, 383–389
Feeheley site, 144, 145
Felton site, 219
Fiber-tempered pottery, 209
Fisher culture, 300, 361
Fisher site, 94
Flambeau phase, 122–123, 125
Fluted points, *see* Paleo-Indian
Folsom culture, 84, 86
Fort Ancient culture, 300
Fort de Buade, 386
Fort Michilimackinac site, 290, 399
Fort Ouiatenon, 404
Fort Ponchartrain, 386
Foxes (tribe), 10, 402
Frontenac, Governor, 397, 398
Frontenac Island site, 174–180, 206
Frontenac phase, 174–180, 206
Frost Island culture, 205–209, 216, 227

G

Garoga phase, 332, 334
Gens de Terre, 390
Geography, 50–55
George Lake 1 and 2 sites, 123–125, 129, 172
Gibson points, 251
Girdled Road site, 227–229
Glacial Kame culture, 193, 224–226, 234
Glacial Lakes, 72–75, 89–91, 116
  Arkona, 72
  Chicago, 72
  Duluth, 75
  Frontenac, 74
  Grassmere, 74
  Iroquois, 74, 89
  Keweenaw, 73
  Lundy, 74
  Maumee, 72
  Saginaw, 72
  Warren, 74, 90–91, 116
  Wayne, 74, 116
  Whittlesey, 72

Glen Meyer culture, 300, 322–323, 324, 336–340, 344, 346
Graham Cave site, 114
Grand River (Oneota) phase, 356, 359, 362, 363, 364
Grand River (Princess Point) focus, 321
Green Bay phase, *see* Mero complex
Green Point Hopewellian phase, 254, 256
Green Point site, *see* Schultz site
Green Point Ware, 254–256, 258
Griffon, 396–399, 403, 404
Grossilliers, Médart, 398

H

Half-Moon Cordmarked pottery, 216
Hardaway points, 113, 129
Hart site, 145
Havana culture, 239
Havana Ware, 247, 248, 276, 277, 322
Heins Creek complex, 295, 301–306, 312, 315, 319, 353, 354
Heins Creek Corded-stamped, 303–305
Heins Creek Cordwrapped-stick, 303–305
Heins Creek site, 301–303
Hell Gap points, 116
Hennepin, Louis, 398
Heron Bay site, 290
Hickory Hill Marsh site, 206
Hi-Lo points, 114, 129
Hi-Lo site, 114
Historic Period, 373–406
Holcombe site, 97, 99, 102–104
Hopewell culture, 219, 238–239, 241–244, 258, 259
Hopewell Ware, 247, 254, 259
Hopewellian culture, 239–241, 243–259, 260, 269, 271–272, 277, 292, 295, 322
Hopewellian interaction sphere, 244, 251, 259, 276
Houghton stage, 76–77
Howlett Hill site, 332
Huber culture, 300, 361
Hunter's Home phase, 272, 319–321, 324, 334
Hurons, 6, 21, 37, 39, 42, 45, 235, 340, 344, 375, 381, 383–386, 387, 391, 398, 401, 403, 404
Hussey site, 94

I

Ice Age, *see* Pleistocene
Illinois (tribe), 12
Inverhuron Archaic culture, 263, 272

Inverhuron–Lucas site, 261–262
Iowas, 355
Iroquoian languages, 5–6
Iroquoian societies, 5–6, 36–46
Iroquois, League of the, 5–6, 39, 43–46, 332, 340, *see also* New York Iroquois
Itasca site, 99, 129–131

J

Jack's Reef Corner-notched points, 273
Jack's Reef Pentagonal points, 273
Juntunen phase, 318, 350–353
Juntunen site, 318–319, 350–353, 386, 387

K

Kanawha points, 129
Kantzler site, 258
Kaskaskias, 12
Keinouches, 8
Kichesipirini, 5
Kickapoos, 10
Kipp Island phase, 272–275, 319, 320–321
Kirk points, 116, 129
Kiskakons, 8
Koens–Crispin Ware, 209
Koshkonong phase, 359, 362, 363, 364
Kutsch site, 91

L

Lake Algonquin, 66–67, 74, 75–76, 91–92, 103–104, 123, 124
Lake Chippewa, 77
Lake Clinton, 103
Lake Erie, 54–55, 76
Lake Huron, 54–55, 258
Lake Michigan, 50–51, 54–55
Lake Nokomis Trailed, 277
Lake Ontario, 54–55
Lakes phase, 295, 312–313, 315, 353–354
Lake Stanley, 77, 123
Lake Superior, 54–55
Lake Winnebago phase, 356, 359, 362, 363, 364, 365
Lake Winnebago Trailed pottery, 357
Lamoka culture, 147–160, 161, 172, 174, 180, 186, 206
Lamoka Lake site, 155–158, 186
Language, *see* Algonquian; Iroquoian; Siouan
La Salle, Robert, 396, 398–399, 401
Lasanen site, 386–389, 396
Lasleys Point site, 357

Late Archaic, 112, 133, 136, 137, 141–199
Late Ontario Iroquois, *see* Ontario Iroquois
Late Paleo-Indian, 111–126, 133, 136
Late Woodland period, 295–372
Late Woodland I period, 295–296, 300–324
Late Woodland II period, 296, 324–372
Laurel Bossed pottery, 289
Laurel culture, 260, 276, 281, 284–292
Laurel Dentate pottery, 289
Laurel Oblique pottery, 289
Laurel Pseudo-scallop Shell pottery, 289
Laurentian culture, 160–180, 186, 195–197, 209, 272
Lawton site, 276
Le Croy points, 129
Leimbach Cordmarked, 230
Leimbach culture, 227–232, 234, 235
Leimbach site, 204, 229–232
Leimbach Thick pottery, 229–230
Leimbach Ware, 216
Levanna points, 273, 329, 334
Le Vesconte Mound site, 259
Longhouse social organization, 40–42
Long Sault Island site, 217, 218
Lux site, 92

M

McCluskey site, 290
Macgillvray site, 290
Mackinac phase, 318–319, 346, 350
Mackinac Ware, 319, 351, 390
McKinstry phase, 289
McKinstry site, 290
Madison Cord Impressed pottery, 304–306, 312
Madison Fabric Impressed pottery, 306
Madison Plain pottery, 306
Madison points, 330, 334, 379
Madison Ware, 304–308, 317, 319
Manitoba focus, 393, 394
Maramegs, 9, 390
Marcey Creek Plain pottery, 209
Marion Thick pottery, 216, 217, 224, 230
Maritime Archaic, 167, 186, 213
Marshall site, 378
Mascoutens, 10
Mason-Quimby Line, 98
Meadowcroft Rockshelter, 106–107
Meadowood culture, 209–217, 218, 222, 224, 227, 234, 261
Medicine, *see* Religion
Men of the Land, 390
Menominis, 10, 11

Mero complex, 357, 362, 363, 365
Mero site, 278, 301, 357
Miamis, 11–12
Michigan Ware, 390, 393
Michipicoten site, 391, 393, 403
Middle Archaic, *see* Early Archaic
Middle Mississippian, *see* Mississippian culture
Middle Ontario Iroquois, 340, 352
Middleport substage, 340, 342–344, 352
Middlesex culture, 217–219, 232, 244
Middle Tier Middle Woodland, 256, 259–284
Middle Woodland culture, 237–293
Midewiwin Society, 26, 36
Mikinacs, 9
Milnesand points, 125
Minocqua phase, 122–123, 125
Minong stage, 75, 125
Missisaugas, 9, 31
Mississippian culture, 238, 299–300, 344, 350, 352, 358, 361, 366–370
Modoc Rockshelter, 114
Mohawks, 5, 42, 334, 379, 389
Morrison's Island-6 site, 195–197
Mound Builder myth, 237–238

N

Nahrwold No. 2 site, 209
Naomikong Point site, 290
Nassauaketons, 8
Neutrals, 6, 37, 340, 344, 381, 389, 398
Neville points, 129
New York Iroquois, 324, 329, 330–334, 346, *see also* League of the Iroquois
Nicolet, Jean, 12–13
Nipissing Great Lakes, 67, 78, 115, 145, 192–193, 194
Nipissings, 8, 30, 210
Nokomis culture, 260, 276–278, 281–284, 286
Nopemings, 9, 390
North Bay culture, 260, 271, 276–284
Northern Tier Middle Woodland, 260, 276, 284–292
Norton Corner Notched points, 251
Norton Incised, 251
Norton Mound Group, 244–252, 256
Norton pottery, 247–251, 254
Norton Zoned Corded, 251
Norton Zoned Cordwrapped Stick, 251
Norton Zoned Dentate Stamped, 251
Noquets, 9
Nutimik focus, 284
Nyman site, 389–390, 391

O

Oak Hill phase, 300, 324, 332, 333, 340
Oberlander No. 2 site, 212
Oconto site, 189, 190, 191–193, 194, 196, 211
Ojibwas, 8, 9–10, 11, 19, 27–32, 36, 210, 389–394, 395, 396, 402
Old Copper culture, 166, 181–194, 195–196, 197, 211, 227
Omahas, 355
Onangizes, 397–398
Oneidas, 5, 378
O'Neil site, 206
Oneota culture, 300, 312, 352, 353, 354–371
Onondagas, 5, 45, 334, 379, 389
Onontchataronon, 5
Ontario Iroquois, 344, 350
O'pimittish Ininiwac, 390
Orr phase, 359, 362, 363, 364, 365
Osceola site, 189, 190–191, 192, 193, 194
Ossossane site, 383–386, 388, 389, 396
Otaguottouemin, 5
Otos, 355
Ottawas, 8–9, 30, 210, 386–389, 398, 401, 402, 403, 404
Otter Creek points, 129, 172, 191
Ouasouarinis, 9, 31
Outchibous, 9
Owasco culture, 295, 319, 321, 324–330, 332, 334, 336

P

Paleo-Indian, 81–110
Palmer points, 129
Parker Festooned pottery, 350
Parkhill site, 94–97, 102
Parsons site, 375, 379, 389, 396
Peninsular Woodland pottery, 390–391
Peorias, 12
Perrot, Nicolas, 398
Peterson Farm site, 220, 222–224
Petuns, 6, 37, 340, 344, 389, 391, 398, 401, 403, 404
Piankashaws, 11
Pickering culture, 300, 322–323, 324, 336–340, 344, 390
Pic River site, 389–391, 393
Pike Bay phase, 289
Plainview points, 125
Plano cultures, 112, 116, 120, 125, 136, 137
Pleistocene epoch, 61–79, 103–104
  climate, 67–69
  fauna, 69–70, 74
  flora, 67–69
  geomorphology, 61–67, 70–71
  glacial chronology, 62–64, 71–79, 103–104
Point Pelee focus, 321
Point Peninsula culture, 258, 259, 260, 269, 271–276, 319, 320–321, 336
Point Peninsula pottery, 272–273
Point Peninsula I culture, *see* Meadowood culture
Point Sauble Collared pottery, 304–306, 312, 350
Pomranky complex, 224
Pope site, 120
Population estimates, Iroquoian groups, 37
Porte des Morts site, 278–281, 284
Potawatomis, 10–11, 32–36, 396–398, 400–403, 404
Potts site, 89–90
Princess Point complex, 295, 319, 321–324, 334, 336
Protohistoric period, 382
Proto-Ojibwa, *see* Ojibwa

R

Radisson, Pierre, 398
Ramey Incised pottery, 352
Rappuhn site, 101
Reagen site, 103
Red Ocher culture, 212, 219–226, 227, 234
Reigh site, 189, 193, 194, 197, 211
Renier site, 117–121, 123, 125, 129, 172
Richter site, 284
Ritchie–Fitting Hypothesis, 132–133
Riverhaven No. 2 site, 209, 210
Riverside Cemetery site, 194, 226–227
Rivière au Vase site, 346
Rivière Ware, 346
Robinson site, 123
Rock art, 394–396
Rock Island Site II, 188, 284, 316, 365, 396–404
Rosencrans site, 219

S

Sables, 8
Sagard, Gabriel, 383
Saginaw Bay Hopewellian, *see* Eastern Michigan Hopewellian
St. Albans points, 129
St. Lawrence Iroquois, 336
Sanders I site, 355
Santee Dakota, 12
Satchell complex, 120, 129

Index

Saugeen culture, 260, 261–271, 272, 273, 276, 281
Sauks, 10–11
Saulteurs, 9
Sawmill site, 115–116, 120, 125
Scaccia site, 209
Schmidt site, 145
Schultz site, 204, 230, 232–234, 254–258
Schultz Thick pottery, 216
Scioto culture, 239
Scottsbluff points, 116, 120, 121, 123, 125
Selkirk pottery, 315, 317, 390, 393
Senecas, 5, 37, 42, 378–381
Serpent Mound site, 272
Shawnee–Minisink site, 93–94
Shebishikong site, 389–390, 391
Sheguiandah site, 123–125, 129, 172
Shield Archaic, 113, 133–139, 144, 147, 154, 166, 187
Sidey–Mackay site, 403
Silver Lake site, 99
Simonsen points, 129
Simonsen site, 130
Sinagos, 8
Sinking Ponds site, 210
Siouan languages, 5, 12, 355
Sioux, 12, 394
Sissung site, 344–345
Smith Mounds site, 290–292, 314
Smith phase, 289, 290
Snyders points, 251
Social organization, general, 4–13
Southern Tier Middle Woodland, 240, 244–259, 295
Spicer Creek site, 210
Springwells phase, 346
Squawkie Hill phase, 240, 258–259, 260, 272
Squaw Rock Shelter, 116, 129
Squirrel River phase, 133, 187–188
Stanley points, 129
Steatite bowls, see Stone bowls
Steatite-tempered pottery, 208–209
Stone bowls, 206, 207–208, 209
Summer Island site, 290
Susquehanna Broad Spearpoints, 207
Susquehanna Soapstone culture, 206
Susquehannocks, 6

T

Tahontaenrat, 6
Thede site, 261, 270–271
Thompson's Island site, 117

Thurston site, 378
Tionnontaté, see Petuns
Tittabawassee Hopewellian phase, 254
Tittabawassee Plain Noded, 254
Tittabawassee Ware, 254
Tobacco Nation, see Petuns
Trade, 20–21
Transitional period, 201–236, 266
Tribes, general nature of, 4–13
Turin points, 129
Turkey-tail blades, 212, 220–222, 224, 226
Tuscaroras, 5

U

Upper group beaches, 76, 123
Upper Mississippian, see Mississippian culture; Oneota culture
Uren substage, 340, 352

V

Valderan stadial, 63, 73–75
Vergennes phase, 167, 172, 191
Vinette 1 pottery, 208, 209, 212, 216–217, 218, 224, 230, 234, 266, 272
Vinette 2 pottery, see Point Peninsula pottery
Vinette site, 272
Vosburg phase, 167, 172

W

Warfare, general nature of, 22–24
Waukesha focus, 239–240
Wayne tradition, 344
Wayne Ware, 319, 346
Weas, 11, 404
Weaver Ware, 322
Wenroronans, see Wenros
Wenros, 6, 340, 344
Weskarini, 5
Western Basin complex, 321, 340–350
Western Michigan Hopewellian, 244–252
Whittlesey culture, 346
Winnebagos, 10, 12–13, 309, 355, 364, 365, 389
Wisconsin glacial stage, 62–64, 66–76
Wolf phase, 346–350
Woodfordian stadial, 63, 71–73
Wyandots, 6, 398, 401, 404

Y

Younge phase, 346
Younge site, 346
Younge tradition, see Western Basin complex